Lecture Notes in Computer Science 8631

Commenced Publication in 1973
Founding and Former Series Editors:
Gerhard Goos, Juris Hartmanis, and Jan van Leeuwen

T0213768

Xian-he Sun   Wenyu Qu   Ivan Stojmenovic
Wanlei Zhou   Zhiyang Li   Hua Guo
Geyong Min   Tingting Yang   Yulei Wu
Lei Liu (Eds.)

Algorithms and Architectures for Parallel Processing

14th International Conference, ICA3PP 2014
Dalian, China, August 24-27, 2014
Proceedings, Part II

 Springer

Volume Editors

Xian-he Sun
Illinois Institute of Technology, Chicago, IL, USA, e-mail: sun@iit.edu

Wenyu Qu
Dalian Maritime University, China, e-mail: wenyu@dlmu.edu.cn

Ivan Stojmenovic
University of Ottawa, ON, Canada, e-mail: ivan@site.ottawa.ca

Wanlei Zhou
Deakin University, Burwood, VIC, Australia, e-mail: wanlei.zhou@deakin.edu.au

Zhiyang Li
Dalian Maritime University, China, e-mail: lizy0205@gmail.com

Hua Guo
BeiHang University, Beijing, China, e-mail: hguo@buaa.edu.cn

Geyong Min
University of Bradford, UK, e-mail: g.min@brad.ac.uk

Tingting Yang
Dalian Maritime University, China, e-mail: yangtingting820523@163.com

Yulei Wu
Chinese Academy of Sciences, Beijing, China, e-mail: yulei.frank.wu@gmail.com

Lei Liu
Shandong University, Jinan City, China, e-mail: l.liu@sdu.edu.cn

ISSN 0302-9743   e-ISSN 1611-3349
ISBN 978-3-319-11193-3   e-ISBN 978-3-319-11194-0
DOI 10.1007/978-3-319-11194-0
Springer Cham Heidelberg New York Dordrecht London

Library of Congress Control Number: 2014947719

LNCS Sublibrary: SL 1 – Theoretical Computer Science and General Issues

Typesetting: Camera-ready by author, data conversion by Scientific Publishing Services, Chennai, India
Printed on acid-free paper
Springer is part of Springer Science+Business Media (www.springer.com)

Preface

Welcome to the proceedings of the 14th International Conference on Algorithms and Architectures for Parallel Processing (ICA3PP 2014) held in Dalian, China.

ICA3PP 2014 is the 14th in this series of conferences started in 1995 that are devoted to algorithms and architectures for parallel processing. As applications of computing systems have permeated in every aspect of daily life, the power of computing system has become increasingly critical. This conference provides a forum for academics and practitioners from countries around the world to exchange ideas for improving the efficiency, performance, reliability, security, and interoperability of computing systems and applications.

It is our great honor to introduce the program for the conference. Thanks to the Program Committee's hard work, we were able to finalize the technical program. In the selection process, each paper was assigned to at least 4 PC members as reviewers. The authors and those PC members from the same institution were separated in the reviewing process to avoid conflicts of interests. We received 285 submissions from all over the world. The large number of submissions indicated continued excitement in the field worldwide. The manuscripts have been ranked according to their original contribution, quality, presentation, and relevance to the themes of the conference. In the end, 70 (24.56%) papers were accepted as the main conference papers and inclusion in the conference.

ICA3PP 2014 obtained the support of many people and organizations as well as the general chairs whose main responsibility was various tasks carried out by other willing and talented volunteers. We want to express our appreciation to Professor Xian-He Sun for accepting our invitation to be the keynote/invited speaker.

We would like to give our special thanks to the program chairs of the conference for their hard and excellent work on organizing the Program Committee, outstanding review process to select high-quality papers, and making an excellent conference program. We are grateful to all workshop organizers for their professional expertise and excellence in organizing the attractive workshops/symposia, and other committee chairs, advisory members and PC members for their great support. We appreciate all authors who submitted their high-quality papers to the main conference and workshops/symposia.

We thank all of you for participating in this year's ICA3PP 2014 conference, and hope you find this conference stimulating and interesting.

July 2014

Ivan Stojmenovic
Wanlei Zhou

Organization

General Chairs

Ivan Stojmenovic	Ottawa University, Canada
Wanlei Zhou	Deakin University, Australia

Program Chairs

Xianhe Sun	Illinois Institute of Technology, USA
Wenyu Qu	Dalian Maritime University, China

Publicity Chairs

Jaime Lloret Mauri	Polytechnic University of Valencia, Spain
Al-Sakib Khan Pathan	International Islamic University Malaysia, Malaysia

Publication Chair

Yang Xiang	Deakin University, Australia

Steering Committee Chairs

Andrzej Goscinski	Deakin University, Australia
Yi Pan	Georgia State University, USA
Yang Xiang	Deakin University, Australia

Workshop Chairs

Mianxiong Dong	National Institute of Information and Communications Technology, Japan
Lei Liu	Shandong University, China

Local Organizing Chair

Zhiyang Li	Dalian Maritime University, China

Registration Chair

Weijiang Liu   Dalian Maritime University, China

Finance Chair

Zhaobin Liu   Dalian Maritime University, China

Web Chairs

Yang Shang   Dalian Maritime University, China
Tingting Wang   Dalian Maritime University, China

Program Committee Members

Zafeirios Papazachos   Queen's University of Belfast, UK
Paolo Trunfio   University of Calabria, Italy
Chao-Tung Yang   Tunghai University, Taiwan
Yong Zhao   University of Electronic Science and Technology
                              of China, China
Xingquan (Hill) Zhu   Florida Atlantic University, USA
Giandomenico Spezzano   ICAR-CNR, Italy
Yasuhiko Takenaga   The University of Electro-Communications,
                              Japan
Sushil Prasad   University of Georgia, USA
Tansel Ozyer   TOBB University of Economics and
                              Technology, Turkey
Deng Pan   Florida International University, USA
Apostolos Papadopoulos   Aristotle University of Thessaloniki, Greece
Eric Pardede   La Trobe University, Australia
Karampelas Panagiotis   Hellenic American University, Greece
Paul Lu   University of Alberta, Canada
Kamesh Madduri   Penn State University, USA
Ching-Hsien Hsu   Chung Hua University, Taiwan
Muhammad Khurram Khan   King Saud University, Saudi Arabia
Morihiro Kuga   Kumamoto University, Japan
Weiwei Fang   Beijing Jiaotong University, China
Franco Frattolillo   Università del Sannio, Italy
Longxiang Gao   Deakin University, Australia
Javier García   University Carlos III, Spain
Michael Glass   University of Erlangen-Nuremberg, Germany
David E. Singh   Universidad Carlos III de Madrid, Spain
Marion Oswald   TU Wien, Austria
Rajkumar Buyya   The University of Melbourne, Australia

Luca Tasquier   Second University of Naples, Italy
Rafael Santos   National Institute for Space Research, Brazil
George Bosilca   University of Tennessee, USA
Esmond Ng   Lawrence Berkeley National Lab, USA
Laurent Lefevre   Laurent Lefevre, Inria, University of Lyon,
                                France
Giuseppina Cretella   Second University of Naples, Italy
Gregoire Danoy   University of Luxembourg, Luxembourg
Bernabe Dorronsoro   University of Lille 1, France
Massimo Ficco   Second University of Naples, Italy
Jorge Bernal Bernabe   University of Murcia, Spain

Computing, Communication and Control Technologies in Intelligent Transportation System (3C in ITS 2014)

Security and Privacy in Computer and Network Systems (SPCNS 2014)

Table of Contents – Part I

The 1st International Workshop on Emerging Topics in Wireless and Mobile Computing (ETWMC 2014)

The 5th International Workshop on Intelligent Communication Networks (IntelNet 2014)

The 5th International Workshop on Wireless Networks and Multimedia (WNM 2014)

Parallel Data Processing in Dynamic Hybrid Computing Environment Using MapReduce

Bing Tang[1], Haiwu He[2], and Gilles Fedak[2]

[1] School of Computer Science and Engineering,
Hunan University of Science and Technology,
Xiangtan 411201, China
btang@hnust.edu.cn
[2] University of Lyon, LIP Laboratory,
UMR CNRS - ENS Lyon - INRIA - UCB Lyon 5668,
46 allée d'Italie, 69364 Lyon Cedex 07, France
{haiwu.he,gilles.fedak}@inria.fr

Abstract. A novel MapReduce computation model in hybrid computing environment called HybridMR is proposed in the paper. Using this model, high performance cluster nodes and heterogeneous desktop PCs in Internet or Intranet can be integrated to form a hybrid computing environment. In this way, the computation and storage capability of large-scale desktop PCs can be fully utilized to process large-scale datasets. HybridMR relies on a hybrid distributed file system called HybridDFS, and a time-out method has been used in HybridDFS to prevent volatility of desktop PCs, and file replication mechanism is used to realize reliable storage. A new node priority-based fair scheduling (NPBFS) algorithm has been developed in HybridMR to achieve both data storage balance and job assignment balance by assigning each node a priority through quantifying CPU speed, memory size and I/O bandwidth. Performance evaluation results show that the proposed hybrid computation model not only achieves reliable MapReduce computation, reduces task response time and improves the performance of MapReduce, but also reduces the computation cost and achieves a greener computing mode.

Keywords: Hybrid Computing Environment, Distributed File System, MapReduce, Volunteer Computing, Fault-tolerance.

1 Introduction

In the past decade, Desktop Grid and Volunteer Computing Systems (DGVCS's) have been proved an effective solution to provide scientists with tens of TeraFLOPS from hundreds of thousands of resources. DGVCS's utilize free computing, network and storage resources of idle desktop PCs distributed over Intranet or Internet environments for supporting large-scale computation and storage. DGVCS's have been one of the largest and most powerful distributed computing systems in the world, offering a high return on investment for applications

X.-h. Sun et al. (Eds.): ICA3PP 2014, Part II, LNCS 8631, pp. 1–14, 2014.

from a wide range of scientific domains, including computational biology, climate prediction, and high-energy physics [1] [2] [9].

MapReduce is an emerging programming model for data intensive application which was first introduced by Google in 2004 [4], and has attracted a lot of attentions recently. Hadoop is an open-source implementation of MapReduce, which is widely used in Yahoo, Facebook and Amazon.

Recently, there are some other MapReduce implementations that are designed for large-scale parallel data processing specialized on desktop grid or volunteer resources in Intranet or Internet, such as BitDew-MapReduce [12], MOON [8], P2P-MapReduce [10], VMR [3], etc. However, because there exists the correlation of volunteer or desktop failures, in order to achieve long-term and sustained high throughput, MapReduce implementations adapted to volatile desktop environments can not lack the support of high reliable cluster nodes.

To this end, this paper presents a hybrid computing environment, in which the cluster nodes and the volunteer computing nodes are integrated. For this hybrid computing environment, we propose and implement a MapReduce parallel computation model that takes advantages of the computing capability of these two kinds of resource to execute reliable MapReduce tasks.

The main challenges include three aspects: the first is how to deal with task failures caused by unreliable volunteer computing node failures, and the second is how to store the input data, the intermediate data and the final results for MapReduce applications, and the third is how to achieve MapReduce task scheduling.

To solve the above problems, we proposed HybridMR, a new MapReduce implementation for hybrid computing environment. Similar to the design of Hadoop, HybridMR is also decomposed into two layers, namely, data storage layer and MapReduce task scheduling and execution layer. First, a hybrid storage system called HybridDFS composed of cluster nodes and volunteer nodes is implemented, then MapReduce task scheduling is implemented. In order to solve the volatility of volunteer nodes, we designed and implemented a node fault-tolerance mechanism based on the "heartbeat" and time-out method. Furthermore, an optimized scheduler taking into account performance differences between cluster nodes and volunteer desktop nodes is also implemented.

2   Background and Related Work

2.1   MapReduce

MapReduce model borrows some ideas from functional programming. MapReduce applications are based on a master-slave model. A MapReduce system includes two basic computing units, Map and Reduce. The MapReduce programming model allows the user to define a Map function and a Reduce function to realize large-scale data processing and analyzing. In the first step, input data are divided into chunks and distributed in a distributed file system, such as HDFS, GFS. In the second step, Mapper nodes apply the Map function on each file chunk. Then, the Partition phase achieves splitting the keys space on Mapper node, so that each Reducer node gets a part of the key space. This is typically done by applying a hash function to the keys although programmers can define their own partition function. The new data produced are called the intermediate results. In short, the Map function processes a (key, value) pair and returns a list of intermediate (key, value) pairs:

$$map(k1, v1) \rightarrow list(k2, v2). \tag{1}$$

During the Shuffle phase, intermediate results are sent to their corresponding Reducer. In the Reduce phase, Reducer nodes apply the Reduce function to merge all intermediate values having the same intermediate key:

$$reduce(k2, list(v2)) \rightarrow list(v3). \tag{2}$$

At the end, all the results can be assembled and sent back to the master node, and this is the Combine phase.

2.2 MapReduce on Non-dedicated Computing Resources

Besides the original MapReduce implementation by Google [4], several other MapReduce implementations have been realized within other systems. Some focused on providing more efficient implementations of MapReduce components, such as the scheduler [13] and the I/O system, while others focused on adapting the MapReduce model to specific computing environments, like shared-memory systems, graphics processors, multi-core systems, volunteer computing environments and Desktop Grids [12].

BitDew-MapReduce proposed by Tang et al. [12] is specifically designed to support MapReduce applications in Desktop Grids, and exploits the BitDew middleware [5], which is a programmable environment for automatic and transparent data management on Desktop Grid, Grid and Cloud. BitDew relies on a specific set of metadata to drive key data management operations, namely life cycle, distribution, placement, replication and fault-tolerance with a high level of abstraction.

Marozzo et al. [10] proposed P2P-MapReduce which exploits a peer-to-peer model to manage node churn, master failures, and job recovery in a decentralized but effective way, so as to provide a more reliable MapReduce middleware that can be effectively exploited in dynamic Cloud infrastructures.

Another similar work is VMR [3], a volunteer computing system able to run MapReduce applications on top of volunteer resources, spread throughout the Internet. VMR leverages users bandwidth through the use of inter-client communication, and uses a lightweight task validation mechanism.

Another system that shares some of the key ideas with HybridMR is MOON [8]. It is a system designed to support MapReduce jobs on opportunistic environments. It extends Hadoop with adaptive task and data scheduling algorithms to offer reliable MapReduce services on a hybrid resource architecture.

There are also some work about using node availability prediction method to enable Hadoop running on unreliable Desktop Grid or using non-dedicated computing resources [6] [7].

3   System Architecture

In this section we describe the architecture of HybridMR. First, we present an overview of the system, then we focus on the algorithms and implementation of the main components of HybridMR and we highlight the main scheduling algorithm.

3.1   General Overview

HybridMR is composed of reliable cluster nodes and volatile desktop PCs, which is simple but effective. MapReduce applications can be run in this hybrid environment to analyze and process large amounts of datasets. The architecture of proposed hybrid MapReduce computing system is shown in Fig. 1.

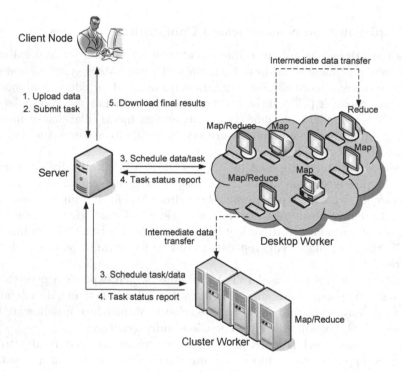

Fig. 1. Architecture of hybrid MapReduce computing system

As is shown in Fig. 1, the system is designed with a hierarchical architecture. The top layer is the user layer, and the middle layer is the service layer, and the bottom layer is the resource layer. Four different service components are implemented in service layer, namely, data storage service, metadata service, data scheduler service, Map/Reduce task scheduler service. Resource layer contains two types of resource: the first is reliable cluster nodes (Cluster Workers), and the second is large number of unreliable volunteer nodes (Desktop Workers), which join the system in a voluntary way. These two types of resource are both computing and storage resources,

Similar to existing MapReduce systems, data storage layer and MapReduce task scheduling layer are also separated in our proposed model. The proposed model relies on a hybrid distributed file system, called HybridDFS, which can also be run independently as a sub-component. HybridDFS has similar characteristics with HDFS and GFS that data are stored in block. The difference is that HybridDFS defines two different types of data storage nodes, the reliable cluster nodes and unreliable volunteer nodes. To sum up, in our proposed model we implemented:

- *ClientNode*, provides interface to access data and submit jobs;
- *NameNode*, provides metadata services;
- *DataNode*, provides data storage services;
- *WorkerNode*, provides Map/Reduce task computing services;
- *TrackerNode*, provides Map/Reduce task monitoring services.

Among them, DataNode and WorkerNode can be deployed in cluster nodes or volunteer nodes, while NameNode and TrackerNode can only be configured in server. The main working principle of the system is shown as follows:

- **Step 1:** ClientNode uploads input data that will be analyzed and processed to HybridDFS;
- **Step 2:** ClientNode submits task, specifying the data stored in HybridDFS which will be processed;
- **Step 3:** Scheduled by data scheduler and MapReduce scheduler, the Map tasks and Reduce tasks are allocated to cluster nodes and volunteer nodes. In the meanwhile, MapReduce scheduler controls the transmission of intermediate data;
- **Step 4:** Cluster nodes and volunteer nodes regularly send "heartbeat" signals to MapReduce scheduler to report task status;
- **Step 5:** Once all of the tasks have completed, ClientNode can download final results from HybridDFS.

3.2 Design Overview of HybridDFS

In HybridDFS, each node contributes a certain space to store files. As we can see in Fig. 2, large file is first separated into chunks, then all chunks stored in different locations. As volunteer nodes are volatile, the chunks stored in volunteer nodes may become unavailable. Therefore, replication approach is utilized to achieve fault-tolerance.

HybridDFS is designed to support large files. A file is split into one or more blocks and these blocks are stored in a set of DataNodes. All blocks in a file except the last block are the same size. The blocks of a file are replicated for fault-tolerance. The block size and replication factor are configurable per file, and a typical block size is 64 MB. Users or applications can define the replication

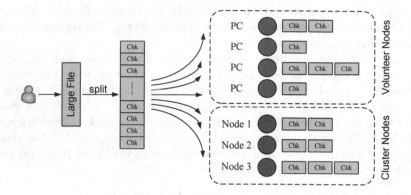

Fig. 2. The principle of file separation and storage for large files in HybridDFS

factor $Rs{:}Rv$ at file creation time in HybridDFS, where Rs means the number of replicas of the file stored in cluster nodes, and Rv means the number of replicas of the file stored in volunteer nodes. For example, 1:2 means storing one copy in cluster nodes, and two copies in volunteer nodes at the same time.

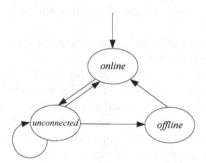

Fig. 3. Node status migration chart

Unlike previous systems, HybridDFS doesn't differentiate transient failure from permanent failure particularly [11]. We define three node statuses: *online*, *offline*, and *unconnected*, and the status migration chart is shown in Fig. 3. Different with others which usually consider the status *dead*, there is a special *unconnected* status. The failure detection is achieved by the method of periodically synchronization ("heartbeat"). It uses a simple timeout threshold approach to detect both short-term failure and long-term failure. We define two thresholds in this model: Synchronization Interval Time (SIT) and Failure Timeout Time (FTT). If the failure timeout period has expired, a node failure is detected (that becomes *offline*). In order to tolerate node failures, especially the volunteer node failures, HybridDFS uses a *Timeout* method to detect node failures.

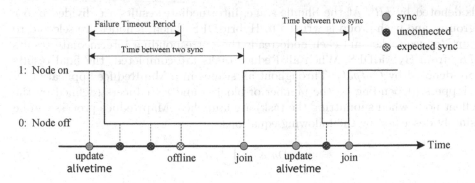

Fig. 4. Node synchronization and timeout-based node failure detection method. The detailed migration of three situations: 1) node migration from *online* to *offline*; 2) node migration from *offline* to *online*; 3) re-join (recover) in a short-time from *unconnected* to *online*.

As the response of "heartbeat" report, the replicas of file blocks are distributed to different volunteer PCs or cluster nodes.

Volatile nodes declare their availability to the system through periodical synchronization (an interval of SIT) with the server. During each synchronization, the value of variable *alivetime* is updated to the current time. If the difference between the value of variable *alivetime* and the current time exceeds FTT, this node becomes *offline*. The detailed migration of three situations are demonstrated in Fig. 4. The green dots stand for periodically node synchronization or node joining to the system, and there is also a updating of the variable *alivetime* associated with each green dot. The blue dots stand for *unconnected*, while the red dots stand for *offline* which means an node failure is detected. Both the blue dots and red dots indicate that a node synchronization is expected, because the node has already lost the communication with the server.

MapReduce applications demand advanced requirements for HybridDFS. HybridDFS acts as the data storage layer, while storage nodes should also run MapReduce tasks. HybridDFS encapsulates methods and interfaces, which allow MapReduce applications get to know how the data is separated, and the physical location of blocks can be queried, and the tasks are scheduled to storage nodes by MapReduce scheduler.

3.3 MapReduce Algorithm and Implementation

The client submits the job that specifies the data to be processed which has already been stored in HybridDFS. By calling HybridDFS API interface, data blocking method and the physical storage location of each data block are obtained. According to the file replication attributes $Rs:Rv$, one copy of each data block in chosen to run Map task. The large data to be analyzed and processed is denoted by *Data*, which is divided into n blocks, and each block is denoted by d_i. The intermediate results for selected blocks when Map task completed is denoted by IR^i. At the Shuffle stage, intermediate results are divided into r groups, and each group is written to HybridDFS. Then, r nodes are selected to run Reduce tasks, and each node reads the corresponding intermediate results IR_j from HybridDFS. When all Reduce tasks are completed, the final results are denoted by $Output_j$. Throughout all stages in a MapReduce application, n Mappers (depending on the number of blocks) and r Reducers (defined by the client node when submitting the task) are launched. MapReduce process can be simply described by the following equations:

$$Data = \bigcup_{i=1:n} d_i \tag{3}$$

$$Map(Data) = \bigcup_{i=1:n} Map(d_i) \tag{4}$$

$$Map(d_i) = \bigcup_{j=1:r} IR_j^i \tag{5}$$

$$Reduce(\bigcup_{i=1:n} IR_j^i) = Output_j \tag{6}$$

In designing the runtime of HybridMR, the general fast/slow nodes detection and fast/slow tasks detection approaches are not fit for this hybrid heterogenous environment, because CPU speed of cluster nodes are always faster than desktop PCs. In existing MapReduce computing models for desktop grid environment, such as BitDew-MapReduce [12], the FIFO scheduling policy is usually employed when processing "heartbeat" report, that the data chunks are assigned in the order that "heartbeat" arrived, without other biases or preferences. In HybridMR implementation, we developed a new node priority-based fair scheduling (NPBFS) algorithm. In the hybrid heterogenous environment, hardware configurations of WorkerNodes or DataNodes are diverse, which proposes an urgent need of a fair algorithm that the node with stronger computing capability should process more jobs.

Therefore, using NPBFS algorithm, the objective is to achieve two kinds of balance in HybridMR: data placement balance (adaptively balances the amount of data stored in each node considering storage capability of each node) and job assignment balance (adaptively balances the task queue length in each node considering computing capability of each node). In HybridMR implementation, job priority isn't considered, instead we focus on node priority, and developed a node rank method considering the hardware configurations. We quantify CPU speed, memory size, network and disk I/O bandwidth, then calculate the R_{weight} for each DataNode and WorkerNode, according to the equations as follows:

$$R_{capacity} = \alpha * R_{cpu} * R_{core} + \beta R_{mem} + \delta R_{bandwidth} \tag{7}$$

$$R_{storageload} = \sum_i (BlockNum[i].datasize) \tag{8}$$

$$R_{workload} = \sum_i (TaskNum[i].datasize) \qquad (9)$$

$$R_{weight} = \frac{R_{workload} + R_{storageload}}{R_{capacity}} \qquad (10)$$

where α, β, and δ are three weight coefficients used to quantify node capacity, and $R_{storageload}$ denotes the total size of chunk stored in a DataNode, and $R_{workload}$ denotes the total size of data to be processed by Map tasks and Reduce tasks in a WorkerNode, so the value of $R_{workload}$ reflects approximatively the length of task queue. Both cluster nodes and desktop PCs are usually configured as DataNode and WorkerNode simultaneously, therefore we use R_{weight} to measure the degree of balance between capacity and load in heterogeneous environment. When a node sends the "heartbeat" report, the updated R_{weight} value is capsulated in the report. The server receives and stores all R_{weight} value, and all nodes are then sorted by their R_{weight} value. A smaller value of R_{weight} means a higher node priority, and therefore more jobs should be assigned to it, or more file chunks should be placed on it. In this algorithm, R_{cpu} is measured in GHz, and R_{mem} is measured in GB, while $R_{bandwidth}$ is measured in 100Mbps. Both $BlockNum[i].datasize$ and $TaskNum[i].datasize$ are measured in GB.

We define a threshold Th_{weight} to distinguish overloaded nodes as follow,

$$Th_{weight} = \xi \left[\max(R_{weight}[j]) - \min(R_{weight}[j])\right] + \min(R_{weight}[j]) \qquad (11)$$

where ξ is an adjustment factor. When a node sends the "heartbeat", if $R_{weight} > Th_{weight}$, the server must stop placing new chunks or allocating new Map/Reduce tasks to this overloaded node; otherwise, it means that this is not an overloaded node which can accept more jobs.

4 Performance Evaluation

4.1 Platform Description

The prototype system of HybridMR is implemented by Java. In order to evaluate the performance, we performed our experiments in the campus local area network environment, and hadoop-0.21.0 is used for comparison. Both HybridMR and Hadoop ran on Ubuntu Linux system. In order to evaluate NPBFS algorithm, the parameters are set to empirical values. Three weight coefficients α, β, and δ are set to 0.4, 0.2, 0.4, respectively, and the value of adjustment factor ξ is 0.6. Our experimental hardware platforms are described as follows:

(1) Both the NameNode and TrackerNode are configured with Xeon E5-2603 Quad-Core 1.8GHz CPU, 4GB memory, and 1Gbps ethernet.

(2) We used 24 cluster nodes, and each node is configured with AMD Opteron 8378 Quad-Core 2.4GHz CPU, 8GB memory, and 1Gbps ethernet.

(3) In the students' laboratory, we used 72 desktop PCs, configured with Intel Core 2 Duo E6300 1.86GHz CPU, 1GB memory, and 100Mbps ethernet for each.

4.2 Throughput of HybridDFS I/O

We have implemented a set of micro-benchmarks, and have measured the achieved throughput as more and more concurrent clients access HybridDFS. Since that MapReduce applications need the "write-once-read-many" model, we evaluated the I/O performance when a single client writes data and concurrent clients read data. We also compared HybridDFS with HDFS.

Scenario 1: Single Writer, Single File. We first measure the performance of HybridDFS when a single client writes a file whose size gradually increases. The size of data chunks in HybridDFS is 64 MB. This test consists in sequentially writing a unique file of $N*64$ MB(N goes from 1 to 192). Block allocation is also based on the node priority-based fair scheduling policy which is explained before, in order to achieve placing data across DataNodes in balance. We measure the time spend for file separation and file distribution, and then calculate the write throughput. We measure the write throughput in three conditions:

- HybridDFS - 24 cluster nodes and 72 desktop PCs;
- HDFS - 24 cluster nodes and 72 desktop PCs;
- HDFS - 24 cluster nodes only.

The results can be seen on Fig. 5(a). The value of SIT and FTT are set to 10s and 30s, respectively. The file replication attribute setting is $Rs:Rv$=1:2, which means that storing one copy in cluster nodes and two copies in desktop nodes. Therefore, the total number of blocks of a large file stored in HybridDFS is $N*3$. As the file size increases, the change of throughput is very tiny. Obviously, we obtain the worst results when only 24 cluster nodes are used, and HDFS achieves higher throughput than HybridDFS when 24 cluster nodes and 72 desktop PCs are used. Because HybridDFS uses NPBFS to realize storage balance, it delays the write client, that is the main reason why HybridDFS is inferior.

Scenario 2: Concurrent Readers, Shared File. In this scenario, N clients read parts from the file concurrently; each client reads different 64 MB chunks. This pattern where multiple readers request data is very common in the "map" phase of a Hadoop MapReduce application, where the mappers read the input file in order to parse (key, value) pairs. When a single client finished writing a file of 192*64 MB to HybridDFS, for each given number N of clients varying from 1 to 192, we executed the experiments and calculated the average throughput. The total size of chunks read by N clients is exactly 192*64 MB. Fig. 5(b) shows the results of average throughput of concurrent read clients. When the number of concurrent clients is more than 64, less than 3 chunks are allocated to each client in average. As the increase of concurrent read clients, the metadata query load and data traffic increases, which causes a decrease of average throughput. The same as Scenario 1, HDFS also outperforms HybridDFS when 24 cluster nodes and 72 desktop PCs are used, but there is only little difference between average throughput of HybridDFS and HDFS. HybridDFS reaches a relatively high throughput.

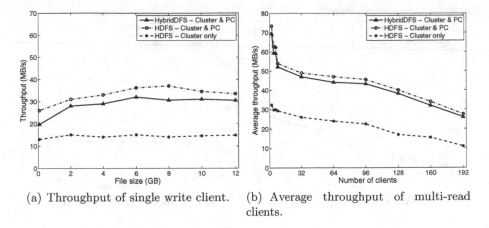

(a) Throughput of single write client.   (b) Average throughput of multi-read clients.

Fig. 5. Throughput of HybridDFS I/O

4.3 MapReduce Job Completion Time

In order to evaluate how well HybridDFS performs in the role of storage layer for real MapReduce applications, we select two standard MapReduce applications *WordCount* (reads text files and counts how often words occur) and *Distributed Grep* (extracts matching strings from text files and counts how many times they occurred). For these two applications, the chunk size of input text files is still 64 MB.

We evaluated MapReduce job completion time as the size of input text file changes. The same as read/write throughput evaluation, in order to compare HybridMR with Hadoop, we also measured three conditions.

The results for WordCount and Distributed Grep are shown in Fig. 6(a) and 6(b), respectively. The maximal size of text file is 12 GB in our experiments. Distributed Grep application has a different MapReduce pattern compared with WordCount application. For WordCount application, the Reduce stage is complex, and takes more time than the Map stage. For Distributed Grep application, the Reduce stage is very simple, and it just collects and sums up the intermediate results. As you can see from these two figures, as the increase of input text file size, job completion time also increases. From these two figures, we can see that there is also only little performance difference between HybridDFS and HDFS.

4.4 Scheduler Optimization

In this scenario, experiments on WordCount application and Distributed Grep application have also been performed to testify the efficiency of the node priority-based fair scheduling (NPBFS) algorithm. We also evaluated job completion time, while we compared two scheduling policies: 1) using NPBFS scheduler; 2) not using NPBFS scheduler. We measure how many performance improvements are caused by NPBFS scheduler. If the NPBFS scheduler is not used, the server

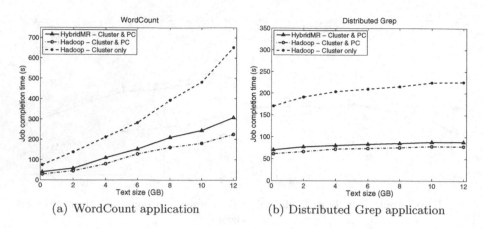

(a) WordCount application   (b) Distributed Grep application

Fig. 6. Job completion time for WordCount and Distributed Grep

doesn't consider any information or attributes of nodes and all nodes are treated equally, which may cause the problem that assigning a lot of tasks to slow desktop PCs. HybridMR is deployed on 24 cluster nodes and 72 desktop PCs, then we run WordCount and Distributed Grep again, and measure the job completion time, varying the input text file size from 2 GB to 10 GB. The results are shown in Fig. 7(a) and 7(b), respectively. These two figures indicate that NPBFS scheduler improves the whole system and makes it more balanced, decreases the overall job response time. When the text file size is 10 GB, the performance improvement is 26.6% for WordCount, while it is 19.9% for Distributed Grep.

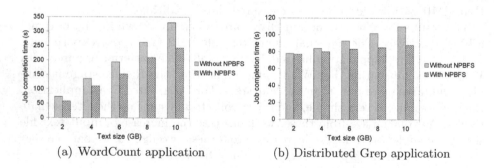

(a) WordCount application   (b) Distributed Grep application

Fig. 7. Performance improvements when the node priority-based fair scheduling policy is used

4.5 Fault-Tolerance

In this scenario, we compare HybridMR with Hadoop in terms of fault-tolerance performance, in order to justify the robustness of HybridMR. We emulate node crashes through generating failures by randomly selecting desktop PCs and killing the MapReduce process, during the MapReduce tasks execution period. Failures are independents and occur sequentially. During the experiment, both Hadoop and HybridMR are deployed on a hybrid environment composed of 24 cluster nodes and 72 desktop PCs. We run the WordCount and Distributed Grep, which represents two different realistic situations, and the input text file size is 12 GB. The results are shown in Fig. 8(a) and 8(b), respectively.

When the number of failures injected are varied from 10 to 40, we measure the job completion time, which are then compared with the normal situation that without any failures. The interval between two failure injections is 60s. We observe that HybridMR outperforms Hadoop in terms of fault-tolerance performance. Compared with the normal situation, in the worst situation that 40 nodes are crashed, for WordCount application, the job completion time increases by around 252.7% for Hadoop and only 43.8% for HybridMR; for Distributed Grep application, it increases by around 313.8% for Hadoop and only 127.1% for HybridMR. The improvement of HybridMR over Hadoop in terms of fault-tolerance performance is quite clear when the number of failure injected is beyond 30. This reveals the robustness of HybridMR, which can accept a large number of faults with reasonable performance overhead.

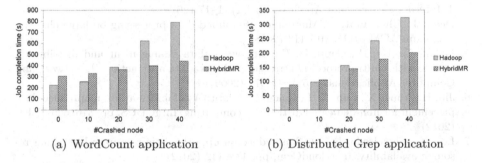

(a) WordCount application   (b) Distributed Grep application

Fig. 8. Fault-tolerance performance comparison between HybridMR and Hadoop

5   Conclusion

This paper presented a MapReduce parallel model for data-intensive computing in dynamic hybrid computing environments, integrating the idle desktop PC resources in the Internet or Intranet with high reliable and high performance cluster nodes to form a hybrid computing environment. The proposed new MapReduce model consists of HybridDFS layer, a new hybrid distributed file system, and MapReduce task scheduling layer. Data replication and replacement mechanism are utilized to guarantee the reliability of storage and computing. Security issues will be considered in the future. Performance test results show that the new model is not only able to achieve a higher throughput and efficiency, but also able to achieve the "green computing" goal. Companies and schools can leverage existing idle desktop PC resources running MapReduce job for massive data analysis, and the proposed method also reduces the computational cost overhead, which has a great potential.

Acknowledgments. This work is supported by the French Agence Nationale de la Recherche through the MapReduce grant under contract ANR-10-SEGI-001-01, as well as INRIA ARC BitDew. This work is also supported by Scientific Research Fund of Hunan Provincial Education Department under grant no. 12C0121, Hunan University of Science and Technology Research Fund under grant no. E51097.

References

1. Anderson, D.P.: Boinc: A system for public-resource computing and storage. In: Buyya, R. (ed.) GRID, pp. 4–10. IEEE Computer Society (2004)
2. Cappello, F., Djilali, S., Fedak, G., Hérault, T., Magniette, F., Néri, V., Lody-gensky, O.: Computing on large-scale distributed systems: Xtremweb architecture, programming models, security, tests and convergence with grid. Future Generation Comp. Syst. 21(3), 417–437 (2005)
3. Costa, F., Veiga, L., Ferreira, P.: Internet-scale support for map-reduce processing. J. Internet Services and Applications 4(1), 1–17 (2013)
4. Dean, J., Ghemawat, S.: Mapreduce: Simplified data processing on large clusters. Commun. ACM 51(1), 107–113 (2008)
5. Fedak, G., He, H., Cappello, F.: Bitdew: A data management and distribution service with multi-protocol file transfer and metadata abstraction. J. Network and Computer Applications 32(5), 961–975 (2009)
6. Jin, H., Yang, X., Sun, X.H., Raicu, I.: Adapt: Availability-aware mapreduce data placement for non-dedicated distributed computing. In: ICDCS, pp. 516–525. IEEE (2012)
7. Lee, K., Figueiredo, R.J.O.: Mapreduce on opportunistic resources leveraging resource availability. In: CloudCom, pp. 435–442 (2012)
8. Lin, H., Ma, X., Chun Feng, W.: Reliable mapreduce computing on opportunistic resources. Cluster Computing 15(2), 145–161 (2012)
9. Litzkow, M.J., Livny, M., Mutka, M.W.: Condor - a hunter of idle workstations. In: ICDCS, pp. 104–111 (1988)
10. Marozzo, F., Talia, D., Trunfio, P.: P2P-Mapreduce: Parallel data processing in dynamic cloud environments. J. Comput. Syst. Sci. 78(5), 1382–1402 (2012)
11. Tang, B., Fedak, G.: Analysis of data reliability tradeoffs in hybrid distributed storage systems. In: IPDPS Workshops, pp. 1546–1555. IEEE Computer Society (2012)
12. Tang, B., Moca, M., Chevalier, S., He, H., Fedak, G.: Towards mapreduce for desktop grid computing. In: Xhafa, F., Barolli, L., Nishino, H., Aleksy, M. (eds.) 3PGCIC, pp. 193–200. IEEE Computer Society (2010)
13. Zaharia, M., Konwinski, A., Joseph, A.D., Katz, R.H., Stoica, I.: Improving mapreduce performance in heterogeneous environments. In: Draves, R., van Renesse, R. (eds.) OSDI, pp. 29–42. USENIX Association (2008)

Fast Scalable k-means++ Algorithm
with MapReduce

Yujie Xu[1], Wenyu Qu[1], Zhiyang Li[1], Changqing Ji[1,2],
Yuanyuan Li[1,3], and Yinan Wu[4]

[1] School of Information Science and Techology,
Dalian Maritime University, Dalian, China, 116026
{yujiex.dlmu,eunice.qu,lizy0205}@gmail.com
[2] School of Physical Science and Technology,
Dalian University, Dalian, China, 116622
jcqgood@gmail.com
[3] School of Software,
Dalian Jiaotong University, Dalian, China, 116028
lyy3232312@sohu.com
[4] Department of Equipment, Unit 91550 of PLA,
Dalian, China, 116023
wyn03021w@163.com

Abstract. K-means++ is undoubtedly one of the most important initializing algorithms for k-means owing to its provable approximation guarantee to the optimal solution. However, due to its sequential nature, k-means++ requires a large number of iterations to complete the initialization and it becomes inefficient as the size of data increase. Even though scalable k-means++ can drastically reduce the iterations and can be easily applied to the MapReduce systems, but due to its sequential nature, it still requires two MapReduce jobs in each round. Moreover, it takes a large number of I/O cost and it is time-consuming. In this paper, we propose Oversampling and Refining (OnR) method which can improve efficiency of scalable k-means++ by using only one MapReduce job to obtain $\Omega(k)$ centers in each round. Except for the oversampling factor ℓ of scalable k-means++, OnR uses another oversampling factor o to further increase the number of chosen centers. Oversampling is executed on the Mapper phase, and in Reducer phase, one Reducer is responsible for removing the oversampled centers generated from o and outputs a set of centers which is the same as the output of scalable k-means++. To reduce the expensive network cost caused by too large o, OnR estimates the global cost by the local clustering cost and uses it to remove some wrong points in Mapper phase. Extensive experiments on real data are conducted and the performance results indicate that OnR outperforms scalable k-means++ in the aspect of I/O cost and running time.

1 Introduction

Clustering has been applied in many areas of computer science and its related fields, such as data mining, pattern recognition and image retrieval [1–4]. K-means

X.-h. Sun et al. (Eds.): ICA3PP 2014, Part II, LNCS 8631, pp. 15–28, 2014.
© Springer International Publishing Switzerland 2014

is one of the most widely used clustering methods, but it suffers from the well-known problem that converges to a local optimum. Due to the reason that it is highly dependent upon the chosen of initial centers. In recent years, many researches have focused on improving its initialization method [5,6]. An important piece of work in this direction is the k-means++ [7]. This algorithm is fast with small data in practice. Moreover, it obtains an $O(logk)$ approximation solution to the optimal result of k-means and gives a theoretical guarantee firstly.

However, the era of big data poses new challenges for k-means++ algorithm. Although it can be run on the MapReduce [8], and there are also many clustering algorithms [9–12] run on MapReduce platform efficiently in practice, k-means++ is an exception. The fundamental reason is that k-means++ is a sequential algorithm and it is lack of scalability. That is the probability a point is chosen to be a center strongly depends on the previous centers. K-means++ algorithm chooses one center in each round and it needs k rounds over the data to produce the expected initial centers. This requires many iterative computations. For a single computer, iterative computation is common and it is easily implemented. While for the MapReduce framework, it does not directly support these iterative data analysis applications. Instead, we must implement iterative programs by manually issuing multiple MapReduce jobs and this renders the data must be re-loaded and re-processed at each iteration, wasting I/O, network and CPU resources [13,14].

To reduce the number of rounds of k-means++, Bahman Bahmani et al. proposed scalable k-means++ algorithm [15]. We show it in Section 3 in more detail. It is a parallel version of the inherently sequential k-means++. Instead of choosing one point in each round, scalable k-means++ uses the oversampling method to choose $\ell = \Omega(k)$ points. Hence, it can drastically reduce the iteration rounds from k to approximate $O(log\psi)$. Scalable k-means++ enhances the scalability of k-means++ and it is easily paralleled in MapReduce framework. Another merit of it is that it achieves an $O(logk)$ approximation to the k-means objective.

However, scalable k-means++ does not thoroughly break the inherent sequential nature of k-means++. Thus, it is embarrassingly parallel and can not be executed on MapReduce-based systems efficiently. Considering that there is no communication between Mappers, MapReduce scalable k-means++ requires two MapReduce jobs to complete in each round. The first job chooses ℓ centers and combines them. The second one is responsible for computing the clustering cost. Therefore, it has to iterate $O(log\psi)$ rounds and at least $2 * O(log\psi)$ MapReduce jobs to choose the initial centers. As mentioned above, MapReduce does not directly support iterative analysis applications, when $log\psi$ is large, it is time-consuming and we cannot put up with so many MapReduce jobs. In addition, it incurs large amount of network and I/O overhead.

This paper proposes an efficient parallel scalable k-means++ algorithm which is called Oversampling and Refining (OnR) in the situation of big data by virtue of MapReduce. The main idea of OnR is to use only one MapReduce job, instead of two jobs, to complete the task of choosing new centers and computing clustering cost. For lack of communication in Mapper phase, we could not compute the total clustering cost of the centers chosen from the previous round in Mapper phase, thus each Mapper chooses centers with the clustering cost of the centers chosen from before the previous round. Since this clustering cost is smaller than the real value, except for oversampling factor ℓ, OnR uses another oversampling factor o to further increase the number of points in Mapper phase. Since, each Mapper has obtained the centers chosen from the previous round, another important work of each Mapper is to calculate the local clustering cost of these centers. In Reducer phase, one Reducer adds all local clustering cost, and uses it to remove the oversampled points generated from o.

The major contributions of this paper are:

1. We propose Oversampling and Refing method which is an efficient scalable k-means++ algorithm with MapReduce. It uses only one MapReduce job to complete the task of choosing centers and computing clustering cost in each round, avoiding too many jobs on multiple machines and thus reducing a large number of I/O cost.
2. To reduce the network cost and the running time caused by too large oversampling factor o, our method OnR estimates the global cost by the local clustering cost and uses it to remove some oversampling points in Mapper phase. This measure also reduces the workload of Reducer.
3. Extensive experiments on real data are conducted. Comparing with scalable k-means++, experimental results indicate that without increasing the network cost, OnR reduces a large amount of I/O cost. It also saves more than 50% time and provides a good approximation to k-means.

The rest of this paper is organized as follows. Section 2 presents the useful preliminaries. The details of our method are discussed in Section 3, where we first describe MapReduce scalable k-means++ algorithm in Section 3.1, and then present Oversampling and Refining method int Section Section 3.2. Finally, we give some discussion and analysis in Section 3.3. Section 4 reports the experimental results. Finally, Section 5 concludes the paper.

2   Preliminaries

To provide a technical context for the discussion in this paper, we begin with preliminaries. First, we give the definition of clustering cost. Then, we describe the scalable k-means++ algorithm in more detail.

Given a data set $X = \{x_1, x_2, ..., x_n\}$ in d-dimensional space and let $||x_i - x_j||$ denote the Euclidean distance between x_i and x_j, the centers set $C = \{c_1, ..., c_k\}$ divides X into k exhaustive clusters and the following function is the clustering cost.

$$\phi_X(C) = \sum_{x \in X} \min_{c \in C} ||x - c||^2$$

Scalable k-means++ [15] modifies the initialization setup of k-means++ [7] and obtains an efficient parallel version. Seeing the following algorithm, instead of choosing one point as a center, it uses the oversampling method and chooses $\ell = \Omega(k)$ centers in each round. Firstly, it uniformly at random chooses an initial center and computes the initial clustering cost ψ of this center. Then, this method iterates $O(log\psi)$ times. In each iteration, given the current set C of centers, each point x is chosen to be a center with probability $\ell * d^2(x, C)/\phi_X(C)$. The sampled points are then added to C. Finally, the algorithm updates $\phi_X(C)$ and the iteration continues. Since the number of chosen points is more than k (the expected number of points in C is $\ell * O(log\psi)$) after the $O(log\psi)$ iterations, it uses a weighted k-means++ to obtain the final k centers.

Algorithm 1. Scalable k-means++ Initialization

Input : k, the number of clusters.

$X = \{x_1, x_2, \ldots, x_n\}$, a set of data points.

ℓ, oversampling factor

Output: $C = \{c_1, c_2, ..., c_k\}$.

1 $C \leftarrow$ sample a point uniformly at random from X

2 $\psi \leftarrow \phi_X(C)$

3 **for** $O(log\psi)$ **times do**

4   C' sample each point $x \in X$ independently with probability

    $p_x = \frac{\ell d^2(x,C)}{\phi_X(C)}$

5      $C \leftarrow C \cup C'$, compute $\phi_X(C)$

6 For $x \in C$, set w_x to be the number of points in X closer to x than any other point in C

7 Recluster the weighted points in C into k clusters

---

3 Our Method

In this section, we first introduce the Parallel Scalable k-means++ with MapReduce (PSKM++), and then present our improved version of PSKM++, Oversampling and Refining (OnR). Finally, we give some discussion and analysis about OnR. Table 1 shows the symbols and definitions used in this section.

3.1 Parallel Scalable k-means++ with MapReduce

The parallel scalable k-means++ algorithm has two steps: (1) computing the initial cost ψ, (2) iterative process. A MapReduce job has at least two modules: Map and Reduce. PSKM++ algorithm partitions the input data through the Mapper phase and merges centers and clustering cost in the Reducer phase.

Figure 1 illustrates the process of parallel scalable k-means++ with MapReduce. It starts with the first MapReduce job (Job1) from phase **P1** to **P3** and it is used to compute the initial clustering cost ψ. In phase **P1**, each Mapper reads the input data X_i and the first random center c_1, then computes the squared distance between each point $x \in X_i$ and c_1, $d^2(x, c_1)$, finally outputs

Table 1. Symbols and Definitions

Symbols	Definitions
X	The set of all data points
X_i	The set of data points processed by Mapper i
c_1	The first center chosen uniformly at random
C_i	Centers chosen from Mapper i
U_0	$U_0 = \{c_1\}$
U_j	The union of centers until jth iteration
$\phi_{X_i}(U_0)$	Clustering cost computed by Mapper i with centers U_0, i.e., $\phi_{X_i}(c_1)$
$\phi_X(U_0)$	Clustering cost with centers U_0, i.e., $\phi_X(c_1)$ and ψ (seeing in Alg. 1)
$\phi_{X_i}(U_j)$	Clustering cost computed by Mapper i with centers U_j
$\phi_X(U_j)$	clustering cost computed by one Reducer with centers U_j

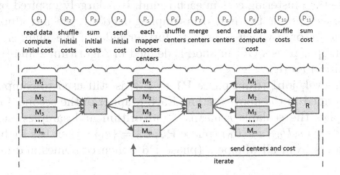

Fig. 1. Parallel Scalable k-means++ with MapReduce

$\langle$key, $\phi_{X_i}(c_1)\rangle$. All elements are shuffled to the same Reducer in phase **P2**. The Reducer sums all $\phi_{X_i}(c_1)$ and outputs the $\phi_X(c_1)$, i.e., ψ. The iterative process includes Job2 (from phase **P4** to **P7**) and Job3 (from phase **P8** to **P11**). Job2 is used to choose new centers and Job3 is response for computing the clustering cost of this iteration. They correspond to the step 4 and step 5 in Algorithm 1 respectively. For jth iteration, the Mapper i of Job2 reads the input data X_i, the clustering cost $\phi_X(U_{j-1})$ and the centers U_{j-1} from the $(j-1)$th iteration, then chooses the point x as a center based on the probability $\ell * d^2(x, U_{j-1})/\phi_X(U_{j-1})$ (phase **P5**). All these centers are transferred to the same Reducer (phase **P6**) and combined by this Reducer (phase **P7**). Job3 is similar to Job1.

PSKM++ achieves the parallel of k-means++ and reduces the number of iterations from k to $O(log\psi)$. However, for the sequential relationship between Job2 and Job3, it still needs too many MapReduce jobs. Generally speaking, it requires at least $2 * O(log\psi)$ MapReduce jobs to choose the initial centers. When $log\psi$ is enormous, we cannot put up with so many MapReduce jobs. Furthermore, in the above section, we have shown that MapReduce does not directly support the iterative operation and the more MapReduce jobs the more cost. As shown in Figure 1, the network cost of PSKM++ is small and there is only $\bigcup_{i=1}^{m} C_i + \bigcup_{i=1}^{m} \phi_{X_i}(U_j)$ in each iteration, but the I/O cost is huge because the whole input has to read twice. In the next section, we present our improved scalable k-means++ algorithm that uses only one MapReduce job to choose centers and compute clustering cost in each iteration.

3.2   Oversampling and Refining

Since there is no communication among all Map tasks, one Map task can not see the centers chosen from other Map tasks, therefore it is impossible to compute the $\phi_{X_i}(U_j)$ in these Map tasks. It requires another MapReduce job to compute $\phi_X(U_j)$ after choosing new centers. In this section, we propose Oversampling and Refining method which uses only one MapReduce job to choose ℓ centers and compute the clustering cost in each round. It is largely inspired by scalable k-means++, except for the first oversampling factor ℓ, we introduce another oversampling factor o which is used to further enlarge the number of chosen centers in Mapper phase. Our method is defined in Algorithm 2 and the process is illustrated in Figure 2.

At a high-level, job1 (from phase **P1** to **P3**) is still used to compute ψ and we have described in the above section. Each Mapper of the second Job (phases **P4-P7**) applies the scalable k-means++ algorithm and samples each x with probability $\ell * d^2(x, U_0)/\phi_X(U_0)$ (phase **P5**, $U_0 = \{c_1\}$), then the Reducer reads the new centers from all Mappers (phase **P6**), then combines and outputs U_1 (phase **P7**).

The iterative process starts from phase **P8** to **P11**. For jth iteration, since each Mapper does not know the previous clustering cost $\phi_X(U_{j-1})$, our method chooses each x with the cost from $(j-2)$th iteration, i.e., $\phi_X(U_{j-2})$. However, because the number of centers of $(j-2)$th iteration is smaller than that of $(j-1)$th iteration, clustering cost $\phi_X(U_{j-2})$ is usually larger than the real value $\phi_X(U_{j-1})$ and the probability $\ell * d^2(x, U_{j-1})/\phi_X(U_{j-2})$ becomes smaller. This decreases the number of centers chosen in jth iteration. To address the above problem, our method uses another oversampling factor o to further enlarge the probability, i.e., the chosen probability of x is $p_x = o * \ell * d^2(x, U_{j-1})/\phi_X(U_{j-2})$. In this situation, the expected number of points chosen by all Mappers in each iteration is more than ℓ which is the expected number of points chosen by scalable

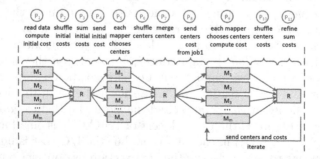

Fig. 2. Oversampling and Refing with MapReduce

k-means++ in each iteration. Thus, our method requires a refining method to remove the oversampled centers in Reducer phase.

Algorithm 2. Oversampling and Refining

Input: k, X, ℓ, o, c_1
Output: initialing centers
/* job 1: Computing ψ */
1 m Mappers read X in parallel and read $U_0 = c_1$. Each of them computes $\phi_{X_i}(U_0)$.
2 All costs $\phi_{X_i}(U_0)$ are shuffled to one Reducer.
3 One Reducer sums all $\phi_{X_i}(U_0)$.
4 Outputs $\psi = \phi_X(U_0)$.
   /* job 2: Oversampling   */
5 m Mappers read X in parallel and $\phi_X(U_0)$. Each of them chooses centers with $p_x = \ell * d^2(x, U_0)/\phi_X(U_0)$.
6 All centers C_i are shuffled to one Reducer.
7 One Reducer merges all the centers $C = \bigcup_{i=1}^{m} C_i$.
8 Outputs $U_1 = C \bigcup U_0$.
   /* iterative job   */
9 **for** $j = 2$; $j \leq \log \psi$; $j++$ **do**
       // Oversampling
10   m Mappers read X in parallel, U_{j-1} and $\phi_X(U_{j-2})$. Each of them chooses centers with $p_x = o * \ell * d^2(x, U_{j-1})/\phi_X(U_{j-2})$ and computes $\phi_{X_i}(U_{j-1})$.
11   All centers C_i, all costs $\phi_{X_i}(U_{j-1})$, p_x^r and $\ell * d^2(x, U_{j-1})$ for each new center are shuffled to one Reducer.
       // Refining by one Reducer
12   Computes $\phi_X(U_{j-1})$ and merges $C = \bigcup_{i=1}^{m} C_i$.
13   **if** $\ell * d^2(x, U_{j-1})/\phi_X(U_{j-1}) < p_x^r$ **then**
14   x is removed from C.
15   Output $U_j = C \bigcup U_{j-1}$ and $\phi_X(U_{j-1})$.
16 Output U_j

The detailed process is as follows. In phase **P9**, each Mapper uses p_x to choose new centers and compute the local real clustering cost $\phi_{X_i}(U_{j-1})$. Then, all the chosen centers C_i, all the local real clustering costs $\phi_{X_i}(U_{j-1})$, the random probability value p_x^r and $\ell * d^2(x, U_{j-1})$ of each chosen center are shuffled to one Reducer (phase **P10**). The refining operation is executed on a single Reducer (phase **p11**). It merges all centers $C = \bigcup_{i=1}^{m} C_i$, sums all local real clustering costs $\phi_{X_i}(U_{j-1})$ and obtains the global real clustering cost of $(j-1)$th iteration $\phi_X(U_{j-1})$. We also obtain the real probability for each chosen center, i.e., $p_x' = \ell * d^2(x, U_{j-1})/\phi_X(U_{j-1})$. If p_x' is still larger than p_x^r, then this center is still kept in C, otherwise, it is removed from C. The output of this iteration is U_j and $\phi_X(U_{j-1})$, then they become the input of the next iteration. As mentioned above, the network cost of OnR in each iteration includes 4 parts, all chosen centers $\bigcup_{i=1}^{m} C_i$, all local clustering costs $\bigcup_{i=1}^{m} \phi_{X_i}(U_{j-1})$, random value p_x^r and $\ell * d^2(x, U_{j-1})$ for each chosen center. Comparing with the network cost of PSKM++, i.e., $\bigcup_{i=1}^{m} C_i$ and $\bigcup_{i=1}^{m} \phi_{X_i}(U_j)$, the main benefit of OnR approach is that it dramatically reduces the I/O cost (read input data X only once), at the cost of shuffling a bit more data in each iteration.

3.3   Discussion

Except for ℓ, OnR uses another oversampling factor o to further enlarge the number of centers in Mapper phase. While the expected number of points is still ℓ after the refining phase in each iteration. Considering the jth iteration, OnR uses the probability $p_x = o_j * \ell * d^2(x, U_{j-1})/\phi_X(U_{j-2})$ to choose centers, while the real probability should be $p'_x = \ell * d^2(x, U_{j-1})/\phi_X(U_{j-1})$. Ideally, we expect that the centers chosen by OnR in each iteration are the same as that chosen by PSKM++. Meanwhile, the network cost is smallest. That is,

$$p_x = p'_x \tag{1}$$

and

$$\frac{o_j * \ell * d^2(x, U_{j-1})}{\phi_X(U_{j-2})} = \frac{\ell * d^2(x, U_{j-1})}{\phi_X(U_{j-1})} \tag{2}$$

Therefore, the optimal value of o_j is

$$o_j = \frac{\phi_X(U_{j-2})}{\phi_X(U_{j-1})} \tag{3}$$

The number of points in U_{j-2} contains is smaller than that in U_{j-1}, therefore $\phi_X(U_{j-2}) \geq \phi_X(U_{j-1})$ and $o_j \geq 1$. However, it is difficult to determine o exactly; if o is too large, there generates too many centers in each Mapper, causing high network cost and heavy workload of the Reducer; while o is set to a small value, the expected number of chosen centers in Reducer may be less than ℓ and the clustering quality is bad, i.e., $\phi_X(C)$ is large. In this section, we propose a method to solve this problem.

From the above analysis we know, each center chosen in Mapper phase will be resampled in Reducer phase. Ideally, for the smallest network cost, the best probability p_x^b of each center in the Mapper phase should be

$$p_x^b = \frac{d^2(x, U_{j-1})}{\phi_X(U_{j-1})} \tag{4}$$

For each point x, if $p_x^b > p_x^r$, it is chosen in Mapper phase. And in the Reducer phase, it is not removed from the result. Seeing From Eq. (4), in Mapper phase, for lack of communication, the global clustering cost $\phi_X(U_{j-1})$ is unknown, but we know the local clustering cost $\phi_{X_i}(U_{j-1})$. Thus, we use the following equation to estimate $\phi_X(U_{j-1})$.

$$\hat{\phi}_X(U_{j-1}) = \frac{n}{m} * \phi_{X_i}(U_{j-1}) \tag{5}$$

n is the total number of points X contains, m is the number of points processed by Mapper i. $\phi_{X_i}(U_{j-1})/m$ is the average clustering cost each point contributes and it is unbiased. Therefore, in the Mapper phase, no matter how large o is, our method can remove some of points with Eq. (5) in advance, and it can also reduce the network cost and Reducer workload of the Reducer.

4   Experiments

In this section, we present the experimental setup and experimental results for evaluating OnR. Note that the main merits of our method OnR are: (1) OnR reduces the number of rounds from $O(log\psi)$ to $0.5 * O(log\psi)$, thus OnR takes less running time when compared to PSKM++. (2) Although the number of points in Mapper phase of OnR is more than that of PSKM++, some of these points will be removed in Reducer phase of OnR and the result is the same as PSKM++. Thus, both of them has the same clustering cost. (3) By another oversampling factor o, OnR method uses only one MapReduce job in each round, therefore, OnR further reduces the I/O cost without increasing the network cost. (4) For there is a refining operation in Mapper phase and the large parallelism of Mapper phase, the running time and clustering cost of OnR are almost the same when o varies.

All experiments are performed on a homogeneous Hadoop cluster running the stable version of Hadoop 0.20.2. The cluster consists of 12 machines with 1 master node and 11 slave nodes. Each node has 2 AMD Opteron 2212 2.00 GHz CPUs, 8 GB of RAM, 80 GB SCSI HDD, Intel 82551 10/100 Mbps Ethernet Controller. The operating system of each node is Ubuntu 10.10 server 64 bit and per Hadoop daemon is allocated 1 GB memory. This cluster has 1 TaskTracker and 1 DataNode daemon running on each slave, and a single NameNode and JobTracker daemon on the master. All machines are directly connected to a 100 Mbps switch. We configure 2 Map slots and 2 Reduce slots on each node. The DFS chunk size is 64 MB.

We use Oxford Buildings DataSet to conduct the experiments. This is a real dataset consists of 5062 images collected from Filckr by searching for particular Oxford landmarks. A large number of 128-dimension SIFT features is extracted from each image and there are more than 17 million features in total. In order to speed up all the experiments, we only use 32-dimension data of each feature. Its size is about 2.6 GB and it is split to 42 chunks in our experiments.

The following aspects are evaluated in the experiments:

1. Running time of PSKM++ and OnR.
2. Clustering cost of PSKM++ and OnR.
3. I/O cost of PSKM++ and OnR.
4. Running time and Clustering cost of OnR while o varies.

4.1   Running Time

In this experiment, we compare the running time of PSKM++ and OnR algorithm. We now describe the parameter settings for this group experiments. o is set to 5, $k \in \{500, 1000\}$, $\ell \in \{0.1k, 0.5k, 1k, 2k, 5k, 10k\}$. We randomly choose one point and both PSKM++ and OnR use this point as the first center, therefore they have the same ℓ and the iteration round. In our experiments, both algorithms iterates $r = 12$ rounds. The results are summarized in Fig. 3 and we can see from it, no matter $k = 500$ and $k = 1000$, the running time of both PSKM++ and OnR is getting longer as ℓ varies from $0.1k$ to $10k$, but OnR takes less running time than PSKM++ and this trend gradually slows down. For example, when $\ell = 0.1k, 0.5k, 1k$, OnR saves more than 50% running time than PSKM++ for both $k = 500$ and $k = 1000$. The maximum time saving is about 58% when $\ell = 0.1k$ for both $k = 500$ and $k = 1000$. Furthermore, the running time of OnR is almost the same when ℓ varies from $0.1k$ to $1k$. However, when ℓ varies from $2k$ to $10k$, the number of chosen points in each round becomes larger and so does the the number of computation times. Thus, the time savings reduce and they are about 30%, 26%, 19% ($k = 500$) and 40%, 18%, 11% ($k = 1000$).

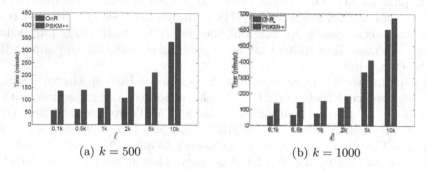

(a) $k = 500$ (b) $k = 1000$

Fig. 3. Running Time: $o = 5$, ℓ varies

4.2 Clustering Cost

In this section, we compare the clustering cost of PSKM++ and OnR. The parameter configuration is the same as the above experiment, i.e., $o = 5$, $k \in \{500, 1000\}$, $\ell \in \{0.1k, 0.5k, 1k, 2k, 5k, 10k\}$. We also randomly choose one point for both algorithms and the iteration round of them is still 12. The results are shown in Fig. 4. It can be seen from it, when ℓ varies from $0.1k$ to $10k$, there is little difference in clustering cost of OnR and PSKM++. The minimum difference and the maximum difference are $4.37e8$ ($\ell = 1k$) and $4.25e9$ ($\ell = 10k$) when $k = 500$. These values are $9.61e5$ ($\ell = 0.1k$) and $1.77e9$ ($\ell = 1k$) when $k = 1000$. Since both OnR and PSKM++ choose each point with a certain probability, they still have the random characteristic. Thus, we observe that OnR takes more clustering cost sometimes, e.g., $\ell = 1k$, $2k$ ($k = 500$) and $\ell = 2k$ ($k = 1000$). But in most cases, e.g., $\ell = 0.1k, 0.5k, 5k, 10k$ ($k = 500$) and $\ell = 0.5k, 1k, 5k, 10k$ ($k = 1000$), the clustering cost of OnR is less than that of PSKM++. Recall that in order to reduce the MapReduce jobs in each round, OnR uses another oversampling factor o, thus OnR chooses more points than

PSKM++ in each round and it has more chances to obtain the better result. From Fig. 4, we also find out both OnR and PSKM++ obtain the worst result when $\ell = 0.1k$ for $k = 500$ and $k = 1000$. Due to the reason the number of points chosen by OnR and PSKM++ is too small when iteration round completes. The expected number of points are 600 ($k = 500$) and 1200 ($k = 1000$) for both OnR and PSKM++. Because it could not obtain a good result when using 600 and 1200 centers to represent such large number of points, let along $k = 500$ and $k = 1000$.

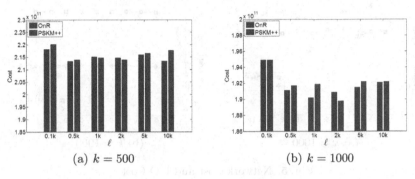

(a) $k = 500$ (b) $k = 1000$

Fig. 4. Cost: $o = 5$, ℓ varies

4.3   I/O Cost and Network Cost

As mentioned above, OnR completes one iteration round by one MapReduce job, but compared with PSKM++, the network cost is almost the same. The main advantage of OnR is that its I/O cost is drastically reduced.

In this section, we evaluate OnR and compare it with PSKM++ in I/O cost and Network cost. Firstly, we present the experiment setup and parameter settings for them. We test OnR and PSKM++ when $k = 1000, \ell = 1k$, o is set to 5 for OnR. We still choose one point randomly as the first center and $r = 12$. For both OnR and PSKM++, the I/O cost and network cost from iterating operation are account for the largest proportion of the whole I/O cost and network cost. Thus, we only record the I/O cost and network cost in each round. The experimental results are summarized in Figure 5. From Fig. 5(a) we can see, for each round, the network cost of both OnR and PSKM++ are small and they are in $[140KB, 200KB]$. However, except for the first round, the network cost of OnR is larger than that of PSKM++, due to the reason that OnR chooses more centers (the expected number of chosen points is $o * \ell$) in Mapper phase than PSKM++ (the expected number of chosen points is ℓ). When $r = 1$, because OnR does not use the parameter o, the expect number of chosen points by OnR is still ℓ and the network cost of it is similar to PSKM++ (about $150KB$). From Fig. 5(b), expect for $r = 1$, the I/O cost of PSKM++ is about 2 times bigger than OnR for each round (about $3.7e10$ vs. $1.8e10$). Due to the reason that OnR read the input data once, while PSKM++ read twice. When $r = 1$, OnR only chooses ℓ points and does not compute the distance of each point to the new centers, the distance computation is completed by the Mapper phase of the next round, thus there is no distance output and the difference is big in this round (about $2.0e10$ vs. $3.1e9$).

From the above analysis, although OnR takes more network cost than PSKM++, it is fairly small. We draw the conclusion that OnR drastically reduce the I/O cost without increasing the network cost.

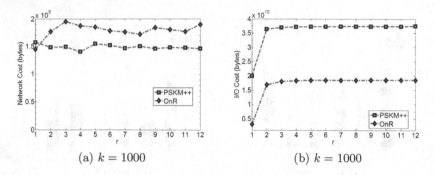

(a) $k = 1000$ (b) $k = 1000$

Fig. 5. Network Cost and I/O Cost

4.4   Running Time and Clustering Cost with Different o

Recall that in order to guarantee the number of points after each iteration is no less than ℓ, we usually set o to a larger value, but this increases the network cost. To solve this issue, OnR estimates the global clustering cost and uses the refining in Mapper phase to remove some points. This section tests the running time and clustering cost for OnR when o varies. In these experiments, we use $k \in \{500, 1000\}$, $\ell = 1k$, $o \in \{3, 5, 7, 15, 50, 250\}$, $r = 12$. The experimental results are summarized in Table 2 and Table 3. From them we observe that, no matter how the parameter o varies, there are few changes in running time and clustering cost. When o varies from 3 to 250, the number of chosen points in

Table 2. Execution Time (minutes)

	$o = 3$	$o = 5$	$o = 7$	$o = 15$	$o = 50$	$o = 250$
$k = 500$	66.65	66.88	66.6	66.75	67.18	66.9
$k = 1000$	75.15	75.57	75.6	75.63	75.7	75.32

Table 3. Clustering Cost, $\times 10^{11}$

	$o = 3$	$o = 5$	$o = 7$	$o = 15$	$o = 50$	$o = 250$
$k = 500$	2.147	2.138	2.143	2.145	2.139	2.131
$k = 1000$	1.915	1.902	1.901	1.905	1.908	1.904

Mapper phase becomes large, but owing to the large parallelism of Mapper, the running time of OnR is almost the same.

5 Conclusion

This paper proposed an efficient MapReduce scalable k-means++ algorithm-OnR. Compared with the MapReduce scalable k-means++, OnR uses only one MapReduce job to choose $\Omega(k)$ centers and compute the clustering cost in each round. The main idea of OnR is that except for the oversampling factor ℓ, OnR uses another oversampling factor o to further increase the number of centers in Mapper phase, and in Reducer phase, one Reducer removes the oversampled centers generated from o. OnR saves a large amount of I/O cost and drastically reduces the running time. In order to reduce the expensive network cost and heavy workload of Reducer caused by too large o, OnR estimates the global cost by the local clustering cost and uses it to remove some oversampled centers in Mapper phase. Experimental results indicate that OnR outperforms the MapReduce scalable k-means++ in the aspect of I/O cost and running time.

Acknowledgment. This work is supported by the National Science Foundation for Distinguished Young Scholars of China under grant No. of 61225010, National Nature Science Foundation of China (Nos. 61173162, 61173165, 61370199, 61300187, 61300189 and 61370198), New Century Excellent Talents (No. NCET-10-0095), the Fundamental Research Funds for the Central Universities(Nos. 31322013044, 31322013029 and 2012TD008).

References

1. Chandra, E., Anuradha, V.P.: A survery on clustering algorithms for data in spatial database management systems. Computer Applications 24(9), 19–26 (2011)
2. Xu, Z., Ke, Y., Wang, Y., Cheng, H., Cheng, J.: A model-based approach to attributed graph clustering. In: Proceedings of the 2012 ACM SIGMOD International Conference on Management of Data, pp. 505–516 (2012)
3. Moise, D.: D, Shestakov, G. Gudmundsson, L. Amsaleg.: Indexing and searching 100m images with map-reduce. In: Proceedings of the 3rd ACM Conference on International Conference on Multimedia Retrieval, pp. 17–24 (2013)
4. Jin, Y., Li, K.: An optimal multimedia object allocation solution in multi-powermode storage systems. Concurrency and Computation: Practice and Experience 22(13), 1852–1873 (2010)
5. Celebi, M.E., Kingravi, H.A., Vela, P.A.: A Comparative Study of Efficient Initialization Methods for the K-means Clustering Algorithm. Expert Syst. Appl. 40(1), 200–210 (2013)
6. Onoda, T., Sakai, M., Yamada, S.: Careful Seeding Method based on Independent Components Analysis for k-means Clustering. Emerging Technologies in Web Intelligence 4(1), 51–59
7. Arthur, D., Vassilvitskii, S.: K-means++: The Advantages of Careful Seeding. In: Proceedings of the 8th Annual ACM-SIAM Symposium on Discrete Algorithms, pp. 1027–1035 (2007)

8. Dean, J., Ghemawat, S.: MapReduce: Simplified Data Processing on Large Clusters. In: Proceedings of the 6th Conference on Symposium on Opearting Systems Design and Implementation, pp. 137–150 (2004)
9. Papadimitriou, S., Sun, J.: DisCo: Distributed Co-clustering with Map-Reduce: A Case Study Towards Petabyte-Scale End-to-End Mining. In: Proceedings of the 2008 Eighth IEEE International Conference on Data Mining, pp. 512–521 (2008)
10. Zhao, W., Ma, H., He, Q.: Parallel K-means clustering based on mapReduce. In: Jaatun, M.G., Zhao, G., Rong, C. (eds.) Cloud Computing. LNCS, vol. 5931, pp. 674–679. Springer, Heidelberg (2009)
11. Ene, A., Im, S., Moseley, B.: Fast Clustering Using MapReduce. In: Proceedings of the 17th ACM SIGKDD International Conference on Knowledge Discovery and Data Mining, pp. 684–689 (2011)
12. Cordeiro, F., Leonardo, R., Caetano Jr., T., Traina, M., Juci, A., López, J., Kang, U., Faloutsos, C.: Clustering Very Large Multi-dimensional Datasets with MapReduce. In: Proceedings of the 17th ACM SIGKDD International Conference on Knowledge Discovery and Data Mining, pp. 690–698 (2011)
13. Bu, Y., Howe, B., Balazinska, M., Ernst, M.D.: HaLoop: Efficient Iterative Data Processing on Large Clusters. VLDB Endow 3(1-2), 285–296 (2010)
14. Ekanayake, J., Li, H., Zhang, B., Gunarathne, T., Bae, S.-H., Qiu, J., Fox, G.: Twister: A Runtime for Iterative MapReduce. In: Proceedings of the 19th ACM International Symposium on High Performance Distributed Computing, pp. 810–818 (2010)
15. Bahmani, B., Moseley, B., Vattani, A., Kumar, R., Vassilvitskii, S.: Scalable K-Means++. VLDB Endow 5(7), 622–633 (2012)

Acceleration of Solving Non-Equilibrium Ionization via Tracer Particles and MapReduce on Eulerian Mesh

Jian Xiao[1], Xingyu Xu[1], Jizhou Sun[1], Xin Zhou[2], and Li Ji[2]

[1] School of Computer Science and Technology,
Tianjin University, Tianjin, China
{xiaojian,xingyuxu,jzsun}@tju.edu.cn
[2] Purple Mountain Observatory,
Chinese Academy of Sciences, Nanjing, China
{xinzhou,ji}@pmo.ac.cn

Abstract. Non-equilibrium ionization (NEI) is an important phenomenon related to many astrophysical processes, but the traditional method, which tightly couples the NEI solver with Eulerian mesh infrastructure, introduced high overhead on computing, memory and communication. In order to overcome the shortcomings of the pure Eulerian scheme, a new approach employing tracer particles and MapReduce model to solve the NEI problem was proposed. We introduce (1) a particle-dumping scheme for tackling the problem of large amounts of small particle snapshots continuously generated at each evolution step, (2) a parallel method based on the MapReduce model to solve the NEI equations along the particle trajectories. Both post-processing and non-intrusive in-situ schemes are supported in the paper's approach. The approach was prototyped and tested based on the FLASH multiphysics simulation framework, and it is easily adapted to other simulations modeling reactive flow on Eulerian mesh. Evaluations on up to 192 cores show that our approach can improve the end-to-end performance of a real world simulation by 3-fold above.

Keywords: non-equilibrium ionization, tracer particle, AMR, MapReduce.

1 Introduction

Non-equilibrium ionization (NEI) is an important phenomenon related to many astrophysical processes, and is generally used in models of small-scale phenomena such as shocked gas in solar flares, supernova remnants and stellar cluster winds etc, as well as large-scale phenomena such as galactic superwinds, active galactic nucleus outflows and intergalactic medium etc. The equation groups governing the astrophysical simulations with NEI effects take the following form [9,5].

$$\frac{\partial \rho}{\partial t} + \nabla \cdot (\rho \mathbf{v}) = 0, \tag{Eq.1}$$

X.-h. Sun et al. (Eds.): ICA3PP 2014, Part II, LNCS 8631, pp. 29–42, 2014.

$$\frac{\partial \rho \mathbf{v}}{\partial t} + \nabla \cdot (\rho \mathbf{v} \mathbf{v}) + \nabla P = \rho \mathbf{g}, \tag{Eq.2}$$

$$\frac{\partial \rho E}{\partial t} + \nabla \cdot [(\rho E + P) \mathbf{v}] = \rho \mathbf{v} \cdot \mathbf{g} \, [+S] \,, \tag{Eq.3}$$

$$\frac{\partial n_i^Z}{\partial t} + \nabla \cdot n_i^Z \mathbf{v} = R_i^Z \; (i = 1, \cdots, N_{spec}) \,, \tag{Eq.4}$$

Eq.1–Eq.3 are the classic Euler equations for gas dynamics and Eq.4 is the set of additional advection equations for all the ion species, where ρ is the fluid density, t is the time, v is the fluid velocity, P is the pressure, E is the sum of the internal energy and kinetic energy per unit mass, and $\mathbf{g}$ is the acceleration due to gravity, and S represents the source item, n_i^Z is the number density of the ion i of the element Z, N_{spec} is the total number of species, R is described by Eq.5,

$$R_i^Z = N_e \left[n_{i+1}^Z \alpha_{i+1}^Z + n_{i-1}^Z S_{i-1}^Z - n_i^Z \left(\alpha_i^Z + S_i^Z \right) \right], \tag{Eq.5}$$

where N_e is the electron number density, $\alpha_i^Z = (N_e, T)$ are the collisional and dielectronic recombination coefficients, and $S_i^Z = S(N_e, T)$ are the collisional ionization coefficients.

In the classic Eulerian scheme, which usually employs the adaptive mesh refinement (AMR) technique for a good balance between performance and accuracy, in order to integrate the continuity equations of the ion species, the Eq.4 is split into two equations given by Eq.6 and Eq.7, where X_i^Z is the mass fraction of the ion i of the element Z. For each time step, the homogeneous hydrodynamic advection equations given by Eq.1 and Eq.6 are solved by hydrodynamics solver, and after each transport step, the ordinary differential equations (ODE) for the NEI problem (Eq.7) are integrated by NEI solver.

$$\frac{\partial \rho X_i^Z}{\partial t} + \nabla \cdot \left(\rho X_i^Z \mathbf{v} \right) = 0 \; (i = 1, \cdots, N_{spec}) \tag{Eq.6}$$

$$\frac{\partial n_i^Z}{\partial t} = R_i^Z \; (i = 1, \cdots, N_{spec}) \tag{Eq.7}$$

In many cases, integrating a large number of stiff ODEs at each time step will dominate the total wall-clock time of a simulation [16], but fortunately in this case the NEI solver, which only integrates several small sets of ODEs(≤ 27), is very lightweight, comparing with the much more complex PDE (partial differential equation) solvers, such as hydro solver and thermal conduction solver (diffuse). So in practice the computing time of NEI itself is only a small fraction (less 10%) of the whole simulation time, but the overhead introduced by the classic approach can no longer be ignored as the number of ion species increasing.

As illustrated in Fig.1.(a), there are only approximate 15 double-precision variables in solution space and three PDEs(Eq.1–Eq.3) needing to be solved by hydrodynamic solver. However as one chemical element containing **n** protons is added, **n+1** variables and **n+1** advection equations (Eq.6) will be introduced

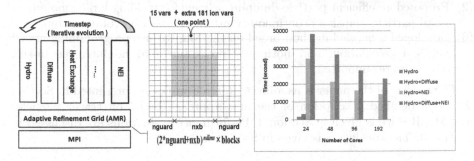

Fig. 1. Solving NEI in pure Eulerian scheme. The left(a): Time-splitting iteration and the grid data structure in Eulerian mesh. The right(b): Performance comparison between simulations with or without NEI (All tests were built on the FLASH code and evolved 1000 timesteps).

according to the classic method. As a result, considering the twelve most abundant elements in the universe plus fully ionized hydrogen and electrons, totally 181 extra variables need to be stored and another 181 advection equations need to be solved at every grid point. Except the increased computing workloads introduced by additional advection equations, it will use up to roughly 15 times of system memory more than the case without NEI, and the following high communication overhead between neighbor processes is unavoidable eithor.

For example of the block-based adaptive mesh refinement–PARAMESH [5,13], each core usually handles a $16 \times 16 \times 1000$ (1000 is the number of blocks) points subdomain in a common 2D simulation, and the grid data structure will need roughly 65MB and 880MB RAM respectively with or without NEI [9,11]. As illustrated in Fig.1.(b), the traditional method caused heavy performance degradation(15-fold slow) when all the ion species are added. Considering common multi-physics simulations involving multiple solvers for different physical processes, except the hydro solver and NEI solver, other solvers also have to endure the overhead introduced by the NEI problem although these solvers never care these ion species. In Fig.1.(b), as the diffuse solver is added, the performance degradation becomes larger, and using increasing number of cores is not very helpful. Moreover, as the grid refines during evolution, the performance degradation will be exacerbated further. For three-dimension simulations, memory and communication overhead will be increased by one order of magnitude, much more computing resources must be employed for sharing such high burden. Astrophysical simulations usually have long running circles, typically 50k iterations above, then the total simulation time may become unacceptable. The main contributions of this study are summarized as follows:

(1) Decoupled the NEI solver from the Eulerian mesh by employing tracer particles, and maximally reduced the high overload on computing, memory and communication introduced by the traditional approach.

(2) Proposed an efficient particle-dumping scheme for tackling large amounts of small particle snapshots continuously produced at each evolution step.
(3) Developed a parallel method based on the MapReduce programming model for NEI calculation, and both post-processing and nonintrusive in-situ scheme were supported.

The outline of the paper is as follows. Related works are presented in Section 2, and a detailed description of the new approach based on tracer particles and MapReduce is given in Section 3. Performance evaluations are discussed in Section 4. The conclusion is given in Section 5.

2   Background and Related Works

As mentioned above, fundamentally the high overhead introduced by the pure Eulerian scheme is due to the tight coupling between the NEI solver and the underlying mesh. It is possible to overcome this drawback of the mesh-based NEI implementation by introducing Lagrange tracer particles. By recording the thermo-dynamical history of individual fluid particles, the NEI calculation can be migrated to the post-processing phase, and totally independent from the Eulerian mesh. Hence, in the thermo-dynamical evolution without NEI, there is no need for extra space to hold all ion species, and sequently the numerous partial advection equations (Eq.6) are also 'disappeared'.

Tracer particle and post-processing method have been widely used in astro-physical simulations and computational fluid dynamic (CFD) domain, and the MapReduce technique is successfully used by several projects for massive parallel trajectories analyses at recent years [17,15]. However the NEI problem has two distinct characteristics that common tracer particle schemes seldom address, (1) usually particle data are dumped at a relative larger interval comparing to the timestep, but the particle data of NEI must be dumped at each evolution step, the frequent dumping will lead to large amounts of small files and heavy IO burden, moreover, it is not an easy task of reconstructing particle trajectory from large files base, (2) most MapReduce-style schemes for analyzing simulation trajectories mainly focus on statistical calculation, such as extreme value, distribution of physical quantities etc., but the NEI calculation must be performed along each trajectory in a strictly time ascending order.

The paper's approach is implemented and tested based on the FLASH code, which is a publicly available multiphysics simulation framework running in massive parallel environments [5]. The FLASH code integrated the traditional NEI solver since version 2.5 and introduced Lagrangian tracer particles on top of its Eulerian hydrodynamics infrastructure since version 3.3 [4,9]. The FLASH can output particle snapshots with either serial IO or parallel IO. But to our best knowledge, no separate effort is made to tackle such frequent snapshot dumping posed by NEI in the current implementation of the FLASH.

Our approach is motivated by several excellent previous studies that can be divided into two topics. The first is map-reduce schemes for analyzing particle trajectories. The second is space-partition method for IO acceleration and in situ analysis.

2.1   MapReduce Model for Reconstructing and Analyzing Particle Trajectories

The MapReduce programing model is proposed by Google for large-scale data processing in a distributed computing environment [1]. Ekanayake et al. [7] proposed a steaming-based MapReduce implementation written in the Java language, which eliminates the overheads associated with communicating via a file system and send the intermediate results directly from its producers to its consumers. The steaming-based idea is widely adopted by the HPC community, and our approach is no exception.

Tu et al. [17] firstly proposed a dedicated MapReduce framework called Hi-Mach built on top of the ubiquitous distributed-memory message-passing interface (MPI), and their framework made a dramatic performance promotion on analyzing terascale molecular dynamics simulation trajectories. Plimpton's group [15,14] made a series of systematic studies about map-reduce libraries on top of MPI for use in large-scale graph analytics. They contributed the MapReduce-MPI (MR-MPI) library and the PHISH framework to the HPC community. Within the PHISH framework, streaming MapReduce operations can be organized in a net, which specifies the sequence of computations and the topology of data flow [15]. Following the idea of the PHISH framework, an in situ scheme for NEI calculation was implemented in the paper.

2.2   Space-Partition Method for IO Acceleration and in Situ Analysis

In the traditional time-partitioning model, usually a simulation must stop to perform extra tasks, such as dumping the snapshots. Reconstructing trajectory of each particle requires snapshots from every timestep in the simulation, and the one-snapshot per-timestep will introduce heavy IO burden even for a modest case with one million particles and 50k iterations [15,6]. With the acceleration of take-up of multicore architecture in modern HPC systems in the last decade, the ideas using space-partitioning approach to relieve the network and file system contention are proposed by several research groups.

Li et al. [12] developed a novel functional partitioning runtime environment that allocates dedicated cores to specific tasks, particularly for I/O activities. Dorier's group [2] proposed the Damaris I/O middleware, which avoids synchronization between cores by overlapping I/O with computation and gathering data into large files. Dorier's approach gives the in-situ analyses the capability of working on raw in-memory data without performing any copy [3]. However in our case, the NEI analysis must follow the continuously moving particles, not the 'fixed' points on the underlying Eulerian grid. So the paper proposed an in situ scheme for running the NEI analysis on dedicated nodes near the simulation cluster.

Except the in-situ scheme, the paper's post-processing scheme also borrowed ideas from space-partition methods. In general, parallel access to a single file will provide the best parallel IO performance unless the number of processors is very large, But Fisher's work [8] shows that none of the parallel I/O libraries available with FLASH, effectively scaled to more than 1024 processors. So a node-level direct I/O approach is adopted in the following post-processing scheme.

3   Method

Our approach includes two independent schemes, post-processing scheme and in situ scheme. The advantage of post-processing schemes is that all snapshots can be reserved, and used repeatedly for various analyses, not only for NEI. Particularly it is very useful for some general simulations, such as turbulence, the data set can be open to the community [8]. While the advantage of in situ scheme is bypassing the lagging IO system and reducing the amount of data stored by large-scale simulations, moreover, in situ analysis can be used for computational steering.

3.1   Architecture

The architecture of the system is described in Fig.2 and Fig.3. Our system consists of discrete components that filter, aggregate, scatter the particles' data (map), perform NEI calculation (reduce), and generate statistical results. It is modular and pluggable, for example, it can be easily adapted for nucleosynthesis [16] analysis only by developing a dedicated reducer. Similar with the net of the PHISH framework [15], components are assembled into workflows, where data flow from component to component. Components can be divided into two groups according whether they are located within the simulation nodes or not. Inner components are designed as a plug-in of the simulation. While outer components, which are loosely coupled with the evolving simulation, can be easily replaced or extended to offer a wide range of features.

Data Filter: mainly used for reducing the data size. Usually post-processing only needs a subset of particle attributes. A data filter continuously receives streaming data from the simulation, and only deliver the data that just necessary for reconstructing trajectories. By default, particles are defined to have

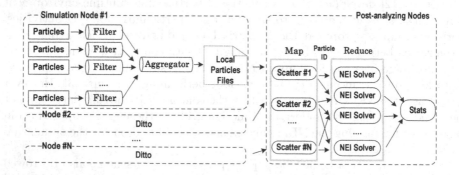

Fig. 2. Post-processing scheme with direct I/O mode

eight properties that are necessary for moving on the grid: 3 positions in x, y, z; 3 velocities in x, y, z; the current block identification number; and a tag which uniquely identifies the particle; additionally three custom attributes are included for NEI calculation: density, temperature and the current timestep. All the properties are double precision, and for a common configuration of one million particles evolving 100k timesteps will generate at least 8TB snapshot files. In fact only five properties are needed in NEI calculation phase, and three position properties are only used in statistical analysis and visualization usually performed at a relative large interval. Because the position data can be extracted from the overall checkpoint files dumped at the same interval with statistical analysis, and the timestep can be shared for all particles within the same snapshot, so the filter can reduce 70% volume of data by removing 8 properties, including 3 velocities, 3 positions, the block ID and redundant timesteps.

Aggregator: mainly used for reducing the data size further and avoiding large amounts of small snapshot files to be generated. Aggregator components only used in post-processing schemes. Usually the simulation writes one snapshot per file, and these snapshots are self-contained, which means metadata included. As a result, the default mechanism will produce too many small snapshots and a lot of redundant metadata information. An aggregator collects the data distilled by the upstream filter, and appends the stream data into several large aggregate files in a time ascending order. The properties with the same value on a snapshot will be written only once, such as timestep, and the metadata is no longer put into the snapshot, but described by a public configuration file.

Configuration File: mainly used to reduce redundant information of the original snapshots and increase the flexibility and adaptability of the system. The configuration file describes meta data and control options, including a full definition of particle data structure, filter options, the max number of snapshot files contained in one aggregate file and IO schemes etc.

Scatter: sends the particle data to a unique NEI solver (reducer) determined by hashing on the particle ID. The hash algorithm used in the paper is very simple, just the modulo operation on particle ID and the count of the reducers (NEI solvers). It ensures that all data from one trajectory will be sent to the same solver. The particle data comes from either aggregate snapshots in post-processing scheme or the filters of in situ scheme. In order to avoid reconstructing long trajectories in system memory, scatters ensure that data from the same particle is sent in a strictly time ascending order.

Reducer(NEI Solver): solving the ordinary differential equations of the NEI problem (Eq.7). The core algorithm of the solver is extracted directly from the traditional implementation of FLASH code. Intermediate results can be aggregated and saved to disk for later analysis or directly sent to the downstream statistical tools. As mentioned in the first section, a data structure is necessary for holding all variables of ion species within each particle. Each particle needs 181×8 bytes, for one million particles, approximate 1.5GB of storage globally is needed. Comparing with the traditional implementation tightly coupled with the grid, the most important advantage of the scheme is that neither extra memory for holding guard points nor the guard points exchange between neighbor processes is needed.

Statistical Tool: mainly used for global analysis, for example, demonstrating the spatial distribution of ionization state. As mentioned in data filter, these analyses usually need additional information only founded in the full checkpoint files, hence the limitation of these analysis is that it must be invoked on existing checkpoints and cannot be performed on the fly.

3.2   Post-processing Scheme

As illustrated in Fig.2, in the scheme, the whole simulation is performed by two phases: the on-line simulation, and the off-line NEI analysis. Two I/O modes are supported in the scheme. The first is the simple serial I/O mode, where each simulation process connecting with a dedicated filter, but only one aggregator exists, and all the filters move the data to the single aggregator for output. In the serial I/O mode, all files are written into a global sharing file system space.

The second is direct I/O mode, and its performance had been verified by Fisher's work on terascale turbulence simulation [8]. An improvement was made based on the space-partitioning ideas [12,2]. As shown is the Fig.2, in order to avoid file system contention from processes within the same node when snapshots written at the same time, in each node a dedicated process is allocated for gathering the data from other processes within the same node, and then writing its portion of the global data to its local file system.

3.3   In Situ Scheme

Considering the NEI calculation is lightweight compared to the whole simulation workload, if a small portion of computing resources is allocated to perform the NEI calculation as the simulation runs, the impact on the overall performance is trivial. As shown in the Fig.3, most of computing resources are allocated to the

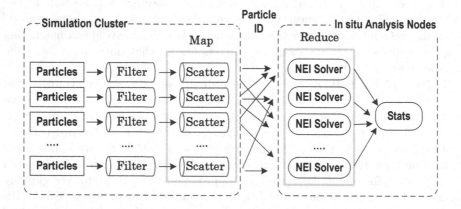

Fig. 3. In situ scheme using MPI inter-communicator

simulation, and just a few cores are reserved for in situ NEI analysis. The filter directly puts the particle data into its private scatter, and then the scatter sends the data to a NEI solver depending on the hash-value of particle ID. The in situ scheme will not introduce disk storage overhead, but a balance strategy must be made for properly allocating computing resources between the simulation and the in-situ analysis, and this is simulation specific. In NEI experiments, the in-situ portion is nearly 10%.

3.4 Implementation

The paper's approach was prototyped based on the FLASH framework, and programmed in FORTRAN 90. By employing the particular directory-based inheritance hierarchy of the FLASH [5], our system can be connected to the simulation in a nonintrusive way just through the particle IO interface of FLASH. The implementation puts minimal impact on the simulation code, so that few code changes is required for users adopting our approach in their simulations. To use the new feature, they only need to make a few configurations and rebuild the code.

The implementation of the MapReduce model in this paper is based on MPICH2. In order to ensure a strict time ascending sequence in NEI calculation, synchronization must be performed carefully. In the post-processing phase, it needs force synchronization at each timestep when scattering the particle snapshots to the NEI reducers. In in-situ scheme, there is no need to make special effort to ensure time sequence, due to the inner synchronization mechanism of the FLASH. It is worth pointing out that in the in-situ scheme, the simulation and the NEI solvers resident in two independent MPI contexts respectively, which will not impact each other, so that it makes the scheme more robust and adaptable.

4 Evaluation

In this section, the paper's approach was evaluated with a real world simulation– W49B built upon the FLASH code, using a Linux cluster, which provides 10 nodes of 4 Intel 2.6GHz CPUs, 6 cores/CPU, 48 GB RAM. One node is reserved for in-situ analysis, and another for management and job submission; therefore in fact totally eight nodes are used for running simulation.

The physical model of W49B describes the evolution of an originally spherical supernova remnant (SNR) expanding through an inhomogeneous medium. The detailed information about the simulation can be found in [18]. For simplicity, the evolution is modeled by numerically solving fluid dynamic equations (Eq.1-Eq.3), taking into account the effects of thermal conduction (diffuse) and NEI (Eq.4). All the particles located within a $0.5 \times 0.5(pc)$ circle region at the center of the $9 \times 12(pc)$ simulation domain ($1pc \doteq 3.0e18cm$). It is worth mentioning that the unbalance of particle load distribution may slow down our approach at the early stage of the evolution, but it will not impact the following performance analysis.

The experiments use 1 million particles and initial $16 \times 16 \times 20k$ AMR points (cells) spread over 12, 24, 48, 96 and 192 processors. In theory, the AMR data structure will take up 18GB and1.3 GB global memory with or without NEI solver coupled. It is worth pointing out that for one million total count of the particles, only one hundred megabytes of storage are required globally in the simulation phase, but in the NEI analysis phase, the memory overhead introduced by NEI can not be avoided totally. The particle data structure will take up 1.5GB global memory for containing all the ion mass fractions, however there is no need for extra memory containing large amounts of ghost points (guard cells) and frequent information exchanges between neighbor processes.

Because the real world simulation has a long running circle (according our previous work [18], only Fe element contained, evolving 400k timesteps, about 20 days on 72 cores), so each evaluation run was limited to 1k timesteps, and the running time varied from 0.5 to 25 hours approximately for different tests. The performance data was collected by the timer and profiler tools of FLASH.

Five groups of tests were conducted, including the basic hydro-thermal simulation without NEI (marked with 'AMR without NEI'), the traditional approach coupling NEI with Eulerian mesh (marked with 'AMR with NEI'), the post-processing approaches with serial IO and direct IO modes (marked with 'particle serial IO' and 'direct IO' respectively), and the in situ scheme (marked with 'particle in situ').

4.1 Performance Analysis

The Fig.4 illustrates the total times used by each test evolving 1k iterations. The three schemes of our approach have similar performance curves, all of them get the maximum acceleration at 48 cores, and then as the cores increase, performance degradation is exacerbated. The same phenomenon occurred more obviously for the basic test (AMR without NEI). The reason is that for a selected workload, simply increasing number of cores does not provide corresponding improvement, and due to the limitation of the test environment, the size of the experiments is fixed to a moderate value.

As mentioned above, due to tightly coupled NEI with the grid, the traditional approach (AMR with NEI) introduced at least one order of magnitude performance degradation. Though as the cores increasing from 12 to 192, the total time dropped from 85k seconds to 22k seconds, it is still 6 folds of the basic case at 24 cores, and 4 folds of our approach at 48 cores. Moreover the acceleration becomes slower as the cores increase, it can be concluded that simply increasing number of cores have few effect on further performance improvement. Comparing with the best result of the tradition method (at 192 cores), the direct IO scheme achieved approximate 4.5-fold performance improvement but only using a half number of cores, and for in-situ scheme, the maximum acceleration is near 3-fold. For a real world simulation evolving 100k iterations, the traditional method will take 28 days at least even using 192 cores according the current experiments; therefore the improvement will save a lot of computing resources in practice. It must be pointed out that as simulation evolves, the mesh will

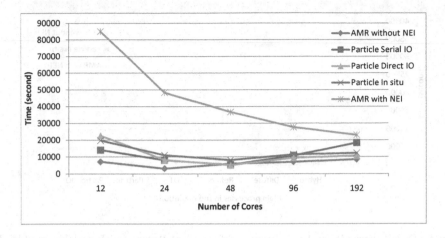

Fig. 4. Total evolving time for 1k iterations at a global workload of 1 million particles and initial $16 \times 16 \times 20k$ AMR points

become more refined, and consequently it will lead to more computing workload and more memory usage. In the original W49B simulation, at the end the global number of cells (points) had increased to 10 times of that at the start. So it's believed that the end-to-end performance improvement will be still better than the experiments show.

4.2 Overhead Introduced by Tracer Particles

As shown in Fig.4, compared to the basic test (AMR with NEI), the overhead still existed in our approach, but much lower than that of the tradition method. The main impacts on performance introduced by tracer particles are (1) particle I/O, (2) particle advance on Eulerian mesh, (3) computing the timestep for ensuring that any particle travels no more than some numerical constraints during a single step, and (4) the grid refinement operation when particle count used as one of grid refinement criteria. For the three latter overheads, all the three schemes of our approach are approximately equivalent in both theory and practice. For the former overhead, particle I/O, the simple serial IO scheme will inevitably encounter the scalability problem due to the bottleneck of network communication as the number of cores increasing, while both of the direct I/O scheme and in situ scheme can totally ignore the time used by outputting particles.

Fig.5 shows a detailed comparison of the times used by each main process of three representative tests performed at 96 cores respectively. In the traditional method, the hydro solver and diffuse solver have to sustain the high overhead on computation and communication introduced by tightly coupling NEI and AMR, and the total time increased 600%. By contrast, in our approach the four main overheads introduced by particle totally account for less than 50% of the overall execution time.

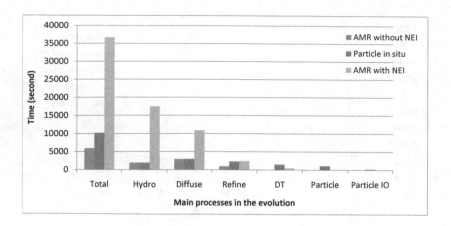

Fig. 5. Detailed profile for 1k iterations performed at 96cores with a global workload of 1 million particles and approximate $16 \times 16 \times 20k$ AMR points

4.3   Overhead Introduced by Post-processing

Large disk storage is the main overhead for saving particle snapshots. Though some efforts (Filter, Aggregator and configuration file etc.) were made to decrease the size of snapshots, for one million particles advancing 10k iterations, it will generate 230GB files, and for a moderate 100k iterations required by common astrophysical simulations, it will occupy 2.3TB of disk capacity.

In our approach, the NEI solver is separated from the Eulerian mesh, but the above performance statistic did not yet contain the time used by NEI calculation in our approach. Experiments showed that a single process needs 0.2s to perform NEI calculation on one trajectory of 1k iterations, and consequently for one million particles, the time is $0.2e6$s. Unlike the traditional approach, because there is no need to exchange information between the neighbor processes, the NEI calculation can get a nearly linear speedup as the number of cores increasing. In our experiments, the total time was 1160s for analyzing one million trajectories of 1k iterations at 192 cores. Plus the minimum evolution time (5120s, as shown in Fig.4) that the redirect IO scheme had achieved, the end-to-end performance improvement of the direct IO scheme was approximate 3 folds.

In summary, by employing proper particle-dumping strategies and the MapReduce programming model, our approach successfully controlled the overhead introduced by NEI within a small scope. In fact, there is another advantage of our method. The traditional approach can easily lead to inconsistent advection of ion species during fluid dynamic evolution, which will break the simulation due to large numerical errors [9]. While the tracer particle method can easily bypass the consistent multi-fluid advection problem, which many reactive flow simulations have to tackle carefully.

5   Conclusion and Future Work

In the paper, we proposed a new approach employing tracer particles and MapReduce model to solve the NEI problem in astrophysical simulations. Some optimization mechanisms were developed for tackling the frequent output of large amounts of snapshots, including data filter, file aggregator, direct I/O and in-situ processing.Comprehensive theoretical analysis and experiments were conducted to demonstrate the efficiency and scalability of the approach, and experiments shown that it can reduce overall execution time of a real world simulation by 3 folds at least. Our system is component-based and nonintrusive, so that it can be easily adapted to other astrophysical simulation frameworks, or extended for accelerating other multi-species related simulations, such as nucleosynthesis [16].

A limitation exists in the current implementation. Our approach is not totally self-consistent, because the contribution of the ionization and recombination to the energy equation is not accounted for [9]. In the traditional Eulerian scheme, because all the solvers share a unified solution space on the top of AMR, the energy generated by NEI can be directly used to the energy conservation equation. But in our approach where NEI and AMR are totally decoupled, there is no effective way to send back data to the running simulation.

Our future work will focus on optimization algorithms for particles moving on Eulerian mesh by taking the advantage of multi-core architecture. We also plan to integrate some new tracer particle schemes, like Monte Carlo tracers [10] for both accuracy and performance improvement.

Acknowledgments. The authors thank Prof. Orlando for his kind guide about the timestep of NEI solver, and Min Long and Shikui Tang for the great help they provided. This work was supported in part by National Natural Science Foundation of China (NSFC) through grant U1231108, and Chinese Academy of Sciences (XXH12503-05-05).

References

1. Dean, J., Ghemawat, S.: Mapreduce: simplified data processing on large clusters. Communications of the ACM 51(1), 107–113 (2008)
2. Dorier, M., Antoniu, G., Cappello, F., Snir, M., Orf, L.: Damaris: how to efficiently leverage multicore parallelism to achieve scalable, jitter-free i/o. In: 2012 IEEE International Conference on Cluster Computing (CLUSTER), pp. 155–163. IEEE Press, New York (2012)
3. Dorier, M., Sisneros, R., Peterka, T., Antoniu, G., Semeraro, D.: Damaris/viz: A nonintrusive, adaptable and user-friendly in situ visualization framework. In: 2013 IEEE Symposium on Large-Scale Data Analysis and Visualization (LDAV), pp. 67–75. IEEE Press, New York (2013)
4. Dubey, A., Antypas, K., Daley, C.: Parallel algorithms for moving lagrangian data on block structured eulerian meshes. Parallel Computing 37(2), 101–113 (2011)
5. Dubey, A., Antypas, K., Ganapathy, M.K., Reid, L.B., et al.: Extensible component-based architecture for flash, a massively parallel, multiphysics simulation code. Parallel Computing 35(10), 512–522 (2009)

6. Dubey, A., Calder, A.C., Daley, C., Fisher, R.T., et al.: Pragmatic optimizations for better scientific utilization of large supercomputers. International Journal of High Performance Computing Applications 27(3), 360–373 (2013)
7. Ekanayake, J., Pallickara, S., Fox, G.: Mapreduce for data intensive scientific analyses. In: IEEE Fourth International Conference on eScience, pp. 277–284. IEEE Press, New York (2008)
8. Fisher, R., Kadanoff, L., Lamb, D., Constantin, P., et al.: Terascale turbulence computation on bg/l using the flash3 code. IBM Journal of Research and Development v52 i1/2, 127–137 (2006)
9. FLASH Center for Computational Science, University of Chicago. FLASH User's Guide (2012)
10. Genel, S., Vogelsberger, M., Nelson, D., Sijacki, D., Springel, V., Hernquist, L.: Following the flow: tracer particles in astrophysical fluid simulations. Monthly Notices of the Royal Astronomical Society 435(2), 1426–1442 (2013)
11. Latham, R., Daley, C., Liao, W.K., Gao, K., Ross, R., Dubey, A., Choudhary, A.: A case study for scientific i/o: Improving the flash astrophysics code. Computational Science & Discovery 5(1), 15001 (2012)
12. Li, M., Vazhkudai, S.S., Butt, A.R., Meng, F., et al.: Functional partitioning to optimize end-to-end performance on many-core architectures. In: Proceedings of the 2010 ACM/IEEE International Conference for High Performance Computing, Networking, Storage and Analysis(SC), pp. 1–12. IEEE Press, New York (2010)
13. MacNeice, P., Olson, K.M., Mobarry, C., de Fainchtein, R., Packer, C.: Paramesh: A parallel adaptive mesh refinement community toolkit. Computer Physics Communications 126(3), 330–354 (2000)
14. Plimpton, S.J., Devine, K.D.: Mapreduce in mpi for large-scale graph algorithms. Parallel Computing 37(9), 610–632 (2011)
15. Plimpton, S.J., Shead, T.: Phish library, http://www.sandia.gov/~sjplimp/phish.html
16. Timmes, F.X., Hoffman, R.D., Woosley, S.E.: An inexpensive nuclear energy generation network for stellar hydrodynamics. The Astrophysical Journal Supplement Series 129(1), 377–398 (2000)
17. Tu, T., Rendleman, C.A., Borhani, D.W., Dror, R.O., et al.: A scalable parallel framework for analyzing terascale molecular dynamics simulation trajectories. In: Proceedings of the 2008 ACM/IEEE International Conference for High Performance Computing, Networking, Storage and Analysis(SC), pp. 1–12. IEEE Press, New York (2008)
18. Zhou, X., Miceli, M., Bocchino, F., Orlando, S., Chen, Y.: Unveiling the spatial structure of the overionized plasma in the supernova remnant w49b. Monthly Notices of the Royal Astronomical Society 415(1), 244–250 (2011)

A Continuous Virtual Vector-Based Algorithm for Measuring Cardinality Distribution

Xuefei Zhou, Weijiang Liu*, Zhiyang Li, and Wenwen Gao

School of Information Science and Technology,
Dalian Maritime University,
Dalian, Liaoning, China
wjliu@dlmu.edu.cn

Abstract. The host cardinality is the number of distinct destinations that a host communicates with. Host cardinality is an important metric for high-speed network profiling. With the development of internet, network attacks occur frequently such as worm spreading, DDoS attack and port scanning and so on. One common characteristic of these attacks is that they usually generate a lot of traffic connections in a short time which will lead the host cardinality distribution to change. Hence we can detect these attacks according to the host cardinality distribution. In this paper, we present an algorithm based on continuous virtual vector to estimate the host cardinality distribution. Through experiments using real internet traces, we demonstrate that our algorithm can estimate the host cardinality distribution accurately while using little storage.

1 Introduction

With the rapid development of internet, the number of users and kinds of applications are also expanding in high speed. Hence the traffic volume increases continually and network behaviors become more and more complicated, these bring many challenges for traffic measuring. Even though existing so many challenges many solutions have been proposed [1][2][3].

Chen et al proposed that due to the large traffic volume in the high-speed network, it is high efficient to derive some succinct summary information that can characterize the traffic behavior pattern as a whole [4]. And the network feature distribution can describe the aggregate behavior pattern. Due to the prior work has focused primarily on distributions concerning traffic volume, such as flow size distribution in [5][6][7], or packet contents distribution in [8], hence Chen et al proposed another characterization of network feature called host cardinality distribution: given a number n, how many hosts communicate with n different destination or have n number of flows in observed traffic. They also developed an algorithm to estimate the cardinality distribution based on continuous Flajolet-Martin (FM) sketches. The algorithm is the first approach for estimating cardinality distribution.

---

* Corresponding author.

X.-h. Sun et al. (Eds.): ICA3PP 2014, Part II, LNCS 8631, pp. 43–53, 2014.

Now Internet plays a very important role in our daily life, but it has also revealed a lot of security problems. When these problems occur they usually cause the host cardinality changing [9] [10]. Knowing how the host cardinality distribute can help us detect various types of internet security attacks such as distributed denial-of-service (DDoS) attack and worm spreading. When a DDoS attack happens, attackers will send attack packets to the victim, if these attackers use spoofed IP addresses, then the number of cardinality of size 1 increases. For the worm spreading, each infected host will try to connect to other hosts to spread the worm as quickly as possible. So we will observe a large number of cardinalities of a particular size around the same time. Knowing cardinality distribution can also help us engineer the usage pattern of traffic. For example, the cardinality of many hosts increases over time that may indicate that the number of P2P hosts is increasing. Knowing cardinality distribution can provide us much other information. But estimating the cardinality distribution is not a relaxed job. Existing methods for estimating the host cardinality distribution either need large storage space or have high computation complexity.

In order to address the aforementioned problems, we propose a new algorithm for measuring cardinality distribution. The data structure of the proposed algorithm is a continuous virtual vector. This algorithm is able to record and process large amounts of packets in the high-speed internet with small space and time consumption. We can derive the estimation of the host cardinality distribution according to these packets information. The main contributions of our work are as follows:

(1) We design a new data structure, called continuous virtual vector, which only need one bit to record a packet. This guarantees the memory efficient of our method.
(2) We derive a reasonable formula for estimating the size of host cardinality, and the formula can give an accurate estimation of cardinality size.
(3) The algorithm can get the host cardinality distribution with small space and time consumption. We demonstrate its performance through experiments using real internet traces.

The rest of this paper is organized as follows. Some related work is provided in Section 2. In Section 3, we present our algorithm for estimating the host cardinality distribution and analysis its performance. Section 4 is the experiment result. Finally, we conclude in Section 5.

2 Related Work

2.1 Bitmap

Bitmap is a bit array used for counting the number of distinct elements [11]. It uses a hash function that maps each element to a bit location of the bit array. Assume a Bitmap with size m, namely the Bitmap is consisted of m bits, at the begin all of its bits are initialized to 0. Whenever an element arrives, the corresponding bit location mapped to is set to 1. Because of hash collision, it is possible that one bit may be set multiple times, while only the first setting is effective the rest has no effect on the bit. Hence we could not use the number of "1" as the estimation of the number of distinct elements, and we get the estimation mathematically. Assume the actual number of the distinct elements is n, the number of bits which are not set to 1 is U. Then the probability that a specific bit in the Bitmap is not set to 1 is $prob=(1-\frac{1}{m})^n$. We use the expected value of U, $E(U)=m*prob$, to derive the estimation number of distinct elements. And the estimating result is $\hat{n}=-m*ln(\frac{U}{m})$. In network measurement domain, Bitmap has been used to count the number of flows [12]. It has low space consumption than other structures.

2.2 Virtual Vector

For estimating host cardinality accurately, Yoon et al create a virtual vector for each source host by taking bits uniformly at random from a bit array. The bits in virtual vector are selected by a set of hash functions, $H_0(), H_1(), ..., H_{s-1}$. For example, there is a bit array B of size m, and the ith bit in the array is denoted as $B[i]$, then a virtual vector $X(src)$ of size s for a specific source address src can be denoted as

$$X(src) = (B[H_0(src)], B[H_1(src)], ..., B[H_{s-1}(src)]).$$

The size of host cardinality can be estimated by using formula $\hat{k} = s*ln(\frac{U_m}{m}) - s*ln(\frac{U_s}{s})$, where U_m and U_s are the number of "0" in bit array and virtual vector respectively. It is need s hash functions to get a virtual vector, so this method has high computing complexity. In order to decrease the computing complexity, we design a new data structure, called continuous virtual vector in this paper. Regard the bit array as a circular bit sequence. We only use a hash function to map to a specific bit of the bit array. A continuous virtual vector consists of s continuous bits starting from the mapped bit. We will describe the continuous virtual vector in detail in the next section.

3 Our Algorithm

In order to adapt the high-speed network, and to meet the requirement of real-time tracking and measuring online, we propose an algorithm based on continuous virtual vector to estimate the host cardinality distribution. Our algorithm consists of two phases: online processing and offline processing. The online processing uses three continuous virtual vector to record flow information of all hosts in the high-speed network. The offline processing obtains the estimation of host cardinality according to those flow information recorded in the online processing phase. The final estimation result will be output as the tuple form of <host cardinality: host number>. The overall architecture of our algorithm is shown in Figure 1.

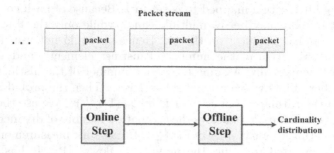

Fig. 1. Overall architecture of our algorithm

3.1 Online Processing

The online processing consists of two modules: flow processing module and source host recording module. And the two modules process packets parallelly in the network.

A. Flow Processing Module

In this module, we use three bit arrays with size m, $B_1[m]$, $B_2[m]$, $B_3[m]$, to record all flow information. What's more, we allocate a continuous virtual vector with size s for every distinct source host to record its cardinality information. In the offline phase, we will estimate the cardinality of a host according to the three bit arrays and the corresponding continuous virtual vectors. When a packet comes, we first extract its source IP address, sip, and its destination IP address, dip. The sip is hashed by three hash functions, $hash_1()$, $hash_2()$, $hash_3()$, which are used to determine the starting location of the host's continuous virtual vectors in $B_1[m]$, $B_2[m]$, $B_3[m]$. Let s be the size of the continuous virtual vector. Then fetch s bits in each bit array continuously, if there are less than s bits remained, complement s bits from the first bit in the bit array. In this way, we get the continuous virtual vectors of sip. Here we use three bit arrays and three hash functions so that we can get three vectors for every distinct sip. Assume that, $i=hash_1(sip)$, $j=hash_2(sip)$, $k=hash_3(sip)$, then the three continuous virtual vectors of the sip are as follows:

$$X_1(Sip) = (B_1[i], B_1[i+1], \dots, B_1[(i+s-1)modm]),$$
$$X_2(Sip) = (B_2[j], B_2[j+1], \dots, B_2[(j+s-1)modm]),$$
$$X_3(Sip) = (B_3[k], B_3[k+1], \dots, B_3[(k+s-1)modm]).$$

Another hash function, $hash_4()$, is used to map dip into the vector. According the result of $hash_4()$, the corresponding bit in the vector is set to 1. For example, $p=hash_4(dip)$, then $B_1[(i+p) \bmod m]$, $B_2[(j+p) \bmod m]$, $B_3[(k+p) \bmod m]$ are set to 1. After this procedure the cardinality information of sip is recorded.

B. Source Host Recording Module

In this module another array, $distinctIP[n]$, is used to record those different source hosts. For a *sip* extracted from each arrival packet, if the *sip* has been recorded, we discard it directly, otherwise it is inserted into *distinctIP*[n].

A detailed description of the online processing phase is presented in Algorithm 1.

Algorithm 1. Online Processing

1: Initialize
2:   B1[i], B2[i], B3[i]:=0; i=1,2,3, ... , m
3:   n:=0;
4: Update
5:   Upon the arrival of a packet *pkt*, extract *sip*, *dip* from it
6:     i:=hash1(sip);
7:     j:=hash2(sip);
8:     k:=hash3(sip);
9:     p=hash4(dip);
10:    B1[(i+p) mod m]:=1;
11:    B2[(j+p) mod m]:=1;
12:    B3[(k+p) mod m]:=1;
13: Insert
14: **if** sip∉distinctIP[n] **then**
15:     distinctIP[n++]=sip;
16: **end if**
17: end

3.2 Offline Processing

In this phase, we estimate the cardinality of each source host recorded in array *distinctIP*[n] according to its three vectors $X_1(sip)$, $X_2(sip)$, $X_3(sip)$ and $B_1[m]$, $B_2[m]$, $B_3[m]$. At last we preserve the results in array *output*[t], where the index value t denotes the size of a cardinality and the value of element *output*[t] is the number of source hosts whose cardinality is t. We estimate the cardinality as follows: for every *sip* in the array *distinct*[n] which represents an exclusive source host in the high-speed network, we first use the three hash functions $hash_1()$, $hash_2()$, $hash_3()$ mentioned in the online processing phase to derive three continuous virtual vectors $X_1(sip)$, $X_2(sip)$, $X_3(sip)$. Then make these vectors do "and" operation, we get another vector $X(sip)$. Namely:

$$X(sip) = X_1(sip) \& X_2(sip) \& X_3(sip).$$

Let U_s denote the number of "0" bits in the vector $X(sip)$. Let V_s be the fraction of "0" bits in $X(sip)$, hence

$$V_s = \frac{U_s}{s}.$$

And U_{m1}, U_{m2}, U_{m3} are the number of "0" bits in $B_1[m]$, $B_2[m]$, and $B_3[m]$, respectively. Let V_{m1}, V_{m2}, V_{m3} be the fraction of "0" bits in $B_1[m]$, $B_2[m]$, $B_3[m]$, respectively. It is easy to get that:

$$V_{m1} = \frac{U_{m1}}{m},$$
$$V_{m2} = \frac{U_{m2}}{m},$$
$$V_{m3} = \frac{U_{m3}}{m}.$$

The following formula is used to estimate the cardinality of host sip:

$$\hat{k} = \sum_{i=1}^{3}(p * s * lnV_{mi} - s * lnV_s) \tag{1}$$

Below we will derive (1) mathematically. Some additional notations are given as follows: let n be the number of distinct pairs $<sip, dip>$ from all source hosts during the measurement period. Define C_{j1} be the event that the jth bit in $B_1[m]$ is still zero when the measurement ends. For a source host with cardinality size k, each of the k distinct pairs is hashed to an arbitrary bit in the vector $X_1(sip)$ with probability $\frac{1}{s}$. And the probability that the bit is mapped by a pair of other source hosts is $\frac{1}{m}$. Hence the probability that event C_{j1} occurs is

$$Prob(C_{j1}) = (1 - \frac{1}{m})^{n-k}(1 - \frac{1}{s})^k, \forall j \in [0, s-1] \tag{2}$$

Let l_{Cj1} be a random variable that takes on the value 1 if event C_{j1} occurs, 0 otherwise. So the number of "0" in vector $X_1(sip)$ can be denoted by $U_{s1} = \sum_{j=0}^{j=s-1} l_{Cj1}$. Hence we can get the expected value of V_{s1} :

$$E(V_{s1}) = \frac{1}{s}E(U_{s1}) = \frac{1}{s}\sum_{j=0}^{j=s-1} E(l_{Cj1}) = \sum_{j=0}^{j=s-1} Prob(C_{j1})$$
$$= \frac{1}{s} * s * (1 - \frac{1}{m})^{n-k}(1 - \frac{1}{s})^k = (1 - \frac{1}{m})^{n-k}(1 - \frac{1}{s})^k \tag{3}$$
$$\simeq e^{-\frac{n-k}{m}} * e^{-\frac{s}{k}} , \text{ as } (n-k), m, k, s \to \infty$$
$$\simeq e^{-\frac{n}{m}-\frac{k}{s}} , \text{ as } k \ll m$$

From (3) we can get the cardinality value k as:

$$k \simeq -s * \frac{n}{m} - s * ln(E(V_{s1})) \tag{4}$$

According to [11] we can get the relation between n and m as follows:

$$n \simeq -m * ln(E(V_{m1})) \tag{5}$$

Hence (4) can be written as:

$$k \simeq s * ln(E(V_{m1})) - s * ln(E(V_{s1})) = s * ln(V_{m1}) - s * ln(V_{s1}) \qquad (6)$$

In (6) the second term is the number of distinct pairs mapped into vector $X_1(sip)$, but it does not equal to the number of distinct pairs of sip, because it has noise made by pairs of other hosts. And the first term is the noise. In our algorithm we let vectors $X_1(sip)$, $X_2(sip)$, $X_3(sip)$ do "and" operation to get the vector $X(sip)$. So the vector $X(sip)$ has eliminated fraction of those noises, we introduce the factor p (where $0 < p < 1$) to eliminate the rest noise. We get the optimal value of p through experiments. Then we can get (1). When k is small, it may happen with a small probability that $\hat{k}$ is less than one, in this case we set $\hat{k}$ to 1.

After derive the cardinality of each source host, we will estimate the cardinality distribution as $output[t]++$. The pseudo-code of the offline processing phase is shown in Algorithm 2.

Algorithm 2. Offline Processing

1: Upon the sip stored by Source IP storing module in array $distinctIP[n]$
2: **for** m=0 to n **do**
3:     sip=distinctIP[m];
4:     Xi(src)=(Bi[hashi(sip)],....,Bi[(hashi(sip)+s-1)mod m]);i=1,2,3
5: **end for**
6: X(src)=X1(src)&X2(src)&X3(src);
7: Us=countbit(X(src));
8: Umi=countbit(Bi[m]);
9: Vs=Us/s;
10: Vmi= Umi/m;
11: $k = \sum_{i=1}^{3}(p * s * lnV_{mi} - s * lnV_s)$;
12: **if** k<1 **then**
13:     k=1;
14: **else**
15:     k=int(k);
16: **end if**
17: output[k]++;
18: end

3.3 Performance Analysis

In order to know of the property of our algorithm, we analyze the space consumption and estimating error theoretically in this section.

A. Space Consumption

The space consumption (SRAM) of the algorithm is mainly determined by the online processing. The arrays $distinctIP[n]$ and $output[t]$ work in the DRAM, their influence to the space consumption can be ignored. Hence the main space consumption comes from the three bit arrays $B_1[m]$, $B_2[m]$, $B_3[m]$. Each bit array only needs one bit to record a flow, so the space consumption of each bit array is $\frac{1}{8}*m$ Bytes, where m is the size of a bit array. So the total space consumption of our algorithm is $\frac{3}{8}*m$ Bytes.

B. Error Analysis

In online processing phase each bit array provides a continuous virtual vector with size s for every source host. For the high cardinality hosts, s bits can't record their all pairs. Two or more pairs can be mapped to the same bit. Therefore the estimation is bigger than the true value. As mentioned above, bits of each bit array can be shared by multiple vectors. Therefore the value of U_s will decrease when the measurement ends and the estimation will be bigger than the true value especially for the low cardinality hosts. In our algorithm, we eliminate this kind of error through "and" operation. From (1), the value of $\hat{k}$ can not be always integer. In our algorithm we set $\hat{k}$ to k (k is the max-integer which is no more than $\hat{k}$). So every value between k and $k+1$ will be set to k. Therefore the number of hosts with cardinality size k is bigger than the true value.

4 Experiment

In this section, we use the continuous virtual vector algorithm to estimate the cardinality distribution using some real traces. Then we compare the estimation distributions with the actual cardinality distributions.

4.1 Data Source

We use different traffic traces gathered from real internet to test our algorithm. These traces are from MAWI Working Group of the WIDE Project (MAWI) [14], Jiangsu provincial network border of China Education and Research Network (CERNET) [15]. The trace from MAWI was collected on a trans-Pacific line (150Mbps link), on March 30, 2009 at 00:00 am. The IPv6 packets of MAWI are filtered out in our experiments. The CERNET traces were collected at Jiangsu provincial network border of China Education and Research Network (CERNET) on April 17, 2004.It includes TR1, TR2 and TR3. The backbone's capacity is 1000 Mbps, and mean traffic per day is 587 Mbps.

4.2 Parameter Analysis and Setting

For the size of bit array m, if it is big enough that the probability of hash collision is low, in such way the result will be relatively accurate. But limited by the memory capacity, m can not be too large. Here we set the size of m to be 65536. For the size of continuous virtual vector s, if it is large that the probability of different source hosts share one or more bits in the bit array is low, this will reduce measuring accuracy. But from (1), we can infer that s determines the maximum value that the algorithm can measure. So the small size of s will limit the measurement range of host cardinality. Considering these two reasons, we set s to be 128. We compute the weighted mean relative difference (WMRD) using MAWI trace to get the optimal value of p. We use (7) to compute the WMRD, where n_i denotes the actual host number with cardinality size n_i and n_i^* denotes the estimation number.

$$WMRD = \frac{\sum(n_i - n_i^*)}{\sum(\frac{n_i + n_i^*}{2})} \qquad (7)$$

When p is 0.75 the WMRD is the smallest as is shown in Table 1. In other words when p is 0.75 the algorithm is relatively accurate, so in our experiments we set p to be 0.75. The finally experiment results are shown in section 4.3.

Table 1. The deviation of algorithm using different p values

p	0.3	0.5	0.75	0.9
WMRD	1.432	1.397	1.175	1.268

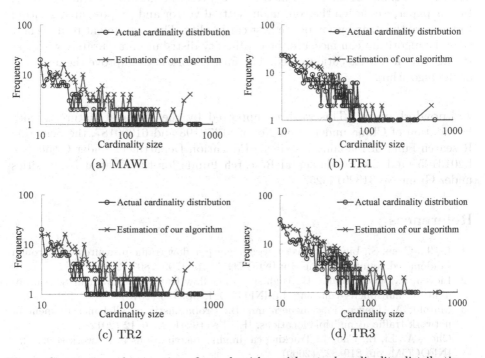

Fig. 2. Comparison of estimation of our algorithm with actual cardinality distribution, (a) MAWI, (b) TR1, (c) TR2, (d) TR3

4.3 Experiment Results

In this section, we compare the cardinality distribution measured by our algorithm with the actual cardinality distribution. In every experiment one million packets are used. The experiment results are shown in Figure 2. The x-coordinate is the cardinality size, and the y-coordinate denotes the number of hosts with the cardinality size x. We can see that for most low cardinality hosts, the estimation result is really bigger than the actual result as we analysed in section 3.3. In actual application such as attack detection, we are usually interested in those high cardinality hosts. And the experiment results show that the estimation of those high cardinality hosts is close to the actual result. So our algorithm can be used in actual application.

5 Conclusion

Because of the huge traffic in the high-speed network, network monitoring system is limited by storage and processing capabilities, it can not record all of the packets information. So getting the overall behavior of network traffic is very necessary for network monitoring and traffic engineering. The host cardinality distribution is one of the useful metrics to express the network overall behavior. In this paper, we design the continuous virtual vector and propose an algorithm to measure the distribution of the host cardinality. The experiment results show that the algorithm can measure the cardinality distribution accurately with less storage and faster execution speed. The future work is to improve the accuracy of the algorithm.

Acknowledgment. This work is supported by the National Nature Science Foundation of China under grant No. of 61370198 and 61300187, the Scientific Research Fund of Liaoning Provincial Education Department under Grant No. L2013195, and the Fundamental Research Funds for the Central Universities under Grant No.3132014325.

References

1. Li, T., Chen, S., Ling, Y.: Fast and compact per-flow traffic measurement through randomized counter sharing. In: INFOCOM, pp. 1799–1807 (2011)
2. Lieven, P., Scheuermann, B.: High-speed per-flow traffic measurement with probabilistic multiplicity counting. In: INFOCOM, pp. 1–9 (2010)
3. Marold, A., Lieven, P., Scheuermann, B.: Probabilistic parallel measurement of network traffic at multiple locations. IEEE Network 26, 6–12 (2012)
4. Chen, A., Li, L., Cao, J.: Tracking cardinality distributions in network traffic. In: INFOCOM, pp. 819–827 (2009)
5. Duffield, N., Lund, C., Thorup, M.: Estimating flow distributions from sampled flow statistics. In: SIGCOMM, pp. 325–336 (2003)
6. Yang, L., Michailidis, G.: Sampled based estimation of network traffic flow characteristics. In: INFOCOM, pp. 1775–1783 (2007)

7. Kumar, A., Sung, M., Xu, J.J., Wang, J.: Data streaming algorithms for efficient and accurate estimation of flow size distribution. In: SIGMETRICS, vol. 32, pp. 177–188 (2004)
8. Karamcheti, V., Geiger, D., Kedem, Z., Muthukrishnan, S.: Detecting malicious network traffic using inverse distributions of packet contents. In: SIGCOMM, pp. 165–170 (2005)
9. Chen, W., Liu, Y., Guan, Y.: Cardinality change-based early detection of largescale cyber-attacks. In: INFOCOM, pp. 1788–1796 (2013)
10. Guan, X., Wang, P., Qin, T.: A new data streaming method for locating hosts with large connection degree. In: GLOBECOM, pp. 1–6 (2009)
11. Whang, K.Y., Vander-Zanden, B.T., Taylor, H.M.: A linear-time probabilistic counting algorithm for database applications. ACM Transactions on Database Systems 15, 208–229 (1990)
12. Estan, C., Varghese, G., Fisk, M.: Bitmap algorithms for counting active flows on high speed links. In: SIGCOMM, pp. 153–166 (2003)
13. Yoon, M., Li, T., Chen, S., Peir, J.K.: Fit a spread estimator in small memory. In: INFOCOM, pp. 504–512 (2009)
14. Wide: http://tracer.csl.sony.co.jp/mawi/samplepoint-f/20090330/200903300000.html (2014)
15. Jslab: http://ntds.njnet.edu.cn/data/index.php (2014)

Hmfs: Efficient Support of Small Files Processing over HDFS

Cairong Yan, Tie Li, Yongfeng Huang, and Yanglan Gan

School of Computer Science and Technology,
Donghua University,
201620 Shanghai, China
cryan@dhu.edu.cn

Abstract. The storage and access of massive small files are one of the challenges in the design of distributed file system. Hadoop distributed file system (HDFS) is primarily designed for reliable storage and fast access of very big files while it suffers a performance penalty with increasing number of small files. A middleware called Hmfs is proposed in this paper to improve the efficiency of storing and accessing small files on HDFS. It is made up of three layers, file operation interfaces to make it easier for software developers to submit different file requests, file management tasks to merge small files into big ones or extract small files from big ones in the background, and file buffers to improve the I/O performance. Hmfs boosts the file upload speed by using asynchronous write mechanism and the file download speed by adopting prefetching and caching strategy. The experimental results show that Hmfs can help to obtain high speed of storage and access for massive small files on HDFS.

Keywords: HDFS, small files, middleware, asynchronous write, prefetching.

1 Introduction

Hadoop, an open-source software framework developed for reliable, scalable, distributed computing and storage, is successfully used by many companies including Yahoo, Amazon, Facebook, and New York Times [1]. Hadoop distributed file system (HDFS), as the primary storage system of Hadoop, is a portable, high reliability, high throughput, and open source distributed file system. It is primarily designed for streaming access of big files. Reading through small files normally causes lots of seeks and lots of hopping from one DataNode to another DataNode to retrieve each small file, all of which is an inefficient data access pattern [2].

The low efficiency of storing and accessing small files on HDFS (which is called small files problem for simplicity in this paper) is majorly caused by: (1) the small files will produce a lot of metadata on HDFS NameNode so that too much memory space will be occupied when HDFS is working; (2) the file access mechanism of HDFS is not suitable for a large number of small files; and (3) HDFS lacks of I/O optimization mechanism such as file prefetching and caching [2,3].

X.-h. Sun et al. (Eds.): ICA3PP 2014, Part II, LNCS 8631, pp. 54–67, 2014.
© Springer International Publishing Switzerland 2014

The most popular idea of solving the small files problem is to combine small files into big ones, establish index mechanism to map the small files to HDFS blocks, prefetch and cache the related small files when one of them is accessed. These existing research methods mainly focus on optimizing the storage structure or the access mechanism of HDFS [3-14].

In this paper, without making any change of HDFS, we design and implement a middleware Hmfs (Hadoop-based middleware for file system) on top of HDFS for addressing the small files problem by providing the following features:

- Hmfs is a middleware running on HDFS. It is easy to be transplanted to some more advanced versions of HDFS in the future.
- Hmfs saves the space of HDFS NameNode by storing the index data in an in-memory database instead of HDFS.
- Hmfs optimizes the file upload operation on HDFS by applying asynchronous write mechanism.
- Hmfs adopts a prefetching and caching strategy to fasten the file download speed.

The remainder of the paper is organized as follows: section 2 reviews some related work; section 3 analyzes the problems of small files processing over HDFS; section 4 introduces the design of Hmfs; section 5 describes the optimization strategy of Hmfs; section 6 presents the experimental results; and section 7 concludes the paper.

2   Related Work

A small file is the one that is significantly smaller than the HDFS block size (default 64MB). Recently, research on small files problem of HDFS has attracted significant attention. Shvachko et al from Yahoo! described the design and implementation of HDFS where every file, directory, and block is represented as an object in the NameNode's memory, each of which occupies 150 bytes [2]. It is designed mainly for the streaming access of big files not small files.

There are some general approaches based on HDFS to solve the small files problem. Hadoop Archives (HAR files) were introduced to HDFS in 0.18.0 to alleviate the problem of lots of files putting pressure on the NameNode's memory. HAR files work by building a layered file system on top of HDFS. However, reading through files in HAR is no more efficient than reading through files in HDFS, since each HAR file access requires two index file reads as well as the data file is read [7]. SequenceFile provides a persistent data structure for binary key-value pairs. It uses file name as the key and file contents as the value, and supports compressing and decompressing at record level or block level [8]. However, it may be slow to convert existing data into SequenceFiles. Unlike HAR files there is no way to list all the keys in a SequenceFile. A MapFile is a type of sorted SequenceFiles with an index to permit lookups by key. It consists of an index file and a data file. The data file stores key-value pairs as records, which are sorted in key order. The index file stores key-location information and the location is the offset where the first record containing this key is located in data file. HBase stores data in MapFiles (indexed SequenceFiles), and is a good choice if you need to do MapReduce style streaming analyses with the occasional random look up [9]. These approaches improve the storage efficiency of HDFS by changing the storage structure.

There are also some approaches based on HDFS for special application files. Reference [4] took the file correlations and access locality into consideration, and proposed a two-level prefetching mechanism to improve the efficiency of accessing powerpoint files. Reference [5,6] packed the related GIS data into big files and stored them into HDFS. These researches made full use of the relationship between files. Some approaches focused on cached the metadata and position of blocks to reduce the access to NameNode or DataNode. Some approaches aimed at optimizing the access of small files by storing the index data in the memory, database or in-memory database [10-14].

Compared with these existing researches, Hmfs proposed in this paper is a middleware based on HDFS, and it's easy to be transplanted to the advanced versions of HDFS in the future. The merged big files only contain file data while the index data of small files is stored in an in-memory database. That improves the memory utilization and simplifies the operation of file update and delete. Furthermore, the asynchronous write mechanism helps to improve the response time of jobs.

3   Small Files Problem in HDFS

HDFS has many similarities with existing distributed file systems. However, the differences from others are significant. It supports tens of millions of files in a single instance, and it has been designed to be easily portable from one platform to another. So it is widely used for big-scale file storage.

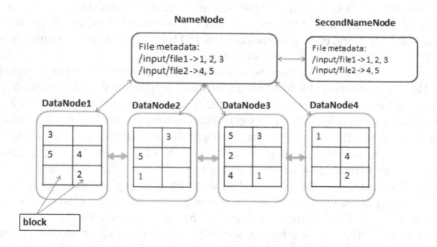

Fig. 1. The architecture of HDFS

As shown in Fig. 1, HDFS is composed of NameNode and DataNodes. NameNode manages file system namespace which is called as metadata, and regulates client accesses. DataNodes provide block storage, serve I/O requests from clients, and perform block operations upon instructions from NameNode. SecondNameNode which is responsible for backing up all data on NameNode is optional.

When we download a file from HDFS, the time cost is composed of the following parts. (1) A client sends an access request to NameNode. Assume the time is T_1. (2) NameNode looks up the metadata of the requested file in memory. Assume the time is T_2. (3) NameNode returns the block addresses to the client. Assume the time is T_3. (4) The client accesses data from DataNodes one by one. Here the time is made up of three parts, T_{4a}, T_{4b}, and T_{4c}. First, the client sends the blockId to DataNode. The time is T_{4a}. Then DataNode gets the blockId and fetches the file data from the hard disk. The time is T_{4b}. Finally, the DataNode returns the data to the client. The time is T_{4c}.

Suppose that there are n files to be downloaded and each file is divided into m blocks, the total time cost can be represented as formula (1):

$$T_n = \sum_1^n (T_1 + T_2 + T_3 + \sum_1^m T_4), \quad T_4 = T_{4a} + T_{4b} + T_{4c} \tag{1}$$

When the size of the files is less than the size of a block, m is 1. The total time consumption can be represented as formula (2):

$$T_n = \sum_1^n (T_1 + T_2 + T_3 + T_4) \tag{2}$$

When n is very big and m is 1, the metadata in NameNode will increase rapidly and NameNode may be overloaded. So it is necessary to minimize the size of metadata so as to reduce the access time in NameNode. Furthermore, if we fetch the files from HDFS in advance, the response time of the job will decrease. The file prefetching and caching strategies are efficient to improve the throughput of the job. When the total size of n files is less than the size of a block, it is a challenge to decrease the total time consumption to $T_1 + T_2 + T_3 + T_4$. This paper will focus on it.

When we upload a file to HDFS, the time cost is composed of the following parts. (1) A client sends an access request to NameNode. Assume the time is T_1'. (2) NameNode creates metadata for the file. Assume the time is T_2'. (3) NameNode returns the data output stream to the client. Assume the time is T_3'. (4) The client sends data to the output stream and stores the data in DataNode, DataNode informs NameNode the place, and the client closes the output stream. Assume the time is T_4'.

Suppose that there are n files needing to be uploaded and each file is divided into m blocks. Then the total time cost can be represented as formula (3):

$$T_n' = \sum_1^n (T_1' + T_2' + T_3' + \sum_1^m T_4') \tag{3}$$

When the size of files is less than the size of a block, m is 1. Then the total time consumption can be represented as formula (4):

$$T_n' = \sum_1^n (T_1' + T_2' + T_3' + T_4') \tag{4}$$

If the total size of n files is less than the size of a block, we can merge the small files in advance so that the total access time consumption can be decreased to $T_1' + T_2' + T_3' + T_4'$. It is also a challenge and this paper will also focus on decreasing the file upload time.

4   The Design of Hmfs

In order to improve the efficiency of storing and accessing small files in HDFS, we propose Hmfs, a middleware supporting file operations over HDFS including upload, download, update, and delete.

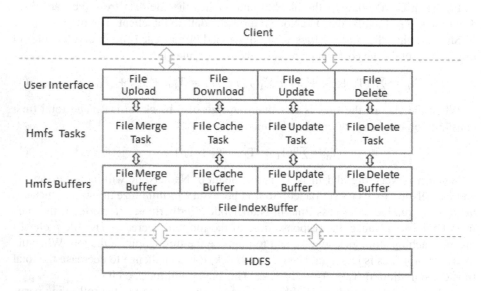

Fig. 2. The architecture of Hmfs

Fig. 2 shows the architecture of Hmfs which consists of three layers, user interface, Hmfs tasks, and Hmfs buffers.

The client can upload, download, update, and delete files according to the user interface layer without thinking about the size of the files. If the files are small, they will be merged in Hmfs tasks layer according to the size of HDFS block. The upload, update, and delete operations are executed asynchronously so that the clients do not need to wait a long time.

Hmfs tasks layer, the core component of Hmfs, is responsible for four kinds of file processing tasks. File merge task is used to combine the small files into big ones, build index for the small files, and upload the big files to HDFS. File cache task is to cache the related files when a small file is accessed. File update task is used to update files. File delete task is used to delete files.

The bottom is the Hmfs buffers layer. Hmfs uses five kinds of buffers in memory to store the uploaded files, indexing files, caching files, and other data. File merge buffer is to store the files that are uploaded by the clients and waiting for merging. File cache buffer is to store the related files when a file is accessed. File index buffer is to store the index data that maps the small files to HDFS blocks. It includes file length, file start position, and HDFS block path. File update buffer is to store the data that needs to be updated, and waits to be stored in HDFS. File delete buffer is to store fileIds that need to be deleted, and wait to be deleted from HDFS later.

All the tasks run as the daemon processes, so Hmfs can process the client request and the file merging, caching and updating operation in parallel. The brief overview of the relationship between Hmfs tasks and HDFS buffers is as follows. File merge task is responsible for merging small files in the file merge buffer to form big files, building index for each small file, and storing the index data in the file index buffer. File cache task prefetches the related files when a small file is accessed and stores the files in the file cache buffer. File update task gets the information in the file update buffer, updates the related block in the HDFS, and forward the updated block to the file merge buffer. File delete task fetches information from the file delete buffer to know which files need to be deleted, then deletes the files in HDFS block and forwards the updated block to the file merge buffer.

4.1   File Operation Interface

Hmfs supports the basic file operations including upload, download, update, and delete. Fig. 3 shows their workflow. The following is the detailed description of these interfaces provided by Hmfs.

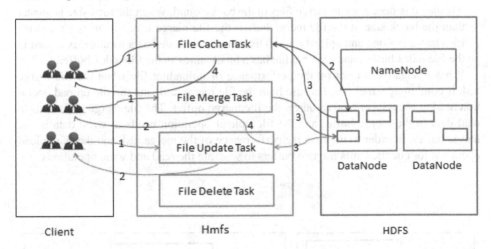

Fig. 3. File upload(red line), download(blue line), and update(green line)

- **FileUpload().** This function will receive a request from a client, generate an identifier fileId for the file, upload the fileId and its data to the file merge buffer, and return the fileId to the client.

- **FileDownload().** This function will check the file according to fileId in the file index buffer, the file delete buffer, the file update buffer, the file merge buffer, and the file cache buffer one by one. If the file is found, the function will return its content. If the file does not exist, the function will check the file in HDFS. After the file is downloaded, the function will trigger the file cache task.
- **FileUpdate().** When a client submits an update request, Hmfs does not update the file in HDFS immediately. The function will check the file in the file index buffer and the file merge buffer, then store the fileId and its new data in the file update buffer.
- **FileDelete().** When a client submits a delete request, Hmfs will check whether the file exists in the file index buffer, the file merge buffer, or the file update buffer. If it exists, Hmfs will store the fileId in the file delete buffer. Or an error will be returned.

From the process of file upload, update, and delete, we can see that these operations will not submit the requests to HDFS immediately; instead, the files and operations will be stored in the buffers and wait for processing by the file tasks. The asynchronous write mechanism is adopted in Hmfs to boost the file operations speed.

4.2   File Tasks

There are four tasks running in the background to implement the file operations.

- **File merge task.** The file merge task will regularly scan the file merge buffer to detect whether it is necessary to merge files in the background. When the total size is greater than the block size in the file merge buffer, the file merge task will merge the small files into a big one and upload it to HDFS. Each small file has a local index record in the file index buffer, and each big file has a block index in the file index buffer.

  It has a negative impact on the performance of uploading file when the file merge task is combining small files because both the file merge task and the file upload operation need to access a critical resource, the file merge buffer. The file merge task needs to read data in the merge buffer and the file upload operation needs to write data in the merge buffer. In order to improve the performance of the merge task and the file upload operation for clients, Hmfs use two buffers to separate the read and write operations.

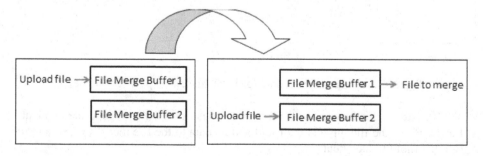

Fig. 4. Buffers switch

As shown in Fig. 4, there are two file merge buffers. When a client is uploading a file to Hmfs and Hmfs is uploading the file to the file merge buffer, the file merge task will not do the merge task. When the file merge task is performing the merge task, the places of buffer 1 and buffer 2 are exchanged. Then buffer 1 is used to read for the file merge task and buffer 2 is used to write for the file upload operation. When the file merge task executes the next task, the places of two buffers are switched again. In this way, the buffers are switched back and forth so that the functions of read and write are split.

- **File update task.** Because HDFS does not support file update operation currently, if we want to update a file, it needs to delete the old file and add the new one. So the file update task will send the old fileId to the file delete task and send the new file to the file merge task.
- **File delete task.** Hmfs delete task will regularly scan the file delete buffer and submit the delete request to HDFS.
- **File cache task.** Hmfs cache task executes the optimization process. The related algorithms will be described in the next section.

4.3 Buffer Structure

There are five kinds of buffers in Hmfs. The data in the buffer is stored in the form of <key, value>. They are the key of improving performance for Hmfs.

- Hmfs index buffer is the basic and most important. When a client uploads a file to Hmfs, it will return a fileId according to some rules. It is necessary to generate index between the small files and the block in HDFS. There are two kinds of index data. For each small file, there is a pair of <key, value> in the index buffer, where key is fileId and value is HDFS path. For each block in HDFS, we store all the related index of small files in the block, which concludes fileIds and their size.
- In the file cache buffer, data is a list which stores the cached file group by block. In order to avoid conflicting, we need to save the latest access time of the block.
- In the file merge buffer, data is stored in the form of <fileId, fileContent>, where fileContent is the content of the file to be merged.
- In the file update buffer, data is stored in the form of <fileId, newContent>, where newContent is the updated content of the file.
- In the file delete buffer, data is stored in the form of <fileId, delTime>, where delTime is used for conflict detection.

5 Optimization Strategy

5.1 File Prefetching and Caching

Prefetching is a widely used storage optimization technique. It hides visible disk I/O cost and improves response time by exploiting access locality and fetching data into cache before they are requested. Currently, HDFS does not provide prefetching function.

It is important to decide when to prefetch the files. For different applications, there are many prefetching strategies to reduce the access time and improve the response speed. In this paper, we assume that there is no relationship between files and the files are merged in accordance with the order of upload time. So the files in one block may share the similar update time. Once a client accesses a small file, Hmfs will fetch the whole block from HDFS to get the small files. Hmfs will store the block in the file cache buffer. If a client accesses another file in this block, Hmfs will obtain it from the cache buffer. It is much faster than from HDFS.

Based on the above analysis, when a client accesses a file with a fileId, we adopt the following prefetching and caching strategy in Hmfs.

Algorithm 1. File prefetching

Input: fileId
Output: cacheList<k,v>
Step 1: Hmfs looks up the file index buffer to get the path of fileId in HDFS.
Step 2: Hmfs downloads the content of the file in HDFS, and sends a request to the file cache task.
Step 3: When the file cache task receives the cache request, it will fetch the rest of the files belong to the same HDFS block and add <fileId, fileContent> to cacheList which will be stored in the file cache buffer.
Step 4: Return cacheList.

5.2   Buffer Replacement Mechanism

Since the memory is limited, it is impossible to cache all the HDFS blocks in the file cache buffer. A buffer replacement mechanism is necessary for data eliminating according to the size of the file cache buffer.

Hmfs adopts the least recently used algorithm to eliminate the longest unused blocks. When a client request hits a block in the file cache buffer, the block's latest access time in the file cache buffer will be updated. Or Hmfs needs to determine whether the number of blocks in the file cache buffer is greater than N (the maximum cache block number). If so, Hmfs sorts the whole block in the file cache buffer by the latest access time and removes the longest unused block.

When a new block needs to be cached in the file cache buffer, we adopt the following mechanism to assign the space for it.

Algorithm 2. Buffer replacement

Input: blockList<k1, v1>, k ,N // k1 is the blockId, v1 is the access time, k is the new request, and N is the capacity of the file cache buffer
Output: blockList<k2, v2> // new blockId and access time
Step 1: Check k in blockList. If k is in blockList, update its access time. Goto Step 4.
Step 2: If the file cache buffer is full, sort the elements in blockList according to v1, and delete the element with the smallest v1.
Step 3: Add <k, currentTime> to blockList. Goto Step 4.
Step 4: Return blockList.

6 Experimental Evaluation

6.1 Experimental Environment

The test platform is built on a cluster with 5 nodes. One node acts as NameNode, which has 2 Intel Xeon CPU (2.40GHz), 16 GB memory, and 1 TB disk. One node runs Hmfs middleware, which has 2 Intel Core CPU (i5-3470, 3.20GHz), 8GB memory, and 1TB disk. The other three nodes act as DataNodes. Each of them has 2 Intel Xeon CPU (2.00GHz), 16 GB memory, and 2 TB disk.

In each node, Ubuntu server 12.04 with the kernel of version 3.2.0-24 is installed. Hadoop version is 1.2.1 and Java version is 1.6.0. The number of replicas is set to 3 and HDFS block size is 64 MB by default.

The small files for test are generated randomly. The minimum size of these small files is 10 KB, and the maximum size is 1024 KB.

6.2 Memory Usage Analysis

The memory usage is an important metric to evaluate the distributed file system. In the experiment, we use AMUPF, average memory usage per file, to evaluate the memory usage of Hmfs. AMUPF = M/N. Here, M stands for the used memory of HDFS NameNode and N stands for the number of files stored in HDFS.

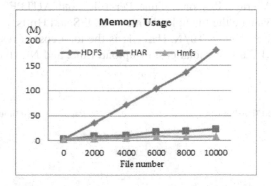

Fig. 5. NameNode memory usage of HDFS, HAR, and Hmfs

Fig. 5 shows the memory usage comparison among HDFS, HAR, and Hmfs. The number of small files are 2000, 4000, 6000, 8000, and 10,000. Their size is distributed randomly. The values of AMUPF for HDFS, HAR, and Hmfs are 0.018, 0.0022, and 0.0008 respectively. From this figure, we can see that, HAR and Hmfs spend much less memory space than HDFS. The main reason why Hmfs has the best performance among these three approaches is that the index of the small files is stored in the Hmfs index buffer.

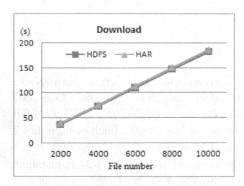
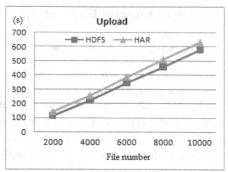

Fig. 6. Download and upload time of HDFS and HAR

Fig. 6 shows the download and upload time of HDFS and HAR. They almost spend the same download time while HDFS spend less upload time because it does not need to combine the small files into big ones. However, HDFS spends more space to store the metadata of the small files individually. Considering this, the following analysis will focus on the performance comparison between HDFS and Hmfs.

6.3   Upload Efficiency Analysis

We use ARTPF (Average Response Time Per File) and AUTPF (Average Upload Time Per File) to evaluate the file upload time of HDFS and Hmfs.

ARTPF = Tr/N, AUTPF = Tu/N. Here, Tr is the total cost of response time when N files are uploaded, Tu is the total cost of upload time, and N is the number of files to be uploaded.

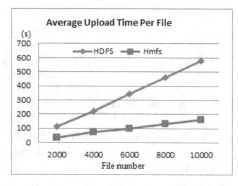
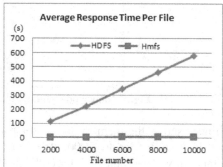

Fig. 7. Upload time of HDFS and Hmfs

Fig. 7 shows the upload time and response time comparison between HDFS and Hmfs. The number of small files are 2000, 4000, 6000, 8000, and 10,000. Their size is distributed randomly.

From this figure, we find that the response time of Hmfs is much less than HDFS. This is mainly because of the asynchronous write mechanism of Hmfs. That is, when a client submits an upload request to Hmfs, Hmfs will create a fileId and send back to the client immediately. The real file upload operation will be completed by the file merge task in background.

When N is 10,000, the value of AUTPF for HDFS is 0.056 while it is 0.016 for Hmfs, and the value of ARTPF for HDFS is 0.056 while it is 0.0006 for Hmfs. Such a big gap is caused because AUTPF takes the file upload time and the file merge time into consideration. So for Hmfs, the value of AUTPF is bigger than that of ARTPF.

6.4   Download Efficiency Analysis

We use ADTPF (Average Download Time Per File) to evaluate the file download time of HDFS and Hmfs. ADTPF = Td/N. Here, Td stands for the total time consumption and N is the number of files.

For different operations such as sequential download and random download, the execute time of HDFS and Hmfs is totally different. This is related to the size of the file cache buffer. Here, we set the capacity of the file cache buffer is 10.

Sequential Download. We first upload 10,000 small files to HDFS and Hmfs respectively, then download 2000, 4000, 6000, 8000, 10,000 files to the local disk by the upload order. Fig. 8 shows the experimental results. The values of ADTPF for HDFS and Hmfs are 0.018 and 0.020 respectively.

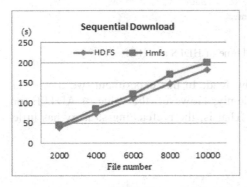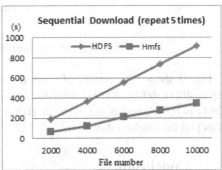

Fig. 8. Sequential download time of HDFS and Hmfs

From Fig. 8, we can see that the sequential download speed of Hmfs is a little slower than HDFS. That's determined by the mechanism of Hmfs prefetching and caching. In Hmfs, when a client submits a request to download a file, Hmfs will get the content of the file from HDFS and return the file to client. Meanwhile, the file cache task will fetch the rest of the files which belong to the same HDFS block and store them in the file cache buffer asynchronously. The strategy of caching files by the asynchronous file cache task affects the response speed of a single file. So the download speed of a single file in Hmfs is slower than HDFS.

66   C. Yan et al.

Prefetching and caching is a popular technology to improve the I/O performance in the file systems. In Hmfs, the prefetching and caching strategy will speed up the next file download speed if they are in the same block with the first file. In order to experience the advantage brought by the optimization strategy, we download N files in sequential, and repeat the process five times. The experimental result is shown on the right side of Fig. 8. The value of ADTPF for Hmfs is 0.007 while it is 0.018 for HDFS. The download speed of Hmfs is much faster than HDFS.

Random Download. The above experiment demonstrates that the prefetching and caching strategy can bring high efficiency for sequential file download when we download a big amount of files. Generally, this optimization strategy will have side effects on random download because it is difficult to predict the next files and an unreasonable prefetching strategy may result in low efficiency.

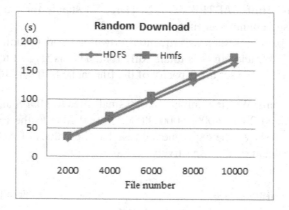

Fig. 9. Random download time of HDFS and Hmfs

Fig. 9 shows the results of random download. In this experiment, we download 2000, 4000, 6000, 8000, 10000 files randomly. However, the value of ADTPF for Hmfs is 0.018, and it is 0.016 for HDFS. That is, the prefetching strategy has little effect on the random download.

7   Conclusion

HDFS is expert in handling big files while it is inefficient to deal with small files. This is mainly caused by the logic structure of HDFS and its access mechanism.

In this paper, we propose Hmfs, a middleware based on HDFS to solve the small files problem in HDFS. Some contributions are outlined as follows. First, Hmfs provides a general solution for all kinds of small files such as text, image, and video segment. It supports four basic file operations including upload, download, update, and delete. It can run on different versions of HDFS as long as the read and write interfaces of HDFS are not changed. Second, the asynchronous write mechanism makes it unique and can bring rapid response for clients. Third, the prefetching and caching strategies with in-memory database improve the efficiency of file access.

In future work, we will consider the relationship between files and focus on content-based file merge method with the aim of improving the speed of related file access.

Acknowledgment. This research is supported by the Fundamental Research Funds for the Central Universities of China (grant No. 14D111210), the National Natural Science Foundation of China (grant No. 61300100), and the Natural Science Foundation of Shanghai (grant No. 13ZR1451000).

References

1. Hadoop, http://hadoop.apache.org/
2. Shvachko, K., Kuang, H.: Radia. S.: The hadoop distributed file system. In: IEEE 26th Symposium on Mass Storage Systems and Technologies (MSST 2010). Incline Village, Nevada (2010)
3. Dong, B., Zheng, Q., Tian, F., et al.: An optimized approach for storing and accessing small files on cloud storage. Journal of Network and Computer Applications 35(6), 1847–1862 (2012)
4. Dong, B., Qiu, J., Zheng, Q., et al.: A novel approach to improving the efficiency of storing and accessing small files on hadoop: a case study by powerpoint files. In: IEEE International Conference on Services Computing (SCC 2010), Miami, Florida, USA (2010)
5. Liu, X., Han, J., Zhong, Y., et al.: Implementing WebGIS on hadoop: a case study of improving small file I/O performance on HDFS. In: IEEE International Conference on Cluster Computing and Workshops (CLUSTER 2009), New Orleans, LA, USA (2009)
6. Cui, J., Zhang, Y., Li, C., Xing, C.: A packaging approach for massive amounts of small geospatial files with HDFS. In: Gao, H., Lim, L., Wang, W., Li, C., Chen, L. (eds.) WAIM 2012. LNCS, vol. 7418, pp. 210–215. Springer, Heidelberg (2012)
7. Hadoop Archives, http://hadoop.apache.org/common/docs/r0.20.2/hadoop_archive
8. Sequence File, http://wiki.apache.org/hadoop/SequenceFile
9. Hbase, http://hbase.apache.org/
10. Gohil, P., Panchal, B.: Efficient ways to improve the performance of HDFS for small files. Computer Engineering and Intelligent Systems 5(1), 45–49 (2014)
11. Wang, Y., Zhang, S., Liu, H.: The design of distributed file system based on HDFS. Applied Mechanics and Materials 423, 2733–2736 (2013)
12. Mao, Y., Min, W.: Storage and accessing small files based on HDFS. In: Patnaik, S., Li, X. (eds.) 4th International Conference on Computer Science and Information Technology (CCSIT 2014). AISC, vol. 255, pp. 565–573. Springer, Heidelberg (2014)
13. Chandrasekar, S., Dakshinamurthy, R., Seshakumar, P., et al.: A novel indexing scheme for efficient handling of small files in hadoop distributed file system. In: 2013 International Conference on Computer Communication and Informatics, ICCCI 2013 (2013)
14. Mackey, G., Sehrish, S., Wang, J.: Improving metadata management for small files in HDFS. In: IEEE International Conference on Cluster Computing and Workshops (CLUSTER 2009), New Orleans, Louisiana, USA (2009)

Utilizing Multiple Xeon Phi Coprocessors on One Compute Node

Xinnan Dong[1], Jun Chai[1], Jing Yang[1], Mei Wen[1], Nan Wu[1], Xing Cai[2,3],
Chunyuan Zhang[1], and Zhaoyun Chen[1]

[1] School of Computer Science, National University of Defense Technology
Changsha, Hunan 410073, China
xinnandong@126.com,
{chaijun200306,estella,meiwen,nanwu,cyzhang,chenzhaoyun}@nudt.edu.cn
[2] Simula Research Laboratory
P.O. Box 134, 1325 Lyakser, Norway
xingca@simula.no
[3] Department of Informatics, University of Oslo.
P.O. Box 1080 Blindern, 0316 Oslo, Norway

Abstract. Future exascale systems are expected to adopt compute nodes that incorporate many accelerators. This paper thus investigates the topic of programming multiple Xeon Phi coprocessors that lie inside one compute node. Besides a standard MPI-OpenMP programming approach, which belongs to the symmetric usage mode, two offload-mode programming approaches are considered. The first offload approach is conventional and uses compiler pragmas, whereas the second one is new and combines Intel's APIs of *coprocessor offload infrastructure* (COI) and *symmetric communication interface* (SCIF) for low-latency communication. While the pragma-based approach allows simpler programming, the COI-SCIF approach has three advantages in (1) lower overhead associated with launching offloaded code, (2) higher data transfer bandwidths, and (3) more advanced asynchrony between computation and data movement. The low-level COI-SCIF approach is also shown to have benefits over the MPI-OpenMP counterpart. All the programming approaches are tested by a real-world 3D application, for which the COI-SCIF approach shows a performance upper hand on a Tianhe-2 compute node with three Xeon Phi coprocessors.

1 Introduction

For the field of high-performance computing, energy efficiency considerations have prompted modern supercomputers to adopt accelerators, such as general-purpose GPUs and many-integrated-core (MIC) coprocessors. A good example is Tianhe-2, which is currently ranked No. 1 on the TOP500 List [1]. Three Intel Xeon Phi coprocessors can be found in each of Tianhe-2's 16,000 compute nodes [2]. However, with this unconventional multi-coprocessor-per-node setup come challenges of programming. Apart from ensuring the performance of each

X.-h. Sun et al. (Eds.): ICA3PP 2014, Part II, LNCS 8631, pp. 68–81, 2014.

coprocessor, there arises a new challenge of joining the force of several coprocessors within one compute node. The most important issue in the latter subject concerns implementing data transfers between the coprocessors, to achieve high performance with acceptable coding difficulty.

The Xeon Phi coprocessors from Intel adopt the MIC architecture and support a modified x86 instruction set, thereby providing the programmability of a full-fledged multicore CPU [3–5]. A coprocessor-enhanced compute node has always a CPU *host* consisting of one or more multicore CPU sockets that share a memory address space. There can be one or more coprocessor cards, each connected to the host as a *device* via a PCIe bus. The cores on each coprocessor have access to a shared device memory space that is disjoint from both the host and the other coprocessors.

For a multi-coprocessor compute node, two usage modes can be adopted: *offload* and *symmetric* [6]. In the offload mode, the code is first started on the CPU host, whereas compute-intensive blocks of the code are offloaded to the coprocessors. In the symmetric mode, the coprocessors are considered as independent nodes of a mini-supercomputer. For example, MPI can be used to start the code simultaneously on the coprocessors, and possibly also the CPU host. This MPI approach in the symmetric mode is simple and has the best code portability. However, one major disadvantage with a pure MPI approach is the excessive overhead in memory footprint due to the large number of MPI processes. A remedy is to use one MPI process per coprocessor while adopting OpenMP threads for intra-coprocessor parallelism.

Due to the possible shortcoming of the MPI-based symmetric usage mode, we also want to consider the offload usage mode. The usual approach is to insert an `offload` pragma in front of each code block that is to be offloaded. The resulting coprocessor-coprocessor data transfers are actually relayed through the host. In this paper, we present a new offload programming approach, which allows each coprocessor to run an independent sub-program, while bi-directional and asynchronous coprocessor-coprocessor data transfers are directly enabled by Intel's low-level APIs of *coprocessor offload infrastructure* (COI) [20] and *symmetric communication interface* (SCIF) [21]. The choice of this offload programming approach is motived by performance. We believe this paper is a first effort in studying how to efficiently program multiple Xeon Phi coprocessors within one compute node, by comparing the two offload programming approaches against the MPI-OpenMP counterpart.

The remainder of the paper is organized as follows. Some background information is presented in Section 2, and the related work is surveyed in Section 3. Section 4 explains the two offload programming approaches, using a simple example of 3D stencil computation. Section 5 quantifies the performance advantages of the low-level COI-SCIF approach, in terms of both bandwidth measurements and time usages of a real-world 3D application. All the experiments have been done on a compute node of Tianhe-2, with three Xeon Phi coprocessors.

2   Background

2.1   Xeon Phi Coprocessor

Intel's Xeon Phi coprocessor has up to 61 x86-based Intel CPU cores on a single chip. Each core supports 512-bit SIMD vector computing, and has 32 KB private L1 data cache and 512 KB shared L2 cache. Four hardware threads can be enabled on each core to give up to 244 threads per chip. Each coprocessor has its own device memory and is connected to the CPU host via PCIe bus.

2.2   Pragma-Based Offloading

In this pragma-based programming approach [18], the CPU host controls the entire execution of a code. Blocks of the code can be delegated to the coprocessors for execution. Since memory is not shared between the host and any of the coprocessors, variables and arrays needed in the offloaded code block also have to be allocated on the target coprocessors. The content of the coprocessor data can be transferred back to the host if desired. Below is an example of the directive that combines code offload with host-coprocessor data transfers.

```
#pragma offload target(mic:id) \
        in(input_msg: length(N)) out(output_msg: length(N))
```

Here, `id` is an integer specifying the target coprocessor. The content of array `input_msg` (of length N), which is marked by the `in` specifier, is copied from the host at the start of offload. Similarly, the content of array `output_msg` is copied back to the host at the end of offload. A third possible data specifier is `inout`, which marks a variable or array as both input and output. A fourth possible data specifier is `nocopy`, which only marks variables that will be used on the target coprocessor, but without any host-coprocessor data movements (by assuming that these variables persist on the coprocessor). For a code block that is offloaded iteratively, to save the cost of repeatedly allocating/deallocating the same data storage, the modifiers `alloc_if(arg)` and `free_if(arg)` can be used.

To initiate asynchronous host-coprocessor data transfers, such that computations have the possibility of being simultaneously carried out, the `signal` clause can used together with the `offload` pragma or another pragma named `offload_transfer`. The compiler directive only initiates an asynchronous data transfer without offloading any computation to the target coprocessor. A matching `offload_wait` pragma should be used to complete the asynchronous data transfer. An example is as follows:

```
#pragma offload_transfer target(mic:id) \
        out(output_msg: length(N)) signal(output_msg)
                       ...
#pragma offload_wait target(mic:id) wait(output_msg)
```

Although asynchronous data transfers are achievable with pragma-based programming, one major disadvantage is that data transfers between two coprocessors always have to be relayed through the host. The second disadvantage is the offload start-up cost, especially for a code block that is offloaded iteratively.

2.3 COI and SCIF

To realize direct coprocessor-coprocessor data transfers in connection with offload programming, while also avoiding the overhead related to repeated offload start-ups, we use two low-level APIs: COI and SCIF, provided by Intel's MPSS software stack [19]. They provide the programmer with a finer control of code offloading and data transfers.

Two of COI's key abstractions, namely *COIEngine* and *COIProcess*, are important for the following implementations. The first abstraction represents a COI-capable device, e.g., the host or a coprocessor, whereas the second one encapsulates a process created by COI on a remote engine. These two abstractions can be used together to offload computations to multiple coprocessors within one compute node.

SCIF is a low-level API that provides a low-latency communication channel between *clients*, which can be either the host or coprocessors. Efficiency of SCIF is due to direct use of the PCIe bus for bi-directional data transfers between two coprocessors (or between the host and a coprocessor). The following is a list of abstractions used by SCIF:

- *Node*: It is a physical node in SCIF network. Both the host and an MIC card can be seen as a node.
- *Port*: An SCIF port on a node is represented as a 16-bit integer, which is a logical endpoint on the SCIF node similar to an IP port.
- *Endpoint*: The port for a connection is defined as an endpoint, which is similar to a socket.
- *Registered memory*: This is a registered memory driven by SCIF, and is held for the connected endpoints.

For small-amount data transfers (<4KB) between two SCIF clients, the scif_send and scif_recv functions should be employed, which can also be used for synchronizing the two clients. SCIF also provides remote direct memory access (RDMA) semantics. More specifically, the scif_register function exposes local memory on a device for remote access by another device. Then, either function scif_readfrom or function scif_writeto can be used to initiate asynchronous and zero-copy data transfers (≥4KB) between two devices. Finally, the scif_fence_signal function can ensure the completion of an asynchronous RDMA-based data transfer.

2.4 Coprocessor-Only Usage Mode

Strictly speaking, the symmetric usage mode means that the CPU host is used simultaneously with the coprocessors [6], i.e., a form of hybrid computing. We will however loosen the definition of symmetric usage to also include the scenario of only using the coprocessors. This is because if the CPU host is not involved, an existing MPI code can be readily run on multiple coprocessors without the worry of sophisticated load balancing. As mentioned in Section 1,

OpenMP threads can be used to exploit the intra-coprocessor parallelism, giving rise to an MPI-OpenMP programming approach. This is for avoiding the pure MPI approach's excessive overhead in memory footprint, due to the large number of MPI processes.

3   Related Work

Many researchers have focused on single-MIC programming. There are, however, not many publications on programming multiple MIC coprocessors or MIC clusters. As introduced in Section 2, pragma-based offload mode (combined with OpenMP) and MPI-based native/symmetric mode are two existing programming approaches. For the default MPI version included in MPSS, there have been reported bandwidth bottlenecks in intra-node and inter-node MPI communication between a MIC and the host or between two MICs, see [15, 16].

Due to the Intel MPI bandwidth problem in MIC clusters, some researchers proposed alternative MPI implementations for improving the communication performance for the native/symmetric mode. DCFA-MPI [8] is an MPI library implementation for direct inter-node InfiniBand communication between MIC coprocessors. MPICH2-1.5 [9] is an MPI implementation that uses shared memory, TCP/IP, and SCIF-based communication for MIC clusters. The research group of D. K. Panda at The Ohio State University has investigated the communication within a node that consists of a CPU host and one MIC coprocessor [17]. They proposed MVAPICH-PRISM [16], an MPI implementation that is a proxy-based communication framework using InfiniBand and SCIF for MIC clusters. All the above MPI implementations targeted MIC clusters with only one MIC coprocessor per node.

In addition, to solve the MPI bandwidth problem in its early version, Intel MPI has also implemented a proxy-based design that allows hybrid utilization of InfiniBand and SCIF, depending on the actual communication scenario [10].

Some researchers have studied the use of COI and SCIF APIs. COSMIC [11] is a user-level middleware for automatically managing MIC coprocessor resources by scheduling COI processes and their offloads, which can improve both performance and reliability of multiprocessing on MIC coprocessors. Dokulila et al. [12] created a library that supports hybrid execution in C++ applications using MIC coprocessors, where SCIF is used for synchronization and data transfers.

High performance has been achieved on coprocessors for many kernels and some applications. Schulz et al. [13] ported existing scientific applications and micro-kernels to a single MIC coprocessor. Pennycook et al. [14] explored SIMD for molecular dynamics applications on a MIC coprocessor. Rosales [15] has summarized the critical skills for pursuing high performance on Xeon Phi. By offloading the Linpack benchmark to MIC coprocessors, Heinecke et al. [7] achieved over 76% efficiency on a 100-node cluster with two MIC coprocessors per node.

Although COI and SCIF are two established APIs, we believe that our work represents a first effort in combining COI and SCIF for programming multiple MIC coprocessors within one compute node.

4   Two Implementations of a Simple 3D Stencil

This section serves to demonstrate the two offload-based programming approaches and their related data transfers. This will be done through parallelizing a very simple example of 3D stencil computation, to make use of multiple coprocessors within one compute node. The MPI-based programming approach is the same as for the scenario of a CPU cluster, thus not discussed here.

The stencil example involves a box-shaped computational grid that has in total $(n_x+2) \times (n_y+2) \times (n_z+2)$ mesh points. The entire computation is assumed as an iterative loop (over time). During each iteration a 3D array named C1 is computed by applying a 7-point stencil operator over another 3D array named C0. Values of C1 are prescribed on the entire boundary, so the actual computation per iteration computes the $n_x \times n_y \times n_z$ inner points of C1 as follows:

```
for (k=1; k<=nz; k++)
    for (j=1; j<=ny; j++)
        for (i=1; i<=nx; i++)
            C1[k][j][i]=a*C0[k][j][i]
                +b*(C0[k][j][i-1]+C0[k][j][i+1]
                +C0[k][j-1][i]+C0[k][j+1][i]
                +C0[k-1][j][i]+C0[k+1][j][i]);
```

Parallelism between the coprocessors can be enforced by dividing the 3D computational grid (and C0/C1 arrays) into subdomains, each being assigned to one coprocessor. Between two neighboring subdomains, values on each other's respective internal boundary layer have to be exchanged through data transfers. It is also customary that the subdomain grid is extended with a layer of ghost points towards each neighbor. An example of 1D grid decomposition can be found in Figure 1.

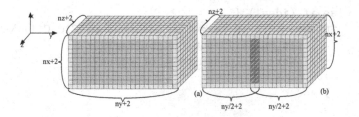

Fig. 1. An example of 1D decomposition (in y-direction) of a 3D grid into two subdomains. (a) Original 3D grid, (b) two subdomains after the decomposition.

The work on each subdomain consists of at least the following tasks per iteration. For each of its neighbors, first pack an "outgoing" buffer (1D array) by copying from respective (possibly non-contiguous) entries of the subdomain 3D array C0 and then unpack an "incoming" buffer (1D array) by copying its content to respective (possibly non-contiguous) entries of C0; compute all the entries of the subdomain 3D array C1 (except its boundary entries), by applying a 7-point stencil over the entries of C0; swap the subdomain array pointers C0 and C1 before proceeding to the next iteration. The actual coprocessor-coprocessor data transfers may be mediated by the host, or asynchronously initiated by the coprocessors themselves, depending on the chosen approach of programming.

For simplicity, let us only consider the case of two coprocessors. In the beginning of both implementations, four 3D arrays C00, C10, C01, C11 are allocated on the host side, such that the first two are duplicated on coprocessor 0, and the latter two duplicated on coprocessor 1. It should be obvious from the names that C00 and C01 together constitute the global 3D array C0, which no longer needs a physical storage. The same idea applies to C10, C11 and C1. It is only after all the iterations are done that values of C00, C10, C01, C11 are copied from the coprocessors back to the host.

4.1 Implementation Based on Pragmas

In this implementation, the host also needs to allocate two 1D arrays, in_buffer0 and out_buffer0, on coprocessor 0. Similiarly, in_buffer1 and out_buffer1 are on allocated coprocessor 1. The following code segment shows the actions that happen during each iteration:

```
#pragma omp parallel num_threads(2) {
    int id = omp_get_thread_num();
    if (id==0) {
      #pragma offload target(mic:0) nocopy(C00,C01) \
          in(in_buffer0) out(out_buffer0)
      { // work offloaded to coprocessor0
        ...
      }
    }
    else if (id==1) {
      #pragma offload target(mic:1) nocopy(C10,C11) \
          in(in_buffer1) out(out_buffer1)
      { // work offloaded to coprocessor1
        ...
      }
    }
} // end of OpenMP parallel region
swap_pointers(out_buffer0,in_buffer1);
swap_pointers(out_buffer1,in_buffer0);
```

It should be noted that we have omitted some programming details in the offload pragmas, and details of the offloaded work tasks are also skipped. Coding for coprocessor 0 is identical with that for coprocessor 1, except for the slightly different variable names and the different locations of the respective ghost boundary points.

It can be seen from the above code segment that two OpenMP threads on the host *simultaneously* offload work to the two coprocessors. All data transfers are relayed through the host. In particular, the two swappings of the buffer array pointers ensure the needed coprocessor-coprocessor data exchanges. Another important remark is that although overlapping computation with data movement is theoretically possible, we have chosen a non-overlapping approach above. It otherwise will require each coprocessor to split the offload into several parts. These will be initiated by `offload` or `offload_transfer` pragmas together with the `signal` clause, for the purpose of asynchrony. Some extensive modifications are also needed for the offloaded code blocks.

4.2   Implementation Based on COI and SCIF

The COI-SCIF implementation uses an independent sub-program per coprocessor. At the same time, the host main program is quite different from the previous implementation, i.e., a pair of `COIEngine` and `COIProcess` will be created and connected to each coprocessor. Thereafter, the host can choose not to disturb the two coprocessors, which will carry out the needed computation iterations, interleaved with bi-directional and asynchronous data transfers directly between themselves. That is, data transfers do not pass through the host. As shown in Figure 2, each coprocessor can independently initiate `scif_writeto` towards the other. By paying some extra effort in coding the coprocessor sub-programs, we can obtain several advantages. First, the repeated cost of offload start-ups of the pragma-based implementation is avoided. Instead, using COI and SCIF APIs can make the single-time device code loading and launching more efficient. Second, bi-directional and asynchronous coprocessor-coprocessor data transfers result in higher bandwidths than the host-mediated data transfer approach. Third, the more advanced asynchrony, due to RDMA data accesses such as `scif_readfrom` and `scif_writeto`, make it easier to overlap computation with communication. This possibility of overlapping is illustrated in Figure 3.

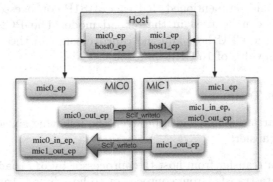

Fig. 2. The coupling between two coprocessors, with a COI-SCIF implementation

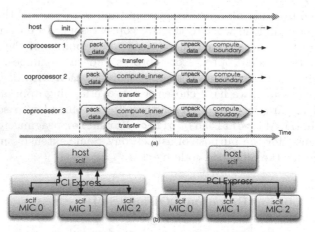

Fig. 3. (a) Overlapping computation and coprocessor-coprocessor data transfers. (b) Data transfers between multiple coprocessors with (left) or without host (right) relay.

5   Experiments and Results

We will report in this section measurements of a set of experiments involving data transfers between multiple Xeon Phi coprocessors. The purpose is to demonstrate the advantages of the COI-SCIF approach, which provides both higher bandwidths and lower overhead related to offload start-ups. Moreover, we want to quantify the resulting performance benefits in connection with solving a real-world 3D reaction-diffusion problem [22] that consists of 7-point stencil computations and additional numerical operations.

5.1   Hardware Platform

One compute node of Tianhe-2 was used as the test hardware platform, having three Intel Xeon Phi 31S1P coprocessors and two Intel Ivy Bridge 12-core E5-2692 CPUs. It should be mentioned that each 31S1P coprocessor has 57 cores, where 56 of them can be used in the offload mode. The PCIe 2.0 bus with 16 lanes between the CPU host and the coprocessors can theoretically offer a bi-directional bandwidth of 16 GB/s in total.

5.2   Bandwidth Tests

Figure 4(a) compares the bandwidth between the following six scenarios of uni-directional data transfer:

- offload-in: data transfer from host to coprocessor by offload_transfer;
- offload-out: data transfer from coprocessor to host by offload_transfer;
- MIC-Host-r: host-initiated data transfer from coprocessor to host, using the scif_readfrom function;

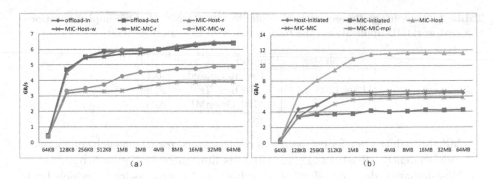

Fig. 4. Measured bandwidths, as functions of the transferred data size, (a) for six scenarios of uni-directional data transfers, (b) for five scenarios of bi-directional data transfers. Details can be found in Section 5.2.

- MIC-Host-w: host-initiated data transfer from host to coprocessor, using the scif_writeto function;
- MIC-MIC-r: data transfer from one coprocessor to another (without host involvement), using the scif_readfrom function;
- MIC-MIC-w: data transfer from one coprocessor to another (without host involvement), using the scif_writeto function.

It can be seen from Figure 4(a) that the first four scenarios enjoy roughly the same bandwidth, which is higher than that of the latter two. Nevertheless, if data need to be transferred from one coprocessor to another, it is still beneficial to use the MIC-MIC-w approach, because otherwise data have to first travel from one coprocessor to the host, then from the host to the other coprocessor.

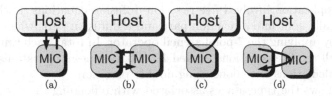

Fig. 5. Four scenarios of bi-directional data transfers: (a) both independently initiate data transfer between MIC and Host, (b) both independently initiate data transfer between MIC and MIC, (c) only host initiates data transfer between MIC and Host, (d) only one MIC initiates data transfer between MIC and MIC

Figure 4(b) shows the bandwidth differences between the following five scenarios of bi-directional data transfer:

- MIC-Host: data transfer between host and coprocessor, for which host and coprocessor independently initiate scif_writeto, as illustrated in Figure 5(a);

Table 1. Time usage (in seconds), by a single coprocessor, of three implementations of a real-world 3D application. The total number of time steps is 1000.

Mesh size	Programming mode	Total
	Pragma-based	30.12
$112 \times 1200 \times 142$	COI-SCIF	26.66
	MPI-OpenMP	26.52

- MIC-MIC: data transfer between two coprocessors, for which each coprocessor independently initiates scif_writeto, as illustrated in Figure 5(b);
- Host-initiated: data transfer between host and coprocessor, for which both scif_readfrom and scif_writeto are initiated on the host side, as illustrated in Figure 5(c);
- MIC-initated: data transfer between two coprocessors, for which both the scif_readfrom and scif_writeto are initiated on the same coprocessor, as illustrated in Figure 5(d);
- MIC-MIC-mpi: data transfer between two coprocessors, for which utilizing MPI_Isend and MPI_Irecv.

In the case of two coprocessors, it is always better to let both coprocessors simultaneously initiate scif_readfrom, instead of letting one coprocessor initiate both scif_readfrom and scif_writeto.

5.3   Performance of a Real-World 3D Application

We used a real-world 3D application [22] to test the two implementations of offloading, as described in Sections 4.1 and 4.2. Both implementations used OpenMP threads for intra-coprocessor parallelism. The performance of an MPI-OpenMP implementation is also included for comparison. More specifically, the real-world application involved five reaction-diffusion equations. Each equation was numerically split into a reaction part and a diffusion part, where the latter was solved by applying the 7-point stencil operator. In total, each time iteration for solving all the five equations needed 150 floating-point operations per mesh point. All calculations were done using double precision.

Table 1 shows the time usages associated with offloading the computational work to a single Xeon Phi coprocessor. The performance difference is due to the fact that the pragma-based offloading approach induced repeated start-up costs, once every time iteration. Note that no data transfers were needed for this single-coprocessor scenario, therefore no performance difference between the COI-SCIF programming approach and the MPI-OpenMP counterpart.

Table 2 summarizes the time usages associated with employing two or three Xeon Phi coprocessors. Unlike Table 1, the costs of data transfers and packing/unpacking data buffers are now present. The pragma-based offload implementation was considerably slower than the COI-SCIF implementation. There are two reasons for this performance difference. The first reason is due to the repeated offload start-up costs, as we have already experienced for Table 1. The

Table 2. Time usage (in seconds) of four implementations of a real-world 3D application. The version of "COI-SCIF*" refers to relaying data transfers via the host. Number of time steps: 1000, global mesh size: $112 \times 1200 \times 142$.

		Pragma-based	COI-SCIF*	MPI-OpenMP	COI-SCIF
	Pack/unpack	0.41	0.41	0.40	0.40
2 Coprocessors	Data trans	1.27	1.26	0.98	0.80
	Total	19.34	15.08	14.91	14.62
	Pack/unpack	0.40	0.40	0.40	0.40
3 Coprocessors	Data trans	1.21	1.31	0.99	0.76
	Total	12.63	10.22	9.72	9.43

second reason is due to the less efficient data transfers of the pragma-based implementation, demonstrated by the "Data trans" row in Table 2.

We recall that the COI-SCIF implementation adopts bi-directional and asynchronous coprocessor-coprocessor data transfers, thereby capable of hiding (a part of) the data transfer costs. The MPI-based symmetric implemetation also has the advantages in asynchronous data transfers between coprocessors, but the extra overhead of MPI communication leds to a lower performance than the low-level COI-SCIF implementation. For comparison purposes, Table 2 also includes another implementation based on using the COI and SCIF APIs. This third implementation, denoted as COI-SCIF*, relayed data transfers through the host. It thereby closely resembled the pragma-based implementation with respect to data transfers, and also that no overlap happened between data transfer and computation.

6   Conclusions

This paper has focused on two offload programming approaches that can be used for a single compute node with multiple coprocessors. An MPI-based symmetric programming approach is included for comparison purposes. The three approaches, MPI-based, pragma-based and COI-SCIF-based, have rather different characteristics. While the first two are easier to use, the latter one gives better performance but requires more involved programming. For a real-world 3D application, the best performance was achieved by the COI-SCIF approach, where bi-directional and asynchronous data transfers were enabled directly between the coprocessors. The low-level COI-SCIF approach also resulted in lower communication overhead, in comparison with the MPI-based approach. It should be remarked that this programming approach is not limited to stencil computation on regular meshes. Our findings not only shed some light on this new topic of using multiple Xeon Phi coprocessors within one compute node, but provide a good starting point for fully utilizing Tianhe-2 in future.

References

1. Top500, China's Tianhe-2 Supercomputer Takes No.1 Ranking on 41st TOP500 List, http://www.top500.org/blog/lists/2013/06/press-release/
2. Dongarra, J.: Visit to the National University for Defense Technology Changsha, http://www.netlib.org/utk/people/JackDongarra/PAPERS/tianhe-2-dongarra-report.pdf
3. Intel Corporation, Intel Xeon Phi Coprocessor Instruction Set Architecture Reference Manual. Reference number 327364-001 (2012)
4. Jeffers, J., Reinders, J.C.: Intel Xeon Phi Coprocessor High-Performance Programming. Morgan Kaufmann, Walthman (2013)
5. Intel MIC Architecture, http://software.intel.com/en-us/articles/intel-xeon-phi-coprocessor-codename-knights-corner
6. Intel Corporation, Intel Xeon Phi System Software Developer's Guide. Reference number 328207-001EN (2012)
7. Heinecke, A., Vaidyanathan, K., Smelyanskiy, M., Kobotov, A., Dubtsov, R., Henry, G., Chrysos, G., Dubey, P.: Design and implementation of the Linpack benchmark for single and multi-node systems based on Intel Xeon Phi coprocessor. In: IPDPS (2013), doi:10.1109/IPDPS.2013.113
8. Si, M., Ishikawa, Y., Direct, M.P.I.: library for Intel Xeon Phi Co-Processors. In: 27th IEEE International Parallel and Distributed Processing Symposium Workshops & PhD Forum (IPDPSW), Boston, MA, USA (2013), doi:10.1109/IPDPSW.2013.179
9. MPICH: High-performance and Portable MPI, http://www.mpich.org/
10. OFS for Xeon Phi, https://www.openfabrics.org/images/docs/2013Dev_WorkshopnewlineMon_0422/2013_Workshop_Mon_1430_OpenFabrics_OFS_software_for_Xeon_Phi.pdf
11. Cadambi, S., Coviello, G., Li, C., Phull, R., Rao, K., Sankaradass, M., Chakradhar, S.: COSMIC: Middleware for high performance and reliable multiprocessing on Xeon Phi coprocessors. In: Proceedings of the 22nd Int'l Symposium on High-Performance Parallel and Distributed Computing, HPDC 2013 (2013), doi:10.1145/2462902.2462921
12. Dokulila, J., Bajrovica, E., Benknera, S., Pllanaa, S., Sandriesera, M., Bachmayerb, B.: High-level support for hybrid parallel execution of C++ applications targeting Intel Xeon Phi coprocessors. In: 2013 International Conference on Computational Science, ICCS 2013 (2013), doi:10.1016/j.procs.2013.05.430
13. Schulz, W., Ulerich, K., Malaya, R., Bauman, N., Stogner, T.P., Simmons, R., Early, C.: experiences porting scientific applications to the many integrated core (MIC) platform. In: TACC-Intel Highly Parallel Computing Symposium, Tech. Rep. (2012), doi:10.1145/2016741.2016764
14. Pennycook, J., Hughes, S., Smelyanskiy, J.C., Jarvis, M., Exploring, A.S.: SIMD for molecular dynamics, using Intel Xeon processors and Intel Xeon Phi coprocessors. In: IEEE Int'l Parallel & Distributed Processing Symposium (2013), doi:10.1109/IPDPS.2013.44
15. Rosales, C.: Porting to the Intel Xeon Phi: Opportunities and challenges. In: Extreme Scaling Workshop, XSCALE 2013 (2013)
16. Potluri, S., Bureddy, D., Hamidouche, K., Venkatesh, A., Kandalla, K., Subramoni, H., Panda, D.K.: MVAPICH-PRISM: A Proxy-based Communication Framework using InfiniBand and SCIF for Intel MIC Clusters. In: Int'l Conference on Supercomputing (2013)

17. Potluri, S., Venkatesh, A., Bureddy, D., Kandalla, K., Panda, K.: D., Efficient intra-node communication on Intel-MIC clusters. In: 13th IEEE Int'l Symposium on Cluster Computing and the Grid, CCGrid 2013 (2013), doi:10.1109/CCGrid.2013.86
18. The Heterogeneous Offload Model for Intel Many Integrated Core Architecture, http://software.intel.com/sites/default/files/article/326701/heterogeneous-programming-model.pdf
19. Intel Manycore Platform Software Stack (MPSS), http://software.intel.com/en-us/articles/intel-manycore-platform-software-stack-mpss#downloads
20. Intel Corporation, MIC COI API Reference Manual 0.65. Monday December 17 12:12:33 (2012)
21. Intel Corporation, MIC SCIF API Reference Manual 0.65 for User Mode Linux. Mon Dec17 12:05:03 (2012)
22. Chai, Jun, Hake, Johan, Wu, Nan, Wen, Mei, Cai, Xing, Lines, T., Glenn, Yang, Jing, Su, Huayou, Zhang, Chunyuan, Liao, Xiangke, S.: Towards simulation of subcellular calcium dynamics at nanometre resolution. International Journal of High Performance Computing Applications (2013)

HPSO: Prefetching Based Scheduling to Improve Data Locality for MapReduce Clusters

Mingming Sun, Hang Zhuang, Xuehai Zhou, Kun Lu, and Changlong Li

Computer Science University of Science and
Technology of China, Hefei, China
{mmsun,zhuangh,local,liclong}@mail.ustc.edu.cn, xhzhou@ustc.edu.cn

Abstract. Due to cluster resource competition and task scheduling policy, some map tasks are assigned to nodes without input data, which causes significant data access delay. Data locality is becoming one of the most critical factors to affect performance of MapReduce clusters. As machines in MapReduce clusters have large memory capacities, which are often underutilized, in-memory prefetching input data is an effective way to improve data locality. However, it is still posing serious challenges to cluster designers on what and when to prefetch. To effectively use prefetching, we have built HPSO (High Performance Scheduling Optimizer), a prefetching service based task scheduler to improve data locality for MapReduce jobs. The basic idea is to predict the most appropriate nodes to which future map tasks should be assigned and then preload the input data to memory without any delaying on launching new tasks. To this end, we have implemented HPSO in Hadoop-1.1.2. The experiment results have shown that the method can reduce the map tasks causing remote data delay, and improves the performance of Hadoop clusters.

Keywords: Data locality, MapReduce clusters, prefetching, task scheduler.

1 Introduction

MapReduce [1] has been highly successful as a parallel distributed processing framework in implementing large-scale data-intensive applications on commodity cloud computing plateforms such as Amazon EC2 and Windows Azure. MapReduce enables hiding the details of the underlying parallel processing to provide a simple programming interface for developing distributed application. There are many different implementations of MapReduce framework such as Hadoop[2], Disco, Phoenix, etc.

In most state-of-the-art cluster systems, a key challenge is to increase the utilization of MapReduce clusters. If map tasks are scheduled to nodes without input data, these tasks will issue remote I/O operations to copy the data to local nodes. This data transfer delay is primarily on the execution time cost of map phase, while map phase often dominates the execution time of the MapReduce jobs. So data locality becomes one critical factor to affect performance of MapReduce framework. In practice, not only clusters are shared by multiple users, but

X.-h. Sun et al. (Eds.): ICA3PP 2014, Part II, LNCS 8631, pp. 82–95, 2014.

also there is a limitation in the number of nodes a user can use. In this case, it is not easy to guarantee good data locality to all map tasks. The process will cause remote data access delay, thus degrading the performance of MapReduce. Workloads from Facebook and Microsoft Bing datacenters show that this remote I/O operations phase constitutes 79% of a job's duration [3]. So in this paper, we focus on the optimizing the map phase. Obviously, the performance of MapReduce clusters is closely tied to its task scheduler. Zaharia [4][5] proposed a delay scheduling algorithm to reduce the map tasks executing remote I/O operations. A next-k-node scheduling method is proposed to improve the data locality [6]. However, in both methods task fairness withered as the cost.

Data prefetching [7] is a data access latency hiding technique, which decouples and overlaps data transfers and computation. And machines in MapReduce clusters have large memory capacities, which are often underutilized; the median and 95 percentile memory utilizations in the Facebook cluster are 10% and 42%, respectively [3]. In light of this trend, we investigate memory locality to speed-up MapReduce jobs by prefetching and caching their input data. Seo et al. [8] designed a intra-block and inter-block prefetching scheme to improve data locality of map tasks, which are assigned to nodes without input data. A data prefetching mechanism in heterogeneous or shared environments [9] is proposed. However, both techniques not only cannot reduce the occurrence of such map tasks, but also do not consider the remote access delay of the first data block split.

The prefetching accuracy is the key factor that affects performance. In MapReduce clusters, task scheduler determines the mapping between tasks and nodes. To this end, we design HPSO, a prefetching service based task scheduler to improve performance for MapReduce clusters. The method first predicts the execution time of map tasks and further evaluates the sequence that nodes free busy slots. According to this node sequence, HPSO predicts and assigns the most suitable map tasks to nodes ahead of time. Once such scheduling decisions are made, nodes preload the related input data from remote nodes or local disk to memory before tasks is launching. In this way, input data prefetching is carried out concurrently with data processing, thus data transfer overhead is overlapped with data processing in the time demension. In summary, in this paper we claim following contributions:

- We provide a novel prefetching mechanism to coordinately manage prefetching input data blocks.
- We exploit task scheduler to determine what and when to prefetch. This method can greatly improve the efficiency of map tasks.
- We have built a Hadoop cluster system to evaluate the HPSO method.

The remainder of the paper is structures as follows. Section 2 introduces some technology background necessary to understand the MapReduce and scheduler, and motivation. Section 3 describes the prefetching technique. The design and implementation of HPSO are illustrated in Section 4. Section 5 evaluates HPSO. Related work is described in Section 6. Finally, conclusion is given in Section 7.

2   Background and Motivation

2.1   MapReduce Programming Framework

Computations in MapReduce framework are divided into map and reduce phases, separated by an internal grouping of the intermediate results. After user submits a job, MapReduce jobs run as follows. Firstly, input data is divided into several fixed-size blocks, each of which runs a map task. Then after all map tasks are finished, the intermediate data is reassigned to reduce tasks according to different keys generated in map phase. In our paper, we chose Hadoop since it is an open-source implementation of MapReduce model. Furthermore it has been used by many companies such as Yahoo!, Amazon, Facebook duo to its high performance, reliability, and availability. Specially, Hadoop manages computing resources by the term of slot, the basic resource allocation unit. The precise number of slots of each slave in Hadoop cluster depends on the number of cores and the amount of memory. Each slave node provides a number of slots for map tasks and a number of slots for reduce tasks, and these are set independently. Each slot can only run a task simultaneously. Hadoop Distributed File System (HDFS)[10] is designed to provide high bandwidth for MapReduce by replicating and partitioning files across many nodes. The partition is the basic data unit in HDFS, the size of which by default is 64MB.

2.2   Hadoop Scheduler

Fig. 2 (a) illustrates the work mechanism of Hadoop running a MapReduce job. Hadoop clusters have one JobTracker, which coordinates the job run, and a number of TaskTrackers, which is in charge of running jobs and periodically heartbeats the JobTracker. When a TaskTracker indicates that it has an idle map slot by heartbeat, job scheduler will allocate it a map task, otherwise, it will select a reduce task. A computation requested by a job will be performed much more efficiently if it is executed near the data it operates on. However, as HDFS files are divided across all nodes, some map tasks must read data over the network. For a map task, it takes into account the TaskTracker's network location and picks a task whose input data is as close as possible to the TaskTracker. The scheduling policy preferentially selects the tasks with data locality. In the optimal case, map task is data-local, that is, running on the same node that input data resides on. Alternatively, map task may be assigned to TaskTracker node with the input data in the same rack, but not the same node, called rack locality. Some map tasks retrieve their data from a different rack, rackoff locality.

2.3   Motivation

TaskTracker will not process a map task until its input data is loaded into the tasktracker node's memory. Map tasks with rack locality or rackoff locality cause remote data transmission overhead. And the network bisection bandwidth in a large cluster is much lower than the aggregate bandwidth of the disks in the nodes, so data locality issue becomes crucial for performance. Especially, data locality issue suffers in two situations: concurrent jobs and small jobs[4]. It is necessary to research a method to hide data transmission overhead.

Data prefetching is an efficient way to solve this problem. Prefetching can hide data transmission delay by preloading the expected data ahead of time. The key challenge, however, is how to improve prefetching rate. That is to determine what and when to prefetch. Some approaches use prediction algorithms based on history of data accesses or cache misses [11][12]. However, in MapReduce clusters, task scheduler determines to assign tasks to tasktracker nodes. So our method researches prefetching mechanism using task scheduler. Another reason motivated this method is that history information of data is not well reflect the future access to data in cloud computing. We design a scheduling policy which predicts the most appropriate tasktracker nodes to assign tasks.

3   Prefetching

In this section, we present data prefetching mechanism in detail. HPSO is to preload the input data before map task is running on tasktracker node. As a result, prefetching can hide data transmission delay and further improve MapReduce performance. The emphasis of this section is not on the syntactical details of HPSO, but on how to simply and effectively manage the memory buffer for prefetching data.

3.1   Buffer Management

The process of data prefetching mechanism is shown as following. When a tasktracker node receive a prefetching request from HPSO, the node will load expected data block to a buffer in memory called prefetching buffer. When the corresponding map task arrives, it will process data of prefetching buffer. Obviously, this process is typical producer-consumer model, where data prefetching thread is the producer and corresponding map task is the consumer. The following issues must be addressed in the prefetching mechanism.

One issue is the size of prefetching buffer. Intuitively, bigger prefetching buffer means better performance. But in fact, according to the producer-consumer model, two buffer units for each map slot are enough. And with the development of technology, memory capacity is increasing. Therefore the memory utilization of the two buffers is unnoticeable to affect the overall performance.

Another issue is how to manage prefetching buffer. Fig. 1 illustrates the prefetching buffer structure and management strategy. Each slot of the tasktracker node has at most two buffer units. One is processing block using by the running map task. The other may be prefetching block, which has been preloaded for the next map task, or null. Fig. 1 (a) shows that all slots have preloaded the data blocks for the following map tasks, and maintain two buffer units into a list. This strategy is convenient to manage prefetching buffer and reuse buffer data. Specifically, a particular data block may be used simultaneously by multiple map

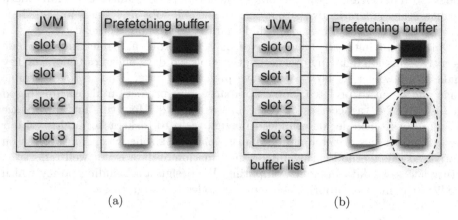

Fig. 1. Prefetching buffer structure and management. The tasktracker node has four map slots. The white box represents a processing block by map task. The black box represents a prefetching block for the following map task, and the gray corresponds a processed block by the previous map task.

tasks. For example, in Fig. 1 (b), *slot 0* and *slot 1* share the same prefetching block. Alternatively, data block which is being processed or has processed may be prefetching block for other slot such as *slot 2* and *slot 3* in Fig. 1 (b). Then the remaining buffer units will be linked into the buffer list. When a buffer unit is needed to store new prefetching data, the method get a buffer unit from buffer list using LRU.

4   HPSO Design and Implementation

In this section, we present the HPSO design issues and implementation, and discuss the techniques required to achieve our goal. Our design seeks to minimize total execution time of applications and improve the performance of MapReduce clusters. The emphasis of this section is that how to effectively design prefetching requests based scheduling policy.

4.1   Framework

As shown in Fig. 2 (b), HPSO consists of three main modules: the prediction module, the scheduling optimizer and the prefetching module. The role of scheduling optimizer is to predict the most appropriate tasktracker nodes to which future map tasks should be assigned. Once the scheduling decisions are made before map tasks are scheduled, HPSO will trigger the prefetching module to load expected input data. Then our method can explore the underutilized disk bandwidth or network bandwidth in CPU-intensive process. Such pipelining can hide away data transfer latency. To implement pipelining, the prediction module

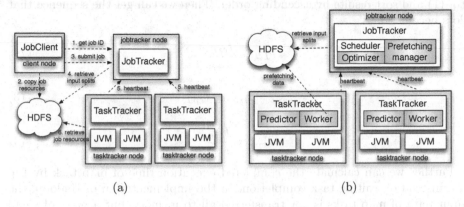

Fig. 2. (a) How Hadoop runs a MapReduce job. (b)The architecture and framework of HPSO.

in each tasktracker node predicts the remaining execution time of map tasks and further evaluates the sequence that slot become idle. The prefetching module consists of a central prefetching manager in JobTracker and a set of worker threads located at tasktracker nodes. The function of prefetching manager is to monitor the status of worker threads and coordinate the prefetching process for map tasks. Each worker thread can automatically finish loading data block by itself before the map task is received. When prefetching manager achieves prefetching instructions from scheduling optimizer, prefetching manager triggers worker threads to load data to memory. Prefetching manager also reports scheduling optimizer the data blocks in tasktracker nodes' prefetching buffer.

4.2 Node Prediction

In Hadoop, tasktracker node requests a map task when it frees a busy slot. And the sooner a tasktracker node has an idle slot, the earlier the node requests a new map task. So tasktracker to issue a request can be predicted according to the time of each tasktracker to complete tasks. That it can be measured by the remaining time of map tasks running on the node. Hadoop monitors task process using a process score, which is a number from 0 to 1. For a map, the score is the fraction of input data read. We estimate the remaining time of an executing map task based on current process using Eq. (1), which is proposed in Ref. [14].

$$RT_m = \frac{t_{exe}}{s_{exe}} * (1 - s_{exe}) \qquad (1)$$

In the method, RT_m is the time left of map task, and t_{exe} is the execution time of the task when the process is up to s_{exe}. In MapReduce framework, a node normally runs multiple tasks simultaneously. For each slot, we compute

Eq. (1) and sort results by ascending order. Then we can get the sequence that slots become idle.

$$T_m = \frac{t_{exe}}{s_{exe}} \tag{2}$$

$$t_{exe} = t_{tran} + t_{cpu} \tag{3}$$

$$T_{cpu} = \frac{t_{cpu}}{s_{exe}} \tag{4}$$

Further we can calculate the completed execution time of map task by Eq. (2), instead of waiting task completion. In the implementation of Hadoop, the input data of map tasks is not transferred all to memory, but a mass of small slices instead. When the processing of the data slice is completed, map tasks will transfer and process another data slice. The data transmission and data processing happens in sequence. So the execution time of map tasks is composed of the data transmission time and the data processing time as shown as Eq. (3). The total data processing time can be estimated by Eq. (4). With the completion of map tasks of same job, we calculate the average of the completed execution time of map tasks as the predicted execution time, assuming that each node processes tasks at a roughly constant speed.

4.3 Scheduling Policy

In Hadoop, task scheduler maintains a complete view of which tasks are running on which tasktracker nodes and job waiting queue. HPSO combines this view with the slot sequence predicted in Section 4.2 to map appropriate tasktracker nodes with future tasks from job waiting queue, and then triggers the prefetching module to preload input data for map tasks without input data.

Algorithm 1 outlines the basic steps of scheduling optimized algorithm. HPSO considers the data blocks in prefetching buffer. If input data block of map task has been in prefetching buffer of certain node, we called this buffer-local and preferentially assign the task to this node. The data in prefetching buffer is equivalent to one replica, which in turn increases the chances of achieving data locality. If a node-local task is found, HPSO will trigger prefetching module to cache data from disk. Unfortunately if we must select rack-local or rack-off task, HPSO will make prefetching instructions and trigger prefetching module to preload data from remote node. The prefetching instructions contain expected data block list and the corresponding destination tasktracker nodes, and where the required data blocks are located.

HPSO guarantees all map task with data locality to the maximum extent. One important principle is that the method does not affect the priotiry of jobs. In this paper we suppose that map tasks in the same priority can be executed out of order. However, inaccurate prediction may cause that low priority tasks will be executed earlier than high priority tasks. To address this problem, when a tasktracker node is ready to request map tasks, task scheduler calculates Eq. (5) for the high priority map task whose RT_n is longest. RT_n is the waiting time left. T_{tran} is the data transmission time. If u is positive, we will remove the map task from original slot waiting queue and assign to idle tasktracker node. Otherwise, HPSO will select a low priority task. To this end, HPSO does not affect the priotiry of jobs. Another issue is fault tolerance. HPSO's failure does not hamper the job's execution as input data can always be read from remote nodes or local disk.

$$u = RT_n - T_{tran} \tag{5}$$

Algorithm 1. Scheduling Optimizer Algorithm

Input:
 1: Array N: the predicted slot sequence that slots become idle;
 2: Array J: job waiting queue.
Begin:
 3: **while** ! (All slots have at least one waiting task or J has no waiting job) **do**
 4:     n: the head slot of N
 5:     **for** j in J **do**
 6:         **if** j has a buffer-local task t for n **then**
 7:             Map t with n; inform prefetching module of the mapping
 8:             Break
 9:         **else**
10:             **if** j has a node-local task t for n **then**
11:                 Map t with n; trigger prefetching module to prefetch input data
12:                 Break
13:             **else if** j has a rack-local task t for n **then**
14:                 Map t with n; trigger prefetching module to prefetch input data
15:                 Break
16:             **else**
17:                 Map t with n; trigger prefetching module to prefetch input data
18:             **end if**
19:         **end if**
20:     **end for**
21:     $RT_n = RT_n + T_{cpu}$ (RT_n: the time left that n becomes idle, T_{cpu}: the processing time of t)
22:     Ascendingly reorder array N;
23: **end while**

4.4   Prefetching Module

The prefetching manager constructs a list known as the data list for each task-tracker node, a collection of all data blocks stored in prefetching buffer. It is worth noting that network bandwith is one of the critical factors to affect performance of MapReduce cluster. To this end, HPSO combines these data information to make scheduling decisions in order to minimize the network transmission traffic. For example, it can reduce the cost of loading the released data at

Table 1. Configurations of single jobs in experiments

Job ID	Workload	map taks	reduce tasks	input file size	input split size	nodes
1	Word count	16	1	1GB	64MB	15
2	Word count	8	1	512MB	64MB	15
3	Word count	4	1	256MB	64MB	15
4	Word count	2	1	128MB	64MB	15
5	Word count	4	1	512MB	128MB	15
6	Word count	4	1	1GB	256MB	15
7	Word count	4	1	256MB	64MB	10
8	Word count	4	1	256MB	64MB	20

the previous round for iterative applications. Upon the arrival of a prefetching request from HPSO, prefetching manager triggers worker threads in tasktracker nodes to start loading corresponding input data to prefetching buffer according to prefetching instructions. The worker thread's main role is to serve cached blocks illustrated in Section 3, as well as prefetch new data blocks. The worker thread periodically informs the prefetching manager of data block updates as the part of heartbeat message. The prefetching manager uses these updates to maintain data lists.

5   Evaluation

We are going to evaluate HPSO in term of performance and scaling. The performance metric is measured as the improvement over default Hadoop. The scaling metric is measured as a different number of cluster nodes. To measure HPSO's performance, we have built a Hadoop cluster, which has one master and 20 machines. A common gigabit Ethernet switch connected each node. We installed Hadoop 1.1.2 and configured that HDFS maintains three replicas for each data block in this cluster. And every node was limited to run at most four map tasks and four reduce tasks simultaneously. We performed our evaluations with word-count, one of the main benchmarks used for evaluating Hadoop performance. Table 1 depicts the eight types of job sets. In the paper, these benchmarks ran varying numbers of jobs based on the job size so as to take 20-30 minutes in total.

5.1   Performance of HPSO

Firstly, we designed this test to evaluate HPSO's performance. Hadoop employed a simple FIFO scheduling policy, which assigns the earliest submitted job to execute, then the second, etc. There is also a priority policy for putting jobs into higher-priority queues. We compared the performance of HPSO with that of default Hadoop as a different number of input data size. Fig. 3 (b) shows normalized running times of the workload in Table 1, while Fig. 3 (a) shows

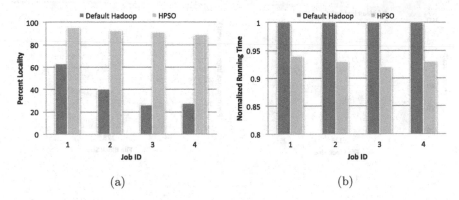

Fig. 3. Comparison for different job settings. (a) comparison of the map tasks processed with data locality. (b) comparison of normalized running time. The horizontal axis shows the Job ID in Table 1.

locality achieved by default Hadoop and HPSO. We can observe that our method shows significantly higher data locality than default Hadoop for all of test sets in Fig. 3 (a). HPSO raised data locality to at least 88.7%, and at most 95.6%. HPSO increased throughout by at most 8% for job ID 3 and at least 6% for job ID 1. The throughput gain is lower for job ID 1 than other jobs because locality with job ID 1 is fairly good even without data prefetching. However, the gain for the smallest job ID 4 is lower than for job ID 2 and job ID 3, because at small job sizes, job initialization becomes a bottleneck in Hadoop. Virtually all the gains are due to preloading the input data for rack-local or rackoff tasks. This would increase throughput in a more bandwidth-constrained environment.

Fig. 4 (b) shows the performance improvement when the data block size of HDFS is set with different values. HPSO has increasingly improved the performance greatly as the data block size becomes larger, from 7.9% to 18.11%. That is because the data transmission time becomes longer with block size increasingly. Our method improves the percentage of map tasks with data locality by prefetching as shown as Fig. 4 (a). We can observe that our method is not substantially affected by the size of the data block. In summary, HPSO raises the percentage of map tasks with data locality by prefetching. Therefore it improves the performance compared with default Hadoop.

However, our approach has not yet reached ideal data locality. Although prefetching is performed simultaneously with computation, the performance is also affected by disk overhead or network congestion. Another reason is ineffective prefetch duo to prediction error. But our method can raise data locality to at least 88.7%, which is fairly high and acceptable for most state-of-the-art literatures.

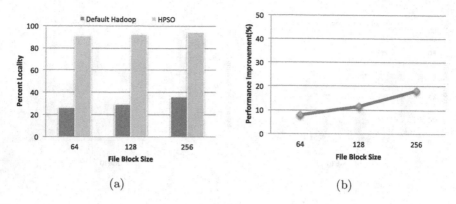

(a)   (b)

Fig. 4. Comparison for different block size for job ID 3, job ID 5 and job ID 6 respectively. (a) comparison of the map tasks processed with data locality. (b) performance improvement of HPSO compared to default Hadoop. The horizontal axis shows the data block size in HDFS.

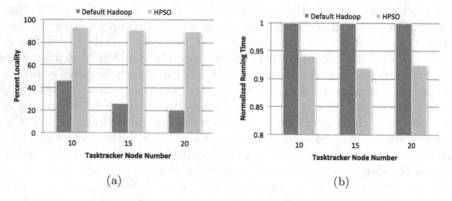

(a)   (b)

Fig. 5. Comparison for different tasktracker node number for job ID 7, job ID 3 and job ID 8, respectively. (a) comparison of the map tasks processed with data locality. (b) comparison of normalized running time. The horizontal axis shows the number of tasktracker nodes.

5.2   Scaling Performance

We explored the scalability of HPSO, growing with the number of nodes. In our tests, we vary the number of tasktracker nodes from 10 to 20. Fig. 5 suggests that HPSO outperforms default Hadoop with different nodes. HPSO reduces the map tasks without data locality by 6.9% for job ID 7 and by 8.9% for job ID 3 and by 10.5% for job ID 8. The improvement in data locality for 10 nodes is lowest because locality with job ID 7 in this smallest cluster is fairly good. The performance gain for job ID 8 is higher than other jobs since the improvement in data locality is the most.

Of course, the only way to conclusively evaluate HPSO's performance at scale will be to deploy it on a large cluster. But in light of this trend, our experiments suggest that HPSO will continue to perform well at scale.

6   Related Work

Recently, prefetching and scheduling technology has been used to slove the data locality problem of MapReduce. Zaharia [4][5] presented a delay scheduling algorithm, which addresses the conflict between locality and fairness in shared MapReduce clusters. A next-k-node scheduling method [6] is similar to delay scheduling algorithm, and considers k candidate nodes for each tasks. However both algorithms do not consider other map tasks without data locality and task fairness withered as the cost. Our work optimizes all map tasks.

Considerable work has been carried out on prefetching methods to reduce I/O latency. Yong [11] proposed an Algorithm-level Feedback-controlled Adaptive (AFA) data prefetcher to address data-access delay in High-Performance computing by analyzing the data-access history cache. A real-time data prefetching algorithm [12] is proposed based on sequential pattern mining and adopts predictive prefetching technology predict related data objects of data object on demand. Both algorithms focus on analyzing the historical data access records and require to predict uses' behavior. Performance improvement has relationship with the uses' behavior. Our method combines prefetching with task scheduler and prefetches input data of the next running map task ahead of time to hide the data transmission delay. Seo et al. [8] designs a prefetching scheme and a pre-shuffling scheme. However, it cannot reduce the total number of the map tasks without node locality, and the method occupies much network bandwidth, so system performance may be decreased. Compared with the Seos method, our method can hide the remote access delay of the first data block and handle all map tasks without data locality. A data prefetching mechanism [9] in heterogeneous or shared environments is proposed, but the method also does not consider the first data block transfer delay. The method only deal with intra-block prefetching for map tasks. A predictive scheduler and prefetching mechanism [13] are proposed to improve the performance of MapReduce by assigning two tasks to each slot. Unfortunately, it affects the priotiry of jobs.

Caching technology also has been used to improve MapReduce performance. PACMan [3] is an in-memory caching system for parallel jobs. Ref. [18] proposed a distributed high-performance storage in memory. Zhang et al. [20] designs a new method to improve the performance by using distributed memory cache as a high speed access between map tasks and reduce tasks. Map outputs sent to the distributed memory cache can be gotten by reduce tasks as soon as possible.

7   Conclusion

This paper presents HPSO, which exploits task scheduler to preload required input data prior to launching tasks to TaskTracker. Our method hides the waiting period of map tasks with rack and rackoff locality and shortens the completion time for MapReduce jobs. HPSO integrates a prediction module and a prefetching module with scheduling optimizer. A scheduling optimizer is integrated into HPSO to improve prefetching rate. We use wordcount workload to demonstrate that our method can outperform default Hadoop at least 6%, and improve data locality at least 88.7%. In light of these results, we believe that HPSO can achieve better utilization of node resources and a high system throughout in MapReduce clusters.

Acknowledgment. Our work could not have been implemented without the assistance of many individuals and teams. Especially our work was supported by the National Science Foundation of China under grants No. 61272131 and No. 61202053, China Postdoctoral Science Foundation grant No. BH0110000014, Fundamental Research Funds for the Central Universities No. WK0110000034, and Jiangsu Provincial Natural Science Foundation grant No. SBK201240198.

References

1. Dean, J., Ghemawat, S.: MapReduce: simplified data processing on large clusters. Communications of the ACM 51(1), 107–113 (2008)
2. White, T.: Hadoop: The definitive guide. O'Reilly Media, Inc. (2009)
3. Ananthanarayanan, G., Ghodsi, A., Warfield, A., Borthakur, D., Kandula, S., Shenker, S., Stoica, I.: PACMan: Coordinated Memory Caching for Parallel Jobs. In: NSDI, pp. 267–280 (2012)
4. Zaharia, M., Borthakur, D., Sarma, J.S., Elmeleegy, K., Shenker, S., Stoica, I.: Job scheduling for multi-user mapreduce clusters. EECS Department, University of California, Berkeley, Tech. Rep. UCB/EECS-2009-55 (2009)
5. Zaharia, M., Borthakur, D., Sen Sarma, J., Elmeleegy, K., Shenker, S., Stoica, I.: Delay scheduling: A simple technique for achieving locality and fairness in cluster scheduling. In: Proceedings of the 5th European Conference on Computer Systems, pp. 265–278. ACM (2010)
6. Zhang, X., Zhong, Z., Feng, S., Tu, B., Fan, J.: Improving data locality of mapreduce by scheduling in homogeneous computing environments. In: 2011 IEEE 9th International Symposium on Parallel and Distributed Processing with Applications (ISPA), pp. 120–126. IEEE (2011)
7. Byna, S., Chen, Y., Sun, X.H.: A taxonomy of data prefetching mechanisms. In: International Symposium on Parallel Architectures, Algorithms, and Networks, I-SPAN 2008, pp. 19–24. IEEE (2008)
8. Seo, S., Jang, I., Woo, K., Kim, I., Kim, J.S., Maeng, S.: HPMR: Prefetching and pre-shuffling in shared MapReduce computation environment. In: IEEE International Conference on Cluster Computing and Workshops, CLUSTER 2009, pp. 1–8. IEEE (2009)
9. Gu, T., Zuo, C., Liao, Q., Yang, Y., Li, T.: Improving MapReduce Performance by Data Prefetching in Heterogeneous or Shared Environments. International Journal of Grid & Distributed Computing 6(5) (2013)
10. Shvachko, K., Kuang, H., Radia, S., Chansler, R.: The hadoop distributed file system. In: 2010 IEEE 26th Symposium on Mass Storage Systems and Technologies (MSST), pp. 1–10. IEEE (2010)

11. Chen, Y., Zhu, H., Sun, X.H.: An adaptive data prefetcher for high performance processors. In: 2010 10th IEEE/ACM International Conference on Cluster, Cloud and Grid Computing (CCGrid), pp. 155–164. IEEE (2010)
12. Li, J., Wu, S.: Real-time Data Prefetching Algorithm Based on Sequential Patternmining in Cloud Environment. In: 2012 International Conference on Industrial Control and Electronics Engineering (ICICEE), pp. 1044–1048. IEEE (2012)
13. Xie, J., Meng, F., Wang, H., Pan, H., Cheng, J., Qin, X.: Research on Scheduling Scheme for Hadoop Clusters. Procedia Computer Science 18, 2468–2471 (2013)
14. Zaharia, M., Konwinski, A., Joseph, A.D., Katz, R.H., Stoica, I.: Improving MapReduce Performance in Heterogeneous Environments. In: OSDI, vol. 8(4), p. 7 (2008)
15. Ranger, C., Raghuraman, R., Penmetsa, A., Bradski, G., Kozyrakis, C.: Evaluating mapreduce for multi-core and multiprocessor systems. In: IEEE 13th International Symposium on High Performance Computer Architecture, HPCA 2007, pp. 13–24. IEEE (2007)
16. Chen, R., Chen, H., Zang, B.: Tiled-MapReduce: Optimizing resource usages of data-parallel applications on multicore with tiling. In: Proceedings of the 19th International Conference on Parallel Architectures and Compilation Techniques, pp. 523–534. ACM (2010)
17. Ganapathi, A., Kuno, H., Dayal, U., Wiener, J.L., Fox, A., Jordan, M.I., Patterson, D.: Predicting multiple metrics for queries: Better decisions enabled by machine learning. In: IEEE 25th International Conference on Data Engineering, ICDE 2009, pp. 592–603. IEEE (2009)
18. Zaharia, M., Chowdhury, M., Das, T., Dave, A., Ma, J., McCauley, M., Stoica, I.: Resilient distributed datasets: A fault-tolerant abstraction for in-memory cluster computing. In: Proceedings of the 9th USENIX Conference on Networked Systems Design and Implementation, pp. 2–2. USENIX Association (2012)
19. Zhang, Y., Gao, Q., Gao, L., Wang, C.: Priter: a distributed framework for prioritized iterative computations. In: Proceedings of the 2nd ACM Symposium on Cloud Computing, p. 13. ACM (2011)
20. Zhang, S., Han, J., Liu, Z., Wang, K., Feng, S.: Accelerating MapReduce with distributed memory cache. In: 2009 15th International Conference on Parallel and Distributed Systems (ICPADS), pp. 472–478. IEEE (2009)

Service Scheduling Algorithm
in Vehicle Embedded Middleware

Juan Luo, Xin Jin, and Feng Wu

College of Computer Science and Electronic Engineering,
Hunan University, Changsha, Hunan 410082, China
juanluo@hnu.edu.cn

Abstract. Due to different hardware environments of different vehicle electronic control units, the reusability of vehicle electronic software is reduced, which hinders the development of vehicle electronics. First, in this paper, we proposed a SOA-based middleware for vehicular embedded system, which makes it possible for each ECU to dispatch and receive data on the bus by service, it will hide the underlying heterogeneity. Second, on the basis of the vehicular service scheduling algorithm, a priority allocation algorithm based on criticality level is proposed. This algorithm makes the transmission of all interior services more efficient. Third, simulation results show that our algorithm has a higher scheduling ratio when the number of tasks is increased to a certain amount.

Keywords: OSGi, middleware, SOA, vehicle.

1 Introduction

In recent years, for the increasing demand for greater vehicle safety, comfort, and entertainment, etc., the functions of vehicle electronics becomes much more powerful. Now,vehicular electronic systems [1] can help the driver control not only the driving, steering, brakes, engines and other systems, but also the lights, wipers, doors and entertainment control systems. And all of these functions are achieved by the electronic control unit (ECU). Premium vehicles have more than 70 ECUs which could exchange multiple signals. So this is a great challenge since the vehicular network has to offer low delay and high reliability. Instant response is a mandatory for embedded systems. The reason is that for many applications consequences can be disastrous if those applications cannot work within deadline. For example, in order to ensure the real-time performance, safety and reliability of systems in emergency situation, the anti-lock system must take effect and function within the deadline, which is closely related to priorities of ECU tasks.

Controller Area Network (CAN) is a simple, effective, robust communication bus [2] that inside the vehicle network. Nowadays, most of transmissions among vehicle ECUs are accomplished via the CAN bus. CAN is a multi-master asynchronous serial data bus that could access the bus through the Carrier Sense Multiple Access/Collision Detection (CSMA/CD) mechanism. CAN bus protocol specifies that nodes can transmit information only when the CAN bus is

X.-h. Sun et al. (Eds.): ICA3PP 2014, Part II, LNCS 8631, pp. 96–107, 2014.
© Springer International Publishing Switzerland 2014

free. If two or more nodes need to transmit their information simultaneously, the CAN message with minimum number identifiers takes priority. And the other nodes can not send their information until the bus is available again. In fact, CAN nodes transmit information through a fixed-priority and non-preemptive scheduling approach, and the ID of each message is its priority.

Service-Oriented Architecture (SOA) [3], aiming to provide a unified interface for functional units of each application, enables each functional system to satisfy their mission requirements collaboratively and independently at the same time. As a component model, the design of SOA consists of functional units in the form of low-coupling, and the functional unit is the so-called service. SOA-based middleware embedded into vehicular systems abstracts functions attributes of electronic control units as services, and meets the needs of the upper application by providing a unified interface.

OSGi (Open Service Gateway initiative) [4] is not only a typical service-oriented components system, but also a dynamic, light-weighted middleware platform. Applications or components in the form of bundles for deployment can be remotely installed, started, stopped, updated, and uninstalled without requiring a reboot. Application life cycle management is done via APIs that allow remote downloading of management policies. The service registry allows bundles to detect the addition of new services, or the removal of services, and adapt accordingly. OSGi technology has improved the Java defects in modular programming, and created a dynamic modular system. OSGi framework mainly consists of three components: *Framework*, *Bundle* and *Service*. *Framework* architecture is on the Java VM (Java Virtual Machine), *Bundle* is executed on the application over *Framework*, and *Service* is interface service that provided(export) or required(import) by *Bundle*. Class loading, life cycle management, service registry and standardize services provided by OSGi framework are all for *Bundles*. *Bundle* is actually a *jar* file that meets specific form. Security mechanism of OSGi extends the Java security mechanisms, so that the module is running in a secure environment through access control module and life cycle management. With the help of OSGi, we can reuse resources that were used in the framework, which will reduce a great deal of cost.

In existing intelligent vehicles, the increasing number of ECUs satisfies the growing requirements, but different ECUs have different hardware environments, which reduces vehicle electronics software reusability and restricts the development of vehicle electronics. Existing researches on intelligent vehicles focused more on vehiclular ad hoc network (VANET) and operating system-level studies, and less on service content of in-vehicle or vehicle-vehicle system. Therefore, it will be an important subject for embedded vehicular middleware to improve software reusability and reach mandatory targets of real-time vehicular systems.

In this paper, we deployed a light-weighted OSGi middleware into vehicular systems in the form of plug-ins. Abstracting ECU services and non-functional properties as services by taking advantage of the service features of OSGi to achieve interoperability among ECUs. In vehicular electronics systems, however, real-time and high efficiency are mandatory targets to reach, and scheduling algorithm is the key to achieve high levels of system performance. So it is essential to schedule tasks within deadline. Therefore, considering a number of factors, including the priority assignment, we propose an OSGi-based service scheduling algorithm to satisfy the real-time vehicular electronics and high efficiency requirements.

2   Related Work

Many efforts in research literature have extended the study and realization of traditional distributed OSGi platform. Rellermeyer [5] achieved the interoperability of OSGi applications by extending the traditional centralized and industry-standard OSGi platform to a distributed middleware on, which greatly simplifies the development of distributed applications with low overhead of performance. But it is invasive to the OSGi programming model, and cannot interact with non-OSGi system. Shi *et al.* [6] proposed CORBA-based distributed OSGi model, which supports interoperability among multiple OSGi applications and between non-OSGi and OSGi, and it reaches the goal of low invasiveness and high scalability.

Lai *et al.* [7] analyzed the P2P multimedia sharing mechanism of home network and he found that the transmission could only be achieved with the use of P2P networks, but when the content server and the client have adopted this mechanism, the transmission speed of the internal network could not increase any more. To solve this problem, the OSGi middleware was added to the DLNA-based multimedia sharing system to expand the network to an OSGi-based P2P one, which effectively improves the quality of service for users. For the smart home service network with limited or unreachable resources, Cheng *et al.* [8] designed a service management mechanism based on priority scheduling algorithm by embedding the middleware into the service gateway to ensure the quality of service and better dealing with emergency situations. But this priority-based service management platform cannot be called among multiple platforms, and thus its scope of application is limited.

CAN bus is widely used in the field of vehicular applications. So information scheduling of vehicles has always been a research hotspot. As for the worst case response time of the vehicular systems, Tian *et al.* [9] proposed a fixed priority scheduling algorithm in the message transfer model based on CAN bus, and its core idea is to determine the priority based on deadline of node information. The shorter the deadline is, the more urgent the task will be, and the higher priority will be assigned. In this way, time and resource can be fully used to complete the task before its deadline. And the results of the experiment showed that this method has improved network utilization in CAN network. However, this method has disadvantage when many tasks are triggered at the same time, the scheduling ratio is not ideal. As for the problem of interconnection between processors in multi-processor systems, in other words, there exist data dependencies among multiple tasks.

Qiu *et al.* [10] presented the dynamic B Level first (DBLF) algorithm based on heterogeneous distributed systems by introducing a weighted directed acyclic graph (DAG) model and the dynamic path mechanisms to optimize communication resources, this algorithm takes the communication behavior of real-time system into account, namely there is competition among communications devices while accessing to each other, so compared with existing algorithms, it is much more practical and accurate.

Davis *et al.* [11] pointed out that the analysis of existing literature on CAN networks are based on the priority scheduling, in fact, many transmissions of tasks are based on FIFO (First In First Out) queue in CAN network. Therefore, this literature introduced the method of response time analysis based on FIFO for task scheduling. Experiments proved that the proposed method has a high utilization of network. Mubeen *et al.* [12] indicated that the node will send two types of messages in CAN network: periodic messages or sporadic messages. At the same time, there are two scheduling modes in CAN network: FIFO-based scheduling and priority-based scheduling. Finally, the literature verified transmission performance through these two scheduling methods, which proved that priority-based scheduling method is superior to FIFO-based scheduling method.

Davis *et al.* [13] pointed out that there is something wrong with the original analysis of CAN bus information scheduling, because it cannot ensure the information reaches the destination node within deadline. Zheng [14] proposed a model-based architecture design in vehicular electronic systems because ECU have to perform more and more complicated function. It also analyzed time-triggered scheduling and event-based trigger scheduling model, and proposed a mapping from signal to information and task to ECU.

3   Architecture of Service-Oriented Vehicular Middleware

OSGi-based service-oriented vehicular middleware is shown in Fig.1, which can not only shield the different underlying hardware environment, but also facilitate the further development of the applications.

Schedule center is the key module in our middleware, which manages the service scheduling for vehicular system. In our framework, the coordination between service schedule component and multiple components could reduce collision rate when multiple tasks are simultaneously transmitted in bus. When the access collision rate is decreased, then the number of repeated requests will be reduced, and so does the number of service request. In addition, service scheduling management can effectively help the whole system quickly complete the task.

SocketCAN is a communication interface between the applications and the underlying hardware in Linux kernel. This module allows underlying SocketCAN framework to be a service in OSGi framework, which exchanges data in CAN bus.

The Data Mapper bundle is used to convert the received byte arrays into data with application-defined meaning. It provides utilities for converting bytes to Java object and vice versa. The Data Mapper bundle converts the raw data in OSGi environment according to the rules of defined XML-based bus definitions file.

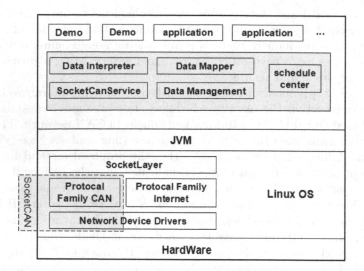

Fig. 1. Overall Framework of OSGi based middleware

Data Interpreter is an information translator. Data Interpreter is mainly used for processing data from the underlying CANSocket, and translating data into java language that can be recognized by various components of the OSGi framework. It also implements the applications to send and to receive vehicle information without considering the underlying structure of vehicles.

Data Management manages data by OSGi DMT (Date Management Tree), and it provides a pattern to access the vehicular data. DMT is used to store and manage vehicle information. DMT provides appropriate metadata for applications. The application running in a local environment can also get the vehicular sensor data via data center module.

4 Service Scheduling Algorithm

4.1 Basic Concepts and Definitions

Service is the set of attributes input and output by the Electronic Control Unit (ECU) in vehicular network. Let S denotes the set of service, $S_m = (I_m, O_m)$ is the mth service in S, where I_m is the set of input attributes, and O_m represents the set of output attributes.

In fact, the OSGi middlewares consist of bundles, so services input or output by ECU are all in the form of bundles. And the information mentioned above is contained in bundles.

Service Priority is the execution sequence of services under the condition of ensuring reliability and service performance. Let P_m represent the priority of service m. The value of P_m is a positive integer, and the service with a bigger value has a higher priority (e.g. service m with the lowest priority satisfies $P_m = 1$).

As for service m $(S_m = (I_m, O_m))$ and service n $(S_n = (I_n, O_n))$, if S_m is transmitted on the CAN bus before S_n, the priority of S_m is higher than that of S_n, i.e. $\mathrm{P_m} > \mathrm{P_n}$.

In real-time intelligent vehicular systems, the service transmitted on the CAN bus must satisfy the real-time requirement. In this case, each service has a fixed deadline, which is the time allowed between a service being sent and received.

D_m is the deadline of service m, and it is an intrinsic property. If transmission time is beyond the deadline, it can not guarantee the real-time character of a service.

We assume that each service has a worst-case response time, which is the maximum time interval between sending and receiving a service. W_m represents the worst-case response time of service m. The service m is schedulable only if $\mathrm{W_m} \leq \mathrm{D_m}$, and it means that m satisfies the real-time requirement.

Therefore, $\mathrm{W_m} \leq \mathrm{D_m}$ is the sufficient and necessary conditions for schedulability of service m. The worst-case response time[15] is

$$W_m^{n+1} = \max(B_m, C_m) + \sum_{\forall k \in hp(m)} \left\lceil \frac{w_m^n + J_k + \tau_{bit}}{T\kappa} \right\rceil C_k \tag{1}$$

In Eq.(1), J_k is the queuing jitter of service k and represents the maximum delay time that a released service k should wait until it can be executed. And k is a service whose priority is higher than m, since the value of J_k is typically small, so it evaluates to 0.

T_k is the minimum time interval that service k would be triggered. Therefore, as time goes on, T_k will still be able to satisfy the scheduling requirements under the condition that each T_k satisfies scheduling requirements right now.

B_m is the blocking time. Since service scheduling is non-preemptive, B_m represents the time that service m with higher priority should wait while service with lower priority being transmitted. It results from the order of those services being triggered, that is, service with lower priority occupies the CAN bus.

C_m (or C_k) represents the transmission time of service m (or k) on the CAN bus.

τ_{bit} is the time required to transmit 1 bit service message.

If a service has a low criticality level, this service instance will be dumped to save resource and ensure the complement of other instances with high criticality level when the criticality level of system is switched to a high one. Therefore, the definition of worst-case response time is modified as

$$W_m^{n+1} = \max(B_m, C_m) + \sum_{\forall k \in hp(m)} \left\lceil \frac{w_m^n + J_k + \tau_{bit}}{T\kappa} \right\rceil C_k(L) \tag{2}$$

Where $C_k(L)$ is the transmission time of service S_k whose criticality level is L.

Equation (2) indicates that the worst-case response time of a service is the sum of the transmission time of all service instances with high priority and the larger one of B_m and C_m.

The task of CAN node is transmitted on CAN bus in the form of service instance, which is a component of OSGi, namely bundle. The character of SOA hides the heterogeneity of different hardware and enhances the reusability of software. In the end, high-priority service nodes send messages firstly and low-priority service nodes send messages till bus is free. Different transmit order leads to different scheduling results, as shown in Fig.2.

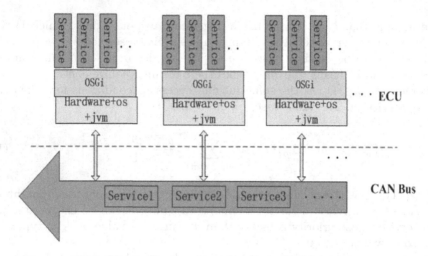

Fig. 2. Service transmission on CAN bus

4.2   Priority Allocation Algorithm Based on Criticality Level

We proposed a priority allocation algorithm based on criticality level as follows:

1. Determine transmission time C, detection period T and the deadline of every service instance S_m with high or low criticality level in set S of service instances.
2. Determine the lowest priority P1. Select service instance which has the biggest deadline from low criticality level or high criticality level instances as candidate value, then iterate Eq.(2) till W_m^{n+1} will not change.
3. If $W_m^{n+1} \leq D_m$, then we can determine priority Pm=1,otherwise, return to step 2.
4. Continue allocating priority and selecting the service instance which has the biggest deadline from low criticality level or high criticality level instances, then iterate Eq.(2) till W_i^{n+1} will not change.
5. If $W_i^{n+1} \leq D_i$, then we can determine priority P_i=2, otherwise, return to step 4.
6. Determine the priority of each service instance according to above methods.

Each service is transmitted in a state of low criticality level. If the transmission time of some services exceeds their deadline, then the service is switched to a high criticality level and transmission time of it will increase to prevent it over its deadline, which lead to failure of this service. With the determined criticality level of a service, we could determine its priority. This algorithm makes more services with high criticality level to be successfully transmitted on bus.

5   Experimental Analysis

In order to verify the execution efficiency of priority allocation algorithm based on criticality level, we use multiple service instances to get it at the aspect of scheduling ratio in this paper. Employing a dynamic task generation algorithm to generate service instances randomly in order to simulate the influence of the real-time variable vehicular interior network environment on experiments. This algorithm is implemented in C programming language.

Since two or more nodes will send messages in experiments, so high-priority nodes will send messages firstly and low-priority nodes will send messages till bus is available. Thus, experiments select bus utilization as the independent variable to denote the time of bus being occupied in unite timed and scheduling ratio as dependent variable, which means the rate of tasks executed successfully while system criticality level changes from low to high with a part of low criticality level tasks being discarded.

5.1   Experiment Parameter

Some of parameters in experiments are initiated as follows:

The bus utilization u is randomly produced by task allocation function: u=c/T;

Task cycle T can be produced by random distribution function and set to be [10ms, 1s];

This paper employs double criticality level L ,namely 0 represents low criticality level and 1 represents high criticality level;

Transmission time of task with low criticality level is : $c(0) = u * T$;

Transmission time of task with high criticality level is : $c(1) = CF * c(0)$, where the fixed parameter CF is greater than 1;

The deadline D equals T;

$CP(L)$ means the probability of criticality level L ,where $CP(0)+CP(1) = 1$;

Experiments in this paper can be expressed by $n, L, CF, (CP(0), CP(1))$, where n is the number of experimental samples that being employed, bus utilization and scheduling ratio of every sample are both statistic calculated by multiple messages; each service instance has L criticality levels, and transmission speed of message with high criticality level is CF times as much as that of messages with low criticality level, $CP(0)$ is the probability of instance with low criticality level and $CP(1)$ is the probability of instance with high criticality level.

5.2   Experimental Analysis

In this section, we evaluate the performance of the proposed priority allocation algorithm based on criticality through comparing with the traditional one in terms of scheduling ratio, as shown in Fig.3. Our algorithm is named as new optimal assignment algorithm (NOPA), and the traditional one is called optimal assignment algorithm (OPA) [15] which is designed at the level of processor aiming at improving the processing successful ratio of CPU while dealing with tasks. Bus utilization(network utilization) is the independent variable and scheduling ratio is the dependent variable.And since we concern about the impact on the scheduling of critical level, so the value of CF is set to be 2, with the same value as [15].

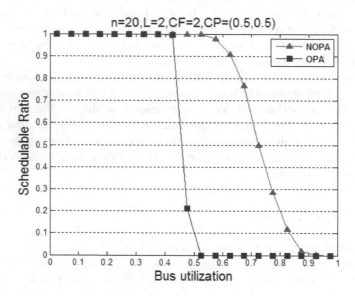

Fig. 3. Comparison about two algorithms

As shown in Fig.3, bus utilization changes from 0 to 0.4, scheduling ratio of these two algorithms are both very high and nearly equal to 1. This indicates that when there are less tasks transmitted on bus ,namely bus utilization is very low, tasks will be executed successfully. With the increasing of bus utilization, scheduling ratio of OPA will suffer a sharp decrease, since the number of tasks increases gradually and more tasks will be abandoned to make sure that high-priority tasks can be executed within deadline, so scheduling ratio will decrease. In contrast, scheduling ratio of NOPA will slowly decrease with the increasing of bus utilization. This experiment shows that NOPA has significant performance overhead over OPA.

Fig.4 and Fig.5 indicate that scheduling ratio has different values with different proportion of high to low criticality level, namely $CP = (0.7, 0.3)$ and $CP = (0.3, 0.7)$. But compared to traditional priority allocation algorithm, the

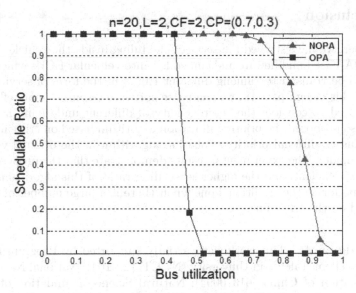

Fig. 4. Comparison with CP=(0.7,0.3)

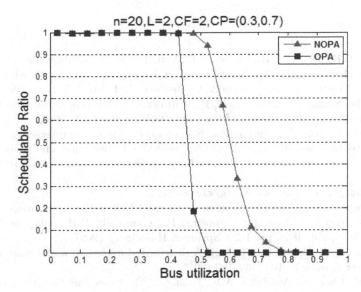

Fig. 5. Comparison with CP=(0.3,0.7)

scheduling ratio of NOPA will decrease more slowly after bus utilization is higher than 0.5 as shown in last two figures. We can conclude that NOPA outperforms traditional priority allocation algorithm. With the increasing number of experimental samples, scheduling ratio of NOPA will always higher than that of OPA though the values of them will both decrease.

6   Conclusion

In this paper, we have studied the service scheduling inside the vehicle. We proposed a SOA-based middleware and embedded into vehicular ECUs which allows messages to be transmitted among different ECUs in the form of service. With the help of this design pattern, we can reuse software resources more effectively and don't need to consider the heterogeneity of different underlying hardware. We have also proposed the priority allocation algorithm based on criticality level by improving traditional priority allocation algorithm in the original vehicular scheduling model. The experimental results demonstrate that the proposed algorithm is very efficient, and the higher scheduling ratio of this algorithm showed that it outperforms the traditional one when there is a large number of services transmitted on the CAN bus.

Acknowledgments. This work was partially supported by Program for New Century Excellent Talents in University (NCET-12-0164); National Natural Science Foundation of China (61370094); Natural Science Foundation of Hunan (13JJ1014); National Key Technology R&D Program(2012BAD35B06).

References

1. Nilsson, D.K., Phung, P.H., Larson, U.E.: Vehicle ecu classification based on safety-security characteristics. In: Road Transport Information and Control-RTIC 2008 and ITS United Kingdom Members' Conference, IET, pp. 1–7. IET (2008)
2. Navet, N., Song, Y., Simonot-Lion, F., Wilwert, C.: Trends in automotive communication systems. Proceedings of the IEEE 93(6), 1204–1223 (2005)
3. Guinard, D., Trifa, V., Karnouskos, S., Spiess, P., Savio, D.: Interacting with the soa-based internet of things: Discovery, query, selection, and on-demand provisioning of web services. IEEE Transactions on Services Computing 3(3), 223–235 (2010)
4. OSGi, http://en.wikipedia.org/wiki/OSGi
5. Rellermeyer, J.S., Alonso, G., Roscoe, T.: R-osgi: Distributed applications through software modularization. In: Cerqueira, R., Campbell, R.H. (eds.) Middleware 2007. LNCS, vol. 4834, pp. 1–20. Springer, Heidelberg (2007)
6. Shi, D., Wu, Y., Ding, B.: Starosgi: A distributed extension middleware for osgi. Computer Science 38(01), 162–189 (2011)
7. Lai, C.F., Chen, M., Vasilakos, A.V., Huang, Y.M.: Extending the dlna-based multimedia sharing system to p2p network on osgi frameworks. In: 2010 IEEE Global Telecommunications Conference (GLOBECOM 2010), pp. 1–5. IEEE (2010)
8. Cheng, S.T., Chou, C.L., Horng, G.J.: Priority-oriented architecture service management on osgi home-service platform. Wireless Personal Communications 71(1), 611–628 (2013)
9. Tian, J., Huang, Y., Wang, L.: Application of fixed priority schedule algorithm in can bus. Computer Engineering 32(23), 94–96 (2006)
10. Qiu, W., Chen, Y., Li, J., Peng, C.: A task scheduling algorithm for real-time heterogeneous embedded systems. Journal of Software 15(4), 504–511 (2004)

11. Davis, R.I., Kollmann, S., Pollex, V., Slomka, F.: Controller area network (can) schedulability analysis with fifo queues. In: 2011 23rd Euromicro Conference on Real-Time Systems (ECRTS), pp. 45–56. IEEE (2011)

12. Mubeen, S., Maki-Turja, J., Sjodin, M.: Response-time analysis of mixed messages in controller area network with priority-and fifo-queued nodes. In: 2012 9th IEEE International Workshop on Factory Communication Systems (WFCS), pp. 23–32. IEEE (2012)

13. Davis, R.I., Burns, A., Bril, R.J., Lukkien, J.J.: Controller area network (can) schedulability analysis: Refuted, revisited and revised. Real-Time Systems 35(3), 239–272 (2007)

14. Zheng, W.: Architectural Synthesis Techniques for distributed automotive system. PhD thesis, University of California, Berkeley (2009)

15. Baruah, S.K., Burns, A., Davis, R.I.: Response-time analysis for mixed criticality systems. In: 2011 IEEE 32nd Real-Time Systems Symposium (RTSS), pp. 34–43. IEEE (2011)

Similar Samples Cleaning in Speculative Multithreading[*]

Yuxiang Li, Yinliang Zhao, and Bin Liu

Department of Computer Science and Technology,
Xi'an Jiaotong University,
Xi'an, China
liyuxiang@stu.xjtu.edu.cn, zhaoy@mail.xjtu.edu.cn,
liubin2010@gmail.com

Abstract. Speculative multithreading (SpMT) is a thread-level automatic paral-lelization technique to accelerate sequential programs on multi-core. Too large and too dense samples can not be able to effectively promote the effectiveness of thread partition, parallel thread evaluation, etc. Selection of appropriate samples is of vital importance. The appropriateness reflects in two points. First, redundant samples never exist. Second, similarity between any two samples is not high. We express a sample with one feature vector of fixed length. We extract sample feature vectors using profiler in Prophet during compile time when running programs. Such profiles are created by feature extraction routines which map each program onto a tuple $(N_1, N_2, N_3, N_4, N_5, N_6)$ where N_i is a count of an occurrence of a particular feature. A comparison routine is then invoked which detects similarities amongst tuples. According to the program features, similarity values between samples are calculated to assess the similar degree. In this paper, we introduce a novel way of assessing the similarity of two program samples using Theory of Fuzzy. We firstly calculate the Euclidean Distance of two different program samples as the input, and then assess the overall similarity degrees as well as respective similarity degrees, using corresponding Fuzzy Functions. Based on them, we clean the similar samples. With multidimensional samples generated virtually, we get that average density of samples decreases, so that a more effective collection of samples are created.

Keywords: Theory of Fuzzy, Similarity Assessment, code features.

1   Introduction

In previous work, static or dynamic features have been represented as structured data, usually as fixed-length feature vectors. Also, previous work has shown that models using dynamic characterizations out-perform the ones with static characterizations [1]. However, dynamic characterizations have disadvantages over static characterizations. To collect this dynamic information from a program, the application must be at

---

[*] This work is supported by National Natural Science Foundation of China through grants No.61173040 and Doctoral Fund of Ministry of Education of China under Grant No.2013021110012.

X.-h. Sun et al. (Eds.): ICA3PP 2014, Part II, LNCS 8631, pp. 108–121, 2014.

least once, which increases training time to construct prediction models and adds an additional cumbersome profiling step to the compilation process. Moreover, dynamic characterizations are sensitive to a program's input because the information was collected during a program run.

In this paper, we introduce a novel method to assess the similarity of program samples using Fuzzy Theory. Firstly we produce the program's graph-based intermediate representation (IR) from the original program. A program's graph-based IR is a static characterization technique because it is collected during the compilation of the program. Then, we use fixed-length feature vectors to present the static characterizations. Finally, Euclidean Distance is brought to calculate the similarity distance between two vectors and Fuzzy Theory is also introduced to assess the similarity values.

In conclusion, this work first calculates the fuzzy similarity values between samples, and adjusts the similarity thresholds as well as eliminates similar samples, to realize the preprocessing, providing efficient input samples for sample analysis process.

This paper is organized as follows. In Sections 2, we characterize the program, mainly included in a feature table. In Section 3, we assess the overall similarity. In Section 4, we perform the experiment. In Section 5, we explain and compare it with related work. Section 6 presents our conclusion and future work.

2   Characterizing the PROG

Compiler researchers have used fixed-length representations of the program's source code features or (IR) intermediate representations [2-4]. These representations are straight-forward to extract from a program and can be collected during compilation time. Other researchers have proposed using dynamic characterizations of programs; however, techniques (e.g. performance counters [1] and reactions [5, 6]) are expensive and require running the program, which limits their practical use.

Table 1. Sample Procedure

```
1     main()
2     {
3            int i, s;
4            i = 0, s = 0;
5            if( i<=10 )
6            {
7                    s = s+i^2;
8            }
9            else
10           {
11                   s = s-i;
12           }
13           printf(("s=%d",s);
14    }
```

2.1   Extracting Feature Vectors

In this section, we motivate the applicability of using the program's source code as input for finding the program features. Table 1 shows an example of source codes.

With regard to a program, we first establish the corresponding structured diagram. Then, we extract the features from the structured diagram. Figure 2 shows the associative process of collecting sample features. How can we characterize a program is to be solved. We need extract features to represent it. As we use the static characters to stand for a procedure, we use the features shown in Table 2 [7] to form the vectors.

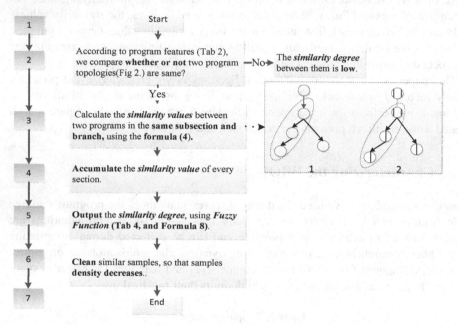

Fig. 1. Flow chart of similar samples cleaning

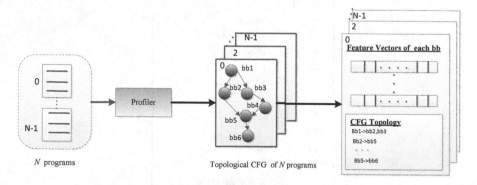

Fig. 2. Collecting different program features

Table 2. A collection of eight different features for each node (basic block) in CFG

variables	Features	Descriptions
N_1	Number of basic blocks	Number of basic blocks in a function
N_2	Number of instructions	Number of dynamic instructions in basic block
N_3	Loop probability	The probability of loop to jump test part
N_4	Branch probability	The probability of branch to be taken and not taken
N_5	DDC	Data dependence counts between two basic blocks
N_6	DDD	Data dependence distance between two basic blocks

Thread size, load balance, data and control dependence are the main factors affecting program's speedup. Generally speaking, we use six features shown in Table 2 to express programs.

Features are extracted from Olden benchmarks by SUIF compiler and data flow analysis framework with program profiling. When dealing with a program, SUIF IR is firstly constructed. Then, features are extracted from SUIF IR and the corresponding features are saved in the matrix M and array A. For a given function, we obtain a fixed-length feature vector, shown in formula (1), where F_k is used to characterize a program.

Prophet can convert any C programs, and change C programs to SUI IRs (SUIF Intermediate Representation) after syntax and semantic analysis. Then, IRs are optimized to create low-grade SUIT IRs, which are sent to Profiler modules to get the feature information. All feature analysis is performed at the high-level intermediate representation of SUIF (high-SUIF). Features are counted based on the CFG of function and CFG can be expressed by matrix $M_{n \times n}$, where n is the number of basic blocks. The matrix elements are defined as follows:

$$M_{i \times j} = (l, b, < d_1, ..., d_n >, n)   \quad (1)$$

where l is the loop branch probability, b is the branch probability, d_k is the k_{th} data dependence distance and n is the data dependence count between node i and node j in CFG. Matrix M stores inter-block features that contain data dependence counts, data dependence distance, branch probability and loop information. Different inter-block features are attached to matrix M in order, as shown in Figure 3. Block features, such as the number of dynamitic instructions are stored in array A. Matrix M and array A are used to represent features of a function.

2.2   Presenting the Solving Scheme

This section provides a brief flow chart of solving scheme, shown in the Figure 1. The whole scheme is divided into five steps. The first step is starting to input two compared programs. The second step is to judge whether or not the topologies of two programs are the same. The third one is to calculate the similarity values between two programs in the same subsection and branch. The fourth step is to accumulate the similarity value of every part of program. The fifth step is to calculate the fuzzy function values between two compared programs. The sixth step is to clean the similar samples.

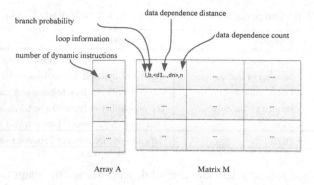

Fig. 3. Features representation

In Figure 3, we show the process of extracting our graph-based characterizations [8]. We use Prophet [9] to extract control flow graphs based on analysis of basic blocks. From the CFG, we generate graph-based characterizations, which include (1) a feature vector for each basic block in the CFG as shown in Table 2 and (2) a list of directed edges in the graph. Prophet [10, 11] can be used to extract other graph-based IRs too.

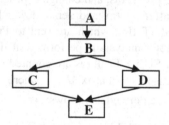

Fig. 4. Control Flow Graph of main() procedure shown in Table 1

3   Assessing the Overall Similarity

In Figure 4, we use Prophet to produce the CFG topologies and features (related with the Table 2) of each node for n-1 programs. The meanings of N_i ($1 \leqslant i \leqslant 8$) have been shown in Table 2. The rightmost of Figure.1 shows two separate parts, one is feature vectors for each *bb* (basic block), and the other shows the CFG topology (CFG: Control Flow Graph).   Features   which correspond to a row in M_{ij} are expressed as follows.

$$F_k = <N_1^k, N_2^k, N_3^k, N_4^k, N_5^k, N_6^k, N_7^k, N_8^k>, k \in N \tag{2}$$

Make a definition, as follows.

$$F_k(i) = N_{i+1}^k, i = 0, 1, 2, 3, 4, 5, 6, 7 \tag{3}$$

Then, we form the comparison vectors A_i or B_i, which is expressed in the following way.

$$A_i = [F_1(i), F_2(i), F_3(i), \ldots, F_n(i)]^T, \ (n \geq 1) \,\&\, (n \in N), \ (0 \leq i \leq 7) \,\&\, (i \in N) \quad (4)$$

Assume two vectors $A_{i,}$ and B_i, we calculate the similarity distance between A_i and B_i using the following algorithm.

$$F_n = \sum_{i=0}^{7} \sqrt{\sum_{k=1}^{n} (A_i(k) - B_i(k))^2} \quad (5)$$

To calculate the distance of two vectors and evaluate the similarity degree of two vectors we have proposed, we meet the challenge in two stages. First, we give a mechanism of similarity calculation. Second, model of similarity assessment is given.

3.1 Mechanism of Similarity Calculation

Now that we have owned the features to calculate the similarity degree, the first step is to determine how these features should be compared. We formulize the comparison by defining distance functions. Due to features that are represented in vector formats (e.g., static instruction mix), we use the Euclidean Distance between two vectors to measure their similarity. For two vectors A and B both with length n, Euclidean distance [12] is defined as:

$$\sqrt{\sum_{i=1}^{n} (A_i - B_i)^2} \quad (6)$$

3.2 Model of Respective Similarity Assessment

Compared to the section 3.1 of this paper, this part aims to assess the respective similarity degree, while the section 3.1 focuses on the overall similarity of two feature vectors. Before we take consideration into the process of assessing the similarity of two features, the process of collecting features is firstly presented. As is shown in Figure 5, we assess the similarity between two feature vectors in three separated stages, including feature collection, analysis, and fuzzy function used to get the specific similarity values.

In the Figure 6, programs are related to the samples, which are used to extract features. In the studying stage, programs are associated with studying samples, while programs are relevant with testing samples in the testing stage. FEATURE Database corresponds to an assemble of features, shown as follows.

$$FEATURE \ Database = \{F_n \mid n \in N, F_n = <N_1, N_2, N_3, \ldots, N_8>\} \quad (7)$$

In the analysis stage, we figure out the similarity distances, corresponding to the following matrix.

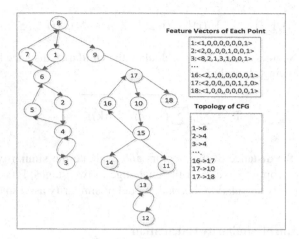

Fig. 5. Collecting different program features

Table 3. Similarity Caculation between Two Blocks. A collection of similarity function f_{ij} between basic blocks is given. As the similarity between B_i and B_j. equals to the one between B_j and B_i.. The annotation '-' denotes the symmetrical values, which can be gotten from the corresponding values in another half matrix. Each element's inherent meaning is shown in the formula (7).

	B_1	B_2	B_3	B_4	B_5	B_6
B_1	1	f_{12}	f_{13}	f_{14}	f_{15}	f_{16}
B_2	-	1	f_{23}	f_{24}	f_{25}	f_{26}
B_3	-	-	1	f_{34}	f_{35}	f_{36}
B_4	-	-	-	1	f_{45}	f_{46}
B_5	-	-	-	-	1	f_{56}
B_6	-	-	-	-	-	1

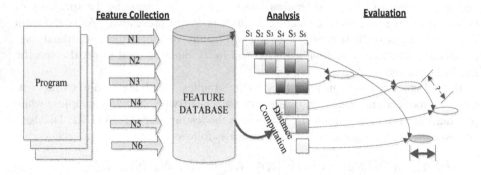

Fig. 6. Procedure of assessing similarities involves three stages: feature collection, analysis and evaluation. In feature collection, features involved in program are assembled. Analysis uses these features to compute distance between two vectors, in turn using distance data to estimate the similarity degree. Finally, we use Fuzzy Function to figure out the similarity values (0~1), and to determine which sample will be cleaned

$$f_{ij} = \sqrt{\sum_{m=1}^{6} (N_m^i - N_m^j)^2} \qquad (8)$$

From formula (8), we can see that $f_{ij} = 0$, while $i=j$; and $f_{ij} = f_{ji}$. So we can get the following similarity matrix.

The Half Similarity Matrix in Table 3 is mapped to the "analysis" process. In the process of analysis, the similarity values are normalized. The values are rounded to be a series of discrete values {0.0,0.1,0.2,0.3,0.4,0.5,0.6,0.7,0.8,0.9,1.0}. The eleven discrete values are mapped to eleven cubes with varying degrees of black. For example, ■ corresponds to the value 1.0; ■corresponds to the value 0.9; ■ is related to the value 0.8; ■ is associated with the value 0.7; ■ is associated with the value 0.6; ■ is associated with 0.5; □ is connected with 0.4; □corresponds to 0.3; □ is related to the value 0.2; □ is associated with 0.1; □ corresponds to the value 0.0.

3.3   Similarity Measurement Using Fuzzy Function

Once the similarity value between two program feature vectors is obtained, we can get the similarity degree for them using a fuzzy function in Figure 7 and formula (8). The input variable represents the similarity values, while the output variable denotes the degree of similarity. The input variables are shown along the x-axis, while the output variables are denoted along the y-axis. S_{low} represents the low similarity value, while S_{large} represents the high similarity value. Using the Fuzzy Function, we can get the result table, namely Table 3.

According to the Table 4, the similarity degree (low or high, or moderate) of two programs is gotten. Figure 8 gives an example of how to clean a similar sample. $S(,)$ is the similarity function between adjacent nodes, and is equal to $D(,)$ in the Table 4.

Table 4. Similarity values of two program feature vectors corresponding to formula (9)

Conditions	Similarity values
$D(V_A,V_B) <= D_{low}$	0
$D_{low} =< D(V_A,V_B) <= D_{larg}$	$D(V_A,V_B)-D_{low}$
$D(V_A,V_B) >= D_{high}$	1

If the value of $S(,)$ is lower than a certain threshold, we will randomly clean a sample. This process is corresponding to "Evaluation" in Figure 6.

$$D = \begin{cases} D_h & S \le S_{low} \\ \dfrac{D_h - D_l}{S_{low} - S_{l\,arg}}(S - S_{l\,arg}) + D_l & S \ge S_{low} \,\&\&S \le S_{l\,arg} \\ D_l & S \ge S_{l\,arg} \end{cases} \qquad (9)$$

Similarity calculation is completed with the formula (8).

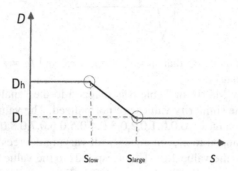

Fig. 7. Fuzzy Function between Similarity and Degree of fuzziness. The x-axis represents simi-larity value, S_{low} denotes the low similarity value and S_{large} denotes the large similarity value. The y-axis denotes degrees of corresponding similarity over the similarity values between two vectors, D_h represents a high degree and D_l represents a low degree.

3.4   Cleaning of Similar Samples

After assessing the similarity degree between two samples, the operation of cleaning similar samples will be performed.   The principles for the operation involve: (1) similarity values (obtained from formula (9)) are sorted in descending order. (2) The more similar two samples are, the more likely they will be cleaned. (3) Once similari-ty degree is fixed, the sample to be cleaned is random.   The specific cleaning process is shown in Figure 8.

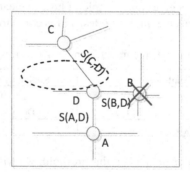

Fig. 8. Samples correlation graph. A,B,C,D,etc are sample nodes. S(,) are similarity degree, ranging from 0 to 1.

4   Experimental Evaluation

4.1   Experimental Setup

We have implemented similar samples cleaning process on the Prophet developed based on SUIF/MACHSUIF. All the compiler analysis is performed at the high-level intermediate representation (IR) of SUIF. A profiler is implemented to produce profiling information from SUIF-IR as forms of annotations. The profiler interprets and executes SUIF programs and provides information such as control flow path prediction, data value prediction, the number of dynamic instructions of loops and subroutines. The Prophet simulator [9] models a generic SpMT processor with four pipelined MIPS-based R3000 processing elements (PEs). The simulator is an execution-driven simulation and executes binaries generated by the Prophet compiler. Each PE has its own program counter, fetch unit, decode unit, and execution unit and it can fetch and execute instructions from a thread. Each PE can issue up to four instructions per cycle in an in-order fashion. Each PE also has private multi-versioned L1 cache with 2 cycles access latency. Multi-version L1 cache is used to buffer the speculation results for each PE and performs cache communication, and the four PEs share a write-back L2 cache via a snoopy bus.

In this section, we use Olden benchmarks to evaluate our approach. Olden benchmarks [15] are popular benchmarks for the study of irregular programs, which have complex control flow and irregular, pointer-intensive data structures. These programs have dynamic structures such as trees, lists and DAGs so that they are hard to be parallelized by the conventional approaches.

4.2   Static Features Extraction

According to the second part of paper, we can refer ten collection of   virtual samples generated using feature sets and abstract syntax tree [16] and establish the feature sets (corresponding to Table 2), shown in Table 5.

Table 5. Seldom Collection of Feature Vectors

Items	N_1	N_2	N_3	N_4	N_5	N_6
1	10	102	0.50	0.30	12	8
2	8	56	0.60	0.60	3	6
3	6	48	0.10	0.20	5	7
4	3	63	0.60	0.30	7	6
5	25	78	0.70	0.80	9	3
6	14	59	0.90	0.60	10	8
7	10	34	0.50	0.70	13	9
8	11	87	0.30	0.90	8	7

As depicted above, we take an example to seldom choose two vectors from the table 6 and assign them to N_1, N_2.

$$N1 = \left(N_1^1, N_2^1, N_3^1, N_4^1, N_5^1, N_6^1, N_7^1, N_8^1 \right) = \left(25, 78, 0.70, 0.80, 9, 3 \right);$$
$$N2 = \left(N_1^2, N_2^2, N_3^2, N_4^2, N_5^2, N_6^2, N_7^2, N_8^2 \right) = \left(14, 59, 0.90, 0.60, 10, 8 \right). \tag{10}$$

As every feature in vectors has different value ranges, so our first task before obtaining the similarity distance is to normalize every feature value.

4.3   Similarity Calculation

Using the formula (5), we can calculate the similarity value

$$Y = \sqrt[2]{\sum_{i=1}^{8} (\frac{N_1(i) - N_2(i)}{MAX(N_x(i))})^2}, \, x \geq 1 \, \& \, \& \, x \leq \text{count}(N(i)), x \in N \quad (11)$$

$$N_1(i) = N_i^1, N_2(i) = N_i^2, i = 1, 2, \ldots, 8 \quad (12)$$

Where, count(N(i)) is the number of N_i, ,so we get the value of Y= $\sqrt{0.6416} \approx 0.801$.

4.4   Similarity Assessment

In the Table 4, we take an example to set the threshold values of S_{low} and S_{large} to be (1,10). Note that the values of S_{low} and S_{large} are given just for an example. Accordingly, they need to be in depth study to get the precise values.

According to the formula (11), we figure out that $S(N_1,N_2)$=0.801, as 0.801>0.5(S_{low}), so the similarity degree for N_1 and N_2 is high shown in the Figure 7. Once two samples have high similarity, the operation of sample cleaning will be done. Moreover, the setting of fuzzy threshold is adaptive. How fuzzy thresholds be adaptively adjusted will be finished in the next stage.

4.5   Similar Samples Cleaning and Evaluation

According to the formula (9), we get that the similarity of N_1 and N_2 is high, so that we must clean one of them .Moreover, we define similarity density to evaluate the similarity degree of two samples.

$$D = \frac{\sum_{i=1}^{n} S(N_i, N_i')}{\text{Count}()} \quad (13)$$

D is density of all samples, $S(N_i, N_i')$ is similarity of two adjacent samples N_i and N_i' .and   Count() is the total sample number. We make use of 10000*20 samples from our Prophet samples (including Quad-core samples and Octa-core samples) to realize the approach. Results show in Table 6.

Table 6. Density of Sample before and after cleaning

Items	Before cleaning	After cleaning
Results	8.2434	8.0012

4.6   Analysis of the Models

This section analyzes the advantages of our approach against other models, including Artificial Neural Network (ANN) [14]   and Support Vector Machine (SVN) [14].

This work is based on the scheme "sample selection->features extraction->similarity calculation->fuzziness analysis->similar samples cleaning". In the process of "fuzziness analysis", half a trapezoidal distribution function is adopted, so that value settings of top and bottom edges of trapezoid are adaptive. Different applications may need adaptive upper limit and bottom limit of trapezoids (Corresponding to the values of D_l and D_h in Figure 1), in order to adaptively modify sample density. However, this approach also incurs the overheads of mistakenly elimination, and just using Euclidean distance to measure sample similarity can not fully exhibit the contribution degree of single sample.

5   Related Work

There have also been some researches on improving the program characterization to be used with machine learning for selecting good optimizations. In particular, Leather et al. [15] used compiler's IR and genetic programming to construct automatically new features from the GCC RTL representation of loops to improve a machine learning algorithm's performance on loop unrolling. However, the static features discovered are those that can be summarized into a fixed-length feature vector. Also, their technique only outperforms static source code features (such as, SRC) by only a couple of percent on average. Fursin et al. [16] also use the program's intermediate representation along with source code information in the Milepost GCC project [16] . These features are used to construct models that predict good optimization strategies according to metrics desired by the user (e.g., performance or code size). The authors collect summary statistics about the different instructions and from the control flow graph for each function, but again, these features are summarized into a fixed-length feature vector.

Wang et al. [17] also used an intermediate representation called the streaming graph to extract static program features. In this work, they focus on streaming programs, and they constructed a model that automatically predicts the ideal partitioning structure of each streaming program. Their program feature includes two sets of feature, one is the summary characteristics of streaming program, e.g., instruction mix, and other characteristics of critical path extracted from stream IR. Again, these features are summarized in a fixed-length feature vector. They developed a tool that automatically generated small training examples for this predictive model.

In contrast to these previous works, we firstly extract topological information from the program's control flow graph, and then we cite the coarse-grained statistics [7] in the graph-based characterization corresponding to each node in the CFG.

6   Conclusions and Future Work

Speculative multithreading (SpMT) is a thread-level automatic parallelization technique to accelerate sequential programs on multi-core. Too large and too dense samples can't be able to effectively promote the effectiveness of thread partition, parallel thread evaluation, etc. Selection of appropriate samples is of vital importance.

In this paper, the main contributions involve four distinct aspects: (1) Solution of assessing the similarity degree of feature vectors is proposed, based on graphical intermediate program representations. (2) To do so, we need first develop expressive means of characterizing the program being optimized. We use the technique for characterizing programs, using a fixed-length feature vector collected by performance counters when running the program. (3) According to the program features, similarity values are calculated to assess the similar degree.   (4) We also introduce a novel way of assessing the similarity of program samples using Theory of Fuzzy, which calculates the Euclidean distance of two different program samples as the input, and assess the similarity values using corresponding Fuzzy Function. Using the results of similarity degrees, we realize to clean the similar samples.

Although our approach in certain extent handle the issue that similarity degrees amongst samples are calculated to assess the similarity of them. However, just using Euclidean distance to assess the similarity amongst samples is obviously too straightforward, unable to fully express the contribution degree of single sample to the whole group, so easily leading to operations of mistakenly cleaning.

References

1. Cavazos, J., Fursin, G., Agakov, F., Bonilla, E., O'Boyle, M.F., Temam, O.: Rapidly selecting good compiler optimizations using performance counters. In: International Symposium on Code Generation and Optimization, CGO 2007, San Jose, pp. 185–197 (2007)
2. Agakov, F., Bonilla, E., Cavazos, J., Franke, B., Fursin, G., O'Boyle, M.F., Thomson, J., Toussaint, M., Williams, C.K.: Using machine learning to focus iterative optimization. In: Proceedings of the International Symposium on Code Generation and Optimization, pp. 295–305 (2006)
3. Monsifrot, A., Bodin, F., Quiniou, R.: A machine learning approach to automatic production of compiler heuristics. In: Scott, D. (ed.) AIMSA 2002. LNCS (LNAI), vol. 2443, pp. 41–50. Springer, Heidelberg (2002)
4. Stephenson, M., Amarasinghe, S.: Predicting unroll factors using supervised classification. In: International Symposium on Code Generation and Optimization, CGO 2005, pp. 123–134 (2005)
5. Fursin, G.G., Temam, O.: Collective optimization. In: Seznec, A., Emer, J., O'Boyle, M., Martonosi, M., Ungerer, T. (eds.) HiPEAC 2009. LNCS, vol. 5409, pp. 34–49. Springer, Heidelberg (2009)
6. Park, E., Cavazos, J., Pouchet, L., Bastoul, C., Cohen, A., Sadayappan, P.: Predictive modeling in a polyhedral optimization space. International Journal of Parallel Programming 41, 704–750 (2013)

7. Park, E., Cavazos, J., Alvarez, M.A.: Using graph-based program characterization for predictive modeling. In: Proceedings of the Tenth International Symposium on Code Generation and Optimization, pp. 196–206 (2012)
8. Wilson, R.P., French, R., Wilson, C., Amarasinghe, S., Anderson, J., Tjiang, S., Liao, S., Tseng, C., Hall, M., Lam, M.: The SUIF compiler system: A parallelizing and optimizing research compiler: Computer Systems Laboratory. Stanford University (1994)
9. Dong, Z., Zhao, Y., Wei, Y., Wang, X., Song, S.: Prophet: A speculative multi-threading execution model with architectural support based on CMP. In: International Conference on Scalable Computing and Communications; Eighth International Conference on Embedded Computing, SCALCOM-EMBEDDEDCOM 2009, pp. 103–108 (2009)
10. Chen, Z., Zhao, Y.-L., Pan, X.-Y., Dong, Z.-Y., Gao, B., Zhong, Z.-W.: An overview of Prophet. In: Hua, A., Chang, S.-L. (eds.) ICA3PP 2009. LNCS, vol. 5574, pp. 396–407. Springer, Heidelberg (2009)
11. Demme, J., Sethumadhavan, S.: Approximate graph clustering for program characterization. ACM Transactions on Architecture and Code Optimization (TACO) 8, 21 (2012)
12. Carlisle, M.C., Rogers, A.: Software Caching and Computation Migration in Olden. Journal of Parallel and Distributed Computing 38, 248–255 (1996)
13. Liu, B., Zhao, Y., Li, M., Liu, Y., Feng, B.: A Virtual Sample Generation Approach for Speculative Multithreading Using Feature Sets and Abstract Syntax Trees. In: 2012 13th International Conference on Parallel and Distributed Computing, Applications and Technologies (PDCAT), pp. 39–44 (2012)
14. Wang, Z.O., Boyle, M.: Mapping parallelism to multi-cores: a machine learning based approach. In: PPoPP, pp. 75–84. ACM (2009)
15. Leather, H., Bonilla, E., O'Boyle, M.: Automatic feature generation for machine learning based optimizing compilation. In: International Symposium on Code Generation and Optimization, CGO 2009, pp. 81–91 (2009)
16. Fursin, G., Kashnikov, Y., Memon, A.W., Chamski, Z., Temam, O., Namolaru, M., Yom-Tov, E., Mendelson, B., Zaks, A., Courtois, E.: Milepost gcc: Machine learning enabled self-tuning compiler. International Journal of Parallel Programming 39, 296–327 (2011)
17. Wang, Z., O'Boyle, M.F.: Partitioning streaming parallelism for multi-cores: A machine learning based approach. In: Proceedings of the 19th International Conference on Parallel Architectures and Compilation Techniques, pp. 307–318 (2010)

Equi-join for Multiple Datasets
Based on Time Cost Evaluation Model

Hong Zhu, Libo Xia, Mieyi Xie*, and Ke Yan

School of Computer Science and Technology,
Huazhong University of Science and Technology,
Wuhan, Hubei, 430074, P.R. China
{zhuhong,xiemeiyi}@hust.edu.cn

Abstract. MapReduce is an important programming model for processing big data with a parallel, distributed algorithm on a cluster. In big data analytic application, equi-join is an important operation. However, it is inefficient to perform equi-join operations in MapReduce when multiple datasets are involved in the join. In this paper, a time cost evaluation model is extended for an equi-join by considering the time cost of calculation. In addition, the sub-joins in an equi-join are classified into star pattern sub-joins on single attribute and chain pattern sub-joins. Based on the extended model, optimization methods are presented and an equi-join plan with lower time cost is chosen for the equi-join. The optimization methods include: the star pattern sub-joins on one attribute are first processed; next, a chain pattern sub-join with minimal scale of intermediate results (i.e. the number of tuples in intermediate results) is processed; at last, a chain pattern sub-join is decomposed into several MapReduce jobs or single MapReduce job by dynamic programming to obtain an optimal scheme for the chain pattern sub-join. We conducted extensive experiments, and the results show that our method is more efficient than those methods such as MDMJ, Hive and Pig.

Keywords: Join, MapReduce, Dynamic Programming.

1 Introduction

With the development of information technology, massive amount of data are collected in many fields, such as medical, finance, communication, and governments. Nowadays, there are urgent needs for analyzing big data in these applications. However, solutions based on conventional distributed or parallel databases are difficult to meet the needs of big data analysis. MapReduce is an important programming model for processing big data with parallel, distributed algorithms on a cluster [3]. Nowadays, thousands of projects for big data processing have been implemented by this model, including large-scale image processing, machine learning as well as many other areas. In data analytical queries, equi-join is an important operation. However, it is not efficient to perform an equi-join

---

* Corresponding author.

X.-h. Sun et al. (Eds.): ICA3PP 2014, Part II, LNCS 8631, pp. 122–135, 2014.

operation in MapReduce when multiple datasets are involved in the join. Although several approaches performing an equi-join are presented in literatures [1, 5–10], these approaches have advantages for the equi-joins on some special datasets and most of them are not general on any datasets.

The approaches for equi-joins are classified into two groups: Map-side join and Reduce-side join [5]. The Broadcast-Join and its improved approaches Semi-Join and Per-Split Semi-Join are all Map-side joins [2]. However, the performances of these approaches for equi-joins decrease seriously when the scales of datasets involved in equi-joins increase, because the efficiencies of these methods depend on the hardware of the clusters. There are also several approaches for Reduce-side joins on multiple datasets, such as the equi-join method with multiple MapReduce jobs (MRJs) [7, 9], multi-dimensional Reducer matrix based multi-join (MDMJ) [1], and modifying original MapReduce frameworks [8, 10]. These methods have different advantages when specific datasets are joined. Amongst these approaches, an equi-join is processed by a series of MRJs or single MRJ. However, it is difficult to determine whether an equi-join should be processed by single MRJ or by multiple MRJs. If we are able to evaluate the time cost for disk I/O, communication and calculation of an equi-join, we could choose a plan with time cost as low as possible from different schemes of the equi-join. Then the efficiency of the equi-join can be improved. We think this is an issue.

The contributions of this paper are listed in the following.

1. The time cost of calculation for an equi-join is extended based on the time cost model in literature [11]. Therefore, time cost for an equi-join consists of three parts: disk I/O, communication, and calculation.

2. Based on the time cost model, optimization methods are presented and an equi-join plan with lower time cost is chosen. Then the performance of the equi-join is improved. The optimization methods include: the star pattern sub-joins on one attribute are first processed; next, a chain pattern sub-join with minimal scale of intermediate results (the number of tuples in intermediate results) is processed; at last, an optimal plan for the chain pattern sub-join is obtained by dynamic programming.

3. We conduct extensive experiments to verify the efficiency of our method. Experimental results show that the performance of our approach is better than that of other methods such as MDMJ, Hive and Pig.

The rest of this paper is organized as follows. Related work is briefly introduced in Section 2. The extended cost model is illustrated in Section 3. The optimization methods for equi-joins are presented in Section 4. In Section 5, experiments are illustrated and at last in Section 6 we summarize the conclusion.

2   Related Work

2.1   Equi-join on Single Attribute

Equi-join on single attribute is an equi-join based on multiple datasets and one attribute. For example, $R_1(a, b_1) \infty R_2(a, b_2) \infty \cdots \infty R_L(a, b_L)$ is a typical equi-join on one attribute a. During Map phase, the Map() function produces

$\langle key, value \rangle$ pairs based on a value of the equi-join attribute a (as key) and name of a dataset and values of other attributes $[R_i, (a + b_i)]$ (as value). During Reduce stage, the *reduce()* function receives a $\langle key, valuelist \rangle$ each time, then the values in *valuelist* are classified according to the dataset and are joined. Here the *valuelist* is the list of *values* with the same *key* (in $\langle key, value \rangle$ pair). Finally, the results are obtained and collected.

2.2 Equi-join on Multiple Attributes

The equi-join on multiple attributes is a join based on multiple datasets and several attributes. Existing approaches for equi-joins focus on Reduce-side join and we briefly summarize them in the following.

In multiple MRJs approach, the equi-join is processed in a series of MRJs. At first, two datasets are joined and the intermediate results are written into HDFS(Hadoop Distributed File System) as an input dataset of next MRJ. In the next MRJ, the results from the previous MRJ are read from HDFS, and a new dataset is chosen to join. Thus, for an equi-join with n datasets, n-1 MRJs are needed.

In MDMJ method [1], Reduce nodes are divided into a multi-dimensional Reducer matrix. When an equi-join is processed, tuples in a dataset are copied from a Map node to Reduce nodes repeatedly. In Reduce stage, intermediate results are saved in buffer, and then the time cost for disk I/O is reduced. The datasets are joined in the order specified in an original SQL statement. By this way, the equi-join can be implemented in one MRJ and the performance is improved. When the number of attributes, the number of Reduce nodes and the scales of the datasets increase, the time cost for communication would be exponentially increases and the performance of the equi-join decreases seriously.

In the approach for joining datasets with bloom filters [6], a bloom filter is constructed for an input dataset, and the redundant tuples are filtered out in another input dataset involved in the equi-join in Map phase. Thus, the number of tuples involved in the equi-join is reduced and the performance of the equi-join is improved.

In Network-aware multi-way join for MapReduce (NAMM) [8], tuples are redistributed directly between Reduce nodes with an intelligent network aware algorithm so that the workload is redistributed amongst Reduce nodes. By considering network distance and workloads of Reduce nodes, datasets are chosen to join, and then the workload of each Reduce node is alleviated and the performance of an equi-join is improved.

Yang et al proposed a Map-Reduce-Merge join [10]. Merge phase is added to MapReduce so that the partitioned and sorted data could be merged and then the final results can be obtained. The model could express relational algebra operators, and several equi-join algorithms are implemented for the model. However, they did not demonstrate experimental results of their method.

The equi-join algorithms in [6, 8, 10] improve the performance of an equi-join in single MRJ. They only optimize single MRJ to improve performance and the improvement is limit, especially when the scales of datasets increase.

3   The Extended Time Cost Model for Equi-join

3.1   The Time Cost Model for Single MRJ

In Map stage, datasets are read from HDFS, and data blocks with $\langle key, value\rangle$ pairs are produced and stored into local disk. In Reduce phase, the data copied from Map tasks through network are aggregated, sorted and calculated, then the final equi-join results are written on HDFS. Therefore, the total time cost of a MRJ consists of the disk I/O in Map phase, copying data in the network and calculation in Reduce phase.

The Time Cost in Map Phase. In Map phase, assume there are m Map tasks and t_M is the time cost for each Map task, and T_M is the time cost in Map phase. If we define the total scales of input datasets of an equi-join for a MRJ is S_I, the total scales of input datasets in each Map task for read is $\frac{S_I}{m}$. The time cost for a Map task is $t_M = t_{in} + t_{out}$, where t_{in} and t_{out} are the time cost of read and write respectively. For the Reduce-side join mthods, we have $t_{in} = C_1 \times S_I/m$, where C_1 is a constant factor about disk I/O capability for read, $t_{out} = (p + C_2) \times \alpha \times S_I/m$, where α denotes the output ratio of a Map task, which is query specific and can be computed with the selectivity estimation, C_2 is a constant factor about disk I/O capability for write and p is a random variable for partitioning and sorting and compressing the data in buffer. The time cost for a Map Task is:

$$t_M = C_1 \times \frac{S_I}{m} + C_2 \times \frac{\alpha \times S_I}{m} + p \times \frac{\alpha \times S_I}{m} \qquad (1)$$

The time cost for the Map phase is: $T_M = t_M \times \frac{m}{m'}$ [11], where m' is the current number of Map tasks running in parallel in the system.

Time Cost for Copying Data in Network. The time cost for copying data from Map tasks to Reduce tasks is related to scales of data produced by Map tasks. It consists of the cost of data copying in network as well as overhead of serving network protocols. Assume there are n Reduce nodes in the system, and t_{CP} stands for the time cost for copying the output data from single Map task to n Reduce nodes. For a Map task, $t_{CP} = C_3 \times \alpha \times S_I/m \times (1/n) + q \times n$, where C_3 is a constant factor denoting the efficiency of data copying over network, q is a random variable which represents the cost of a Map task serving n connections from n Reduce tasks. After the data copying ends, Reduce tasks begin to process the data received. Suppose that T_{CP} denotes the time of copying output data from Map tasks to n Reduce nodes, then we have $T_{CP} = t_{CP} \times \frac{m}{m'}$. Assume the time when Reduce tasks begin is T_{RS}, T_{RS} is determined by the time when the last Map task ends data copying. If $t_M \geq t_{CP}$, and when the last Map task ends copying output data, then $T_{RS} = T_M + t_{CP}$. If $t_M \leq t_{CP}$, and when the last Map task ends, some Reduce nodes are still copying output data, then $T_{RS} = t_M + T_{CP}$.

The Time Cost in Reduce Phase. Assume S_R^i is the dataset that the ith Reduce node received, the time cost of Reduce phase is composed of the cost of reading, calculation and writing: $T_{R_i} = (p + C_1) \times TS(S_R^i) + FO(S_R^i) \times C_4 + C_2 \times \beta \times TS(S_R^i)$, where $TS(x)$ is a function that returns the scale of a dataset x. $(p + C_1) \times TS(S_R^i)$ is the time cost consists of pre-processing data from Map nodes (including shuffle, merge and sort) and sending the data from disk to *reduce()* function. $C_2 \times \beta \times TS(S_R^i)$ is the time cost of writing final results on HDFS. β denotes the output ratio of a Reduce task. $FO(S_R^i) \times C_4$ is the time cost of calculation for the equi-join in a Reduce node. Obviously, the time cost of calculation should not be ignored because the time cost of calculation depends on the equi-join algorithms and scales of datasets. Comparing with the time cost model in literature [11], we consider the time cost of calculation in our model.

Assume T_R stands for the time cost in Reduce phase. The time cost for Reduce tasks depends on the time which the last Reduce task spends. Therefore, T_R is determined by the end time of the Reduce task with maximal scale S_R^x of data. Then we have:

$$T_R = (C_1 + p) \times TS(S_R^x) + FO(S_R^x) \times C_4 + C_2 \times \beta \times TS(S_R^x) \qquad (2)$$

After all, the time cost model for a MRJ is:

$$T = \begin{cases} T_M + t_{CP} + T_R, & t_M \geq t_{CP} \\ t_M + T_{CP} + T_R, & t_M < t_{CP} \end{cases} \qquad (3)$$

Although the formula (3) is the same as the time cost in [11], T_R is different from the T_R in [11]. When we consider time cost of calculate for a MRJ, we need determine the values for α, β, S_R^x and $FO(S_R^x)$. In the following discussion, we will give these values for an equi-join in single MRJ on single attribute and multiple attributes.

3.2 The Time Cost of an Equi-join for Single MRJ on Single Attribute

Suppose we join datasets $R_1, R_2, \cdots, R_L$. In Map phase, a tuple is read in *map()* function and is changed into a $\langle key, value \rangle$ pair. Therefore, the sum of scales for input datasets $R_1, R_2, \cdots, R_L$ is equal to the total number of tuples in output datasets, then $\alpha = 1$. In Reduce phase, the tuples are classified in *reduce()* function according to the dataset which the tuples come from, and then Cartesian product is calculated. The total cost of computation for a Reduce node x is:

$$FO(S_R^x) = \sum_{i=1}^{L} TS(SR_i^x) + TS(SR_1^x \infty SR_2^x \infty \cdots \infty SR_L^x) \qquad (4)$$

As the number of tuples in output is the number of tuples in results, the output ratio is:

$$\beta = TS(SR_1^x \infty SR_2^x \infty \cdots \infty SR_L^x) / \sum_{i=1}^{L} TS(SR_i^x), \qquad (5)$$

Where SR_i^x stands for the number of tuples in dataset R_i which is received by a Reduce node x. Assume the data distribution in each dataset R_i is uniform, and we can preprocess the dataset such that the number of tuples which each

Reduce task receives is almost equal. Then we have $TS(S_R^x) = \sum_{i=1}^{L} TS(SR_i^x)$ and $TS(SR_i^x) = TS(R_i)/n$, where n is the number of Reduce nodes.

3.3   The Time Cost of an Equi-join for Single MRJ on Multiple Attributes

In this section, we evaluate the time cost of an equi-join for MDMJ. Before a MRJ is executed, Reduce nodes are divided into a multi-dimensional Reducer matrix according to the scales of datasets involved in the equi-join. Because a tuple in a dataset will be useful for the result of multiple tuples, and these tuples are distributed on different nodes. Therefore, the input tuples would be copied several times in $map()$ function, and a partition function would calculate which reduce nodes the tuple should be copied to for each attribute involved in the equi-join. The total scale of input datasets for the equi-join S_I is the sum of scales for all datasets, and the scale of output in Map phase is related to the number of times copying tuples, if we define cpT_i as the times of copying datasets R_i, then we have:

$$\alpha \times S_I = \sum_{i=1}^{N}(TS(R_i) \times cpT_i) \tag{6}$$

The cpT_i can be calculated by Lagrange formula.

In Reduce phase, after copying data from different Map Tasks, the tuples stored on local disk are partitioned by keys, and are sorted according to the first joining attribute specified in the equi-join. In $reduce()$ function, the tuples from the first dataset are read into the buffer, and when the tuples from the second dataset come, we just check whether there are suitable tuples (which have the same joining keys with the tuples from the second dataset) in the buffer. If there are suitable tuples, we join the tuples in the buffer and from the second dataset, and the intermediate results are stored into another buffer and sorted according to the attribute which would join with the next dataset. Then we check the intermediate results and continue the join following above steps. Because the tuples in buffer are sorted in advance, when we check whether there are suitable tuples in the buffer, we only traverse the data once. Therefore, the tuples received from different datasets are joined in the order specified in the equi-join.

Suppose we have a typical equi-join $R_1(a_1)\infty R_2(a_1, a_2)\infty \cdots \infty R_L(a_{L-1})$. For each Reduce node x, tuples from dataset $R_i(1 \leq i \leq L)$ are sorted. According to the description above, we first finish the equi-join $R_1 \infty R_2$, then we sort their results according to next joining attribute a_2, and so on. The time cost of computation for this procedure is:

$$FO(S_R^x) = \sum_{i=2}^{L}(TS(MidR_{1i-1}^x + TS(SR_i^x) + TS(MidR_{1i}^x)) + \sum_{i=2}^{L-1} TS(MidR_{1i}^x) \times log(TS(MidR_{1i}^x)) \tag{7}$$

Where SR_i^x stands for the data in R_i received by Reduce node x. $MidR_{1i}^x$ denotes intermediate results of joining from SR_1^x to SR_i^x. At last, the amount of data written into HDFS is equal to the scale of results, namely the output ratio is the same as formula (5).

After analysis the time cost of an equi-join, we have following Theorem 1.

Theorem 1. The time cost of an equi-join for single MRJ is a monotone increasing function of the total scales of input datasets S_I.

Proof. From the formula (1) and (3), we first prove that the total time cost of Map phase and copying data in network phase is the monotone increasing function of S_I: for $T_M + t_{CP}$, we have:

$$T_M + t_{CP} = (C_1 \times \frac{S_I}{m} + C_2 \times \frac{\alpha \times S_I}{m} + p \times \frac{\alpha \times S_I}{m}) \times \frac{m}{m'} + C_3 \times \frac{\alpha \times S_I}{m} \times \frac{1}{n} + q \times n;$$

for $t_M + T_{CP}$, we have:

$$t_M + T_{CP} = C_1 \times \frac{S_I}{m} + C_2 \times \frac{\alpha \times S_I}{m} + p \times \frac{\alpha \times S_I}{m} + (C_3 \times \frac{\alpha \times S_I}{m} \times \frac{1}{n} + q \times n) \times \frac{m}{m'};$$

Therefore, the total time cost for Map phase and copying data in network phase is linear dependent to S_I and is the monotone increasing function of S_I.

For the time cost in Reduce phase, from formula (2), where $\beta \times TS(S_R^i)$ is related to the scale of the final results.

Next, we only prove $FO(S_i^x)$ is also a monotone increasing function of S_I.

For single attribute, by replacing the formula (4) in above formula, we can prove that time cost of an equi-join in single MRJ is a monotone increasing function of the total scales of input datasets S_I.

For multiple attributes, according to results estimation method for an equi-join in [4] and formula (7), we have:

$$MidR_{1i}^x = \frac{MidR_{1i-1}^x \times R_i^x}{max(min(MidR_{1i-1}^x, difR_{i-1}^x), difR_i^x)}$$

where $difR_{i-1}^x$ is the number of different attribute values in R_{i-1}^x involved in an equi-join.

Suppose $MidR_{1i-1}^x \geq difR_{i-1}^x$, then we have:

$$MidR_{1i}^x = \frac{MidR_{1i-1}^x \times R_i^x}{max(difR_{i-1}^x, difR_i^x)} \geq \frac{MidR_{1i-1}^x \times R_i^x}{max(MidR_{1i-1}^x, R_i^x)} \geq min(MidR_{1i-1}^x, R_i^x)$$

Otherwise, if $MidR_{1i-1}^x \leq difR_{i-1}$, because the number of different attribute values is less than the number of attribute values in a dataset, then $difR_{i-1}^x = MidR_{1i-1}^x$.

$$MidR_{1i}^x = \frac{MidR_{1i-1}^x \times R_i^x}{max(MidR_{1i-1}^x, difR_i^x)} \geq \frac{MidR_{1i-1}^x \times R_i^x}{max(MidR_{1i-1}^x, R_i^x)} \geq min(MidR_{1i-1}^x, R_i^x)),$$

Therefore, we have: $MidR_{1i}^x \geq min(MidR_{1i-1}^x, R_i^x), \cdots$, as $MidR_{12}^x \geq min(MidR_{11}^x, R_2^x) = min(R_1^x, R_2^x)$, $MidR_{1i}^x \geq min(R_1^x, R_2^x, \cdots, R_i^x)$. Then the formula (7) is changed into:

$$FO(S_R^x) \geq \frac{\alpha \times S_I}{n} + 2 \times L \times min(R_1^x, R_2^x, \cdots R_i^x) + L \times min(R_1^x, R_2^x, \cdots R_i^x) \times log(min(R_1^x, R_2^x, \cdots R_i^x))$$

Therefore, the time cost in the Reduce phase is the monotone increasing function of the scale of input datasets S_I.

4   The Optimization Methods for an Equi-join

For an equi-join, the problem is in what order the datasets be joined such that the total time cost is as low as possible. When we choose an optimal equi-join plan with lowest time cost, a naive method is enumerating and evaluating the time costs of all possible equi-join schemes, and the method is a NP-hard problem [11]. There are two types of sub-joins in an equi-join: star pattern sub-joins and chain pattern sub-joins. In a star pattern sub-join, a dataset (star-center) is joined with all of other datasets (the star-angle) on single attribute. In a chain pattern sub-join, a typical sub-join is described as $R_1(a_1) \infty R_2(a_1, a_2) \infty \cdots \infty R_L(a_{L-1})$. For a chain pattern sub-join $R_i(a_{i-1}, a_i) \infty R_{i+1}(a_i, a_{i+1}) \infty \cdots \infty R_j(a_{j-1}, a_j)(1 < i \leq j < L)$, we call it a sub-chain of $R_1(a_1) \infty R_2(a_1, a_2) \infty \cdots \infty R_L(a_{L-1})$. If a chain pattern sub-join is not a sub-chain of any other chain pattern sub-join of the equi-join, the chain pattern sub-join is called a complete chain pattern sub-join.

Our optimization methods for an equi-join have following three steps:

1. A star pattern sub-join should be first processed and replaced by the set of intermediate results of the star pattern sub-join in an original equi-join.

2. A complete chain pattern sub-join could be searched, and then the chain pattern sub-join with minimal number of tuples in results would be processed. The complete chain is also replaced by the set of intermediate results.

3. The time cost of a complete chain pattern sub-join obtained in step 2 is evaluated by dynamic programming, and then an optimal equi-join scheme is chosen. The set of intermediate results are added to the equi-join after step 1, and then the equi-join is further modified. The step 2 is repeated. From the associative law for the join operation, the final results of the equi-join are correct.

4.1 Optimization Methods for Star Pattern Sub-joins and Chain Pattern Sub-joins

A star pattern sub-join should be processed in single MRJ. We have following *Property 1*.

Property 1. Assume there is a star pattern equi-join J_a. Suppose J_a is processed with several MRJs and the time cost is T_{MJ}, and J_a is also implemented with a MRJ and the time cost is T_S. Then we have $T_S \leq T_{MJ}$.

Property 1 is obvious according to Theorem 1. From *Property 1* above, a star pattern sub-join should not be divided into several MRJs.

After processing all star pattern sub-joins, the equi-join consists of several chain pattern sub-joins. Then we have *property 2*.

Property 2. Suppose two chain pattern sub-joins cross in an equi-join. If the chain pattern sub-join, which would produce less number of tuples in results, is first joined, and then the total time cost for the equi-join would be decreased.

We will use these two properties to simplify the equi-join and reduce the time cost. Due to space limitation, we will not give their proofs. Actually, they will be verified in our experiments.

4.2 The Optimization Method by Dynamic Programming

We will use the time cost evaluation model in Section 3 and dynamic programming to choose an optimal plan for chain pattern sub-joins. In dynamic programming, all of the time costs for possible join schemes are evaluated for a chain pattern sub-join and a join scheme with minimal time cost is chosen.

Assume a chain pattern equi-join $R_1(a_1)\infty R_2(a_1, a_2)\infty \cdots \infty R_L(a_{L-1})$, and $fcost(i, j)$ stands for the minimal time cost of joining from dataset R_i to dataset R_j. If a chain pattern equi-join from R_i to R_j is decomposed into two sub-chains, namely the final results would be obtained by joining the intermediate results of R_i to R_k and the intermediate results of R_{k+1} to R_j, then the minimal time cost is $fcost(i, j) = min(fcost(i, k) + fcost(k+1, j) + fjoincost(midR(i, k), midR(k+1, j)))$, $i \leq k \leq j - 1$, where $fjoincost(x, y)$ stands for the time cost of joining datasets x with y, $midR(i, j)$ denotes intermediate results by joining dataset R_i to dataset R_j. For example, if a chain pattern equi-join is divided into three sub-joins, then the formula is: $fcost(i, j) = min(fcost(i, k_1) + fcost(k_1 + 1, k_2) + fjoincost(midR(i, k_1), midR(k_1 + 1, k_2), midR(k_2 + 1, j)))$, $i \leq k1 < k2 \leq j - 1$. The same methods could be used for the equi-join with four sub-chains, five sub-chains, and so on. In addition, it is possible that the time cost for MDMJ is minimal in some cases. Therefore, we could choose one scheme from all of the possible schemes:

$$fcost(1, L) = min(\begin{cases} fcost(1, k) + fcost(k + 1, L) + fjoincost(midR(i, k), midR(k + 1, L)); \\ when 1 \leq k \leq L - 1 \\ fcost(1, k_1) + fcost(k_1 + 1, k_2) + fcost(k_2 + 1, L) + \\ fjoincost(midR(1, k_1), midR(k_1 + 1, k_2), midR(k_2 + 1, L)); \\ when 1 \leq k_1 \leq k_2 \leq L - 1 \\ \cdots \\ fjoincost(R_1, R_2, \cdots, R_i, \cdots, R_L); otherwise \end{cases}$$

We can obtain the optimal join scheme with lowest time cost by dynamic programming. The time cost (e.g. $fjoincost$) of joining datasets in single MRJ can be calculated by formula (3). If two datasets join on single attribute, the time cost can be computed by the method in Section 3.2. If several datasets join, the cost can be calculated by the method in Section 3.3. Actually, the number of datasets and attributes involved in an equi-join is determined by configuration of hardware and the number of Reduce nodes. We can specify the maximum number of datasets in single MRJ to improve the efficiency of search in above formula.

5   Experiments

5.1   The Environment in Experiments

In this section, we will verify the efficiency of our approach and compare with other equi-join algorithms. As NAMN and MapReduceMerge algorithms modified MapReduce framework, they are not comparable to our method. Then we will compare the MDMJ and multiple MRJs algorithms with our method. In addition, Pig and Hive are two databases based on Hadoop and need to compare with our method. The experiments are based on Hadoop platform, the hardware in experiments consists of 1 Master node and 3 slave nodes, all of the nodes are

Table 1. Hardware and software lists in experiments

Hardware	Software
CPU:Intel Xeon(R) 2.13GHz*4 Memory: 8G Disk:300GB	Operating System: Ubuntu-12.04 LTS Type of OS: 64bit Hadoop: Hadoop-1.0.1

Table 2. SQL statements in experiments

NO.	SQL statements
Q1	SELECT * FROM T1, T2, T3, T4, T5 WHERE T1.T1_COL1=T5.T5_COL1 AND T2.T2_COL1=T5.T5_COL2 AND T3.T3_COL1=T5.T5_COL3 AND T4.T4_COL1=T5.T5_COL3
Q2	SELECT * FROM T1, T2, T3, T4, T5 WHERE T1.T1_COL1=T5.T5_COL1 AND T2.T2_COL1=T5.T5_COL2 AND T3.T3_COL1=T5.T5_COL3 AND T4.T4_COL1=T5.T5_COL4
Q3	SELECT * FROM T1, T2, T3, T4, T5 WHERE T4.T4_COL1=T5.T5_COL4 AND T3.T3_COL1=T5.T5_COL3 AND T2.T2_COL1=T5.T5_COL2 AND T1.T1_COL1=T5.T5_COL1
Q4	SELECT * FROM T1, T2, T3, T4, T5 WHERE T1.T1_COL1=T2.T2_COL1 AND T2.T2_COL2 =T3.T3_COL1 AND T3.T3_COL2=T4.T4_COL1 AND T4.T4_COL2=T5.T5_COL1
Q5	SELECT * FROM T1, T2, T3, T4, T5 WHERE T4.T4_COL2=T5.T5_COL1 AND T3.T3_COL2=T4.T4_COL1 AND T2.T2_COL2 =T3.T3_COL1 AND T1.T1_COL1=T2.T2_COL1

blade servers. The hardware and software environment in experiments are listed in Table 1.

The experiments consist of three types of equi-joins: hybrid join with star pattern sub-joins, hybrid join without star pattern sub-joins, and chain pattern equi-joins. The datasets are produced randomly by specifying the scope of the data and the different number of tuples for different join attributes. In the following discussion, our method is denoted as JoinStrategy and multiple MRJs as MutipleJob.

5.2 The Experiments for a Hybrid Equi-join with Star Pattern Sub-joins

In the experiments (EXP1 for short), we will have two tests for the SQL statements Q1 in Table 2. For the equi-join, the number of tuples in each dataset is shown in Table 3 and Table 4 respectively. Compared with Table 3, the scales of datasets in star-center (dataset T5) in Table 4 are changed. The results of experiments are shown in Fig.1 and Fig.2 in which the scales (1-5) in x-axis are shown in Table 3 and Table 4 (from No.1 to No.5) respectively. From the experiments, the joinStrategy is more efficient than that of other methods.

Comparing Fig.1 with Fig.2, whether the scales of datasets in star-center or in star-angle are changed, JoinStrategy is the most efficient approach among these methods. The reason is that in one MRJ only star pattern sub-joins are

Table 3. In experiment EXP1.a, the number of tuples in datasets and the final results

No.	T1($\times 10^6$)	T2($\times 10^6$)	T3($\times 10^6$)	T4($\times 10^6$)	T5($\times 10^6$)	Results
1	6	6	2	2	2	2444916
2	6	6	2	4	2	2453824
3	6	6	2	6	2	2448719
4	6	6	2	8	2	2457335
5	6	6	2	10	2	2467211

Table 4. In experiment EXP1.b, the number of datasets in join and the final results

No.	T1 ($\times 10^6$)	T2($\times 10^6$)	T3($\times 10^6$)	T4($\times 10^6$)	T5($\times 10^6$)	Results
1	2	2	2	2	2	2453578
2	2	2	2	2	4	4910520
3	2	2	2	2	6	7378282
4	2	2	2	2	8	9822087
5	2	2	2	2	10	12290426

processed so that large amount of redundant disk I/O is avoided. However, the methods for MutipleJob, Hive and Pig decompose star pattern sub-joins into several MRJs, the time costs of them are more than that of JoinStrategy. In Fig.2 the time cost for MDMJ is almost the same as JoinStrategy when the scales of datasets are small, but when the scales of datasets increase, the time cost for MDMJ is more than that of JoinStrategy. The reason is that when the scales of datasets are small the JoinStrategy process the star pattern sub-joins first, then the JoinStrategy chooses MDMJ to process rest of datasets.

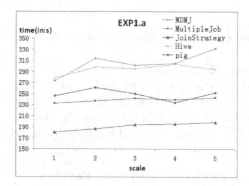
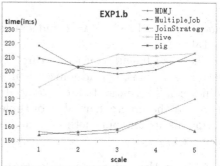

Fig. 1. Time cost for datasets in Table 2   **Fig. 2.** Time cost for datasets in Table 3

From the experimental results above, the JoinStrategy are more efficient than that of other methods as the star pattern sub-join is processed first. The results indicate that the *Property1* in Section 4.1 is correct and effective.

5.3   Experiments for Hybrid Equi-joins without Star Pattern Sub-joins

For the experiments in this section (EXP2 for short), we will test the efficiencies of queries Q2 and Q3 in Table 2. The difference of the two SQL statements is that the orders of datasets in the two equi-joins are different, and the order of joining datasets in our approach would be rearranged according to the optimization method: the chain pattern sub-joins with smaller intermediate results are processed after star pattern sub-joins are processed.

The experimental results are illustrated in Fig.3 and Fig.4, and the scales of datasets and results for the equi-joins are illustrated in Table 5.

Table 5. In experiment EXP2, the number of tuples in datasets and final results

No.	T1 ($\times 10^6$)	T2($\times 10^6$)	T3($\times 10^6$)	T4($\times 10^6$)	T5($\times 10^6$)	Results
1	2	2	2	2	6	89915
2	2	2	2	6	6	271685
3	2	2	2	10	6	271142
4	2	2	6	10	6	825062
5	2	2	10	10	6	820939
6	2	6	10	10	6	2458097
7	2	10	10	10	6	2453931
8	6	10	10	10	6	7386461

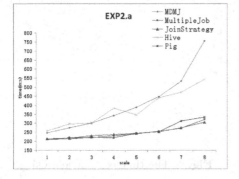 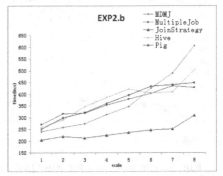

Fig. 3. The time cost for the join Q2   **Fig. 4.** The time cost for the join Q3

Comparing the experimental results in Fig.3 and Fig.4, when we changed the order of datasets in an equi-join, the efficiency of MDMJ and JoinStrategy is unchanged but the performances of other methods decrease obviously. The reason is that MDMJ and JoinStrategy optimize the order of joining datasets while other methods only join datasets in the order specified in SQL statements. Once the order of joining datasets is unreasonable, the performance would decrease obviously. From the experimental results in Fig.4, the performance of an equi-join is improved when the chain pattern sub-joins with smaller intermediate results are processed first. The results indicates that *Property2* in Section 4.1 is suitable.

5.4 Experiments for Chain Pattern Joins

We will verify that the plan produced by dynamic programming would improve the efficiency of an equi-join in the experimental (EXP3 for short). Like the experiments for hybrid equi-join without star pattern sub-joins, this experiment will test the joins with different order, the SQL statements Q4 and Q5 are illustrated in Table 2.

Table 6. In experiment EXP3, the number of tuples in datasets and final results

No.	T1($\times 10^6$)	T2($\times 10^6$)	T3($\times 10^6$)	T4($\times 10^6$)	T5($\times 10^6$)	Results
1	2	2	2	2	2	2459063
2	2	2	2	2	6	2447277
3	2	2	2	2	10	2455207
4	2	2	2	6	10	2458453
5	2	2	2	10	10	2458784
6	2	2	6	10	10	2453944
7	2	2	10	10	10	2455965
8	2	6	10	10	10	2462062
9	2	10	10	10	10	2461461

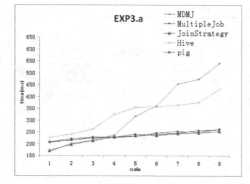

Fig. 5. The time cost for join Q4

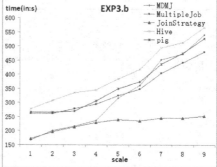

Fig. 6. The time cost for join Q5

The experiment results are illustrated in Fig.5 and Fig.6. The experimental results are similar to the results in Section 5.3. From the results in Fig.5, the efficiency of the JoinStrategy is almost the same as Pig and Multiplejob, the reason is that the order of datasets in SQL statement in Fig.5 is close to the order of joining datasets by our optimization methods. However, in Fig.6, the order of joining datasets is unreasonable in Multiplejob and Pig, and the efficiencies of Pig and Multiplejob decrease. Moreover, as the data scales are small before the datasets of No.4 in Table 6, in Fig.5 and Fig.6, MDMJ is more efficient than that of MultipleJob, so we choose MDMJ for multiple datasets in single MRJ by dynamic programming. Therefore, before the datasets No.4 in Table 6, JoinStrategy is more close to MDMJ. When the scales of datasets increase and the cost for copying data in network increases in MDMJ, performance of MDMJ decreases. At this time, the plan for the equi-join tends to choose multiple MRJs. Therefore, from the datasets No.5 in Table 6, the optimal plan obtained from dynamic programming is the multiple MRJs. From the results, the performance of our method is more efficient.

6   Conclusion

An new equi-join method is presented in this paper. A time cost evaluation model is extended for equi-joins on multiple datasets and multiple attributes by considering the time cost of calculation. Then optimization methods is presented: star pattern sub-joins are first processed, then the intermediate result-set replaces the star pattern sub-joins and the original equi-join can be simplified; next, the scale of results for each chain pattern sub-join is estimated and the chain pattern sub-joins with minimal scale of results are processed; at last, for chain pattern sub-joins time costs are evaluated for each MRJ by dynamic programming and an optimal plan is chosen. We conducted extensive experiments and verified the efficiency of our approach. In the future, we will study on how to solve the problem of theta-join based on this model.

References

1. Afrati, F.N., Ullman, J.D.: Optimizing joins in a map-reduce environment. In: Proceedings of the 13th International Conference on Extending Database Technology, pp. 99–110. ACM (2010)
2. Blanas, S., Patel, J.M., Ercegovac, V., Rao, J., Shekita, E.J., Tian, Y.: A comparison of join algorithms for log processing in mapreduce. In: Proceedings of the 2010 ACM SIGMOD International Conference on Management of Data, pp. 975–986. ACM (2010)
3. Dean, J., Ghemawat, S.: Mapreduce: simplified data processing on large clusters. Communications of the ACM 51(1), 107–113 (2008)
4. Garcia-Molina, H., Ullman, J.D., Widom, J.: Database system implementation, vol. 654. Prentice Hall, Upper Saddle River (2000)
5. Lee, K.H., Lee, Y.J., Choi, H., Chung, Y.D., Moon, B.: Parallel data processing with mapreduce: A survey. AcM sIGMoD Record 40(4), 11–20 (2012)
6. Lee, T., Kim, K., Kim, H.J.: Exploiting bloom filters for efficient joins in mapreduce. Information an International Interdisciplinary Journal 16(8), 5869–5885 (2013)
7. Olston, C., Reed, B., Srivastava, U., Kumar, R., Tomkins, A.: Pig latin: A not-so-foreign language for data processing. In: Proceedings of the 2008 ACM SIGMOD International Conference on Management of Data, pp. 1099–1110. ACM (2008)
8. Slagter, K., Hsu, C.-H., Chung, Y.-C., Park, J.H.: Network-aware multiway join for mapreduce. In: Park, J.J(J.H.), Arabnia, H.R., Kim, C., Shi, W., Gil, J.-M. (eds.) GPC 2013. LNCS, vol. 7861, pp. 73–80. Springer, Heidelberg (2013)
9. Thusoo, A., Sarma, J.S., Jain, N., Shao, Z., Chakka, P., Anthony, S., Liu, H., Wyckoff, P., Murthy, R.: Hive: A warehousing solution over a map-reduce framework. Proceedings of the VLDB Endowment 2(2), 1626–1629 (2009)
10. Yang, H.C., Dasdan, A., Hsiao, R.L., Parker, D.S.: Map-reduce-merge: Simplified relational data processing on large clusters. In: Proceedings of the 2007 ACM SIGMOD International Conference on Management of Data, pp. 1029–1040. ACM (2007)
11. Zhang, X., Chen, L., Wang, M.: Efficient multi-way theta-join processing using mapreduce. Proceedings of the VLDB Endowment 5(11), 1184–1195 (2012)

Identifying File Similarity in Large Data Sets by Modulo File Length

Yongtao Zhou, Yuhui Deng*, Xiaoguang Chen, and Junjie Xie

Department of Computer Science, Jinan University, Guangzhou, 510632, P.R. China
y.t.zhou@foxmail.com, tyhdeng@jnu.edu.cn, {iczabg,xiejunjiejnu}@gmail.com

Abstract. Identifying file similarity is very important for data management. Sampling files is a simple and effective approach to identify the file similarity. However, the traditional sampling algorithm(*TSA*) is very sensitive to file modification. For example, a single bit shift would result in a failure of similarity detection. Many research efforts have been invested in solving/alleviating this problem. This paper proposes a Position-Aware Sampling(*PAS*) algorithm to identify file similarity in large data sets by modulo file length. This method is very effective in dealing with file modification when performing similarity detection. Comprehensive experimental results demonstrate that PAS significantly outperforms a well-known similarity detection algorithm called simhash in terms of precision and recall. Furthermore, the time overhead, CPU and memory occupation of PAS are much less than that of simhash.

Keywords: file similarity, large data sets, position shifted, simhash.

1 Introduction

In 2013, IDC predicts[13]that the digital data created in 2014 will reach 4ZBytes. This leads to a 50% growth in contrast to the data volume in 2012. IBM employs volume, variety, velocity, value, and veracity to summarize the features of those data. This indicates that the characteristics of this data are very complex. For example, the data sets could contain structured, semi-structured, and unstructured data. The characteristics of data sets pose many challenges to the existing data management technologies. File similarity detection plays a very important role in the data management. For example, clustering similar data is crucial for data mining, adopting similarity to improve the performance of data backup[3][17][29], employing similarity to enhance the cache hierarchy in clouds[4][14].

Although the community has made important strides in identifying data similarity, effectively detecting the data similarity is still facing many challenges. We summarize the challenges as follows:

1. **Reducing the computing overhead of similarity detection:** Traditional similarity identification algorithms belong to I/O bound and CPU-bound tasks. Calculating the eigenvalues of similar files requires lots of CPU

---

* Corresponding author.

X.-h. Sun et al. (Eds.): ICA3PP 2014, Part II, LNCS 8631, pp. 136–149, 2014.
© Springer International Publishing Switzerland 2014

cycles and memory space, and incurs comprehensive disk accesses, when us
ing the traditional algorithms. Furthermore, the disk accesses are normally
random accesses, which results in a significantly performance degradation.
What's more, the computing overhead normally increases with the growth
of data sets.

2. **Reducing the time of similarity detection:** Traditional similarity identify algorithms normally require a large amount of time for detecting, which
   results in long delays especially with large data sets. This makes it difficult
   to apply the algorithms to some applications requiring real time and high
   throughput.

3. **Achieving both the efficiency and accuracy:** It is a challenge to achieve
   both the efficiency and accuracy of the similarity detection. The traditional
   algorithms have to make a tradeoff between the efficiency and accuracy.

In this paper, we propose a Position-Aware Similarity (PAS) identification
algorithm to detect the similar files in large data sets by modulo file length.
This method is very effective in dealing with file modification when performing similarity detection. Comprehensive experimental results demonstrate that
PAS significantly outperforms a well-known similarity detection algorithm called
simhash in terms of precision and recall. Furthermore, the time overhead, CPU
and memory occupation of PAS are much less than that of simhash. This is because the overhead of PAS is relatively stable. It is not increases with the growth
of data size.

The remainder of this paper is organized as follows: we present related work
in section 2. In section 3 we describe some background knowledge. Section 4
introduces the basic idea of PAS algorithm. Section 5 shows the evaluation results
of PAS algorithm. Section 6 draws conclusions.

2   Related Work

The research efforts focusing on data similarity detection can be divided into
five categories.

The first one is similar web page detection with web search engine. Detecting
and removing similar web pages can save network bandwidth, reduce storage
consumption, and improve the quality of web search engine index. Andrei et al
[7][8] proposed a similar web page detection technique called shingle algorithm.
The shingle algorithm detects similarity by using set operations. This algorithm
is applied to AltaVista web search engine.

The second one is similar file detection in storage system. In storage systems,
data similarity detection and encoding can greatly improve the resource utilization. Forman[12] presented an approach for finding similar files and applied to
document repositories. This approach greatly reduces storage space consumption. Manber[18] implemented a tool, called SIF, for detecting similar files in a
file system. Ouyang[22] presented a large-scale file compression technique based
on cluster by using shingle similarity detection technique.

The third one is plagiarism detection. Digital information can be easily copied and retransmitted. This feature causes owner copyright violated. In order to protect copyright and other related rights, we need plagiarism detection. Baker[2] ddescribed a program called dup which can be used to locate instances of duplication or near duplication in a software. Shivakumar[27] presented a data structures for finding overlap detection between documents and implemented these data structures in SCAM. Brin et al[6] described an algorithms for copy detection, either complete copies or partial copies. Brin also implemented a working prototype, called COPS.

The forth one is remote file backup. Traditional remote file backup approaches take high bandwidth and consume a lot of resources. Similarity detection applied to remote file backup can greatly reduce bandwidth consumption. Teodosiu et al[28] proposed an algorithm to efficiently find the client files that are the most similar to a given server file. Teodosiu implemented this algorithm in DFSR. Experimental results suggest that these optimizations may help reduce the bandwidth required to transfer file updates across a network. Muthitacharoen et al[21] presented LBFS which exploits similarity between files or versions of the same file to save bandwidth. Cox et al[11] presented a similarity-based mechanism for locating a single source file to perform peer-to-peer backup and implemented a system called Pastiche.

The fifth one is similarity detection for specific domain. Hua et al[14] explored and exploited data similarity which supports efficient data placement for cloud. They designed a novel multi-core-enabled and locality-sensitive hashing that can accurately capture the differentiated similarity across data. Biswas et al[4] proposed a novel cache architecture called *Mergeable*. *Mergeable* detects data similarities and merges cache blocks. This results in substantial savings in cache storage requirements. Experimental results suggested that *Mergeable* reduces off-chip memory accesses and overall power usage. *Mergeable* also can increase the performance of applications.

3   Background

3.1   Simhash Algorithm

Charikar proposed a Simhash[10] algorthim. Manku et al[19] applied the simhash algorithm to identify similarity in web documents belonging to a multi-billion page repository. Simhash is a member of the local sensitive hash[15]. It is different from traditional hash functions whose signature values are discrete and uniform distributed. When using the traditional hash functions, if two files differ just a bit, their hash signature values are almost different. Simhash has the property that the fingerprints of similar files differ in a small number of bit positions. It can map a file into f-bit fingerprints. Figure 1 shows the computing process of m-bit simhash fingerprints. It can be described as follows:

1. Employ chunk algorithm to split files into a set of data blocks: $C_1, C_2, \ldots, C_n$
2. Define an m-dimension vector V, every dimension is initialized as zero.

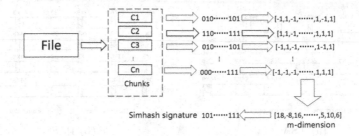

Fig. 1. Process of Calculating simhahs fingerprint

3. Calculate m-bit signature of every data block by using traditional hash functions. If the i-th bit of a signature is positive, then the i-th dimension V should plus 1. Otherwise, it minus 1.
4. Generate a m-bit simhash fingerprint f according to each dimension of vector V. If the i-th dimension of V is a positive number, then the i-th bit of f is 1. Otherwise, it will be 0.

After calculating the simhash fingerprints of files, we can determine the similarity of files by working out their Hamming distance.

4 Position-Aware Similarity Algorithm

In order to quickly identify similarity in large data sets with less overhead, we propose a similarity detection algorithm PAS. The symbols used in the following sections are summarized in Table 1.

4.1 Traditional Sampling Algorithm

Suppose we sample N data blocks of file A, each data block sizing Lenc is injected to a hash function. We then can obtain N fingerprint values that are collected as a fingerprint set $Sig_A(N, Lenc)$. In this scenario, similarity detection problem can be transformed into a set intersection problem. By analogy, we will have a fingerprint set $Sig_B(N, Lenc)$ of file B. According to equation (1),

Table 1. Symbols and the corresponding means used in the following sections

Symbol	Meaning
Lenc	The length of sampling data blocks length
N	The number of sampling data blocks
FileSize	File size
LenR	The distance between two sampling data blocks
T	Sampling position impact factor of PAS
δ	The threshold of PAS

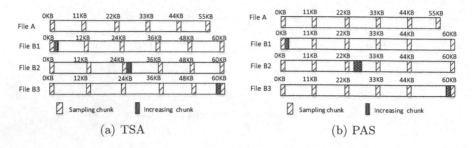

(a) TSA   (b) PAS

Fig. 2. The Sampling positions of TSA and PAS

the degree of similarity between file A and file B can be described as equation (1), where $Sim(A, B)$ ranges s between 0 and 1. If $Sim(A, B)$ is reaching 1, it means the similarity of file A and file B are very high, vice verse. After selecting a threshold δ of the similarity, we can determine that file A is similar to file B when $Sim(A, B) \geq \delta$ is satisfied. This TSA is described in algorithm 1. by using pseudo-code.

$$Sim(A, B) = \frac{|Sig_A(N, Lenc) \cap Sig_B(N, Lenc)|}{|Sig_A(N, Lenc) \cup Sig_B(N, Lenc)|} \tag{1}$$

TSA is simple, but it is very sensitive to file modifications. A small modification would cause the sampling positions shifted, thus resulting a failure. Suppose we have a file A sizing 56KB. We sample 6 data blocks and each data block sizes 1KB. According to Algorithm 1, file A has $N = 6, Lenc = 1KB, FileSize = 56KB, LenR = 10KB$. If we add 5KB data to file A to form file B, file B will have $N = 6, Lenc = 1KB, FileSize = 61KB, LenR = 11KB$ in terms of algorithm 1..

Algorithm 1. Traditional Sampling Algorithm

---

function TRADITIONALSAMPLING(fd, N, $Lenc$)

   $LenR = (FileSize - Lenc*N)/(N - 1)$//Calculate distance between the sampling data blocks

   for $i = 1$ to N **do**

      $offset = (i - 1)*(Lenc + LenR)$//Calculate the sampling offset

      lseek(fd, $offset$, $SEEK_SET$) //Set the sampling offset

      read(fd, buf, $Lenc$)

      Md5(buf, $Lenc$, $Md5Val$)

      put($Md5Val$, $SigA$)   //Put the fingerprint to the $Sig_A(N, Lenc)$

   end for

end function

Adding 5KB data to file A has three situations including the begging, the middle, and the end of the file A. File B1, B2, and B3 in figure 2(a) represent

Algorithm 2. PAS Sampling Algorithm

function PASSAMPLING(fd, N, $Lenc$, T)
    $FileSize = (FileSize/T)T$
    $LenR = (FileSize - Lenc*N)/(N - 1)$
    $LenR = LenR > 0$? $LenR$: 0
    for $i = 1$ to $N - 1$ **do**
        $offset = (i - 1)*(Lenc + LenR)$
        lseek(fd, $offset$, $SEEK_SET$)
        read(fd, buf, $Lenc$)
        Md5(buf, $Lenc$, $Md5Val$)
        put($Md5Val$, $SigA$)
    end for
    lseek(fd, $-Lenc$, $SEEK_END$)
    read(fd, buf, $lenc$)
    Md5(buf, $Lenc$, $Md5Val$)
    put($Md5Val$, $SigA$)
end function

these three different situations. We can find that the above file modifications cause the sampling position shifted and result in an inaccuracy of similarity detection. For example, the six sampling positions of file A are $0KB$, $11KB$, $22KB$, $33KB$, $44KB$, and $55KB$ $((1 - 1) * (1 + 10) = 0KB, (2 - 1) * (1 + 10) = 11KB, (3 - 1) * (1 + 10) = 22KB, (4 - 1) * (1 + 10) = 33KB, (5 - 1) * (1 + 10) = 44KB, (6 - 1) * (1 + 10) = 55KB)$, respectively. However, due to the added $5KB$ data, the six sampling positions of file B1,B2, and B3 are shifted to $0KB, 12KB, 24KB, 36KB, 48KB$, and $60KB((1 - 1) * (1 + 11) = 0KB, (2 - 1) * (1 + 11) = 12KB, (3 - 1) * (1 + 11) = 24KB, (4 - 1) * (1 + 11) = 36KB, (5 - 1) * (1 + 11) = 48KB, (6 - 1) * (1 + 11) = 60KB)$, respectively. Although the $Sim(A, B)$ is far from actual value when using TSA, the sampling method is very simple and takes much less overhead in contrast to the shingle algorithm and simhash algorithm.

4.2 PAS Algorithm

FPP[17] exploits prefetching fingerprints belonging to the same file by leveraging file similarity, thus improving the performance of data deduplication systems. The experimental results suggest that FPP increases cache hit ratio and reduces the number of disk accesses greatly. FPP samples three data blocks in the beginning, the middle, and the end of files to determine that a forthcoming file is similar to the files stored in the backed storage system, by using the TSA. This method is sample and effective. However, as explained in section 4.1, a single bit modification would result in a failure. Therefore, PAS is proposed to solve this problem.

Definition 1. *Given a positive integer p for any integer n must be existing equation $n = kp + r$. There k, r is an integer and $0 \leq r < p$, k is quotient n divided by p, r is remainder n divided by p.*

Suppose $n = 150, p = 100$, we have $150 = 1100 + 50$ in terms of Definition 1, where r and k equal to 50 and 1, respectively. The k always equals to 1 for $-50 < r \leq 50$. Then we have $k \times p \equiv p$. Therefore, the changing of r keeps n unchanged.

We can apply this simple method to the identification of file similarity. This mechanism is illustrated in algorithm 2. with pseudo-code.

In order to detect similarity accurately, we sample two data blocks in the beginning and in the end of files, respectively. The remaining sampling positions are calculated by using algorithm 2.. After choosing an appropriate parameter T according to algorithm 2., we can avoid the shifting of sampling positions due to slight file modifications

We take the same example used in Section 4.1 to illustrate the basic idea of PAS. Suppose file A sizes $56KB$, and file B is achieved by adding $5KB$ data to file A. We also sample six data blocks and the length of each data block is $1KB$. We take T as $28KB$. This is because in order to avoid the shifting of sampling positions incurred by adding the $5KB$ data, T should be bigger than $5KB$. Other numbers of T are also applicable. For example, T could be $6KB, 7KB, 8KB, 9KB$ and so on. We will discuss how to determine an optimal T in Section 5.2. Then, the file A has $N = 6, FileSize = 56KB, LenR = 10KB, T = 28KB$. According to Algorithm 2., file B will have $N = 6, FileSize = 61KB, LenR = 10KB, T = 28KB$.

Consider adding $5KB$ to file A in the beginning, the middle, and the end of the file, we will have file B1, B2, B3 illustrated in Figure 3. We can find that the sampling positions of file B are $0KB, 11KB, 22KB, 33KB, 44KB((1-1) * (1 + 10) = 0KB, (2-1)*(1+10) = 11KB, (3-1)*(1+10) = 22KB, (4-1)*(1+10) = 33KB, (5-1) * (1+10) = 44KB)$, and $60KB$, respectively. In contrast to the sampling positions of file A, the only difference is the last sampled data block at the position $60KB$. This is because we fix two sampling position in the beginning and the end of the corresponding files. According to the above analysis, we can conclude that the PAS algorithm can effectively avoid the shifting of sampling positions due to slightly file modifications.

Fig.2(b) shows that the sampling positions when using PAS algorithm. It also illustrates that the file modifications incur a shift of some sampled file contents. For example, the modification of file B1 is at the beginning of the file, although the sampling positions are the same as that of file A, all the sampled contents have been shifted except the first sample. However, this problem will be alleviated when the modification gradually moves from the beginning to the end of the file. For instance, all the sampled contents of file B3 are the same as that of file A except the last one occurring at the end of file B3.

Data deduplication systems [24][26][25] normally employ fixed-sized partition algorithm to obtain data chunks. In this scenario, most of the striped data chunks of file A and file B1 are not identical due to the modification at the beginning of file B1. Therefore, the mapped fingerprints of the data chunks are not identical as well. Even if file A and file B1 are actually similar, prefetching the fingerprints cannot improve the hit ratio of the fingerprints accesses when using the fixed-sized partition algorithm. According to the above analysis, we can determine that PAS matches the problem of data deduplication systems when the fixed-sized partition algorithm is adopted. Therefore, we believe that the PAS algorithm is applicable although it contains defects mentioned before.

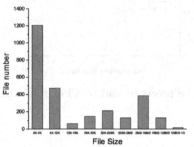

Fig. 3. The file size distribution of data set D1

Table 2. The profile of data set D1

	Popularity		Storage Space	
Rank	Ext.	%Occur	Ext.	%Storage
1	h	55.30	pdf	77.52
2	pdf	14.70	mkv	4.38
3	jpg	5.34	rar	4.24
4	c	4.28	mp3	4.01
5	mp3	3.48	zip	2.39
Total	–	83.1	–	92.54

5 Evaluation

5.1 Evaluation Environment

The experiments in this paper are performed in a Ubuntu operation system (kernel version is 2.6.32) at VirtualBox(4.3.8.r92456) with virtual machine software. The virtual machine consists of 1GB memory, 2.0GHZ Intel(R) Pentium(R) CPU. We use Tokyo Cabinet(1.4.48)[16] to store PAS results.

In order to measure the performance of PAS algorithm, we employed two data sets D1 and D2 to perform the evaluation. Data set D1 is collected from a Linux server in our research lab and a personal cloud DropBox. D1 has 2756 files with total size of $11.5GB$. Table 2 summarizes the profile of D1. It shows that the top five popular files are the files with the suffix of .h, .pdf, .jpg, .c and .mp3. Tables 2 also indicates that the files with suffix .pdf consumes the highest portion of storage capacity. Fig.3 shows the distribution of file size. It implies that the highest portion of file size ranging between 0KB to 4KB. The file size distribution in Fig.3 is consistent with the investigation of Agrawal et al[1] and Meyeret et al[20]. Therefore, we believe that data set D1 is very representative.

In order to determine the optimal parameters of PAS, we build another data set D2. The files in D2 consist of original files and the augmented files that are modified in the begging, the middle, and the end of the corresponding original files. D2 is made up of 14 txt files. It total size is $128MB$.

5.2 Parameters Selection

Since the parameters T and threshold δ have a significant impact on the performance of PAS, it is important to determine the optimal parameters. We compare

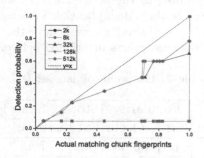 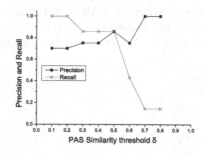

(a) The impact of T on the detection probability($Lenc = 32byte$, $N = 8$, $T = 2KB, 8KB, 32KB, 128KB, 512KB$)

(b) The precision and recall of PAS algorithm

Fig. 4. Parameters selection of PAS

the detection probability of PAS algorithm against the actual portion of matching chunks in data set D2. Because the actual portion of matching chunks is the up bound of the similarity between two files, the optimal parameters should make the detection probability of PAS get close to the actual portion of matching chunks. The Fix-Size Partition algorithm first split files into predefined fixed size chunks[5], then maps these chunks into fingerprints by using hash functions and obtains a fingerprint set. The chunk size is defined as $4KB$ in our experiments. Applying this method to file A and file B, we have two fingerprint sets $Finger(A)$ and $Finger(B)$. The actual portion of matching chunk fingerprints of file A and file B is described with equation (2), where $Match(A, B)$ lies between 0 to 1. This is consistent with equation (1). If $Match(A, B)$ reaches 1, this indicates that most of chunks of file A and file B are matching, vice verse.

$$Match(A, B) = \frac{|Finger(A) \cap Finger(B)|}{|Finger(A) \cup Finger(B)|} \tag{2}$$

By comparing Match(A,B) in equation(2) against $Sim(A, B)$ in equation (1), we can determine optimal parameters. For example, if $Match(A, B) = Sim(A, B)$, this implies that the PAS algorithm catches the real similarity of file A and file B. This scenario can be expressed in mathematical form as $y = x$, where y and x range between 0 and 1. Theoretically, if a curve keeps very close to $y = x$, it means this curve is the best candidate to select optimal parameters. The experiments in this section are all performed with data set D2.

Sampling Position Impact Factor T. Fig.4(a) shows the impact of sampling position impact factor T on the detection probability, where Lenc equals to $32byte$, N equals to 8, and T is determined as $2KB, 8KB, 32KB, 128KB$, and $512KB$. It is very interesting to observe that when T is defined as $2KB$ and $8KB$, the corresponding two curves goes far from the line $Sim(A, B) = Match(A, B)$.

At this point, the values of actual matching chunk fingerprints $Match(A, B)$ range from 0.05 to 0.98, while the values of detection probability $Sim(A, B)$ float around 0.07. In this situation, the failure ratio of detection is very high. Because even though two files most data blocks are identical, detection probability is low. When T is set as $32KB, 128KB$, and $512KB$, the corresponding curves are very close to the line $Sim(A, B) = Match(A, B)$. This indicates $32KB, 128KB$, and $512KB$ are optimal values of T. We take $T = 512KB$ in the following experiments.

Threshold δ of PAS Algorithm. Consider file A and file B, $Sim(A, B) \geq \delta$ indicates that file A is similar to file B, where δ is a threshold of similarity. We employ Precision and Recall introduced in [9][23] to select an optimal threshold δ. The Precision and Recall are defined in equation (3) and equation (4), respectively, where A represents a file set, u denotes the file required to detect similarity among the file set A, $Query(A, u)$ means a file set detected by using PAS algorithm, that file set is similar to the file u among the file set A, $Matchall(A, u)$ indicates a file set that is actually similar to the file u among the file set A, $|Matchall(A, u) \cap Query(A, u)|$ implies that a detection file set is actually similar to file u.

$$Precision = \frac{|Matchall(A, u) \cap Query(A, u)|}{|Query(A, u)|} \tag{3}$$

$$Recall = \frac{|Matchall(A, u) \cap Query(A, u)|}{|Matchall(A, u)|} \tag{4}$$

According to formula (3) and formula (4), precision is the fraction of detection instances which are actually similar, while recall is the fraction of actually similar instances that are retrieved, both values are between 0 to 1. If the precision value is close to 1, it means that most detection instances are actually similar. On the country, if the precision value is close to 0, it indicates that most detection instances are not similar. By analogy, if the recall value is close to 1, it implies that we detect most actually similar instances. If the recall value is close to 0, it denotes that we just detect a few similar instances.

Generally, according to the above analysis, we expect to have very high precision and recall that are close to 1. Unfortunately, this is very hard to achieve. If we want to detect more actually similar files, it means we have to relax the limit of threshold value δ. However, reducing the threshold value δ incurs more actual instances that are not similar to occur in the detection results. This will decrease the precision value. Expecting most detection results are actually similar means that we need to restrict the limit of threshold value δ. This will reduce the actually similar instances detected, thus decreasing the recall value. Therefore, we have to make a tradeoff between the precision and recall.

Fig.4(b) shows the impact of similarity threshold δ on the precision and recall when using PAS algorithm, where T equals to $512KB$, Lenc is $32byte$, and N is defined as 10. It is easy to observe that with the growth of δ, the precision

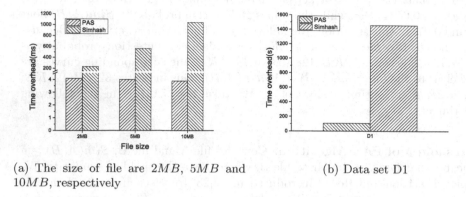

(a) The size of file are $2MB$, $5MB$ and $10MB$, respectively

(b) Data set D1

Fig. 5. The time overhead of PAS and simhash algorithm

increases, while the recall decreases. According to figure 10, We determine that the optimal similarity threshold δ is 0.5, because both the precision and recall can achieve a high value of 0.85. Therefore, if file A and file B satisfy the equation $Sim(A, B) \geq 0.5$, we treat these two file as similar.

5.3 PAS Algorithm Evaluation

We evaluate the time overhead, memory and CPU utilization, precision and recall of PAS against the well-known similarity detection algorithm called simhash. The T, Lenc, N, and δ are set as $512KB$, $32bytes$, 10, and 0.5, respectively. And according to the work in [19], hamming distance is selected as 3, and the number of stored table is determined as 4. All the measurements in this section are performed with data set D1.

In order to reduce the storage consumption and easy to express, the PAS algorithm use 8 bits to store a fingerprint. Therefore, it takes 80 bits for each file. However, the redundant table of simhash needs 256 bits to store the fingerprints of each file.

Time Overhead. The time overhead is evaluated with three different file size including 2MB, 5MB, 10MB. Fig.5(a) shows that the time overhead of PAS is much smaller than that of simhash across the three different file size. The actual time overhead of PAS are 4ms, 4ms, and 3.9ms, while the corresponding time overhead of simhash are 232.198ms, 564.668ms, and 1046.38ms. When using the data set D1, we obtain a similar trend in fig.5(b). The time overhead of PAS and simhash are 105s and 1452.5s, respectively.

CPU and Memory Utilization. Fig.6 illustrates the CPU and memory utilization of PAS algorithm against that of simhash algorithm when employing

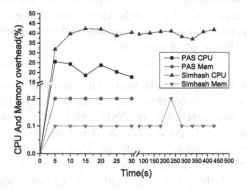

Fig. 6. CPU and memory utilization of *PAS* and simhash with data set D1

data set D1. It shows that the CPU utilization of PAS and simhash are 20%
and 40%, respectively. This indicates that simhash is more computing intensive
than PAS algorithm. However, the memory utilization of PAS and simhash are
2% and 1%, respectively. The reason behind this is because PAS algorithm use
Tokyo Cabinet to store fingerprint sets, and the Tokyo Cabinet maps data files
into memory as much as possible. This makes the PAS algorithm take more
memory space. However, PAS algorithm memory utilization does not increase
with time. Tokyo Cabinet does not store any data in cache. Simhash algorithm
memory utilization increases with time. Simhash algorithm stores all fingerprints
in memory and exists redundance fingerprints. So we think PAS particularly
suitable for limited physical memory environment.

Precision and Recall. In order to illustrate the effectiveness of PAS, we evaluate the precision and recall of PAS against that of simhash with data set D1.
Our experiments demonstrate that the precision and recall of PAS are 0.875 and
1, respectively. However, the measured precision and recall of simhash are 1 and
0.125, respectively.

The Main reason of this result is because simhash employs fixed-size partition
algorithm. This makes the simhash algorithm become very sensitive to the file
modifications. A single bit modification will make the fingerprints of the corresponding two files completely different. Therefore, we believe that the PAS
algorithm is a practical and applicable solution for the file similarity detection.

6   Conclusion

In this paper, we proposed an algorithm PAS to identify file similarity in large
data sets by modulo file length. Comprehensive experiments are performed to
select optimal parameters of PAS. Corresponding analysis and discussion of the
parameter selection are introduced in the paper. The evaluation of precision

and recall demonstrates that PAS is very effective in detecting file similarity in contrast to a well-known similarity detection algorithm called simhash. The experiment results suggest that the time overhead, CPU and memory occupation of PAS are much less than that of simhash.

Acknowledgement. We would like to thank the anonymous reviewers for helping us refine this paper. Their constructive comments and suggestions are very helpful. This work is supported by the National Natural Science Foundation (NSF) of China under grant (No.61272073, No. 61073064), the key program of Natural Science Foundation of Guangdong Province (no. S2013020012865), the Scientific Research Foundation for the Returned Overseas Chinese Scholars (State Education Ministry), the Educational Commission of Guangdong Province (No. 2012KJCX0013), the Creative Engineering for Undergraduates of Jinan University(No.cx13113). The corresponding author of this paper is Yuhui Deng.

References

1. Agrawal, N., Bolosky, W.J., Douceur, J.R., Lorch, J.R.: A five-year study of file-system metadata. ACM Transactions on Storage (TOS) 3(3), 9 (2007)
2. Baker, B.S.: On finding duplication and near-duplication in large software systems. In: Proceedings of 2nd Working Conference on Reverse Engineering,1995, pp. 86–95. IEEE (1995)
3. Bhagwat, D., Eshghi, K., Long, D.D., Lillibridge, M.: Extreme binning: Scalable, parallel deduplication for chunk-based file backup. In: IEEE International Symposium on Modeling, Analysis & Simulation of Computer and Telecommunication Systems, MASCOTS 2009, pp. 1–9. IEEE (2009)
4. Biswas, S., Franklin, D., Savage, A., Dixon, R., Sherwood, T., Chong, F.T.: Multi-execution: Multicore caching for data-similar executions. In: ACM SIGARCH Computer Architecture News, vol. 37, pp. 164–173. ACM (2009)
5. Bitton, D., DeWitt, D.J.: Duplicate record elimination in large data files. ACM Transactions on Database Systems (TODS) 8(2), 255–265 (1983)
6. Brin, S., Davis, J., Garcia-Molina, H.: Copy detection mechanisms for digital documents. In: ACM SIGMOD Record, vol. 24, pp. 398–409. ACM (1995)
7. Broder, A.Z.: On the resemblance and containment of documents. In: Proceedings of the Compression and Complexity of Sequences 1997, pp. 21–29. IEEE (1997)
8. Broder, A.Z., Glassman, S.C., Manasse, M.S., Zweig, G.: Syntactic clustering of the web. Computer Networks and ISDN Systems 29(8), 1157–1166 (1997)
9. Buckland, M.K., Gey, F.C.: The relationship between recall and precision. JASIS 45(1), 12–19 (1994)
10. Charikar, M.S.: Similarity estimation techniques from rounding algorithms. In: Proceedings of the Thiry-fourth Annual ACM Symposium on Theory of Computing, pp. 380–388. ACM (2002)
11. Cox, L.P., Murray, C.D., Noble, B.D.: Pastiche: Making backup cheap and easy. ACM SIGOPS Operating Systems Review 36(SI), 285–298 (2002)
12. Forman, G., Eshghi, K., Chiocchetti, S.: Finding similar files in large document repositories. In: Proceedings of the Eleventh ACM SIGKDD International Conference on Knowledge Discovery in Data Mining, pp. 394–400. ACM (2005)

13. Gens, F.: Top 10 predictions idc predictions Competing on the 3rd platform (2013), http://www.idc.com/research/Predictions13/downloadable/238044.pdf
14. Hua, Y., Liu, X., Feng, D.: Data similarity-aware computation infrastructure for the cloud. IEEE Transactions on Computers p. 1 (2013)
15. Indyk, P., Motwani, R.: Approximate nearest neighbors: towards removing the curse of dimensionality. In: Proceedings of the Thirtieth Annual ACM Symposium on Theory of Computing, pp. 604–613. ACM (1998)
16. Labs, F.: Tokyo cabinet, http://fallabs.com/tokyocabinet/
17. Song, L., Deng, Y., Xie, J.: Exploiting fingerprint prefetching to improve the performance of data deduplication. In: Proceedings of the 15th IEEE International Conference on High Performance Computing and Communications. IEEE (2013)
18. Manber, U., et al.: Finding similar files in a large file system. Usenix Winter 94, 1–10 (1994)
19. Manku, G.S., Jain, A., Das Sarma, A.: Detecting near-duplicates for web crawling. In: Proceedings of the 16th International Conference on World Wide Web, pp. 141–150. ACM (2007)
20. Meyer, D.T., Bolosky, W.J.: A study of practical deduplication. ACM Transactions on Storage (TOS) 7(4), 14 (2012)
21. Muthitacharoen, A., Chen, B., Mazieres, D.: A low-bandwidth network file system. In: ACM SIGOPS Operating Systems Review, vol. 35, pp. 174–187. ACM (2001)
22. Ouyang, Z., Memon, N., Suel, T., Trendafilov, D.: Cluster-based delta compression of a collection of files. In: Proceedings of the Third International Conference on Web Information Systems Engineering, WISE 2002, pp. 257–266. IEEE (2002)
23. Powers, D.M.: Evaluation: from precision, recall and f-measure to roc, informedness, markedness & correlation. Journal of Machine Learning Technologies 2(1), 37–63 (2011)
24. Quinlan, S., Dorward, S.: Venti: A new approach to archival storage. In: FAST, vol. 2, pp. 89–101 (2002)
25. Ruijter, M.: Lessfs, http://www.lessfs.com/wordpress/
26. Sapuntzakis, C.P., Chandra, R., Pfaff, B., Chow, J., Lam, M.S., Rosenblum, M.: Optimizing the migration of virtual computers. ACM SIGOPS Operating Systems Review 36(SI), 377–390 (2002)
27. Shivakumar, N., Garcia-Molina, H.: Building a scalable and accurate copy detection mechanism. In: Proceedings of the First ACM International Conference on Digital Libraries, pp. 160–168. ACM (1996)
28. Teodosiu, D., Bjorner, N., Gurevich, Y., Manasse, M., Porkka, J.: Optimizing file replication over limited bandwidth networks using remote differential compression. Microsoft Research TR-2006-157 (2006)
29. Xia, W., Jiang, H., Feng, D., Hua, Y.: Silo: A similarity-locality based near-exact deduplication scheme with low ram overhead and high throughput. In: Proceedings of the 2011 USENIX Conference on USENIX Annual Technical Conference, pp. 26–28. USENIX Association (2011)

Conpy: Concolic Execution Engine
for Python Applications

Ting Chen[1], Xiao-song Zhang[1], Rui-dong Chen[1], Bo Yang[1], and Yang Bai[2]

[1] School of Computer Science & Engineering, University of Electronic Science and
Technology of China, Chengdu 611731, China
[2] No.30 Research Institute, China Electronics Technology Group Corporation
(CETC), Chengdu 618841, China
chenting19870201@163.com

Abstract. Concolic execution has become a promising technique for
program analysis in recent years, whereas it rarely applies to Python
applications. In this work, we propose a concolic execution engine for
Python applications named Conpy. Conpy is easy to deploy since it is
written in pure Python and it is not dependent on any third-party tools.
Conpy is also easy to use. Anyone with basic knowledge of Python and
concolic execution can quickly get start with Conpy. Besides, Conpy
works in low level and produces human-readable reports which facilitate
subsequent analysis. We then make an elaborate performance testing on
Conpy. Results show that the overhead of Conpy is acceptable, that is
to say, less than one order of magnitude in most cases.

Keywords: Python, concolic execution, easy to deploy, easy to use, low
overhead.

1 Introduction

Concolic execution, or dynamic symbolic execution, which is a variation of traditional symbolic execution proposed in 1970s [1], is now becoming a hot technique
for program analysis. As the name implies, concolic execution combines concrete
execution which runs the programs under analysis (PUA) concretely with symbolic execution which marks symbols, tracks symbols and produces path condition in the meanwhile. So far, concolic execution has applied to software testing,
software bugs finding and malware analysis. A number of concolic execution
tools have been proposed recently, such as SAGE [2], Pex [3], KLEE [4], DART
[5], CUTE [6], Fuzzgrind [7], Catchconv [8], S2E [9], Splat [10], TaintScope [11],
BitBlaze [12], CREST [13], JPF-SE [14] as well as our previous tools SMAFE
[15] and SEVE [16].

However, rare tools can handle Python applications. Python was often used
as a scripting language for web applications, but now it is widely used by large
organizations including Google, Yahoo!, NASA for its high productivity [17]. So
it is meaningful to design and implement a concolic execution tool for Python
applications.

X.-h. Sun et al. (Eds.): ICA3PP 2014, Part II, LNCS 8631, pp. 150–163, 2014.
© Springer International Publishing Switzerland 2014

We have two major contributions in this work. The first, we design and implement a concolic execution engine for Python applications named Conpy. Conpy is written in pure Python and it does not depend on any third-party tools, so it can be released with Python's codebase as a module. Besides, Conpy is easy to use. Typically, the only effort for users is to specify symbol sources, such as the inputs read from files, data comes from Internet, return values of any functions. Conpy runs in low level, so it is able to produce reports containing low-level information, which obviously benefit subsequent analysis. Furthermore, the reports generated by Conpy are human-friendly. So experts can analyze the reports manually or interpret the reports by any third-party tools.

The second contribution is that we test the performance (i.e. overhead) of Conpy extensively. To our knowledge, the overhead issue of existing concolic execution tools has not been studied in depth. Current concolic execution tools are employed in off-line analysis, such as automated test generation, software bugs finding etc., rather than on-line detection or protection. So overhead is not so critical for current usage. The results from performance testing are promising that in most cases the overhead is less than one order of magnitude.

2   Related Work

This section briefly reviews the design and implementation of existing concolic execution tools in order to outline the differences between them and our Conpy. We try to present some typical tools which have got high attention, but we do not intend to present all of them. Readers who are interested in current concolic execution tools can refer to a recent survey [18].

SAGE [2] is proposed by Microsoft Corporation which concolically executes Windows binaries. SAGE is built on top of a trace replay framework, named TruScan. The trace files consumed by TruScan are produced by iDNA framework. So concolic execution in SAGE is according to the following process: (1) executes PUA concretely and gathers trace files by iDNA. (2) executes trace files symbolically with the help of TruScan. The paper [2] reports SAGE is rather slow and it gives an example to illustrate how slow SAGE is. The symbolic execution of Media 2 with wff-3 takes 25 minutes 30 seconds, while concrete execution costs only several seconds.

DART [5], CUTE [6], Splat [10] and CREST [13] are instrumented by a source-to-source translator, named CIL. New source files will be produced by CIL, including original source which performs concrete execution and instrumented functions which perform symbolic execution. Those tools above can handle C programs only when source code is available since CIL requires C source code. JPF-SE [14] is based on Java Pathfinder which applies a similar approach: it utilizes a Java source-to-source translation tool for instrumentation.

Fuzzgrind [7] and Catchconv [8] employ Valgrind to instrument PUA dynamically. That is, the function of symbolic execution is instrumented when PUA is running. TaintScope [11], as well as our previous tools SMAFE [15] and

SEVE [16] do a similar work based on another dynamic instrumentation tool, Pin. Similarly, Minesweeper [19] enhances Qemu with dynamic binary instrumentation. Those tools which are built on dynamic binary instrumentation can handle unmodified binary PUA with the cost of very high overhead. For example, the average overhead introduced by Pin and Valgrind is 2.5 times and 8.3 times respectively even if a simple task for basic-block counting is instrumented. So it is not surprising that orders of magnitude overhead will be incurred by those dynamic-instrumentation-based concolic execution tools.

KLEE [4] itself acts as an interpreter to concolically execute the bytecode produced by LLVM. KLEE runs below PUA and it is in charge of the execution of PUA. KLEE does not instrument PUA in static or dynamic way. Instead, KLEE directly interprets bytecode and maps bytecode to constraints. S2E [9] reuses the symbolic execution engine of KLEE to handle both user-mode and kernel-mode binaries. To translate x86 instructions to the bytecode that KLEE's symbolic execution engine can understand, S2E proposes an x86-to-LLVM backend for QEMU on where the guest OS and S2E run. As mentioned in paper [9], the overhead of S2E in symbolic mode is ~78 times.

Pex [3] adopts a dynamic-instrumentation-based method to concolically execute .NET code. It instruments by .NET profiling API and it enhances .NET virtual machine with symbolic execution. BitBlaze [12] and BitScope [20] implement a plugin for TEMU to mark and track symbols. As PUA runs in TEMU, so those tools have the privilege to interpret the execution of PUA in symbolic mode.

Conpy employs a different design with existing concolic execution tools. Unlike DART, CUTE, Splat, CREST, JPF-SE, no source-to-source translators are required. Compared to Fuzzgrind, Catchconv, TaintScope, SMAFE, SEVE etc., Conpy does not depend on dynamic instrumentation tools. Besides, Conpy does not require virtue machines like Qemu and Temu. Moreover, Conpy does not behave as an interpreter like KLEE. Actually, Conpy does not care about (or even be aware of) the executions which do not involve symbolic computations. Also, in Conpy, symbolic execution is along with concrete execution, so it is different from the replay scheme of SAGE.

This work conducts experiments to measure the overhead of Conpy. We find that only two (i.e. SAGE [2] and S2E [9]) existing concolic execution tools briefly report their overhead that is high. Concretely speaking, paper [2] presents an example to show SAGE's high overhead and paper [9] claims the overhead of S2E in symbolic mode is ~78 times. The overhead evaluation of the two tools considers the whole process of test data generation such as concolic execution, constraint solving, path exploration and so on. Differently, this work measures the overhead of concolic execution only which includes concrete execution and symbolic execution (e.g. symbol marking, symbol tracking, generation of path conditions).

3 Design

3.1 Principles

At first, we present the design principles of Conpy, and then describe the design scheme. The design principles are actually the goals we want to achieve.

1. Conpy should be easy to deploy. That is to say, it is able to run on mainstream hardware platforms and software platforms. Besides, this tool would better not depend on any special third-party tools. Otherwise, if the tool can run on special situations only, its practicability will be impaired.
2. Conpy should be easy to use. The reason is obvious that too much pre-knowledge and complex usage will hinder users from getting start with the tool.
3. Conpy runs in low level and produces reports with low-level information. Even if it is not always so, low-level information is usually richer and more interesting than high-level information. For instance, if Conpy runs in the string level, it can discern whether the two strings are equal or not. But if it runs in the byte level, additional information can be got: if the two strings are not equal, Conpy can tell users which bytes are different.

   Besides, high-level concolic execution tool may produce more false alarms than the low-level counterparts. For example, assume a string $s1$ is a symbol, if the concolic execution tool is now in the string level, the new string $s2$ which is the concatenation of $s1$ and a non-symbol string $s3$ should be symbolized. So consider the string $s4$, which is computed as $s2[len(s2) - len(s3):]$, $s4$ should be symbolized since $s2$ is a symbol. However it is incorrect because $s4$ equals to $s3$ in essence. On the contrary, if the concolic execution tool runs in the byte level, $s4$ will be recognized accurately.

   Additionally, low-level concolic execution facilitates tracking symbols among different data types. For example, in statement $s = $ "%i"%x, x is a symbolized integer. After the execution of this statement, Conpy will map the symbol linked with x to each byte of the string s, thus string s will be symbolized.
4. The overhead of Conpy should be acceptable. Even if current concolic execution tools are applied in off-line analysis, overly high overhead may make them impracticable.

3.2 Scheme

The design of Conpy is based on the claim "everything in Python is an object" [21]. Even the primitive types such as "int", "float", "bool" are objects, which is different from traditional programming languages such as C, C++. The core idea of Conpy consists of extending the Python's objects with an additional attribute termed by *symbol* or *symbol_set* indicating the symbol(s) linked with the objects and enhancing Python's functions with the abilities to track symbols and produce path conditions.

Whether an object links with a symbol or a symbol set depending on whether the object is a primitive type or a container. For example, an integer which is a primitive type links with a symbol but a string that is a container is associated with a symbol set. Each item in the symbol set indicates whether the corresponding item in the container is a symbol or not. Put it another way, if an item in the symbol set is empty, the associated item in the container is not a symbol even if the container itself is already symbolized. In this way, Conpy is able to run in primitive level rather than much higher container level.

Consider the following example, assume a string with length three is symbolized as $s1$, the symbol set of $s1$ is something like ['$b1$', '$b2$', '$b3$'] indicating the three bytes of the string links with three symbols $b1$, $b2$ and $b3$ respectively. If a new string $s2$ is the concatenation of $s1$ and a constant string, say 'abc', the symbol set of $s2$ should be ['$b1$', '$b2$', '$b3$', '', '', '']. Therefore, by looking up the symbol set, Conpy is aware that the last three bytes of $s2$ are actually not dependent on symbols.

The concolic execution of Conpy typically consists of three procedures: marking symbol sources, tracking symbols and producing path conditions. The last two steps are fully automated, only the first one requires human intervention. To mark symbol sources, users is asked to specify which variables are of interested. This step is made by simply calling the interface *symbolize* provided by Conpy. To facilitate users, Conpy can run in a fully automated mode which marks all inputs read from the environment as symbols.

The general principle of symbol tracking is: mapping the effects of statements to the symbols of destination variables if the statements involve symbolic computations. The mapping process should maintain the semantics of the statements. For example, given a statement $y = x + 10$, assuming before its execution, y and x have been symbolized as $i0$ and $i1$ respectively. After its execution, the symbol associated with y should be updated as $i1 + 10$.

Constraints should be produced when the comparisons which involve symbolic computations are made. Like symbolic expressions, constraints should maintain the semantics of comparison statements. A critical step of producing constraints is to discern which statements can produce constraints. In many cases, the statements for comparison are obvious, such as $x == y, x >= y, x! = 0$.

But in some cases, comparisons are implicit. For instance, if Conpy symbolizes a string by invoking the interface *symbolize*, it should produce a constraint like $s1 == b0.'a'.b3$. The constraint contains the following information: the string is symbolized as $s1$; its first byte corresponds to a symbol $b0$; its second byte is a constant 'a'; its last byte links with a symbol $b3$. Let's consider another example, *find* is a build-in function of the *str* type which returns the lowest index where the substring is found. Conpy extends *find* with constraint generation if comparisons in *find* involve symbols.

To get low-level path conditions, Conpy runs in primitive type level. That's to say, Conpy treats a primitive type as an atom which cannot be broken down. While executing a container concolically, Conpy dives into the container and symbolizes primitive variables in the container. For example, Conpy symbolizes each byte of a string. Given a list of integers, Conpy treats each integer of the list as a symbol.

Low overhead can be achieved through our design since only the symbolized variables are manipulated by Conpy. In other words, Conpy does not care about or even not be aware of non-symbol variables. So actually the computations without symbols run in native mode which incurs no overhead. Experiments validate our claim that the overhead of a symbol-intensive program is as high as 46 times, but the overhead of a symbol-non-intensive program is only about 80%.

4 Implementation

This section presents the implementation details as well as some critical code of Conpy. As a representative of primitive type, we present the handling of *int* in Section 4.1. The other primitive types such as *float, bool* are handled similarly.

Then we show the concolic execution of *str* in Section 4.2, which is a frequently-used container in Python. We handle the other containers such as *list, tuple* in a similar way. In fact, we find that the handling of *str* is more intricate than the other containers. One obvious reason is that *str* provides so many build-in functions which require extensions for concolic execution. Additionally, the atomic items of *list, tuple* etc. may be the primitive types we have already handled such as *int, float, bool*. So considerable development effort can be saved. However, the atomic items of *str* is still *str*. So we have to manipulate the *str* type from scratch.

Finally, we show how symbols spread from the *int* type to the *str* type and back in Section 4.3.

4.1 Manipulation of *int*

To mark new integer symbols, users need to invoke the interface *symbolize* with the argument being an integer. After discerning the type of the argument, the corresponding routine *symbolize_int* is called. The function *symbolize_int* is defined as:

```
1   def symbolize_int(val):              3      sym_int.symbol = symbol(0)
2       sym_int = symbol_int(val)        4      return sym_int
```

The integer is passed as the argument *val* in line 1. In line 2, a new object of type *symbolize_int* is created. Actually, the class *symbolize_int* inherits from the primitive type *int*. So all attributes and build-in functions of *int* are also available in *symbolize_int*. Line 3 links the attribute *symbol* of object *symbolize_int* with an object of class *symbol*. Finally the object *symbolize_int* is returned. The code of initializing an object of class *symbol* is:

```
1   class symbol:                        6          self.atom= 'i' + str(symbol.
2       sym_num = 0                                 sym_num)
3       def __init__(self, f_atom):      7          symbol.sym_num += 1
4           if f_atom==0: #atomic symbol 8          self.operand_num = 0
5               self.sign = sign_none    9          self.operands = []
```

The variable *sym_num* which is defined in line 2 denotes the number of symbols. Once an atomic symbol is created, the variable will increase by 1 (line 7). If a new symbol is created from existing symbols (i.e. the predicate in line 4 evaluates as false), the following statements will not be executed. Conpy organizes a symbol as a tree in memory. As an atomic symbol, the sign of the symbol is initialized as *sign_none* (line 5) and its operands are empty (line 8 and line 9).

To track symbols, Conpy overrides the build-in functions which are able to spread symbols. We present the implementation of *__add__* as an example.

```
1   def __add__(first , second):
2      res = int.__add__(first , second)
3      if isinstance(first , symbol_int):
4         if isinstance(second, symbol_int):
5            sym = symbol.__add__(first.symbol, second.symbol)
6         else:
7            sym = symbol.__add__(first.symbol, second)
8         add_int = symbol_int(res)
9         add_int.symbol = sym
10     else: pass
11     return add_int
```

When a statement like $x + y$ executes, the build-in function *__add__* or *__radd__* will be called depending on which operands (x or y or both) are symbols. Specifically, if the first operand is a symbol (no matter whether the second operand is a symbol or not), the function *__add__* will be invoked. In cases when the first operand is not a symbol but the second is, in turn the function *__radd__* will be called. Note that if neither of them are symbols, original function of class *int* will be called, thus no additional overhead will be introduced in this case.

The original function *__add__* of class *int* is invoked to compute the concrete outcome of the statement (line 2). Then the integer *res* is symbolized as *add_int* in line 8. The symbol linked with *add_int* is created by invoking the function *__add__* of class *symbol*. Below is the core code of *symbol.__add__*.

```
1   def __add__(sym1, sym2):          5      add_sym.operands = []
2      add_sym = symbol(1)            6      add_sym.operands.append(sym1)
3      add_sym.sign = sign_plus       7      add_sym.operands.append(sym2)
4      add_sym.operand_num = 2        8      return add_sym
```

A new symbol is created in line 2. As the new symbol is the plus of existing symbols, the argument of class *symbol* should be 1. The sign of the symbol is defined as *sign_plus* (line 3) denoting the symbol results from a plus operation. The symbol has two operands (line 4) and each of them is a symbol or a concrete value. The two operands are appended in the set *operands* as two subtrees of symbol *add_sym* (line 6 and line 7). Finally, the symbol is returned.

Conpy will produce constraints when the comparisons which involve symbolic computations are executed. Consider the following example, when executes the statement $x == y$, the build-in function *__eq__* will be called. So Conpy extends the function with the ability to produce constraints as follows:

```
1   def __eq__(val1, val2):
2      res = int.__eq__(val1, val2)
3      if isinstance(val1, symbol_int)& isinstance(val2, symbol_int):
4         print_sym(val1.symbol)
5         if res == 1:
6            print('==', end = ' ')
7         else:
8            print('!=', end = ' ')
9         print_sym(val2.symbol)
10     elif: # code for the other situations
11     return res
```

The concrete outcome of the comparison is got by invoking original function of class *int* in line 2. If both *val1* and *val2* are symbols, the statements from line 4 to line 9 will be executed. The other situations are handled similarly, so related code does not present here. The symbols of *val1* and *val2* are printed by the function *print_sym*. The function *print_sym* is actually a recursive function which traverses the trees where store symbols. Naturally, depending on the outcome of comparison, '==' or '!=' is printed.

4.2   Manipulation of *str*

To mark a string as a symbol, users invoke the interface *symbolize*. Inside the this function, routine *symbolize_str* is invoked as the argument being a string. Function *symbolize_str* works similar with the function *symbolize_int* except two aspects. First, a symbol set rather than a symbol links with the symbolized string. The symbol set is created by invoking function *create_sym* of class *symbolize_str* which inherits from the build-in class *str*. Related code is:

```
1   def create_sym(s):
2     sym_set = []
3     for i in range(0, len(s)):
4       sym = symbol()
5       sym.sign = sign_none
6       sym.atom = 'b' + str(symbol_str.sym_num)
7       sym_set.append(sym)
8       symbol_str.sym_num += 1
9     return sym_set
```

Conpy links each byte of the string with a symbol through the loop from statement 3 to statement 8. Second, a constraint denoting the string is the concatenation of its bytes is produced through the function *print_create_cons* of class *symbol*.

Conpy tracks the propagation of symbols by overriding build-in functions of class *str*. Consider the example, given a symbolized string *s* with its symbol being $b0.b1.b2$, after the execution of the statement $s = s * 2$, the symbol of *s* should be updated as $b0.b1.b2.b0.b1.b2$. To this purpose, Conpy extends the build-in functions *__mul__* and *__rmul__* with the ability to symbolic execution. We present *__mul__* here.

```
1    def __mul__(s, count):
2      res = str.__mul__(s, count)
3      sym = symbol_str(res)
4      sym.name = 's' + str(symbol_str.str_num)
5      symbol_str.str_num += 1
6      ln = len(s.sym_set)
7      sym.sym_set = [0]*ln*count
8      for i in range(0, count):
9        sym.sym_set[i*ln:(i+1)*ln]=s.sym_set
10     symbol.print_create_cons(sym)
11     return sym
```

The outcome of multiplication is computed by invoking original function *__mul__* of class *str* (line 2). The symbol set of symbolized string is copied from the symbol set of argument *s* by *count* times (line 8 and line 9).

When statements like $x == y, x > y, x! = y$ execute, Conpy will produce constraints if those statements involve symbolic computations. Conpy handles those

158   T. Chen et al.

statements similarly with the manipulations of symbolized integers except that
the comparison of two strings usually produces a number of constraints rather
than only one. Conpy handles *find, rfind, __contains__, index etc.* specially because
those functions can produce constraints besides their original return values. We
do not show associated code here since the code is relatively long. In short, the
basic idea is to use symbolic strings to simulate operations of concrete strings.

4.3 Symbol Propagation between *str* and *int*

Conpy runs in low level making it is able to spread symbols among different types.
This section shows how symbols propagate from *int* type to *str* type through
function *chr* and back through function *ord*. The basic idea is to extend functions
chr and *ord* with the abilities to spread symbols and produce constraints. Look
at the code below:

```
1   def symbol_func(org):                  13        i = args[0]
2     def inner(*args, **kwargs):          14        if isinstance(i, symbol_int):
3       r = org(*args, **kwargs)           15          res = symbolize(r)
4       if org.__name__ == 'ord':          16          print_sym(res.sym_set[0])
5         c = args[0]                       17          print('==', end = ' ')
6         if isinstance(c, symbol_str):     18          print_sym(i.symbol)
7           res = symbolize(r)              19          return res
8           print_sym(res.symbol)          20      return r
9           print('==', end = ' ')         21    return inner
10          print_sym(c.sym_set[0])        22  ord = symbol_func(ord)
11          return res                     23  chr = symbol_func(chr)
12      elif org.__name__ == 'chr':
```

Original functions *chr* and *ord* are enhanced by invoking function *symbol_func*
in line 22 and line 23. In *symbol_func*, original function is invoked first to get the
concrete return value *r* (line 3). If the function is *ord*, the first item in *args* should
be the argument passed to *ord* and then the item is assigned to a variable *c* for
convenience (line 5). If *c* is symbolized, the return value *r* should be symbolized
accordingly (line 7). After that, a constraint indicating the correlation between
the symbol of *res* and the symbol of *c* is produced (lines 8 – 10). Finally, the
symbolized integer *res* is returned. The handling of function *chr* is similar (lines
13 – 19).

5 Experiments

5.1 Setup

Our experiments have two goals. The first is to validate the ability of Conpy to
produce path conditions. The second is to evaluate the performance overhead
of Conpy. We first present test environment. CPU is an Intel Core i7-2760QM
with the frequency of 2.4GHz. The capacity of main memory is 8GB. Operating
system is 64-bit Windows 7 Home Premium. The version of Python installed on
my computer is 3.3.0.

We select ten programs which are all standard modules of Python as benchmarks. The reason for choosing those programs lies in that those modules are
frequently invoked by any other Python programs making experimental results
more valuable. Results as well as corresponding test harnesses are presented in
the following section.

5.2 Results

We first summarize test results in table 1 and then detail each tested program with its test harness. The second column of table 1 shows the length of path condition of each tested program. To measure overheads accurately, we run some of tested programs multiple times. So we get very long path conditions. The last column gives the overhead of each tested program. We can observe that seven out of ten tested programs slow down by less than one order of magnitude. The highest overhead is about 46 times when testing *heapq* module. The overhead can be as low as 80% when testing *imghdr* program. Actually, we can expect even lower overhead after further optimizations of our implementation.

Table 1. Test results

Program	Length of PC	Overhead
heapq	142825	46
calendar	1749090	5.1
random	34662	2.7
bisect	237987	4.1
html.parser	237000	12.1
re	140042	5.1
mimetypes	62000	6.4
urllib.parse	280114	27.6
imghdr	301000	0.8
sndhdr	30000	2.9

heapq. The tested program is *Lib/heapq.py* which provides an implementation of heap queue algorithm. Test harness is shown below. The code for importing Conpy, producing random integers, outputting the statistics of performance overhead *etc.* is omitted.

```
1   #ln = symbolize(ln)
2   h = []
3   for v in ln:
4       heappush(h, v)
5   heappop(h) for i in range(len(h))
```

The list *ln* contains 10000 random integers. After sorting, the result is stored in the list *h*. By uncommenting line 1, the program will run concolically, otherwise, it will run concretely. Time cost for concrete execution is about 6.7ms while the time for concolic execution is about 313.8ms which is roundly **46** times longer than concrete execution. Path condition produced by Conpy is as long as 142825 denoting there are 142825 constraints in the path condition.

calendar. It is a program (*Lib/calendar.py*) allows to output calendars like the Unix Lib *cal* program. Test harness is given below.

```
1   for year in range(1000, 3000):
2       for month in range(1, 13):
3           #year = symbolize(year)
4           #month = symbolize(month)
5           matrix = monthcalendar(year, month)
```

As variable *year* ranges from 1000 to 3000 and variable *month* ranges from 1 to 13, function *monthcalendar* will be called 24000 times. The reason for running *monthcalendar* so many times is that it facilitates to evaluate performance overhead. Time for concrete execution is about 744ms. By uncommenting line 3 and line 4, the program runs concolically. Consequently, time consumption increases to 4538.3ms (i.e. overhead is about **5.1** times). Path condition consists of 1749090 constraints.

random. It is a program (*Lib/random.py*) implements pseudo-random number generators for various distributions. Below presents test harness.

```
1  for i in range(0, 10000):
2     #i = symbolize(i)
3     x = randrange(i)
```

Running the above program, 10000 random integers are generated in about 60.8ms. In concolic mode, the program costs about 223.8ms indicating overhead is about **2.7** times. The length of path condition is 34662.

bisect. It is a program (*Lib/bisect.py*) provides support to maintain a list in sorted order without having to sort the list after each insertion. This module is termed by *bisect* because it uses a basic bisection algorithm to do its work. Below is the test harness.

```
1  for i in range(0, 10000):
2     #r = symbolize(r)
3     bisect(list, r)
4     insort(list, r)
```

The variable r is a random integer. Time for concrete execution is 121.2ms. Concolic execution costs about 612.7ms which is **4.1** times longer than concrete execution. Produced path condition contains as many as 237987 constraints.

html.parser. The module (*Lib/html/parser.py*) defines a class *HTMLParser* which serves as the basis to parse text files formatted in *HTML* or *XHTML*. Here is the test harness.

```
1  for i in range(0, 1000):
2     parser = HTMLParser(strict = False)
3     s = ' <html><head><title>Test</title></head><body><h1>Parse me!</h1></
             body></html> '
4     #s = symbolize(s)
5     parser.feed(s)
```

To evaluate the performance overhead of Conpy accurately, the parsing process repeats for 1000 times. The parsed *html* text is given in line 3 which will be symbolized in line 4. In concrete mode, the program costs about 133.2ms. Switching to concolic mode, time consumption rises to 1748.2ms. In other words, the overhead incurred by Conpy is about **12.1** times. The length of path condition is 237000.

re. This module provides regular expression matching operations. Test harness is shown as following.

```
1  for i in range(0, 10000):     4     #s1 = symbolize(s1)
2     s1 = ' (?<=abc)def '        5     s2 = symbolize(s2)
3     s2 = ' abcdef '             6     m = re.search(s1, s2)
```

Function *search* provided by *re* module is used to look for a location where the regular expression (as shown in line 2) produce a match, and return a corresponding match object. Search process repeats for 10000 times so as to evaluate Conpy's overhead adequately. Time cost by concrete execution is about 159.6ms. The program runs concolically by uncommenting line 4 and line 5. Time consumption in concolic mode is 981ms. So the overhead of Conpy is about **5.1** times. The number of constraints produced by Conpy is as many as 140042.

mimetypes. The *mimetypes* module (*Lib/mimetypes.py*) converts between a filename or a *URL* and the *MIME* type associated with the filename extension. Two functions *guess_type* and *guess_extension* are tested in the following test harness.

```
1   minetypes.init()                   5   res = mimetypes.guess_type(fname)
2   for i in range(0, 1000):           6   ty = res[0]
3       fname = '/ct/ycg/f.tgz'        7   #ty = symbolize(ty)
4       #fname = symbolize(fname)      8   mimetypes.guess_extension(ty)
```

To evaluate performance overhead reliably, test progress repeats 1000 times. Concrete execution costs 70.4ms, while concolic execution spends about 523ms which is **6.4** times longer. The path condition produced by Conpy consists of 62000 constraints.

urllib.parse. This module (*Lib/urllib/parse.py*) defines a standard interface to break *URL* strings up in components, to combine the components back into a *URL* string, and to convert a "relative *URL*" to an absolute *URL* given a "base *URL*". We test function *urlparse* through the following harness.

```
1   for i in range(0, 5000):
2       url = ' http://www.uestc.edu.cn/index.html '
3       #url = symbolize(url)
4       urlparse(url)
```

Time cost for concrete execution is about 45.7ms. By uncommenting line 3, the program runs concolically which spends 1307.4ms. Overhead is about **27.6** times. The length of path condition is 280114.

imghdr. This module (*Lib/imghdr.py*) determines the type of image contained in a file or byte stream. We reuse the test harness included in the source *imghdr.py* by only a few modifications. For example, we insert a line of code $h = symbolize(h)$ after line 13 to symbolize the data read from input file. Test harness recognizes whether the type of files under current path is image. We repeat test process for 1000 times to get accurate information of performance overhead. The result is that concrete execution spends 5326.5ms, while concolic execution costs about 9552ms. That is to say, the overhead of Conpy is about **80%**. The path condition consists of 301000 constraints.

sndhdr. The sndhdr module (*Lib/sndhdr.py*) provides utility functions which attempt to determine the type of sound data which is in a file. We reuse the test harness in the source *sndhdr.py*. Test harness recognizes whether the files under current path are sound files or not. We just make only a few modifications to run the program concolically. For example, we add a line of code $h = symbolize(h)$ after line 44. Additionally, the test process repeats 100 times in order to evaluate overhead. Time consumption for concrete execution is about 663.2ms, while the time for concolic execution is 2591.7ms. So the overhead incurred by Conpy is about **2.9** times. The generated path condition contains 30000 constraints.

6   Conclusion

Concolic execution is a promising technique for program analysis. But so far we have not observed any concolic execution tools for Python applications. In this work, we propose a concolic execution engine named Conpy. Conpy is easy to deploy and easy to use. Besides, Conpy runs in low level which produces meaningful reports. We make preliminary experiments to validate Conpy's capability of producing path conditions. Additionally, experiments show that the overhead of Conpy is low.

References

1. King, J.C.: Symbolic execution and program testing. J. ACM 19(7), 385–394 (1976)
2. Godefroid, P., Levin, M., Molnar, D.: Automated whitebox fuzz testing. In: NDSS, pp. 151–166 (2008)
3. Tillmann, N., de Halleux, J.: Pex-white box test generation for.NET. In: Beckert, B., Hähnle, R. (eds.) TAP 2008. LNCS, vol. 4966, pp. 134–153. Springer, Heidelberg (2008)
4. Cadar, C., Dunbar, D., Engler, D.: Klee: unassisted and automatic generation of high-coverage tests for complex systems programs. In: OSDI, pp. 209–224 (2008)
5. Godefroid, P., Klarlund, N., Sen, K.: DART: directed automated random testing. ACM Sigplan Notices 40(6), 213–223 (2005)
6. Sen, K., Marinov, D., Agha, G.: CUTE: A concolic unit testing engine for C. In: ESEC/FSE, pp. 263–272 (2005)
7. Fuzzgrind: An automatic fuzzing tool, http://esec-lab.sogeti.com/dotclear/index.php?pages/Fuzzgrind
8. Molnar, D.A., Wagner, D.: Catchconv: symbolic execution and run-time type inference for integer conversion errors. Tech. Rep. UC Berkeley EECS, 2007–23 (2007)
9. Chipounov, V., Kuznetsov, V., Candea, G.: S2E: A platform for in-vivo multi-path analysis of software systems. Sigarch Comput. Archit. News 39(1), 265–278 (2011)
10. Xu, R.G., Godefroid, P., Majumdar, R.: Testing for buffer overflows with length abstraction. In: ISSTA, pp. 27–37 (2008)
11. Wang, T.L., Wei, T., Gu, G.F., Zou, W.: TaintScope: A checksum-aware directed fuzzing tool for automatic software vulnerability detection. In: S&P, pp. 497–512 (2010)
12. Song, D., Brumley, D., Yin, H., Caballero, J., Jager, I., Kang, M.G., Liang, Z., Newsome, J., Poosankam, P., Saxena, P.: BitBlaze: A new approach to computer security via binary analysis. In: Sekar, R., Pujari, A.K. (eds.) ICISS 2008. LNCS, vol. 5352, pp. 1–25. Springer, Heidelberg (2008)
13. Burnim, J., Sen, K.: Heuristics for scalable dynamic test generation. In: ASE, pp. 443–446 (2008)
14. Khurshid, S., Păsăreanu, C.S., Visser, W.: Generalized symbolic execution for model checking and testing. In: Garavel, H., Hatcliff, J. (eds.) TACAS 2003. LNCS, vol. 2619, pp. 553–568. Springer, Heidelberg (2003)
15. Chen, T., Zhang, X.S., Zhu, C., Ji, X.L., Guo, S.Z., Wu, Y.: Design and implementation of a dynamic symbolic execution tool for windows executables. J. Softw-Evol. Proc. 25(12), 1249–1272 (2013)
16. Chen, T., Zhang, X.S., Xiao, X., Wu, Y., Xu, C.X., Zhao, H.T.: SEVE: Symbolic execution based vulnerability exploring system. COMPEL. 32(2), 620–637 (2013)

17. Python (programming language),
    http://en.wikipedia.org/wiki/Python_programming_language
18. Chen, T., Zhang, X.S., Guo, S.Z., Li, H.Y., Wu, Y.: State of the art: dynamic
    symbolic execution for automated test generation. Future Gener. Comp. Sy. 29(7),
    1758–1773 (2013)
19. Brumley, D., Hartwig, C., Liang, Z.K., Newsome, J., Poosankam, P., Song, D.,
    Yin, H.: Automatically identifying trigger-based behavior in malware. In: Botnet
    Detection, pp. 65–88 (2008)
20. Brumley, D., Hartwig, C., Kang, M.G., Liang, Z.K., Newsome, J., Poosankam,
    P., Song, D.: BitScope: automatically dissecting malicious binaries. Tech. Rep.
    CMU-CS-07-133 (2007)
21. Dive into python, everything is an object,
    http://www.diveintopython.net/getting_to_know_python/
    everything_is_an_object.html

A Platform for Stock Market Simulation with Distributed Agent-Based Modeling

Chunyu Wang[1], Ce Yu[1,*], Hutong Wu[1], Xiang Chen[1],
Yuelei Li[2], and Xiaotao Zhang[2]

[1] School of Computer Science and Technology, Tianjin University, Tianjin, China
[2] School of Economics and Management, Tianjin University, Tianjin, China
{wangchunyu,yuce,wht}@tju.edu.cn

Abstract. Agent-based modeling (ABM) has been widely used in stock market simulation. However, traditional simulations of stock markets with ABM on single computers are limited by the computing capability as breakthroughs in financial research need much larger amount of agents. This paper introduces a platform for stock market simulation with ABM focusing on large scale parallel agents in a distributed computing environment such as Cluster and MPP. With the customized trade strategies inside the agents, the runtime system of the platform can distribute the massive amount of agents to multiple computing nodes automatically during the execution of the simulation. And agents exchange information with each other and the market through a uniform communication system. With this platform financial researchers can design their own financial model without caring about the complexity of parallelization and related problems. The sample simulation on the platform is verified to be compatible with the data from Euronext-NYSE and the platform shows fair scalability and performance under different parallelism configurations.

Keywords: stock market simulation, agent-based modeling, parallel, distributed environment.

1 Introduction

The simulation of financial markets, such as stock markets, is an important method in behavioral finance to reveal the irrational behavior and decision-making laws. Financial markets can be regarded as complex adaptive systems described by a large number of variables, which are in turn influenced by an even larger number of factors or investors [1], and agent-based modeling (ABM) is an efficient method to simulate complex adaptive systems. In ABM, each agent individually assesses its situation and makes decisions on the basis of a set of rules. The potential system-level consequences of financial market are reflected through the behaviors of sets of agents [2]. With ABM, a financial market is simulated as a collection of autonomous decision-making entities called agents, and a market

---

* Corresponding author.

X.-h. Sun et al. (Eds.): ICA3PP 2014, Part II, LNCS 8631, pp. 164–177, 2014.

in which stocks or bonds are exchanged. ABM has been applied in some simulations of stock market [3][4], but the schedule of agents in these simulations is sequential, which is not corresponding with the situation in real world where the agents (investors participating in stock market) think and behave concurrently. Besides, with the development of behavioral finance, it is needed to expand the amount of agents in a stock market to achieve breakthrough research results. But when number of agents is much larger, these sequential simulations show bad performance. So we adapt traditional ABM method to parallel agent-based modeling, which has been applied in some complex adaptive systems [5].

Massive parallel agents requires greater computing capability beyond single computer server. This paper proposes a platform called PSSPAM (Platform for Stock market Simulation with Parallel Agent-based Modeling) to support the stock market simulation with large amount of parallel agents. The platform is designed for distributed environments with multi processors, which can provide much greater computing capability than a single processor. With the increasing of agent number, the distributed platform shows a good scalability. Also PSS-PAM supports easy customization for new financial models provided by users. For researchers in financial field, they are just concerned with financial items in stock market simulation and try to avoid being trapped in complex computer related stuff. The platform handles parallel programming and completes the frame of a basic stock market so that financial researchers can extend their own algorithms without being confused by the complexity in parallel programming. Another advantage of PSSPAM is its modularity with four loosely coupled modules: i) Communication system, providing message interface for agents to interact with the market and shield the distributed environment from the agents, ii) Agents module, defining agents and their behaviors, iii) Market module, a mimic of a real stock exchange, iv) User interface, handling interaction with users.

The rest of paper is organized as the follows. In section 2, we discuss related works. Section 3 introduces the architecture of the PSSPAM. Section 4 presents the experiments evaluating this platform. And in Section 5, we summarize current work and suggest questions for the future.

2   Related Works

The dynamics of the stock markets results from the behavior of many interacting agents, leading to emergent phenomena that are best understood by using a bottom-up approach: ABM (Agent-Based Modeling) [6]. Since it is proposed in 1980s, the study on financial field with ABM has developed much further.

Traditionally, the stock markets with ABM are on single processor and the agents involved in run sequentially. Such works focus on the financial model and learning algorithms of agents. SFI-ASM (Santa Fe Institute Artificial Stock Market) is a famous achievement among all the works. The first generation SFI-ASM was published in 1994 [7]. The authors said in [8] that the Santa Fe Market is a computer-based model that can be altered, experimented with, and studied in a rigorously controlled way. Most of the artificial market's features are malleable and can be changed to carry out different experiments. But SFI-ASM is not of extensible structure and the financial researchers have to change the source code of SFI-ASM to achieve their own market model. Additionally, running on single processors restricts the amount of agents in the artificial stock market. And all the agents in SFI-ASM are of sequential manner, which cannot reflect the concurrent behaviors of investors in real world. Up to now, there are many researches or improvements on SFI-ASM [9][10], but these works are launched in financial perspective, and cannot solve the problems above.

The development of computer technology, especially in high performance computing, brings new opportunity for ABM to make breakthroughs in multi-processor environments. RepastHPC (Repast for High Performance Computing) is a toolkit for parallel agent-based modeling in distributed environments. It is improved on the base of Repast (Recursive Porous Agent Simulation Toolkit), which is a set of libraries that allows programmers to build simulation environments, create agents in social networks, collect data from simulations automatically, and build user interfaces easily [11]. RepastHPC is a useful and usable framework, a complete ABM simulation platform developed explicitly for larger scale distributed computing systems that leverages modern C++ techniques and the ReLogo language [2]. Communication in RepastHPC is implemented by MPI. Besides RepastHPC, there are several other works [12][13] describe the toolkits for general parallel agent-based modeling. These platforms are not specialized in financial field, and building a stock market simulation with these toolkits seems complex for financial experts who just want to focus on financial items. Artificial Open Market (ATOM) is a highly flexible agent-based model of financial markets in an API form [14]. It allows distributed simulations with many computers interacting through a network as well as localhost. ATOM stresses too much on the equity among all the agents. In ATOM, each agent sends at most one order during a "round table discussion" [14], which makes agents behave in a synchronized way. While in the real world, traders behave concurrently and independently. In this paper, we introduce parallel agents into stock market simulation to mimic the concurrent features of real traders.

PSSPAM in this paper builds the basic skeleton of a stock market simulation, and at the same time, provides the interface for financial researchers to easily extend this simulation with their own algorithms or methods. Furthermore, the platform is designed for distributed environments so that it can support large amount of parallel agents. PSSPAM also introduces a communication system to support different types of logical network topology of agents in distributed environments.

3   PSSPAM Platform for Distributed Environments

The architecture of PSSPAM is based on the Agent-based Modeling method, which generally consists with two parts: individual agents and the environment they interact with. In the platform, the agents represent individual investors, and the environment is the stock market. As in the real world, agents communicate with each other and participate in the market to trade stocks. PSSPAM is also designed for researchers in financial field, hiding the programming details from them. Thus the user interface is ease of use for financial researchers.

3.1   Logical Architecture of PSSPAM

The logical architecture of PSSPAM is depicted in Fig. 1. There are four relatively independent modules in the platform, namely communication system, agents module, market module, and the user interface module. Physical layer is the distributed environment that the platform will run on, such as Cluster, MPP, or other types of distributed computing environment.

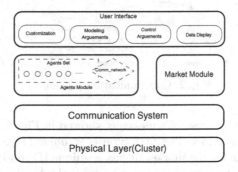

Fig. 1. Logical Architecture of PSSPAM

The communication system provides interaction interface for agents to communicate with each other and with the market. Due to the system, the distributed environment is transparent to agents module and market module. The agents module has two components: the collection of all the agents, and the network. The network defines the logical network topology of all the agents. The agents reside on different nodes, and the number of agents on each node is determined by the control arguments from user interface. The market module is a model of stock market in real world, such as Shanghai Stock Exchange and it is simplified to a market model trading only one stock. It can sustain large amount of concurrent access from agents. The platform is fairly extensible by supporting customization in agents module and market module. The user interface is the top layer to handle the interaction with users, such as configuration and execution of simulations.

3.2   Communication System

As the agents are distributed in different nodes, it's difficult for them to communicate with each other directly. We introduce an efficient communication system to provide message interfaces for the agents module and market module, so that agents can communicate with each other and the market without the knowledge of physical information of the destination. We take a compromise between a centralized communication mode and a point-to-point mode: on each node there is a local server responsible for forwarding the messages of local agents; and all the local servers communicate with each other in a point-to-point mode. The compromised scheme is depicted in Fig. 2. Usually on the market node, there is only the market and the local server. The local server on each node is like a postman whose task is to deliver the message according to the destination. And the local server here is also responsible for parsing the destination, because that the physical location of all the agents and the market is maintained by local servers.

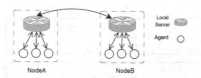

Fig. 2. Communication scheme

During the delivery process of a message, showed in Fig. 3, the destination of the message has three types. The first type is $< agentID >$, which is used in the agents module. As for the market, it has a unique ID to identify itself. When the message comes to the communication system, the local server will parse the destination to the type of $< node, queue >$, where "node" is the name of the node that the destination agent locates in, and "queue" refers to the receive queue of the destination agent. When the message posted from the communication system to physical layer, it comes to the local area network, and the node name will be transferred to IP address. Then the delivery will be done by general network.

After the message arrives at the destination node, a reverse parsing process will be done to get the ID of the destination: an agent or the market. Then the agent or the market can just invoke the message interface to get messages from its own receive queue.

With this mechanism of delivery, the physical layer is transparent to agents module and market module, thus the two modules are physical environment-independent.

3.3   Agents Module

The agents module consists of two submodules: agents set and the communication network model. Agents set is the collection of agents that reside on distributed nodes. Communication network model defines the social relationship of all the agents.

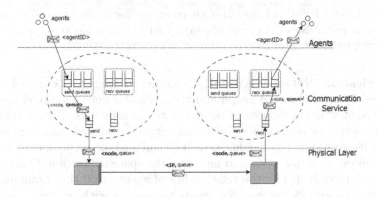

Fig. 3. Communication system

Agents Set. In agent-based modeling, an agent is a complete and independent individual. It receives messages from outside and adapts itself according to the messages. In PSSPAM, we define the agent as investor agent (ItAgent), a simulation for real investors. The structure of ItAgent is depicted in Fig. 4. Kernel specifies the activity flow of an ItAgent during its lifetime. Generally, in the lifetime of an ItAgent, it is continuously repeating the course: making decision and behaving as the result of the decision indicates which can be submitting an order or getting data from the market. MsgInterface contains send/receive methods and send/receive buffers. Actually the message interface is an application of the communication system. Adjacency list contains the agents with which the ItAgent can directly communicate. The list is defined according to the communication network model, which is configurable. Assets as well as history data forms the internal state of ItAgent. Assets refer to all the cash and stock an ItAgent owns. History data is the accumulated data in each course cycle of ItAgent and the content of data varies according to different decision methods, as different algorithms may reference to different history data.

The internal state evolves during the lifetime of ItAgent, which is a concrete manifestation of self-adaptation. Usually an agent achieves self-adaption through continuously learning, and for ItAgent, the learning process embodies in the

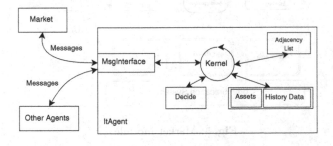

Fig. 4. Investor agent

decide procedure. PSSPAM provides an interface for users to customize their own decision methods, so that the platform can be extended to support agents with varying levels of intelligence.

Communication Network Model. Communication network model can be represented by an undirected graph and the scale of a network model increases with a speed of n^2 as the number of agent denoted by n increases. Due to the large amount of agents, a network model is even larger, so in each agent there is an adjacency list containing its neighbors rather than a whole network model, which avoids unnecessary duplication and improves the space utilization. Communication network models specify the relationship of agents, and the communication system provides an efficient way for agents to interact with neighbors specified in network models, which indicates that the communication is compatible with various network models. In PSSPAM, we also provide the interfaces for users to customize the network.

3.4 Market Module

Market is a simple model of the real exchange market. It has the basic functions of a real market, namely, matching orders, storing data, and displaying data. As it shows in Fig. 5, there are three separate areas in the market module, and they are loosely coupled, which makes the market module easily extended. The register area maintains a global ID table, and allocates a unique ID for each agent participated in the market. Agent response area is responsible for all the requests from agents. It parses the requests, and calls the corresponding handler to handle the request. As it may have additional requests in the customized decision method, we provide the interface for users to define new handlers. Trading area matching orders sent by agents. The data generated during the register and trade process is stored in database, and there is a user interaction handler to deal with the data display request from the user interface.

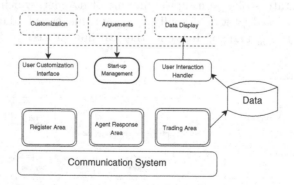

Fig. 5. Market module

Agent Response Area. Agent response area is the port of market module. Messages sent to market are treated as requests by this area and it parses various requests and then invokes different handlers to handle them. Due to the large number of parallel agents, there will be large amount of requests queuing in the receive queue of the market. To deal with the large amount of requests efficiently, we introduce a worker pool to agent response area, as it shows in Fig. 6. Each time a request is fetched from the receive queue, the area will take a worker to deal with this request. Parsing request is done concurrently in each worker rather than being done sequentially before a worker is taken. In this way, the requests in the receive queue will be consumed as quickly as possible. After parsing the request, the worker invokes corresponding handler to handle the request. Predefined handlers in the system include register handler and order handler. Users can also define their own request handlers to coordinate with customized decision methods of agents module.

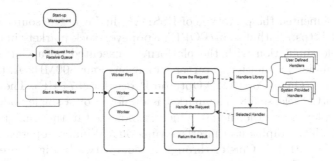

Fig. 6. Agent response area

Trading Area. In a real market, the auction mechanism defines the occasion of matching orders. Generally there are two kinds of auction mechanism, namely Call Auction mechanism and Continuous mechanism. With Call Auction mechanism, the matching just happens at the end of a trading period. With Continuous Auction mechanism, the matching happens each time when an order is submitted to the market. Trading area supports both auction mechanisms. Different auction mechanisms usually go with varies matching rules which specify the conditions under which two orders can be matched. To customize a matching rule, users need to specify the matching conditions as well as how to insert an order into sell/buy queues according to the matching conditions. Sell/buy queues are the shared field of all the order handlers, and can be concurrently accessed by multi handlers, as it shows in Fig. 7. To ensure the operations on sell/buy queues, we implement the safety insert and get operations on the queues and package them as interface. So that the users need only focus on the matching rule, without being trapped in the details of concurrent visit to a shared field.

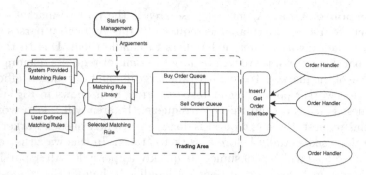

Fig. 7. Trading area

4   Experiments

We have implemented the prototype of PSSPAM in Java. The source codes can be fetched at https://github.com/POPEYEpopeye/stock-market-simulation.

The sample simulation with the platform is executed on a Cluster with 5 nodes. Each node is a multi-core server which has four 800MHz AMD processors with 4cores (Quad-Core AMD Opteron Processor 8374 HE). The operating system is CentOS release 5.8. The market is deployed on a single node, and the agents are deployed on other nodes, which is indicated in the configuration file of xml format. The graphic user interface runs on a Windows operating system, communicating with this Cluster through a local network. Fig. 8 presents this graphic interface. Fig. 8(a)is the control panel, managing the simulation configurations, and Fig. 8(b) is the data panel, displaying the trading results in real time.

We conduct experiments respectively to verify the validity of the simulation platform and evaluate the scalability and performance of the platform. In these experiments, the market is customized with Continuous Auction mechanism [15] and agents use a random strategy [15].

Firstly, we ran the sample simulation to verify whether PSSPAM can generate major stylized facts that are usually found in real-world stock markets. These

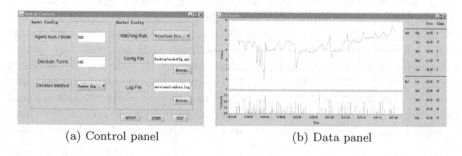

(a) Control panel   (b) Data panel

Fig. 8. Graphic user interface

stylized facts are reposted in [15], and for the sake of simplicity we only present a form of the classical departure from Normality of asset returns. The distribution of asset returns does not follow the normal distribution, but appears the property of sharp peaked and heavy tailed [15]. Sharp peaked indicates that the peak value (frequency near mean returns) is higher than the theoretical value estimated with normal distribution, while heavy tailed means that the frequency at the end is also higher than the theoretical value estimated with normal distribution, indicating that low probability events are more likely to happen in real world. Fig. 9(b) is the distribution of asset returns of a specific stock on Euronext-NYSE. The curve is the fitted result of asset returns using normal distribution and the histogram is the exact frequency distribution of asset returns, which shows a typical feature of sharp peaked and heavy tailed.

Fig.9(a) depicts the departure from normality of asset returns when using random strategy, and shows the sharp peaked, heavy tailed property of stock market, suggesting that PSSPAM produces stylized facts in line with those observed for a specific stock on Euronext-NYSE. This experiment results prove that PSSPAM is a valid mimic of stock markets.

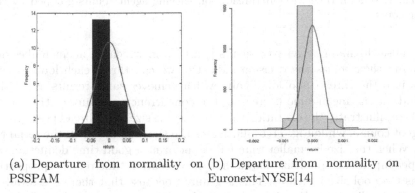

(a) Departure from normality on PSSPAM

(b) Departure from normality on Euronext-NYSE[14]

Fig. 9. PSSPAM produces stylized facts in line with those observed on Euronext-NYSE

Secondly, we ran a series of experiments to evaluate the performance and scalability of PSSPAM. For simplicity there is no communication among agents in these experiments. In agents module, there are two methods to implement the running of all the agents. The first one is that each thread takes care of one agent, executing the kernel of that agent, so the threads are as many as the number of agents. To test the scalability of the simulation platform with this method, we present the execution time for varying agent counts grouped by computing cores, depicted in Fig. 10. The abscissa is the total number of agents running in the simulation, representing the scale of the simulation. For same agent counts the platform achieves a good time reduction with increasing cores, and this trend keeps well as agent counts increase. It also shows that PSSPAM scales weakly at smaller number of agents but scales well at larger numbers, as with agents increasing, the computation time instead of the cost of creating and scheduling threads conducts the execution time. This means that PSSPAM performs a good scalability in distributed environments. But when the number of agents exceeds 1600, there will be too much agents connecting the market at the same time, resulting in timeout error at market. To overcome this problem, we proposed another method of using thread pool to coordinate all the agents.

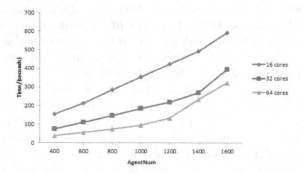

Fig. 10. Execution time without threadPool, varying agent counts grouped by computing cores

Because the main activity of agents is a loop in which an agent makes decisions and then act as the decision indicates, we can throw each loop of every agent into the thread pool randomly, which achieves same results as the first method, at the mean time decreasing the concurrency pressure of the market. Fig. 11(a) illustrates the execution time for varying sizes of a thread pool grouped by agent counts, while Fig. 11(b) illustrates the speedup based on the serial running. When the size is smaller than 64, it performs a good time deduction, and the speedup at each pool size shows that the execution time reduces proportionally as the pool size increases. This is granted because that there are totally 64 cores in the distributed environment, so that the time consumption is mainly donated by the computing of each agent, with rarely threads scheduling costs. This property keeps well as agent counts increase, presenting a good scalability of the platform. When the pool size exceeds 64, there is still a time reduction as pool size increases, but the growth rate of speedup is evidently slower. This results due to the threads scheduling in each processor, and this cost increases as there are more threads. The trend of slower growth rate lasts to 256 threads for agent counts less than 1200, while for agent counts larger than 1200, this trend keeps till 128 threads. And then it finally reaches a roughly stable execution time for each agent count, which is limited by the concurrent and synchronized processing in the market. During the stable stage, the average concurrent connections to market should be generally stable. While with the same pool size, the total connections increase with the agent counts increasing, bringing much more scheduling cost, resulting that the speedup decreases as the agent counts

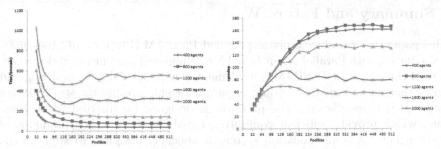

(a) Execution time for varying pool sizes grouped by agent counts

(b) Speedup for varying pool sizes grouped by agent counts

Fig. 11. Execution result using threadPool

increase. To further enhance the performance of this platform, more optimization needs to be done at the market.

Fig. 12 shows the comparison of the minimum execution time at various agent counts respectively with the two methods. When agent counts is less than 1200, the execution time with each method is nearly the same and when agent counts is larger, the method using thread pool is more efficient than the first method. This results from that there is much less threads creation and scheduling consumption when using thread pool and when agent counts is smaller, the total execution time is mainly donated by computing and these consumption can be neglected; but when the agent counts is larger, these consumption in the first method is much greater than that in the method using thread pool. What's more, too much concurrent threads will bring heavy connection pressure for market, which is more likely to generate timeout errors. So we can conclude that using a thread pool to implement the execution of agents is a better way rather than running them directly with newly created threads.

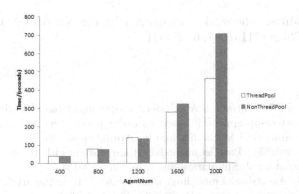

Fig. 12. Execution time comparison of the two methods at various agent counts

5   Summary and Future Work

In this paper, we introduce a platform called PSSPAM (Platform of Stock market Simulation with Parallel Agent-based Modeling) and present the architecture design of this platform. PSSPAM is implemented with agent-based modeling and extends this method to large amount of parallel agents, so that the stock market simulation is more efficient. The platform is designed for distributed environments, which provide sufficient computing capability for the large amount of parallel agents. A communication system is specially designed to support the interaction of agents and the market residing on distributed environments and it is compatible with various communication network models that define the social relationship of all the agents. Another contribution of the PSSPAM is that financial researchers can use this platform to customize their own algorithms of decision methods and matching rules without considering details of parallel programming. Users can specify the decision method of agents and the auction mechanism, either by selecting pre-defined methods or programming their own methods. To support fair extensibility, PSSPAM also allows users to customize different network structure in agents module, and more request handlers in market module. In addition, this platform provides a graphical user interface, so that researchers on finance can easily extend this stock market and conveniently control the configuration of deployment and running through parameters. We conduct a series of experiment to verify the correctness of the simulation and evaluate the performance and scalability of the platform.

The paper gives a detailed design scheme of PSSPAM and a referenced implementation of the platform. PSSPAM is still under development and needs more supplements and improvements in the future. For instance, the communication system is under evaluated and the market is also need to be optimized for better scalability. There is still much work to be done to enhance the system's robustness and performance. It is also hoped that more graphical tools can be provided to simplify users customization.

Acknowledgments. The work is sponsored by the National Natural Science Foundation of China (71131007, 61303021).

References

1. Lye, R., Tan, J.P.L., Cheong, S.A.: Understanding agent-based models of financial markets: A bottom-up approach based on order parameters and phase diagrams. J. Physica A: Statistical Mechanics and its Applications 391, 5521–5531 (2012)
2. Collier, N., North, M.: Parallel agent-based simulation with Repast for high performance computing. J. Simulation 89, 1215–1235 (2013)
3. Johnson, P.E.: Agent-based modeling: what I learned from the artificial stock market. J. Social Science Computer Review 20, 174–186 (2002)
4. Chen, S.H., Yeh, C.H.: Evolving traders and the business school with genetic programming: A new architecture of the agent-based artificial stock market. J. Journal of Economic Dynamics and Control 25, 363–393 (2001)

5. Deissenberg, C., Van Der Hoog, S.: EURACE: A massively parallel agent-based model of the European economy. J. Applied Mathematics and Computation 204, 541–552 (2008)
6. Bonabeau, E.: Agent-based modeling: Methods and techniques for simulating human systems. J. Proceedings of the National Academy of Sciences of the United States of America 99, 7280–7287 (2002)
7. LeBaron, B.: Building the Santa Fe artificial stock market. J. Physica A (2002)
8. Arthur, W.B.: Asset pricing under endogenous expectations in an artificial stock market. Diss. Brunel University, London (1996)
9. LeBaron, B.: Evolution and time horizons in an agent based stock market. J. Macroeconomic Dynamics 5, 225–254 (2001)
10. Ehrentreich, N.: The Santa Fe artificial stock market re-examined-suggested corrections. Technical report, Computational Economics series of EconWPA (2002)
11. Gilbert, N., Bankes, S.: Platforms and methods for agent-based modeling. J. Proceedings of the National Academy of Sciences of America 99, 7197–7198 (2002)
12. Kiran, M., Richmond, P., Holcombe, M., Chin, L.S., Worth, D.: FLAME: Simulating large populations of agents on parallel hardware architectures. In: 9th International Conference on Autonomous Agents and Multiagent Systems, pp. 1633–1636. International Foundation for Autonomous Agents and Multiagent Systems, Toronto (2010)
13. Scheutz, M., Schermerhorn, P., Connaughaton, R., Dingler, A.: SWAGES: an extendable distributed experimentation system for large-scale agent-based ALife simulations. J. Proceedings of Artificial Life X 412–419 (2006)
14. Mathieu, P., Brandouy, O.: A Generic Architecture for Realistic Simulations of Complex Financial Dynamics. In: Demazeau, Y., Dignum, F., Corchado, J.M., Pérez, J.B. (eds.) Advances in PAAMS. AISC, vol. 70, pp. 185–197. Springer, Heidelberg (2010)
15. Cont, R.: Empirical properties of asset returns: Stylized facts and statistical issues. J. Quantitative Finance 1, 223–236 (2001)

C2CU : A CUDA C Program Generator for Bulk Execution of a Sequential Algorithm

Daisuke Takafuji, Koji Nakano, and Yasuaki Ito

Department of Information Engineering,
Hiroshima University,
Kagamiyama 1-4-1, Higashi Hiroshima, 739-8527 Japan

Abstract. A sequential algorithm is oblivious if an address accessed at each time does not depend on input data. Many important tasks including matrix computation, signal processing, sorting, dynamic programming, and encryption/decryption can be performed by oblivious sequential algorithms. Bulk execution of a sequential algorithm is to execute it for many independent inputs in turn or in parallel. The main contribution of this paper is to develop a tool that generates a CUDA C program for the bulk execution of an oblivious sequential algorithm. More specifically, our tool automatically converts a C language program describing an oblivious sequential algorithm into a CUDA C program that performs the bulk execution of the C language program. Generated C programs can be executed in CUDA-enabled GPUs. We have implemented CUDA C programs for the bulk execution of bitonic sorting algorithm, Floyd-Warshall algorithm, and Montgomery modulo multiplication. Our implementations running on GeForce GTX Titan for the bulk execution can be 199 times faster for bitonic sort, 54 times faster for Floyd-Warshall algorithm, and 78 times faster for Montgomery modulo multiplication, over the implementations on a single Intel Xeon CPU.

Keywords: GPGPU, CUDA, bulk execution, oblivious algorithms, Floyd-Warshall algorithm, Montgomery modulo multiplication.

1 Introduction

A Graphics Processing Unit (GPU) is a specialized circuit designed to accelerate computation for building and manipulating images [1–3]. Latest GPUs are designed for general purpose computing and can perform computation in applications traditionally handled by the CPU. Hence, GPUs have recently attracted the attention of many application developers [1, 4–7]. NVIDIA provides a parallel computing architecture called *CUDA* (Compute Unified Device Architecture) [8], the computing engine for NVIDIA GPUs. CUDA gives developers access to the virtual instruction set and memory of the parallel computational elements in NVIDIA GPUs. In many cases, GPUs are more efficient than multicore processors [9], since they have hundreds of processor cores and very high memory bandwidth.

X.-h. Sun et al. (Eds.): ICA3PP 2014, Part II, LNCS 8631, pp. 178–191, 2014.

CUDA uses two types of memories in the NVIDIA GPUs: *the shared memory* and *the global memory* [8]. The shared memory is an extremely fast on-chip memory with lower capacity, say, 16-48 Kbytes. The global memory is implemented as an off-chip DRAM, and thus, it has large capacity, say, 1.5-6 Gbytes, but its access latency is very long. The efficient usage of the shared memory and the global memory is a key for CUDA developers to accelerate applications using GPUs. In particular, we need to consider *the bank conflict* of the shared memory access and *the coalescing* of the global memory access [6, 9, 10]. The address space of the shared memory is mapped into several physical memory banks. If two or more threads access the same memory bank at the same time, the access requests are processed in turn. Hence, to maximize the memory access performance, CUDA threads should access the distinct memory banks to avoid the bank conflicts of the memory accesses. To maximize the bandwidth between the GPU and the DRAM chips, the consecutive addresses of the global memory must be accessed at the same time. Thus, CUDA threads should perform coalesced access and avoid stride access when they access the global memory. However, it is not an easy task for CUDA developers to design efficient parallel algorithms that does not perform stride memory access.

The bulk execution of a sequential algorithm is to execute it for many independent inputs in turn or in parallel. For example, suppose that we have p arrays $b_0, b_1, \ldots b_{p-1}$ of n points each. We can execute the Fourier transform of each b_j ($0 \leq j \leq p-1$) by executing the FFT algorithm for n points on a single CPU in turn or on a parallel machine in parallel. The bulk execution of an FFT is frequently used in the area of image processing and signal processing. Further, the bulk execution is widely used in many applications. For example, plain text is partitioned into substrings with the same size when we encrypt it. The substrings are encrypted in turn to obtain encrypted text.

Intuitively, a sequential algorithm is *oblivious* if an address accessed at each time unit is independent of the input. For example, the prefix-sums of an array b of size n can be computed by executing $b[i] \leftarrow b[i] + b[i-1]$ for all i ($1 \leq i \leq n-1$) in turn. This prefix-sum algorithm is oblivious because the address accessed at each time unit is independent of the values stored in b. The readers may think that the oblivious memory access is too restricted, and most useful algorithms are not oblivious. However, many important and complicated tasks including many matrix computations, signal processing, sorting, dynamic programming, and encryption/decryption can be performed by oblivious sequential algorithms.

In our previous paper [11], we have introduced an algorithmic technique performing the bulk execution of a sequential algorithm on the GPU and evaluated the performance using the Unified Memory Machine (UMM). The UMM is a theoretical parallel computing machine used to evaluate the performance of the computation on the GPU. The resulting implementation on the UMM performs the bulk execution for p independent inputs in $O(\frac{pt}{w} + lt)$ time units using p threads on the UMM if a sequential algorithm is oblivious, where w is the number of threads in a warp, l is the global memory access latency, and t is the running time of a sequential algorithm. It also proved that this implementation is time optimal. Further, it implemented the prefix-sum algorithm and the dynamic programming algorithm using this algorithmic technique and obtained a speedup factor of 150 over the sequential computation by a single CPU. However, developers need to write CUDA C programs for the bulk execution of a sequential algorithm. Since it needs deep knowledge of CUDA programming and GPU architecture to optimize CUDA C programs, it is not an easy task to write efficient CUDA C programs for the bulk execution.

The main contribution of this paper is to present a tool, *C2CU*, that converts a sequential C program into a CUDA C program with no stride memory access. More specifically, a sequential program written by C programming language is given to C2CU. C2CU converts it into a CUDA C program that performs the bulk execution of a sequential program on CUDA-enabled GPUs. The CUDA C program thus obtained performs no stride global memory access of GPUs. Hence, even developers with few knowledge of CUDA C programming and GPU architecture can automatically generate a CUDA C program for the bulk execution. Once they write a C program for a sequential algorithm, they can obtain a CUDA C program for the bulk execution using our tool C2CU.

To see the performance of CUDA C programs generated by our C2CU converter, we have measured the running time of the bulk execution of three oblivious sequential algorithms: bitonic sort [12, 13], Floyd-Warshall algorithm [14–16], and Montgomery modulo multiplication [17–19]. For this purpose, we first have written sequential algorithms for these three algorithms by C programming language. We then have converted them into CUDA C programs using our C2CU converter. CUDA C programs thus obtained have been executed on GeForce GTX Titan. They run 199 times faster for bitonic sort, 54 times faster for Floyd-Warshall algorithm, and 78 times faster for Montgomery modulo multiplication, over the implementations on a single Intel Xeon CPU.

2   The Bulk Execution of Sequential Algorithms on the UMM

The main purpose of this section is to review the bulk execution of sequential algorithms on the Unified Memory Machine(UMM). Please see [11] for the details.

Intuitively, a sequential algorithm is *oblivious* if an address accessed in each time unit is independent of the input. More specifically, there exists a function $a : \{0, 1, \ldots, t-1\} \to \mathcal{N}$, where t is the running time of the algorithm and $\mathcal{N}$ is a set of all non-negative integers such that, for any input of the algorithm, it accesses address $a(i)$ or does not access the memory at each time i ($0 \leq i \leq t-1$). In other words, at each time i ($0 \leq i \leq t-1$), it never accesses an address other than $a(i)$.

Let us see an example of oblivious algorithms. Suppose that an array b of n integers are given. The prefix-sum computation is a task to store each i-th prefix-sum $b[0] + b[1] + \cdots + b[i]$ in $b[i]$. Let r be a register variable. The following algorithm computes the prefix-sum of n numbers.

[Algorithm Prefix-sums]
$r \leftarrow 0$
for $i \leftarrow 0$ to $n - 1$ do
  $r \leftarrow r + b[i]$
  $b[i] \leftarrow r$

Since $b[0]$, $b[1]$, ..., $b[n-1]$ are added to r in turn, the prefix-sums are stored in b correctly when this algorithm terminates. Let us see the address accessed in each time unit to confirm that this algorithm is oblivious. For simplicity, we ignore access to registers and local computation such as addition and we assume that such operations can be done in zero time unit. Clearly, memory access operations performed in this algorithm are: read $b[0]$, write $b[0]$, read $b[1]$, write $b[1]$, ..., read $b[n-1]$, and write $b[n-1]$. Hence, the memory access function a is $a(2i) = a(2i+1) = i$ for all i ($0 \leq i \leq n-1$), and thus, this algorithm is oblivious.

Suppose that we need to execute a sequential algorithm for many independent inputs on a single CPU in turn or on a parallel machine at the same time. We call such computation the *bulk execution*. For example, suppose that we have p arrays $b_0, b_1, \ldots, b_{p-1}$ of size n each on the UMM. The goal of the bulk execution of the prefix-sums is to execute the prefix-sums of every b_j ($0 \leq j \leq p-1$) on the UMM in parallel. We use p threads and each thread j ($0 \leq j \leq p-1$) executes the prefix-sums of b_i by Algorithm Prefix-sums. Let r_j ($0 \leq j \leq p-1$) be a register of thread j. The prefix-sums can be computed in parallel by the following algorithm:

[Parallel Algorithm Prefix-sums]
for $j \leftarrow 0$ to $p-1$ do in parallel
  $r_j \leftarrow 0$
  for $i \leftarrow 0$ to $n-1$ do
    $r_j \leftarrow r_j + b_j[i]$
    $b_j[i] \leftarrow r_j$

In our previous paper [11], we have evaluated the running time of the bulk execution of the prefix-sums algorithm for column-wise arrangement on the Unified Memory Machine (UMM) [20, 21]. The UMM captures the essence of the global memory access of CUDA-enabled GPUs. The UMM has three parameters: the number p of threads, width w, and memory access latency l. Each thread is a Random Access Machine (RAM) [22], which can execute fundamental operations in a time unit. Threads are executed in SIMD [23] fashion, and run on the same program and work on the different data. The p threads are partitioned into $\frac{p}{w}$ groups of w threads each called *warp*. The $\frac{p}{w}$ warps are dispatched for the memory access in turn, and w threads in a dispatched warp send the memory access requests to the memory banks (MBs) through the memory management unit (MMU). We do not discuss the architecture of the MMU, but we can think that it is a multistage interconnection network in which the memory access requests are moved to destination memory banks in a pipeline fashion. Note that the UMM with width w has w memory banks and each warp has w threads.

MBs constitute a single address space of the memory. A single address space of the memory is mapped to the MBs in an interleaved way such that the word of data of address i is stored in the $(i \bmod w)$-th bank $B[i \bmod w]$, where w is the number of MBs. In the UMM, a single set of address lines from the MMU is connected to the MBs. Hence, the same address value is broadcast to every MB, and the same address of the MBs can be accessed at each time unit. Also, we assume that MBs are accessed in a pipeline fashion with latency l. In other words, if a thread sends a memory access request, it takes at least l time units to complete it. A thread can send a new memory access request only after the completion of the previous memory access request and thus, it can send at most one memory access request in l time units. Let $A[j] = \{j \cdot w, j \cdot w + 1, \ldots, (j + 1) \cdot w - 1\}$ denote the j-th address group. In the UMM, if multiple memory access requests by a warp are destined for different address groups, they are processed separately. Figure 1 illustrates the memory access by two warps $W(0)$ and $W(1)$. Since memory access requests by $W(0)$ are destined for three address groups, they occupy three pipeline stages. On the other hand, those by $W(1)$ are destined for the same bank, they occupy only one stages. Thus it takes $3(\text{stages}) + 1(\text{stage}) + 5(\text{pipeline stages}) - 1 = 8$ time units to complete memory access requests in Figure 1.

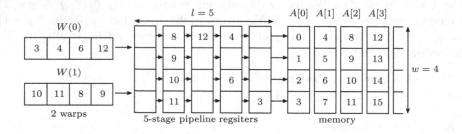

Fig. 1. The memory access of Unified Memory Machine (UMM) with width $w = 4$ and latency $l = 5$

Suppose that each element $b_j[i]$ $(0 \le i \le n - 1, 0 \le j \le p - 1)$ is arranged in address $i \cdot p + j$ of the global memory as illustrated in Figure 2. Suppose that the bulk execution of an oblivious algorithm running in t time units is performed for p inputs with column-wise arrangement on the UMM. Clearly, pt memory access operations are performed at all and all memory access operations by all warps are coalesced. Also, each thread on the UMM performs t memory access operations, each of which takes l time units. Thus, we have the following theorem:

Theorem 1 ([11]). *A column-wise oblivious computation of size $n \times p$ runs $O(\frac{pt}{w} + lt)$ time units using p threads on the UMM with width w and latency l, where t is the running time of the corresponding oblivious sequential algorithm.*

Please see [11] for the details of the proof of Theorem 1.

0	1	2	3	4	5	6	7
$b_0[0]$	$b_1[0]$	$b_2[0]$	$b_3[0]$	$b_4[0]$	$b_5[0]$	$b_6[0]$	$b_7[0]$
8	9	10	11	12	13	14	15
$b_0[1]$	$b_1[1]$	$b_2[1]$	$b_3[1]$	$b_4[1]$	$b_5[1]$	$b_6[1]$	$b_7[1]$
16	17	18	19	20	21	22	23
$b_0[2]$	$b_1[2]$	$b_2[2]$	$b_3[2]$	$b_4[2]$	$b_5[2]$	$b_6[2]$	$b_7[2]$
24	25	26	27	28	29	30	31
$b_0[3]$	$b_1[3]$	$b_2[3]$	$b_3[3]$	$b_4[3]$	$b_5[3]$	$b_6[3]$	$b_7[3]$
32	33	34	35	36	37	38	39
$b_0[4]$	$b_1[4]$	$b_2[4]$	$b_3[4]$	$b_4[4]$	$b_5[4]$	$b_6[4]$	$b_7[4]$
40	41	42	43	44	45	46	47
$b_0[5]$	$b_1[5]$	$b_2[5]$	$b_3[5]$	$b_4[5]$	$b_5[5]$	$b_6[5]$	$b_7[5]$

Fig. 2. Column-wise arrangement of $p = 8$ arrays of $n = 6$ elements each

3   Our C2CU Converter

The main purpose of this section is to describe C2CU converter, that converts a sequential algorithm written by C programming language into CUDA C program for the bulk execution on CUDA-enabled GPUs.

Figure 3 illustrates the behavior of C2CU converter. A sequential program written by C programming language is converted into a CUDA C program. The converted C program accepts p independent inputs. They are copied to the device memory (global memory) of the GPU. The CUDA device program with p threads is spawned, and each thread executes the sequential program for one input. After all threads terminate, p outputs obtained by all threads are copied to the host memory.

Let us see how C2CU converter generates CUDA C program using Floyd-Warshall algorithm [14–16] as an example. Floyd-Warshall algorithm is a well known graph theoretic algorithm that computes the distances of the shortest paths of all pairs of nodes in a directed graph. It uses a 2-dimensional array D of size $n \times n$ for an n-node graph. We assume that, initially, $D[i][j]$ $(0 \leq i, j \leq n-1)$

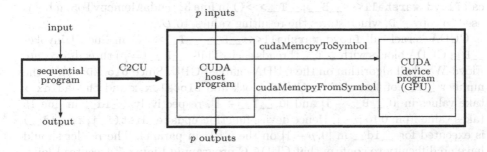

Fig. 3. The behavior of C2CU converter

stores the distance of an edge from node i to j if it exists and $+\infty$ otherwise. Floyd-Warshall algorithm is described as follows:

[**Algorithm Floyd-Warshall**]
for $k \leftarrow 0$ to n do
  for $i \leftarrow 0$ to n do
    for $j \leftarrow 0$ to n do
      if ($D[i][j] > D[i][k] + D[k][j]$)
        $D[i][j] \leftarrow D[i][k] + D[k][j]$

After termination of the algorithm, $D[i][j]$ stores the distance of the shortest path from node i to j. If there is no such path, it stores $+\infty$.

Figure 4 shows a C program for Floyd-Warshall algorithm. It should be clear that this C program computes the all-pairs shortest distance by Floyd-Warshall algorithm. The values of D is updated by calling `update_dist`, although it is not necessary to be a function. The reason is to show our C2CU converter supports function calls. The C program in Figure 4 is a direct implementation of Floyd-Warshall algorithm except that it has a directive `#pragma kernel` in line 22. Most C compilers such as GNU C compiler ignores this directive. Hence, this C program can be compiled correctly, and it computes all-pairs shortest distance in an input graph by Floyd-Warshall algorithm. A directive `#pragma kernel` is used to specify a function for the bulk execution on the GPU. A function call just after directive `#pragma kernel` will be executed on the GPU in the CUDA C program obtained by C2CU.

Figure 5 shows a CUDA C program generated by our tool C2CU from the C program in Figure 4. Users can specify the number p of inputs (i.e. the number p of threads) and the number of threads in each CUDA block, by using options for C2CU. These values are defined as `__P__` $(= p)$ and `__T__` in lines 2 and 3. In Figure 5, they are 2048 and 64, respectively. Thus, 32 CUDA blocks with 64 threads each are spawned by CUDA kernel call `floyd_warshall<<<__B__,__T__>>>()` in line 31. Since the generated CUDA C program accepts p inputs, a 3-dimensional array D of size $N \times N \times p$ allocated in the host memory are used to store them. Also, a 3-dimensional array `__D` of the same size allocated in the device memory (i.e. the global memory of the GPU) are used. In line 30, cudaMemcpyToSymbol is used to copy p inputs stored in D to `__D`. After the bulk execution by CUDA kernel call `floyd_warshall<<<__B__,__T__>>>()` in line 31, cudaMemcpyToSymbol is used to copy `__D`, which stores the resulting values, to D.

CUDA kernel call `floyd_warshall<<<__B__,__T__>>>()` in line 31 invokes `__B__` CUDA blocks with `__T__` threads each. Thus, `__P__` $(= p)$ threads execute Floyd-Warshall algorithm on the CUDA-enabled GPU. Since `blockDim.x` is the number `__B__` of threads in a CUDA block and `blockIdx.x` and `threadIdx.x` take values in $[0, \text{\_\_B\_\_} - 1]$ and $[0, \text{\_\_T\_\_} - 1]$, respectively, `__id__` in line 15 takes value from 0 to $p - 1$. Hence device function `update_dist(i,j,k,__id__)` is executed for `__id__` in $[0, p - 1]$ on the GPU in parallel. The reader should have no difficulty to confirm that CUDA C program in Figure 5 executes Floyd-Warshall algorithm for p inputs in parallel.

```
1: #define N 1024
2: float D[N][N];
3: void update_dist(int i, int j, int k){
4:   if( D[i][j] > D[i][k] + D[k][j] ) {
5:     D[i][j] = D[i][k] + D[k][j];
6:   }
7: }
8:
9: void floyd_warshall(){
10:   int i,j,k;
11:   for(k=0;k<N;k++) {
12:     for(i=0;i<N;i++) {
13:       for(j=0;j<N;j++) {
14:         update_dist(i,j,k);
15:       }
16:     }
17:   }
18: }
19:
20: int main(int argc, char *argv[]){
21:   input_array();
22: #pragma kernel
23:   floyd_warshall();
24:   ...
```

Fig. 4. A C program of the Floyd-Warshall algorithm

Let us see how C2CU converts a C program into a CUDA C program for general cases and confirm that the generated CUDA C programs performs coalesced memory access. If an original C program uses d dimensional array a of size $s_1 \times s_2 \times \cdots \times s_d$, a CUDA C program generated by C2CU uses $d+1$ dimensional array a of size $s_1 \times s_2 \times \cdots \times s_d \times p$. If the original C program accesses $a[i_1][i_2] \cdots [i_d]$ then each thread with ID id of the corresponding CUDA C program accesses $a[i_1][i_2] \cdots [i_d][\_\_id\_\_]$. Since $a[i_1][i_2] \cdots [i_d][0]$, $a[i_1][i_2] \cdots [i_d][1]$, ..., $a[i_1][i_2] \cdots [i_d][p-1]$ are allocated in consecutive addresses, these memory accesses by p threads are coalesced.

4   Experiment Results

The main purpose of this section is to show experimental results on GeForce GTX Titan. GeForce GTX Titan has 14 streaming multiprocessors with 192 cores each. Hence, it can run 2688 threads in parallel. Note that, a single kernel call to GeForce GTX Titan can run more than 2688 threads in a time sharing manner using CUDA [8] parallel programming platform. All input and output data are stored in the global memory of the GPU and we do not use the shared memory of the streaming multiprocessors.

```
 1: #define N 1024
 2: #define __P__ 2048
 3: #define __T__ 64
 4: #define __B__  __P__/__T__
 5: float D[N][N][__P__];
 6: __device__ float __D[N][N][__P__];
 7:
 8: __device__ void update_dist(int i, int j, int k, int __id__){
 9:    if( __D[i][j][__id__] > __D[i][k][__id__] + __D[k][j][__id__] ) {
10:       __D[i][j][__id__] = __D[i][k][__id__] + __D[k][j][__id__];
11:    }
12: }
13:
14: __global__ void floyd_warshall(){
15:    int __id__ = blockIdx.x * blockDim.x + threadIdx.x;
16:    int i,j,k;
17:    for(k=0;k<N;k++) {
18:       for(i=0;i<N;i++) {
19:          for(j=0;j<N;j++) {
20:             update_dist(i,j,k,__id__);
21:          }
22:       }
23:    }
24: }
25:
26: int main(int argc, char *argv[])
27: {
28:    input_array();
29: #pragma kernel
30:    cudaMemcpyToSymbol(__D, D, sizeof(float)*N*N*__P__, 0);
31:    floyd_warshall<<<__B__,__T__>>>();
32:    cudaMemcpyFromSymbol(D, __D, sizeof(float)*N*N*__P__, 0);
33:    ...
```

Fig. 5. A CUDA program for the bulk execution of Floyd-Warshall algorithm generated by C2CU

We have used three sequential algorithms as follows:

- bitonic sort [12, 13],
- Floyd-Warshall algorithm [14–16], and
- Montgomery modulo multiplication [17–19].

Bitonic sort is a well-known parallel sorting algorithm developed by K.E. Batcher [12]. It can be described as a sorting network with comparators as illustrated in Figure 6. Since elements compare-exchanged in each stage are fixed, bitonic sort can be written as an oblivious sequential algorithm.

Montgomery modulo multiplication is used to speed the modulo multiplication $X \cdot Y \cdot 2^{-R} \bmod M$ for R-bit numbers X, Y, and M. The idea of Montgomery

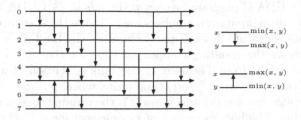

Fig. 6. Bitonic sort for $n = 8$

modulo multiplication is not to use direct modulo computation, which is very costly in terms of the computing time and hardware resources. By iterative computation of Montgomery modulo multiplication, the modulo exponentiation P^E mod M can be computed, which is a key operation for RSA encryption and decryption [24]. Since R is at least 1024 to use Montgomery modulo multiplication for RSA encryption and decryption, addition/multiplication is repeated to perform R-bit addition/multiplication. Figure 7 illustrates how the product $a \cdot b$ of two integers a and b of large bits is computed. Both a and b are partitioned into four integers and the sum of pair-wise products is computed. Using this idea, we can design an oblivious sequential algorithm to compute the product of two integers with large bits in an obvious way. Since Montgomery modulo multiplication repeats computation of the product and the sum of two large integers, it can also be computed by an oblivious sequential algorithm.

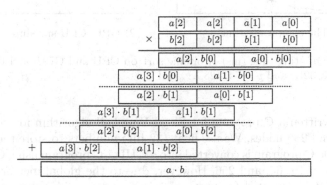

Fig. 7. Multiplication of two integers with large bits

We have written a C program for bitonic sort that sorts $n = 32$, 1K ($=$ 1024), and 32K ($=$ 32768) float (32-bit) numbers. We have converted into a CUDA C program for the bulk execution of bitonic sort with parameter $p =$ $64, 128, \ldots, 4$M. However, due to the global memory capacity of the GPU, it is executed for up to $p = 128$K and $p = 4$K when $n = 1$K and $n = 32$K, respectively. The CUDA C program invokes p threads in $\frac{p}{64}$ CUDA blocks with 64 threads each to sort p inputs of n numbers each. To see the speedup factor, the original C program is repeatedly executed p times on the Intel Xeon (2.66GHz)

Figure 8 (1) shows the resulting computing time for the bulk execution of bitonic sort. Recall that, from Theorem 1, the bulk execution of a sequential algorithm can be computed in $O(\frac{pt}{w} + lt)$ time units, where p is the total number of threads, l is the memory access latency, and t is the running time of the original sequential algorithm. The bulk execution of bitonic sort for $n = 32$ takes about 0.13ms when $p \leq 1$K. Further, the computing time is proportional to p when $p \geq 16$K and it runs 65.1ms when $p = 4$M. Thus, we can think that $O(lt) = 0.13$ms and $O(\frac{pt}{w}) = (15.5p)$ns. More specifically, the bulk execution of bitonic sort for $n = 32$ and p can be computed in approximately 0.13ms+(15.5p)ns. Figure 8 (2) shows the speedup factor of the GPU over the CPU. We can see that the bulk execution of bitonic sort on the GPU can achieve a speedup of factor more than 180 when $n = 32$ and $p \geq 128$K. Further, when $n = 32$ and $p = 4$M, the GPU is 199 times faster than the CPU.

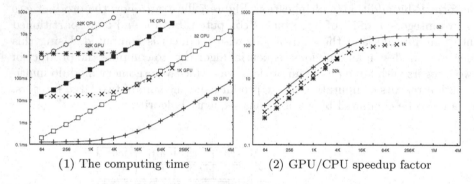

(1) The computing time   (2) GPU/CPU speedup factor

Fig. 8. The computing time (ms) of bitonic sort on CPU and GPU, and the speedup for $n = 32$, 1K, 32K, and $p = 64$, 128, ..., 4M

We have written a C program for Floyd-Warshall algorithm for graphs with $n = 16$, 64, and 256 nodes. We use float (32-bit) numbers to store the length of each edge. The C program is converted into a CUDA C program using C2CU with parameters $p = 16$, 64, and 256. However, due to the global memory capacity of the GPU, it is executed for up to $p = 16$K and $p = 1$K when $n = 64$ and $n = 256$, respectively.

Figure 9 (1) shows the resulting computing time for the bulk execution of Floyd-Warshall algorithm. We will verify $O(\frac{pt}{w} + lt)$ time units shown in Theorem 1. The bulk execution of Floyd-Warshall algorithm for $n = 16$ takes about 3.4ms when $p \leq 512$. Also, the computing time is proportional to p when $p \geq 4$K and it runs 42.6ms when $p = 128$K. Thus, we can think that $O(ln^3) = 3.4$ms and $O(\frac{pn^3}{w}) = (325p)$ns. More specifically, the bulk execution of the Floyd-Warshall algorithm for $n = 32$ and p can be computed in approximately 3.4ms+(325)ns.

Figure 9 (2) shows the speedup factor of the GPU over the CPU. We can see that the bulk execution on the GPU can achieve a speedup of factor more than 30 when $n = 16$ and $p \geq 8K$. Further, when $n = 16$ and $p = 128K$, the GPU is 54 times faster than the CPU.

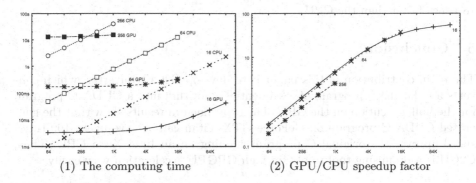

(1) The computing time   (2) GPU/CPU speedup factor

Fig. 9. The computing time (ms) of the Floyd-Warshall algorithm on CPU, and GPU and the speedup for $n = 16$, 64, 256, and $p = 64$, 128, ..., 128K

Finally, we have written a C program for Montgomery modulo multiplication for $n = 512$, 16K ($= 16384$), and 1M ($= 1048576$) bits. We use C2CU to convert it into a CUDA C program with parameter $p = 64, 128, \ldots, 2M$. However, due to the global memory capacity, it is executed for up to $p = 64K$ and $p = 2K$ when $n = 16K$ and $n = 1M$, respectively.

Figure 10 (1) shows the resulting computing time for the bulk execution of the Montgomery modulo multiplication. Again, we will verify $O(\frac{pt}{w} + lt)$ time units shown in Theorem 1. The bulk execution of the algorithm for $n = 512$ takes about 0.45ms when $p \leq 512$. Also, the computing time is proportional to p when $p \geq 128K$ and it runs 124ms when $p = 2M$. Thus, we can think that

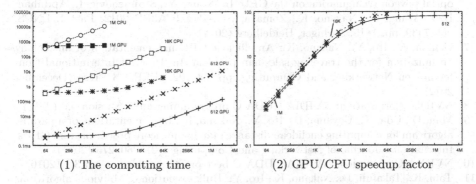

(1) The computing time   (2) GPU/CPU speedup factor

Fig. 10. The computing time (ms) of the Montgomery modulo multiplication on CPU, and GPU. and the speedup for $p = 64$, 128, ..., 4M.

$O(ln^2) = 0.45$ms and $O(\frac{pn^2}{w}) = (59.1p)$ns. More specifically, the bulk execution of the algorithm for $n = 512$ can be computed in approximately 124ms$+(5.9p)$ns. Figure 9 (2) shows the speedup factor of GPU computation using the GPU over the CPU. We can see that the GPU can achieve a speedup of factor more than 70 when $n = 512$ and $p \geq 32$K. Further, when $n = 512$ and $p = 2$M, the GPU is 78 times faster than the CPU.

5   Conclusion

The main contribution of this paper is to develop C2CU converter, which converts a C language program of a sequential algorithm into a CUDA C program for the bulk execution on the GPU. The experimental results show that the generated CUDA C program on GeForce GTX Titan can achieve up to 199 times speed-up over the original C program running on an Intel Xeon CPU. Thus, C2CU is a promising tool to obtain high GPGPU acceleration very easily.

References

1. Hwu, W.W.: GPU Computing Gems Emerald Edition. Morgan Kaufmann (2011)
2. Man, D., Uda, K., Ito, Y., Nakano, K.: A GPU implementation of computing Euclidean distance map with efficient memory access. In: Proc. of International Conference on Networking and Computing, pp. 68–76 (December 2011)
3. Uchida, A., Ito, Y., Nakano, K.: Fast and accurate template matching using pixel rearrangement on the GPU. In: Proc. of International Conference on Networking and Computing, pp. 153–159. CS Press (December 2011)
4. Ogawa, K., Ito, Y., Nakano, K.: Efficient Canny edge detection using a GPU. In: Proc. of International Conference on Networking and Computing, pp. 279–280. IEEE CS Press (November 2010)
5. Nishida, K., Ito, Y., Nakano, K.: Accelerating the dynamic programming for the matrix chain product on the GPU. In: Proc. of International Conference on Networking and Computing, pp. 320–326 (December 2011)
6. Nishida, K., Nakano, K., Ito, Y.: Accelerating the dynamic programming for the optial poygon triangulation on the GPU. In: Xiang, Y., Stojmenovic, I., Apduhan, B.O., Wang, G., Nakano, K., Zomaya, A. (eds.) ICA3PP 2012, Part I. LNCS, vol. 7439, pp. 1–15. Springer, Heidelberg (2012)
7. Uchida, A., Ito, Y., Nakano, K.: An efficient GPU implementation of ant colony optimization for the traveling salesman problem. In: Proc. of International Conference on Networking and Computing, pp. 94–102. IEEE CS Press (December 2012)
8. NVIDIA Corporation: NVIDIA CUDA C programming guide version 5.0 (2012)
9. Man, D., Uda, K., Ueyama, H., Ito, Y., Nakano, K.: Implementations of a parallel algorithm for computing euclidean distance map in multicore processors and GPUs. International Journal of Networking and Computing 1(2), 260–276 (2011)
10. NVIDIA Corporation: NVIDIA CUDA C best practice guide version 3.1 (2010)
11. Tani, K., Takafuji, D., Nakano, K., Ito, Y.: Bulk execution of oblivious algorithms on the unified memory machine, with gpu implementation. In: Proc. of International Parallel and Distributed Processing Symposium Workshops, pp. 586–595 (May 2014)

12. Batcher, K.E.: Sorting networks and their applications. In: Proc. AFIPS Spring Joint Comput. Conf., vol. 32, pp. 307–314 (1968)
13. Akl, S.G.: Parallel Sorting Algorithms. Academic Press (1985)
14. Floyd, R.W.: Algorithm 97: Shortest path. Communications of the ACM 5(6), 345 (1962)
15. Warshall, S.: A theorem on boolean matrices. Journal of the ACM 9(1), 11–12 (1962)
16. Cormen, T.H., Leiserson, C.E., Rivest, R.L.: Introduction to Algorithms. MIT Press (1990)
17. Montgomery, P.L.: Modular multiplication without trial division. Mathematics of Computation 44(170), 519–521 (1985)
18. Shigemoto, K., Kawakami, K., Nakano, K.: Accelerating montgomery modulo multiplication for redundant radix-64k number system on the FPGA using dual-port block RAMs. In: Proc. of International Conference on Embedded and Ubiquitous Computing (EUC), pp. 44–51 (2008)
19. Bo, S., Kawakami, K., Nakano, K., Ito, Y.: An RSA encryption hardware algorithm using a single DSP block and a single block RAM on the fpga. International Journal of Networking and Computing 1(2), 277–289 (2011)
20. Nakano, K.: Simple memory machine models for GPUs. International Journal of Parallel, Emergent and Distributed Systems 29(1), 17–37 (2014)
21. Nakano, K.: Sequential memory access on the unified memory machine with application to the dynamic programming. In: Proc. of International Symposium on Computing and Networking, pp. 85–94 (December 2013)
22. Aho, A.V., Ullman, J.D., Hopcroft, J.E.: Data Structures and Algorithms. Addison Wesley (1983)
23. Flynn, M.J.: Some computer organizations and their effectiveness. IEEE Transactions on Computers 21, 948–960 (1972)
24. Blum, T., Paar, C.: High-radix montgomery modular exponentiation on reconfigurable hardware. IEEE Trans. on Computers 50(7), 759–764 (2001)

Dynamically Spawning Speculative Threads to Improve Speculative Path Execution*

Meirong Li, Yinliang Zhao, and You Tao

Department of Computer Science, Xi'an Jiaotong University 710049 Xi'an, China
meirongli.xjtu@gmail.com, zhaoy@mail.xjtu.edu.cn,
taoyou8115@stu.xjtu.edu.cn

Abstract. Branch misprediction, as one of scaling bottlenecks, has a significant effect on the performance of thread-level speculation. Due to ambiguous control and data dependences, it is still hard for the compiler to extract more efficient threads from the hard-to-predict branches by means of either conservative single path-based thread selection or aggressive thread optimization. Thus, this paper proposes a novel dynamic speculative path scheme to dynamically determine the right speculative path at runtime. It relies on compiler to select and optimize all frequent subpaths greedily, and attempts to generate speculative threads on them using the modified FP-growth algorithm. Based on the path-based performance prediction, the best speculative path is always dynamically chosen to parallelize. We have examined our approach using ODLEN benchmarks. Compared to the single speculative path scheme, it can achieve comparable or better performance.

Keywords: Branch misprediction, Thread-level speculation, Path-based performance Prediction.

1 Introduction

As the exploitation of thread-level parallelism, various sophisticated parallel execution models have been explored on multi-core architectures. Thread-level speculation (TLS)[5],[16],[20], as one of such execution models, can extract multiple dependent threads from irregular sequential programs, and allow them to execute speculatively to improve performance. In case a branch misprediction occurs, speculative threads along the incorrect path will be squashed, and the correct path will be taken to serialize directly. This thread behavior not only causes few spawned threads to be parallelized, but also results in performance losses.

Most efforts have been done on improving the branch prediction accuracy or reducing the branch execution penalty in the speculation[9],[10],[12],[22]. The path execution frequency[5],[6],[19] derived from profiling is often used for the compiler to estimate the most likely speculative path on the hard-to-predict

---

* This work is supported by National Nature Science Foundation of China(NSFC) under Grant No.61173040 and Doctoral Fund of Ministry of Education of China under Grant No.20130201110012.

X.-h. Sun et al. (Eds.): ICA3PP 2014, Part II, LNCS 8631, pp. 192–206, 2014.
© Springer International Publishing Switzerland 2014

branches. And it is common that only the most frequent successor of a branch node is chosen to parallelize while other less frequent ones are discarded. Thus, few subpaths are selected to parallelize. Without consideration of the relation between branch nodes, speculative threads that are executed logically later are usually spawned more aggressively under an out-of-order thread spawn[17]. Once a mispredicted branch is encountered, it will result in all spawned threads along the path to be postponed or serialized forever. However, it is more adaptive for the hardware-based branch prediction schemes[10],[22], which focus on recognizing branching patterns and are extremely effective for some branches that are not data-dependent on relatively random data. But they often suffer from few extractable threads due to the lack of source-level information and TLS-enhancing optimization. Although it is desirable for the hardware-based multi-path execution[22], it is not cost-effective for TLS execution since all idle processor cores are employed to predict the correct path in case of a hard-to-predict branch. Therefore, other sophisticated techniques are needed to explore more efficient speculation on branches.

This paper presents a dynamic adaptive scheme for speculative path selection on the hard-to-predict branches. The compiler is responsible for selecting all frequent subpaths of each branch node greedily. Based on them, we take advantage of the FP-growth algorithm to reveal the relation between branch nodes, and then extract a subset of the most frequent subpaths to generate speculative threads. In case of a hard-to-predict branch, the right speculative path is further decided by the runtime performance profiles of speculative threads. These performance profiles are obtained from our prediction, where the hardware-based branch detection scheme is employed to dynamically collect the information of each speculative path and make a decision for the best speculative path. Two policies are also used to improve the efficiency of our dynamic path selection.

The rest of the paper is organized as follows: Section 2 describes the framework of dynamic speculative path scheme. Section 3 details frequent path selection and the relative path-based thread partitioning algorithm. Section 4 describes the runtime hardware-based scheme for speculative path prediction and thread scheduling. Section 5 presents the experimental results. Section 6 discusses related work and Section 7 concludes the paper.

2   Overview of Dynamic Speculative Path Scheme

The dynamic speculative path scheme consists of compile-time and run-time two phases. Figure 1 shows the crucial components of these two phases. In the compiler phase, each procedure will be proceeded on the frequent path selection, and we can obtain several most frequent subpaths of each branch node. Based on the path-based thread partitioning algorithm, all of them are then extracted and generated a set of speculative threads. They are further compiled and optimized in both the thread creation and TLS-enhancing optimization modules.

In the runtime phase, these thread candidates are dynamically chosen and executed on the basis of TLS execution model, where the construction of dynamic

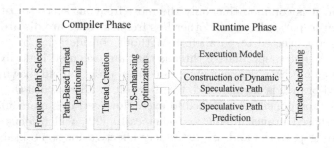

Fig. 1. The framework of dynamic speculative path scheme

speculative path module always provides the right set of speculative threads for the TLS execution. Both speculative path prediction and thread scheduling modules are used to collect the information of all parallelized paths and make a decision for the best speculative path.

3   Compiler Phase

3.1   Frequent Path Selection

Due to ambiguous control and data dependences, it is hard for traditional single speculative path[5],[13],[19] to extract sufficient threads from the hard-to-predict branches. Instead, we assume that all possible paths of each branch node can be dynamically parallelized by means of control flow edge profiling[5],[6]. However, it is common that the occurrence of some branches is associated with others, and even depends on the results of them. To make an aggressive speculation, it is necessary to understand the relationship between branch nodes, and thus reduce the branch misprediction overhead incurred by them.

For each procedure, we consider the traces of different paths as the frequent itemset, which is used to explore the relation between branch nodes using association rules. But different algorithms will cause different costs and performance. FP-growth algorithm[1], taking advantage of the FP-tree construction, has been proved to be efficient for all associated rules with different lengths. Therefore, it is used for our frequent path selection.

Figure 2 describes the structure of a branch FP-tree, which can be seen as a multi-branch tree. Each node represents the control flow of two consecutive branch nodes in the control flow graph(CFG). It is further expressed as Node(branch_node$\langle b\_id1, b\_id2 \rangle$,control_flow$\langle con1, con2 \rangle$). Both b_id1 and b_id2 correspond to the unique identification number of branch nodes, which can be easily obtained from control flow edge profiling[5],[6]. The relative control flows are indicated as $con1$ and $con2$, respectively. There are at most six possible results, such as $\langle T,T \rangle, \langle T,F \rangle, \langle T,\emptyset \rangle, \langle F,T \rangle, \langle F,F \rangle$ and $\langle F,\emptyset \rangle$. Here T and F are the control flow transfers in the CFG, where each branch node is allowed to have no more than two successors[4]. T is the *taken* successor while F is the *fall-through* successor. And $\emptyset$ means that no successors have been executed no matter whether

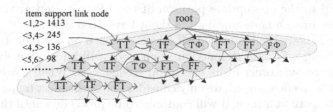

item support link node
<1,2> 1413
<3,4> 245
<4,5> 136
<5,6> 98

Fig. 2. The structure diagram of a branch FP-tree

the chosen branch is taken or not. Meanwhile, the edge between two nodes represents the control flow of branch nodes in the branch FP-tree. The path execution frequency is also included as the value of minimal support of branch nodes, and used to construct the branch FP-tree. More details of the FP-tree generation are described in Algorithm 1.

Algorithm 1. Branch FP-tree generation

INOUT: the traces of branch nodes from control flow edge profiling, D
OUTPUT: the built branch FP-tree, T_{root}
 1: **function** create_FP_tree(D)
 2:      *Ordered* ← sort the traces of branch nodes in D;
 3:      create T_{root} as the root of branch FP-tree if it doesn't exist;
 4:      **for all** Trace T in *Ordered* **do**
 5:          *Head* ← find the first pair of branch nodes in Trace T;
 6:          insert_tree(*Head*,T_{root});
 7:      **end for**
 8: **end function**

 9: **function** insert_tree(*Head*,T_{root})
10:      **if** T_{root} has a child T_{child} equal to *Head* **then**
11:          add up the execution frequency of Head to T_{child};
12:      **else**
13:          create a new node in T_{root};
14:      **end if**
15:      *Head* ← find the next pair of branch nodes in Trace T;
16:      insert_tree(*Head*,T_{root});
17: **end function**

In Algorithm 1, function *create_FP_tree* is responsible for the construction of branch FP-tree. To improve the efficiency of this algorithm, all traces of branch nodes have been proceeded in the non-increasing order of their execution times, and the same branches are also sorted in the non-increasing order of their edge execution frequencies. For each trace, a *root* node has to be established before all other branch nodes are inserted. The insertion of branch nodes is in the form of node pairs using *insert_tree* function. In case of an existing FP-tree node, its frequencies will be added instead. Otherwise, a new node will be created and connected to the appropriate position of the FP-tree. Repeat this step for inserting other branch nodes until all of them have been done.

Algorithm 2 shows the frequent path selection based on the built branch FP-tree. In the *branch_FP_growth* function, each node will be recursively searched by the non-increasing order of its execution frequencies. When more than one successor has been encountered, we only consider one of the most frequent ones to be a candidate path at a time. It will continue to be proceeded until the minimal support of its successors is less than the predefined threshold. The threshold of the minimal support is set to 25%, which has been proved to be effective in our approach. In case an infrequent node is executed, we will choose the successor with the maximum execution frequencies to continue and thus maximize the coverage and speedup of the whole program.

Algorithm 2. Frequent path selection

INOUT: the root of branch FP-tree, T_{root}; the value of minimal support, *minSupport*
OUTPUT: a list of all selected frequent paths, *worklist*

1: **function** branch_FP_growth(T_{root})
2:    **for all** Node T_{node} in T_{root} **do**
3:        Path *path*=*path*∪T_{node};
4:        **if** T_{node}→ support≥*minSupport* **then**
5:            branch_FP_growth(T_{node});
6:        **else**
7:            T_{node} ← the child of T_{node} with the maximum execution frequencies;
8:            branch_FP_growth(T_{node});
9:        **end if**
10:        *worklist*=*worklist*∪*path*;
11:    **end for**
12: **end function**

Based on the frequent path selection, lots of procedures are able to select at least two candidate paths. All these paths are included in the list of *worklist* in the non-increasing order of their execution frequencies. Our approach only focuses on the exploitation of two successive conditional branch nodes. The main reason is that the deeper the speculation is, the less likely the speculated path will be executed. Thus, to make an efficient speculation, more alternative paths can be dynamically parallelized and to some extent reduce such branch misprediction costs. The overhead of our frequent path selection primarily depends on the number of branch nodes in the FP-tree, and is simply estimated as O($\log n$).

3.2   Path-Based Thread Partitioning

In order to partition multiple frequent paths, we propose a path-based thread partitioning algorithm, which is extended from the single speculative path selection[13]. It can deal with one procedure at a time. Two critical factors are needed in this algorithm. One is the degree of inter-thread data dependences, both intra- and inter-procedural data dependences are considered in our thread selection. The other is the thread size, which is used to determine the granularity of a thread and reduce the cost of load imbalance. To create threads on all frequent paths, each of them will be proceeded due to their order in the *worklist*. The more frequent the path is, the more likely it will be chosen to parallelize.

When it comes to the identification of different paths, we name each path with a unique identification number and it is denoted as Path($procName$, $begin_{b\_id1}$, end_{b_id2}, $length$, $rank\_level$). The $procName$ indicates where a path belongs to. Both $begin_{b\_id1}$ and end_{b_id2} correspond to the first and last basic blocks along the path, respectively. The $length$ is the length of a path. The $rank\_level$ represents the order of path speculation, which is derived from the *worklist*. We attempt to partition all these selected paths from the most frequent one to the least frequent one within each procedure. The procedure of thread partitioning is described in Algorithm 3.

Algorithm 3. Path-based thread partitioning algorithm

INOUT: a list of all selected paths, *worklist*
OUTPUT: a set of all partitioned paths
 1: **function** partition_thread(*worklist*)
 2:     **for all** Path *path* in *worklist* **do**
 3:         /*$start\_block$ and end_block are the beginning and end of Path *path*, and $curr\_thread$ is the position of the current thread*/
 4:         $curr\_thread$=partition_subpath($start\_block, end\_block, path, curr\_thread$);
 5:     **end for**
 6: **end function**

Function *partition_subpath* attempts to generate threads for each path recursively in the top-down manner. For each path, it is always proceeded on the inputs of the position of the current thread, the path information, as well as the boundaries of the chosen path. Both the data dependences and thread size are used to dynamically determine the appropriate position of a thread. Due to the limitation of length, more details of thread partitioning on the non-region are discussed in [13]. When a subpath is too large for a thread, the first basic block of it will be further decided. Otherwise, a smaller subpath will be directly included into the current thread until it is large enough for a thread. When a thread is found, it will be attached with the path information to facilitate the identification of different speculative paths. The overhead of this algorithm is estimated as $O(\log n)$. Particularly, this algorithm only focuses on branch nodes in the non-loop region. Because each loop iteration is often considered as a thread, and thus all branch nodes of the same iteration will be serialized.

3.3   Thread Creation and TLS-Enhancing Optimization

For a thread, it is necessary for the compiler to point out the beginning and end of the thread before TLS execution. Thus, both spawn point(SP) and control quasi-independent point(CQIP) are applied in our approach. SP is used to initiate a thread on an idle processor core while CQIP points to where the thread is ready to execute. To understand the performance impact of different speculative paths, both SP and CQIP points are annotated with the path information, i.e., Thread($path,targetAddr$). The $path$ indicates where the thread belongs to while $targetAddr$ is the target address of instruction execution.

Pre-computation slice(p-slice)[16] is used to reduce the potential of inter-thread data dependence violation. It is responsible for calculating the live-ins(the data consumed by the current thread but produced by its predecessors) of a thread on the assumption that the input values are always correct. All of these live-ins are inserted at the entry of the thread. To guarantee the correctness of p-slice, the underlying hardware mechanism can detect and recover those violated threads from mis-speculation.

4   Runtime Phase

4.1   TLS Execution Model

Our TLS execution model is similar to the out-of-order TLS execution model[17]. Only speculative threads from the same path are allowed to be executed speculatively since we devote all processor cores to one path at a time, and are expected to make an aggressive speculation. All threads are maintained in an immediate successor(IS) list due to their relative sequential order. The least speculative thread is the unique non-speculative thread while others are speculative threads. The relation between two consecutive threads in the list is defined as predecessor and successor. All speculative states of threads are buffered in the L1 D-cache using speculative versioning cache(SVC)[21]. In case a control violation occurs, the violated thread and its successors will be squashed immediately. Otherwise, the successor will be verified and committed by the non-speculative thread at the end of execution. Once done, the successor will become the non-speculative thread to continue.

The main difference between them is that the speculative path in our approach is further decided by the runtime path prediction. Our approach can explore a large amount of parallelism even if a branch misprediction occurs. As illustrated in Fig. 3, we assume the speculative path is shown by the dotted lines. When a mispredicted branch is encountered on the path A→B, the traditional single speculative path scheme will suffer from branch misprediction as described in Fig. 3(a). Thus, the parallel overhead T_{par} consists of parallelizing the incorrect path and serializing the correct path(i.e., $T_{incorrect\_path}$ and $T_{correct\_path}$), as well as cycles stalled for the delayed spawnee which isn't executed by the current branch but spawned aggressively by one of its successors. But the correct path can also be parallelized in our approach, such as both the $spawn\_1$ and $spawn\_2$ spawn points. As shown in Fig. 3(b), the execution time of other branches is also overlapped due to the potential of speculation on the path A→C. Hence the parallel overhead T_{par} is largely reduced.

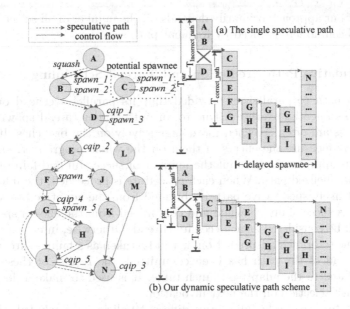

Fig. 3. An example of dynamic speculative path execution

4.2 Construction of Dynamic Speculative Path

In the TLS execution, we should dynamically decide the most frequent speculative path for each procedure. Thus, a hardware-based adaptive branch table is built on each processor core, which is a content-addressable memory(CAM) indexed by a unique identification number associated with each candidate path. Each table entry contains two fields: a *taken counter*, which is incremented if the chosen speculative path has been proved to be correct and decremented otherwise. Initially, the information of each candidate path is obtained from frequent path selection, and it will be dynamically updated by different thread scheduling policies as the number of invocations increases. Another is *path performance summary*. It is used to keep track of the performance profiles of all parallelized paths, i.e., the accumulative differences between the number of successful and failure threads.

In case of a hard-to-predict branch, this table will be requested for making a decision for the right speculative path. A decline response will fail to initiate speculative threads from those less frequent speculative paths. Otherwise, when all threads along the parallelized path have been done, the information of the chosen path will be updated to the adaptive branch table immediately: (1) increase or decrease the relative *taken counter*. (2) summarize the difference between the successful and failure threads due to dynamic path speculation.

The adaptive branch table can be implemented by software or hardware. The aim of our approach is to make an aggressive speculation on different paths and maximize the parallelism of hard-to-predict branches. Thus, the adaptive branch table is maintained on hardware. Compared to the multi-path execution[22], the overhead of our approach primarily depends on the number of all selected paths, which has been largely reduced by frequent path selection.

4.3   Speculative Path Prediction and Thread Scheduling

Choosing a path to parallelize, provided that its parallel overhead outweighs the relative sequential overhead. Due to an out-of-order thread spawn, speculative threads are often spawned more aggressively on the branches. It is hard to accurately measure the effects of them on the whole program. A simple solution of our approach is to count the number of successful and failure threads along the parallelized path. When each procedure is proceeded, the information of the most likely speculative path is obtained from the adaptive branch table. If a thread is successfully spawned and committed from the chosen speculative path, it will be considered as a successful thread. Otherwise, in case a thread is squashed due to branch misprediction, it will be taken as a failure thread. When the last thread of the path has been committed, the results of these threads will be updated to the adaptive branch table. It is used to make a decision for dynamic path selection on the next invocation.

To facilitate thread scheduling, two different policies are included, the latest effective path selection(LEPS) and the most frequent path selection(MFPS). The performance of LEPS primarily depends on the latest speculative paths that have been correctly executed. To doing so, we need to change the way to count the adaptive branch table. The relative *taken counter* will be increased when the speculative path has been proved to be correct and cleared otherwise. It also indicates that the correctness of the latest speculative paths is treated as a metric for thread scheduling in LEPS. The larger the relative *taken counter* is, the more frequent the path is. But the disadvantage of this approach is that it is only effective for branches with regular data accesses, and easily affected by branches that are data-dependent on relatively random data.

However, the most frequent speculative path of MFPS is decided by the quantitative evaluation. The accumulative differences between the number of successful and failure threads are used to weigh different speculative paths. Thus, the path with the maximum value will be considered as the most likely speculative path. When the value of the chosen path becomes negative, it reveals that excessive mispredicted branches have been executed on the path. In such case, other frequent paths will be explored instead. This method utilizes the results of all parallelized paths to decide the next most frequent path. It is more adaptive for hard-to-predict branches in the speculation.

5   Experimental Results

We have evaluated the effectiveness of our approach using 10 programs from OLDEN benchmark suite[2], which is often used in Mitosis[16] and SEED[8]. An additional *rook*, solving the issue of chess placement on the board using binary tree, is also applied. These benchmarks have been proved to have lots

Table 1. Processor parameters

parameter	value
Fetch/Issue/Commit Width	4/4/4
Integer Units	4 units/1 cycle
Floating Point Units	2 units/ 12 cycles
Private L1-Data/Inst Cache	64KB,4-way,32B
Speculative Buffer Size	Fully associated 2KB
Latencies to Remote L1 Data Cache	at least 8 cycles
Unified L2 Cache	2MB,4-way,64B
L1/L2/Memory Latencies	1/80/150 cycles
Thread Spawn/Verify/Commit	5/15/5

of complex control flow and data dependences on branches, and are difficult to be parallelized. The SUIF compiler[3] is responsible for frequent path selection and path-based thread partitioning on them. Under the code generation, the generated MIPS assemble code is extended with a set of TLS-specific instructions to support for our TLS system.

For the simulator, it models a generic speculative multithreading(SpMT) processor with four pipelined MIPS-based R3000 processing cores similar to Stanford Hydra[15]. The processor parameters are shown in Table 1. Each core has its own function units, register file, L1 I-cache, and L1 D-cache. All of them share a unified L2 cache. The private L1 D-cache is used to maintain the semantics of sequential execution using the SVC coherence protocol[21], which allows each cache line has multiple different values in the TLS execution, and is able to identify remote data cache accesses and detect the cross-thread dependence violation. Our simulator is an execution-driven and executes binaries generated by the SUIF compiler. The speculative overhead and the costs of the ineffective speculative path are also included in our experiments.

5.1   Subpath Candidates and Pre-computation

The dynamic speculative path scheme attempts to extract multiple frequent paths from the hard-to-predict branches. It is common that both two sides of the same branch node are selected by our frequent path selection. We compare our approach with the traditional single speculative path selection, which always assumes that the most frequent path of the whole program consists of the ones with the highest execution possibility. Figure 4(a) shows that the total number of all selected paths is relatively smaller in the single speculative path selection, by contrast, most of procedures are able to extract multiple different paths in our approach. Particularly, *perimeter* can find no less than 70 paths from all branch nodes due to complex control and data dependences.

The average path length is also examined in Fig. 4(b). We simply utilize the number of branch nodes to estimate the length of a path. Due to the utilization of FP-growth algorithm, each path is created only if it satisfies the value of the

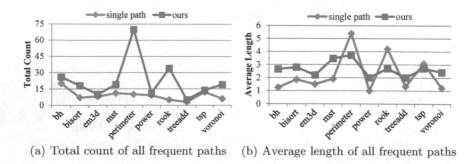

(a) Total count of all frequent paths   (b) Average length of all frequent paths

Fig. 4. Path information of our frequent path selection

minimum support threshold. Thus, the average length of all frequent paths in our approach is quite different from that in the single speculative path selection. Meanwhile, our approach, taking advantage of the relation between branch nodes, can choose more alternative paths to parallelize when speculative threads are executed deeply. To some extent, it avoids the branch misprediction penalty of TLS execution.

To take a detailed analysis of the path-based thread partitioning algorithm, we divide all created threads into *postdominator* and *non-postdominator* two categories due to the position of thread creation in the CFG. The former corresponds to the thread that is executed at the beginning of an immediate postdominator of a branch node while the latter will be dynamically speculated in terms of the outcomes of branches. As described in Table 2, the number of *non-postdominator* threads take up a large proportion of all benchmarks. All of them further dominate the performance of the hard-to-predict branches. Thus, it is critical for our approach to dynamically determine the best speculative path on each branch node. Furthermore, it has been proved that hoisting the *postdominator* threads aggressively on different paths can reduce the potential of all its delayed spawnees on the path.

Table 2. Information of thread creation and pre-computation slice

benchmark	bh	bisort	em3d	mst	perimeter	power	rook	treeadd	tsp	voronoi
postdominator	11	2	8	13	11	3	9	1	0	5
non-postdominator	36	6	15	24	26	15	19	2	9	20
p-slice	4.3	3.5	4.9	4.2	3.2	3.8	4.2	3.3	3.1	3.2
p-slice(%)	6.6	9.9	12.1	10.8	8.7	6.7	10.3	5.8	9.6	6.1

For the p-slice, it consists of live-ins that are extracted from the predecessor thread but consumed by the successor thread. The information of p-slice is shown in Table 2. The average size of p-slice is about 3.77, and the largest p-slice doesn't exceed 20% of the whole thread size. It also indicates that the p-slice takes up a small proportion of the thread. We are expected to reduce the overhead of p-slice that comes from those infrequent paths as well.

5.2   Performance of Dynamic Speculative Path Selection

The dynamic speculative path scheme can allow more than one speculative path to be dynamically chosen to parallelize due to different procedure calls. But different thread scheduling policies have different effects on overall performance. Figure 5 shows the overall speedup of both the LEPS and MFPS policies in the non-loop regions, where all parallelized loops are discarded and serialized. It is because we are expect to reveal the performance impact of these two policies on our dynamic speculative path selection. Based on the determination of the latest speculative path, it is effective for LEPS to find the best speculative path on some invocations. But it is still hard to handle branch nodes that are data-dependent on the random data, such as *bisort*, *perimeter* and *rook*, etc.

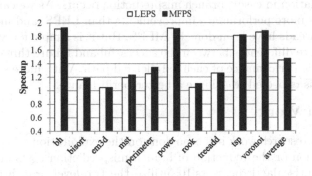

Fig. 5. Performance impact of different policies on the non-loop regions

However, the MFPS policy can achieve better performance in most cases due to the quantitative evaluation of all parallelized paths. The best speculative path will be always the most frequent one on each invocation. Particularly, *mst*, *perimeter* and *rook* benefit from the parallelism of the right speculative path and achieve significant performance gains. But both of LEPS and MFPS always have the same results for *em3d* and *treeadd*. The reason is that most of the execution time of *em3d* only focuses on one single speculative path upon the given input sets, and the performance of *treeadd* is limited by its recursion structure, respectively.

Due to the performance impact of different policies, the speedup of the whole program is also influenced. Figure 6 makes a performance comparison between the traditional single speculative path selection and our dynamic speculative path scheme. It is obvious that our approach outperforms the single speculative path selection. Meanwhile, our approach is more efficient since the overhead of those ineffective paths is largely overlapped when compared to the potential

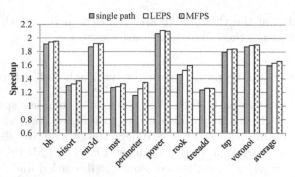

Fig. 6. Performance comparison between single speculative path selection and dynamic speculative path scheme

performance brought by LEPS and MFPS. And speculative threads that are initiated at the immediate post-dominator of the branch node benefit from the potential of multiple spawn points on all subpaths and are able to make an aggressive speculation in case a branch misprediction occurs. As we can see in Fig. 6, MFPS gains more performance improvements than LEPS, and more successful spawned threads have been done by MFPS. But it is simple for MFPS to use the accumulative differences between the successful and failure threads to evaluate the dynamic performance of each parallelized path. With more sophisticated techniques, it is expected to achieve a better performance.

6 Related Work

A great deal of research work has been done on the exploitation of more accurate branch prediction or the reduction of branch misprediction costs on multi-core processors. Multiscalar Processors[10] utilize the two-level branch predictor to improve the accuracy of branch prediction, and it has been proved to be effective for loop-level speculation. ASTEX[14] introduce the concept of hot paths where the helper threads are extracted and allocated with a set of frequent execution traces obtained from gprof profiling tool, and are then in parallel with the main thread to improve performance. Likewise, the branch misprediction resolved by [22] is at the cost of parallelizing all possible paths simultaneously on all idle processor cores when a hard-to-predict branch is encountered.

However, the work in BLP[12] is similar to our work. It attempts to determine the appropriate spawn points of speculative threads by means of keeping track of the potential of control and data dependences, and thus can exploit substantial branch-mispredict level parallelism from hard-to-predict branches. But the differences between them are as follows: (1) We focus on the dynamic speculative path selection where multiple frequent paths are selected greedily from each branch node, by contrast, only one single speculative path has been resolved in BLP. (2) The relation between branch nodes maintained in our approach is used to create multiple different speculative paths. (3) The best speculative path of our approach is dynamically determined by the runtime performance prediction while the simple profiler runs are used in BLP.

In the TLS execution, dynamically identifying the potential of performance bottlenecks can speed up the whole program execution. [11] utilize a set of hardware-based programmable performance counters to predict the sequential execution time of each parallelized loop on each invocation. In case a non-beneficial loop is found, it will be serialized directly to save execution time. Otherwise, it will continue to be parallelized instead. Similarly, [8] present two critical performance counters to dynamically evaluate the parallelism of different loop nesting levels. To make the cost-performance trade-offs, the best speculative path is simply determined by means of the accumulative differences between the successful and failure threads in our approach. Other optimizations for branch misprediction are also explored in [7] and [18]. Both of them focus on the selective branch recovery to reduce the branch misprediction costs.

7   Conclusions

We describe a novel dynamic adaptive scheme for TLS execution to exploit thread-level parallelism from the hard-to-predict branches. The basic idea is to statically extract multiple frequent paths from the built branch FP-tree using the modified FP-growth algorithm. All these selected paths are then proceeded on the path-based thread partitioning to generate speculative threads. In the process of TLS execution, these partitioned paths are dynamically chosen to parallelize in terms of their runtime performance profiles obtained from our prediction. Once each parallelized path has been done, the results of our prediction will be collected and used to decide the best speculative path on the next invocation. Our preliminary results show that our approach can achieve a comparable or better performance when compared to the traditional single speculative path selection. We are also expected to integrate our approach into speculative loop execution and further improve the overall performance of TLS execution.

References

1. Fp-growth algorithm,
   http://en.wikipedia.org/wiki/Association_rule_learning
2. Olden benchmark suite, http://www.cs.preceton.edu/mcc/odlen.html
3. The suif compiler system. suif group, stanford, http://suif.stanford.edu
4. The suif control flow graph library,
   http://www.eecs.harvard.edu/hube/softwa-re/v130/cfg.html
5. Bhowmik, A., Franklin, M.: A general compiler framework for speculative multi-threaded processors. IEEE Transactions on Parallel and Distributed Systems 15(8), 713–724 (2004)
6. Chen, Z., Zhao, Y.-L., Pan, X.-Y., Dong, Z.-Y., Gao, B., Zhong, Z.-W.: An overview of prophet. In: Hua, A., Chang, S.-L. (eds.) ICA3PP 2009. LNCS, vol. 5574, pp. 396–407. Springer, Heidelberg (2009)
7. Gandhi, A., Akkary, H., Srinivasan, S.: Reducing branch misprediction penalty via selective branch recovery. In: Proceedings of the 10th International Symposium on High Performance Computer Architecture, pp. 254–264. IEEE (2004)

8. Gao, L., Li, L., Xue, J., Yew, P.C.: Seed: A statically greedy and dynamically adaptive approach for speculative loop execution. IEEE Transactions on Computers 62(5), 1004–1016 (2013)
9. Iwama, C., Barli, N.D., Sakai, S., Tanaka, H.: Improving conditional branch prediction on speculative multithreading architectures. In: Sakellariou, R., Keane, J.A., Gurd, J.R., Freeman, L. (eds.) Euro-Par 2001. LNCS, vol. 2150, pp. 413–417. Springer, Heidelberg (2001)
10. Jacobson, Q., Bennett, S., Sharma, N., Smith, J.: Control flow speculation in multiscalar processors. In: Proceedings of the IEEE Symposium on High-Performance Computer Architecture, pp. 218–229. IEEE, San Antonio (1997)
11. Luo, Y., Packirisamy, V., Hsu, W.C., Zhai, A., Mungre, N., Tarkas, A.: Dynamic performance tuning for speculative threads. In: Proceedings of the 36th Annual International Symposium on Computer Architecture, pp. 462–473. ACM, New York (2009)
12. Malik, K., Agarwal, M., Stone, S., Woley, K., Frank, M.: Branch-mispredict level parallelism (blp) for control independence. In: IEEE 14th International Symposium on High Performance Computer Architecture, Lake City, UT, pp. 62–73 (2008)
13. Pan, X., Zhao, Y., Chen, Z., Wang, X., Wei, Y., Du, Y.: A thread partitioning method for speculative multithreading. In: Proceedings of the International Conference on Scalable Computing and Communications, pp. 285–290. IEEE (2009)
14. Petit, E., Bodin, F., Papaure, G., Dru, F.: Astex: A hot path based thread extractor for distributed memory system on a chip. In: Proceedings of the 2006 ACM/IEEE Conference on Supercomputing. ACM, New York (2006)
15. Prabhu, M.K., Olukotun, K.: Using thread-level speculation to simplify manual parallelization. In: Proceedings of the ACM SIGPLAN Symposium on Principles and Practice of Parallel Programming, pp. 1–12. ACM, New York (2003)
16. Quiñones, C.G., Madriles, C., Sánchez, J., Marcuello, P., González, A., Tullsen, D.M.: Mitosis compiler: An infrastructure for speculative threading based on precomputation slices. In: Proceedings of the 2005 ACM SIGPLAN Conference on Programming Language Design and Implementation, pp. 269–279. ACM, New York (2005)
17. Renau, J., Tuck, J., Liu, W., Ceze, L., Strauss, K., Torrellas, J.: Tasking with out-of-order spawn in tls chip multiprocessors: Microarchitecture and compilation. In: Proceedings of the 19th Annual International Conference on Supercomputing, pp. 179–188. ACM, New York (2005)
18. Sarangi, S.R., Torrellas, J., Liu, W., Zhou, Y.: Reslice: Selective re-execution of long-retired misspeculated instructions using forward slicing. In: Proceedings of the 38th Annual IEEE/ACM International Symposium on Microarchitecture, pp. 257–270. IEEE Computer Society, Washington, DC (2005)
19. Sohi, G.S., Breach, S.E., Vijaykumar, T.N.: Multiscalar processors. In: Proceedings of the 22Nd Annual International Symposium on Computer Architecture, pp. 414–425. ACM, New York (1995)
20. Steffan, J.G., Colohan, C., Zhai, A., Mowry, T.C.: The stampede approach to thread-level speculation. ACM Transactions Computer Systems 23(3), 253–300 (2005)
21. Vijaykumar, T.N., Gopal, S., Smith, J., Sohi, G.: Speculative versioning cache. IEEE Transactions on Parallel and Distributed Systems 12(12), 1305–1317 (2001)
22. Xekalakis, P., Cintra, M.: Handling branches in tls systems with multi-path execution. In: 2010 IEEE 16th International Symposium on High Performance Computer Architecture, pp. 1–12 (2010)

A Parallel Algorithm of Kirchhoff Pre-stack Depth Migration Based on GPU

Yida Wang, Chao Li, Yang Tian, Haihua Yan, Changhai Zhao, and Jianlei Zhang

School of Computer Science and Engineering,
Beihang University,
Beijing, China
lianayizu@gmail.com

Abstract. Kirchhoff pre-stack depth migration (KPSDM) algorithm, as one of the most widely used migration algorithms, plays an important part in getting the real image of the earth. However, this program takes considerable time due to its high computational cost; hence the working efficiency of the oil industry is affected. The general purpose Graphic Processing Unit (GPU) and the Compute Unified Device Architecture (CUDA) developed by NVIDIA have provided a new solution to this problem. In this study, we have proposed a parallel algorithm of the Kirchhoff pre-stack depth migration and an optimization strategy based on the CUDA technology. Our experiments indicate that for large data computations, the accelerated algorithm achieves a speedup of 8~15 times compared with NVIDIA GPU.

Keywords: Kirchhoff pre-stack depth migration, GPU, CUDA, parallel algorithm, optimization.

1 Introduction

In areas of complex geology, the main goal of earth exploration is to provide the oil and gas industry with knowledge of the earth's subsurface structure to detect where oil can be found and recovered. To do so, large-scale seismic surveys of the earth are performed, and the data recorded undergoes complex iterative processing to extract a geological model of the earth. The data is then interpreted by experts to help decide where to build oil recovery infrastructure [1] [2].

As the most efficient geophysical imaging technique in the oil industry, the 3-D pre-stack depth migration (PSDM) supports people to understand the deep and complex structure of underground. PSDM is one of the most widely used migration methods, which has advantages of flexible input and output data, high efficiency, and good quality of images [4].

However, PSDM is a compute-intensive application. Based on the geological model, it needs repeatedly modifying the model and multiple iterations. Even on a cluster with hundreds of high performance CPUs, it may take days or even weeks to complete the processing and get the final migration image for some practical jobs.

X.-h. Sun et al. (Eds.): ICA3PP 2014, Part II, LNCS 8631, pp. 207–218, 2014.
© Springer International Publishing Switzerland 2014

The Kirchhoff PSDM (KPSDM), which is a frequently-used PSDM algorithm, can be divided into 3 partitions: parameters parsing, travel time calculation, and migration. Particularly the migration may account for more than 50% of the total processing time, which is the most time-consuming partition. So it is necessary to accelerate the migration processing to improve the entire performance of the KPSDM application.

In recent years, driven by the insatiable market demand for real-time, high-definition 3D graphics, the programmable Graphic Processor Unit (GPU) has evolved into a highly parallel, multi-threaded, many-core processor with tremendous computational horsepower and very high memory bandwidth [5]. According to the latest figures, the theoretical floating-point operations per second for GPU have come to thousands of GFLOPS while for CPU the number is hundreds of GFLOPS. Because of its great performance in floating-point operation, GPUs have been used as general platforms to exploit data-level-parallelism (DLP) for non-graphic applications, which are known as general purpose GPUs(GPGPUs). Considerable programming models and runtime environments for GPGPUs have been proposed. Among them, NVidia's compute unified device architecture (CUDA) provides a C-like programming model to leverage the massively parallel processing power of NVidia's GPUs, and it has been a mature and widely adopted platform for GPGPU applications[7].

In areas of complex geology, GPUs have been used widely recently, e.g., [6] provides a new idea based on the GPGPU methodology to reduce the computation time of the MRF algorithm for ASR image segmentation; [7] demonstrates a method to accelerate the PKTM algorithm. All these researches have gained ideal performance improvement. As an SIMT (Single-Instruction, Multiple-Thread) processor, GPU is suitable for the calculation pattern of the migration partition in the KPSDM because it is a compute-intensive application and the tasks in migration have little mutual dependency.

In this study, we propose a new GPU-based KPSDM parallel algorithm (GKPSDM) and its optimizing strategy using CUDA technology. This paper begins with an overview of the CUDA technology (§2). We then present the method of the parallel KPSDM algorithm and its optimizing strategy (§3) followed by the experiments and result analysis (§4). Finally, we discuss the conclusion and future works (§5).

2   Overview of CUDA

Although GPUs have powerful floating-point operating capability, the general approach in the early days of GPU computing was extraordinarily convoluted. Because standard graphics APIs such as Open GL and DirectX were still the only way to interact with a GPU, any attempt to perform arbitrary computations on a GPU would still be subject to the constraints of programming within a graphics API. This is a tough progress and the programmers should have knowledge of the OpenGL or DirectX graphics programming interfaces. To solve these problems, the NVIDIA published the CUDA release to reduce the programming complexity and make it easier for programmers to use GPUs for general purpose.

The CUDA architecture is illustrated in Fig. 1. CPU and GPU are known as the host and the device respectively, and each has its own memory space. CUDA provides a series of APIs to handle the device memory malloc, free, and data transmission between host and device. Generally, data should be transmitted to the device memory from the host memory before calculation. But by using the newest release 6 of CUDA, there is no need to execute the transmitting any more.

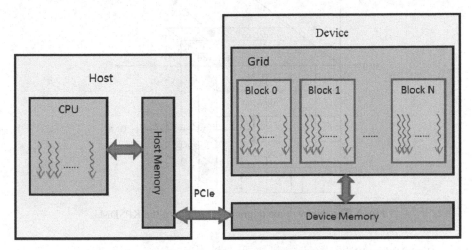

Fig. 1. General architecture of CUDA

CUDA kernels are functions callable from the host that execute asynchronously on the CUDA devices, which means that the host queues a kernel for execution only on GPUs and does not wait for it to finish but rather continues to perform some other work. Although the CUDA kernels cannot return values due to the asynchronous mechanism, CUDA also provides some synchronization interfaces so that the host can determine when the kernel or pipeline has completed [8].

A CUDA thread is a basic executing unit on GPU, which acts as if each thread has its own processor with different registers and thread identity that runs in a shared memory environment. A kernel should utilize many threads to perform the work. The onboard GPU hardware thread scheduler has the responsibility for thread switching and scheduling, which is transparent to the CUDA developers. An execution configuration in the kernel source code defines both the number of threads that will run the kernel and their arrangementina1D, 2D or 3D computational grid [9] [10].

3   KPSDM Parallel Algorithm

3.1   KPSDM Theory

The theory of the migration partition of the KPSDM is illustrated in Fig. 2. The space subsurface can be divided into 3D grid. A mesh on the top surface is defined as a CELL. Imaging points in the depth direction are divided into several point chunks.

For each chunk, the travel time from source (TTS) and receiver (TTR) to the end-points are needed to calculate the total travel time and the interpolation coefficient which are represented by TM and TA respectively in the program. Finally we use these parameters to compute the result of all the imaging points.

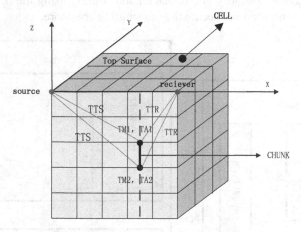

Fig. 2. The theory of the migration partition of the KPSDM

3.2   Serial Algorithm

Fig. 3 presents the pseudocode of a practical KPSDM program. There are three main loops: the first one loops over the input traces and calculates the relative parameters including travel time, trace head, etc. for each trace; the second one loops over the CELLs and calculate some parameters related to one CELL; the last one loops over chunks of a CELL, calculates TM, TA and some other parameters for endpoints of each chunk and then use them to calculate the final image.

```
for all input traces do
  Calculate relative parameters including travel time,
trace head, etc.;
    for all CELLs do
    Calculate relative parameters;
      for all chunks of a CELL do
        Calculate TM, TA and some other parameters;
        Calculate and accumulate the final image result to
the image points;
      end for
    end for
  end for
```

Fig. 3. Pseudocode of a serial KPSDM program

3.3 CUDA Parallel Algorithm

Fig. 4 presents the logic structure of GKPSDM. The first step is to transmit some parameters which are constant through all the migration progress to the constant memory of GPU. Next we have a loop of the input traces on the host. Once getting an input trace, the CPUs will calculate parameters relative to the trace on the host as the serial program does. Then after transmitting these parameters to the global memories of GPUs, the GPUs will complete the following computation using 3 CUDA kernels.

```
Transmit constant parameters to the constant memory;
for all input traces do
   Calculate relative parameters including travel time,
trace head, etc.
   Transmit parameters to global memory;
   (Executed by GPU)Kernel1: every CUDA thread calculates
parameters relative to one CELL;
   (Executed by GPU)Kernel2: every 32 CUDA threads calcu-
late all the TM, TA of one CELL;
   (Executed by GPU)Kernel3: every 32 CUDA threads calcu-
late all the image results of one CELL;
}
end for
Copy the imaging result from GPU memory to host memory
```

Fig. 4. Pseudocode of parallel GKPSDM program

kernel1 : In this kernel, every CUDA thread calculates parameters relative to one CELL and keeps them in the global memory for the later processing. Fig. 5 shows the threads organization and simplified pseudocode of kernel1. CELLNUM is the number of CELLs. DP, OS, and OR is parameters that will be used in other kernels.

```
dim3 dimBlock_kernel1(NCELL_kernel1)
dim3 dimGrid_kernel1((CELLNUM + NCELL_kernel1 - 1) /
NCELL_kernel1)

kernel1(…){
   CellIdx = blockIdx.x * blockDim.x + threadIdx.x
   ......
   DP[CellIdx] = ......
   ......
   OS[CellIdx] = ......
   ......
   OR[CellIdx] = ......
   ......
}
```

Fig. 5. Threads organization and pseudocode of kernel1

kernel2 : In this kernel, every 32 CUDA threads calculate all the TM, TA of one
CELL. There is an inner loop in which each thread fetches a point every other 32
points. The results are stored in the global memory. The reason why we choose 32
threads to deal with one CELL will be explained in the later optimizing strategy. Fig.
6 demonstrates the threads organization of kernel2 and the simplified pseudocode.

```
dim3 dimBlock_kernel2(32,NCELL_kernel2)
dim3 dimGrid_kernel2((CELLNUM + NCELL_kernel2 - 1) /
NCELL_kernel2)

kernel2(...){
  CellIdx = blockIdx.x * blockDim.y + threadIdx.y
  ......
  for(L = 0;L < NTAB ; L += blockDim.x) {
    ......
    TM[CellIdx * ntab + L] = ......
    TA[CellIdx * ntab + L] = ......
    ......
  }
}
```

Fig. 6. Threads organization and pseudocode of kernel2

kernel3 : In this kernel, every 32 CUDA threads calculate all the final image results
of one CELL. There is an inner loop just like the one in the kernel2 in which each
thread fetches a point every other 32 points. The structure of kernel3 is similar with
the one of kernel2, except replacing the TM and TA calculation with the image results
calculation. We don't show the pseudocode here.

After all input traces have been processed, the imaging result will be copied from
the GPU memory to the host memory for the later processing.

3.4   Optimizing Strategy

Although the preceding parallel program has gained better runtime performance than
the serial program, it has not yet taken full advantage of the GPUs' compute capability. So a series of appropriate optimizing methods are necessary to get further improvement.

Based on the GPU architecture and CUDA technology, there are 4 main methods
in our optimizing strategy: processor occupancy, branch divergence, memory access,
and data transmission.

3.4.1   Processor Occupancy
The general NVIDIA GPU architecture is built around a scalable array of multi-
threaded Streaming Multiprocessors (SMs). Each SM contains several Streaming
Processors (SPs). The multiprocessor creates, manages, schedules, and executes

threads in groups of 32 parallel threads called warps. When a multiprocessor is given one or more thread blocks to execute, it partitions them into warps and the warp is the unit of thread scheduling in SMs. Yet there can be more resident warps than SPs in an SM so the CUDA processors could efficiently execute long-latency operations such as global memory accesses. When an instruction executed by the threads in a warp must wait for the result of a previously initiated long-latency operation, the warp is not selected for execution. Another resident warp that is no longer waiting for results is selected for execution. If more than one warp is ready for execution, a priority mechanism is used to select one for execution. With enough warps around, the hardware will likely find a warp to execute at any point in time, thus making full use of the execution hardware in spite of these long-latency operations.

Each CUDA device offers a limited amount of CUDA memory, which limits the number of threads that can simultaneously reside in the streaming multiprocessors for a given application. In general, the more memory locations each thread requires, the fewer the number of threads that can reside in each SM and thus the fewer number of threads that can reside in the entire processor. So it is very important to reduce the use of memory units to improve the processor occupancy.

In our GKPSDM parallel program, the main pullback is the number of registers. The 3 kernels consume more than 60 registers, and consequently, only 30 percent of the threads can reside in the processors. Then we found that the actual parameters including many pointers in the parameter list take up a considerable number of registers.

In this paper, the optimizing method is transmitting these parameters to the constant memory before the kernel invocation. As the constant memory can also be accessed fast, the accessing delay will not increase much. After this, the number of registers used by the 3 kernels all decrease to less than 40, causing more than 60 percent of the threads to reside in the processors, and an improvement of performance can be achieved accordingly.

3.4.2 Branch Divergence

In the CUDA architecture, the hardware executes an instruction for all threads in the same warp, before moving to the next instruction. It works well when all threads within a warp follow the same control flow path when working their data. For example, for an if–then–else construct, the execution works well when either all threads execute the then part or all execute the else part. When threads within a warp take different control flow paths, the simple execution style no longer works well. In our if–then–else example, when some threads execute the then part and others execute the else part, the SIMT execution style no longer works well. In these situations, the execution of the warp will require multiple passes through these divergent paths. One pass will be needed for those threads that follow the then part and another pass for those that follow the else part. These passes are sequential to each other, thus adding to the execution time.

Fig.7 demonstrates some codes in the GKPSDM parallel program. There are two if-then-else constructs in which a branch divergence will cause considerable performance degradation.

```
if ( TTS >= -8.888f && TTR >= -8.888f ) {
    TM1 = … + TTS;
    RTMP1 = … + TTR;
    TM = TM1 + RTMP1 + …;
}
else {
    TM = 0;
}
……
if ( TM > RKP1 ) {……}
else {……}
```

Fig. 7. Code with branch divergence

In this paper, as shown in Fig.8, we remove the if-then-else construct by setting a special value at the invalid position (in our program, -99999 is appropriate), which will make TM an invalid value accordingly. So after analyzing the second if-then-else construct, we will get the same result as the original program. Although the calculation increases, the overall performance of the program benefits from the reduction of branch divergence.

```
Set -99999 at the invalid position of TTS and TTR;
TM1 = … + TTS; //TM1 is invalid because of TTS
RTMP1 = … + TTR;
TM = TM1 + RTMP1 + …;
……
if ( TM > RKP1 ) {……}
else {……}
```

Fig. 8. Code after optimizing

3.4.3   Memory Access

Although GPUs have strong computing power, the memory access, especially the global memory access, is not fast enough to match up with the computation and often becomes the bottleneck of a CUDA program. Therefore, making memory optimization has always been the most important portion of the optimizing process.

In the GKPSDM program we mainly focus on the global memory access. Perhaps the single most important performance consideration in programming for the CUDA architecture is coalescing global memory accesses. Global memory loads and stores by threads of a half warp (for devices of compute capability 1.x) or of a warp (for devices of compute capability 2.x) are coalesced by the device into as few as one transaction when certain access requirements are met.

Global memory should be viewed in terms of aligned segments of 16 and 32 words. If the addresses fall within a 128-byte segment, then a single 128-byte transaction is performed. Otherwise, if a half warp accesses memory split across two 128-byte segments, then two transactions are performed and access time is doubled as a result.

In our early program version, in kernel2 and kernel3, every one thread is in charge of one CELL. The pseudocode of kernel2_old is present in Fig.9. As the number of CELLs is big enough so the occupancy of GPU processors are not decreased and the program structure is simplified. But the travel time table is organized with the CELLs index, none of the threads' memory access fall within a 128-byte segment, as shown in Fig.10. Then we modified the program and used 32 threads to manage a CELL (Fig.6), so that threads in a warp could fetch the data in the global memory in an efficient way. Fig.11 demonstrates the coalescing memory access after the optimization.

```
dim3 dimBlock_kernel2(NCELL_kernel2)
dim3 dimGrid_kernel2((CELLNUM + NCELL_kernel2 - 1) /
NCELL_kernel2)

kernel2_old(…){
  CellIdx = blockIdx.x * blockDim.x + threadIdx.x
  ……
  for(L = 0;L < NTAB ; L ++) {
    ……
    TM[CellIdx * ntab + L] = ……
    TA[CellIdx * ntab + L] = ……
    ……
  }
}
```

Fig. 9. Threads organization and pseudocode of kernel2_old

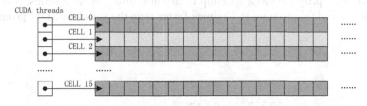

Fig. 10. No coalescing memory access

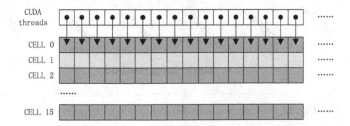

Fig. 11. Coalescing memory access after the optimization

3.4.4   Data Transmission

We use CUDA release 4.2 in our program, so before invoking the kernels on GPUs, data needed for the computation should be transmitted from the host memory to the device memory. Because of the limited PCIe bandwidth, the transmission may cost much time in a job with a huge amount of data.

The method we use in this paper to handle this pullback includes two aspects: using the CUDA stream and using the pinned memory. A stream is a sequence of commands that execute in order. Different streams, on the other hand, may execute their commands out of order with respect to one another or concurrently. Using the CUDA stream with the asynchronous transmitting functions enables the overlap of data transfers with computation.

Using pinned memory, we could attain the highest bandwidth between the host and the device. But pinned memory should not be overused. Excessive use can reduce overall system performance because pinned memory is a scarce resource.

4   Experiments Result and Analysis

We implemented the practical GKPSDM program on NVIDIA Tesla C2050 GPUs, which have more than 2G GPU memory and 448 cores. The host has an Intel's i7 3G CPU with 12G host memory. We have two kinds of contrast experiment to measure the optimizing effectiveness and the speedup of the GKPSDM to the serial KPSDM respectively.

In the first contrast experiment, we use four optimizing methods mentioned above in sequence. Each optimizing method is on the basis of the previous one. For a practical job with 10000 traces and 500 CELLs, the results are demonstrated in Fig. 12. The original GKPSDM program has a speedup of about 6 times. After a series of optimizing, the final GKPSDM program is 14 times faster than the serial KPSDM program.

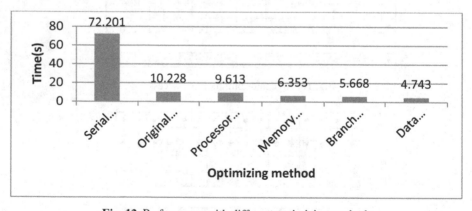

Fig. 12. Performance with different optimizing methods

In the second experiment, we use four different practical jobs with 1000 CELLs and different number of trace to measure the performance with a variety of data volume. Fig.13 demonstrates the speedup times to the serial program. The speedup seems to be limited before the number of trace has come to a high level. That is because with less data, the data transmission and kernel invocation take up a large percentage of the executing time. But when sufficient data is available, these problems seem to be negligible. The speedup could come to and remain stable at high level. As in practical jobs, there can be billions of traces, the performance is acceptable. For different jobs, the speedup can be 8~15 times.

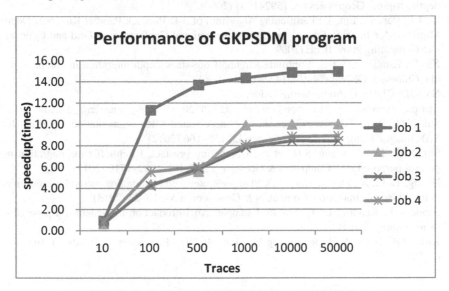

Fig. 13. Performance of GKPSDM program with 4 jobs

5   Conclusion and Future Work

In this paper, we introduce a GPGPU solution for a practical KPSDM algorithm. We present a parallel algorithm and optimizing strategy. Experiments have shown that with GPGPU and CUDA technology we can achieve an acceptable speedup (8 ~15 times). Moreover, the GPUs have several features that we should pay attention to when optimizing a CUDA program, including processor occupancy, branch divergence, memory access, and data transmission.

Although our GKPSDM program has increased the speed of KPSDM, much work remains to be done.

- There are still some optimizing methods that haven't been used in our program, like shared memory, texture memory, etc.
- Some practical jobs have too much data in the travel time table, causing the data transmission to GPU memory to become the bottleneck of the program. An efficient compressing algorithm is imperative.
- Much work can be done by integrating multi-cores CPU and GPUs to avoid wasting any computation resource.

References

1. Deschizeaux, B., Blanc, J.Y.: Imaging Earth's Subsurface Using CUDA, http://developer.download.nvidia.com/books/gpu_gems_3/samples/gems3_ch38.pdf
2. Sun, Y., Qin, F., Checkles, S., Leveille, J.P.: 3-D prestack Kirchhoff beam migration for depth imaging. Geophysics 65, 1592–1603 (2000)
3. Li, J.J., Dan, H., Lin, Y.: Partitioning Algorithm of 3-D Prestack Parallel Kirchhoff Depth Migration for Imaging Spaces. In: Eighth International Conference on Grid and Cooperative Computing 2009. IEEE (2009)
4. Xu, S., Lambar, G.: True amplitude Kirchhoff pre-stack depth migration in complex media. Chinese J. Geophys. 49(5), 1434–1444 (2006)
5. NVIDIA CUDA C Programming Guide, http://docs.nvidia.com/cuda/pdf/CUDA_C_Programming_Guide.pdf
6. Sui, H.G., Peng, F.F., Xu, C., et al.: GPU-accelerated MRF segmentation algorithm for SAR images. Computers & Geosciences 43, 159–166 (2012)
7. Shi, X.H., Li, C., Wang, S.H., et al.: Computing prestack Kirchhoff time migration on general purpose GPU. Computers & Geosciences 37(10), 1702–1710 (2011)
8. Huang, T., Li, X., Zhang, T., et al.: GPU-accelerated Direct Sampling method for multiple-point statistical simulation. Computers & Geosciences 57, 13–23 (2013)
9. Sanders, J., Kandrot, E.: CUDA by Example: An Introduction to General-Purpose GPU Programming (2010)
10. Kirk, D.B., Hwu, W.: Programming Massively Parallel Processors: A Hands-on Approach (2010)

An Algorithm to Embed a Family
of Node-Disjoint 3D Meshes
into Locally Twisted Cubes

Lantao You[1] and Yuejuan Han[2]

[1] Suzhou Industrial Park Institute Of Services Outsourcing,
[2] Center of Information Development and Management, Soochow University,
Suzhou 215000, China
yoult@siso.edu.cn

Abstract. In this paper, embeddings of a family of 3D meshes in locally twisted cubes are studied. Let $LTQ_n(V, E)$ denotes the n-dimensional locally twisted cube. We find two major results in this paper:(1) For any integer $n \geq 4$, two node-disjoint 3D meshes of size $2 \times 2 \times 2^{n-3}$ can be embedded into LTQ_n with dilation 1 and expansion 2. (2) For any integer $n \geq 6$, four node-disjoint $4 \times 2 \times 2^{n-5}$ meshes can be embedded into LTQ_n with dilation 1 and expansion 4. Further, an embedding algorithm can be constructed based on our embedding method. The obtained results are optimal in the sense that the dilations of the embeddings are 1.

Keywords: Interconnection networks, locally twisted cube, 3D mesh, embedding, parallel computing.

1 Introduction

An interconnection network can be represented by a graph $G = (V, E)$, where V represents the node set and E represents the edge set. One of the important properties of interconnection networks is graph embedding ability. Graph embedding problem is to embed a gust graph G_1 to a host graph G_2. Two common measures of effectiveness of an embedding are the dilation and expansion. The dilation of embedding ψ is defined as $\mathrm{dil}(G_1, G_2, \psi) = \max\{\mathrm{dist}(G_2, \psi(u), \psi(v)) | (u, v) \in E_1\}$, where $\mathrm{dist}(G_2, \psi(u), \psi(v))$ denotes the distance between the two nodes $\psi(u)$ and $\psi(v)$ in G_2. The smaller the dilation of an embedding is, the shorter the communication delay that the graph G_2 simulates the graph G_1. The expansion of embedding is defined as $\exp(G_1, G_2, \psi) = |V(G_2)|/|V(G_1)|$, which measures the processor utilization. The smaller the expansion of an embedding is, the more efficient the processor utilization that the graph G_2 simulates the graph G_1. Graph embedding has good applications in transplanting parallel algorithms developed for one network to a different one, and allocating concurrent processes to processors in the network. Paths[5],[6],[7] and cycles[1],[2],[21] are two common fundamental guest graphs used in interconnection network.

X.-h. Sun et al. (Eds.): ICA3PP 2014, Part II, LNCS 8631, pp. 219–230, 2014.

Meshes are common interconnection structures used in parallel computing. Many parallel algorithms with mesh-structured task graphs have been developed. Therefore, it is important to study the problem of how to embed different kinds of meshes into a host graph. Recently, many mesh embedding problems [3],[4],[12],[13],[15],[17] have been studied.

The locally twisted cube LTQ_n is a variant of hypercube, proposed by Yang et al. [16]. It has many attractive features superior to those of the hypercube, such as the diameter is only about half of that of Q_n. Recently, locally twisted cubes were discussed widely [8],[9],[10],[11],[14],[18],[19],[20].

In this paper, embeddings of node-disjoint 3D meshes in locally twisted cubes are studied. We find two major results in this paper: (1) For any integer $n \geq 4$, two node-disjoint 3D meshes of size $2 \times 2 \times 2^{n-3}$ can be embedded in LTQ_n with dilation 1 and expansion 2. (2) For any integer $n \geq 6$, four node-disjoint $4 \times 2 \times 2^{n-5}$ meshes can be embedded in LTQ_n with dilation 1 and expansion 4.

This paper is organized as follows. Section 2 gives some definitions and notations. We provide constructing proofs of the results in Section 3 and Section 4. At last, we conclude the paper in Section 5.

2   Preliminaries

Notation 1. An $r \times s$ mesh M can be denoted by an $r \times s$ matrix

$$\begin{pmatrix} \alpha_{11} & \alpha_{12} & \dots & \alpha_{1s} \\ \alpha_{21} & \alpha_{22} & \dots & \alpha_{2s} \\ \dots & \dots & \dots \\ \alpha_{r1} & \alpha_{r2} & \dots & \alpha_{rs} \end{pmatrix}$$

where $V(M) = \{\alpha_{ij} | 1 \leq i \leq r,$ and $1 \leq j \leq s\}$, $(\alpha_{ij}, \alpha_{i,j+1}) \in E(M)$ for $1 \leq i \leq r$ and $1 \leq j \leq s - 1$, and $(\alpha_{kl}, \alpha_{k+1,l}) \in E(M)$ for $1 \leq k \leq r - 1$ and $1 \leq l \leq s$. $\langle \alpha_{11}, \alpha_{12}, \dots \alpha_{1s} \rangle$ and $\langle \alpha_{r1}, \alpha_{r1}, \dots, \alpha_{rs} \rangle$ are called the row-borders.

If M can be embedded into LTQ_n and $(\alpha_{11}, \alpha_{r1}), (\alpha_{12}, \alpha_{r2}), \dots, (\alpha_{1s}, \alpha_{rs}) \in E(LTQ_n)$, we call the row-borders of M are edge-connected.

Notation 2[3]. A 2D mesh $M = (a_{i,j})_{m \times n}$ of size $m \times n$ is defined as a graph G, where

$V(G) = \{a_{i,j} : 1 \leq i \leq m, 1 \leq j \leq n\}$,

$E(G) = \{(a_{i,j}, a_{i+1,j}) : 1 \leq i \leq m - 1, 1 \leq j \leq n\} \bigcup \{(a_{i,j}, a_{i,j+1}) : 1 \leq i \leq m, 1 \leq j \leq n - 1\}$.

A 3D mesh $M_k = (a_{i,j,k})_{m \times n}$ of size $m \times n \times p$ is defined as a graph G, where

$V(G) = \{a_{i,j,k} : 1 \leq i \leq m, 1 \leq j \leq n, 1 \leq k \leq p\}$

$E(G) = \{(a_{i,j,k}, a_{i+1,j,k}) : 1 \leq i \leq m - 1, 1 \leq j \leq n, 1 \leq k \leq p\}$

$\bigcup \{(a_{i,j,k}, a_{i,j+1,k}) : 1 \leq i \leq m, 1 \leq j \leq n - 1, 1 \leq k \leq p\}$

$\bigcup \{(a_{i,j,k}, a_{i,j,k+1}) : 1 \leq i \leq m, 1 \leq j \leq n, 1 \leq k \leq p - 1\}$.

For any integer k with $1 \leq k \leq p$, let G_k denote a 2D mesh of size $m \times n$ defined as

$V(G_k) = \{a_{i,j,k} : 1 \leq i \leq m, 1 \leq j \leq n\}$,

$E(G_k) = \{(a_{i,j,k}, a_{i+1,j,k}) : 1 \leq i \leq m - 1, 1 \leq j \leq n\}$

$\bigcup\{(a_{i,j,k}, a_{i,j+1,k}) : 1 \leq i \leq m, 1 \leq j \leq n-1\}$,

Thus, the 3D mesh can be denoted by the blocked matrix $M = (M_1 \ M_2 \ ... \ M_p)$.

Notation 3. A binary string x of length n is denoted by $x_1 x_2 ... x_{n-1} x_n$, where x_1 is the most significant bit and x_n is the least significant bit. The ith bit x_i of x can also be written as $bit(x,i)$. Suppose that z is a binary string. z^i denotes the new binary string by repeating z string i times. If $i = 0$, z^i denotes the empty set. For a binary string s and a matrix $Z = (z_{i,j})_{m \times n}$ with binary-string entries, let sZ denote the matrix $(sz_{i,j})_{m \times n}$, where $sz_{i,j}$ is the concatenation of s and $z_{i,j}$.

Notation 4. For any blocked matrix $M = (M_1 \ M_2 \ ... \ M_n)$, we use $\overleftrightarrow{M}$ to denote $(M_n \ M_{n-1} \ ... \ M_1)$.

Similar to the n-dimensional hypercube, the n-dimensional locally twisted cube LTQ_n is an n-regular graph of 2^n nodes. Every node of LTQ_n is identified by a unique binary string of length n. LTQ_n can be recursively defined as follows.

Definition 1 [16]. Let $n \geq 2$. The n-dimensional locally twisted cube, LTQ_n, is defined recursively as follows.

(1) LTQ_2 is a graph consisting of four nodes labeled with 00, 01, 10, and 11, respectively, connected by four edges (00, 01), (00, 10), (01, 11) and (10, 11).

(2) For $n \geq 3$, LTQ_n is built from two disjoint copies LTQ_{n-1} according to the following steps. Let LTQ_{n-1}^0 denote the graph obtained by prefixing the label of each node of one copy of LTQ_{n-1} with 0, let LTQ_{n-1}^1 denote the graph obtained by prefixing the label of each node of the other copy of LTQ_{n-1} with 1, and connect each node $x = 0x_2 x_3 ... x_n$ of LTQ_{n-1}^0 with the node $1(x_2 + x_n)x_3 ... x_n$ of LTQ_{n-1}^1 by an edge, where $'+'$ represents the modulo 2 addition.

Figure 1 and Figure 2 demonstrate LTQ_3, LTQ_4 and LTQ_5, respectively.

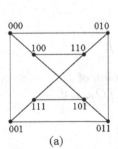 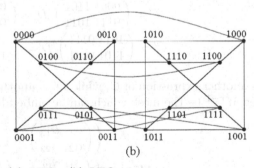

(a)   (b)

Fig. 1. (a) LTQ_3; (b) LTQ_4

3   Embedding Two Node-Disjoint $2 \times 2 \times 2^{n-3}$ Meshes into the n-Dimensional Locally Twisted Cubes

In this section, we discuss the $2 \times 2 \times 2^{n-3}$ mesh embedding in the n-dimensional locally twisted cubes by induction on the dimensional n. We use M_1^n, M_2^n to

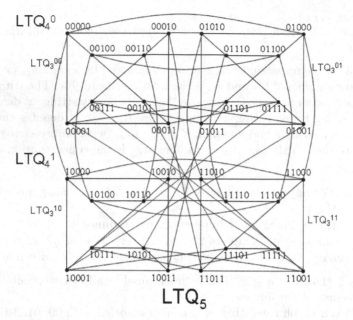

Fig. 2. 5-dimensional locally twisted cube LTQ_5

denote the two node-disjoint meshes of size $2 \times 2 \times 2^{n-3}$ in LTQ_n. For any integer $n \in \{4, 5\}$, by Definition 1, we can easily verify lemmas 1, 2 as follows. To express clearly, we let

$$A = \begin{pmatrix} 0000\ 1000 \\ 0100\ 1100 \end{pmatrix} B = \begin{pmatrix} 0010\ 1010 \\ 0110\ 1110 \end{pmatrix}$$

$$C = \begin{pmatrix} 0001\ 1101 \\ 0111\ 1011 \end{pmatrix} D = \begin{pmatrix} 0011\ 1111 \\ 0101\ 1001 \end{pmatrix}$$

$$C' = \begin{pmatrix} 1011\ 0111 \\ 1101\ 0001 \end{pmatrix} D' = \begin{pmatrix} 1001\ 0101 \\ 1111\ 0011 \end{pmatrix}.$$

C' is another expression of C, while D' is another expression of D.

Let $M^{\tau-1}$ be the mesh which can be embedded into $LTQ_{\tau-1}$, if

$$0M^{\tau-1} = \left(\begin{pmatrix} \alpha_{11}\ \alpha_{12} \\ \alpha_{21}\ \alpha_{22} \end{pmatrix} \cdots \begin{pmatrix} \beta_{11}\ \beta_{12} \\ \beta_{21}\ \beta_{22} \end{pmatrix} \right)$$

$$1M^{\tau-1} = \left(\begin{pmatrix} \gamma_{11}\ \gamma_{12} \\ \gamma_{21}\ \gamma_{22} \end{pmatrix} \cdots \begin{pmatrix} \delta_{11}\ \delta_{12} \\ \delta_{21}\ \delta_{22} \end{pmatrix} \right),$$

and if

$$(\beta_{11}, \gamma_{11}), (\beta_{12}, \gamma_{12}), (\beta_{21}, \gamma_{21}), (\beta_{22}, \gamma_{22}) \in E(LTQ_\tau),$$

then we say $\begin{pmatrix} \beta_{11}\ \beta_{12} \\ \beta_{21}\ \beta_{22} \end{pmatrix}$, $\begin{pmatrix} \gamma_{11}\ \gamma_{12} \\ \gamma_{21}\ \gamma_{22} \end{pmatrix}$ are edge-connected and

$$M^{\tau} = 0M^{\tau-1} + 1M^{\tau-1} = \left(\begin{pmatrix} \alpha_{11} & \alpha_{12} \\ \alpha_{21} & \alpha_{22} \end{pmatrix} \cdots \begin{pmatrix} \beta_{11} & \beta_{12} \\ \beta_{21} & \beta_{22} \end{pmatrix} \begin{pmatrix} \gamma_{11} & \gamma_{12} \\ \gamma_{21} & \gamma_{22} \end{pmatrix} \cdots \begin{pmatrix} \delta_{11} & \delta_{12} \\ \delta_{21} & \delta_{22} \end{pmatrix} \right),$$

which can be embedded into LTQ_τ.

Lemma 1. There are two node-disjoint 3D meshes of size $2 \times 2 \times 2$ in LTQ_4.

Proof. Obviously,
$M_1^4 = (A\ B)$ and $M_2^4 = (C\ D)$
are two $2 \times 2 \times 2$ meshes in LTQ_4 (See Fig. 3). □

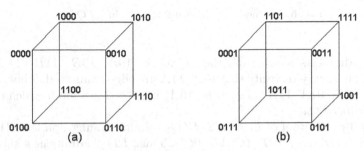

Fig. 3. (a) 3D mesh M_1^4; (b) 3D mesh M_2^4

Lemma 2. There are two node-disjoint 3D meshes of size $2 \times 2 \times 4$ in LTQ_5.

Proof. Obviously,
$M_1^5 = (0A\ 0B\ 1B\ 1A)$ and $M_2^5 = (0C\ 0D\ 1C'\ 1D')$
are two node-disjoint $2 \times 2 \times 4$ meshes in LTQ_5(See Fig. 4, Fig. 5). By Definition 1, $1D'$ and $0C$ are edge-connected. Thus, $(0D'\quad 1C\quad 1D\quad 0C')$ can also be embedded into LTQ_5, whose node set is the same of that of M_2^5(See Fig. 5) . □

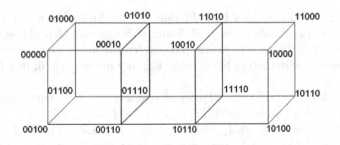

Fig. 4. 3D mesh M_1^5 of size $2 \times 2 \times 4$ in LTQ_5

Lemma 3. There are two node-disjoint 3D meshes of size $2 \times 2 \times 8$ in LTQ_6.

Proof. By Lemma 2, LTQ_5 admits as subgraph the 3D mesh $M_1^5 = (0A\quad 0B\ 1B\ 1A)$. Thus, LTQ_5^0 admits as a subgraph the 3D mesh $(00A\ 00B\ 01B\ 01A)$,

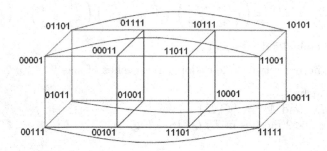

Fig. 5. 3D mesh M_2^5 of size $2 \times 2 \times 4$ in LTQ_5

and LTQ_5^1 admits as a subgraph the 3D mesh (10A 10B 11B 11A). By Definition 1, it is easy to verify that 01A, 11A are edge-connected. Thus, $M_1^6 =$ (00A 00B 01B 01A 11A 11B 10B 10A) is a $2 \times 2 \times 8$ mesh which can be embedded into LTQ_6.

Similarly, by the proof of Lemma 2, LTQ_5 admits as subgraph the 3D mesh (0C 0D 1C' 1D') and (0D' 1C 1D 0C'). Thus, LTQ_5^0 admits as a subgraph the 3D mesh (00C 00D 01C' 01D'), and LTQ_5^1 admits as a subgraph the 3D mesh (10D' 11C 11D 10C'). By Definition 1, it is easy to verify that 01D', 10D' are edge-connected. Thus, $M_2^6 =$ (00C 00D 01C' 01D' 10D' 11C 11D 10C') is a $2 \times 2 \times 8$ mesh which can be embedded into LTQ_6.

Therefore, M_1^6 and M_2^6 are two $2 \times 2 \times 8$ meshes in LTQ_6. It can be easily verified they are node-disjoint.   □

Then, we will prove two main lemmas in the following.

Lemma 4. For any integer n with $n \geq 7$, the meshes of size $2 \times 2 \times 2^{n-3}$ can be embedded into LTQ_n with dilation 1. $M_1^n = (M_1, M_2, M_3, ...M_{2^{n-3}})$, where the least significant bits of all nodes are 0. $M_1 = 0^{n-4}A$, $M_{2^{n-3}} = 10^{n-5}A$.

Proof. We prove this lemma by induction on the dimension n. By Lemmas 1, 2 and 3, this lemma holds when n=4, 5 and 6. Supposing that the lemma holds for $n = \tau - 1$ ($\tau \geq 7$), we will prove that the lemma holds for $n = \tau$.

According to the induction hypothesis. For any integer $n \geq 6$, in $LTQ_{\tau-1}$, we have

$M_1^{\tau-1} = (M_1$ M_2 M_3 ... $M_{2^{\tau-4}})$ of size $2 \times 2 \times 2^{\tau-4}$ such that the least significant bits of all nodes are 0. $M_1 = 0^{\tau-5}A$, $M_{2^{\tau-4}} = 10^{\tau-6}A$.

In $LTQ_{\tau-1}^0$, we have (0M_1 0M_2 0M_3 ...   0$M_{2^{\tau-4}}$). In $LTQ_{\tau-1}^1$, we have (1$M_{2^{\tau-4}},...,$1M_2, 1M_1). Note that the least significant bits are 0, by Definition 1, 0$M2^{\tau-4}$, 1$M2^{\tau-4}$ are edge-connected. Therefore, we have $M_1^\tau =$ (0M_1 0M_2 0M_3 ...   0$M_{2^{\tau-4}}$ 1$M_{2^{\tau-4}}$ ...   1M_2 1M_1) of size $2 \times 2 \times 2^{\tau-3}$ can be embedded into LTQ_τ, where 0$M_1 = 0^{\tau-4}A$ and 1$M_1 = 10^{\tau-5}A$. Thus, the lemma holds for $n = \tau$.   □

Lemma 5. For $n \geq 7$, meshes of size $2 \times 2 \times 2^{n-3}$ can be embedded into LTQ_n. $M_2^n = (M_1$ M_2 M_3 ... $M_{2^{n-3}})$, $N_2^n = (N_1$ N_2 N_3 ... $N_{2^{n-3}})$, where the least significant bits of all nodes are 1. And N_2^n uses exactly the same nodes of M_2^n. $M_1 = 0^{n-4}C$, $M_{2^{n-3}} = 110^{n-6}C$, $N_1 = 010^{n-6}C$, $N_{2^{n-3}} = 100^{n-6}C$.

Proof. We prove this lemma by induction on the dimensional n. By Lemma 3, $M_2^6 = (00C\ 00D\ 01C'\ 01D'\ 10D'\ 11C\ 11D\ 10C')$ is a 3D mesh which can be embedded into LTQ_6. We can easily verify that $(M_2^6)' = (00C'\ 00D'\ 01C\ 01D\ 10D\ 11C'\ 11D'\ 10C)$ is another expression of M_2^6. And by Definition 1, $010C'$, $100C'$ are edge-connected, and $000C'$, $110C'$ are edge-connected. Thus,

$M_2^7 = 0M_2^6 + 1(M_2^6)' = (000C\ 000D\ 001C'\ 001D'\ 010D'\ 011C\ 011D\ 010C'$
$100C'\ 100D'\ 101C\ 101D\ 110D\ 111C'\ 111D'\ 110C)$

$N_2^7 = 0(\overleftrightarrow{M_2^6})' + 1\overleftrightarrow{M_2^6} = (010C\ 011D'\ 011C'\ 010D\ 001D\ 001C\ 000D'\ 000C'$
$110C'\ 111D\ 111C\ 110D'\ 101D'\ 101C'\ 100D\ 100C)$

are two $2 \times 2 \times 2^4$ meshes which can be embedded into LTQ_7 using the same nodes.

By Definition 1, $0110C, 1010C$ are edge-connected and $0010C, 1110C$ are also edge-connected. Thus,

$M_2^8 = 0M_2^7 + 1N_2^7 = (0000C\ 0000D\ 0001C'\ 0001D'\ ...\ 1101D'\ 1101C'$
$1100D\ 1100C)$

$N_2^8 = 0\overleftrightarrow{N_2^7} + 1\overleftrightarrow{M_2^7} = (0100C\ 0100D\ 0101C'\ 0101D'\ ...\ 1001D'\ 1001C'$
$1000D\ 1000C)$ are two $2 \times 2 \times 2^5$ meshes which can be embedded into LTQ_8.

Thus, the lemma holds for $n=7, 8$.

Supposing that the lemma holds for $n = \tau - 1$ ($\tau \geq 8$), we will prove that the lemma holds for $n = \tau$.

According to the induction of hypothesis. For any integer $n \geq 6$, for $LTQ_{\tau-1}$, we have

$M_2^{\tau-1} = (M_1\ M_2\ M_3\ ...M_{2^{\tau}-4})$, $N_2^{\tau-1} = (N_1\ N_2\ N_3\ ...N_{2^{\tau}-4})$, where the least significant bits of all nodes are 1. And $N_2^{\tau-1}$ uses exactly the same nodes in $M_2^{\tau-1}$. $M_1 = 0^{\tau-5}C$, $M_{2^{\tau}-4} = 110^{\tau-7}C$, $N_1 = 010^{\tau-7}C$, $N_{2^{\tau}-4} = 100^{\tau-7}C$.

For $LTQ_{\tau-1}^0$, we have $0M_2^{\tau-1} = (00^{\tau-5}C\quad...\quad0110^{\tau-7}C)$, $0N_2^{\tau-1} = (0010^{\tau-7}C\quad...\quad0100^{\tau-7}C)$, where the least significant bits of all nodes are 1.

For $LTQ_{\tau-1}^1$, we have $1M_2^{\tau-1} = (10^{\tau-5}C\ ...\ 1110^{\tau-7}C)$, $1N_2^{\tau-1} = (1010^{\tau-7}C\ ...\ 1100^{\tau-7}C)$, where the least significant bits of all nodes are 1.

By Definition 1, $0110^{\tau-7}C, 1010^{\tau-7}C$ are edge-connected. Therefore, we have $M_2^{\tau} = 0M_2^{\tau-1} + 1N_2^{\tau-1} = (0^{\tau-4}C\ ...\ 0110^{\tau-7}C\ 1010^{\tau-7}C\ ...\ 110^{\tau-6}C)$ can be embedded into LTQ_{τ}. Similarly, by Definition 1, $0010^{\tau-7}C, 1110^{\tau-7}C$ are edge-connected. Thus, we have $N_2^{\tau} = 0\overleftrightarrow{N_2}^{\tau-1} + 1\overleftrightarrow{M_2}^{\tau-1} = (010^{\tau-6}C\ ...\ 0010^{\tau-7}C\ 1110^{\tau-7}C\ ...\ 10^{\tau-5}C)$ can be embedded into LTQ_{τ}.

Therefore, $M_2^n = (M_1\ M_2\ M_3\ ...M_{2^{n-3}}) = (0^{n-4}C\ ...\ 110^{n-6}C)$ is a $2 \times 2 \times 2^{n-3}$ mesh in LTQ_n, where the significant bits of all nodes are 1. $\square$

Based on these lemmas, we prove one result in this paper as follows.

Theorem 1. For any integer $n \geq 4$, there is two node-disjoint 3D meshes of size $2 \times 2 \times 2^{n-3}$ in LTQ_n.

Proof. By Lemma 1, 2, 3, 4, 5, there are two $2 \times 2 \times 2^{n-3}$ meshes M_1^n and M_2^n in LTQ_n for any $n \geq 4$, such that bit$(x,n)=0$ for all $x \in V(M_1^n)$ and bit$(y,n)=1$

for all $y \in V(M_2^n)$. As a result, $V(M_1^n) \bigcap V(M_2^n) = \emptyset$. Therefore, the theorem holds.   □

According to Theorem 1, we have the following corollary.

Corollary 1. For any integer $n \geq 4$, two node-disjoint $2 \times 2 \times 2^{n-3}$ meshes can be embedded with dilation 1 and expansion 2 in LTQ_n, such that these two meshes cover all nodes of LTQ_n.

4   Embedding Four $4 \times 2 \times 2^{n-5}$ Meshes into the n-Dimensional Locally Twisted Cubes

In this section, the $4 \times 2 \times 2^{n-5}$ mesh embedding in the n-dimensional locally twisted cube is studied. Similar to the $2 \times 2 \times 2^{n-3}$ mesh embedding in the last section, the method adopted is still by induction on n. We use $M_1^n, M_2^n, M_3^n, M_4^n$ to denote the four node-disjoint meshes of size $4 \times 2 \times 2^{n-5}$ in LTQ_n.

To express clearly, we let

$$
A = \begin{pmatrix} 000100\ 000000 \\ 010100\ 010000 \\ 110100\ 110000 \\ 100100\ 100000 \end{pmatrix} \quad
B = \begin{pmatrix} 000110\ 000010 \\ 010110\ 010010 \\ 110110\ 110010 \\ 100110\ 100010 \end{pmatrix}
$$

$$
C = \begin{pmatrix} 001110\ 001010 \\ 011110\ 011010 \\ 111110\ 111010 \\ 101110\ 101010 \end{pmatrix} \quad
D = \begin{pmatrix} 001100\ 001000 \\ 011100\ 011000 \\ 111100\ 111000 \\ 101100\ 101000 \end{pmatrix}
$$

$$
E = \begin{pmatrix} 000111\ 000001 \\ 011111\ 011001 \\ 101111\ 101001 \\ 110111\ 110001 \end{pmatrix} \quad
F = \begin{pmatrix} 000101\ 000011 \\ 011101\ 011011 \\ 101101\ 101011 \\ 110101\ 110011 \end{pmatrix}
$$

$$
G = \begin{pmatrix} 100101\ 100011 \\ 111101\ 111011 \\ 001101\ 001011 \\ 010101\ 010011 \end{pmatrix} \quad
H = \begin{pmatrix} 100111\ 100001 \\ 111111\ 111001 \\ 001111\ 001001 \\ 010111\ 010001 \end{pmatrix},
$$

where A, B, C, D use the nodes labeled by strings ended with 0 and E, F, G, H use the nodes labeled by strings ended with 1. And we can easily verify that A, B, C, D, E, F, G, H use exactly all the 64 nodes in LTQ_6.

Let $M^{\tau-1}$ be the mesh which can be embedded into $LTQ_{\tau-1}$, if $0M^{\tau-1} =$

$$
\left(\left(\begin{matrix} \alpha_{11}\ \alpha_{12} \\ \alpha_{21}\ \alpha_{22} \\ \alpha_{31}\ \alpha_{32} \\ \alpha_{41}\ \alpha_{42} \end{matrix} \right) \cdots \left(\begin{matrix} \alpha_{13}\ \alpha_{14} \\ \alpha_{23}\ \alpha_{24} \\ \alpha_{33}\ \alpha_{34} \\ \alpha_{43}\ \alpha_{44} \end{matrix} \right) \right), 1M^{\tau-1} = \left(\left(\begin{matrix} \beta_{11}\ \beta_{12} \\ \beta_{21}\ \beta_{22} \\ \beta_{31}\ \beta_{32} \\ \beta_{41}\ \beta_{42} \end{matrix} \right) \cdots \left(\begin{matrix} \beta_{13}\ \beta_{14} \\ \beta_{23}\ \beta_{24} \\ \beta_{33}\ \beta_{34} \\ \beta_{43}\ \beta_{44} \end{matrix} \right) \right),
$$

and $(\alpha_{13}, \beta_{11}), (\alpha_{23}, \beta_{21}), (\alpha_{33}, \beta_{31}), (\alpha_{43}, \beta_{41}), (\alpha_{14}, \beta_{12}), (\alpha_{24}, \beta_{22}), (\alpha_{34}, \beta_{32}),$

$(\alpha_{44}, \beta_{42}) \in LTQ_\tau$, we say $\begin{pmatrix} \alpha_{13}\ \alpha_{14} \\ \alpha_{23}\ \alpha_{24} \\ \alpha_{33}\ \alpha_{34} \\ \alpha_{43}\ \alpha_{44} \end{pmatrix} \begin{pmatrix} \beta_{11}\ \beta_{12} \\ \beta_{21}\ \beta_{22} \\ \beta_{31}\ \beta_{32} \\ \beta_{41}\ \beta_{42} \end{pmatrix}$ are edge-connected. Thus,

$$M^{\tau} = 0M^{\tau-1} + 1M^{\tau-1} = \left(\left(\begin{pmatrix} \alpha_{11} & \alpha_{12} \\ \alpha_{21} & \alpha_{22} \\ \alpha_{31} & \alpha_{32} \\ \alpha_{41} & \alpha_{42} \end{pmatrix} \cdots \begin{pmatrix} \alpha_{13} & \alpha_{14} \\ \alpha_{23} & \alpha_{24} \\ \alpha_{33} & \alpha_{34} \\ \alpha_{43} & \alpha_{44} \end{pmatrix} \begin{pmatrix} \beta_{11} & \beta_{12} \\ \beta_{21} & \beta_{22} \\ \beta_{31} & \beta_{32} \\ \beta_{41} & \beta_{42} \end{pmatrix} \cdots \begin{pmatrix} \beta_{13} & \beta_{14} \\ \beta_{23} & \beta_{24} \\ \beta_{33} & \beta_{34} \\ \beta_{43} & \beta_{44} \end{pmatrix} \right) \right),$$

which can be embedded into LTQ_{τ}.

According to Definition 1, we can easily verify the following lemmas.

Lemma 6
$M_1^6 = (A\ B)$, $M_2^6 = (C\ D)$, $M_3^6 = (E\ F)$ and $M_4^6 = (G\ H)$
are four $4 \times 2 \times 2$ meshes in LTQ_6 using different nodes(See Fig. 6).

Lemma 7. By Definition 1, we can easily verify that
$M_1^7 = (0A\ 0B\ 1B\ 1A)$
$M_2^7 = (0C\ 0D\ 1D\ 1C)$
$M_3^7 = (0E\ 0F\ 1G\ 1H)$
$M_4^7 = (1E\ 1F\ 0G\ 0H)$
are four $4 \times 2 \times 4$ meshes in LTQ_7 using different nodes (See Fig. 7).

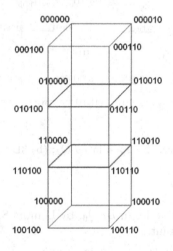

Fig. 6. 3D mesh M_1^6 of size $4 \times 2 \times 2$ in LTQ_6

Lemma 8. For $n \geq 8$, meshes of size $4 \times 2 \times 2^{n-5}$ can be embedded into LTQ_n.
$M_1^n = (00^{n-7}A\ \dots\ 10^{n-7}A) = (M_1\ M_2\ M_3\ \dots\ M_{2^{n-5}})$, where the least significant bits of all nodes are 0.

Proof. We prove this lemma by induction on the dimensional n. By Lemma 7, we know that $M_1^7 = (0A\ 0B\ 1B\ 1A)$ is a 3D mesh of size $4 \times 2 \times 2^2$ in LTQ_7. By Definition 1, 01A, 11A are edge-connected, so $M_1^8 = (00A\ 00B\ 01B\ 01A$
$11A\ 11B\ 10B\ 10A) = 0M_1^7 + 1\overset{\longleftrightarrow}{M_1^7}$ is a 3D mesh of size $4 \times 2 \times 2^3$ in LTQ_8.

Supposing that the lemma holds for $n = \tau - 1$ ($\tau \geq 8$), we will prove that the lemma holds for $n = \tau$.

According to the induction of hypothesis. For $LTQ_{\tau-1}(\tau \geq 8)$, we have $M_1^{\tau-1} = \left(00^{\tau-8}A \ldots 10^{\tau-8}A\right)$. By Definition 1, $010^{\tau-8}A, 110^{\tau-8}A$ are edge-connected. Thus, $M_1^\tau = 0M_1^{\tau-1} + 1\overleftrightarrow{M_1^{\tau-1}} = \{000^{\tau-8}A \ldots 100^{\tau-8}A\} = \{00^{\tau-7}A \ldots 10^{\tau-7}A\}$ is a $4 \times 2 \times 2^{\tau-5}$ mesh which can be embedded into LTQ_τ. □

Lemma 9. For $n \geq 8$, meshes of size $4 \times 2 \times 2^{n-5}$ can be embedded into LTQ_n. $M_2^n = (M_1 \ M_2 \ M_3 \ \ldots \ M_{2^{n-5}}) = (00^{n-7}C \ \ldots \ 10^{n-7}C)$, where the least significant bits of all nodes are 0.

Proof. Beginning with the $4 \times 2 \times 4$ mesh M_2^7 in LTQ_7 in Lemma 7, the proof is similar to Lemma 8, so omitted here. □

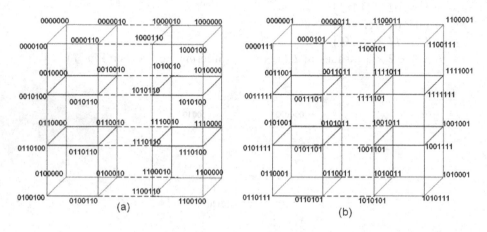

Fig. 7. (a)3D meshes M_1^7 of size $4 \times 2 \times 4$ in LTQ_7; (b) 3D mesh M_3^7 of size $4 \times 2 \times 4$ in LTQ_7

For M_1^6, M_2^6 use different nodes in LTQ_6, by Lemma 8, 9, we can easily verify that M_1^n, M_2^n are node-disjoint.

Lemma 10. For $n \geq 8$, meshes of size $4 \times 2 \times 2^{n-5}$ can be embedded into LTQ_n. $M_3^n = (M_1 \ M_2 \ M_3 \ \ldots \ M_{2^{n-5}}) = \left(0^{n-6}E \ 0^{n-6}F \ldots 110^{n-8}F \ 110^{n-8}E\right)$ $M_4^n = (M_1 \ M_2 \ M_3 \ \ldots \ M_{2^{n-5}}) = \left(10^{n-7}E \ 10^{n-7}F \ldots 010^{n-8}F \ 010^{n-8}E\right)$, where the least significant bits of all nodes are 1.

Proof. By Lemma 7, we know that $M_3^7 = (0E \ 0F \ 1G \ 1H)$, $M_4^7 = (1E \ 1F \ 0G \ 0H)$.

And, by Definition 1, $01H, 10H$ are edge-connected. Thus, we can get:
$M_3^8 = 0M_3^7 + 1\overleftrightarrow{M_4^7} = (00E \ 00F \ 01G \ 01H \ 10H \ 10G \ 11F \ 11E)$.
Still, by Definition 1, $11H, 00H$ are edge-connected. Thus, we can get:
$M_4^8 = 1M_3^7 + 0\overleftrightarrow{M_4^7} = (10E \ 10F \ 11G \ 11H \ 00H \ 00G \ 01F \ 01E)$.
M_3^8 and M_4^8 are two $4 \times 2 \times 2^{8-5}$ meshes in LTQ_8. Thus, the lemma holds for $n=8$.

Supposing that the lemma holds for $n = \tau - 1$ ($\tau \geq 9$), we will prove that the lemma holds for $n = \tau$.

According to the induction of hypothesis. For $LTQ_{\tau-1}(\tau \geq 8)$, we have two meshes $M_3^{\tau-1}$ and $M_4^{\tau-1}$ of size $4 \times 2 \times 2^{\tau-6}$, which can be embedded into $LTQ_{\tau-1}$, where

$M_3^{\tau-1} = \left(0^{\tau-7}E \quad 0^{\tau-7}F \quad \ldots \quad 110^{\tau-9}F \quad 110^{\tau-9}E\right)$

$M_4^{\tau-1} = \left(10^{\tau-8}E \quad 10^{\tau-8}F \quad \ldots \quad 010^{\tau-9}F \quad 010^{\tau-9}E\right)$

Because $0110^{\tau-9}E$ and $1010^{\tau-9}E$ are edge-connected, respectively, we can get:

$M_3^{\tau} = 0M_3^{\tau-1} + 1\overleftarrow{M_4^{\tau-1}}$

$= (0^{\tau-6}E \quad 0^{\tau-6}F \quad \ldots \quad 0110^{\tau-9}F \quad 0110^{\tau-9}E \quad 1010^{\tau-9}E \quad 1010^{\tau-9}F \quad \ldots$
$110^{\tau-8}F \quad 110^{\tau-8}E)$

$M_4^{\tau} = 1M_3^{\tau-1} + 0\overleftarrow{M_4^{\tau-1}}$

$= (10^{\tau-7}E \quad 10^{\tau-7}F \quad \ldots \quad 1110^{\tau-9}F \quad 1110^{\tau-9}E \quad 0010^{\tau-9}E \quad 0010^{\tau-9}F \quad \ldots$
$010^{\tau-8}F \quad 010^{\tau-8}E)$

Therefore, M_3^{τ} and M_4^{τ} are two node-disjoint meshes of size $4 \times 2 \times 2^{\tau-5}$, which can be embedded into LTQ_{τ}. Thus, the lemma holds.

With these lemmas we have the following theorem.

Theorem 2. For any integer $n \geq 6$, there are four node-disjoint meshes of size $4 \times 2 \times 2^{n-5}$ in LTQ_n.

Proof. By Lemma 6, 7, 8, 9, 10, there are four $4 \times 2 \times 2^{n-5}$ meshes M_1^n, M_2^n, M_3^n and M_4^n in LTQ_n for any $n \geq 6$, such that bit$(x,n)=0$ for all $x \in V(M_1^n) \bigcup V(M_2^n)$ and bit$(y,n)=1$ for all $y \in V(M_3^n) \bigcup V(M_4^n)$. As a result, $(V(M_1^n) \bigcup V(M_2^n)) \bigcap (V(M_3^n) \bigcup V(M_4^n)) = \emptyset$.   □

According to the Theorem 2, we have the following corollary.

Corollary 2. For any integer $n \geq 6$, four $4 \times 2 \times 2^{n-5}$ meshes can be embedded with dilation 1 and expansion 4 into LTQ_n, such that there is no node-overlapping between the four embedded meshes(subgraphs) and these four $4 \times 2 \times 2^{n-5}$ meshes cover all nodes of LTQ_n.

Corollary 2 shows that four embedded meshes can work independently in the n-dimensional locally twisted cube without interference to each other, which is a desirable feature in parallel computing.

5   Conclusions

This paper provides embeddings of two kinds of special meshes in locally twisted cubes. Two major results are gained: (1) For any integer $n \geq 4$, two node-disjoint 3D meshes of size $2 \times 2 \times 2^{n-3}$ can be embedded in LTQ_n with dilation 1 and expansion 2. (2) For any integer $n \geq 6$, four node-disjoint $4 \times 2 \times 2^{n-5}$ meshes can be embedded in LTQ_n with dilation 1 and expansion 4. An embedding algorithm can be constructed based on our embedding method. The result are optimal in the sense that the dilations of all embeddings are 1.

References

1. Bae, M.M., Bose, B.: Edge disjoint hamiltonian cycles in k-ary n-cubes and hyper-cubes. IEEE Trans. Computers 52, 1271–1284 (2003)
2. Chang, J.M., Yang, J.S.: Fault-tolerant cycle-embedding in alternating group graphs. Applied Mathematics and Computation 197, 760–767 (2008)
3. Dong, Q., Yang, X., Zhao, J., Tang, Y.: Embedding a family of disjoint 3D meshes into a crossed cube. Information Science 178, 2396–2405 (2008)
4. Fan, J., Jia, X.: Embedding meshes into crossed cubes. Information Sciences 177, 3151–3160 (2007)
5. Fan, J., Lin, X., Jia, X.: Optimal path embedding in crossed cubes. IEEE Trans. Parallel and Distributed Systems 16, 1190–1200 (2005)
6. Fan, J., Jia, X., Lin, X.: Optimal embeddings of paths with various lengths in twisted cubes. IEEE Trans. Parallel and Distributed Systems 18, 511–521 (2007)
7. Fan, J., Jia, X.: Edge-pancyclicity and path-embeddability of bijective connection graphs. Information Sciences 178, 341–351 (2008)
8. Han, Y., Fan, J., Zhang, S., Yang, J., Qian, P.: Embedding meshes into locally twisted cubes. Information Sciences 180, 3794–3805 (2010)
9. Han, Y., Fan, J., Zhang, S.: Changing the diameter of the locally twisted cube. International Journal of Computer Mathematics 90, 497–510 (2013)
10. Hsieh, S.Y., Tu, C.J.: Constructing edge-disjoint spanning trees in locally twisted cubes. Theoretical Computer Science 410, 926–932 (2009)
11. Kung, T.: Flexible cycle embedding in the locally twisted cube with nodes positioned at any prescribed distance. Information Sciences 242, 92–102 (2013)
12. Lai, C.J., Tsai, C.H.: Embedding a family of meshes into twisted cubes. Information Processing Letters 108, 326–330 (2008)
13. Li, T.K., Lai, C.J., Tsai, C.H.: A novel algorithm to embed a multi-dimensional torus into a locally twisted cube. Theoretical Computer Science 412, 2418–2424 (2011)
14. Ma, M., Xu, J.: Panconnectivity of locally twisted cubes. Applied Mathematics Letters 19, 681–685 (2006)
15. Tsai, C.H.: Embedding of meshes in Möbius cubes. Theoretical Computer Science 401, 181–190 (2008)
16. Yang, X., Evans, D.J., Megson, G.M.: The locally twisted cubes. International Journal of Computer Mathematics 82, 401–413 (2005)
17. Yang, P.J., Tien, S.B., Raghavendra, C.S.: Embedding of rings and meshes onto faulty hypercubes using free dimensions. IEEE Trans. Comput. 43, 608–613 (1994)
18. Yang, X., Wang, L., Yang, L.: Optimal broadcasting for locally twisted cubes. Information Processing Letters 112, 129–134 (2012)
19. Yang, H., Yang, X.: A fast diagnosis algorithm for locally twisted cube multiprocessor systems under the MM* model. Computers and Mathematics with Applications 53, 918–926 (2007)
20. Zhang, J., Yang, X., Li, X.: Wavelength assignment for locally twisted cube communication pattern on optical bus network-on-chip. Optical Fiber Technology 20, 228–234 (2014)
21. Hsieh, S.Y., Yu, P.Y.: Cycle embedding on twisted cubes. In: International Conference on Parallel and Distributed Computing Applications and Technologies, pp. 102–104 (2006)

GPU Acceleration of Finding Maximum Eigenvalue of Positive Matrices

Ning Tian[1], Longjiang Guo[1,2,*], Chunyu Ai[3], Meirui Ren[1,2], and Jinbao Li[1,2]

[1] School of Computer Science and Technology, Heilongjiang University, China
[2] Key Laboratory of Database and Parallel Computing, Heilongjiang, China
longjiang_guo@yeah.net
[3] Division of Math & Computer Science, University of South Carolina Upstate, USA

Abstract. Matrix eigenvalue theory has become an important analysis tool in scientific computing. Sometimes, people do not need to find all eigenvalues but only the maximum eigenvalue. Existing algorithms of finding the maximum eigenvalue of matrices are implemented sequentially. With the increasing of the orders of matrices, the workload of calculation is getting heavier. Therefore, traditional sequential methods are unable to meet the need of fast calculation for large matrices. This paper proposes a parallel algorithm named PA-ST to find the maximum eigenvalue of positive matrices by using similarity transformation which is implemented by CUDA (Computer Unified Device Architecture) on GPU (Graphic Process Unit). To the best of our knowledge, this is the first CUDA based parallel algorithm of calculating maximum eigenvalue of matrices. In order to improve the performance, optimization techniques are applied in this paper such as using the shared memory rather than the global memory to improve the speed of computation, avoiding bank conflicts by setting the span index, satisfying the principle of coalesced memory access, and by using single-precision floating-point arithmetic and the pinned memory to reduce the copy operation and obtain higher data transfer bandwidth between the host and the GPU device. The experimental results show that the similarity transformation technique can significantly shorten the running time compared to the sequential algorithm and the speedup ratio is nearly stable when the number of iterations increases. As the matrix order increases, the running time of the sequential algorithm and PA-ST increases correspondingly. Experiments also show that the speedup ratio of the PA-ST is between 2.85 and 35.028.

Keywords: Maximum Eigenvalue, Positive Matrix, Similarity Transformation, GPU, CUDA.

1 Introduction

Matrix computing plays key roles in vibration problems, control systems, and determination of certain critical value in physics. Especially, solving matrix eigenvalues is one common and important calculation in matrix computing [1]. For

---

* Corresponding author.

X.-h. Sun et al. (Eds.): ICA3PP 2014, Part II, LNCS 8631, pp. 231–244, 2014.

a lot of applications, it is not necessary to find all the eigenvalues but only the maximum eigenvalue. The maximum eigenvalue has a crucial role in displaying the nature feature of the matrix, specifically in the digital signal processing. For example, given a particularly large graph, how can we know how many triangles in it [2]? To answer this question, we just need to find out the maximum eigenvalue of the adjacency matrix of the large graph. Some specific processing in radar, sonar, communications, image processing, and other systems often requires real-time calculation of the maximum positive eigenvalue of the positive matrix [3][4]. Therefore, the problem of maximum eigenvalue of positive matrices is an important part of matrix computing.

Nowadays, the size of matrices which people deal with has been increased dramatically in many application fields. The orders of matrices often reach thousands, tens of thousands, or even millions [5]. Thereby, solving maximum eigenvalue of positive matrices becomes one of the most significant computational tasks in high-performance computing [6][7]. However, almost all existing algorithms for solving the maximum eigenvalue are implemented sequentially such as power[8], QR[9], and Oepomo's iteration algorithm [10]. These are some parallel algorithms of QR, but as we know QR is suitable for solving all the eigenvalues of matrix. The speed of these sequential solutions is undoubtedly very slow for large matrices. Some researchers use SMP (Symmetric Multi-Processing) cluster systems or parallel machine systems to accelerate the computing. The computing speed of cluster systems is much faster than the sequential methods. Nevertheless, using cluster systems will cause high costs in equipments and power consumptions.

In recent years, GPU became a famous programming scheme for the large-scale fast calculations. GPU is the abbreviation of Graphic Process Unit[11]. Nvidia and AMD launched its own GPU computing technology–CUDA and ATI Stream. The CUDA technology is an outstanding representative in this area [12]. Researchers regard the GPU and CUDA as a united hardware and software system of data parallel computing. CUDA programming provides us a new way to solve the linear problem [13]. Because GPU has small calculate volume, cheap cost, simple structure, and powerful floating point capability. CUDA implements CPU and GPU hybrid computing scheme. CPU is responsible for performing complex logic processing and transaction management that is not suitable for data-parallel computing, whereas GPU is responsible for large-scale data parallel computing of compute-intensive. Rational use of CPU and GPU resources can achieve the goal of not wasting computing resources.

This paper proposes a parallel algorithm named PA-ST for using GPU acceleration to find maximum eigenvalue of positive matrices. PA-ST is implemented by CUDA (Computer Unified Device Architecture). To the best of our knowledge, this is the first CUDA-based parallel algorithm which is implemented on GPU to solve the maximum eigenvalue of positive matrices by using similarity transformation. The implementation details are shown in Section 3. Compared to the best sequential algorithm which we know, the proposed algorithm has obvious better running time performance. In order to achieve the best performance, we parallelize core operations, design new performance optimization methods, use the division of tasks to solve the sum of every row, adopt single-precision floating-point arithmetic, and call the GPU's *cudaHostAlloc()* function to allocate pinned memory to reduce the copy operation and obtain higher data transfer bandwidth between CPU and GPU devices. Then we use synchronizing function across all thread blocks to ensure that each thread of thread-block performs all operations before the synchronizing function is called. Also, the shared memory is used rather than the global memory to improve the performance and avoid the bank conflict by setting the span index. The algorithm also utilizes the mechanism of coalesced memory access to improve performance.

In experiments, the speedup ratio of the proposed algorithm is between 2.85 and 35.028. As the order of a matrix increases, the running time of sequential algorithms and parallel algorithms increases correspondingly. The experimental results show that the proposed algorithm can save more running time than the sequential algorithm and the speedup ratio is nearly stable while the number of iterations increases.

The paper is organized as follows: Section 2 introduces fundamental knowledge about CUDA. The sequential similarity transformation algorithm and the parallel similarity transformation algorithm are addressed in Section 3. Section 4 studies complexity analysis. Section 5 shows experimental results. Finally, Section 6 concludes the paper.

2   An Overview of CUDA

Traditionally, GPU is only responsible for graphic rendering, and most of other processing tasks are handled by CPU. It is such a waste of GPU's computing resources since GPU has obvious advantages over CPU in processing ability and memory bandwidth. For the same amount of workload, the computation cost and power consumption of GPU is lower. Currently, the single precision floating point processing capacity of mainstream GPUs has reached about 10 times of the same period CPU.

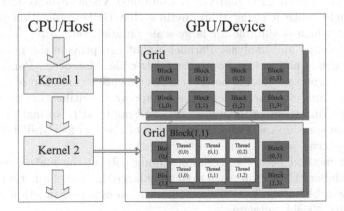

Fig. 1. CUDA Thread Structure

NVIDIA had officially released CUDA in 2007. It is the first developing environment and software system using C-like language instead of graphic API. Compared to the traditional GPU general computing development, CUDA had made a very significant improvement. Moreover, since CUDA uses C-like language, it can be quickly accepted and mastered by programmers. After several years of development, CUDA and CUDA-enabled GPU performance have been significantly improved, as well as functions.

Program code developed on CUDA can be divided into two parts in actual execution. One part is the host code which runs on CPU, and the other part is the device code which runs on GPU. A parallel program that runs on GPU is called a kernel. The CUDA thread structure is shown in Figure 1. Threads of an executing kernel are organized as blocks, and blocks are organized as grids. A block is the execution unit of a kernel. A grid is a collection of blocks which can be executed in parallel. All blocks are executed in parallel. There is no communication and execution order among blocks. Within a block, all threads are also executed in parallel. The same kernel program can be executed in parallel by all the threads of the blocks which are contained in the same grid. Threads in the same block communicate with each other by using the shared memory and are synchronized by calling the _syncthreads() function. This is the two-level block-thread parallel execution model of CUDA.

The memory space of CUDA is divided into register, local memory, shared memory, global memory, constant memory, and texture memory. It is shown in Figure 2. Each thread has its own memory, i.e., registers and local memory, which can be read and written directly. Each block has a shared memory, which can be read and written by the threads in the same block. All the threads in the same grid can access the same global memory. In addition, ROM is accessible by all threads, i.e., constant memory and texture memory, which can help to do the optimization for different applications.

Here we must introduce the NVIDIA Parallel Nsight software, it is the first develop environment which is integrated in the Visual Studio aimed at large-scale parallel computing. It can make programmers finish development in the Visual Studio aimed at both CPU and GPU. Combined Visual Studio and NVIDIA Parallel Nsight make it easier than anytime that GPU application programm development which is suitable for large-scale parallel computing. Through the native GPU debug and analysis, Parallel Nsight can provide the most efficient methods to debug analysis and optimize GPU code. Moreover , Parallel Nsight admit programmers to observe heterogeneous executive condition of application programm by analysis trace function, and improve the utilization of multi-core CPU, the speedup scope of the multi-GPU and multi-API. No matter you want the algorithm speedup ratio or the processing of the graphs,Parallel Nsight can make it come true, and with the most efficient.

Since our method need the iteration among solving the matrix computing, when the number of iteration reach extremely large,the kernel function will have the overtime problem. So we relieve the limitation of kernel function by closing the TDR with Nsight software.

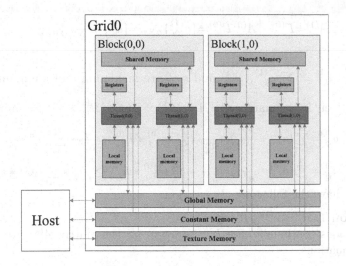

Fig. 2. CUDA Memory Model

3 The Parallel Algorithm of Similarity Transformation (PA-ST)

3.1 Similarity Transformation and Theoretical Foundation

Mathematical Basis. If λ is an eigenvalue of an $n \times n$ matrix A, with the corresponding eigenvector X, then from $(A - \lambda I_n)X = 0$, where $X \neq 0$, and $det(A - \lambda I_n) = 0$, we know that there are at most n distinct eigenvalues of A.

If there is a eigenvalue λ^*, such that $\lambda^* = max\{|\lambda|\}$, then we call λ^* the maximum eigenvalue of the matrix A, we denote λ^* as $\lambda^*(A)$. The eigenvector corresponding to the eigenvalue $\lambda^*(A)$ is denoted by $X^*(A)$. For any real matrix $A = \{a_{i,j}\}_{n \times n}$, if every element $a_{i,j}$ in A, $a_{i,j} > 0$, then A is called a positive matrix.

Key Idea of Sequential Algorithm. Here, we show the key idea of sequential algorithm by using similarity transformation.

For any positive matrix $A = A^{(0)} = \{a_{i,j}^{(0)}\}_{n \times n}$, where $a_{i,j}^{(0)} > 0$, $R_i^{(0)}$ is the sum of ith row of $A^{(0)}$, i.e. $R_i^{(0)} = \sum_{j=1}^{n} a_{ij}^{(0)}$, $R^{(0)}$ and $r^{(0)}$ are maximum and minimum sum of rows respectively, i.e. $R^{(0)} = \max\limits_{1 \leq i \leq n} \{R_i^{(0)}\}$, $r^{(0)} = \min\limits_{1 \leq i \leq n} \{R_i^{(0)}\}$.

$$\text{Let } \Gamma^{(0)} = \begin{bmatrix} R_1^{(0)} & & & \\ & R_2^{(0)} & & \\ & & \ddots & \\ & & & R_n^{(0)} \end{bmatrix}, \text{ then } \Gamma^{(0)^{-1}} = \begin{bmatrix} \frac{1}{R_1^{(0)}} & & & \\ & \frac{1}{R_2^{(0)}} & & \\ & & \ddots & \\ & & & \frac{1}{R_n^{(0)}} \end{bmatrix}.$$

To make a similarity transformation for $A^{(0)}$:

$$A^{(1)} = \Gamma^{(0)-1} A^{(0)} \Gamma^{(0)} = \{a_{i,j}^{(1)}\}_{n \times n} = \{a_{i,j}^{(0)} * \frac{R_j^{(0)}}{R_i^{(0)}}\}_{n \times n}.$$

For $A^{(1)}$, $R_i^{(1)} = \sum_{j=1}^{n} a_{ij}^{(1)}$, $R^{(1)}$ and $r^{(1)}$ are maximum and minimum sum of rows respectively in the matrix $A^{(1)}$, i.e. $R^{(1)} = \max_{1 \le i \le n} \{R_i^{(1)}\}$, $r^{(1)} = \min_{1 \le i \le n} \{R_i^{(1)}\}$.

$$R_i^{(1)} = \sum_{j=1}^{n} a_{ij}^{(1)} = \sum_{j=1}^{n} (a_{i,j}^{(0)} * \frac{R_j^{(0)}}{R_i^{(0)}}) = \frac{1}{R_i^{(0)}} * \sum_{j=1}^{n} (a_{i,j}^{(0)} * R_j^{(0)}) \le \frac{1}{R_i^{(0)}} * \sum_{j=1}^{n} (a_{i,j}^{(0)} * R^{(0)}) = R^{(0)}.$$

$$R_i^{(1)} = \sum_{j=1}^{n} a_{ij}^{(1)} = \sum_{j=1}^{n} (a_{i,j}^{(0)} * \frac{R_j^{(0)}}{R_i^{(0)}}) = \frac{1}{R_i^{(0)}} * \sum_{j=1}^{n} (a_{i,j}^{(0)} * R_j^{(0)}) \ge \frac{1}{R_i^{(0)}} * \sum_{j=1}^{n} (a_{i,j}^{(0)} * r^{(0)}) = r^{(0)}.$$

Thus, we have the following observation:

Observation 1: $r^{(0)} \le r^{(1)} \le R^{(1)} \le R^{(0)}$.

Do iterations continually. For k^{th} iteration for the matrix $A^{(k)}$, we have the following equations:

$$R_i^{(k)} = \sum_{j=1}^{n} a_{ij}^{(k)};$$

$$R^{(k)} = \max_{1 \le i \le n} \{R_i^{(k)}\};$$

$$r^{(k)} = \min_{1 \le i \le n} \{R_i^{(k)}\};$$

$$\Gamma^{(k)} = diag(R_1^{(k)}, R_2^{(k)}, \cdots, R_n^{(k)}).$$

The iteration process is given as follows:

$$A^{(k+1)} = \{a_{i,j}^{(k+1)}\}_{n \times n} = \Gamma^{(k)-1} A^{(k)} \Gamma^{(k)} = \{a_{i,j}^{(k)} * \frac{R_j^{(k)}}{R_i^{(k)}}\}_{n \times n}$$

According to observation 1, we have a further observation:

Observation 2

$$r^{(0)} \le r^{(1)} \le r^{(2)} \cdots \le r^{(k)} \le R^{(k)} \le R^{(k-1)} \cdots \le R^{(1)} \le R^{(0)}.$$

Therefore, we have a result of convergence of iterations due to the fact that the sequence of $r^{(k)}$ is monotonically increasing and the sequence of $R^{(k)}$ is monotonically decreasing, and they both have bounds of $r^{(0)}$ and $R^{(0)}$.

Theoretical Foundation. Some theorems are given as follows.

Theorem 1. [14]: For a positive matrix $A^{(0)} = \{a_{i,j}^{(0)}\}_{n \times n}$, in k^{th} iteration, $R^{(k)} = \max_{1 \le i \le n} \{R_i^{(k)}\}$, $r^{(k)} = \min_{1 \le i \le n} \{R_i^{(k)}\}$, there exists a real number q ($0 < q < R^{(0)}$), where $q = \min\{ a_{i,i}, \min_{i \ne j}\{2\sqrt{a_{i,j}a_{j,i}}\}\}$, such that

$$R^{(k)} - r^{(k)} \leq (R^{(0)} - r^{(0)}) * [(1 - q/R^{(0)})]^k, \ k = (1, 2 \cdots).$$

Theorem 2. [14]: For a positive matrix $A^{(0)} = \{a_{i,j}^{(0)}\}_{n \times n}$, in k^{th} iteration, $R^{(k)} = \max\limits_{1 \leq i \leq n} \{R_i^{(k)}\}$, $r^{(k)} = \min\limits_{1 \leq i \leq n} \{R_i^{(k)}\}$, then $\lim\limits_{k \to \infty} R^{(k)} = \lim\limits_{k \to \infty} r^{(k)} = \lambda^*(A^{(0)})$, where $\lambda^*(A^{(0)})$ is the maximum eigenvalue of the matrix $A^{(0)}$.

Theorem 3. [14] For a positive matrix $A^{(0)} = \{a_{i,j}^{(0)}\}_{n \times n}$, the eigenvector of $\lambda^*(A^{(0)})$ is $X^*(A) = (P_1, P_2, \cdots, P_n)^T$, where $P_i = \prod\limits_{j=0}^{\infty} \frac{R_i^{(j)}}{R^{(j)}}$, $(i = 1, 2, 3, \cdots, n)$.

According to Theorem 1, the termination condition of iterations can be induced as follows. For a given accuracy ε, if $R^{(N)} - r^{(N)} \leq (R^{(0)} - r^{(0)}) *$ $[(1 - q/R^{(0)})]^N < \varepsilon$, then the number of iterations is $N = \left\lceil \frac{\log_2 \frac{\varepsilon}{R^{(0)} - r^{(0)}}}{\log_2 1 - \frac{q}{R^{(0)}}} \right\rceil$. That is if $R^{(N)} - r^{(N)} < \varepsilon$, then $R^{(N)} - \lambda^*(A^{(0)}) < \varepsilon$ because the sequence $r^{(k)}$ is monotonically increasing, it is obvious that $r^{(N)} \leq \lambda^*(A^{(0)})$, therefore $R^{(N)} - \lambda^*(A^{(0)}) \leq R^{(N)} - r^{(N)} < \varepsilon$. Furthermore, according to Theorem 2, $\lambda^*(A^{(0)}) \approx R^{(N)}$. The approximate eigenvector of $\lambda^*(A^{(0)})$ is $X^*(A) = (P_1, P_2, \cdots, P_n)^T$, where $P_i = \prod\limits_{j=0}^{N} \frac{R_i^{(j)}}{R^{(j)}}$, $(i = 1, 2, 3, \cdots, n)$.

An Example of Sequential Algorithm. The following is an example to show the above iterations. Given a positive matrix $A^{(0)} = \begin{matrix} 4 \\ 6 \\ 10 \end{matrix} \begin{pmatrix} 1 & 1 & 2 \\ 2 & 1 & 3 \\ 2 & 3 & 5 \end{pmatrix}$. We compute the sum of each row, and put them on the left of the matrix.

Then $R^{(0)} = 10$, $r^{(0)} = 4$, $q = 1$, $\Gamma^{(0)} = diag(4, 6, 10)$, $\Gamma^{(0)-1} = diag(1/4, 1/6, 1/10)$,

$$A^{(1)} = \begin{matrix} 7.5 \\ 7.33 \\ 7.6 \end{matrix} \begin{pmatrix} 1 & 1.5 & 5 \\ 1.33 & 1 & 5 \\ 0.8 & 1.8 & 5 \end{pmatrix}.$$

After five iterations: $A^{(5)} = \begin{matrix} 7.5311 \\ 7.5311 \\ 7.5311 \end{matrix} \begin{pmatrix} 1 & 1.46890 & 5.06223 \\ 1.36159 & 1 & 5.16955 \\ 0.79017 & 1.74097 & 5 \end{pmatrix}$, $\lambda^*(A) = 7.53$.

Then, we compute the corresponding eigenvectors, P_i $(i = 1, 2, 3)$,

$$P_1 = \prod(R_1^{(k)}/R^{(k)}) = (4/10)*(7.5/7.6)*(7.53334/7.54545)*(7.53097/7.53147)$$

$$*(7.53118/7.53120)*(7.53113/7.53114) = 0.3941, \ (k = 0, 1, 2, 3, 4, 5).$$

$$P_2 = \prod(R_2^{(k)}/R^{(k)}) = (6/10)*(7.333/7.6)*(7.54545/7.54545)*(7.53012/7.53147)*$$

$$(7.53120/7.53120)*(7.53114/7.53114) = 0.5788, \ (k = 0, 1, 2, 3, 4, 5).$$

$$P_3 = \prod(R_3^{(k)}/R^{(k)}) = (10/10)*(7.6/7.6)*(7.52631/7.54545)*(7.53147/7.53147)*$$

$(7.53111/7.53120)*(7.53114/7.53114)=0.9975$, $(k=0,1,2,3,4,5)$.

Thus, $X^*(A)= (P_1, P_2, P_3)=(0.3941, 0.5788, 0.9975)$.

3.2   Parallel Algorithm Using Similarity Transformation (PA-ST)

We use one-dimensional array to store our elements. Because of GPU's better single-precision computing performance compared to double-precision computing performance, we adopt single-precision floating-point arithmetic to obtain better performance.

We call the GPU's function to allocate memory for array *ginput* and array *goutput*. Array *ginput* includes the input elements, and array *goutput* stores the results. Allocate memory for array *ainput*, *binput* and *deva* to implement the whole algorithm. As we know, GPU's basic *cudamalloc()* function allocates pageable memory. A large number of copy operations between the host and the device make us use another method, *cudaHostAlloc()* function, to allocate pinned memory. It implemented the copy between the host and GPU by direct memory accessing technology. By calling the *cudamemcpy()* function, original elements in the host memory are transferred to the device memory. The transmission direction is assigned by the parameter *cudamemcpyHosttoDevice*. After computing, the results are returned with the parameter *cudamemcpyDevicetoHost* to the host.

In the first step, we need compute the sum of all the elements in every row. To improve the performance, the parallel reduction algorithm is adopted. Due to the large size of arrays, we need to be able to use multiple thread blocks to keep all multiprocessors on the GPU busy, and each thread block reduces a portion of the array. Each thread performs a summation operation to deal with two elements. Every thread processes the reduction in parallel. How to implement communication of partial results among thread blocks is an issue. We use synchronization function _*syncthreads()* across all thread blocks to easily reduce large arrays, and it can ensure that each thread of each block performs all the statements while calling the synchronization function, then go to the next step. Since it is expensive to build GPUs with high processor count, CUDA has no global synchronization. _*syncthreads()* enforces instruction synchronization and ensures memory visibility, but only within a block, not across blocks. In the case of reductions, code for all levels for kernel invocation is the same. The related detail of structure is shown in Figure 2.

In our algorithm, we are sticking to power-of-2 matrix orders. Assume that each block has n threads, so finishing the reduction of a block needs $\log(2n)$ iterations. In each iteration, thread i reads two elements in the array, then adds them together and stores the result to the *ith* index. In each iteration, only halve threads participate in the computing, but a synchronization is required, and thread 0 records the final result. Because of the shared memory's higher access speed than the global memory, it is the best choice to store the elements. We use the optimization strategy proposed by Mark Harris [15], such that the algorithm follows the principle of coalesced memory access and we use the span index to eliminate the shared memory bank conflicts. In order to eliminate the situation that half of the threads are idle on the first loop iteration, we set $sdata[tid] = gidata[i] + gidata[i + blockDim.x]$. CUDA supports C++ template parameters on device and host functions to unroll for a fixed block size, therefore, we are sticking to power-of-2 block sizes.

It is notable that each block only can be allocated to the limited number of threads. So when the maximum number of matrix order is over a block's capacity of elements, it needs to be completed by more than one block. Thus, the result of each block needs to be re-combined. For instance, the order of the matrix is 1024×1024. Assume that each block has 64 threads, as each thread deals with two elements, namely a block can process up to 128 elements, then the reduction needs $(1024*1024)/128 = 8192$ blocks.

In summary, we adopt single-precision floating-point arithmetic to obtain better performance and call the GPU's $cudaHostAlloc()$ function to allocate pinned memory to reduce the copy operations. Then we use synchronize function across all thread blocks to ensure that each thread of thread block performs all the operations before the synchronization function is called. Also, we use the shared memory instead of the global memory and eliminate the shared memory bank conflicts by setting the span index. Figure 3 shows the example. The kernel function is described in Algorithm 1. The Parallel Similarity Transformation Algorithm is shown in Algorithm 2.

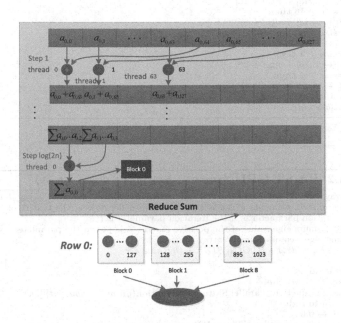

Fig. 3. Parallel Reduction Model

Algorithm 1. Parallel_Statute_Summation_on_GPU$(ginput[\,], goutput[\,], n)$

Input: The array $ginput[\,]$ is used to stored the matrix elements, the matrix order is n:
Output: The array $goutput[\,]$ is used to stored the sum of all the elements in every row:
1: $template < unsignedintblocksize >$
2: $externsharedints[\,]$
3: $unsignedinttid \leftarrow threadidx.x$
4: $unsignedinti \leftarrow blockidx.x * (blocksize * 2) + tid$
5: $unsignedintgridsize \leftarrow blocksize * 2 * griddim.x$
6: $s[\,] \leftarrow 0.0$
7: **while** $i < n$ **do**
8:    $s[tid] \leftarrow s[tid] + g_i nput[i] + g_i nput[i + blocksize]$
9:    $i \leftarrow i + gridsize$
10: call the $syncthreads()$ function.
11: **if** $(blocksize \geq 512)$ **then**
12:    **if** $tid < 256$ **then**
13:       $s[tid] \leftarrow s[tid] + s[tid + 256]$
14: call the $syncthreads()$ function.
15: **if** $(blocksize \geq 256)$ **then**
16:    **if** $tid < 128$ **then**
17:       $s[tid] \leftarrow s[tid] + s[tid + 128]$
18: call the $syncthreads()$ function.
19: **if** $(blocksize \geq 128)$ **then**
20:    **if** $tid < 64$ **then**
21:       $s[tid] \leftarrow s[tid] + s[tid + 64]$
22: call the $syncthreads()$ function.
23: **if** $(tid < 32)$ **then**
24:    **if** $blocksize \geq 64$ **then**
25:       $s[tid] \leftarrow s[tid] + s[tid + 32]$
26:    **if** $blocksize \geq 32$ **then**
27:       $s[tid] \leftarrow s[tid] + s[tid + 16]$
28:    **if** $blocksize \geq 16$ **then**
29:       $s[tid] \leftarrow s[tid] + s[tid + 8]$
30:    **if** $blocksize \geq 8$ **then**
31:       $s[tid] \leftarrow s[tid] + s[tid + 4]$
32:    **if** $blocksize \geq 4$ **then**
33:       $s[tid] \leftarrow s[tid] + s[tid + 2]$
34:    **if** $blocksize \geq 2$ **then**
35:       $s[tid] \leftarrow s[tid] + s[tid + 1]$
36: **if** $(tid == 0)$ **then**
37:    $g\_output[blockidx.x] \leftarrow s[0]$

Algorithm 2. PA_ST_GPU$(ainput[\,], boutput[\,], deva[\,], n, it)$

Input: The array $ainput[\,]$ is used to stored the matrix elements in the host, array $deva[\,]$ is used to stored the matrix elements which is transferred into the device, the matrix order is n, the maximum iteration parameter is it, the iteration parameter is l:
Output: The maximum eigenvalue of the positive matrix A is put in the parameter sum, and the corresponding eigenvectors is in the array $boutput[\,]$:
1: $ThreadID \leftarrow blockidx.x * BLOCKSIZE + threadidx.x$
2: $l \leftarrow 1$
3: **for** $l = 0$ to it **do**
4:    **if** $(ThreadID < n)$ **then**
5:       Call kernel function: Parallel_Statute_Summation$(ginput[\,], goutput[\,], n)$
6:       **for** $j = 0$ to n **do**
7:          $sum \leftarrow 0.0$
8:          $sum \leftarrow b[j * n + j] + b[ThreadID * n + i]$
9:          $a[ThreadID * n + j] \leftarrow a[ThreadID * n + j] * sum$
10:   call the $syncthreads()$ function.
11: Call kernel function: Parallel_Statute_Summation$(ginput[\,], goutput[\,], n, i)$

4 Complexity Analysis

4.1 The Time Complexity of Sequential Algorithm

Firstly, we need to compute the sum of every row, it needs $O(n)$. Since $a_{i,j}^{(k+1)}$ represents the element in the row i and column j of the $(k+1)^{th}$ iteration matrix, according to the previous related conclusion, $a_{i,j}^{(k+1)} = a_{i,j}^{(k)} * (T_j^{(k)}/T_i^{(k)})$, where $T_i^{(k)}$ is the sum of elements in row i^{th} of the kth iteration matrix, $T_j^{(k)}$ is the elements of diagonal matrix, so we just need to solve each element in the $(k+1)^{th}$ iteration from the kth iteration to the $(k+1)^{th}$ iteration, the time complexity is $O(n^2)$. Thus, the total time complexity of the sequential algorithm is $k * O(n^2)$ when the number of iterations is k. The iteration parameter is confirmed as follows: according to Theorem 1, we can obtain the number of iterations k meet $(R^{(0)} - r^{(0)}) * [(1 - q/R^{(0)})]^k < \varepsilon$, where ε is the precision parameter. And the number of iterations is $k = \left\lceil \dfrac{\log_2 \frac{\varepsilon}{R^{(0)} - r^{(0)}}}{\log_2 1 - \frac{q}{R^{(0)}}} \right\rceil$, and where $q = \min_{1 \le i \le n}\{ a_{i,i}, \min_{i \ne j}\{2\sqrt{a_{i,j}a_{j,i}}\}\}$.

4.2 The Time Complexity of Parallel Algorithm

For one iteration, computing the sum of n rows can be finished in parallel. Suppose there are S SM(Streaming Multiprocessors). Each SM has 8 streaming processors. Each row of a positive matrix has n elements. For one sum in each row, the parallel complexity is derived by: $\frac{n}{8S \cdot 2^1} + \frac{n}{8S \cdot 2^2} + \cdots + \frac{n}{8S \cdot 2^y} = \frac{n}{8S} - 1$, where $y = \log_2^{(\frac{n}{8S})}$. For n rows, the time complexity of each iteration of the parallel algorithm is $n * (\frac{n}{8S} - 1)$. According to Theorem 1, we can obtain the number of iterations k meet $(R^{(0)} - r^{(0)}) * [(1 - q/R^{(0)})]^k < \varepsilon$, where ε is the precision parameter. And the number of iterations is $k = \left\lceil \dfrac{\log_2 \frac{\varepsilon}{R^{(0)} - r^{(0)}}}{\log_2 1 - \frac{q}{R^{(0)}}} \right\rceil$, and $q = \min_{1 \le i \le n}\{ a_{i,i}, \min_{i \ne j}\{2\sqrt{a_{i,j}a_{j,i}}\}\}$. Thus, the total time complexity of the parallel algorithm is $O\left(\left\lceil \dfrac{\log_2 \frac{\varepsilon}{R^{(0)} - r^{(0)}}}{\log_2 1 - \frac{q}{R^{(0)}}} \right\rceil * n * (\frac{n}{8S} - 1) \right)$, and $q = \min_{1 \le i \le n}\{ a_{i,i}, \min_{i \ne j}\{2\sqrt{a_{i,j}a_{j,i}}\}\}$.

5 Experimental Results

In our experimental environment, we use Intel Core i5-760 quad-core CPU, NVIDIA GeForce GTX460 card, and Win7 64-bit operating system.In order to use Nsight software to close the TDR, avoiding the kernel function overtime phenomenon, we install another display card in main-card, which is connected into the computer monitor to display, then NVIDIA GeForce GTX460 card is completely for computing. Here the called overtime problem is referred to that kernel function has some time limitation, kernel function will maybe occur the overtime when the iteration numbers reach certain quantity . Nsight software is just to solve the problem. The data of the matrix are randomly generated with a random function. Our environment of compiling and running is Visual Studio 2010 and CUDA 4.0 and Nsight 2.0.

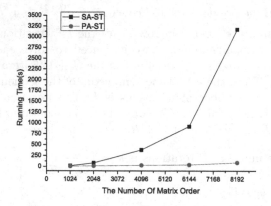

Fig. 4. The Number of Matrix Order and Running Time

Firstly, the number of iterations is set by 1000, we test the running time of the sequential algorithm and parallel algorithm when the order of matrix is 1024×1024, 2048×2048, 4096×4096, 6144×6144, and 8192×8192, respectively. The results are shown in Figure 4. It can be seen that the running time of the sequential algorithm increases with the order of the matrix; however, the running time of parallel algorithm do not increase obviously when the order of matrix increases. Overall, the parallel algorithm has obvious shorter running time compared with the sequential algorithm. So the running time performance of the parallel version is very satisfactory due to the fact that we implement the most part of computation in parallel.

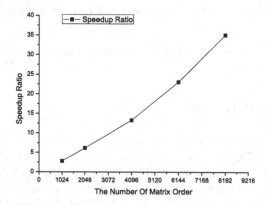

Fig. 5. The Number of Matrix Order and Speedup Ratio

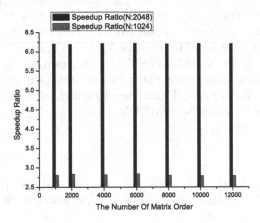

Fig. 6. The Iteration Numbers and Speedup Ratio (The Number Of Matrix Order :1024 and 2048)

Figure 5 shows the speedup ratio according to the running time of the Figure 4. It can be seen that as the order of matrix increases, the speedup ratio increases quickly, the speedup ratio of our algorithm also goes up. The maximum speedup ratio can reach 35.028 when we adopt our compute version is Lenovo M730E ,our display card for computing is NVIDIA GeForce GTX460 card, and the computer memory is four GB, quad-core processor,

Then, we tested the speedup radio with the increasing number of iterations when the orders of matrix are 1024 and 2048 respectively. Figure 6 shows the result. It indicates that our algorithm can obtain very stable speedup when the number of iterations is very large. So our algorithm obtains an impressive speedup ratio, and does not add much computational costs obviously. Our proposed algorithm overcomes this problem as well.

6   Conclusion

This paper proposes a parallel algorithm named PA-ST which is implemented by CUDA (Computer Unified Device Architecture) on GPU (Graphic Process Unit) to solve the maximum eigenvalue of positive matrices. Compared to the best sequential algorithm which we know, the proposed algorithm has obvious better running time performance. The proposed algorithm solves the problem without high computational costs of using cluster systems and save more time than the sequential algorithm. The new algorithm also provides a new way to solve the maximum eigenvalue of a positive matrix. In addition, the experimental results show that the Similarity Transformation algorithm can save more running time than traditional sequential algorithms, and the speedup ratio of the PA-ST is 2.85~35.028. The speedup ratio increases when the order of the matrix increases, but it is nearly stable when the number of iterations increases.

Acknowledgement. This work is supported by Program for New Century Excellent Talents in University under grant No.NCET-11-0955,Programs Foundation of Heilongjiang Educational Committee for New Century Excellent Talents in University under grant No.1252-NCET-011, Program for Group of Science and Technology Innovation of Heilongjiang Educational Committee under grant No.2013TD012, the Science and Technology Research of Heilongjiang Educational Committee under grant No.12511395.

References

1. Wang, T., Guo, L., Li, G., Li, J., Wang, R., Ren, M., He, J.S.: Implementing the jacobi algorithm for solving eigenvalues of symmetric matrices with cuda. In: NAS, pp. 69–78 (2012)
2. Tsourakakis, C.E.: Fast counting of triangles in large real networks without counting: Algorithms and laws. In: ICDM, pp. 608–617 (2008)
3. Gaidhane, V.H., Hote, Y.V., Singh, V.: Article: A new approach for estimation of eigenvalues of images. International Journal of Computer Applications 26(9), 1–6 (2011)
4. Griffiths, J.W.R.: Adaptive array processing: A tutorial. IEE Proceedings F Communications, Radar and Signal Processing 130(1), 3–10 (1983)
5. Luo, X., Lin, J., Wu, W.: A prediction-correction dynamic method for large-scale generalized eigenvalue problems. Abstract and Applied Analysis 2013(SI), 1–8 (2013)
6. Hall, C., Porsching, T.: Computing the maximal eigenvalue and eigenvector of a positive matrix. SIAM J. Numer. Anal. 5(2), 269–274 (1968)
7. Oepomo, T.: Survey of power, qr, and oepomos iterative methods for solution of largest eigenvalue of essentially positive matrices. International Journal of Management Science and Engineering Management 4(1), 3–19 (2009)
8. Faddeev, D., Faddeeva, V.: Computational Methods of Linear Algebra. W. H. Freeman and Company (1973)
9. Wilkinson, J.: Convergence of lr, qr and related algorithms. Comp. Jour. 8(1), 77–84 (1966)
10. Oepomo, T.: A contribution to collatzs eigenvalue inclusion theorem for nonnegative irreducible matrices. ELA 10(1), 31–45 (2003)
11. NVIDIA Corporation: NVIDIA CUDA Programming Guide version 4.2 (2012), http://developer.download.nvidia.com/compute/DevZone/docs/
12. Garland, M., Grand, S.L., Nickolls, J., Anderson, J., Hardwick, J., Morton, S., Phillips, E., Zhang, Y., Volkov, V.: Parallel computing experiences with cuda. IEEE Micro 28(4), 13–27 (2008)
13. Spampinato, D.G., Elster, A.C.: Linear optimization on modern gpus. In: IPDPS, pp. 1–8 (2009)
14. Yeh, L.: Inequalities for the maximal eigenvalue of a nonnegative matrix. Glasgow Mathematical Journal 39(3), 276–284 (1997)
15. Harris, M.: Optimizing parallel reduction in cuda. Technical report, NVIDIA Developer Technology Website/projects/reduction/doc/reduction.pdf (2007), http://developer.download.nvidia.com/compute/cuda/1_1/

Improving Speculation Accuracy
with Inter-thread Fetching Value Prediction

Fan Xu, Li Shen, Zhiying Wang, Hui Guo, Bo Su, and Wei Chen

State Key Lab of High Performance Computing, College of Computer,
National University of Defense Technology,
Dongfeng RD. 190, 410073 Changsha, China
{xufan,lishen,zhywang,guohui,subo,chenwei}@nudt.edu.cn

Abstract. Conventional software speculative parallel models are facing
challenges due to the increasing number of the processor core and the
diversification of the application. The speculation accuracy is one of the
key factors to the performance of software speculative parallel model.
In this paper, we proposed a novel value prediction mechanism named
Inter-thread Fetching Value Prediction(IFVP). It supports a speculative
thread to read the values of conflict variables speculatively from another
speculative thread. This method can remarkably reduce the miss speculation rate in a loop to be parallelized with cross-iter dependencies.
We have proved that the IFVP can improve the speculation accuracy by
about 19.1% on the average, and can improve the performance by about
37.1% on the average, compared with the conventional models without
value prediction.

Keywords: computer architecture, thread level speculation, parallel
computing.

1 Introduction

Exploiting potential thread-level parallelism(TLP) is becoming the key factor
to improving performance of programs on multi-core systems. A series of parallelization tools are developed to make parallel programming more simple and
effective. For a single loop without cross-iter dependency(DOALL loop), conventional parallel tools can divide it into several parts, and assign each part to a
single worker thread. However, a loop with cross-iter dependencies(DOACROSS
or PIPELINE loop) cannot be parallelized simply and smoothly by conventional
tools. Most of the conventional models require programmers to do explicitly
synchronization between threads, which enlarges the programmer's burden, and
makes the performance rely on the programmer's individual skills.

The speculative parallel model provides a new solution to the problem. It
offers simpler programming interfaces, and underlying hardware or software for
correctness checking. Programmers using Transactional Memory(TM)[1][2][3] or
Thread Level Speculation (TLS)[4][5][6] models do not have to know the details
about the dependencies between threads. They can neglect the dependencies

X.-h. Sun et al. (Eds.): ICA3PP 2014, Part II, LNCS 8631, pp. 245–258, 2014.

while they are parallelizing the program, and focus on the algorithm optimization or task partition. The underlying hardware or runtime system will help them to insure the program against errors. Speculative parallel model can drastically exploit parallelism in the program and reach a high performance, without increasing burden of programmers.

However, speculative parallel model has its own defects. For hardware based speculative models, the changes in micro-architecture are costly and less scalable. Software speculative parallel models usually can overcome these defects, but bring more global overhead. Especially for the program with lots of cross-iter dependencies, the paralleled speculative task may rollback frequently due to mis-speculation, producing large global overhead and impacting the performance. Generally speaking, the global overhead of a software speculative parallel model in a period can be present as follows.

$$O_{global} = task\_number \times (\overline{O_{control}} + \overline{O_{rollback}} \times miss\_rate)$$

In the equation above, $task\_number$ stands for the total number of the speculative task executed in the period, the $\overline{O_{control}}$ and $\overline{O_{rollback}}$ stand for the average control and rollback overhead of a single task. $miss\_rate$ stands for the rate of mis-speculation happened in the period. This equation indicates that the miss rate has great impact on the performance of the speculative parallel model.

To reduce the mis-speculation rate, value prediction schemes are introduced in many software speculative parallel models. The basic idea of value prediction is to generate the values of the conflict variables(CVARs), which cause the cross-iter dependencies, before they are committed. The Figure 1 shows a value prediction scheme applied in a software speculative parallel model. Although value prediction scheme may increase the time cost by the speculative read(SRD) operation more or less, proper value prediction scheme can increase the speculative accuracy, and reduce the speculative task rollbacks remarkably, bringing much benefit to the overall performance.

Based on this indication, several value prediction schemes are applied in different software speculative parallel models. Though these schemes can improve the speculative accuracy, they have their own defects, such as large hardware resource consumption, complex compiling support, or additional execution for learning process.

This paper proposed a novel value prediction scheme: Inter-thread Fetching Value Prediction(IFVP). In this mechanism, a speculative thread can fetch a CVAR's value produced by approximate speculative thread while doing SRD operation. This mechanism has 3 advantages.

- IFVP can improve the speculation accuracy remarkably without any additional compiling technology support.
- IFVP has more adaptability for different type of CVAR, not only the CVAR with a regular value changing trace, but also for the CVAR with randomly changing trace.

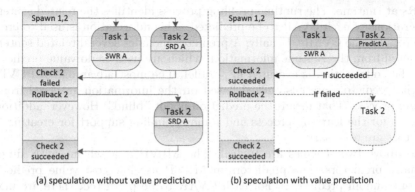

Fig. 1. speculation with/without value prediction.(SRD/SWR means speculative read/write in the task).

- IFVP is a single prediction mechanism. That means a speculative task won't be duplicated and executed for multiple times. Therefore, it won't cost lots of hardware thread.

The rest of the paper is organized as follows: Section 2 introduced some related works of value prediction scheme used in others' software speculative parallel model. Section 3 introduced the stimulation, basic concept, and work flow of the IFVP. Section 4 described the implementation of IFVP on the HEUSPEC. The experiment and result evaluation are shown in Section 5. At last, the conclusions are made in Section 6.

2   Related Works

With the support of GPU's many core architecture, Liu et al from University of California, Irvine were able to apply their Multiple Random Value Prediction(MRVP) scheme on a CPU-GPU platform[8]. In this model, a single task may have several copies executed in different threads with different sets of predicted CVAR values. For each task and its copies, the earliest finished one which passed the correctness checking can submit, while others are discarded. This scheme can improve the speculation accuracy remarkably with a large hardware thread consumption(An task with n CVARs and m possible values for each CVARs may have m^n copies and need the same number of hardware threads to executed them in parallel). Therefore the support from GPU's many-core architecture is necessary.

Tian et al from University of California, Riverside developed their own software speculative parallel model named CorD[7]. The Cord also applied MRVP scheme. Besides, the Pre-computing Value Prediction(PCVP) scheme is also applied on the CorD. Under PCVP, the serial binary code of each code section to be parallelized is executed with Pin in order to analyze the information of

CVARs at runtime. The runtime profiling process identifies the related sentence or operations of each CVAR to be predicted. This information is used to create predictors for the CVARs. Usually, A predictor includes several related sentence abstracted from the runtime information, which are used to do value prediction when the code section is executed in parallel. The most advantage of PCVP is that the predictors are customized based on the information gathered from a learning process. That means the prediction is not "blind". However, additional time cost for the learning process and some compiling support for creating the predictors are necessary.

The above two schemes are typical. The MRVP is a scheme with simple-but-many predictors. The predictors in MRVP use low cost value prediction function(random prediction). For each CVAR to be predicted, there are many predicted values come from many MRVP predictors. These values overlap a large proportion of the CVAR's possible value space. Thus increase the speculation accuracy. The PCVP is a scheme with complex-but-few predictors. For each CVAR, there is only one predictor which created with the information from learning process. The predictor is hard to create, but powerful for prediction.

As a new prediction scheme, Heuristic Value Prediction(HVP) is applied in the HEUSPEC speculative parallel model, which we have proposed in 2013[9]. This scheme is a compromise between the MRVP and PCVP. This prediction scheme aims at the CVARs which has regular value changing traces. For a single CVAR to be predicted, HVP uses multiple predictors to generate a group of predicted values based on the history values of the CVAR. A credit system is applied to evaluate all the prediction results of the predictors in the commit process. A predictor gains one credit if it has done a correct prediction. The prediction result from the predictor with the highest credit is always selected to be the result of an SRD operation. Without learning process and compiling support, the predictors in the HVP is not as "clever" as those in the PCVP, but also not as "blind" as those in the MRVP. Therefore, it has a compromised complexity, and time/space overhead.

3 Inter-thread Fetching Value Prediction

Above 3 typical prediction schemes shows that there is a tradeoff between the complexity of the predictor and the hardware consumption inside the prediction scheme. To insure the level of speculative accuracy, MRVP has to increase the number of predictors. Thus cost lots of processor cores and memory space. The availability of the PCVP is limited by its complexity of the predictor creation. We try to find a novel prediction scheme, with high accuracy, but less complexity and space/hardware consumption. Therefore, we proposed Inter-thread Fetching Value Prediction.

3.1 Thread Isolation

Many software speculative parallel models keep the speculative thread relatively isolated. With the thread isolation mechanism, each speculative thread has its own private space, storing CVARs' copies which are necessary to its own computation work. The CVARs are copied into the private space of each speculative thread via *SRD* operations, and copied out to the shared memory space via speculative write(*SWR*) operations. The shared memory space is maintained by the main thread, storing the committed CVARs. This mechanism has the advantage that it keeps the simplicity of the speculative task code, without many communication or synchronization methods.

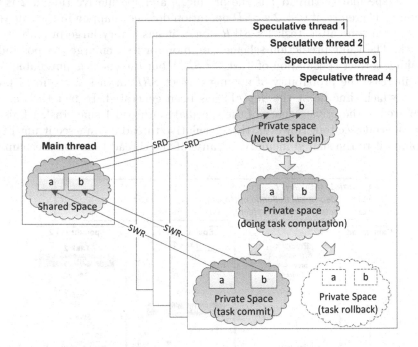

Fig. 2. The thread isolation mechanism

The Figure 2 shows the basic idea of the thread isolation. In the figure, the speculative task in each speculative thread has 4 states. At the beginning of the task, the threads get the values of CVARs through *SRD* operation and copy them into their private spaces. In the middle of the computation, the threads use the CVARs' copy in their own private spaces. If the speculative task passed the correctness checking, it can submit the CVARs to the shared memory space via *SWR* operation. But if the task failed, it will go to the rollback routine, and all the CVARs in the thread will be discarded.

Under the thread isolation mechanism, all the speculative threads only need to synchronize with the main thread while its current speculative task is beginning or in the correctness checking. They do not contact with other speculative threads. Most value prediction schemes won't break the thread isolation. The speculative threads generate the CVARs' predicted value by themselves. The prediction schemes such as MRVP, PCVP or HVP are of this kind.

The thread isolation mechanism builds communication walls between the speculative threads. However, it also builds a wall to the performance of the speculative parallel model. Here we use a case-study to explain. The Figure 3 shows a code section to be parallelized under a software speculative parallel model with thread isolation. We assume that speculative task 1 and 2 are spawned almost at the same time, and doing approximate 2 iterations in the loop. Task 1 is executed in speculative thread 1 while task 2 is executed in speculative thread 2. In this case, the speculative thread 1 is the producer, and speculative thread 2 is the consumer. Therefore, if task 2's SRD operation does not happen in the safe time zone(colored zone after Task 1's SWR done), it has a very large probability to rollback. The value prediction scheme can, more or less, enlarge the possibility of making correct speculation of Task 2's SRD, but the effect is unreliable.

To increase the probability of making correct SRD in task 2, we must know that at which time point the $dep(v1)$ has been generated. In fact the $dep(v1)$ has existed in the private space of the speculative thread 1 since task 1 finished $L1$ in the code seciton. However, the speculative thread 2 can't see it until task 1 submits it to the shared memory, because of the thread isolation mechanism.

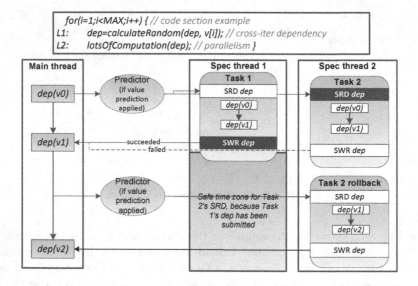

Fig. 3. Speculation under the thread isolation mechanism(in the code section, L1 is a sentence including a cross-iter dependency. L2 is a function call, which is time consumption but can be parallelized. the darken SWR in task 1 and SRD in task 2 have a cross-iter dependency.)

3.2 Fetching CVAR from Another Speculative Thread

We try to break the wall of thread isolation, allowing the speculative thread 2 to fetch the correct value of dep as earlier as possible. Therefore, we proposed the Inter-thread Fetching Value Prediction(IFVP) scheme. The IFVP scheme is based on this idea: There is a probability that the consumer thread can get the correct version of CVAR in the producer thread's private space before the CVAR is submitted to the shared memory space.

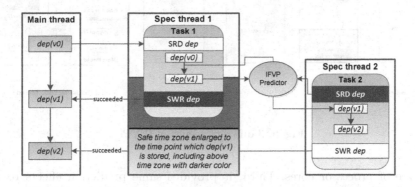

Fig. 4. Speculation with IFVP(the safe time zone enlarged due to the application of IFVP predictor)

The Figure 4 shows the speculative parallel under the model with IFVP scheme, using same code case as the Figure 3 shows. Instead of directly accessing the private space of speculative thread 1, we use an IFVP predictor to be the agent of inter-thread fetching. When thread 2 doing *SRD*, it calls IFVP predictor to access the private space of thread 1. The IFVP predictor will check if there is a new version of *dep* is stored in the private space of thread 1, then return it to the thread 2. The Figure 4 shows that the safe time zone of the *SRD* in the task 2 has been enlarged due to the IFVP predictor. That means the probability of making right speculation is increased. While doing *SRD* under IFVP scheme, there are 3 different scenes at runtime, which are shown in figure 5.

The cases shown in Figure 5(b) and 5(c) are safe, which means the *SRD* in task 2 can get the right value. However, in the case in Figure 5(a), the IFVP predictor has to make choice: to return immediately or wait until the new version of *dep* is created. If the predictor returns the value immediately, no matter if it gets the right value, it is Relaxed IFVP. Or else if the predictor waits until a new version is stored, it is Forced IFVP. The Forced IFVP is actually a implicit synchronization between the two threads. However, the Forced IFVP has a fatal defect. The predictor does not know how many times the producer thread will write the CVAR in the task, until the task is finished. Therefore, the Forced IFVP still can't ensure the result of *SRD* always correct. In our implementation, we chose Relaxed IFVP scheme.

The IFVP has several advantages. First, it is a lightweight prediction scheme, which won't bring much cost of time or space. Second, it does not create additional copies of speculative tasks, which means it does not need lots of additional

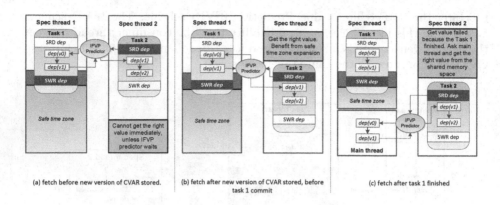

(a) fetch before new version of CVAR stored.

(b) fetch after new version of CVAR stored, before task 1 commit

(c) fetch after task 1 finished

Fig. 5. 3 different scenes of IFVP

resource of processor cores. Third, it provides same prediction effects to the CVARs with random value traces as those with regular value traces. The value traces of the CVARs won't affect the speculative accuracy of IFVP. Finally, it does not need additional compiling supports or learning process.

IFVP scheme uses special IFVP predictor to do indirect accessing to the producer thread's private space. This way of implementation also has several advantages. The IFVP predictor does not destroy the thread isolation mechanism. It just provides a channel between the private space of the producer thread and the consumer thread, but also keeps 0-synchronization between the consumer and producer. Besides, the IFVP predictor can work just like other predictors. Therefore it's easy to be integrated into a software speculative parallel model with another prediction scheme.

4   Implementation of IFVP

We have integrated the IFVP predictor into our HEUSPEC model. It works well with the mechanisms in the model.

4.1   Overview of HEUSPEC

HEUSPEC is a software speculative parallel model. It consists with a source-to-source compiler and a runtime library. The source-to-source compiler can transform the labeled code into HEUSPEC style code, which has one main thread and several speculative threads. The main thread offers all kinds of essential supports for the speculative parallelization, such as task creating, task assignment, value prediction, correctness checking, and result submitting. The speculative threads handle the computation activities of each speculative task. To ensure the correctness of speculative parallel execution, and improve the performance, HEUSPEC adopts three mechanisms. They are Thread Isolation(TI), Heuristic Value Prediction(HVP) and Dynamic Task Granularity Resizing(DTGR). The TI and the

HVP have been mentioned in the former parts of this paper. The DTGR is a mechanism which can adjust the size of the speculative tasks dynamically, in order to control the overhead in a low level.

4.2 Integrating IFVP Predictor with HEUSPEC

As a lightweight prediction scheme, IFVP is easy to be integrated to any software speculative parallel model with value prediction. We implemented IFVP predictor in our HEUSPEC model. When IFVP mode is activated, the model uses IFVP predictor in the *SRD* operations.

The Figure 6 shows how we integrated IFVP predictor into HEUSPEC. When the IFVP prediction is activated, the HEUSPEC will use IFVP predictor instead of HVP predictors. The IFVP prediction in the HEUSPEC works as follows:

The prediction begins with a function call from the consumer thread while doing *SRD*. It calls the IFVP predictor to search the object CVAR of the *SRD* in the private space of the producer thread. The IFVP predictor firstly look up the WR_MAP, which is a table stores all the addresses of the CVARs written by the producer thread while executing current task. If there is a matched address in the WR_MAP, it is surely that the CVAR's value has been updated by the producer thread and stored in the private space. In this case, the IFVP predictor will get the value by the address, and return it to the consumer thread. However, if there is no matched address, there are two possible status. First, the new value has been committed and stored in the shared memory space. Second, the new value has not been generated by the speculative task running in the producer thread because the calculation is not done. In this case, the predictor searches the CVAR Table, which stores the information of committed CVARs, to see if the new value has been committed. If it is committed, the predictor will get the CVAR from the shared memory space. Or else, the predictor will still get the CVAR from the private space of the producer thread(Relaxed IFVP) or wait until the WR_MAP has an matched address.(Forced IFVP).

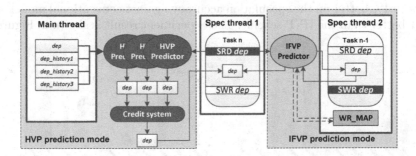

Fig. 6. Integrate IFVP scheme into HEUSPEC model

5   Experiment and Evaluation

We did 3 parts of experiments to test mis-speculation rate, speedup and time/space overhead of HEUSPEC model with IFVP scheme. We chose the conventional model without prediction scheme and HEUSPEC model with HVP scheme as comparisons. The experiments has been done on a platform with 4 Xeon E5-4620 processors(8 cores per processor, 2 way SMT per core). The capacity of the memory is 512GB. The software environment includes a Linux OS (kernel version 2.6.32) and a gcc/g++ compiler (version 4.4). Table 1 lists the benchmarks we used in our experiments. The number of code lines the PCVP scheme will take to the predictor(for highest accuracy) in each benchmark is also listed in the table.

Table 1. The benchmarks used in the experiment

Name	Package	CVAR Number	Total iterations in the loop	Total lines in the loop	Lines need to be identified in PCVP	Favorite Predictor in HVP
Badloop	Self-coded	1	620	5	1	Linear
Kmeans	Rodinia 2.1	8	494020	13	4	Constant
Fluidanimate	Parsec 2.1	1	31	53	42	Constant
183.equake	SPEC 2000	5	30169	50	13	Constant
179.art	SPEC 2000	13	180	281	195	Constant
456.hmmer	SPEC 2006	7	5000	29	10	Linear

5.1   Experiment Results

First, we tested the mis-speculation rate. Because the hardware platform has 32 processor cores, we set the speculative depth(max number of speculative thread at the same period) to 4 different levels: 3, 7, 15 and 31. On the average, the IFVP shows 19.1% better on the speculation accuracy against conventional model, and 11.9% better than the HVP scheme. The experiment result is shown in Figure 7.

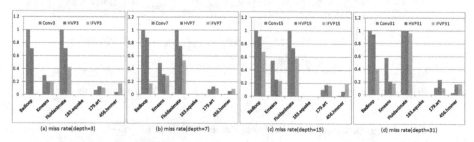

Fig. 7. The mis-speculation rates. ((a) for speculative depth equaling 3, (b) for 7, (c) for 15 and (d) for 31).

Among the 6 benchmarks, the *badloop* shows the largest improvement. Its miss speculation rates under IFVP are much lower than other two schemes on all the speculation depth levels. The section to be parallelized in *badloop* is with a determined dependency, which means the code of the dependency always be executed in each iteration, and cause a conflict. The dependency distance, which means the difference between the consumer and the producer iteration, is 1. The section also includes a lots_of_computation() function to offer a large quantity of potential parallelism. The IFVP handles this kind of dependency very well. Compared with the conventional model, the reduction of miss speculation rate can reach 99% while speculation depth level equals 3. It also has remarkable miss speculation rate reduction while depth level equals to 31, about 61%.

Besides *badloop*, *kmeans* and *fluidanimate* also shows well about the miss speculation rate reduction. The kmeans has a undetermined dependency in the section to be parallelized. And the dependency distance is 1. During the execution, the section to be parallelized is executed for multiple times. Each time the possibility that conflict happens is different from others. Compared with the conventional model, the IFVP reduced the miss speculation rate by about

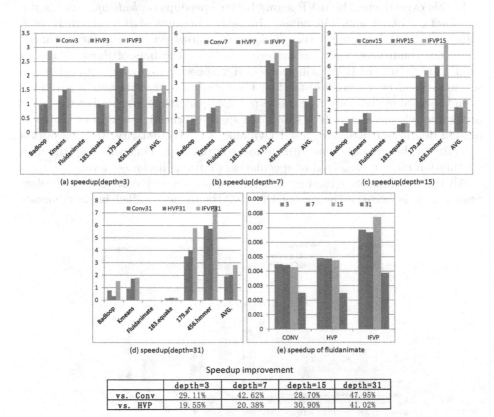

Speedup improvement

	depth=3	depth=7	depth=15	depth=31
vs. Conv	29.11%	42.62%	28.70%	47.95%
vs. HVP	19.55%	20.38%	30.90%	41.02%

Fig. 8. The speedups.(The speedup of *fluidanimate* is shown separately in the subgraph (e). The table shows the average speedup improvement against the other two schemes).

25%, 2% lower than HVP. *fluidanimate* has a cross-iter dependency inside 6 nested loops. It is a undetermined dependency, whose dependency distance is also undetermined. Because loops are nested, this section has a very high average rollback overhead. The IFVP can reduce the miss speculation rate by about 38%, compared with conventional model, and 17%, compared with HVP.

183.equake has a undetermined dependency. However, we have proved that it is a fake dependency, because it does not cause any conflict during the whole execution of the code section. But at the compiling process, this dependency was still treated as a real dependency. Therefore, the miss speculation rate under all conditions equal zero. For *179.art*, the average miss speculation rate of IFVP is about 2% higher than conventional model, but 5% lower than HVP. For *456.hmmer*, the miss speculation rate of IFVP is higher than conventional model at all the conditions. That's because the conventional model can't increase the size of the speculation task. Therefore it can only handle a single iteration of the loop per task. This is not good for the overall performance.

Second, we tested the speedup of all the benchmarks on different level of speculation depth with the 3 different schemes. The result is shown in Figure 8.

In this experiment, the IFVP shows better speedups on *badloop*, *kmeans flu-idanimate*, *179.art* and *456.hmmer*. However, because of the extremely high rollback overhead of single task, *fluidanimate* shows no speedup larger than 1 on all the conditions. Therefore we even can't see the bars of *fluidanimate* on the Figure 8. But the IFVP still shows better speedup compared with other two schemes. We drew Figure 8(e) to show the speedup of *fluidanimate* separately.

In the third experiment, we have tested the space/time overhead of the IFVP prediction scheme. Figure 9(a) shows the space overhead grows up as the speculation depth increases. We closed Dynamic Task Granularity Resizing option to make the benchmarks run with task size equal to 1. Thus will keep the miss speculation rate on each level of speculation depth at its lowest level.

All the benchmarks show very low additional memory cost, except *fluidanimate*. This is because the one of the CVARs to be handled in *fluidanimate*

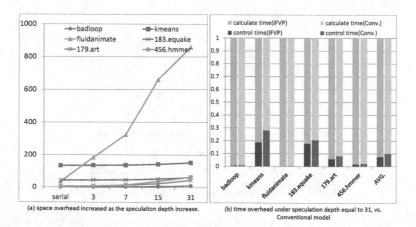

(a) space overhead increased as the speculation depth increase.

(b) time overhead under speculation depth equal to 31, vs. Conventional model

Fig. 9. Space/time overhead

is a large vector. Each vector element takes 832 bytes. And in each iteration, there are multiple vector elements copied to the private space of each speculative thread. Thus cause the memory cost exploded.

Figure 9(b) shows the percentage of the time overhead introduced by HEUSPEC model with IFVP prediction scheme under speculative depth equal to 31. The time overhead introduced on the average is lower than 10% of the whole execution time. It proved that IFVP is a low-cost prediction scheme.

6   Conclusion

In this paper, we have proposed a value prediction scheme for the software speculative parallel model: the Inter-thread Fetching Value Prediction. Compared with other prediction scheme, this prediction scheme has 3 advantages. First, it can improve the speculation accuracy remarkably without any additional compiling technology support. Second, it has more adaptability for different type of CVAR, not only the CVAR with a regular value changing trace, but also for the CVAR with randomly changing trace. Third, it can reach a high speculative accuracy with little processor-core consumption. The IFVP shows better on speculation accuracy and speedup than conventional model and HVP in our experiment. Besides, it has low time and space overhead for most benchmarks.

Acknowledgments. This work is partially supported by the China National 863 Program (No.2012AA010905), the National Natural Science Foundation of China (No.61070037, 61272143, 61103016, 61202121), the NUDT Innovation Foundation for Excellent Postgraduate (No.B120604) and the Hunan Provincial Innovation Foundation For Postgraduate (No.CX2012B209), and the Young Teachers Foundation Project supported by the Doctorate in Higher Education Institutions of Ministry of Education (No.20114307120013).

References

1. Feng, M., Gupta, R., Hu, Y.: SpiceC: Scalable parallelism via implicit copying and explicit Commit. In: 16th ACM SIGPLAN symposium on Principles and practice of parallel programming(PPoPP'11), pp. 69-79, ACM, New York (2011).
2. Moore, K.E., Bobba, J., Moravan, M.J., Hill, M.D., Wood, D.A.: LogTM: log-based transactional memory. In: 12th International Symposium on High-Performance Computer Architecture(HPCA'06), pp. 254-265, IEEE, Piscataway (2006).
3. Saha, B., Adl-Tabatabai, A.-R., Jacobson, Q.: Architectural Support for Software Transactional Memory. In: 39th Annual IEEE/ACM International Symposium on Microarchitecture(MICRO'06), pp. 185-196, IEEE, Piscataway (2006).
4. Prabhu, M.K., Olukotun, K.: Using thread-level speculation to simplify manual parallelization. In: 9th ACM SIGPLAN symposium on Principles and practice of parallel programming(PPoPP'03), pp. 1-12, ACM, New York (2003).
5. Ioannou, N., Cintra, M.: Complementing User-Level Coarse-Grain Parallelism with Implicit Speculative Parallelism. In: 44th Annual IEEE/ACM International Symposium on Microarchitecture(MICRO'11), pp. 284-295, ACM, New York (2011).

6. Ding, C., Shen, X., Kelsey, K., Tice, C., Huang, R., Zhang, C.: Software behavior oriented parallelization. In: 28th ACM SIGPLAN conference on Programming language design and implementation(PLDI'07), pp. 223-234, ACM, New York (2007).
7. Tian, C., Feng, M., Nagarajan, V., Gupta, R.: Copy or Discard execution model for speculative parallelization on multicores. In 41st annual IEEE/ACM International Symposium on Microarchitecture(MICRO'08), pp. 330-341, IEEE, Piscataway (2008).
8. Liu, S., Eisenbeis, C., Gaudiot, J.-L.: Speculative Execution on GPU: An Exploratory Study. In: 39th International Conference on Parallel Processing(ICPP'10), pp. 453-461, IEEE, Piscataway (2010).
9. Xu, F., Shen, L., Wang, Z., Guo, H., Su, B., Chen, W.: HEUSPEC: A Software Speculation Parallel Model. In: 42nd International Conference on Parallel Processing (ICPP'13), pp.621-630, IEEE, Piscataway (2013).

Towards Efficient Distributed SPARQL Queries on Linked Data

Xuejin Li[1], Zhendong Niu[1], and Chunxia Zhang[2]

[1] School of Computer Science, Beijing Institute of Technology
xuejinli7@gmail.com, zniu@bit.edu.cn
[2] School of Software, Beijing Institute of Technology
cxzhang@bit.edu.cn

Abstract. The fast growth of the web of linked data raises new challenges for distributed query processing. Different from traditional federated databases, linked data sources cannot cooperate with each other.
Hence, sophisticated optimization techniques are necessary for efficient
query processing. Source selection and distributed join operations are
key factors concerning performance of linked data query engines. In this
paper, we propose identifier graph based source selection taking into account the logical relationship between triple patterns, and develop effective solutions for distributed join operations to avoid program errors and
to minimize network traffic. In experiments, we demonstrate the practicability and efficiency of our approaches on a set of real-world queries
and data sources from the Linked Open Data cloud. With the implemented prototype system, we achieve a significant improvement in the
accuracy of source selection and query performance over state-of-the-art
federated query engines.

Keywords: Linked Data, Semantic Web, Query Federation.

1 Introduction

In recent years, the World Wide Web has evolved from a global information
space of linked documents to one where both documents and data are linked
[3]. The linked data adopt the general data format (RDF), are described by predefined vocabularies which make them have restrict semantics, and then can be
understood by computers. This kind of Web of Data opens up possibilities for
new types of applications which can aggregate data from different data sources
and integrate fragmentary information from multiple sources to achieve a more
complete view. Transparently querying distributed RDF data sources is a key
challenge for these possibilities.

With the ever-increasing amount of data sources accessible via SPARQL endpoints, federated query approach has attracted more and more attentions. However, federated query systems for Linked Data are still in their infancy. Improving
the query performance of these systems is always in the center of their work. We
outline two key factors concerning the performance of federated query systems:

X.-h. Sun et al. (Eds.): ICA3PP 2014, Part II, LNCS 8631, pp. 259–272, 2014.
© Springer International Publishing Switzerland 2014

Firstly, the decomposition of original queries must be accurate as far as possible; Secondly, distributed join operations should be effectively executed.

In this paper we concentrate on improving performance of federated SPARQL queries over the Web of Linked Data. To provide users with a transparent view for this Web of Data, the only available information for query decomposition is the user query strings. Hence, we argue that the more clues (presented or implied in query strings) are contributed to source selection, the better accuracy of query decomposition will be. Due to the network latency, distributed join operations may lead to poor query performance. Our goal is to provide optimizations for minimizing the number of remote requests and the amount of network traffic. Thus, sophisticated optimization strategies are needed for efficiently executing distributed join operations. Our main contributions are:

- We utilize a novel approach to make the query decomposition to be convenient and accurate.
- We propose optimization strategies for distributed join operations, mainly including join ordering and join execution.
- We implement the presented optimization techniques in our prototype system and perform experiments on a set of real-world queries and data sources.

The remainder of this paper is structured as follows. In Section 2 we review related work. Details of evaluating distributed SPARQL queries are discussed in Section 3. An evaluation of our prototype system is given in Section 4. Finally, we conclude and discuss future directions in Section 5.

2   Related Work

Related work can be divided into two main categories: (a) query decomposition (b) query optimization.

2.1   Query Decomposition

DARQ [17] extends the popular query processor Jena ARQ to an engine for federated SPARQL queries. It requires users to explicitly supply a configuration file which enables the query engine to decompose a query into sub-queries and optimize joins based on predicate selectivity. Stuckenschmidt [20] presents an index structure called source index hierarchy which is used to determine information sources that contain instances of a particular schema path. Given a predicate path in a dataset, an index hierarchy is constructed, where the source index of the indexed path is the root element. Both two approaches require predicates of triple patterns contained in the query string to be bound. SemWIQ [11] requires all subjects must be variables and for each subject variable its type must be explicitly or implicitly defined. Additional information (another triple pattern or DL constraints) is needed to tell the type for the subject of a triple pattern. It uses these additional information and extensive RDF statistics to decompose the original user query. These requirements limit the variety of user queries.

In other cases, users are required to provide additional information to determine the relevant data sources. For instance, [21] theoretically describes a solution called Distributed SPARQL for distributed SPARQL query on the top of the Sesame RDF repository. Users are required to determine which SPARQL endpoint the sub-queries should be sent to by the GRAPH graph pattern. The association between graph names and respective SPARQL endpoints at which they reside is explicitly described in a configuration file. The W3C SPARQL working group has defined a federation extension for SPARQL 1.1 [5]. However, remote SPARQL queries require the explicit notion of endpoint URIs. The requirement of additional information imposes further burden on the user. On the other hand, the proposed approach hardly imposes any restrictions on user queries.

Recently, several attempts have been made to do source selection without local statistics. FedX [19] asks all known data sources by SPARQL ASK query form whether they contain matched data for each triple pattern presented in a user query. FedSearch[14] is based on FedX and extends it with sophisticated static optimization strategies. If the amount of known data sources is very large(it is common in an open setting), the query performance may leave much to be desired. SPLENDID [6] relies on the VOID descriptions existed in remote data sources. However, a VOID description is not an integral part of Linked Data principles. [1].

2.2 Query Optimization

Research on query optimization has a long history in the area of database systems. Concepts in these research areas have been adopted to optimize queries on local RDF stores. OptARQ [2] reorders triple patterns in SPARQL queries based on their selectivity. Hartig [9] adapted the query graph model (QGM) for SQL queries to represent SPARQL queries. Based on SQGMs, SPARQL queries are rewritten for optimization purpose. Due to the triple nature of RDF data, optimization for queries on local repositories has also focused on the use of specialized indices to accelerate the join operations, e.g. [7].

In [17] Quilitz et.al have adopted some of existing techniques from relational systems to federated SPARQL queries. They present a cost based optimization for join ordering. However, their estimation on the result size of joins is inaccurate by simply setting the selectivity factor for the join attributes to a constant. Because unbound queries generally returning a large result set, other join implementations are proposed as an alternative to local nested-loop implementation of joins, such as pipeline join [8] and semijoin [21]. Due to the variety of the Web, none of these approaches can effectively process all user queries. The reasons are discussed in Section 3.3. In this paper, we propose a novel way, called groupjoin, to execute join operations. The size of group can be modified flexibly for enhancing performance of the system in different situations.

3 Federated SPARQL Query

A federated query system has the similar architecture shown in Figure 1. A mediator(also called query federator) analyzes and decomposes the user query into several sub-queries and distributes them to autonomous data sources which execute these sub-queries and return the results, and then integrates intermediate results into query answers. This section describes in detail how to evaluate distributed SPARQL queries.

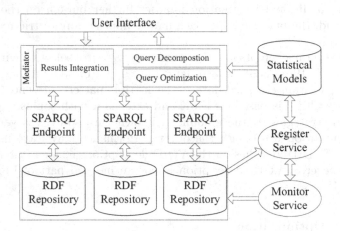

Fig. 1. A common architecture of federated query systems

3.1 Query Decomposition

RDF data is a kind of graph-structured data, and the Web of Linked Data can be seen as a huge distributed RDF graph. SPARQL is a query language for RDF, based on graph patterns and subgraph matching. The simplest graph pattern defined for SPARQL is the triple pattern which is like the RDF triple except that each of the subject, predicate and object may be a variable. The basic graph pattern(BGP) consists of a set of triple patterns which are conjunctive relationship, and also has a graph structure. Other complex graph patterns can be constructed by BGP using SPARQL logical operators(UNION, OPTIONAL). Solutions of a SPARQL query are decided by non-variable parts of triple patterns and the logical relationship between graph patterns. Hence, the decision of query decomposition should be made not only by non-variable parts of triple patterns but also by the logical relationship between graph patterns.

Formal Definitions. Before discussing our approaches, we give formal definitions of concepts used in this section.

Definition 1 (Triple). *Assume that I(IRIs), B(Blank nodes) and L(RDF literals) are pairwise disjoint infinite sets. An RDF statement can be represented*

as a tuple: $(s,p,o) \in (I \cup B) \times I \times (I \cup B \cup L)$. *In this tuple, s is the subject, p is the predicate and o is the object. The tuple representing an RDF statement is called a RDF triple, simply called triple.*

A group of resources with similar characteristics is called a class. The members of a class are instances of the class. In RDF, the predicate rdf:type[1] generally is used to express a source being an instance of a class. For example, P rdf:type C, denotes that P is an instance of C. In the context of this paper, we divide RDF triples into instance triples and class triples. Formally, they are defined as:

Definition 2 (Class Triple). *A RDF class triple (C,p,D) is a RDF triple, both C and D are instances of the rdfs:Class. If c is an instance of C and d is an instance of D, then the triple (c,p,d) is called an instance triple of (C,p,D) and (C,p,D) is called a class triple of (c,p,d).*

Definition 3 (Triple Pattern). *Assume that I(IRIs),B(Blank nodes),L(RDF literals) and V(variables) are pairwise disjoint infinite sets. A triple pattern tp satisfies:* $tp \in (I \cup B \cup V) \times (I \cup V) \times (I \cup B \cup L \cup V)$.

Similarly, we divide RDF triple patterns into RDF class triple patterns and RDF instance triple patterns. Following the definition above, we give the formalized definitions of RDF class triple patterns and RDF instance triple patterns:

Definition 4 (Class Triple Pattern). *Assume that V is a infinite set of variables, for a given triple pattern* (v_1, v_2, v_3), *if* $v_1 \notin V$ *and* v_1 *is a instance of the class C, then* $s = C$, *else* $s = v_1$; *if* $v_3 \notin V$ *and* v_3 *is a instance of the class D, then* $o = D$, *else* $o = v_3$. *The triple pattern* (s, v_2, o) *is called a class triple pattern of the triple pattern* (v_1, v_2, v_3) *and* (v_1, v_2, v_3) *is called an instance triple pattern of* (s, v_2, o).

Source Selection. Before source selection, we previously extract class triples from all known data sources. The RDF graph consisting of all class triples from one data source is named by the URI of the SPARQL endpoint of this data source and stored into a local RDF dataset. A RDF dataset represents a collection of RDF graphs. It comprises one default graph and none or more named graphs, where each named graph is identified by an IRI [16]. Besides, we also compute the total number of instance triples and the number of distinct subjects associated with each class triple. The object values domain for predicates is represented by histograms[15]. Consequently, a Web of Linked Class is built on top of the Web of Linked Data. The former is much smaller than the latter, and can be loaded into memory during the system running.

If all triple patterns contained in a SPARQL query are class triple patterns, then this query is called a class query. If all class triple patterns in a class query

---

[1] In this paper we use the following prefixes: rdf:
http://www.w3.org/1999/02/22-rdf-syntax-ns#
rdfs: http://www.w3.org/2000/01/rdf-schema#

are respectively replaced with an instance triple pattern of them, then the new query is called an instance query of the class query. Before a SPARQL query being evaluated, it is transformed into class queries. Graph patterns containing in class queries are used as identifier graph for source selection.

SPARQL provides the mechanism accessing names of named graphs in a dataset. By using the keyword of GRAPH, a query engine can access the name of a named graph from which the matched data of one or a group of triple patterns come. Our main idea for query decomposition is that firstly translating the original query into class queries; then adding the GRAPH keyword for each class triple pattern; finally evaluating each class query on the statistical model dataset. Classes of an IRI resource can be obtained by dereferencing this IRI. Non-IRI resources are assigned with a common class of rdfs:Literal. SPARQL GRAPH keywords do not change the logical relationships between SPARQL graph patterns. Hence, the result of query decomposition is a comprehensive action of the information of classes, predicates and logical relationships between graph patterns in a query. To the best of our knowledge, there are not any existing approaches considering all these three factors. Hence, we can expect that the presented approach is more accurate than others.

3.2 Cardinality Estimation

Single Triple Pattern. Estimating the cardinality of one single triple pattern $tp = (s, p, o)$ on a data source d includes two steps: Firstly transforming tp into its class triple pattern ctp and evaluating ctp on the class graph dm of d, then a subset d' of d can be decided; the cardinality of tp is estimated on d'.

The cardinality of tp can be estimated by the following function:

$$card_d(tp) = card_{d'}(tp) = |T'| \times sel_{d'}(tp) = |T'| \times sel_{d'}(s) \times sel_{d'}(p) \times sel_{d'}(o) \quad (1)$$

Where $|T'|$ is the total number of triples in d'. $sel_{d'}(s)$, $sel_{d'}(p)$ and $sel_{d'}(o)$ respectively are the selectivity of s, p and o on d'. For s, p and o, if it is a variable, then its selectivity is set to 1. Otherwise, their selectivity are respectively computed by the following functions:

$$sel_{d'}(s) = \frac{1}{|I'|} \quad (2) \qquad\qquad sel_{d'}(p) = \frac{|T'_p|}{|T'|} \quad (3)$$

$$sel_{d'}(o) = \begin{cases} \sum_{s_i \in S} \sum_{p_j \in P_{s_i}} c(s_i, p_j, o_c) & \text{if both } s \text{ and } p \text{ are not bound} \\ \sum_{s_i \in S} c(s_i, p, o_c) & \text{if } s \text{ is not bound and } p \text{ is bound} \\ \sum_{p_j \in P_{s_i}} c(s, p_j, o_c) & \text{if } s \text{ is bound and } p \text{ is not bound} \\ c(s, p, o_c) & \text{if both } s \text{ and } p \text{ are bound} \end{cases}$$

$$\quad (4)$$

where $|I'|$ is the total number of URIs in d', $c(s, p, o_c) = \frac{h_c(s, p, o_c)}{|T'_{(s,p)}|}$, i.e., the frequency of o_c normalized by the number of triples matching s and p, and o_c is the histogram class in which the object o falls into, $|T'_p|$ corresponds to the number of triples matching predicate p in d'. If p is bound, then $|T'_p| = |T'|$. Hence, $sel_{d'}(p) \equiv 1$.

Pattern Groups. The function estimating the cardinality of a group of triple patterns $TP = (tp_1, tp_2, ..., tp_n)$ is:

$$card(TP) = min(m_1, m_2, ..., m_n) \prod_{i=1}^{n} \frac{card(tp_i)}{m_i} \tag{5}$$

Where m_i is the number of different values of tp_i in the joint position. If the joint variable is in subject position, then $m_i = |R'|$. If the joint variable is in predicate position, then m_i is the number of different predicates. If the joint variable is in object position, then m_i is the number of different values of all predicates.

Join Cardinality. We compute the join cardinality as

$$card(q_1 \bowtie q_2) = |R_1||R_2|sel_\bowtie(q_1, q_2) \tag{6}$$

Where $|R_1|$ and $|R_2|$ are respective the cardinality of q_1 and q_2; $sel_\bowtie(q_1, q_2)$ is the join selectivity of q_1 and q_2. It is a reduction factor which depends on the selectivity of the join variable in both datasets. We use the maximum selectivity of the join variable as the join selectivity.

3.3   Join Reordering

The join order determines the number of intermediate results and is thus one of key factor for query performance. For the federated setup, we propose a rule-based join optimizer, which orders a list of subqueries according to a heuristics-based cost estimation. Our algorithm uses a variation of technique proposed in [19] and is depicted in Algorithm 1. Firstly, It selects the subquery with minimum cardinality(line 3) and append it to the result list(line 4). Then, it selects the subquery from remaining subqueries which has minimum join cardinality with the last subquery in the result list (line 7-8) and append it to the end of the result list(line 9).

Algorithm 1. Join Order Optimization

1: order($sqs : list\ of\ n\ joint\ subqueries$)
2: $result \leftarrow \varnothing$
3: $mincard \leftarrow min(card(sqs[1 - n]))$
4: $result \leftarrow result + \{sqs[j]\}$//j is the index of subquery with minimum cardinality
5: $sqs \leftarrow sqs \backslash sqs[j]$
6: **while** $sq \neq \varnothing$ **do**
7:     $q \leftarrow result[result.len - 1]$
8:     $mincost \leftarrow card(q \bowtie sqs[i])$//i is the index of subquery which has the minimum join cardi-
        nality with q
9:     $result \leftarrow result + \{sqs[i]\}$
10:    $sqs \leftarrow sqs \backslash sqs[i]$
11: **end while**
12: **return** $result$

3.4   Join Execution

While pipeline join(PJ) directly passes each solution produced by one operation to the operation that uses it, semijoin(SJ) buffers the obtained variable binding sets and sends them in a batch as conditions in a SPARQL FILTER expression to remote SPARQL endpoints. The former may produce too many concurrent access to remote data sources, and the latter may lead to program errors due to long query strings.

We propose groupjoin(GJ) which restrains the number of the cached solutions in the mediator. In contrast to caching all solutions of the prior sub-query in semijoin, these solutions are divided into some groups, each group contains n solutions. Assume that, q_1 and q_2 are two join query and are respectively evaluated on dataset D_1 and D_2; the cardinality of q_1 is N_1 and the times which D_2 allows one client to access in a period of time is N_C. Then, the size of each group should be $n \geq \frac{N_1}{N_C}$. Again, the maximum length of query string evaluated on D_2 is N_F. Hence, $\frac{N_1}{N_C} \leq n \leq \frac{N_F}{N_T}$, where N_T is the average length of RDF terms in D_2. In practice, n is firstly set to an experimental value between $\frac{N_1}{N_c}$ and $\frac{N_F}{N_T}$. When errors occurred due to too many remote connections, the query engine increases the group size, and thus decreases the number of concurrent threads. When errors occurred due to too many value constraints, the query engine decreases the group size.

The difference between PJ, SJ and GJ lies in the different number of concurrent threads during executing join operations. However, in case of distributed query processing the amount of transferred data has the highest influence on query execution time. Essentially, PJ, SJ and GJ need equal network traffic. For simplicity, we consider the transfer cost of SJ. The cost of a semijoin is estimated as

$$cost_{sj}(q_1 \bowtie q_2) = |R_1||V_1|c_t + |\Pi_V(R_1)||V|c_t + |R_2'||V_2|c_t + 2c_q \qquad (7)$$

Where c_t and c_q are the respective transfer costs for one result tuple[2] and one query; R_1 is the result set of q_1; R_2' is the result set of q_2' which is the query with variables bound with values of a result tuple from q_1; V_1 and V_2 are the respective variable set of q_1 and q_2; V is the intersection of V_1 and V_2, $\Pi_V(R_1)$ is the projection of R_1 on V.

While semijoin projects R_1 on V in the mediator, double semijoin(DSJ)[12] executes this operation in D_1. The cost of a double semijoin is estimated as

$$cost_{dsj}(q_1 \bowtie q_2) = (2|\Pi_V(R_1)| + |\Pi_V(R_2')|)|V|c_t + |R_2'||V_2|c_t + |R_1'||V_1 \setminus V|c_t + 3c_q \qquad (8)$$

Where $|R_1'|$ is the result set of q_1' which is the query with variables bound with values of R_2'.

Distributed join operations are parallel executed in GJ. In each thread, we select the optimal way according to function (7-8).

---

[2] For simplicity, we currently disregard the specific tuple size.

4   Evaluations

We have developed a prototype system(LDMS[3]) implementing the proposed approaches and conducted an experimental study to empirically analyze the effectiveness of it compared with several existing federated SPARQL query systems.

Our evaluation is based on FedBench[4][18]. In contrast to other SPARQL benchmarks[4,13], FedBench focus on testing and analyzing the performance of **federated** query processing strategies on semantic data. It includes two subsets of data sources in the Linked Data cloud: Cross Domain(DBpedia, NYTimes, LinkedMDB, Jamendo, GeoNames) and Life Sciences(KEGG, Drugbank, ChEBI, DBpedia). For each data set, it defines seven queries. In this paper, we discuss the evaluation of graph pattern containing BGP and UNION, omitting other kinds of graph patterns. Hence, thirteen out of fourteen queries are adopted in our experiments. The overview of the data sets is shown in Table 1(a) in terms of number of triples(#Triples), size of statistical models and time taken to create them in hh:mm:ss. Queries are shown in Table 1(b) in terms of number of BGPs and patterns in the WHERE clause and size of results.

Table 1. FedBench datasets and queries used for the evaluation

(a)

Dataset	#Triples	SM Size	SM Time
DBpedia	43.6M	12.8MB	03:55:18
NYTimes	335k	103KB	00:01:27
LinkedMDB	6.15M	368KB	00:27:36
Jamendo	1.05M	33KB	00:5:12
Geo Names	108M	68KB	08:43:47
SW DogFood	104k	646KB	00:00:30
KEGG	1.09M	42KB	00:05:30
Drugbank	767k	195KB	00:02:12
ChEBI	7.33M	23KB	00:25:12

(b)

Query	#BGPs	#Patterns	#Results
CD1	2	3	90
CD2	1	3	1
CD3	1	5	2
CD4	1	5	1
CD5	1	4	2
CD6	1	4	11
CD7	1	4	1
LS1	2	2	1159
LS2	2	3	333
LS3	1	5	9054
LS4	1	7	3
LS5	1	7	393
LS6	1	5	28

The data server was set up using OpenRDF Sesame framework which provides a query service (SPRAQL endpoint) for each data source. Benchmark datasets simulated on the same physical host and were respectively loaded as a single repository with the type of Sesame Native Store. The prototype system(i.e. test client) was on a Windows XP with two Dual-Core Intel Xeon processors (2.8 GHz) and 3GB memory. The server was running a 64 Bit Debian Linux Operation System with two Intel Xeon CPU E7530 processors (each with twelve cores at 2 GHz), 32 GB main memory. The statistical models for data sources were loaded into memory when starting the system.

---

[3] LDMS is available as Java source code(eclipse project) from the SVN repository: https://svn.code.sf.net/p/semwldms/code/LDMS/trunk
[4] FedBench can be downloaded at http://code.google.com/p/fbench/

4.1 Evaluation of Join Execution

Based on LDMS, benchmark queries were respectively evaluated by four ways of execution of join operations: pipeline join(LDMS-PJ), nested loops join(LDMS-NLJ), semijoin(LDMS-SJ) and groupjoin(LDMS-GJ). We measured the query evaluation time to see how different ways of join execution affects the overall performance of the query system. For group-join, the size of group was set to 100. All queries were evaluated five times with the five minutes timeout. Figure 2 shows the average time of returning completed answers.

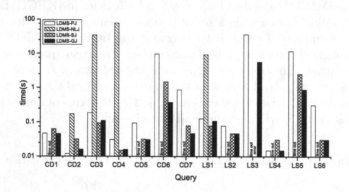

Fig. 2. The Comparison of Time Performance for Different Ways to Execute Join Operations(not including the time for query decomposition)

Due to all intermediate results being transferred over network, the time performance of nested loops join is in the worst situation. However, if all sub-queries have small result sets, it still can be comparable to other ways, i.e. CD2. While pipeline join needing too many remote requests, semijoin suffers from too many intermediate results. When the amount of intermediate results being attached to a sub-query is very large, the internal performance of the remote data sources may become very low, i.e. CD6 and LS5. For LS3 LDMS-SJ sends too long query strings to KEGG data source and encounters program errors. No distributed join operations are concerned in CD1, LS1 and LS2. Hence, LDMS-PJ, LDMS-SJ and LDMS-GJ evaluate these three queries in the same way, and are similar in time performance. For queries that the group size is larger than the size of intermediate result sets, LDMS-SJ is equal to LDMS-GJ, i.e. CD3, CD4, CD5 ,CD7 and LS6. For CD6 and LS4-5, LDMS-GJ is faster than LDMS-SJ.

4.2 Comparison with Other Federated SPARQL Query Systems

Some other state-of-the-art federated SPARQL query systems were deployed in our experimental environments, namely SPLENDID and FedX to which LDMS was compared. Every system evaluates all benchmark queries and returns completed answers. We test the accuracy of query decomposition and time performance for these three systems.

Evaluation of Query Decomposition. We define $R = \frac{N_e}{N_E}$ and $P = \frac{N_e}{N}$ to measure the quality of query decomposition, where N_e is the number of effective query plans generated by query systems and N_E is the number of all effective query plans that a original query should have, N is the number of all query plans generated by query systems. An effective query plan means that it can produce query answers. A poor recall will produces incomplete query answers and a poor precision means unnecessary access to the remote data resources which leads to poor time performance. Therefore, we investigated how different strategies affect the accuracy of the source selection. For each query, we look at the recall and the precision of query plans. We test approaches used in LDMS, SPLENDID and FedX respectively. While the recall of these three systems in term of query decomposition is 100%, the precision is different.

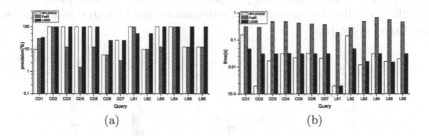

(a)   (b)

Fig. 3. The Precision(a) and Time Performance(b) of Query Decomposition

As shown in Figure 3(a), both LDMS and SPLENDID have 100% precision for CD2-5, LS3-4. The query decomposition strategies of SPLENDID can be approximately seen as the integration of approaches used by DARQ and SemWIQ(reviewed in Section 2.1). For queries with unbound predicates, SPLENDID have to use additional SPARQL ASK queries to refine selected data sources. Nevertheless, for six queries LDMS is better than SPLENDID, i.e. CD1, CD6-7, LS2 and LS5-6. SPLENDID misses consideration of the path information which is common in conjunctive queries. The similar shortcoming is happened to FedX. For example, FedX decides that (?x <owl:sameAs> ?present) and (?present <rdf:type> <dbpedia-owl:President>) in CD3 are relevant to DBpedia which can not give any answers for the conjunctive query comprising these two triple pattern. FedX has 100% precision for only three out of thirteen queries, i.e. CD2, LS1 and LS4.

FedX directly asks all known data sources whether they contain matched data for each triple pattern in a query. On the other hand, LDMS accesses remote data sources when getting types of IRIs in the position of subject and object. As shown in Figure 3(b), for all queries LDMS is better than FedX in terms of query decomposition time. SPLENDID hardly needs remote requests, hence takes just a little time for query decomposition. For CD1 and LS2, FedX is comparable to SPLENDID. The reason is that these two queries contains triple patterns comprising three variables and SPLENDID needs accessing to all remote data sources for their source selection. For CD4, CD6 and CD7, all predicates are bound and no IRIs presented in the position of subject or object, hence, LDMS needs no remote requests, and then is comparable to SPLENDID in term of decomposition time.

Time Performance. We measure the overall time performance for LDMS, SPLENDID and FedX. Again, all queries were evaluated five times and the average time is used for comparisons. Besides of query decomposition, these three systems are different in join optimization strategies. FedX uses heuristics to reordering join operations whereas SPLENDID and LDMS use statistical information to optimize query plans based on dynamic programming. While FedX uses bound join to optimize traditional implementation of semi-join, SPLENDID adopt nested loops join and pipeline join. LDMS reorders joins based on the result of cardinality estimation of sub-queries and executes join operations in the way of groupjoin.

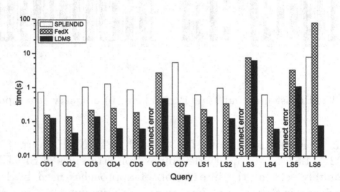

Fig. 4. The Comparison of Time Performance with other state-of-the-art Federated SPARQL Query Systems

The result of the experiment is encouraging, shown in Figure 4. For all queries LDMS is faster than other two systems. However, FedX is comparable to LDMS for queries with a large amount of results, i.e. LS3. It is because that the cost of query decomposition is insignificant for the overall time performance. SPLENDID fails to return results for CD6, LS3 and LS5. The reason is that SPLENDID opens too many connections to data sources and encounters connection errors. For six queries FedX is faster than SPLENDID, i.e. CD1-5, CD7, LS1-2, LS4. For LS6, FedX generates many ineffective query plans and the first sub-query evaluated in some of query plans has non-empty result set. It means that many intermediate results need to be transferred to local federator, but produce no results when join with the next sub-query.

5   Conclusions

We have presented an approach for evaluating SPARQL queries over the Web of Linked Data, based on general statistical models which form a local web of linked classes. We have shown how the statistical model can be used to select relevant sources, and how to optimize distributed join. As revealed by our benchmarks, source selection approaches are effective in terms of accuracy and time performance. We use almost all clues presented or implied in the original user queries to make query decompositions. By decreasing the number of classes of entities, the precision of query decompositions is satisfactory. Compare with the traditional ways of executing join operations, groupjoin makes a compromise between pipeline join and semijoin. By setting an appropriate group size, LDMS is better than or at least comparable to the state-of-art federated SPARQL query systems.

The approach presented in this paper can be seen as a very first step towards a solution for the problems of federated query processing on Linked Data. A number of limitations exist in the current proposal with respect to the generality of the approach and assumptions made. In federation query, query service is necessary for relevant data sources. However, providing a SPARQL endpoint is not required in the Linked Data principles. Both traditional federation query and our approach just omit those datasets not providing query services. For a more general query interface, additional technologies should be considered. The link traversal based query execution [10] is a possible solution.

Though the network communication is the main factor influencing the time performance of systems, the internal efficiency of remote data sources is also important. We aim at providing an infrastructure for developing semantic applications. In a future release, we propose to combine these technologies into a hybrid one.

Acknowledgments. This work is supported by the National Natural Science Foundation of China (No 61272361) and the National Basic Research Program of China (No 2012CB7207002).

References

1. Berners-Lee, T.: Design issues: Linked data (2006),
   http://www.w3.org/DesignIssues/LinkedData.html (2011)
2. Bernstein, A., Kiefer, C., Stocker, M.: OptARQ: A SPARQL optimization approach based on triple pattern selectivity estimation. Citeseer (2007)
3. Bizer, C., Heath, T., Berners-Lee, T.: Linked data-the story so far. International Journal on Semantic Web and Information Systems (IJSWIS) 5(3), 1–22 (2009)
4. Bizer, C., Schultz, A.: The berlin sparql benchmark. International Journal on Semantic Web and Information Systems (IJSWIS) 5(2), 1–24 (2009)
5. Garlik, S.H., Seaborne, A., Prudhommeaux, E.: Sparql 1.1 query language. In: World Wide Web Consortium (2013)

6. Görlitz, O., Staab, S.: Splendid: Sparql endpoint federation exploiting void descriptions. In: COLD (2011)
7. Harth, A., Decker, S.: Optimized index structures for querying rdf from the web. In: Third Latin American Web Congress, LA-WEB 2005, p. 10. IEEE (2005)
8. Hartig, O., Bizer, C., Freytag, J.-C.: Executing sparql queries over the web of linked data. In: Bernstein, A., Karger, D.R., Heath, T., Feigenbaum, L., Maynard, D., Motta, E., Thirunarayan, K. (eds.) ISWC 2009. LNCS, vol. 5823, pp. 293–309. Springer, Heidelberg (2009)
9. Hartig, O., Heese, R.: The sparql query graph model for query optimization. In: Franconi, E., Kifer, M., May, W. (eds.) ESWC 2007. LNCS, vol. 4519, pp. 564–578. Springer, Heidelberg (2007)
10. Ladwig, G., Tran, T.: Linked data query processing strategies. In: Patel-Schneider, P.F., Pan, Y., Hitzler, P., Mika, P., Zhang, L., Pan, J.Z., Horrocks, I., Glimm, B. (eds.) ISWC 2010, Part I. LNCS, vol. 6496, pp. 453–469. Springer, Heidelberg (2010)
11. Langegger, A., Wöß, W., Blöchl, M.: A semantic web middleware for virtual data integration on the web. In: Bechhofer, S., Hauswirth, M., Hoffmann, J., Koubarakis, M. (eds.) ESWC 2008. LNCS, vol. 5021, pp. 493–507. Springer, Heidelberg (2008)
12. Mokadem, R., Hameurlain, A., Morvan, F.: Performance improving of semi-join based join operation through algebraic signatures. In: International Symposium on Parallel and Distributed Processing with Applications, ISPA 2008, pp. 431–438. IEEE (2008)
13. Morsey, M., Lehmann, J., Auer, S., Ngonga Ngomo, A.-C.: Dbpedia sparql benchmark–performance assessment with real queries on real data. In: Aroyo, L., Welty, C., Alani, H., Taylor, J., Bernstein, A., Kagal, L., Noy, N., Blomqvist, E. (eds.) ISWC 2011, Part I. LNCS, vol. 7031, pp. 454–469. Springer, Heidelberg (2011)
14. Nikolov, A., et al.: Fedsearch: Efficiently combining structured queries and full-text search in a sparql federation. In: Alani, H., Kagal, L., Fokoue, A., Groth, P., Biemann, C., Parreira, J.X., Aroyo, L., Noy, N., Welty, C., Janowicz, K. (eds.) ISWC 2013, Part I. LNCS, vol. 8218, pp. 427–443. Springer, Heidelberg (2013)
15. Piatetsky-Shapiro, G., Connell, C.: Accurate estimation of the number of tuples satisfying a condition. In: ACM SIGMOD Record, vol. 14, pp. 256–276. ACM (1984)
16. Prud'hommeaux, E., Seaborne, A., Laboratories, H.P.: Sparql query language for rdf. W3C Recommendation 15 (January 2008)
17. Quilitz, B., Leser, U.: Querying distributed rdf data sources with sparql. In: Bechhofer, S., Hauswirth, M., Hoffmann, J., Koubarakis, M. (eds.) ESWC 2008. LNCS, vol. 5021, pp. 524–538. Springer, Heidelberg (2008)
18. Schwarte, A., Haase, P., Hose, K., Schenkel, R., Schmidt, M.: FedX: Optimization techniques for federated query processing on linked data. In: Aroyo, L., Welty, C., Alani, H., Taylor, J., Bernstein, A., Kagal, L., Noy, N., Blomqvist, E. (eds.) ISWC 2011, Part I. LNCS, vol. 7031, pp. 585–600. Springer, Heidelberg (2011)
19. Schwarte, A., Haase, P., Hose, K., Schenkel, R., Schmidt, M.: Fedx: Optimization techniques for federated query processing on linked data. In: Aroyo, L., Welty, C., Alani, H., Taylor, J., Bernstein, A., Kagal, L., Noy, N., Blomqvist, E. (eds.) ISWC 2011, Part I. LNCS, vol. 7031, pp. 601–616. Springer, Heidelberg (2011)
20. Stuckenschmidt, H., Vdovjak, R., Houben, G.J., Broekstra, J.: Index structures and algorithms for querying distributed rdf repositories. In: Proceedings of the 13th International Conference on World Wide Web, pp. 631–639. ACM (2004)
21. Zemánek, J., Schenk, S., Svatek, V.: Optimizing sparql queries over disparate rdf data sources through distributed semi-joins. In: International Semantic Web Conference, Posters & Demos (2008)

MRFS: A Distributed Files System
with Geo-replicated Metadata

Jiongyu Yu, Weigang Wu, Di Yang, and Ning Huang

Department of Computer Science, Sun Yat-sen University, Guangzhou 510006, China
{yujiongy,yangdi5}@mail2.sysu.edu.cn, wuweig@mail.sysu.edu.cn

Abstract. Distributed file system is one of the key blocks of data centers. With the advance in geo-replicated storage systems across data centers, both system scale and user scale are becoming larger and larger. Then, a single metadata server in distributed file system may lead to capacity bottleneck and high latency without considering locality. In this paper, we present the design and implementation of MRFS (Metadata Replication File System), a distributed file system with hierarchical and efficient distributed metadata management, which introduces multiple metadata servers (MDS) and an additional namespace server (NS). Metadata is divided into non-overlapping parts and stored on MDS in which the creation operation is raised, while namespace and directory information is maintained in NS. Such a hierarchical design not only achieves high scalability but also provides low-latency because it satisfies a majority of requests in local MDS. To address hotspot issues and flash crowds, the system supports flexible and configurable metadata replication among MDSs. Evaluation results show that our system MRFS is effective and efficient, and the replication mechanism brings substantial local visit at the cost of affordable memory overhead under various scenarios.

Keywords: Distributed file system, Metadata management, data replication.

1   Introduction

With the emergence and development of large-scale geo-replicated application, distributed file system, as a general storage infrastructure, has attracted more and more attentions in the past years. One of the key challenges in distributed file system lies in big data processing. Data has become of greater importance, and storage demand also has an explosive growth, which has increased exponentially exceeding petabytes and getting close to exabytes in certain applications [1].

Consequently, high scalability and providing low-latency response have been two critical factors in the design of distributed file system for geo-replicated applications. Since metadata transactions account for over 50% of all file system operations [2], most modern distributed file systems decouple the metadata transactions from actual data accesses so as to achieve scalability and availability. Dedicated metadata server (MDS) is deployed to process metadata transactions while storage nodes are to store actual data. Metadata management then becomes a critical issue in file systems.

X.-h. Sun et al. (Eds.): ICA3PP 2014, Part II, LNCS 8631, pp. 273–285, 2014.
© Springer International Publishing Switzerland 2014

However, in most of existing distributed file systems, there is usually only single MDS node, which is prone to be a bottleneck if the number of files is very large [3]. Though a few designs introduce distributed metadata model, it is costly to maintain a global and consistent namespace. Besides, these works consider only single datacenter, which are not suitable for systems that spread across multi-datacenters, i.e. geo-replicated systems.

To solve the issues discussed above, this paper presents a two-tiered metadata management scheme with metadata across multiple metadata servers (MDSs). We separate the file metadata and namespace information and store them in MDS (metadata server) and NS (namespace server), respectively. File metadata is initially stored in the MDS where the creation operation is raised. We call such MDS as primary MDS of the metadata in the rest of the paper. Based on the rule of locality and visit pattern of applications, we assume that a majority of client requests are satisfied in the primary MDS and therefore will not cost high network latency among different datacenters. In addition, multiple MDSs can serve requests simultaneously and potentially improve the performance and concurrency. Moreover, NS maintains a global and consistent namespace which supports fast response for directory lookup and modification requests from clients. Such operation is supposed to cause high delay in other designs since the namespace is scattered among different MDSs and involved entries should be located and merged upon each query.

We propose to extend MooseFS, a well-known open source distributed file system, by modifying the entire metadata module and introducing a new role, namespace server. More precisely, we refer to the basic blocks of MooseFS, like communication mechanism and client module, but recode the whole metadata service module, i.e., redesign the data structure of file metadata and namespace information and implement the replication mechanism. The metadata of the file system is dynamically partitioned into non-overlapping parts upon clients' creation request. Namely, each metadata node is in charge of one subset of the whole metadata in file system. It should be clarified that, in the context of MRFS, clients are applications or front-end servers that issue read/write operations on behalf of real world users. All processes and interaction with NS hiding behind the primary MDS are transparent to clients.

On the other hand, to alleviate flash crowds and hotspot issues, we implement a flexible and configurable replication mechanism. Popular metadata entries are replicated to other MDSs that query them frequently during a pre-defined period. The replication threshold and time interval are both configurable to meet diverse requirements. With replication, high-latency access across MDSs is reduced and load balance among the overall system is enhanced.

MRFS is tested in real deployment. Experiments have been conducted under several scenarios to validate our design and evaluate the performance of the new file system. The results show that our design is effective and efficient. Besides, the newly-added replication mechanism largely reduces the across-datacenter communication at the cost of affordable memory overhead.

The rest of the paper is organized as follows. We briefly review existing works on metadata management for distributed file systems in Section 2. Section 3 describes the design and implementation of MRFS. The experiments and results are reported in Section 4. In the last section, we conclude the paper and discuss about future works.

2   Related Work

According to the metadata server type, we categorize existing works on metadata management into three classes, i.e., centralized metadata management, distributed metadata management, and implicit metadata management.

Most of popular and famous distributed file systems, i.e., HDFS [4], GoogleFS [5] and MooseFS [6], use a centralized metadata server. The advantage of such design lies in easy implementation and management. However, the drawback is also obvious. Since metadata is maintained in main memory, as the scale of file count increases to extremely large, it may become a bottleneck and limit the scalability of overall system.

Quite a number of distributed metadata management schemes have been introduced to solve the problems of centralized ones. With static subtree partitioning, metadata is divided in to non-overlapped parts and distributed into individual MDSs by system administrator. This approach is simple and relatively efficient and used by many famous implementations like Coda [7] and Sprite [8]. However, it may face workload imbalance among MDSs. Besides, when namespace need to be re-divided, system administrator is involved again.

Hashing-based namespace partitioning removes the issue of unbalanced workloads in static partitioning. In general, path name of file and directory is hashed and then assigned to corresponding servers, i.e., Lazy Hybrid [9]. System can quickly locate the requested metadata utilizing the path name and hashing function. This approach causes tremendous overhead when node is added to or deleted since system should re-calculate the hashing-function and relocate most of the metadata. Traversal of a directory is also inefficient in such design.

Dynamic subtree partitioning [10] is proposed to address the load imbalance problem in static partitioning, i.e., Ceph [11]. The metadata of the whole file system is partitioned by hashing directories near the root of the directory hierarchy, each of which is undertaken by a node in a MDS cluster. By migrating heavily loaded metadata automatically and overlapping popular parts, the load among different MDSs can be balanced dynamically. However, because of the existence of overlapped metadata, the maintenance of the consistency between different MDSs becomes more significant and critical, and consequently, the system becomes very complex and costly to realize and execute. Moreover, balancing load will cause metadata redistribution when the user access pattern or the MDS set changes. This results in additional overhead.

Hierarchical Bloom-filter Array (HBA) is an approach based on bloom filter [12]. In HBA, each metadata server constructs a bloom filter to store the path name of metadata that it hosts. Exploiting the temporal access locality, HBA uses another bloom filter to store some frequently accessed path. Although bloom filter is space-efficient, it returns a probabilistic answer and cannot guarantee the location of a file.

In the third class of metadata management, there is no dedicated metadata sever at all. GlusterFS [13] is a representative of this class, which replaces the metadata module, i.e. MDS, with an elastic hash algorithm. That is, there is in fact no explicit MDS, and client is in charge of locating data according to file's absolute path. Therefore, the bottleneck and single point of failure issues in server side is eliminated too, and high scalability and parallelism is simply achieved. However, such approach also has trouble when traversing a directory and maintaining the consistency of namespace. Additionally, lack of specialized MDS causes more workloads and responsibility at client nodes.

As for the replication of metadata, the Hadoop extension by MapR Inc. [14] is the only existing work to the best of our knowledge. In this system, metadata is replicated like common data to achieve for high availability and better performance. Our work differs from the work of MapR Inc. in the overall system architecture and the management method of replication management.

3   The Design and Implementation of MRFS

3.1   Overview of MRFS

MRFS (Metadata Replication File system) is mainly composed of four components: Metadata Server (MDS), Namespace Server (NS), Client and Chunk Server (CS). Several MDSs distribute in different geography locations, and store actual file metadata. On the other side, there is only one single NS maintaining a global namespace and managing the whole file system. Clients connect and conduct operations to their primary MDSs. Chunk servers are nodes that provide storage for file data.

MRFS aims to provide low latency for a majority of client requests of metadata under different scenarios. It is assumed that clients have higher interest in metadata that they created, which means that requests are more probably satisfied in clients' primary MDS. A small portion of requests cannot be handled locally and therefore primary MDS inquires NS for the location of that metadata and then forward the request to corresponding MDS containing the requested metadata. In case of special states, like hotspots or flash crowds, replication is used to reduce such across-MDS interactions noticeably, and in consequence, improve the overall performance and load balance.

Taking advantage of the locality of metadata and client behavior, such design avoids the inherently existing drawbacks of other methods like static subtree partitioning and hashing design, and provides low-latency access for clients in most situations. Moreover, by means of replication, MRFS addresses the work balance issue.

In the rest of this section, we present the details of the design and implementation of MRFS. The architecture of MRFS is shown in Fig 1, which is the basis of the following description.

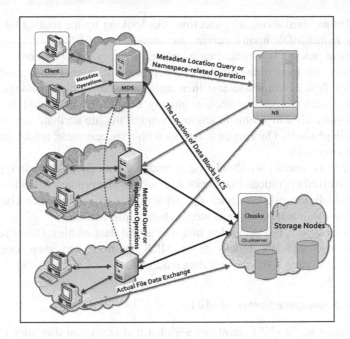

Fig. 1. The architecture of MRFS

3.2   The Client Module of MRFS

The client of MRFS is built on FUSE [15], a loadable kernel module that provides library API to create a file system in user space. We implement interfaces that are essential to build a practical file system. These interfaces are listed in table 1.

Table 1. Implemented interfaces in MRFS

Name	Description
fsinit	initiating process for file system
getattr	retrieve attributes of file or directory
create	create a file
unlink	remove a file
mkdir	create a directory
rmdir	remove a directory
read	read a file
write	write a file
readdir	read a directory, i.e., *ls* operation
chmod	change modes of file or directory

When initiated, client connects and registers with its primary MDS, which has a lowest latency for client requests. Client communicates with its primary MDS through a long-lived TCP connection. Such design eliminates the process of figuring out the closest MDS and initializing a connection, like looking up the routing table and then connecting to that MDS, upon receiving any request from FUSE.

After client process is mounted on a certain directory, all operations conducted in this directory are transmitted to the client process through FUSE module. Client identifies the type of command and then sends a corresponding message directly to the primary MDS via the connection already established. It should be noted that FUSE automatically call *getattr* function to acquire the file attribute for existence and access privilege check. Only when it returns with a success code, actual operation can be executed onwards.

Two types of operations should be considered individually. First type is only-metadata-involved operations like create and unlink. The primary MDS is in charge of handling the whole workflow. Such operations come to an end when client receives the execution result and/or the requested metadata information.

The second type is operation that involves actual data of files. Client retrieves the storage location of data blocks from MDS at first, and then interacts with corresponding storage nodes for real data read/write.

3.3   The Namespace Server of MRFS

The namespace server (NS) maintains a global and consistent directory tree in main memory. All metadata servers connect to NS when starting up, and forward all namespace-related operations, i.e., creating or removing a file, to NS. Since NS uses a single-thread model, we don't need to worry about the annoying consistency issues. By novelly separating the namespace from traditional metadata service, unlike other distributed metadata management, MRFS is able to provide much more efficient and straightforward response for directory query, i.e., ls operation.

Additionally, NS stores the mapping between metadata entry of each file and its primary MDS, identified by the absolute path name of files. Therefore, MDS can acquire the location of every metadata entry along with its path name. Though absolute path may cause extra memory overhead, the overall system is benefited from its faster locating and traversal of the directory. As a workaround, we can use the prefix-compression algorithm on path name to reduce memory usage, at the cost of longer delay of processing.

To realize replication mechanism, NS also records the replicas information. With this, NS provides more flexibility and useful functionalities, like restricting the total number of replicas and computing the popularity of entries.

3.4   The Metadata Server of MRFS

The MDS module in MooseFS is originally designed as a central node that bundles metadata and namespace service together. So we extend it to support distributed metadata model. There are multiple metadata servers in system and each of them is in charge of managing a part of the metadata. The metadata of the whole file system is divided into non-overlapping parts in accordance with the client's creation operation. Fig 2 and Fig 3 illustrate the creation process and the consequent namespace.

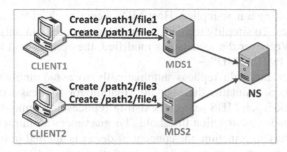

Fig. 2. Clients create different files

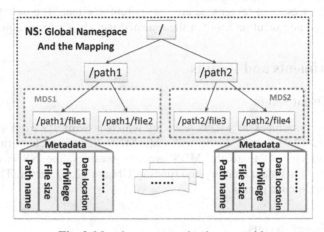

Fig. 3. Metadata construction in server side

Client1 and client2 create files respectively and send command to their own primary MDSs. MDS stores that metadata entry is called Host MDS, i.e., MDS1 is the Host MDS of */path/file1*. To complete the command, MDS should inform NS of the creation operation, so that new files are added into the namespace. As a result, namespace and file metadata are stored in NS and MDS separately. For MDS, it constructs a hash table in memory to store all local file metadata, so as to accelerate the query speed.

Each MDS serves multiple clients simultaneously. When a request from client is coming, primary MDS scans the hash table to check whether the requested entry exists locally. If so, MDS returns directly; or else, it should forward the query to NS for a global query. If the path exists in other MDS, NS will return its location. Then primary MDS connects to the Host MDS (for the first time of connection) and queries for the actual metadata. This procedure introduces an extra RTT, but such situation is supposed to be rare.

In case that there are hotspot issues or flash crowds, we implement the replication mechanism among MDSs. It uses a server-initiated model. Host MDS pushes the copy of popular metadata entries to other MDSs that have queried the metadata beyond a configurable threshold in a specific time interval. Replicas are distributed in different MDSs to improve the workload balance for servers and a low latency for clients. When creating a new replica, Host MDS keeps track of the replica MDS for subsequent updates. To simplify the design, metadata updates can only be executed in the Host MDS. Whenever the metadata is modified, the updates will be pushed to all available replicas by Host MDS.

MRFS removes the stale replicas automatically to avoid unlimited increase of replicas. Each MDS maintains the visit information for replicas. At intervals of a configurable period, each MDS scans all existing replicas and removes those that are old enough and under the deletion threshold. To guarantee the fairness and decrease the impact of history information, the concept of decay is applied in our design. Each decay period the history visit count is decayed at a rate, whose value can be set according to different requirements.

At last, all processes in server side are transparent to client. The only thing clients concern about is the execution result or the returned metadata information.

4   Experiments and Results

4.1   Experiment Setup

We deploy four machines as MDSs, each of which is with 1G main memory and running Ubuntu 12.04 Server. Along with each MDS, there is a client running at the same node and connecting to the MDS process. Besides, the NS is deployed at another node with 8G main memory and running Ubuntu 12.10 Server. The local-disk file system at each node is ext4.

4.2   Experiment Results

We use four different metrics to measure the performance of metadata service. Firstly, we measure the memory overhead of MDS and NS without replicas. Then we create replicas in one MDS on purpose to measure the replica's impact on memory usage. Secondly, the execution time of creation in different situation is measured. At last, we use NumPy [16] and Python to simulate the visit pattern of web applications. By this, we can measure the efficiency of replicas and the performance enhancement it brings.

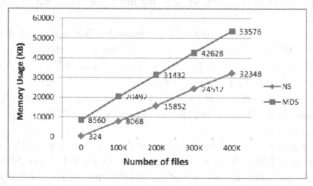

Fig. 4. Memory usage of NS and MDS process changes as the number of created files increases

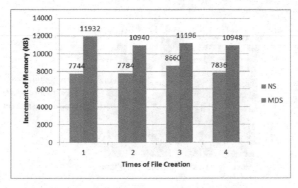

Fig. 5. Increment of memory usage of NS and MDS process in each creation operation

Fig 4 and Fig 5 show the memory usage and increment in NS and MDS along with the increasing of the number of created files. Obviously, the memory usage increase linearly with the file count. Each entry in MDS costs about 110 bytes, while that of NS is about 30% less. This can be explained because NS doesn't store the file information but the directory tree and mapping. Although MDS may take up more memory, in real environment, there are multiple MDS in different locations, workload will be distributed among them and MDS is unlikely to have a bottleneck in memory. It should be clarified that the reason why MDS takes much more memory than NS is that process allocates the memory to hash table in advance.

We run another experiment with two MDS and a NS to demonstrate the impact of replicas. Initially, we create 100K files in MDS2, and then make MDS1 create all files' replica locally. The *dmap* command is used to monitor the memory usage of each process in different stages. Fig 6 shows some features of MRFS. The creation in one MDS won't affect other MDS, which means MDS is able to work individually. The replica creation will introduce extra memory overhead in all three machines. NS increases a tiny amount of memory as it only keeps track of the replica MDS's ip for further use. As the Replica MDS, MDS1 increases about 85% of the primary metadata copy in MDS2. This is because Replica MDS doesn't store the information of remote visit but local visit. As the Primary MDS, MDS2 need to record the replica MDS's information, and therefore its memory usage increases about 20% compared to the original.

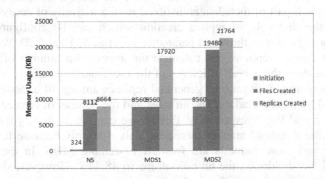

Fig. 6. Comparison of memory usage before and after creating replicas

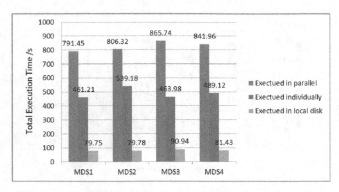

Fig. 7. Total execution time of creating 100K files in four MDS

Each MDS applies the creation of 100K files for three times. More precisely, creation is firstly operated in parallel and then individually and lastly executed in local file system. Fig 7 shows that local file system provides the best performance with the total execution time of 80 seconds. For MRFS, due to the network latency, the elapsed time is about 5 times slower than local file system. Averagely, each creation operation costs about 5ms. When executed in parallel, the average execution time is a little longer, for the reason that each MDS should interchange with NS to finish the operation and the single-thread design of NS limits the throughput. Fortunately, all metadata and namespace information are stored in main memory and this inherent advantage leads to a fast processing. Therefore, network latency takes up most of the elapsed time, and even in parallel mode, the average time of 8ms for each creation is efficient enough for a distributed file system. This result meets our design expectation.

To measure the effectiveness of replication, we firstly create 500 disjoint files in each MDS, and then use Python script and the NumPy library to simulate the access pattern of metadata. Each Client executes 40K access operations through their Primary MDS, and every operation is carried out at a time interval of 10ms.

The local/remote access ratio is set in the script, i.e., ratio=0.2 means that local access takes up 20% of all access while remote access of other MDS takes up 80%. All accesses conform to the Pareto Distribution, which is a power-like distribution and can be used as a model for many read-world problems [17][18]. For MRFS, that means only a small part of metadata is involved with a majority of accesses. Another parameter is the threshold of replica creation which can be configured in MDS module. In our experiment, threshold parameter is set as 5, 10 and 20. We also count the number of created replicas, and calculate the average hit number of all replicas. This metric can show the overall efficiency of the metadata replication.

We can calculate the hit ratio of generated replicas among all accesses that could not be satisfied by local metadata. The hit rates and the number of created replicas are plotted in Fig 8 and Fig 9 respectively. Firstly, we can see obviously the hit ratio is decreasing as the threshold number increases. This is simply because fewer replicas are generated and more requests are forward to remote MDS. In the worst case (ratio=0.8 and threshold=20), the hit ratio drops to 48.44%. However, since the total remote accesses account for 20% of all accesses, the actual forward operations take up only 10.29%. Secondly, with the value of ratio increases, which reflects more requests are handled locally, the percentage of replica hit falls on the contrary. The reason is that with the same value of threshold, fewer remote accesses will lead to fewer replicas according to the feature of Pareto distribution, and consequently a greater number of requests will be forward to other MDS.

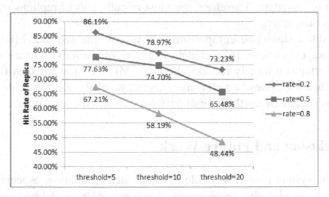

Fig. 8. Hit rate of replicas with various parameters

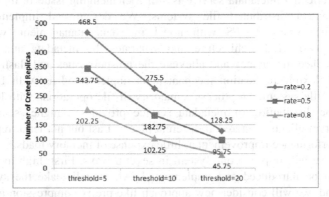

Fig. 9. Number of generated replicas with various parameters

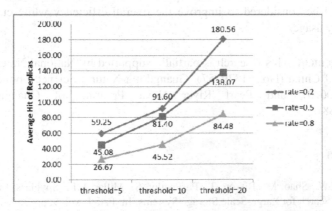

Fig. 10. Average hit count of replicas with various parameters

Besides the hit ratio of replicas, we use the average hit count to measure the efficiency of replicas. As can be observed in Fig 10, one replica serves more visit requests while the total number of replicas declines. This can be explained by the basic properties of Pareto distribution, that is a majority of access only involve with a small amount of metadata. Therefore, the most popular part of replicas will take over more requests than others.

From the discussions and comparisons above, we can see that MRFS performs efficiently and effectively in metadata service in various scenarios. And the replication mechanism largely reduces the cross-MDS visit at the cost of affordable memory overhead. Besides, we can take advantage of the flexible configuration to achieve the balance between the overall performance and memory usage.

5   Conclusion and Future Work

Distributed file system plays a key role in distributed computing, especially in cloud computing systems with high requirement of storage volumes and performance. High scalable and effective metadata service is still a challenging issue in the design and implementation of distributed file systems. We design and implement a real distributed file system MRFS with novel metadata management, which takes advantage of two-tiered architecture and separates the metadata and namespace service. To reduce the latency and alleviate the hotspot issues and flash crowds, an efficient and flexible replication mechanism is implemented as well. Experiments show that the file system can process a majority of file operations with low latency. Moreover, the distribution of metadata service provides a higher scalability and efficiently serves clients scattered at different places. Last but not least, replicas bring substantial performance improvement at little expense of memory loads.

In future, we will improve our system in several ways. First, high availability of metadata will be introduced and implemented, which will make the system more robust. Second, we will consider new approach like prefix-compression algorithm to reduce the memory overhead in namespace server. Third, new replica placement strategies will be considered to improve the overall efficiency while cutting down more memory usage.

Acknowledgement. This research is partially supported by National Natural Science Foundation of China (No. 61379157), Guangdong Natural Science Foundation (No. S2012010010670), and Pearl River Nova Program of Guangzhou (No. 2011J2200088)

References

1. Leung, A.W., Shao, M., Bisson, T., Pasupathy, S., Miller, E.L.: Spyglass: Fast, Scalable Metadata Search for Large-Scale Storage Systems. In: FAST, vol. 9, pp. 153–166 (2009)
2. Roselli, D.S., Lorch, J.R., Anderson, T.E.: A Comparison of File System Workloads. In: USENIX Annual Technical Conference, General Track, pp. 41–54 (2000)

3. Traeger, A., Zadok, E., Joukov, N., Wright, C.P.: A nine year study of file system and storage benchmarking. ACM Transactions on Storage (TOS) 4(2), 5 (2008)
4. Shvachko, K., Kuang, H., Radia, S., Chansler, R.: The hadoop distributed file system. In: 2010 IEEE 26th Symposium on Mass Storage Systems and Technologies (MSST), pp. 1–10. IEEE (2010)
5. Ghemawat, S., Gobioff, H., Leung, S.T.: The Google file system. In: ACM SIGOPS Operating Systems Review, vol. 37(5), pp. 29–43. ACM (2003)
6. MooseFS, http://www.moosefs.org
7. Satyanarayanan, M., Kistler, J.J., Kumar, P., Okasaki, M.E., Siegel, E.H., Steere, D.C.: Coda: A highly available file system for a distributed workstation environment. IEEE Transactions on Computers 39(4), 447–459 (1990)
8. Rosenblum, M., Ousterhout, J.K.: The design and implementation of a log-structured file system. ACM Transactions on Computer Systems (TOCS) 10(1), 26–52 (1992)
9. Brandt, S.A., Miller, E.L., Long, D.D., Xue, L.: Efficient metadata management in large distributed storage systems. In: 2013 IEEE 10th International Conference on Mobile Ad-Hoc and Sensor Systems, pp. 290–290 (2003)
10. Weil, S.A., Brandt, S.A., Miller, E.L., Maltzahn, C.: CRUSH: Controlled, scalable, decentralized placement of replicated data. In: Proceedings of the 2006 ACM/IEEE Conference on Supercomputing, p. 122. ACM (2006)
11. Weil, S.A., Brandt, S.A., Miller, E.L., Long, D.D., Maltzahn, C.,, C.: A scalable, high-performance distributed file system. In: Proceedings of the 7th Symposium on Operating Systems Design and Implementation. USENIX Association (2006)
12. Zhu, Y., Jiang, H., Wang, J.: Hierarchical bloom filter arrays (hba): A novel, scalable metadata management system for large cluster-based storage. In: 2004 IEEE International Conference on Cluster Computing, pp. 165–174 (2004)
13. GlusterFS, http://www.gluster.org
14. MapR, http://www.mapr.com
15. FUSE, http://fuse.sourceforge.net
16. NumPy, http://www.numpy.org
17. Arnold, B.C.: Pareto distribution. John Wiley & Sons, Inc. (1985)
18. Reed, W.J.: The Pareto, Zipf and other power laws. Economics Letters 74(1) (2001)

An Advanced Data Redistribution Approach to Accelerate the Scale-Down Process of RAID-6

Congjin Du, Chentao Wu, and Jie Li

Shanghai Key Laboratory of Scalable Computing and Systems,
Department of Computer Science and Engineering, Shanghai Jiao Tong University,
Shanghai, China 200240
ducongjin@gmail.com, {wuct,lijie}@cs.sjtu.edu.cn

Abstract. Nowadays RAID is widely used with the increasing requirements of the reliability in storage systems and the fast development of
cloud computing. Among various levels and implementations of RAID
systems, RAID-6 is one of the most significant category with the ability
to tolerate concurrent failures of any two disks. However, the scalability
of RAID-6 is a big challenge. Although many approaches are proposed to
accelerate the scaling process and reduce the overhead, how to efficiently
remove disks (refers to scale-down process) from existing array is still an
open problem.

To address the scalability problem, we propose an Advanced Data
Redistribution (ADR) approach. The basic idea of ADR is to reorganize
previous stripes in RAID-6 systems to achieve higher scalability. ADR
is a stripe-level scheme and can be combined with other approaches as
SDM and MDS-Frame. It can minimize the overhead of data migration
and parity modification. We have conducted mathematical analysis by
comparing ADR to various popular RAID-6 codes. The results show
that, compared to typical approach (Round-Robin), ADR decreases more
than 52.1% migration I/O operations, saves the migration time by up to
63.5%, and speeds up of the scaling process by up to 1.91.

Keywords: RAID-6, MDS Code, Performance Evaluation, Scalability,
Scale-Down, Reliability.

1 Introduction

With the increasing requirements for storage systems and the fast development
of cloud computing, **R**edundant **A**rrays of **I**nexpensive (or **I**ndependent) **D**isks
(**RAID**) [15] [5] becomes popular due to its ability to provide both high performance and high reliability for cloud computing services. In recent years, scalability, especially scale-down (removing disks), becomes an important issue [1] in
RAID systems because of the following reasons.

- By removing some inefficient disks from a disk array, the power consumption
  can be reduced, and the system can be more power-efficient.

X.-h. Sun et al. (Eds.): ICA3PP 2014, Part II, LNCS 8631, pp. 286–299, 2014.
© Springer International Publishing Switzerland 2014

- Removing disks from a disk array can shorten parity chains, and the reliability and the speed of recovery can be improved.
- Typically, RAID is widely used in various online services such as cloud computing [1]. High scalability can avoid the extremely high downtime cost [14].
- Bidirectional scaling is critical in data centers. RAID-based architectures are widely used for clusters and large scale storage systems, where scalability plays an important role [11] [19].

RAID-6 has received more attention than ever, with higher possibility of double disk failures [20] [16]. There are many implementations of RAID-6 based on various erasure code technologies, of which **M**aximum **D**istance **S**eparable (**MDS**) codes are the most popular. MDS codes can be categorized into horizontal codes [18] [2] [6] [3] [17] and vertical codes [4] [25] [26] [12] [24] [22].

However, existing solutions in disk arrays scaling [29] [28] are insufficient for RAID-6 scaling under scale-down condition. There are two reasons as follows,

- Most scaling approaches [8] [23] are designed for scale-up (extending disks), while scale-down (removing disks) is significant as well. Removing inefficient disks can save energy consumption.
- Typical scaling approaches under scale-down condition are based on **R**ound-**R**obin (**RR**) approach, which is insufficient to provide efficient scaling [29] [21]. It is because RR approach has extremely high overhead in terms of migration I/O, computation cost and migration time.

To solve the above problems, we propose a novel scaling approach named **A**dvanced **D**ata **R**edistribution approach (**ADR**) to accelerate RAID-6 scaling. ADR is an advanced approach to reorganize previous stripes in RAID-6 systems to achieve higher scalability. We make the following contributions in this work:

- We propose a scaling (ADR) approach to address RAID-6 scalability problems under scale-down condition, which is a significant issue in large scale data storage systems.
- ADR accelerates RAID-6 scaling process, in terms of the number of modified parities, the total number of XOR operations, the total number of I/O operations and the migration time.
- ADR provides fast data addressing algorithm.

The rest of this paper continues as follows: Section 2 discusses the motivation of this paper and details the background of existing scaling methods. ADR is described in detail in Section 3. Section 4 gives the quantitative analysis on scalability. Finally we conclude the paper in Section 5.

2   Background and Motivation

In this section we discuss the background of our work, problems in existing RAID-6 scaling schemes and our motivation. To facilitate our discussion, we summarize symbols used in this paper in Table 1.

2.1 Desired Scaling Features in RAID-6

To scale a disk array, some data need to be migrated to achieve a balanced data distribution. During data migration, we prefer to keep an evenly distributed workload and minimize the data/parity movement. Combined with existing scaling approaches [29] and the real cases in RAID-6, the following four features are typically desired,

Feature 1 (*Uniform Data Distribution*): Each disk should have the same amount of data blocks to maintain an even workload.

Feature 2 (*Minimal Data & Parity Migration*): By removing m disks from a RAID-6 system with n_d data disks storing B data blocks, the expected total number of data movements is $m \times B/n_d$ [23].

Feature 3 (*Fast Data Addressing*): The locations of blocks in the array should be efficiently computed.

Feature 4 (*Minimal Parity Computation & Modification*): A movement on data block could bring modification cost on its corresponding original parities and computation cost on new parities, so movements on data blocks should be limited in the original parity chain and thus parity blocks should be retained without any change.

Table 1. A List of Symbols in This Paper

Symbols	Description
n, n'	number of disks in a disk array before/after scaling
m	number of removed disk(s)
B	total number of data blocks (data elements)
p	a prime number
P, Q	parity blocks before scaling
P', Q'	parity blocks after scaling
S, S'	total number of stripes before/after scaling
$n_d, n_{d'}$	number of data disks before/after scaling
S_{id}, S'_{id}	stripe ID before/after scaling
i, i'	row ID in a stripe before/after scaling
j, j'	column ID (disk ID) in a stripe before/after scaling
R_d	data migration ratio
R_p	parity modification ratio
n_{io}	total number of I/O operations
T_b	access time of a read/write request to a block
T_m	migration time

2.2 Existing Fast Scaling Approaches

Existing approaches to improve the scalability of RAID systems include Round-Robin (RR) [9] [13] [27], Semi-RR [8], ALV [28], MDM [10], FastScale [29], etc.

To clearly illustrate various strategies in RAID-6, we use P/Q (e.g., P_1 and Q_1) to delegate various parity blocks before scaling and P'/Q' (e.g., P'_1 and Q'_1) for the parity blocks after scaling. If the parity block is still presented by P/Q after scaling, it means that parity is retained.

Traditional RR and Semi-RR approaches are used in RAID-6 under two restrictions. First, all data blocks are migrated based on round-robin order in the scaling process. Second, all parity blocks are retained without any movement.

For a traditional RR scaling approach (as shown in Figure 1), obviously, all parities need to be modified and recalculated after data migration. Although RR is a simple approach to implement on RAID-6, it brings high overhead.

Based on RR approach, Brown [13] designed a reshape toolkit in the Linux kernel (MD-Reshape), which writes mapped metadata with a fixed-size window. Due to the limitation of RR approach, metadata are frequently updated by calling MD-Reshape function, which is inefficient.

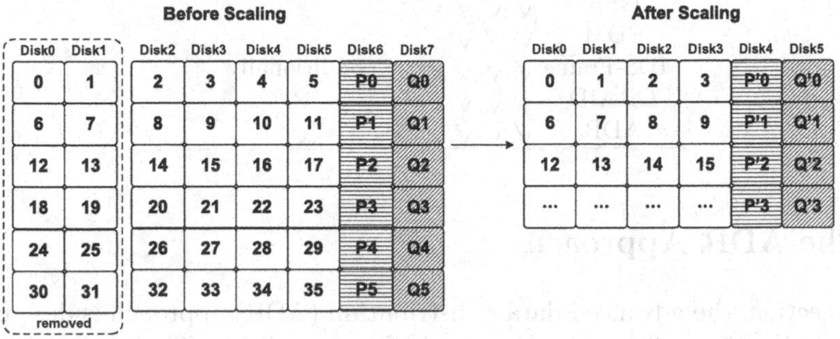

Fig. 1. RAID-6 scaling in RDP from 8 to 6 disks using RR approach (all data blocks are migrated)

Semi-RR [8] is proposed to decrease high migration cost in RR scaling. Unfortunately, by extending multiple disks, the data distribution is not uniform after scaling, which causes unbalanced workload and decrease the performance. SDM [23] can provide high scalability by extending specific number of disks. However, SDM cannot be applied under scale-down condition. MDS-Frame [30] approach has the ability of bidirectional scaling, but the scaling is limited to the same p among different erasure codes. Scaling on several levels of RAID can be achieved by CRAID [31], but this method cannot be used in scale-down scenario.

McPod [32] is used in RAID-4 scaling, ALV [28], MDM [10] and GSR [21] are RAID-5 scaling approaches, Fastscale [29] accelerates the scaling process of RAID-0. They take advantages of both RR and Semi-RR approaches, and improve the migration efficiency. However, they cannot be applied in RAID-6.

2.3 The Motivation

We summarize the existing fast scaling approaches in Table 2. It shows that existing scaling approaches are difficult to conduct scaled-down process in RAID-6 systems, which is caused by the complex layout of RAID-6 codes. Therefore, existing scaling approaches are insufficient to satisfy the desired features listed in Section 2.1, which motivates us to propose a new approach for RAID-6 scaling under scale-down condition.

Table 2. Summary on Various Fast Scaling Approaches

Name	Features 1 2 3 4	Support Scale-down in RAID-6?
RR	✓ × ✓ ×	conditionally
Semi-RR	× × ✓ ×	×
ALV	✓ × ✓ ×	×
MDM	× ✓ ✓ ✓	×
FastScale	✓ ✓ ✓ ✓	×
GSR	✓ ✓ ✓ ✓	×
SDM	✓ ✓ ✓ ✓	×
MDS-Frame	✓ ✓ ✓ ✓	conditionally
CRAID	✓ ✓ ✓ ✓	×
ADR	✓ ✓ ✓ ✓	✓

3   The ADR Approach

In this section, the advanced data redistribution (ADR) approach is designed to accelerate the RAID-6 scaling under scale-down condition. The purpose of ADR is to minimize the parity migration, modification and recalculation according with a global view on the two types of parities and single/multiple stripe(s).

The corresponding stripes during scaling process can be categorized into two types, old stripe and new stripe, which are defined as follows,

Old Stripe: A used stripe before scaling.

New Stripe: A new stripe generated in the scaling process.

There are several critical steps for ADR approach, disk labeling, stripe generation and scaling, and they are shown as follows,

1. Disk Labeling: According to the layouts before and after scaling, a cost-effective way can be find to handle the scaling process in an old stripe, and the disks should be labeled before the following steps.

2. Stripe Generation New stripes are generated in this step to place data blocks in removed disks before scaling.

3. Scaling: Based on the scaling approach in Step 1, migrate data blocks for each stripe and update parities in every parity chains.

Typically, without any special instructions, a data/parity block (in logical address view) corresponds to a data/parity element (in parity layout view) in a stripe. In this section, we use RDP [6], a typical MDS code, as an example to show how ADR works in RAID-6, scaling from 8 to 6 disks. The corresponding parity layouts are shown in Figure 2.

3.1   Disk Labeling

For RAID-6 scaling under scale-down condition, there are four rules compared to the current and future parity layouts. We propose different rules for a RAID-6 scaling under scale-down condition.

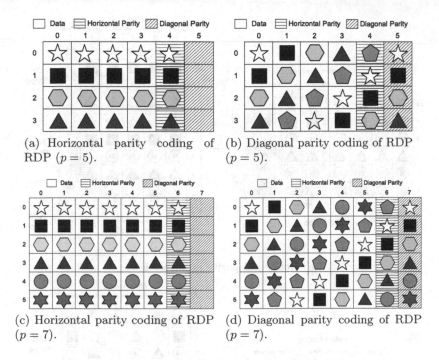

(a) Horizontal parity coding of RDP ($p = 5$).

(b) Diagonal parity coding of RDP ($p = 5$).

(c) Horizontal parity coding of RDP ($p = 7$).

(d) Diagonal parity coding of RDP ($p = 7$).

Fig. 2. RDP Code (for $p + 1$ disks)

- **(Disk Labeling)** There are always two parity disks, so the parity disks are retained and removed disks are all data disks. They are labelled based on the number of the removed disks.
- **(Row Process)** If an Old Stripe contains n_r rows, the first $n_r - m$ rows are retained in the corresponding stripe after scaling.

For example, if we want to scale a RAID-6 array using RDP from 8 to 6 disks, compared to the layouts in Figure 2, we have the following strategies according to the above rules (shown in Figure 3, assume disks 4 and 5 are removed).

- **(Disks Labeling)** Label the parity disks as disks 4 and 5 and data disks as their original labels.
- **(Row Process)** The first 4 rows are retained after scaling.

3.2   Stripe Generation

Although we retain the original parity chains as much as possible, there are still several parity chains and rows need to be removed to adapt the new layout after scaling. The data blocks in these chains should be handled according to the two different cases as follows, and new stripes are generated to store them.

Case 1: In the removed disk(s), these data blocks are migrated to the retained disks;

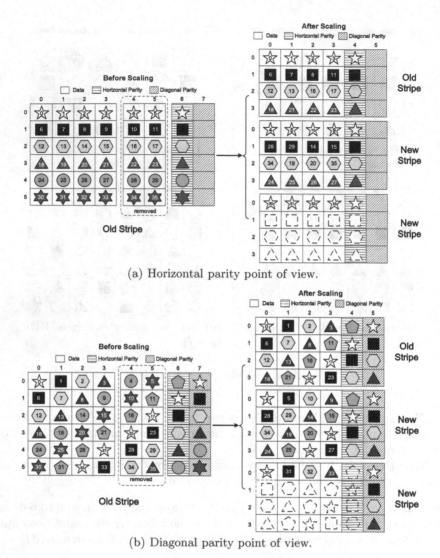

(a) Horizontal parity point of view.

(b) Diagonal parity point of view.

Fig. 3. RAID-6 scaling in RDP from 8 to 6 disks using ADR approach

Case 2: In the retained disk(s), these data blocks need to be remapped to new stripes.

According to the layouts of the disk array before and after scaling, a part of data blocks migrated and remapped in this step are used to generate new stripes, and the others remain in the old stripe. To ensure that there are as many parity chains retained as possible, the data blocks migrated and remapped in the first $n - m$ rows are limited to the least. Therefore, the modification of the old stripe can be minimized. In addition, data blocks used to form new stripes also need to retain as many parity chains as possible to take advantage of the original parities.

For example, as shown in Figure 3, blocks 9, 14, 15 are remapped to generate new stripes.

3.3   Scaling

In ADR, the scaling is the process of data migration, which is based on retaining the original parity chains as many as possible, with the following rules.

Rule 1: In the retained parity chain(s), these blocks are migrated to the old stripes.

Rule 2: Not in the retained parity chain(s), these blocks are migrated to generate new stripes.

For example, as shown in Figure 3, blocks 11, 16 and 17 are migrated to the old stripes, and blocks 29, 34 and 35 are migrated to the new stripes.

After data migration, stale parities should be updated.

According to the migration process shown in Figure 3, we can calculate the total number of migrated data blocks. In the figure, 12 blocks are needed to be migrated and the total number of migrated blocks is $12 \times B/36 = B/3$, which is the same results as presented in Feature 2 in Section 2.1 ($2B/6 = B/3$). It demonstrates that ADR can minimize the data migration in the scale-down process.

3.4   Data Addressing

From Figure 3, the data addressing is easily calculated as previous literatures [29] [21] [23], which satisfies fast addressing feature in Section 2.1. According to the discuss in Section 3.2 and 3.3, the data addressing algorithm in RDP code can be generated in Algorithm 1, and the algorithm for other erasure codes can be generated in this way. In addition, for a continuous scaling process on a disk array, for example, a disk array scaling from 12 to 8 then to 6 disks by using RDP code, our algorithms can be used multiple times by saving the initialization information.

3.5   Properties of ADR

The desired features on RAID-6 scaling-down are listed in Section 2 and Table 2, and all of them can be satisfied by our ADR approach. From the discussions in Section 3.2 to 3.4, it is clear that ADR satisfies the features 1-3, which guarantees uniform data and parity distribution, minimal migration of data and parity elements and fast data addressing, of RAID-6 scaling defined in Section 2.1. ADR also satisfies Feature 4: minimal modification and computation cost of the parity elements, which is discussed in detail in Sections 4.

4   Scalability Analysis

In this section, we evaluate the scalability of various MDS codes by using different approaches.

Algorithm 1. Data Addressing Algorithm in RDP code

Set n and m from the number of disks in RAID systems before and after scaling.
$n' = n - m$.
if $(i + j \leq n' - 3)$ *or* $((i > n' - 3)$ *and* $(j < n' - 2))$ **then**
    $j' = j$.
    if $i + j \leq n' - 3$ **then**
        Conserve this block on the same place during scaling.
        $i' = i$.
    end
    else
        Migrate this block to a new stripe.
        $i' = i + m(n-2)/(n'-2) \mod (n'-2)$.
    end
end
else
    if $i + j > n' - 1$ **then**
        Migrate this block on the same row in the old stripe.
        $i' = i$.
        $j' = j - 2$.
    end
    else
        Migrate these blocks to form new stripes.
    end
end

4.1   Evaluation Methodology

We compare the ADR approach to the RR [9] [13] [27] approach. Note that Semi-RR[8], ALV [28], MDM [10], FastScale [29], GSR [21], SDM [23], MacPod [32] and CRAID [31] cannot be used in RAID-6 scaling-down , so they are not evaluated.

We also propose an ideal fast scaling method as a baseline. The ideal case is based on Feature 2 (Section 2.1) with minimal data movements to maintain a uniform workload in the enlarged new used stripe. We assume this case doesn't involve any parity migration, modification and computation as in RAID-0. Because no movement in dedicate parity disks (e.g., for RDP code), actually the number of ideal movements is $m \times B/n_d$, where n_d is the number of data disks.

Several popular MDS codes in RAID-6 are selected for comparison,

1) **Codes for $p - 1$ disks:** HDP [22];
2) **Codes for p disks:** X-Code [26];
3) **Codes for $p + 1$ disks:** RDP code [6] and H-Code [24];
4) **Codes for $p + 2$ disks:** EVENODD code [2].

Suppose the total number of data blocks in a disk array is B, the total number of stripes in a disk array before scaling is S, we can derive the relationship between these two parameters. For example, for RDP code when $p = 5$, $B = 16S$; when $p = 7$, $B = 36S$.

We define **Data Migration Ratio** (R_d) as the ratio between the number of migrated data/parity blocks and the total number of data blocks. **Parity Modification Ratio** (R_p) delegates the ratio between the number of modified parity blocks (including the number of new generated parity blocks) and the total number of data blocks. For the example of RDP and P-Code shown in Section 3, $R_d = \frac{12S}{36S} = 33.3\%$ and $R_p = \frac{21S}{36S} = 58.3\%$.

In RAID-6 scaling, each data or parity migration only costs two I/O operations, and the modification of each parity also has two I/Os. Based on the data migration ratio (R_d) and parity modification ratio (R_p), the total number of I/O operations is $n_{io} = 2 \times R_d \times B + 2 \times R_p \times B$. According to this equation, the total number of I/O operations for RDP example in Section 3 is $2 \times B \times 33.3\% + 2 \times B \times 58.3\% = 1.83B$.

If we ignore the computation time and assume the same time on a read or write request to a block (denoted by T_b), and suppose the migration I/O can be processed in parallel on each disk. From the example, we can see that the diagonal parity disks have the largest number of I/Os, which indicates the longest migration time. So the migration time T_m for RDP example is $T_m = 12ST_b = BT_b/3$.

4.2   Numerical Results

In this section, we give the numerical results of scalability using different scaling approaches and various erasure codes. In the following Figures 4 to 8, a two-integer tuple (n, m) denotes the original number of disks and the removed number of disks. For example, RDP $(8, 2)$ means a RAID-6 scaling from 8 to $8 - 2 = 6$ disks using RDP code.

Data Migration Ratio. First, we calculate the data migration ratio (R_d) among various fast scaling approaches under different cases as shown in Figure 4. Our ADR approach has the approximate migration ratio compared to Semi-RR and the ideal case in RAID-0.

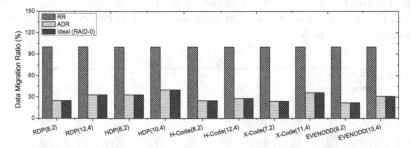

Fig. 4. Comparison on data migration ratio under various RAID-6 scaling approaches

Parity Modification Ratio. Second, parity modification ratio (R_p) among various RAID-6 scaling approaches under different cases is presented in Figure 5. Compared to other schemes with the same p and m, ADR sharply decreases the number of modified parities by up to 48.0%.

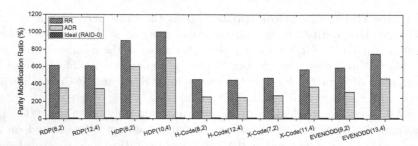

Fig. 5. Comparison on parity modification ratio under various RAID-6 scaling approaches

Total Number of I/O Operations. Next, total number of I/O operations are calculated in these cases. If we use B as the baseline, the results of total I/Os are shown in Figure 6. By using ADR approach, $33.3\% - 52.1\%$ I/Os are reduced.

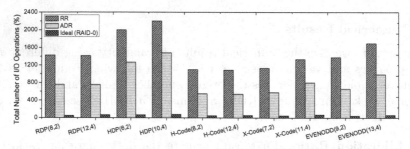

Fig. 6. Comparison on total I/Os under various RAID-6 scaling approaches (The number of B I/O operations is normalized to 100%)

Computation Cost. The total number of XOR operations are calculated as shown in Figure 7. Compared to other approaches, ADR can decreases the computation cost by up to 52%.

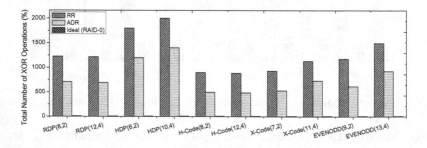

Fig. 7. Comparison on total number of XOR operations under various RAID-6 scaling approaches (The number of B XOR operations is normalized to 100%)

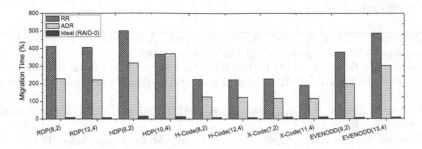

Fig. 8. Comparison on migration time under various RAID-6 scaling approaches (The time $B \times T_b$ is normalized to 100%)

Migration Time. Migration time is evaluated as shown in Figure 8. Compared to other approaches, ADR performs well in multiple disks extension, decreases the migration time by up to 63.5%, and speeds up the scaling process by up to 1.91.

4.3 Analysis

From the results in Section 4.2, compared to RR, ADR has great advantages. There are several reasons to achieve these gains. First, ADR takes advantages of GSR and SDM approaches, which are global management on multiple stripes according to the priorities of data movements. They can reduce the parity modification cost, computation cost, total I/Os. Second, compared to other approaches, ADR scheme distributes the migration I/Os more evenly among data and parity disks, which accelerates the scaling process in parallel.

5 Conclusions

In this paper, we have proposed a novel Advanced Data Redistribution (ADR) approach to achieve high scalability for RAID-6. Our comprehensive mathematic analysis shows that ADR achieves better scalability compared to other approaches in the following aspects: less I/O operations by $33.3\% - 52.1\%$ and shorter migration time and faster scaling process by up to 1.91.

Acknowledgements. We thank anonymous reviewers for their insightful comments. This work is partially sponsored by the National Natural Science Foundation of China (NSFC) (No. 61332001, No. 61303012, No. 61272099, and No. 61261160502), the Program for Changjiang Scholars and Innovative Research Team in University (IRT1158, PCSIRT), the Shanghai Innovative Action Plan (No. 13511504200), the Shanghai Natural Science Foundation (No. 13ZR1421900), the Scientific Research Foundation for the Returned Overseas Chinese Scholars, and the EU FP7 CLIMBER project (No. PIRSES-GA-2012-318939).

References

1. Armbrust, M., Fox, A., et al.: Above the Clouds: A Berkeley View of Cloud Computing. Technical Report, UCB/EECS-2009-28 (2009)
2. Blaum, M., Brady, J., et al.: EVENODD: An Efficient Scheme for Tolerating Double Disk Failures in RAID Architectures. IEEE Trans. Computers 44, 192–202 (1995)
3. Blaum, M., Roth, R.: On Lowest Density MDS Codes. IEEE Trans. Information Theory 45, 46–59 (1999)
4. Cassuto, Y., Bruck, J.: Cyclic Lowest Density MDS Array Codes. IEEE Trans. Information Theory 55, 1721–1729 (2009)
5. Chen, P., Lee, E., et al.: RAID: High-Performance, Reliable Secondary Storage. ACM Computing Surveys 26, 145–185 (1994)
6. Corbett, P., English, B., et al.: Row-Diagonal Parity for Double Disk Failure Correction. In: 3rd USENIX Conference on File and Storage Technologies, pp. 1–14. USENIX Press, San Francisco (2004)
7. Ghandeharizadeh, S., Kim, D.: On-line Reorganization of Data in Scalable Continuous Media Servers. In: Thoma, H., Wagner, R.R. (eds.) DEXA 1996. LNCS, vol. 1134, pp. 751–768. Springer, Heidelberg (1996)
8. Goel, A., Shahabi, C., et al.: SCADDAR: An Efficient Randomized Technique to Reorganize Continuous Media Blocks. In: 18th International Conference on Data Engineering, pp. 478–482. IEEE Press, San Jose (2002)
9. Gonzalez, J., Cortes, T.: Increasing the Capacity of RAID5 by Online Gradual Assimilation. In: 2004 International Workshop on Storage Network Architecture and Parallel I/O, Antibes, Juan-les-pins, pp. 17–24 (2004)
10. Hetzler, S.: Storage Array Scaling Method and System with Minimal Data Movement. US Patent 20080276057 (2008)
11. Hwang, K., Jin, H., Ho, R.: RAID-x: A New Distributed Disk Array for I/O-Centric Cluster Computing. In: 9th IEEE International Symposium on High Performance Distributed Computing, pp. 279–286. IEEE Press, Pittsburgh (2000)
12. Jin, C., Jiang, H., et al.: P-Code: A New RAID-6 Code with Optimal Properties. In: 23rd International Conference on Supercomputing, pp. 360–369. ACM Press, New York (2009)
13. Brown, N.: Online RAID-5 Resizing. drivers/md/raid5.c in the Source Code of Linux Kernel 2.6.18, http://www.kernel.org/
14. Patterson, D.: A Simple Way to Estimate the Cost of Downtime. In: 16th USENIX Conference on Systems Administration, pp. 185–188. USENIX Press, Philadelphia (2002)
15. Patterson, D., Gibson, G., Katz, R.: A Case for Redundant Arrays of Inexpensive Disks (RAID). In: 1988 ACM SIGMOD International Conference on Management of Data, pp. 109–116. ACM Press, Chicago (1988)
16. Pinheiro, E., Weber, W., Barroso, L.: Failure Trends in a Large Disk Drive Population. In: 5th USENIX Conference on File and Storage Technologies, pp. 17–28. USENIX Press, San Jose (2007)
17. Plank, J.: The RAID-6 Liberation Codes. In: 6th USENIX Conference on File and Storage Technologies, pp. 97–110. USENIX Press, San Jose (2008)
18. Reed, I., Solomon, G.: Polynomial Codes over Certain Finite Fields. Journal of the Society for Industrial and Applied Mathematics 8, 300–304 (1960)

19. Saito, Y., Frolund, S., et al.: FAB: Building Distributed Enterprise Disk Arrays from Commodity Components. In: 11th International Conference on Architectural Support for Programming Languages and Operating Systems, pp. 48–58. ACM Press, Boston (2004)
20. Schroeder, B., Gibson, G.: Disk Failures in the Real World: What does an MTTF of 1,000,000 Hours Mean to You? In: 5th USENIX Conference on File and Storage Technologies, pp. 1–16. USENIX Press, San Jose (2007)
21. Wu, C., He, X.: GSR: A Global Stripe-Based Redistribution Approach to Accelerate RAID-5 Scaling. In: 41st International Conference on Parallel Processing, pp. 460–469. IEEE Press, Pittsburgh (2012)
22. Wu, C., He, X., et al.: HDP code: A Horizontal-Diagonal Parity Code to Optimize I/O Load Balancing in RAID-6. In: 41st IEEE/IFIP International Conference on Dependable Systems and Networks, pp. 209–220. IEEE Press, Hong Kong (2011)
23. Wu, C., He, X., et al.: SDM: A Stripe-Based Data Migration Scheme to Improve the Scalability of RAID-6. In: 2012 IEEE International Conference on Cluster Computing, pp. 284–292. IEEE Press, Beijing (2012)
24. Wu, C., Wan, S., et al.: H-Code: A Hybrid MDS Array Code to Optimize Partial Stripe Writes in RAID-6. In: 25th IEEE International Symposium on Parallel and Distributed Processing, pp. 782–793. IEEE Press, Anchorage (2011)
25. Xu, L., Bohossian, V., et al.: Low-Density MDS Codes and Factors of Complete Graphs. IEEE Trans. Information Theory 45, 1817–1826 (1999)
26. Xu, L., Bruck, J.: X-Code: MDS Array Codes with Optimal Encoding. IEEE Trans. Information Theory 45, 272–276 (1999)
27. Zhang, G., Shu, J., et al.: SLAS: An Efficient Approach to Scaling Round-Robin Striped Volumes. ACM Trans. Storage 3, 1–39 (2007)
28. Zhang, G., Zheng, W., Shu, J.: ALV: A New Data Redistribution Approach to RAID-5 Scaling. IEEE Trans. Computers 59, 345–357 (2010)
29. Zheng, W., Zhang, G.: FastScale: Accelerate RAID Scaling by Minimizing Data Migration. In: 9th USENIX Conference on File and Storage Technologies, pp. 149–161. USENIX Press, San Jose (2011)
30. Wu, C., He, X.: A Flexible Framework to Enhance RAID-6 Scalability via Exploiting the Similarities among MDS Codes. In: 42nd International Conference on Parallel Processing, pp. 542–551. IEEE Press, Lyon (2013)
31. Miranda, A., Cortes, T.: CRAID: Online RAID Upgrades Using Dynamic Hot Data Reorganization. In: 12th USENIX Conference on File and Storage Technologies, pp. 133–146. USENIX Press, Santa Clara (2014)
32. Zhang, G., Wang, J., et al.: Redistribute Data to Regain Load Balance during RAID-4 Scaling. IEEE Trans. Parallel Distrib. Syst. 25 (2014)

Thread Mapping and Parallel Optimization
for MIC Heterogeneous Parallel Systems

Tao Ju[1], Zhengdong Zhu[1], Yinfeng Wang[2], Liang Li[1], and Xiaoshe Dong[1]

[1] School of Electronics and Information Engineering, Xi'an Jiaotong University
710049 Xi'an, China
[2] Shenzhen Institute of Information Technology, 518172 Shenzhen, China
immensewaves@163.com, {zdzhu,xsdong}@mail.xjtu.edu.cn,
{wangyinfeng,liliang199}@gmail.com

Abstract. There is no dedicated thread mapping method for Many Integrated Core (MIC) heterogeneous system in the traditional multithread programming model. The unreasonable thread mapping will lead the promising computing power of MIC coprocessor not to be fully exploited. In order to fully exploit the computing potential of MIC coprocessor, this paper discussed effective multi threads mapping strategies through comparing the computing performance and analyzing the performance differences between various mapping methods. Meanwhile, for the further exploiting the high computing power of MIC heterogeneous system, the specific program porting and performance optimization strategies were explored by using the k-means application program. Experimental results show that the proposed mapping and parallel optimization strategies are effective, which can be guide the programmer to port and optimize applications effectively to MIC heterogeneous parallel system.

1   Introduction

The overall system architecture development trend in Top 500 RANK [1] implies that the heterogeneous system will be the mainstream development direction in future high performance computer systems. With the emergence of new coprocessor technologies, the heterogeneous architecture will play important role in the following Petascal and Exascal super computing systems [2]. Heterogeneous computing has been recognized as the third era after the single core and multi-core ear. It will break Moore's law, and can effectively handle the energy consumption, scalability and other related issues [3].

The current two types of mainstream heterogeneous parallel systems, namely CPU+GPU and CPU+MIC, have different application characteristics. For the CPU+GPU heterogeneous system, its programing commonality is very limited due to the CPU and GPU apply the different instruction set system. Though the CUDA proves the general API and syntax feature for GPU programing, the programmers still need to clearly understand the characteristics and limitations of various underlying computing sources, which greatly constricted the GPU commonality. Meanwhile, a lot of research works have been done to explore how to reduce the difficulty of GPU programming [4-7], however, which did not fundamentally solve the difficult problem of programming. To address above problem, Intel has announced the Many Integrated Core (MIC)

X.-h. Sun et al. (Eds.): ICA3PP 2014, Part II, LNCS 8631, pp. 300–311, 2014.

architecture. The most significant merit of this architecture is to run existing X86 application programs, not need to port the program to a completely new programming environment, which greatly facilitates programmers to develop the heterogeneous programs [8].

In MIC heterogeneous system, programmers can directly use the common existed programming model to develop the parallel applications, but they may at the same time face the dilemma of no dedicated thread mapping strategy for Mangy Integrated Core in common multi-threaded programming model. The irrational thread mapping will greatly reduce computing performance, and not beneficial to exploit the high computing power of Many Integrated Core processor. To fully exploit the computing potential of Many Integrated Core, the paper studies the performance effect of thread mapping to different processing cores. Through comparing the computing performance and analyzing the performance differences between various thread mapping methods, we obtain the rational multi threads mapping schemes. Meanwhile, for further exploit the high computing power of MIC heterogeneous system, we explore the effect factors of performance when the application is ported to the MIC heterogeneous system, as well as propose the corresponding optimization strategies. Finally, we verify the validity of the proposed specific optimization strategy using different Benchmarks.

The remainder of this paper is organized as follows. Section 2 provides overview the MIC architecture and programing method. Section 3 describes thread mapping pattern to deduce the rational thread mapping scheme on the MIC heterogeneous parallel system. Section 4 discusses the details of porting and optimizing strategy on MIC heterogeneous system and evaluates the proposed strategies. Section 5 reviews related work and Section 6 concludes the paper.

2   Overview of the MIC

2.1   MIC Architecture

MIC (Many Integrated Core), a new type of many-core coprocessor architecture, is announced by Intel in 2011.This architecture extends the traditional microprocessor vector, and integrates many microprocessors onto single chip, aiming to compose the MIC processor for further improving computing power. The Intel®Xeon Phi™ co-processor, codenamed Knights Corner (KNC), is the first commercial release of the MIC architecture. Unlike the previous microprocessors from Intel, KNC works on a PCI-E card with GDDR5 memory and offers extremely high memory bandwidth. After the MIC card is installed on server, it can combine with Xeon processors on the server to constitute a parallel computing cluster. The MIC card collaborates computing with CPU, so as to further improve the computing performance. Fig.1 shows the architecture of MIC heterogeneous system.

2.2   MIC Programming Pattern

MIC integrates many cores onto the single die, each core can be programed using standard C, C++, and FORTRAN. MIC architecture has many advantages such as the compatibility, high parallelism, and programming controllability against the existing

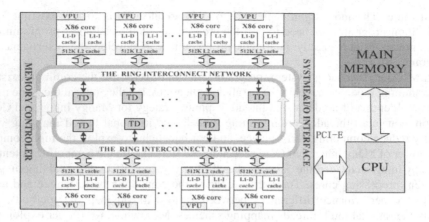

Fig. 1. MIC heterogeneous system architecture

heterogeneous many-core architecture. There is no fundamental difference of programming methods between MIC and CPU. MIC program only extends the pragma statement to indicate the specific data transfer operation between device and processor side. The detailed operation is completely realized by the compiler and transparent to the users. MIC architecture has a flexible programming pattern, which can be used as a coprocessor, also can be used a separate computing node. In general, there are three types of programming patterns in MIC heterogeneous system [8]: (1) the offload pattern; (2) the native pattern; (3) the symmetric pattern.

3   Thread Mapping on MIC

Currently, more than 50 processing cores are integrated on one MIC chip, each of processing cores supporting 4 hardware threads. Intel®Xeon Phi™ Coprocessor consisting of 61 processing cores supports total 244 hardware threads. How to reasonably map different computing loads to the hardware thread of processing core to take full advantage of the MIC high computing power becomes the challenging problem. Two aspects should be simultaneously considered when mapping computing loads in multiple threads programming: one aspect is to consider of mapping the computing load to thread, another aspect is mapping the threads to different processing cores. In this paper, we mainly focus on the performance effect of different mapping threads onto processing core in MIC coprocessor.

3.1   Different Thread Mapping Methods

To achieve the high parallel computing capability of many-core processor, the program must use corresponding parallel programming model. The OpenMP is one of the most commonly used model, which provides the special environment variables to control specific thread mapping to different processing cores. There are three mapping methods as follows:

(1) Compact mapping. This method aims to fully utilize each of processing cores. During mapping, the method first makes one hardware core as much as possible to obtain adequate threads, and then allocates the remaining threads to the next one, and to do so until all the threads to be allocated out. Fig.2(a) depicts the detailed schematic diagram, where the white areas represent idle resources, and the maximum number of threads is 2n.

(2) Scatter mapping. In this mapping a thread is first allocated to the processing core which has lightest load. The schematic diagram as shown in Fig.2(b).

(3) Balanced mapping. This method takes into account the load balancing and data locality simultaneously, to ensure the threads are distributed uniformly to different processing cores while the adjacent threads are allocated in the same processing core. The schematic diagram is presented in Fig. 2(c).

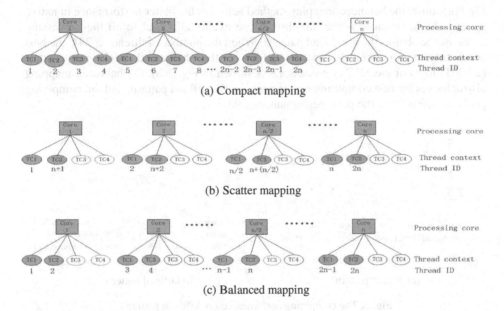

(a) Compact mapping

(b) Scatter mapping

(c) Balanced mapping

Fig. 2. Different thread mapping methods

3.2   Measurement and Findings

3.2.1   Measurement Environment and Schemes

Measurement Environment. The MIC heterogeneous platform consists of two-socket eight-core E5-2670 CPUs, and two Xeon Phi 7110P MIC coprocessors, a 64G memory, and a 300G disk. The PCI-E x16 bus connects the main memory and coprocessor. The OS is Red Hat Enterprise Linux Server release 6.3, the soft development environment is Intel parallel_studio_xe_2013_update3_intel64.

Measurement Schemes. The offload and native programming pattern are used separately to measure the computing performance of simulating calculation of linear equation $y = mx + b$ by different thread mapping methods. For the native pattern, we measure the performance at different mapping methods (compact, scatter, and balanced), using different numbers of threads: 61, 122, 244, and 305. Since the Xeon Phi 7110P MIC coprocessor has total 61 processing cores, each can support up to 4 hardware threads, in order to better reflect the actual usage of processing cores when mapping, the number of threads is set to be of integer multiple of processing cores. For the offload pattern, the total number of the used computing processing cores is 60, one of the cores is used to run μOS, which is in charge of the control and management the interaction between CPU and MIC coprocessor. During measurement, the number of threads is set to be of integer multiple of processing core (60,120, 180,240, and 300). The computing load is increased along with the increase of the thread number, but the task for each of threads is fixed.

3.2.2   Measurement Results and Analysis

Fig.3(a) shows the balanced mapping method achieves the better performance in native pattern, the main cause is that the threads are evenly allocated to all the processing cores, hence obtains the good load balance. When the number of threads is 244, the best computing performance is up to 94.6% of the theoretical peak performance (2.130TFlops) of the MIC coprocessor. As shown in Fig. 3(b), the balanced mapping also achieves the best computing performance in the offload pattern, and the computing performance is up to the peak performance of 93.3%.

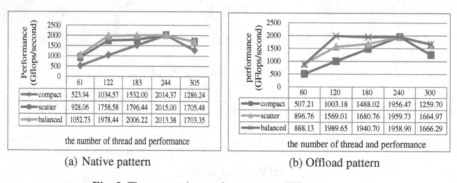

	61	122	183	244	305
compact	523.94	1034.57	1532.00	2014.37	1286.24
scatter	928.06	1758.58	1796.44	2015.00	1705.48
balanced	1052.73	1978.44	2006.22	2013.38	1703.35

the number of thread and performance

(a) Native pattern

	60	120	180	240	300
compact	507.21	1003.18	1488.02	1956.47	1259.70
scatter	896.76	1569.01	1680.76	1959.73	1664.97
balanced	888.13	1989.65	1940.70	1958.90	1666.29

the number of thread and performance

(b) Offload pattern

Fig. 3. The computing performance on different patterns

As compared to the native pattern, the overall performance of offload pattern is slightly worse. Because, in offload pattern, the portion of being accelerated program and data need to be uploaded to the coprocessor before computing and downloaded the computing results to the CPU side after computing finished, which introduces the additional transmission overhead.

3.2.3   Scalability Analysis of MIC Performance

To examine the scalability of the MIC coprocessor, we measured the performance of MIC coprocessor by changing the number of the threads. As shown in Fig.4, when the number of threads increases to 244 from 61, 122, and 183, the performance of all methods increases along with the increase of the number of threads, the compact mapping performance almost increases linearly against with the number of threads. Overall, the test results demonstrate a good scalability.

Compact mapping obtained the worse performance when the number of threads is less than 244 cases, because the parts of the processing cores are idle. When the number of the threads is reaching to 244, all processing cores are fully used. Three types of mapping achieve nearly same computing performance at this time. If the number of threads is further increased to exceed 244, the computing performance begins to decline. The reason is that when the number of threads exceeding the maximum 244 of hardware threads, there will be inevitable competition of hardware thread context among multiple threads.

As the number of thread continues to increase, the overall computing performance of MIC coprocessor tends to the optimal value. If the number of thread is up to more than 1000, all three mapping methods reach the best performance, where the performance does not changed obviously, and reaches the stable state.

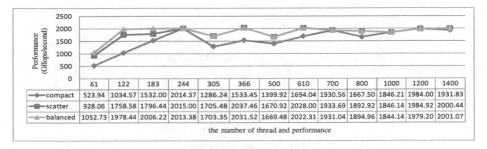

	61	122	183	244	305	366	500	610	700	800	1000	1200	1400
compact	523.94	1034.57	1532.00	2014.37	1286.24	1533.45	1399.92	1694.04	1930.56	1667.50	1846.21	1984.00	1931.83
scatter	928.06	1758.58	1796.44	2015.00	1705.48	2037.46	1670.92	2028.00	1933.69	1892.92	1846.14	1984.92	2000.44
balanced	1052.73	1978.44	2006.22	2013.38	1703.35	2031.52	1669.48	2022.31	1931.04	1894.96	1844.14	1979.20	2001.07

the number of thread and performance

Fig. 4. The scalability under the native pattern using different mapping

3.2.4   Summary

From the above measurement and analysis, we can obtain the following conclusion. The load balancing and data locality should be considered simultaneously when mapping threads to the processing core: (1) if the application has the strong data dependence among each threads, the compact mapping method should be used to make full use of the data locality to reduce the additional communication overhead; (2) If the application has no obvious data dependence among different threads, and the thread number is large, the scatter mapping method should be applied to better handle the load balance between processing cores; (3) If both the data dependency and load balance need to be considered, the balanced mapping method should be used to obtain better performance.

4   Performance Optimization

In order to further analysis different factors that affect application performance of MIC heterogeneous system, we exemplified with a specific k-means clustering applications to explore the porting and optimizing methods on the MIC heterogeneous system.

4.1   Benchmarks

We adopt the k-means program in the Rodinia Benchmark [9] to discuss the detailed porting and optimizing methods. Meanwhile, we used the same strategy to port and optimize the Matrix Multiplication, Monte Carlo, N-body, FFT, Histogram, SPGEMM benchmark program [10], measured and compared the performance differences of those benchmark programs, and verified the effectiveness of porting and optimization schemes.

4.2   Implementation

4.2.1   Direct Parallelization Using Native Pattern

We firstly evaluated the performance on both the CPU and MIC coprocessor with different numbers of threads at different dataset size using native pattern. The experimental configuration is as same as the one in Section 3.2.1, and the experimental results are shown in Fig.5.

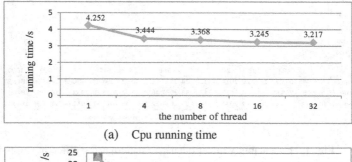

(a)   Cpu running time

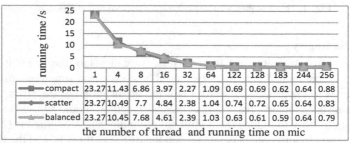

(b) MIC running time

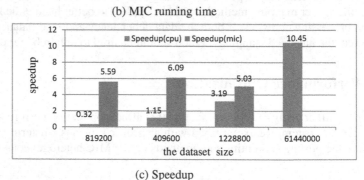

(c) Speedup

Fig. 5. The program running under the native pattern

Fig.5(a) and Fig.5(b) show the program running time when using different numbers of threads at the 819200 dataset on CPU and MIC coprocessor separately. As can be seen from Fig.5(a), the best performance is obtained when the number of thread is 32, the reason for which is that the CPU side is two-socket eight-core processor, and the maximum of the supported hardware threads is 32. For the MIC coprocessor, however, the program execution time is far greater than the one related to the CPU if the number of the threads is less than 32. When the number of the threads is more than 32 in MIC coprocessor, the MIC coprocessor can obtain a better performance. Along with the increase of the number of the threads, program running time will constantly decrease until the number of the thread approaches to120. After that, the program execution time has almost no change if the number of the threads continues to increase, which because the data scale is limited.

To achieve the better computing performance, we further extend the data scale. Fig.5(c) shows the maximal speedup at different dataset size on both CPU and MIC coprocessor compared to the serial program on the CPU side. Overall, the program speedup of MIC coprocessor is superior to the CPU. It is worth noting that a program at data scale of 61440000 cannot be directly run on MIC coprocessor due to the limited MIC memory capacity.

4.2.2   Collaborate Computing CPU and MIC

Due to the limited memory capacity, MIC coprocessor cannot directly deal with the large-scale data set application in native pattern. On the other hand, the CPU is idle when the MIC coprocessor is computing in native pattern, leading to not fully take advantage of the computing resource of the whole heterogeneous computing system.

In order to make full use of the computing resources in the MIC heterogeneous system, and handle the massive data applications, we use offload pattern to make the CPU and MIC coprocessor collaboratively deal with the computing tasks.

A two-level parallelization scheme is designed to achieve the above goals. In the first level parallelism, we employ the MPI between CPU processing cores and MIC coprocessors to realize the process level parallelism. In the second level parallelism, the OpenMP is used to realize thread level parallelism inside the MIC processing core. At the same time, in order to overcome the limit of MIC coprocessor memory capacity, the task partitioning method has been employed, which divides a large-scale data task into many data partitions, so that the CPU and the MIC coprocessor handle different parts of task respectively.

4.3   Comprehensive Performance Optimization

To make full use of the MIC coprocessor computing power to improve computing performance of the program, combined with the MIC architecture characteristics, we further comprehensively optimized the program based on the analysis and reference performance optimization methods in literature [11-13].

1) Memory management optimization. We let the data to be as the shared variables that can be used by all threads in same MIC coprocessor to effectively use the MIC memory. It is beneficial for improving the usage efficiency of memory, since each thread no needs to save independent data copies.

2) Data transformation optimization. In the CPU and the MIC coprocessor collaborative computing pattern, the data transmission between the two processors will occupy many part of the additional overhead during the program execution. We use the statement *nocopy(), in(), out()* combined with the corresponding control statement *alloc_if(), free_if()* to control the data and memory space to be reused in the iterative part of program. In addition, we use the asynchronous transformation to further reduce the delay overhead of communication. By designing the pipeline to handle the data transformation and computing of MIC coprocessor, we realized the data transmission and computing overlap to make full use of computing resource for improving the program performance.

3) Vectorization. The MIC vectorization has two main ways: the automatic vectorization and the SIMD instruction. In order to reduce the programming difficulty, this work directly inserts the corresponding directive statements into the program to realize an automatic vectorization.

4) Load balance. We consider the load balance on two levels: the first level load balance is between CPU and MIC coprocessor, and another level is the one between processing cores inside MIC coprocessor.

4.4   Experimental Results and Analysis

This section measures the optimized program at different datasets to evaluate the optimization effects of the proposed specific optimization strategies. The experimental configuration is presented in section 3.2.1. The measurement results are as follows.

Fig.6 shows the running time and the best speedup compared to the serial program using the different mapping methods at the 409600 dataset of k-means program. Due to the data scale is small, the speed efficiency is not ideal, which is only up to 7.4. Fig.6 (a) shows that the performance of compact mapping is superior to the scatter and balanced mapping, the computing performance keeps improving along with the increase of the number of threads. The program performance is nearly stable when the thread increases to 120. There is almost no improvement on performance when the number of the threads continues to increase due to be restricted by the size of the data.

Fig.7(a) shows the running time of K-means program on the 61440000 dataset. With the increase of the number of threads, the program speedup increase obviously. When the number of the threads exceeds 120, the acceleration effect tends to be stable. Fig.7(b) shows the best speedup compared to the serial program using the proposed comprehensive optimizing, which is up to 85.56. At the same dataset, the best speedup of CPU side is only up to 10.45.

Fig.8 shows the best speedup of different Benchmark programs compared to the serial program on CPU platform and MIC heterogeneous platform using the optimizing scheme proposed previously. The average speedup achieved for six Benchmark programs is up to 20.66 on the MIC heterogeneous platform, but the average speedup is only up to 8.47 on the CPU platform. Overall, the Benchmark programs achieve the better performance on the MIC heterogeneous parallel system.

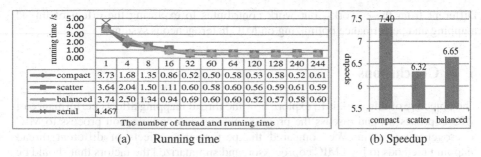

(a)   Running time

(b) Speedup

Fig. 6. The running time and speedup of 409600 data set of k-means

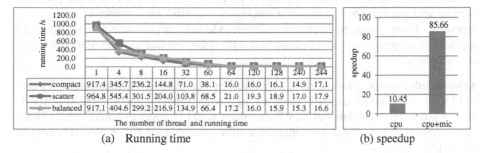

(a)   Running time

(b) speedup

Fig. 7. The running time and speedup of 61440000 dataset of k-means

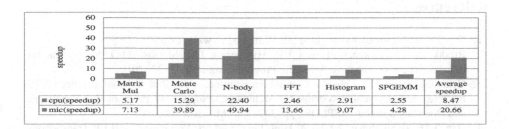

Fig. 8. The speedup of different benchmarks

5   Related Work

Due to the tremendous computing power as well as x86 programing compatibility, the Intel MIC architecture has been attracting the great attention from academia and industry. S. Saini et al.[17] conducted an early performance evaluation of the Xeon Phi. Potluri S [15] proposed and evaluated design alternatives for efficient communication on a node with Xeon Phi coprocessor. Si M.et al. [16] implemented an MPI library to provide direct Xeon Phi coprocessor to Xeon Phi coprocessor inter-node MPI communication. D. Schmidl et al [18] compared a Xeon-based two-socket compute node with the Xeon Phi stand-alone in scalability and performance. Liu X et al. [14] described an efficient implementation of SpMV on the Intel Xeon Phi[TM] Coprocessor.

Different from these works, our work contributes to exploring the effect of thread mapping and performance optimizing on MIC heterogeneous system.

6   Conclusions

The objective of this work is to explore how the thread mapping affects performance of MIC coprocessor, and discuss the program porting and optimization process to MIC heterogeneous system. We compared the performance effects of different thread mapping methods to Intel MIC coprocessor, and summarized the factors that should be considered when mapping thread on MIC heterogeneous system. At the same time, through analyzing the different factors of performance effect, the specific program porting and performance optimizing strategies on MIC heterogeneous system are proposed. These proposed strategies may provide certain guidance and reference to application programmer when porting and optimizing applications on MIC heterogeneous system.

Acknowledgements. This work is supported by the NSF of China (under Grants 61173039, 61202041), the 863 Program of China (under Grants 2012AA010904, 2012AA01A306), the National Key Technology R&D Program of China (under Grant 2011BAH04B03), and the Shenzhen Scientific plan (under Grant No. JCYJ20120 615101127404).

References

1. Top 500 supercomputer sites (June 2013), http://www.top500.org/
2. Brodtkorb, A.R., Dyken, C., Hagen, T.R., Hjelmervik, J.M., Storaasli, O.O.: State-of-the-art in heterogeneous computing. Scientific Programming 18(1), 1–33 (2010)
3. Gelado, I., Stone, J.E., Cabezas, J., et al.: An asymmetric distributed shared memory model for heterogeneous parallel systems. In: Architectural Support for Programming Languages and Operating Systems (ASPLOS), pp. 347–358 (March 2010)
4. Han, T.D., Abdelrahman: hiCUDA: High-Level GPGPU Programming. IEEE Transactions on Parallel and Distributed Systems 22(1), 78–90 (2011)
5. Brodtkorb, A.R., Hagen, T.R., et al.: Graphics processing unit (GPU) programming strategies and trends in GPU computing. Journal of Parallel and Distributed Computing 73(1), 4–13 (2013)
6. Pusukuri, K.K., Gupta, R., Bhuyan, L.N.: ADAPT: A framework for coscheduling multi-threaded programs. ACM Transactions on Architecture and Code Optimization 9(4), Article 45 (2013)
7. Jablin, T.B., Prabhu, P., Jablin, J.A., Johnson, N.P., Beard, S.R., August, D.I.: Automatic CPU-GPU communication management and optimization. In: Proc. ACM Programming Language Design and Implementation (PLDI), pp. 142–151 (June 2011)
8. Jeffers, J., Reinders, J.: Intel's Xeon Phi Coprocessor High-Performance Programming. Elsevier Inc., USA (2013)
9. Che, S., Boyer, M., Meng, J., Tarjan, D., Sheaer, J.W., Lee, S.H., Skadron, K.: Rodinia: A benchmark suite for heterogeneous computing. In: Proceedings of IISWC, pp. 44–54 (2009)

10. Stratton, C., Rodrigues, I., et al.: Parboil: A Revised Benchmark Suite for Scientific and Commercial Throughput Computing. IMPACT Technical Report, University of Illinois at Urbana-Champaign Center for Reliable and High-Performance Computing (March 2, 2012)
11. Yang, Y., Xiang, P., Mantor, M., Zhou, H.: CPU-Assisted GPGPU on Fused CPU-GPU Architectures. In: 18th International Symposium on High Performance Computer Architecture, pp. 1–12 (2012)
12. Lee, J., Lakshminarayana, N.B., Kim, H., et al.: Many-thread aware prefetching mechanisms for gpgpu applications. In: Proceeding of the 43rd Annual IEEE/ACM International Symposium on Microarchitecture (MICRO), pp. 213–224 (2010)
13. Liu, W., Lewis, B., Zhou, X., et al.: A balanced programming model for emerging heterogeneous multicore systems. In: Proceedings of the 2nd USENIX Conference on Hot Topics in Parallelism (2010)
14. Liu, X., Smelyanskiy, M., Chow, E., et al.: Efficient sparse matrix-vector multiplication on x86-based many-core processors. In: Proceedings of the 27th International ACM Conference on International Conference on Supercomputing, pp. 273–282 (2013)
15. Potluri, S., Venkatesh, A., Bureddy, D., et al.: Efficient Intra-node Communication on In-tel-MIC Clusters. In: Proceeding of the 13th IEEE/ACM International Symposium on Cluster, Cloud and Grid Computing, pp. 128–135 (2013)
16. Si, M., Ishikawa, Y., Tatagi, M.: Direct MPI Library for Intel Xeon Phi Co-Processors. In: Proceeding of the 27th IEEE International Parallel and Distributed Processing Symposium Workshops & PhD Forum (IPDPSW), pp. 816–824 (2013)
17. Saini, S., Jin, J., Jespersen, D., et al.: An early performance evaluation of many integrated core architecture based SGI rackable computing system. In: Proceedings of the ACM International Conference for High Performance Computing, Networking, Storage and Analysis (2013)
18. Schmidl, D., Cramer, T., Wienke, S., Terboven, C., Müller, M.S.: Assessing the performance of OpenMP programs on the intel xeon phi. In: Wolf, F., Mohr, B., an Mey, D. (eds.) Euro-Par 2013. LNCS, vol. 8097, pp. 547–558. Springer, Heidelberg (2013)

Efficient Storage Support for Real-Time Near-Duplicate Video Retrieval

Zhenhua Nie, Yu Hua, Dan Feng, Qiuyu Li, and Yuanyuan Sun

Wuhan National Lab for Optoelectronics (WNLO),
School of Computer Science and Technology,
Huazhong University of Science and Technology,
Wuhan, Hubei 430074, China
{niezhenhua,csyhua,dfeng,liqiuyu,sunyuanyuan}@hust.edu.cn

Abstract. Near-duplicate video retrieval in a real-time manner is important to offer efficient storage services, and becomes more challenging due to dealing with the rapid growth of multimedia videos. Existing work fails to efficiently address this important problem due to overlooking the storage property of massive videos. In order to bridge the gap between storage system organization and application-aware videos, we propose a cost-effective real-time video retrieval scheme, called FastVR, which supports fast near-duplicate video retrieval. FastVR has the salient features of space- and time-efficiency in large-scale storage systems. The idea behind FastVR is to leverage space-efficient indexing structure and compact feature representation to facilitate keyframe based matching. Moreover, in the compact feature representation, FastVR transforms the frames into feature vectors in the Hamming space. The indexing structure in FastVR uses Locality Sensitive Hashing(LSH) to support fast similar neighboring search by grouping similar videos together. The conventional LSH unfortunately causes space inefficiency that is well addressed by a cuckoo hashing scheme. FastVR uses a semi-random choice to improve the performance in the random selection of the cuckoo hashing scheme. We implemented FastVR and examined the performance using a real-world dataset. The experimental results demonstrate the efficiency and significant performance improvements.

1 Introduction

According to the report of International Data Corporation (IDC) in 2011, the amount of data in our whole world reaches 1.8 Zettabytes and its growth rate is about doubling every two years. The amount of data produced will increase to 40ZB by 2020 [5]. The unstructured data, typically represented by videos and images, is growing faster than structured data. The percentage of unstructured data is about 90 percent of all data created in the next decade [5].

The number of online videos has experienced an exponential growth in recent decades, especially when social video sharing sites appear. In YouTube, over 6 billion hours of video are watched each month, and there are 100 hours of video being uploaded each minute in 2014 [1]. These videos in a variety of formats contain duplicate copies and exhibit similarity from the content view [20]. Near-duplicate video retrieval is important in the era of big data.

X.-h. Sun et al. (Eds.): ICA3PP 2014, Part II, LNCS 8631, pp. 312–324, 2014.
© Springer International Publishing Switzerland 2014

In order to improve storage performance when handling massive videos, data centers are utilized by service providers and developers. However, the centralized data storage model becomes potential performance bottleneck when dealing with the highly redundant videos. Although the cache techniques on chip-multiprocessors [25] are used, data centers still consume substantial energy and system resources to offer storage services. In the meantime, highly redundant videos increase query delay and jeopardize the quality of storage services. In practice, existing work proposes efficient query schemes to deal with metadata management in storage systems, such as Spyglass [14], SmartStore [6], flash-based multiple Bloom filters [19] and BloomStore [16]. These retrieval methods mainly address the exact-matching query in the metadata search, rather than the near-duplicate retrieval for videos in a real-time manner.

In general, near-duplicate video retrieval contains the following operations. First, the extracted keyframes of videos are classified by time sampling, shot based detection algorithms or sliding window so that every video is represented by a sequence of keyframes [8]. Second, these keyframes are represented by their visual features including global features and local features [9,24]. Specifically, a global feature consists of color and spatial and temporal features extracted from a keyframe. A local feature is represented by local keypoints extracted from a keyframe in a high dimensional vector. Third, the system constructs an indexing structure via organizing extracted visual features (global and local features), like the prevalent inverted index [22]. Fourth, we compute the similarity between the queried videos and the video library by using visual features. The whole extracted visual features are taken as the representation of video library. The final results include the most similar videos that are compared with the query video. In this paper, we address two challenges, i.e., inefficient feature representation and performance bottleneck of indexing, to support real-time near-duplicate video retrieval.

Inefficient Feature Representation. In order to support real-time video retrieval, existing work proposes a variety of feature extraction based schemes for efficient video representation to facilitate the near-duplicate video retrieval. These approaches can be classified into two categories: global feature based schemes [21], and local feature based schemes [28]. Specifically, the global feature schemes can extract color, spatial and temporal signatures to deal with almost identical videos, while the local feature schemes can extract the local keypoints to tolerate more photometric and spatial transformations. The global feature based methods have rapid processing speed but low accuracy, while the local feature based methods obtain high accuracy by extracting local keypoints. In practice, these schemes mainly concentrate on improving the retrieval accuracy via extracting more features from the videos or the keyframes to represent the features. Due to overlooking the property of storage, these approaches always consume too much in-memory space, thus failing to support real-time video retrieval.

Performance Bottleneck of Indexing. To support real-time query performance, it is important to construct an efficient indexing structure, which is space-efficient and obtains low query latency. Only a few studies focus on the real-time retrieval in the large scale near-duplicate videos. Many methods are used to construct the indexing structure in real-time near-duplicate video retrieval, such as tree-structures [2], cluster, spectral hashing [23], and the variations of the search engine technology like the inverted table [4]. Locality Sensitive Hashing (LSH)[3] [10] is often used to implement the fast similarity query by mapping the approximate points into a same bucket to narrow the query scope. LSH has the salient features in efficiency of hashing computation and stabilization of data locality. LSH has the property that the similar items can be hashed into the same buckets with high probability. Although LSH can be used to maintain the near-duplicate relationships among keyframes in the indexing structure, performing real-time LSH-based near-duplicate video retrieval needs to address two main problems. *(1) LSH suffers from low space-efficiency and low-speed I/O access, (2) LSH has an unbalanced load in the hash table storage.*

The conventional LSH unfortunately causes space inefficiency that is well addressed by a cuckoo hashing scheme. The cuckoo hashing scheme obtains worst-case constant query time and high utilization of hash tables. Cuckoo hashing recursively kicks items out of their positions and uses multiple hash functions for resolving hash collisions during insertion operation. The random selection in cuckoo hashing incurs a large number of repeated relocations in the kicking-out processes. The reason of repeated relocations is that the item frequently kicks similar items, thus incurring repetitions and loops with a high probability.

This paper has made the following contributions.

Compact Feature Representation. In order to obtain the real-time near-duplicate video retrieval, we propose a compact feature representation. Our feature representation only extracts the local feature to obtain high accuracy, and to avoid the complex computation of the extraction operations which combine the global feature and local feature. By using a feature-aware Bloom filter, we map the local keypoints (extracted from a keyframe) to a feature vector in the Hamming space. Hence, this keyframe is represented by a feature vector. The space of feature vector is much smaller than that of local keypoints.

Semi-random Holistic Hashing. The indexing structure is constructed by the semi-random holistic hashing, which addresses the space-efficiency and load imbalance for the LSH-based method in the near-duplicate video retrieval. The conventional LSH unfortunately causes space inefficiency that is well addressed by a cuckoo hashing scheme. FastVR uses a semi-random choice to improve the performance in the random selection of the cuckoo hashing scheme. We show that the effective combination of LSH and Cuckoo Hashing can accelerate the near-duplicate video retrieval.

Real Prototype Implementation. We have implemented all the components and algorithms of FastVR in our prototype system. We compared it with state-of-the-art work, including NEST [7], ViDeDup [11] and the baseline approach. The baseline approach is the traditional LSH without cuckoo hashing. Furthermore, we use a real and large dataset collected from the popular campus networks of universities in China to evaluate the performance.

The rest of paper is organized as follows. Section 2 presents the backgrounds and related work. Section 3 shows our FastVR model. Section 4 shows the performance evaluation. We conclude our paper in Section 5.

2   Backgrounds and Related Work

This section presents the research backgrounds about feature representation in near-duplicate video retrieval, locality sensitive hashing scheme and cuckoo hashing scheme.

2.1   Feature Representation

In recent decade, various feature extraction methods are proposed by researchers to represent a keyframe. These features are mainly grouped into two categories, global feature based schemes and local feature based schemes.

The global feature schemes extract color, spatial and temporal signatures to represent the keyframes extracted from a video. For example, HSV is extracted to represent the keyframe, and this method receives fast query performance [24]. The compact spatiotemporal feature can be represented by using relative gray-level intensity distribution in a frame and temporal structure of videos [21]. The global feature based methods are less robust in the videos which has spatially and temporally variation, and the experimental performance of the global feature based methods is not as good as the local feature based methods.

Because of the shortage of the global feature based methods, the local feature based methods obtain more attentions [4][13][22]. Some of the popular methods based on local features are SIFT [15] and PCA-SIFT [12]. In [22], the local keypoints can be extracted by SIFT to represent keyframes. The visual keywords are quantized by the local keypoints, then the inverted index is used to index the visual keywords. The correlated work [4] based on visual keywords and inverted index presents excellent experimental results.

2.2   Locality Sensitive Hashing

Locality Sensitive Hashing (LSH) [10] has the property that the similar items can be hashed into the same bucket with high probability. Formally, each hash function $h(v): R^\theta \to Z$ maps a θ dimensional vector to a real number. The domain S denotes the point sets, and the distance measure D denotes the distance between two points, so an LSH family is defined as:

Definition 1. *LSH family,* $H = \{h : S \to U\}$ *is called* (r, cr, P_1, P_2)-*sensitive for distance function* D *if for any* $p, q \in S$

- *If* $D(p,q) \le r$ *then* $Pr_H[h(p) = h(q)] \ge P_1$,
- *If* $D(p,q) > cr$ *then* $Pr_H[h(p) = h(q)] \le P_2$.

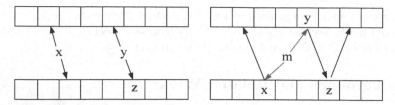

Fig. 1. An example of cuckoo hashing structure

Due to the use of LSH, the settings should be $P_1 > P_2$ and $c > 1$. We define a function family $\Gamma = \{g{:}S{\to}U^k\}$. Then we need to illustrate another two parameters, d, the number of hash tables and k, the number of hash functions in function family. We have $g(v)=(h_1(v),\ldots, h_k(v))$, where v is a θ dimensional vector and $h_i(v) \in H$.

LSH uses the hash collisions to support the approximate queries. As a result, it suffers from low space-efficiency utilization in hash tables and unbalanced load in the storage of hash tables. The multi-probe LSH [17] is proposed to illustrate the similarity with adjacent buckets. The last level caches can leverage the temporal and spatial capacity demands to narrow the gap between processor cores and main memory [26] [27]. This can partially address the time-inefficiency in real-time near-duplicate video retrieval.

2.3 Cuckoo Hashing

To address the low space-efficiency utilization and unbalanced load in hash tables of LSH, the cuckoo hashing scheme can be used to address this problem very well. Cuckoo hashing [18] is a simple dynamic dictionary for resolving hash collisions in a hash table, with achieving worst case constant query time by providing several possible locations in the hash table for each key. Cuckoo hashing can efficiently support query services and has high utilization of hash tables.

In order to describe the detailed implementation of cuckoo hashing principle, Figure 1 shows an example of the standard cuckoo hashing. Each item has two possible positions and it can be inserted directly into the hash table if either of the candidate positions is empty, as the items x, y shown in Figure 1(a). Figure 1(b) illustrates the case of inserting a new item m when both of its candidate positions are occupied(which are filled by "x" and "y"). The item m will kick either item ("x" and "y" will be selected randomly) for getting a position, likewise, the repeated kicking-out operations will be accomplished by addressing an empty bucket. A rehashing operation is required if an endless loop appears. The case of $d = 2$ has a low utilization of hash tables, hence we introduce the case of $d > 2$ to improve the space utilization to meet the needs of the real-world near-duplicate video retrieval.

The standard cuckoo-driven locality-sensitive hashing design constructs the indexing structure [7], called NEST, to support real-time near-duplicate video retrieval and partially addresses the load imbalance and low space efficiency of hash tables. NEST leverages the LSH and cuckoo hashing to find similar items

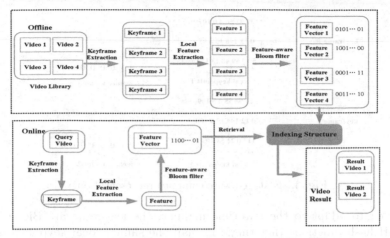

Fig. 2. The framework of our proposed FastVR

that are placed closely to obtain balanced load in hash tables. NEST uses random selection in cuckoo hashing among its kicking-out process. The random selection increases the time overhead, which is unsuitable in real time near-duplicate video retrieval.

3   The Design of FastVR

Our proposed framework is shown in Figure 2, which consists of two main parts. The first part depicts our compact feature representation, which includes the offline and online modules. Using the feature-aware Bloom filter, the local keypoints extracted from a frame are mapped into the feature vectors in Hamming space. The second part is the indexing structure using the semi-random holistic hashing. It uses the semi-random selection to accelerate the insertion of the cuckoo hashing.

The important problems to be addressed in this paper are *(1)How to construct the feature representation, (2)How to build an efficient indexing structure to accelerate query and keyframe matching.* In this section, we show the details of the two problems.

3.1   Compact Feature Representation

Our compact feature representation uses the feature-aware Bloom filter to construct the feature vectors as shown in Figure 3. Unlike the conventional hash function, the feature-aware Bloom filter is a Bloom filter which using LSH as hash function. The feature-aware Bloom filter is used to handle the hundreds or even thousands keypoints in a frame. A feature vector produced by the feature-aware Bloom filter belongs to one keyframe, not all keyframes. In our work, we use SIFT to extract local keypoints of 128 dimensions from a keyframe. The numbers of local keypoints in a keyframe may be hundreds or even thousands, and the number of local keypoints between keyframes are different.

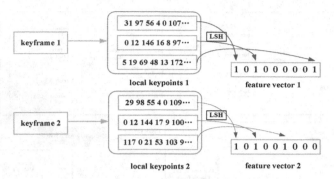

Fig. 3. Feature-aware compact representation

In order to adapt to the real-time manner, the feature-aware Bloom filter uses LSH hash functions that they can map the similar local keypoints to the same position. In the example denoted in Figure 3, we use the first three local keypoints to present the problems. The first two local keypoints of the keyframes are similar, and it is confirmed by the expressions in the local keypoints in Figure 3. Considering the first three dimensions of the local keypoints, the first local keypoints in the two keyframes are "31, 97, 56" and "29, 98, 55" and the corresponding values("31" and "29", "97" and "98", "56" and "55") are similar to each other respectively. Hence we use LSH hash functions to get the same hash values from the similar local keypoints. We introduce the feature vectors, that all the local keypoints in a frame can be represented by the resulting feature vectors thus the similarity in videos will be transformed into the same bit in feature vectors, that the first bit and the third bit in the two feature vectors are set "1". However, the third local keypoints in the two keyframes are not similar so the values obtained by LSH hash functions are different. Hence the feature vectors hashed by LSH hash functions are efficient to represent the similarity of the keyframes.

The advantage of compact feature representation is that the local keypoints of a frame are mapped to a feature vector, and then a keyframe corresponds to a feature vector. In our FastVR, the indexing structure directly organizes the feature vectors as items. This indexing structure can significantly reduce the storage space and can be more suitable in the large scale near-duplicate videos. Moreover, the keyframe matching in Hamming space is faster than in Euclidean space, hence the compact feature representation can significantly improve the performance of keyframe matching.

3.2   The Semi-random Holistic Hashing

Our FastVR combines the LSH and cuckoo hashing to construct the indexing structure and we denote MaxLoop as the maximum kicking-out count, and the kicking-out count is initialized to 0. Then we optimize the efficiency of kicking-out process in cuckoo hashing. First, when the kicking-out count is under MaxLoop/2, we use the random selection in cuckoo hashing to address the

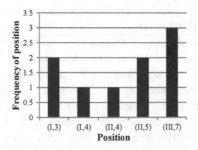

Fig. 4. The frequency of positions occurrence in a kicking-out path

kicking-out process. Meanwhile, we record the count of position occurrences. Second, when the kicking-out count is greater than MaxLoop/2 and under MaxLoop, we do not use the random selection to select the item to be moved if the potential positions are all occupied for current item. We pick the minimum frequency of the potential positions of the current item for the next "kicking out". Third, our indexing structure uses a random cuckoo hashing in the last step, i.e. the MaxLoop step, to jump out the similar group.

For example, we assume that the size of 3 hash tables, I, II and III, is 10, and we use (II, 7) to represent the 7th position in Table II. The MaxLoop is 5. The count of position occurrence is added to 1 when the position is one of the candidate positions in a kicking-out path. Figure 5(a) presents the kicking-out process in the indexing structure. Suppose item t will be inserted into the indexing structure, and its candidate positions are all occupied. Then the kick-out operations have experienced the path $e \rightarrow c \rightarrow a$, and the candidate positions of e, c, a are [(I,4)(II,5)(III,7)], [(I,3),(II,5),(III,7)], [(I,3),(II,4),(III,7)] respectively. Hence, the count of position occurrences has a statistic in Figure 4. Until now, the kicking count is 2, and the kicking operations use the random selection. The next step's kicking count is 3 > MaxLoop/2, and we will select the minimum frequency of the candidate positions of item a. From Figure 4, the count of position occurrences of a are 2,1 and 3, and the a will select the position (II,4) as the next position to kick out. Then the item a will kick the item d in position (II,4), and so on.

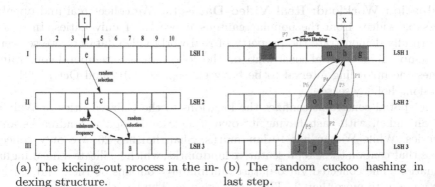

(a) The kicking-out process in the indexing structure.

(b) The random cuckoo hashing in last step.

Fig. 5. The kicking operations in semi-random selection

Figure 5(b) presents the random cuckoo hashing in the third step. The item x will be inserted into the hashing structure. We assume that all the items are similar items. The candidate positions of x and the adjacent positions are all occupied. Then the position which item h occupied is selected to start the kicking process in cuckoo hashing schemes. P1 means the first kicking operation in the procedure of inserting the item x. The kicking path from P1 to P6 has two circles and the last item may kick another item. The reason is that all the items are the similar items which calculated through the LSH, and all the items form a similar group. Then the items will kick each other in the similar group, and this insert operation will fail. The cuckoo hashing can only partly address the unbalanced load in the LSH based hash table. As to the problem of circle kicking in the similar group, we use the random cuckoo hashing to jump out the similar group to further address this problem.

The semi-random selection is used to optimize the kicking-out path through the history information of the kicking-out position. The random cuckoo hashing in the last step is used to jump out the similar group. Our indexing structure uses LSH to classify the near-duplicate items. Then we use the semi-random selection and the random cuckoo hashing in last step to accelerate the insertion process. It can significantly improve the utilization rate of hash tables and speed up the insertion.

4   Performance Evaluation

This Section presents the experimental results in a real cloud system in terms of multiple evaluation metrics.

4.1   Experiment Setup

We implemented a FastVR prototype on a 128-node cluster. Each node has a quad-core CPU running at 2.4GHz, with a 16GB RAM, a 500GB 7200RPM hard disk and a Gigabit network interface card. To drive the FastVR prototype evaluation, we use a real and large dataset collected from the cloud. Initially, the video dataset is randomly distributed among the nodes.

Evaluation Workload: Real Video Datasets. We collect real and openly assessable videos from the popular campus networks of universities. In order to faithfully demonstrate the property of real-world video datasets, we set certain temporal and spatial constraints on the collection. The temporal constraint defines the uploading interval to be between Sep. 30, 2012 and Oct.7, 2012, a week-long holiday season.

The spatial constraint confines the locations to the Chinese cities of Wuhan and Shanghai, with each having its own unique and popular landmarks and sceneries. While Wuhan has 10 landmarks, Shanghai has 20. We only collect videos that contain these representative landmarks, which facilitate a meaningful evaluation. The collected video dataset ultimately contains 50 thousand videos that amount to more than 2.5TB in storage size. The key characteristics of the video dataset are summarized in Table 1.

Table 1. The Properties of Collected Video Sets

Dataset Name	No. Videos	Total Size	No. Landmarks
Wuhan	21.2 thousand	1.34 TB	10
Shanghai	28.8 thousand	1.16 TB	20

Evaluation Comparisons and Parameters. To evaluate the efficiency of our method, we compare the performance of FastVR, ViDeDup, NEST, and the baseline approach. For meaningful and fair comparisons, we mainly examine the performance of their query functionality. Since there are no complete open-source code of ViDeDup, we choose to re-implement it. ViDeDup [11] proposes a framework for video de-duplication based on an application-level view of redundancy. We implement its main components, including video signature generation, video segmentation, video sequence comparison, clustering, centroid selection and video segment indexing and referencing. Moreover, NEST [7] is the standard cuckoo-driven locality sensitive hashing scheme. The baseline approach is the traditional LSH without cuckoo hashing. All above functionalities are implemented in the Linux environment. In addition, we evaluate different parameter settings to obtain high space- and time-efficiency. By analyzing the actual experimental results, we use d=10, k=8, ω=4, and Δ=3 to obtain higher query accuracy and smaller storage space.

4.2 Results and Analysis

The evaluation metrics include the query latency and space overhead.

Query Latency. Figure 6 shows the average query latency. We examine the query performance as a function of the number of query requests from 1000 to 5000 with an increment of 1000. The latency of Baseline, at 30min on average, is almost one order of magnitude better than 3.6min in NEST and 5.2min in ViDeDup. NEST makes use of cuckoo-driven hashing to execute flat addressing and quickly identify the queried results. ViDeDup reduces the query latency due to its similarity detection in the application level, and however, its 2-phase video

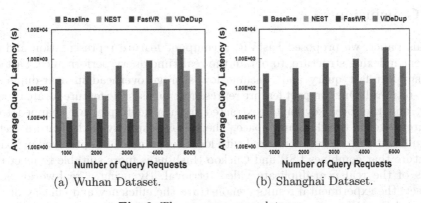

(a) Wuhan Dataset.   (b) Shanghai Dataset.

Fig. 6. The average query latency

comparison exacerbates the query performance due to the increase of operation complexity.

FastVR requires the smallest latency, around 10 seconds. The advantage of FastVR is to leverage the cuckoo hashing to obtain the load balance on hash tables. The hash tables based on FastVR save the storage space and can be effectively loaded into the high-speed memory, thus alleviating frequent access to the low-speed hard disks. FastVR hence mitigates the I/O costs to obtain low the query latency. Moreover, compared with NEST, the kicking-out path of cuckoo hashing in FastVR is optimized by semi-random selection to accelerate the insertion in the hash tables. This acceleration can further reduce the query latency to make FastVR more suitable for the real-time query in near-duplicate video retrieval.

Space Overhead. Table 2 summarizes the space overheads of Baseline, NEST, ViDeDup and FastVR, normalized to that of Baseline. By reducing the number of dimensions to be processed and the use of load-balanced design, NEST achieves a space saving of about 20% from Baseline. To support application-aware deduplication, ViDeDup leverages similarity detection and trades CPU for storage, thus obtaining about 30% space savings.

Table 2. Space Overhead normalized to Baseline

Video Datasets	Baseline	NEST	FastVR	ViDeDup
Wuhan	1	0.85	0.11	0.72
Shanghai	1	0.77	0.09	0.67

FastVR makes use of the semi-random selection to significantly improve the kicking-out path of cuckoo hashing, thus obtaining the space savings. FastVR requires about 10% space overhead and is able to store more index information into the main memory, which is helpful to significantly improve the query performance.

5 Conclusion

In this paper, we proposed FastVR, a compact feature representation and an efficient indexing structure, to obtain the real-time query performance. FastVR can support fast query and consume low storage overhead in near-duplicate video retrieval. Our compact feature representation uses the feature-aware Bloom filter, and the local keypoints (extracted from a keyframe) are mapped to a feature vector in the Hamming space. The storage capacity in the feature vector is significantly decreased, compared with local keypoints. The optimized indexing structure that combines LSH and Cuckoo Hashing is more suitable to meet the needs of the real near-duplicate video retrieval. By using a real-world video dataset, the experimental results demonstrate the efficiency and efficacy of our proposed FastVR in terms of query latency and accuracy, and space overhead.

Acknowledgment. This work was supported in part by NSFC 61173043; National Basic Research 973 Program of China 2011CB302301; NSFC 61025008, 61232004; The Seed Project of Wuhan National Laboratory for Optoelectronics (WNLO).

References

1. YouTube Statistics (2014), http://www.youtube.com/yt/press/
2. Böhm, C., Berchtold, S., Keim, D.A.: Searching in high-dimensional spaces: Index structures for improving the performance of multimedia databases. ACM Computing Surveys (CSUR) 33(3), 322–373 (2001)
3. Datar, M., Immorlica, N., Indyk, P., Mirrokni, V.S.: Locality-sensitive hashing scheme based on p-stable distributions. In: Proc. Annual Symposium on Computational Geometry. ACM (2004)
4. Douze, M., Gaidon, A., Jegou, H., Marszałek, M., Schmid, C., et al.: Inria-lears video copy detection system. In: TREC Video Retrieval Evaluation, TRECVID Workshop (2008)
5. Gantz, J., Reinsel, D.: The Digital Universe in 2020: Big Data, Bigger Digital Shadows, and Biggest Growth in the Far East. In: International Data Corporation (IDC) iView (December 2012)
6. Hua, Y., Jiang, H., Zhu, Y., Feng, D., Tian, L.: Smartstore: A new metadata organization paradigm with semantic-awareness for next-generation file systems. In: Proceedings of the Conference on High Performance Computing Networking, Storage and Analysis. IEEE (2009)
7. Hua, Y., Xiao, B., Liu, X.: Nest: Locality-aware approximate query service for cloud computing. In: Proceedings of IEEE International Conference on Computer Communications, INFOCOM (2013)
8. Huang, Z., Shen, H.T., Shao, J., Cui, B., Zhou, X.: Practical online near-duplicate subsequence detection for continuous video streams. IEEE Transactions on Multimedia 12(5), 386–398 (2010)
9. Huang, Z., Shen, H.T., Shao, J., Zhou, X., Cui, B.: Bounded coordinate system indexing for real-time video clip search. ACM Transactions on Information Systems (TOIS) 27(3), 17 (2009)
10. Indyk, P., Motwani, R.: Approximate nearest neighbors: towards removing the curse of dimensionality. In: Proc. ACM Symposium on Theory Of computing. ACM (1998)
11. Katiyar, A., Weissman, J.: ViDeDup: An application-aware framework for video de-duplication. In: Proceedings of the 3rd USENIX Conference on Hot Topics in Storage and File Systems, HotStorage (2011)
12. Ke, Y., Sukthankar, R.: Pca-sift: A more distinctive representation for local image descriptors. In: Proceedings of the 2004 IEEE Computer Society Conference on Computer Vision and Pattern Recognition, CVPR 2004, vol. 2, pp. II–506. IEEE (2004)
13. Law-To, J., Chen, L., Joly, A., Laptev, I., Buisson, O., Gouet-Brunet, V., Boujemaa, N., Stentiford, F.: Video copy detection: a comparative study. In: Proceedings of the 6th ACM International Conference on Image and Video Retrieval, pp. 371–378. ACM Press (2007)
14. Leung, A.W., Shao, M., Bisson, T., Pasupathy, S., Miller, E.L.: Spyglass: Fast, scalable metadata search for large-scale storage systems. In: Proceedings of the Conference on File and Storage Technologies (FAST), pp. 153–166 (2009)

15. Lowe, D.G.: Distinctive image features from scale-invariant keypoints. International Journal of Computer Vision 60(2), 91–110 (2004)
16. Lu, G., Nam, Y.J., Du, D.H.: BloomStore: Bloom-filter based memory-efficient key-value store for indexing of data deduplication on flash. In: Proc. IEEE 28th Symposium on Mass Storage Systems and Technologies (MSST). IEEE (2012)
17. Lv, Q., Josephson, W., Wang, Z., Charikar, M., Li, K.: Multi-probe lsh: Efficient indexing for high-dimensional similarity search. In: Proceedings of the 33rd International Conference on Very Large Data Bases, pp. 950–961. VLDB Endowment (2007)
18. Pagh, R., Rodler, F.F.: Cuckoo hashing. Journal of Algorithms 51(2), 122–144 (2004)
19. Park, D., Du, D.H.: Hot data identification for flash-based storage systems using multiple Bloom filters. In: Proc. IEEE 27th Symposium on Mass Storage Systems and Technologies (MSST). IEEE (2011)
20. Poullot, S., Crucianu, M., Buisson, O.: Scalable mining of large video databases using copy detection. In: Proceedings of the 16th ACM International Conference on Multimedia, pp. 61–70. ACM (2008)
21. Shang, L., Yang, L., Wang, F., Chan, K.P., Hua, X.S.: Real-time large scale near-duplicate web video retrieval. In: Proceedings of the International Conference on Multimedia, pp. 531–540. ACM (2010)
22. Sivic, J., Zisserman, A.: Video google: A text retrieval approach to object matching in videos. In: Proceedings of the Ninth IEEE International Conference on Computer Vision (ICCV), pp. 1470–1477. IEEE (2003)
23. Weiss, Y., Torralba, A., Fergus, R.: Spectral hashing. In: Advances in Neural Information Processing Systems, pp. 1753–1760 (2008)
24. Wu, X., Hauptmann, A.G., Ngo, C.W.: Practical elimination of near-duplicates from web video search. In: Proceedings of the 15th International Conference on Multimedia, pp. 218–227. ACM (2007)
25. Zhan, D., Jiang, H., Seth, S.C.: Exploiting set-level non-uniformity of capacity demand to enhance cmp cooperative caching. In: Proceedings of the 2010 IEEE International Symposium on Parallel & Distributed Processing (IPDPS), pp. 1–10. IEEE (2010)
26. Zhan, D., Jiang, H., Seth, S.C.: Stem: Spatiotemporal management of capacity for intra-core last level caches. In: Proceedings of the 43rd Annual IEEE/ACM International Symposium on Microarchitecture (MICRO), pp. 163–174. IEEE (2010)
27. Zhan, D., Jiang, H., Seth, S.C.: Locality & utility co-optimization for practical capacity management of shared last level caches. In: Proceedings of the 26th ACM International Conference on Supercomputing, pp. 279–290. ACM (2012)
28. Zhao, W.L., Tan, S., Ngo, C.W.: Large-scale near-duplicate web video search: Challenge and opportunity. In: Proceedings of the IEEE International Conference on Multimedia and Expo (ICME), pp. 1624–1627. IEEE (2009)

Repairing Multiple Data Losses by Parallel Max-min Trees Based on Regenerating Codes in Distributed Storage Systems

Pengfei You, Yuxing Peng, Zhen Huang, and Changjian Wang

College of Computer, National University of Defense Technology,
410073 Changsha, China
hbypf@outlook.com, {yooroc,huangzh,wangcj}@gmail.com

Abstract. Due to high storage efficiency, erasure codes are recently used to provide high data reliability in distributed storage systems. When multiple data loses in system, regeneration time for them demands to be as short as possible so as to keep data availbility and reliability. Common way is to repair them one by one, which prolongs the regeneration time. Tree-structured regeneration may reduce regeneration time when regenerating one single node failure by relaying the network traffic, and is also extended to regenerate multiple data losses. In this paper, based on regenerating codes which achieve minimal network traffic during the regeneration, we consider reducing regeneration time by using multiple max-min trees to parallel regenerate multiple data losses. And we proposed an algorithm: bandwidth-sharing max-min algorithm (BSM2RC) to construct multiple parallel max-min trees. It realizes efficient bandwidth utilization by maximizing the minimal bottleneck edge weight of multiple regeneration trees, thus improve regeneration efficiency. Our simulation experiment shows that multiple parallel max-min trees reduce total regeneration time for multiple data losses significantly, and thus enhance system reliability, compared with existing regeneration scheme.

Keywords: Distributed storage System, Data regeneration, Regenerating codes, Regeneration tree, Max-min tree, Maximum spanning tree.

1 Introduction

Distributed storage systems, such as Total Recall [15] and OceanStore [1] etc. have been becoming very popular since they can provide large-volume storage services for users. In such systems, due to frequent node departures and failures, data losses are deemed as normal state. Frequent data losses jeopardize data availbility and reliability [4], which is usually recovered by data redundancy technology.

Replication is one of the most common redundancy techniques, where each file has n copies and each copy is placed at an individual node [6]. Another common redundancy technique is a (n, k) erasure code $(n>k)$, where each file is split into k fragments with equal size and they are encoded into n fragments, each of which is stored at an individual node. The original file can be reconstructed from any k fragments, which

X.-h. Sun et al. (Eds.): ICA3PP 2014, Part II, LNCS 8631, pp. 325–338, 2014.
© Springer International Publishing Switzerland 2014

makes erasure codes be able to provide the same reliability as replication requiring much less storage space [7]. Therefore, erasure codes become a popular redundancy solution in distributed storage systems recently.

Data availbility and reliability are achieved by keeping the same redundancy level of the system. That is, when data losses, the lost data needs to be recovered, which is called regeneration. In regeneration, a node in the distributed storage system, referred to as a newcomer, receives coded data from active storage nodes, referred to as providers, and finally becomes a new storage node, so the lost data are regenerated. Regeneration time is expected to be as little as possible, so as to provide high data availbility and reliability [12]. There are two ways to reduce regeneration time. One is to reduce the network traffic in the regeneration, such as applying regenerating code [10]. The other is to take into account heterogeneity of bandwidth capacity between nodes in data transmission for regeneration [11].

In real systems, there are many common situations for regenerating multiple nodes failure. On one hand, multiple nodes fail simultaneously and frequently in real storage systems, such as churn. On the other hand, to reduce the management cost and keep performance, system prefers to launch a recovery only when the total amount of failed nodes reaches a given threshold [15]. To cope with multiple nodes failure, the sequential regeneration schemes are proposed, and the regeneration time is long [14]. To reduce regeneration time, MCR [13] regenerates multiple failed nodes in parallel, but the single node regeneration is still in star-structure. TPR [14] uses tree-structure to regenerate multiple failed nodes in parallel, but the structure is based on maximum spanning tree which greedy selects maximal edges and incurs the minimal bottleneck edge among all the trees. In addition, the construction for tree is restricted to fixed k providers for general random linear codes which do not further reduce network traffic.

In this paper, inspired by the case that bottleneck edge weights of multiple trees interact each other and the construction scheme for tree could impact the minimal bottleneck edge weight of multiple trees, we consider using multiple max-min trees based on regenerating codes to parallel regenerate multiple data losses so as to further reduce total regeneration time. We propose a construction algorithm for parallel max-min regeneration trees: bandwidth-sharing max-min algorithm based on regenerating codes (BSM2RC). In the algorithm, multiple parallel regeneration trees based on regenerating code are constructed, each of which is independently responsible for one data loss. Due to Minimum-storage regenerating (MSR) code [10, 12], the network traffic on each link is only $\dfrac{M}{k(r-k+1)}$ bytes ($k \le r \le n-1$), which is the least and less than M/k bytes in TPR.

The main contribution for BSM2RC is that max-min tree rather than maximum spanning tree is created, which does not always select maximal edges in construction and could leave them in the construction for next tree, thus extends space for next tree to select larger bottleneck edge. Especially, to make minimal bottleneck edge weight of multiple trees as large as possible, we realize the construction for the max-min tree whose weight sum of all edges is as small as possible.

In addition, different from [12], when utilizing MSR code in trees, an optimized adjusting strategy for in-degree of tree root is adopted to ensure large enough edge could be further left for next tree so as to achieve maximal bottleneck edge of multiple trees.

BSM2RC enhances selection chance for larger bottleneck edge among all regeneration trees by constructing max-min trees with minimal weight sum of all edges and reduces network traffic by using MSR code, thus the entire regeneration time is reduced significantly. Our simulation experiment shows that BSM2RC improve the data availbility and reliability of the system remarkably, compared with some existing regeneration solutions for multiple nodes failure.

The reminder of the paper is organized as follows. In Section 2 we introduce the related work. We describe the basic network model for regenerating multiple data losses in Section 3. In Section 4, we present BSM2RC for constructing multiple parallel regeneration trees. The experiment and analysis of BSM2RC is performed in Section 5. Finally, we conclude the paper in Section 6.

2   Related Work

Compared with replica, erasure codes provide higher data availability and have been used in many distributed systems, such as Windows Azure [2], HDFS [3], etc. In order to maintain data availability and reliability, the system should regenerate lost data as soon as possible. There are two ways to reduce regeneration time for the lost data. One is to reduce network traffic, the other is to construct optimal network topology to by-pass bottleneck link for data transmission.

A common (n, k) erasure code, such as Reed–Solomon codes [7] or random linear codes [8] etc., stores redundant data for a file sized M bytes in n storage nodes, each node with M/k bytes data, where $n>k$. When a node failures, k providers participate in the regeneration, each of which transmits M/k bytes data to the newcomer. That is, the network traffic is M/k bytes on each link. Dimakis $et\ al.$ [9] propose regenerating code, which reduces the amount of data transmitted in regeneration by accessing more than k providers [8]. Wu $et\ al.$ [10] propose minimum-storage regenerating (MSR) codes which is proved to realize minimal network traffic in the regeneration over all erasure codes, and the network traffic on each link is $\dfrac{M}{k(r-k+1)}$ bytes, where r is the number of providers and satisfies $k \le r \le n-1$.

When transmitting data in regeneration, the conventional scheme is star-structured network topology, in which the newcomer receives coded blocks directly from each provider, thus the regeneration time depends on the minimal edge connecting to the newcomer. As showed in left part of Fig. 1, in star-structured regeneration scheme, the bandwidth bottleneck link is the edge connecting to the newcomer and provider A, and the actual transmission rate during the regeneration process is 10KB/s. In order to quicken data transmission in regeneration, Li $et\ al.$ propose tree-structured network topology based on random linear codes in [11] and based on regenerating codes in [12] respectively. In the tree-structured regeneration scheme, the child node sends data to its parent node, and the parent node encodes the received data with the data it stores and then sends the encoded data to its parent node. If the transmission is pipelined, the bandwidth bottleneck is the edge with the narrowest bandwidth in the tree [12]. As showed in right part of Fig. 1, by constructing a regeneration tree, bandwidth bottleneck link is the edge connecting to the newcomer and provider C, and the actual transmission rate during the regeneration process is 30KB/s, which reaches higher speed than that in the left part of Fig. 1. A maximum spanning tree is proved an optimal regeneration tree [11], which achieves maximal bottleneck bandwidth when regenerating single node. In [11] the network traffic between nodes is still M/k bytes,

while in [12] it is down to $\dfrac{M}{k(r-k+1)}$ bytes by constructing a regeneration tree for
MSR code whose in-degree of the root must be at least adjusted to $r - k + 1$, and thus
the regeneration time is further reduced. Because only consider single node failure, in
[12] some edges are randomly removed when adjusting in-degree of the tree root.

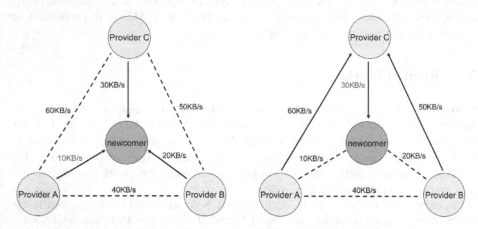

Fig. 1. Star-structured network topology & tree-structured network topology

The above regeneration works are for single node failure. For multiple nodes failure, there are sequential regeneration schemes and parallel regeneration schemes.
Sequential schemes include sequential Star-Structured Regeneration (referred to as
SSR) [11] and sequential Tree-Structured Regeneration (TSR) [11] etc., which regenerate multiple newcomers one by one and thus prolong the total regeneration time. To
parallel regenerate multiple failed nodes, Hu *et al.* [13] propose a Mutually Cooperative Recovery (MCR) mechanism, in which the lost data are regenerated cooperative-
ly and simultaneously by all the newcomers. But in MCR data is still transferred by
the star structure, thus the network bandwidth capacity is not utilized maximally to
speed up regeneration. To increase network bandwidth capacity for regenerating multiple data losses, Sun et al. [14] proposes Tree-structured Parallel Regeneration (TPR)
mechanism which constructs multiple trees to regenerate parallel. In TPR, each regeneration tree is rooted by an individual newcomer and responsible for regenerating
its lost data, thus multiple data losses are regenerated in parallel. However, data
transmission scheme for TPR is based on the tree-structured topology in [11] suitable
for random linear codes, in which, the provider number must be k for each newcomer,
thus the network traffic between nodes is actually still M/k bytes and not reduced
further. In addition, TPR applies maximum spanning tree (MST) [11] which greedy
selects maximal edges from available edges set. In fact, one MST achieves maximal
bottleneck edge only when repairing single node. When repairing multiple failed
nodes, the similar greed selection will construct two MSTs, one is with very large
bottleneck edge and the other with very small bottleneck edge, which prolongs the
entire regeneration time.

3   Network Model for Regenerating Multiple Data Losses

In a distributed system applying a (n, k) MSR code, an original file sized M bytes is divided into k blocks and then encoded into n coded blocks, each of which is M/k bytes in size. All blocks are stored in n storage nodes, each node with one block. When s nodes failures, s idle nodes are selected as newcomers, each of which downloads one block from each of r providers and regenerates its lost block, where $s \leq n - k$ and $k \leq r \leq n - s$. Each newcomer and all r providers form one regeneration tree rooted by the newcomer. By the relay of providers, the newcomer will finally get a linear combination of r coded blocks of r providers to regenerate the lost data [11]. The network traffic on each edge is $\dfrac{M}{k(r-k+1)}$ bytes in the tree based on MSR code, and the regeneration time is determined by the edge with bottleneck bandwidth in the tree [12]. When s regeneration tree are constructed, the entire regeneration can be performed parallel.

Assume that the storage node set for a file is $N = \{ N_1, N_2, \ldots, N_n \}$, (N_i, N_j) is the undirected edge connecting N_i and N_j, and $\omega(N_i, N_j)$ is the weight of edge (N_i, N_j) which represents the bandwidth capacity between N_i and N_j, where $1 \leq i, j \leq n$ and $i \neq j$. We denote the network model for regenerating multiple data losses as an undirected complete graph $G(s; n, k, r / N)$, in which there is no edge between any two of s newcomers.

4   Parallel Regeneration for Multiple Data Losses Using Max-min trees Based on MSR Code

In this section, we present how to construct multiple max-min trees based on MSR code to parallel regenerate multiple data losses in the network model above. First, we show parallel regeneration scheme for multiple max-min trees. Second, we analysis the characteristics for max-min tree as well as maximum spanning tree (MST) and prove that max-min tree has less regeneration time than MST when parallel regenerating multiple data losses, then discuss the root feature of max-min tree based on MSR code. Last we realize construction algorithm for multiple parallel max-min trees based on regenerating codes: bandwidth-sharing max-min algorithm (BSM2RC).

4.1   Parallel Regeneration Scheme for Multiple Max-min Trees

The bottleneck edge or bandwidth is the minimal weighted edge in a regeneration tree. The bottleneck edge or bandwidth of multiple trees is the minimal bottleneck edge over all the trees.

Assume that multiple regeneration trees are T_i $(1 \leq i \leq s)$, bottleneck bandwidth of each T_i is ω_i; t_{para} and t_i denote entire regeneration time for parallel multiple trees and each T_i respectively.

In construction for multiple trees, they are finished in turn, in which each of them is assigned some part of bandwidth of all edges in $G(s; n, k, r /N)$ and aims at one data loss. They share all network edges in $G(s; n, k, r /N)$, that is, for all i and j, where $1 \le i, j \le s$ and $i \ne j$, one edge in T_i may appear in T_j and the two trees could occupy some part of bandwidth of the edge respectively, which is similar to edge sharing strategy in [14].

In parallel regeneration for multiple data losses, each tree based on MSR code regenerates one data loss individually, thus $t_i = \dfrac{M}{k(r - k + 1)\omega_i}, 1 \le i \le s$ [12]. Since s failed nodes are regenerated simultaneously, the total regeneration time of parallel regeneration trees depends on the minimum bottleneck bandwidth of all regeneration trees, and then $t_{para} = \max\limits_{1 \le i \le s}\{t_i\}$.

4.2   Max-min Tree vs. Maximum Spanning Tree

Max-min Tree: we define it as a spanning tree of a graph G whose smallest edge (bottleneck edge) weight is maximum over all spanning trees of G.

Maximum spanning tree (MST) is a spanning tree where the weight sum of all edges is maximal. Because MST must be max-min tree [11], it is used to find bottleneck edge in existing tree-structured regeneration schemes. However, max-min tree is not necessary MST. For example, as showed in Fig. 2, tree A and B are Max-min trees with the same bottleneck edge whose weight is 3. But B is also a MST, while A is not. Weight sum of all edges of tree A is 20, while that of tree B is 24. Obviously, the weight sum of all edges of max-min tree is not more than maximum spanning tree.

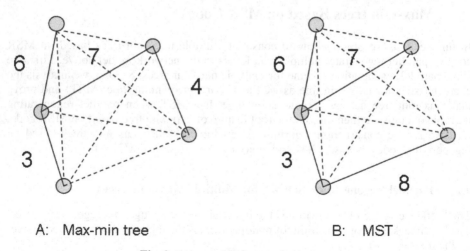

A: Max-min tree   B: MST

Fig. 2. tree-structured network topology

Lemma 1: Based on the same network graph model $G(s; n, k, r /N)$ above, when constructing the same amount of multiple tees respectively, the minimal or final bottleneck bandwidth for multiple max-min trees is not less than that for MST.

Analysis: According to the regeneration scheme, each tree achieves its maximal bottleneck edge from the remaining network bandwidth after its previous tree is constructed, while the entire regeneration time depends on the tree whose bottleneck edge weight is minimal over all trees. It shows the bottleneck edge weight for each tree is interactional, and the minimal bottleneck edge weight of trees is impacted by the construction scheme for trees.

Proof: Based on $G(s; n, k, r /N)$ above, assume s max-min trees MMT_i and maximum spanning tree MST_i are respectively constructed in turn, where $1 \le i \le s$; the weight sum of all edges for MMT_i and MST_i is $MMTW_i$ and $MSTW_i$ respectively; the bottleneck edge weight is $MMTB_i$ and $MSTB_i$ respectively. $MMTW_1 - MMTB_1 \le MSTW_1 - MSTB_1$ since $MMTW_1 \le MSTW_1$ and $MMTB_1 = MSTB_1$. That is, MST_1 selects some unnecessary edges which have larger weights than that of MMT_1. In addition, MST_1 uses greedy algorithm to select maximal edges from edge set of G, which leaves minimal edges into G. Therefore, when constructing the second tree, MMT_2 has space to select larger weighted bottleneck edge from remainder edges of G than that of MST_2, which incurs $MMTB_2 \ge MSTB_2$.

For example, in Fig. 2, within the same graph there are two spanning trees represented by solid lines. The bottleneck edge weight is 3 in the two trees, while MST also includes the maximal edge whose weight is 8. When constructing the next tree, max-min tree could select the maximal edge, but MST can not. Similarly, $MMTB_i \ge MSTB_i$, so the minimal or final bottleneck weight of s max-min trees MMT_i is not less than that of MST_i, $i=0,1,2,...s$.   ∎

Lemma 1 shows the regeneration time for max-min tree is not more than that of MST when network traffic between nodes is same. In the worst case, the regeneration time is same.

In addition, in parallel regeneration each max-min tree is built on MSR code which can reduce the regeneration traffic by increasing provider number. However, in TPR the network traffic can not be changed since the provider number must be k according to random linear code. In one max-min tree based on MSR code with r providers, where $k \le r \le n-1$, each provider sends its parent node $\dfrac{M}{k(r-k+1)}$ bytes block generated by encoding M/k bytes block stored in it. Finally the newcomer receives r encoded blocks, and encodes them into M/k bytes block, thus at least r $k + 1$ providers must be directly linked to the newcomer. That is, the root node in-degree of each max-min tree based on MSR code must be at least r $k + 1$ in regeneration [12].

Based on above analysis, it is concluded that the bottleneck edge weight of a max-min tree depends on the construction of its previous tree. After excluding the previous tree, if the bandwidth of remaining edges in original graph is more, the bottleneck edge weight of current tree could be more. That is, if weight sum of all edges of the max-min tree is as small as possible, the bottleneck edge weight for next tree could be as large as possible. The construction for max-min tree with minimal weight sum is introduced in next section.

4.3   Bandwidth-Sharing Max-min Algorithm for Parallel Regenerating Multiple Data Losses

In this section, aiming at multiple data losses, we introduce the construction algorithm for multiple parallel max-min trees based on regenerating codes: bandwidth-sharing max-min algorithm (BSM2RC).

BSM2RC includes a recursive sub-procedure *GetMax-minTree* (G), which returns a max-min tree T of graph G. It is showed as follows:

```
T  GetMax-minTree(G)
{
1: E ←  list the edges of G in ascending order
2: if ( |E| == 1)
3: return E
4: b ← weight(E(⌊|E|/2⌋))
5: G' ← remove all edges whose weight < b from G keeping
vertices
6: F ← get components of G' by performing depth first
search of G
7: For i = 1 to |F|
8: minTᵢ ← find minimum spanning tree of F(i)
9: Nᵢ ← all nodes of minTᵢ
10: End for
11: If (|F| == 1)
12: Return GetMax-minTree(G')
13: Else
14: G* ← G - edges of G' keeping vertices
15: G" ← collapse G* into { N₁, N₂, ... , N|F| }
16: Return minT₁ ∪ minT₂ ∪...∪ minT|F| ∪ GetMax-minTree(G")
17: End else
}
```

The sub-procedure is a modification version for min-max tree construction algorithm in [16]. The new method is that we construct one minimum spanning tree for each component of G and then add it to edge set of the max-min tree, whose weight sum could be minimal while bottleneck edge weight remains unchanged. That is, it makes weight sum of all edges of max-min tree as small as possible, which leaves the larger edges into construction for next max-min tree as many as possible so as to make the bottleneck edge for next tree as large as possible. The sub-procedure has 3 steps as followed:

1. sort the edges of G into edge set E in ascending order and remove all edges whose weight are less than median edge weight b of E to get remaining graph G' while keeping all vertices of G *(line 1 to line 5)*

2. get all components of G' by depth first search algorithm and find one minimum spanning tree of each component by Prime algorithm (*line 5 to line 10*)
3. if G' is connected, recall sub-procedure using G' as input; else add trees of step 2 into max-min tree and recall sub-procedure using G'' which is achieved by collapsing $G*$ (*line 11 to line 17*)

Note, in collapsing $G*$ of step 3, shrink each connected component of G' as one vertex of G''; the edges of G'' are the largest weight edge that goes between the corresponding components.

Without loss of generality, we assume the newcomers are N_j, and the current edges set of tree T_j is E_j, where $1 \le j \le s$. The BSM2RC algorithm is described as follows:

Algorithm for BSM2RC: Construction of multiple max-min trees T_1, T_2,...,T_s for parallel regeneration. Define $RootE_j = \{(N_j, N_i) \mid i = s + 1, s + 2, \ldots, n\}, j = 1, 2, \ldots s$.

```
1: for j ← 1 to s do
2: T_j ← φ
3: CandE_j = RootE_j
4: E_j = GetMax-minTree(G(CandE_j))
5: α = | RootE_j ∩ E_j |
6: for i ← α + 1 to r - k + 1 do
7: e_m ← select the smallest edge from RootE_j - E_j which
is larger than min (E_j)
8: If (e_m == φ)
e_m ← select the largest edge from RootE_j - E_j
9: e_n ← select the largest edge from E_j - RootE_j making
T_j ∪ {e_m} - {e_n} a tree rooted by N_j
10: T_j ← T_j ∪ {e_m} - {e_n}
11: end for
12: ω_j = min (E_j)
13: for i ← 1 to r do
14: bw_i -= ω_j
15: end for
16: end for
```

In BSM2RC, Line 2 to Line 5 firstly constructs a max-min tree T_j by calling *GetMax-minTree* (), in which $G(CandE_j)$ is the graph consisting of candidate edges set $CandE_j$. Line 6 to Line 11 then adjusts the in-degree of the tree's root node to be at least $r - k + 1$, which satisfies the regeneration demand in regenerating codes. Especially, to ensure that the bottleneck edge weights for T_j and its next tree are large enough, we select the small enough edge from remaining graph and add it to T_j, then remove the large enough edge in T_j to adjust root in-degree. After each construction of single regeneration tree T_j, the bandwidth bw_i for each edge in T_j is updated by subtracting the minimum bandwidth ω_j of the edge set E_j for T_j so as to make remaining bandwidth be used simultaneously by other trees. The same process above is repeated until all the s regeneration trees have been constructed. As analyzed before, the algorithm ensures the larger bottleneck edge weight when repairing multiple data losses in parallel.

There are two main innovations. First, BSM2RC constructs max-min tree whose weight sum of all edges is as small as possible so as to make bottleneck edge weight for multiple trees as large as possible. Second, different from the random selection strategy in [12], when utilizing MSR code to achieve the minimal network traffic between nodes, an optimized method for adjusting in-degree of tree root is adopted to ensure maximal bottleneck edge of multiple trees. These two aspects further reduce regeneration time for multiple data losses.

5   Simulation Experiment

In this section, we compare BSM2RC with TPR, sequential Star-Structured Regeneration (referred to as SSR), sequential Tree-Structured Regeneration (TSR) and Mutually Cooperative Recovery (MCR) mechanism for multiple data losses in distributed storage systems by an event-driven simulator, which simulates the nodes' activities based on an availability trace file of PlanetLab network [17]. In the simulator, we assume that the weight of the edge in $G(s; n, k, r / N)$ satisfies an uniform distribution $U[0.3Mbps, 120Mbps]$, which reveals the bandwidth between nodes in PlanetLab [9, 12].

We configure 500 nodes for simulation, which lasts for 2000 seconds, and repeats 50 times. The system uses $(9 + k, k)$ MSR coding. In the simulation, when the number of data loss reaches some value, regeneration will be trigged. Equation $t_i = \dfrac{M}{k(r - k + 1)\omega_i}$ shows that the provider number r decides the regeneration time for single failed node. Denote $\mu = r \quad k$, we measure respective regeneration time for different number of data loss by increasing k, s and μ, where k is selected as $4,\ldots,10$, 12, while s is increased from 2 to 6, and μ is increased from 0 to 2. Fig. 3 shows the average regeneration time when the number of failures varies from 2 to 6 and $\mu = 0, 1, 2$ respectively. In the same simulation conditions, we also measure probability of successful regeneration and data availability for each regeneration scheme. The probability of successful regeneration is the ratio of finished regeneration number to total started regeneration number, while data availability is the ratio of data's available time to total simulation time. The simulation results are showed as Fig. 4 and Fig. 5 respectively.

Fig. 3 shows that among all regeneration schemes, BSM2RC gets the minimal regeneration time when repairing the same number of data loss. As the number of failures increases, the differences between BSM2RC and the others becomes more and more obvious. When the failure number equals to 6 the reduced time of BSM2RC is up to about 80%, 70%, 60%, and 30%, compared with SSR, TSR, MCR and TPR. Especially, when $\mu = 0$ (namely $r = k$), BSM2RC has less regeneration time than TPR since the bottleneck weight found by the former is more than the latter. As μ increases, the regeneration time decreases since the network traffic decreases. However, the decrement is not proportionate to μ and becomes less since node number for each regeneration tree becomes more, which may incur less bandwidth bottleneck.

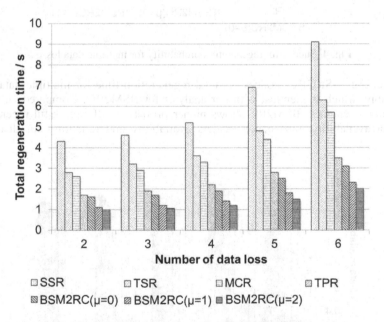

Fig. 3. Regeneration time for multiple data losses

Fig. 4 shows that the probability of successful regeneration of BSM2RC is obviously higher than others. It decreases slightly as the number of failed nodes increases, and is around about 90%. But the others decreases obviously, especially SSR which reaches the lowest probability.

Fig. 5 shows that BSM2RC reaches about 95% of data availability, which is higher than the others. Especially, when failed node number is 6, the data availability increases about 60%, 50%, 40% and 15% respectively, compared with SSR, TSR, MCR and TPR. It does not decrease obviously as the failed node number increases, which reveals nice stability for maintaining system data.

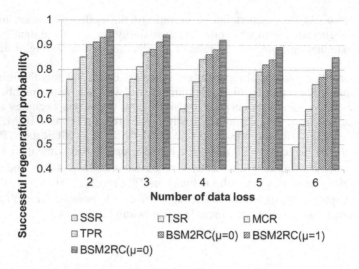

Fig. 4. Successful regeneration probability for multiple data losse

In general, BSM2RC reduces the total regeneration time for multiple data losses remarkably, which is identical with our analysis for BSM2RC. Compared with other regeneration schemes, BSM2RC shows higher probability of successful regeneration and data availability, thus enhances data availability and reliability for distributed systems.

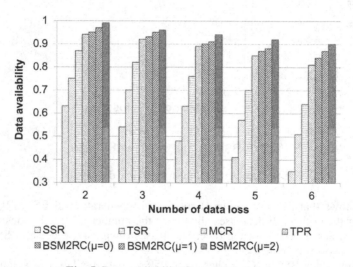

Fig. 5. Data availability for multiple data losse

6   Conclusion

In this paper, we discuss how to reduce regeneration time when regenerating multiple data losses in distributed storage systems using erasure codes; especially analyze the situation that construction scheme for trees would affect final bottleneck bandwidth of multiple trees. We present a construction algorithm for multiple parallel max-min trees based on regenerating codes (BSM2RC) for regenerating multiple data losses in distributed storage systems. We firstly introduce the network model for BSM2RC, and then describe the algorithm mechanism for BSM2RC. The main innovation is that BSM2RC increase minimal bottleneck weight by constructing multiple max-min trees base on regenerating codes, and then speed up parallel regeneration for multiple data losses. Our simulation results show that BSM2RC reduces regeneration time significantly, achieves higher successful regeneration probability and data availability, thus improve data availability and reliability in distributed storage systems, compared with existing regeneration schemes.

Acknowledgments. This research work is supported by National Basic Research Program of China under Grant No.2014CB340303, and National High-Tech R&D Program of China under Grant No.2013AA01A213.

References

1. Rhea, S., Eaton, P., Geels, D., Weatherspoon, H., Zhao, B., Kubiatowicz, J.: Pond: the OceanStore Prototype. In: FAST (2003)
2. Huang, C., Simitci, H., Xu, Y., et al.: Erasure Coding in Windows Azure Storage. In: Proceedings of the 2012 USENIX Conference on Annual Technical Conference. USENIX Association, Boston (2012)
3. Sathiamoorthy, M., Asteris, M., Papailiopoulos, D., et al.: XORing elephants: Novel erasure codes for big data. In: Proceedings of the 39th International Conference on Very Large Data Bases, VLDB Endowment, pp. 325–336 (2013)
4. Ghemawat, S., Gobioff, H., Leung, S.-T.: The Google File System. In: SOSP (2003)
5. Lee, S.-J., Sharma, P., Banerjee, S., Basu, S., Fonseca, R.: Measuring bandwidth between planetLab nodes. In: Dovrolis, C. (ed.) PAM 2005. LNCS, vol. 3431, pp. 292–305. Springer, Heidelberg (2005)
6. Weatherspoon, H., Kubiatowicz, J.D.: Erasure coding vs. replication: A quantitative comparison. In: Druschel, P., Kaashoek, M.F., Rowstron, A. (eds.) IPTPS 2002. LNCS, vol. 2429, pp. 328–337. Springer, Heidelberg (2002)
7. Rodrigues, R., Zhou, T.H.: High availability in DHTs: Erasure coding vs.replication. In: van Renesse, R. (ed.) IPTPS 2005. LNCS, vol. 3640, pp. 226–239. Springer, Heidelberg (2005)
8. Acedanski, S., Deb, S., Medard, M., Koetter, R.: How good is random linear coding based distributed networked storage? In: Proc. 1st Workshop on Network Coding, Riva del Garda, Italy (April 2005)
9. Dimakis, A., Godfrey, P., Wainwright, M., Ramchandran, K.: Network coding for distributed storage systems. In: Proc. of INFOCOM, pp. 2000–2008 (May 2007)
10. Wu, Y., Dimakis, R., Ramch, K.: Deterministic regenerating codes for distributed storage. In: Allerton Conference on Control, Computing, and Communication. Urbana-Champaign, IL (2007)
11. Li, J., Yang, S., Wang, X., Xue, X., Li, B.: Tree-structured Data Regeneration with Network Coding in Distributed Storage Systems. In: Proc. 17th IEEE International Workshop on Quality of Service, IWQoS (2009)

12. Li, J., Yang, S., Wang, X., Li, B.: Tree-structured Data Regeneration in Distributed Storage Systems with Regenerating Codes. In: Proc. INFOCOM (2010)
13. Hu, Y., Xu, Y., Wang, X., Zhan, C., Li, P.: Cooperative Recovery of Distributed Storage Systems from Multiple Losses with Network Coding. IEEE Journal on Selected Areas in Communications 28, 268–276 (2010)
14. Sun, W., Wang, Y., Pei, X.: Tree-structured parallel regeneration for multiple data losses in distributed storage systems based on erasure codes. Journal on China Communications 4, 113–125 (2013)
15. Bhagwan, R., Tati, K., Cheng, Y., Savage, S., Voelker, G.: Total recall: System support for automated availability management. In: Proc. NSDI 2001 (March 2004)
16. Camerini, P.R.: The min-max spanning tree problem and some extensions. Information Processing Letters 7, 10–14 (1978)
17. Planetlab, http://www.planet-lab.org/

Exploiting Content Locality to Improve the Performance and Reliability of Phase Change Memory

Suzhen Wu[1], Zaifa Xi[1], Bo Mao[2,*], and Hong Jiang[3]

[1] Computer Science Department, Xiamen University, Fujian China
[2] Software School of Xiamen University, Fujian China
[3] Department of Computer Science and Engineering, University of Nebraska-Lincoln, USA
maobo@xmu.edu.cn

Abstract. With the explosive growth in data volume, the I/O bottleneck has become an increasingly daunting challenge for big data analytics. The outstanding energy efficiency and scalability characteristics of Phase Change Memory (PCM) make it a potential, attractive alternative to DRAM and traditional storage devices. However, PCM's slow write performance and weak write endurance are the two major weaknesses that prevent its wider applications. Moreover, the slow processing workflow of write requests also causes significant contention for and interferes with read requests, thus affecting the system performance. In this paper, we propose Content Aware PCM (short for CA-PCM) that employs a lightweight data deduplication module to exploit the content locality in memory accesses. CA-PCM is able to effectively reduce write traffic to PCM by removing unnecessary duplicate writes and also substantially extend the lifespan of the PCM device. Our trace-driven simulation results show that CA-PCM improves the performance and reliability significantly.

Keywords: Phase Change Memory, Data Deduplication, Performance, Reliability.

1 Introduction

The demand for memory capacity is escalating with the emergence and wide spread of data-intensive and big data applications. While DRAM remains the dominant main memory technology, its relatively low energy efficiency and low scalability have made it a severe scalability and energy bottleneck [1,2,3,4]. Therefore, memory technologies that promise better scalability and energy efficiency than DRAM have become attractive for designing future memory systems.

The non-volatile memory technologies, such as NAND Flash and PCM, are becoming increasingly mature. The NAND flash has better performance over traditional magnetic hard disks and has been widely deployed in practical storage

---

* Corresponding author.

X.-h. Sun et al. (Eds.): ICA3PP 2014, Part II, LNCS 8631, pp. 339–351, 2014.

systems. However, the performance of NAND flash (in us) is still significantly lower than DRAM (in ns). In contrast, PCM is a scalable technology that has read latency close to that of DRAM, which makes it a promising alternative to the main memory [5]. A performance comparison among DRAM, NAND flash memory and PCM is summarized in Table 1, which reveals that PCM has most of the combined advantages of DRAM and NAND flash.

Table 1. Comparison of DRAM, NAND Flash and PCM [5]

Characteristics	DRAM	NAND Flash	PCM
Cell Size	$6\text{-}8F^2$	$4\text{-}6F^2$	$4\text{-}20F^2$
Read Time	~10ns	5-50μs	**10-100ns**
Write Time	~10ns	2-3ms	**100-1000ns**
Standby Power	Leakage	Zero	Zero
Write Endurance	10^{15}	10^5	$10^8\text{-}10^{12}$
Non-volatility	No	Yes	Yes

Unfortunately, the PCM devices also have their own shortcomings: the long write latency, high write energy, and limited write endurance, besides the severely constrained write bandwidth [10]. First, it takes much more time to program (i.e., write) a PCM cell than a DRAM cell. Second, the programming of a PCM cell takes much more energy than a DRAM write. To provide the same write bandwidth, PCM may require 5 times more power than that of DRAM. The asymmetrical write/read latency makes PCM unsuitable for storing frequently modified data.

Data deduplication is a specialized data compression technique [7]. It divides the data into non-intersecting chunks and employs a cryptographic hash to represent each chunk. By storing only the unique chunk, identified by the corresponding hash value also known as fingerprint, duplicate chunks in data are removed from the write process. Data deduplication has been extensively used in archival and backup systems and primary storage systems, such as VM and flash-based SSDs [8,9], but its benefits to PCM have not been fully explored.

To reduce the number of PCM writes, we propose content aware PCM, or CA-PCM, that employs the data deduplication technology to exploit the content locality in memory accesses. In order to minimize the computing and memory overhead caused by data deduplication, we design a lightweight data deduplication module to speed up fingerprint computing in the hash stores. Moreover, CA-PCM can leverage the abundance of processing power, such as Graphic Processing Unit (GPU) and multi-core processors, in computer systems to compute data chunks' fingerprints in data deduplication. This enables CA-PCM to accurately and quickly eliminate duplicate writes to PCM cells to improve the performance and reliability of PCM systems. To evaluate the efficiency of our proposed CA-PCM scheme, we implement its prototype by integrating it into an open-source PCM simulator PCMSim [20]. The experimental results show that CA-PCM improves the performance and reliability significantly.

The rest of this paper is organized as follows. Background and motivation are presented in Section 2. We describe the design and system architecture of CA-PCM in

Section 3. The performance evaluation and analysis are presented in Section 4. We review the related work in Section 5 and conclude this paper in Section 6.

2   Background and Motivation

2.1   PCM Basics

PCM uses the different resistivity between the crystalline (low resistivity) and the amorphous (high resistivity) phase of the phase change material to store the data. By dividing the large range of resistance into different levels, a PCM cell can store several bits of information. The reset operation changes the PCM cell into the amorphous phase by a large but short-duration current pulse. The set operation changes the PCM cell into the crystalline phase with a medium but long-duration current pulse [4]. Figure 1 shows the set and reset processes in the PCM device.

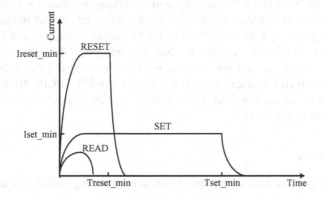

Fig. 1. The set and reset processes of PCM

The read latency of PCM is about 10~100ns, which is close to that of DRAM. The program codes can be directly executed after reading from PCM without the need to put them into RAM. Unlike DRAM, PCM is non-violate, allowing data stored in PCM to be persistent. Moreover, without the frequent fresh operation, the power consumption, a key criterion in today's computer design, can be greatly decreased. Among existing types of random access memory, PCM has obvious advantages over SRAM and DRAM. With a multi-level cell design (MLC), PCM can achieve even greater densities by storing multiple bits in one bit cell. Therefore, PCM can provide much higher capacity than DRAM.

However, PCM also has drawbacks: long write latency, high write energy, and limited write endurance, relative to DRAM. A PCM device may endure around 100 million write cycles and often fails either stuck open or stuck close for a PCM cell. After many rewrites, the PCM cell failures become much easier. It is a more serious problem when applying PCM in applications with frequent writes. Thus, reducing the write operations is critical to both the performance and reliability of PCM devices.

2.2   Data Deduplication

Data deduplication splits files or data blocks into multiple roughly equal-sized data chunks that are each uniquely identified by a fingerprint that is a hash signature of the data chunk. The redundant data chunks in a file or data block are replaced by the pointers that point to their corresponding unique data chunks. When data arrives, it will be split into multiple data chunks, each of which is associated with a computed hash value (i.e., fingerprint). Then the index-lookup process tries to find the redundant data chunks from the index table according to the hash values. When a redundant data chunk is identified, the logic block address (*LBA*) value of the data chunk in the index table will be obtained and kept in the metadata. Then only the unique data chunks are written and the redundant data chunks are replaced with the pointers in the metadata.

Data deduplication has been an essential and critical component in backup and archiving storage systems. It not only reduces the storage space requirements, but also improves the throughput of the backup and archiving systems by eliminating the network transmission of redundant data. Recent studies reveal that moderate to high data redundancy clearly exists in VM (Virtual Machine), enterprise and HPC storage systems. These studies have shown that by applying the data deduplication technology to large-scale data sets, an average space saving of 30%, with up to 90% in VM and 70% in HPC storage systems can be achieved [17,18,19,20]. For example, data deduplication has been applied in the VM servers and SSDs to save storage space and reduce write traffic [8,9].

2.3   Motivation

PCM has a comparable read access speed to and better energy efficiency than DRAM. It relies on analog current and thermal effects and does not require control over discrete electrons. As technologies scale and heating contact areas shrink, programming current scales linearly. As a scalable DRAM alternative, PCM has a great potential for increasing main memory density and capacity. But there are still some existing disadvantages to overcome before this vision becomes reality. Whether as a flash replacement currently or as a DRAM replacement in the future, the write endurance and write latency of the PCM device are the key problems to be solved. Thus, reducing write traffic to PCM devices is critical for both performance and reliability.

On the other hand, data deduplication has been demonstrated in the literature and by commercial products to be an effective technique in backup, archiving, and primary storage systems such as VM servers and flash-based SSDs. Recent studies have shown that moderate to high data redundancy clearly exists in primary storage systems. It can greatly reduce the duplicate writes to the storage devices, thus reducing the response times and saving storage space. However, directly applying data deduplication to PCM devices to reduce write traffic will likely cause computational and memory overhead.

Based on these important observations, we propose content aware PCM that employs a lightweight data deduplication module to exploit the content locality in memory accesses. By exploiting the data redundancy in memory accesses, CA-PCM is able to greatly reduce the amount of programming in PCM cells to improve both the performance and reliability of PCM devices.

3   CA-PCM

3.1   Design Objective

CA-PCM aims to improve the performance and reliability of PCM devices. CA-PCM uses a lightweight data deduplication module to reduce the duplicated data chunks, thus avoiding the repeated write to the memory. CA-PCM not only improves the write performance, but also improves the read performance by freeing up more PCM bandwidth to the read accesses. Moreover, by reducing the write traffic, the PCM cell programming count is also reduced, which significantly enhances the lifespan of the PCM cells and thus the reliability of PCM devices.

3.2   System Overview

Figure 2 shows a system overview of our proposed CA-PCM. CA-PCM consists of two modules: the data deduplicator module and the I/O distributor module. The former is responsible for computing the fingerprints of the incoming write data chunks and updating the Index_table that stores the fingerprints and locations of the data chunks. The latter is responsible for issuing the I/O requests to the corresponding locations based on the Map_table that keeps the data mapping information.

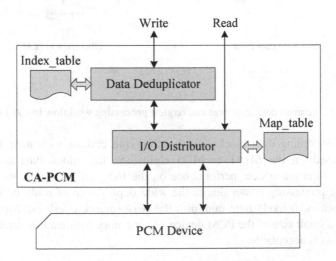

Fig. 2. System overview of CA-PCM

Figure 3 shows the two main data structures and their relationship in CA-PCM: Index_table and Map_table. In the Index_table, the *Key* and physical block address (*Pba*) values in an entry indicate the fingerprint and physical location information of a data chunk. The Count value indicates how many times the data chunk is referenced by other data blocks, i.e., the number of duplicate chunks of the data chunk. The *LBA* value in Map_table indicates the logical address of a user request and the *Pba* value indicates its physical address in the PCM device. The Map_table maps deduplicated write data chunks to their unique counterparts stored in PCM by storing the *LBAs* of the former and the *Pbas* of the latter. This also helps incoming user read requests locate their read data.

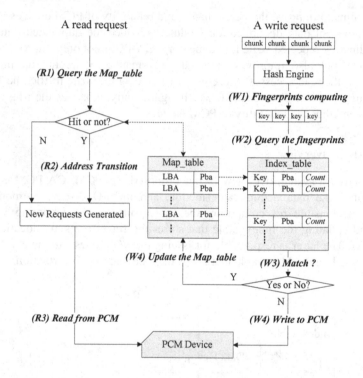

Fig. 3. The main data structures and request processing workflow in CA-PCM

Since the incoming data blocks will be split into chunks with their fingerprints computed based on the SHA1 or MD5 algorithm, the added data deduplication module will affect the system performance on the I/O path. However, the increasing abundance of processing power due to the wide deployment of multi-core and GPU processing units will likely help minimize the performance overhead. Moreover, due to the relative small size of the PCM device, the memory overhead incurred in storing the fingerprints is acceptable.

3.3   Request Processing Workflow

Figure 3 also shows the request processing workflows in CA-PCM. For a read request, CA-PCM first checks the Map_table. If it hits, the data will be fetched from the PCM address pointed to by the matched *Pba* value in the Map_table. Otherwise, the read request is returned with data stored in the requested address.

When a write request arrives, the data deduplicator module in CA-PCM first splits the data into multiple data chunks, calculates their fingerprints, and identifies the redundant data chunks by comparing the fingerprints of these data chunks with those in the Index_table. For the incoming data chunks whose fingerprints find matches in the Index_table, they will not be actually written to the PCM device since they are confirmed redundant. Instead, the Map_table will be updated to record the write data by adding an LBA-Pba entry, also called a redirected log. For all the other write data, CA-PCM processes these requests in the free space with the out-of-place update strategy.

3.4   Data Consistency Issue

Data consistency is critical in the design of new storage systems. Two aspects are carefully considered in CA-PCM: (1) The Map_table must be reliably stored; (2) the user read requests must fetch the up-to-date data.

First, to prevent the loss of the Map_table in the event of a power supply failure or a system crash, CA-PCM stores the contents of the Map_table in a non-volatile memory, such as a certain reserved space in PCM. Since the size of the Map_table is general small, a capacitor may delay shutdown until the RAM content is safely saved to an area of PCM device reserved for the purpose.

Second, since the write data may have been scattered across the PCM from data deduplication, each incoming read request is first checked in the Map_table to fetch all the data chunks to keep the fetched data always up-to-date.

4   Performance Evaluation

4.1   Experimental Setup and Methodology

We have implemented a prototype of CA-PCM by incorporating it into the PCMSim simulator. PCMSim [20] is a block device driver for Linux that simulates the presence of a PCM device in the system installed in one of the DIMM slots on the motherboard. It is implemented as a kernel module for Linux that creates /dev/pcm0 when it is loaded. The experiments are conducted on a single system with an Intel Xeon X3440 CPU. In the system, a Seagate 500GB HDD is used to host the operating system (Ubuntu Linux 2.6.35) and other software. We use a set of trace-driven experiments to evaluate the efficiency of CA-PCM and compare it with a system without any data deduplication ("Native" for short).

The three traces used in our experiments are obtained from the SyLab of FIU [7] covering a duration of three weeks. They are collected from a virtual machine running a file server (Homes), an email server (Mail) and two web servers (Web-vm), respectively. Each request in the traces includes the hash value of the requested data. Because the original request data have been split into several small data chunks with a fixed size (e.g., 4KB or 512B), the original requests are reconstructed according to their timestamp, *LBA* and length. In order to simulate the hash-computing overhead of each data chunk, we added around 100,000 CPU cycles for fingerprint-computing delay to each process of writing a 4KB data chunk, which is an overestimation for the processors in modern computer systems [7]. It is time-consuming to replay the whole three-week's trace, so we chose to replay the 8th day's trace with burst periods. The three traces are shown in Table 2.

Table 2. The characteristics of the three traces

Traces	Write Ratio	I/Os	Average Request Size
Homes	80.5%	64,819	13.1 KB
Mail	78.5%	328,145	40.8 KB
Web-vm	69.8%	154,105	14.8 KB

4.2   Performance Results and Analysis

Figure 4 shows the normalized average response times of the two schemes driven by the three traces. CA-PCM speeds up the Native system in the average response-time performance by a factor of 2.1, 4.8 and 2.5 for the Homes, Mails and Web-vm traces, respectively. The reason is that the write ratios of all the three traces are very high, making the write latency the dominant factor in the overall user response time. Moreover, CA-PCM also improves the read performance indirectly by substantially reducing the write traffic. That is, the significant number of reduced write requests in CA-PCM greatly shortens the length of the I/O queue of PCM cells and relieves its pressure, thus allowing the read requests to be serviced more quickly.

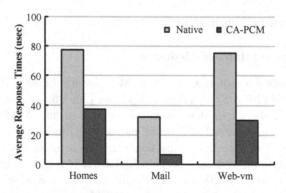

Fig. 4. Average response time driven by the three traces

Figure 5 shows the average response times of two schemes as the three traces are being replayed. We can see that CA-PCM outperform the native scheme in terms of user response times. This is because CA-PCM deduplicates the redundant write data on the I/O path, which effectively shortens the I/O queues and allows the remaining write requests to be serviced on the PCM more quickly. The shortened I/O queues also indirectly improve read performance, especially for the mail trace where the read burstiness and write burstiness are mixed. Moreover, as write requests are very expensive for PCM devices due to the long write latency as that elaborated in Section 2.1, reducing write requests has the effect of freeing up more PCM resources to service the read requests.

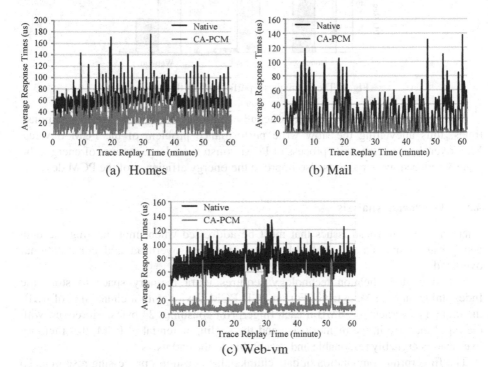

(a) Homes

(b) Mail

(c) Web-vm

Fig. 5. The average response times of two schemes as a function of the replaying time driven by the three traces: (a) Homes, (b) Mail, and (c) Web-vm.

To better understand the reasons behind the significant performance improvement, we also plot the percentage of the I/O requests that are performed on the PCM device, as shown in Figure 6. The actual write requests that are performed on the PCM device is normalized to the Native system. CA-PCM reduces the number of write requests by 48%, 97% and 73% for the Homes, Mail and Web-vm traces, respectively. The number of I/O requests that are performed on the PCM device is reduced significantly, leading to significant reductions in the average response times for the three traces. Generally, a typical cell of PCM can bear at most 10^8 writes before failure strikes, making the lifetime of PCM directly proportional to the number of writes per cell. Thus, these results suggest that CA-PCM is able to at least double the average lifespan of the PCM device. They also suggest that the higher the write redundancy in an application, the higher the improvement in performance and lifespan of the PCM device.

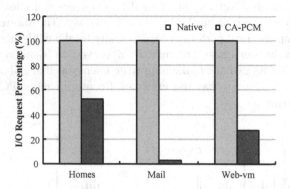

Fig. 6. The I/O requests performed on the device

The reduced write traffic also significantly improves on the user average response times, thus alleviating the slow write performance problem of the PCM devices. Moreover, because the write process of PCM consumes a large amount of energy, the greatly reduced write requests also improve the energy efficiency of the PCM device.

4.3   Overhead Analysis

There are two overhead issues that must be addressed when implementing the data deduplication module into a PCM system: memory overhead and computational overhead.

The data deduplication technology requires extra memory space to store the Index_table and the Map_table. For an 8GB PCM device with a chunk size of 4KB, the memory overhead is 48MB if each fingerprint consumes 24 bytes. Moreover, with the rapid increase in the memory size and the scaling potential of PCM, this memory overhead is arguably reasonable and acceptable to the end users.

The fingerprint computation of data chunks also consumes processing resource. To reduce the computational overhead, CA-PCM uses the low-overhead fix-size chunking scheme, rather than the high-overhead variable size and content-defined chunking schemes, to calculate the fingerprint to identify the redundant data chunks. Moreover, today's GPUs and multi-core processors make the computer systems more powerful, allowing them to extend their capabilities to integrate new techniques, such as data deduplication.

5   Related Work

The limited write endurance and long write-latency are the two main drawbacks of the PCM devices. Many studies have been conducted to address the two problems.

Flip-N-Write [3] uses a simple read-modify-write technique to write either flipped or un-flipped data by comparing the original data and the newly written data to reduce the response time. The two-stage-write scheme [4] separates the write process of a cache line into two different stages: write-1 stage that writes all 1-valued bits of the target cache line, and write-0 stage that writes all 0-valued bits. By leveraging the asymmetric properties for writing "1" and "0", two-stage-write speeds up the write operations of zeros and increases the degree of parallelism for writing ones. The write cancellation and write pausing strategy [6] is proposed to avoid the read performance degradation caused by the slow write process. It services the read request first when a newly arriving read request falls on the same bank with the ongoing write request in the PCM device. By logging changed bytes instead of the entire block, Shortcut-JFS [11] reduces write requests to the PCM device with a Journaling file system. The PCM-aware swap algorithm [14] uses a new cache replacement policy to avoid the unnecessary writes and leverages the wear-leveling to extend the lifetime of a PCM main memory. The start-gap wear-leveling technique [15] uses only two registers to improve the PCM endurance with negligible overhead.

DRAM-PCM hybrid memory systems have become popular in the research community [6], [12], [16]. In these studies, the main idea is to exploit the advantages of both DRAM and PCM and avoid their disadvantages. For example, Qureshiet al. [5] propose a PCM-based hybrid main memory system that uses a small amount of DRAM as a write buffer of the PCM memory in order to prolong the lifetime of PCM and hide the long write latency of PCM. The page-attribute-aware memory allocation policy [13] tries to place read-only pages in PCM, while loads writable pages into DRAM in a hybrid PCM-DRAM memory system, thereby reducing the write requests to the PCM device.

While all these studies on PCM devices address the write endurance and write performance issues, none has exploited, or adequately exploited the content locality in memory accesses. Our proposed CA-PCM uses a lightweight data deduplication module at the system level and leverages the system computing resources to significantly reduce the write traffic to the PCM devices, thus improving both the performance and reliability.

6   Conclusion and Future Work

The PCM technology is a prime alternative or complement to DRAM-based main memory. To address PCM's inherent problems of write endurance and write latency, we proposed CA-PCM that employs a lightweight data deduplication to exploit the content locality in memory accesses to reduce the write traffic. We have implemented a prototype of CA-PCM by integrating it into an open-source PCM simulator PCMSim. The trace-driven simulation results show that CA-PCM improves the performance and reliability significantly.

The CA-PCM study is an ongoing research project in which we are currently exploring several directions for the future work. First, we will add the similarity identification module in the CA-PCM system to further reduce the partial redundant write data blocks. Second, we will use more applications and workloads to investigate the performance and memory overhead of the CA-PCM in our evaluations. Third, we will build a power measurement module to evaluate the energy efficiency of the proposed CA-PCM scheme. Because energy efficiency is an increasingly important system design goal, we believe that CA-PCM will improve the energy efficiency of PCM devices by reducing the write traffic.

Acknowledgement. We thank the SyLab in FIU for providing us with the I/O traces. This work is supported by the China National Natural Science Foundation No. 61100033, the US NSF under Grant No. NSF-CNS-1116606, NSF-CNS-1016609, NSF-IIS-0916859, NSF-CCF-0937993, the Scientific Research Foundation for the Returned Overseas Chinese Scholars, State Education Ministry, and the Fundamental Research Funds for the Central Universities. This work is also sponsored by Huawei Innovation Research Program and the Equipments Donation from Intel Shanghai.

References

1. Schaller, R.: Technological innovation in the semiconductor industry: A case study of the International Technology Roadmap for Semiconductors (ITRS). George Mason University (2004)
2. Raoux, S., Burr, G., Breitwisch, M.: Phase-change random access memory: A scalable technology. IBM Journal of Research and Development 52, 465–479 (2008)
3. Cho, S., Lee, H.: Flip-N-Write: A Simple Deterministic Technique to Improve PRAM Write Performance, Energy and Endurance. In: Proceedings of the 42nd Annual IEEE/ACM International Symposium on Microarchitecture, pp. 347–357. IEEE Press, New York (2009)
4. Yue, J., Zhu, Y.: Accelerating Write by Exploiting PCM Asymmetries. In: Proceedings of the IEEE 19th International Symposium on High Performance Computer Architecture, pp. 282–293. IEEE Press, Shenzhen (2013)
5. Qureshi, M.K., Srinivasan, V., Rivers, J.A.: Scalable high performance main memory system using phase-change memory technology. In: Proceedings of the 36th International symposium on Computer Architecture, pp. 24–33. ACM, New York (2009)
6. Moinuddin, M.F., Qureshi, K., Lastras, L.: Improving Read Performance of PCM via Write Cancellation and Write Pausing. In: Proceedings of IEEE 16th International Symposium on High Performance Computer Architecture, pp. 1–11. IEEE Press, Bangalore (2010)
7. Koller, R., Rangaswami, R.: I/O Deduplication: Utilizing Content Similarity to Improve I/O Performance. In: ACM Transactions on Storage, vol. 6. ACM, New York (2010)
8. Chen, F., Luo, T., Zhang, X.: CAFTL: a Content-aware Flash Translation Layer Enhancing the Lifespan of Flash Memory based Solid State Drives. In: Proceedings of the 9th USENIX Conference on File and Storage Technologies, vol. 11. FAST, San Jose (2011)
9. Gupta, A., Pisolkar, R., Urgaonkar, B., Sivasubramaniam, A.: Leveraging Value Locality in Optimizing NAND Flash-based SSDs. In: Proceedings of the 9th USENIX Conference on File and Storage Technologies, pp. 91–103. FAST, San Jose (2011)
10. Lee, B., Ipek, E.: Architecting Phase Change Memory as a Scalable DRAM Alternative. In: Proceedings of the 36th Annual International Symposium on Computer Architecture, pp. 2–13. ACM, New York (2009)

11. Lee, E., Yoo, S., Jang, J.: Shortcut-JFS: A Write Efficient Journaling File System for PCM. In: Proceedings of the 28th IEEE Conference on Massive Data Storage, pp. 1–6. IEEE Press, San Diego (2012)
12. Ipek, E., Condit, J., Nightingale, E.B., Burger, D., Moscibroda, T.: Dynamically Replicated Memory: Building Reliable systems from Nanoscale Resistive Memories. In: Proceedings of the International Conference on Architectural Support for Programming Languages and Operating Systems, pp. 3–14. ACM, New York (2010)
13. Mogul, J.C., Argollo, E., Shah, M., Faraboschi, P.: Operating system support for NVM+DRAM hybrid main memory. In: Proceedings of the 12th Workshop on Hot Topics in Operating Systems (2009)
14. Ferreira, A., Zhou, M., Bock, S.: Increasing PCM main memory lifetime. In: Proceedings of the Conference on Design, Automation and Test in Europe, pp. 914–919. EDAA, Belgium (2010)
15. Qureshi, M., Karidis, J., Franceschini, M., Srinivasan, V., Lastras, L.: Enhancing Lifetime and Security of PCM-Based Main Memory with Start-Gap Wear Leveling. In: Proceedings of the 42nd Annual IEEE/ACM International Symposium on Microarchitecture, pp. 14–23. ACM, New York (2009)
16. Kim, H., Seshadri, S., Dickey, C., Chiu, L.: Evaluating Phase Change Memory for Enterprise Storage Systems: A Study of Caching and Tiering Approaches. In: Proceedings of the 12th USENIX Conference on File and Storage Technologies, pp. 33–45. FAST, Santa Clara (2014)
17. Mao, B., Jiang, H., Wu, S., Fu, Y., Tian, L.: Read Performance Optimization for Deduplication-based Storage Systems in the Cloud. In: ACM Transactions on Storage, vol. 10. ACM, New York (2014)
18. Mao, B., Jiang, H., Wu, S., Tian, L.: POD: Performance Oriented I/O Deduplication for Primary Storage Systems in the Cloud. In: Proceedings of the 28th IEEE International Parallel & Distributed Processing Symposium (2014)
19. Srinivasan, K., Bisson, T., Goodson, G., Voruganti, K.: iDedup: Latency-aware, Inline Data Deduplication for Primary Storage. In: Proceedings of the 9th USENIX Conference on File and Storage Technologies, vol. 12, pp. 1–14. FAST, San Jose (2012)
20. Elshimi, A., Kalach, R., Kumar, A., Oltean, A., Li, J., Sengupta, S.: Primary Data Deduplication–Large Scale Study and System Design. In: Proceedings of the 2012 USENIX Annual Technical Conference, pp. 285–296. FAST, San Jose (2012)

Application of Support Vector Machine in the Decision-Making of Maneuvering

Zhuang Qi[1], Zheng Chang[2], Hanbang Song[1], and Xinyu Zhang[1]

[1] Navigation College, Dalian Maritime University, Dalian 116026, China
{qizhuang,songhanbang,zhangxinyu}@dlmu.edu.cn
[2] Transportation Management College, Dalian Maritime University, Dalian 116026, China
changzheng@dlmu.edu.cn

Abstract. To get the best course and speed navigating in stormy waves, establish the sea-keeping assessment model based on Support Vector Machine method, verify the accuracy of the model with sea-keeping estimation equation, and finally apply it in decision making of maneuvering. It turns out that the assessment model works well. The conclusions provide references for maneuvering in stormy waves.

Keywords: Support Vector Machine, Sea-keeping, Decision-making of Maneuvering.

1   Introduction

When ships are sailing in the stormy waves, course and speed are the two basic elements in maneuvering, which are very important for the safety of navigation. There are a lot of articles researching on decision-making of course and speed navigating in stormy waves, which analyzed from multiple factors to optimize course and speed, but we found that, due to some reasons, the analysis and research before are not practical and difficult to guide practice through the survey, which did not combine with actual control of the ship well, such as complex calculation process. The author has used the BP neural network to build seakeeping evaluation model [1], the evaluation result is ideal, but the actual calculation time is about two hours, which has certain limitation and it is not suitable for the actual manipulation, so this article is to discuss on ship maneuvering decision making problems based on support vector mechanism (SVM) theory. According to the structural risk minimization criterion, Support Vector Machine theory can improve the ability of learning machine's generalization ability(forecasting), and it is better to solve practical problems such as the small sample, nonlinear high dimension, local minimum point and so on[2]. Relevant scholars have done a lot of comparisons on the BP neural network and SVM [3, 4], and the results show that compared with the BP neural network, SVM theory has unique advantages.

Based on the theory of SVM, this article is to build the seakeeping evaluation model, verify the evaluation model with the seakeeping evaluation equation, and guide the actual manipulation of the ship.

X.-h. Sun et al. (Eds.): ICA3PP 2014, Part II, LNCS 8631, pp. 352–358, 2014.

2   Basic Principle of Support Vector Machine

The basic idea of Support Vector Machine is to make the input space map to a high-dimensional space through nonlinear mapping, put the insensitive function in it, build the optimal hyperplane, and sum up the algorithm of search for optimal hyperplane to a solving constrained convex quadratic problem [5].

Assuming that the training set is $\{(x_1,y_1), \dots , (x_n,y_n)\}$, $x_i \in R^d$, $y \in R$, $F = \{f \mid f : R^d \rightarrow R\}$, So the Support Vector Machine regression problem is to look for a linear function $f \in F$, minimize the expected risk, which is to fit samples with the hyperplane function $f(x) = w \times x + b$. Nonlinear regression estimation function is $f(x) = (w \times \varphi(x)) + b$, in which $\varphi(x)$ is the nonlinear mapping from input space to high dimension space, w is weight coefficient, and b is offset.

In the Support Vector Machine regression, the loss function L is defined as insensitive function, which represents the maximum offset is up to ε between function f(x) and the sample observation value. The ξ_i and ξ_i^* are slack variable, so the problem of looking for optimal hyperplane is converted into the following constrained optimization problem:

$$\min \phi(w,b,\xi_i,\xi_i^*) = \frac{1}{2}\|w\|^2 + c\sum(\xi_i + \xi_i^*) \tag{1}$$

$$s.t.\begin{cases} y_i - w \times \varphi(x_i) - b \le \varepsilon + \xi_i \\ -y_i + w \times \varphi(x_i) - b \le \varepsilon + \xi_i^* \\ \xi_i \ge 0, \ \xi_i^* \ge 0 \end{cases} \tag{2}$$

in which c is the penalty function, which is used to adjust the degree of punishment on ε. The larger the C and the smaller the ε, the higher the training precision is, but the generalization ability is worse.

We can convert the above problem into the dual optimization problem by Lagrange function:

$$\min \frac{1}{2}\sum_{i,j=1}^{n}(a_i - a_i^*)(a_j - a_j^*)(\varphi(x_i)\varphi(x_j)) + \sum_{i=1}^{n}\varepsilon(a_i + a_i^*) - \sum_{i=1}^{n}y_i(a_i - a_i^*) \tag{3}$$

$$s.t.\begin{cases} \sum_{i=1}^{n}(a_i - a_i^*) = 0 \\ 0 \le a_i, \ a_i^* \le c \end{cases} \tag{4}$$

So we can obtain nonlinear regression estimate function:

$$f(x,a,a^*) = \sum_{i=1}^{n}(a_i^* - a_i)k(x_i,x) + b \qquad (5)$$

$(a_i^* - a_i) = m_i$ is Lagrange multiplier, corresponding data point of m_i (non-zero) is the support vector of model. Kernel function is: $k(x_i,x) = \varphi(x_i)\varphi(x_j)$. Therefore when calculating regression estimation function, we can only calculate kernel function and do not need to calculate $\varphi(\bullet)$, so that the complexity of the calculation depends on the number of samples, especially the number of support vector, which avoid the dimension disaster problem of high-dimensional space.

Common functions used to detect the precision of SVM are the relative error function and the root mean square error function. Relative error function is used to detect prediction effect for each test sample of model:

$$Error(n) = \frac{|x(n,true) - x(n,pred)|}{|x(n,true)|} \qquad (6)$$

Root mean square error   function is used to detect overall prediction effect:

$$RMS = Sqrt(\frac{1}{N}\sum_{n=1}^{N}(x(n,true) - x(n,pred))^2) \qquad (7)$$

3   Seakeeping Evaluation Based on Support Vector Machine

3.1   Model of the Process

Figure 1 is the process of the seakeeping evaluation model based on SVM, including four steps: The first step is the determination of evaluation index; the second step is to collect learning samples, including training samples and testing samples. Training samples are used to establish model. Test samples are used to test model prediction ability, normalized to process the sample data, and then the index's linear stretches to [0, 1]. The third step is to select learning parameters and obtain knowledge of the SVM, including nuclear parameter, tolerance error ε, penalty parameter c, nuclear parameter g, and train the selected samples, after adaptive learning, get training support vector and its coefficient values, build the decision function; The last is the establishment of seakeeping evaluation model, and using the decision function to identify the safety status of seakeeping test samples and determine its level.

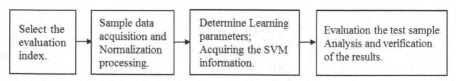

Fig. 1. Evaluation process based on SVM

3.2   Determine the Seakeeping Evaluation Indicators

There are many wave resistance factors influencing the safe navigation of the ship, generally ships' seakeeping indexes contain fore roll, pitch, roll, heave, surge, sway, a transverse section acceleration, hull deck drown, propeller, lateral acceleration, slamming, deck water waves, stall, longitudinal wave bending moment, stability loss, seasick rate and control performance deterioration, etc. Regarding the tanker as the research object and considering the factors offered by the seakeeping criterion of the China ship scientific research center, this article sums up the most important wave resistance factors that affect the safe navigation of the tanker in the stormy waves, respectively: roll, pitch and heave, deck bow wave, propeller water, slamming and vertical acceleration[1].

3.3   The Pretreatment of the Sample Data

In this paper, a total of 30 samples is designed, sample data is derived by the spectrum analysis method of ships in irregular waves and seakeeping evaluation equation [1][7], and regardi 1~25 samples as training samples of support vector machine and 26 ~ 30 samples as test samples to test the model performance.

For the convenience of calculation, first of all, the sample data are normalized processing, and observe the various index score as the input variables of the model, namely $P_1 \sim P_7$ (on behalf of all the seakeeping evaluation index), calculate the value through the evaluation of seakeeping comprehensive evaluation equation and regard it as the output variable, and the R_x is seakeeping evaluation value under the certain course and speed. The smaller the value of R_x, the more dangerous the ship. The input and output vectors constitute model training set, and part of the sample data are shown in table 1.

Table 1. The sample data of ship seakeeping

SERIAL	P_1	P_2	P_3	P_4	P_5	P_6	P_7	R_x
1	0	0.79	0.81	0.08	0.2	0.14	0.04	0.6235
2	0.3	0.54	0.65	0.15	0.1	0.14	0.12	0.5878
3	0.94	0.67	0.81	0.46	0.3	0.43	0.24	0.2156
4	0.67	0	0.01	0.15	0	0	0.44	0.6479
5	0.52	0.79	0.87	0.46	0.4	0.57	0.76	0.2578
6	0.34	0.87	0.65	0	0.5	0.71	0.68	0.3602
7	0	0.59	0.76	0.23	0.4	1	0.56	0.4667
...	...	...	...	...	...	...	...	...
26	0.14	0.78	0.92	0.46	0.9	0.86	0.76	0.27
27	0.89	0.31	0.38	0.23	0	0.29	0.4	0.4263
28	0.89	0.23	0.11	0.31	0.6	0.43	0.28	0.3758
29	0.56	0.69	0.76	0.38	0.3	0.57	0.72	0.3027
30	0.52	0.67	0.87	0.46	0.9	0.71	1	0.1634

3.4   Parameter Selection

Due to the forecast ability of Gaussian radial basis kernel function is not less than high order polynomial kernel function and type-S kernel function, this article chooses the kernel function, and tolerance error is set to $1e$-5 at the same time. The determination of penalty parameter and nuclear parameters is using cross-validation, the results show that when $c = 80$ and $g = 0.8$, root mean square error of the model get the smallest MSE=1.9036e-07, which is the best SVM model at this time.

3.5   Model Training and the Result Analysis

According to the selected model parameters, use Libsvm-3.11 software package in MATLAB to calculate and the coefficient $b = 0.3837$, finally get a total of 12 support vector(the risk of data of the ship), respectively: 1, 2, 4, 7, 8, 9, 11, 15, 18, 20, 21, 27. So get the seakeeping risk prediction model of SVM:

$$f(x,a,a^*) = \sum_{i=1}^{n}(a_i^* - a_i)k(x_i,x) + 0.3837 \tag{8}$$

x_i (i=1,2,4,7,8,9,11,15,18,20,21,27) is a support vector of the model, x is a vector wave resistance index for the evaluation, the value of the Lagrange multiplier is as follows: m_1=0.2398, m_2=0.2041, m_4=0.2642, m_7=0.0830, m_8=0.3000, m_9=0.1865, m_{11}=0.1783, m_{15}=0.2563, m_{18}=0.0290, m_{20}=0.0280, m_{21}=0.3161, m_{27}=0.0426.

Calculate five test samples at the back of all the seakeeping indexes in table 1 and get risk value in table 2. The results show that when use the SVM model, the relative error value of the test sample is smaller(within 1%). It can meet the precision requirement of the ship's seakeeping risk assessment model.

Table 2. Compared the SVM evaluation results with the original data

Sample data	SVM evaluation result	Original data	Relative error
26	0.2636	0.27	-0.0064
27	0.4326	0.4263	0.0063
28	0.3801	0.3758	0.0043
29	0.2968	0.3027	-0.0059
30	0.1694	0.1634	0.006

The evaluation results of the support vector machine and the actual value is very close, and the relative error is within the acceptable range. The result shows that compared with the BP neural network, the generalization ability of SVM theory is stronger, the optimal solution is more precise and convergence speed is faster, about 5 minutes. So the model can be applied to the ship's seakeeping evaluation well and guide practice.

4   Ship Maneuvering Decisions

A 20000-ton ocean liner vessel parameters are: the length over all=170 m, breadth =25.00 m, moulded depth=12.60m, draft=9.5 m, drainage volume V=31331m^3, water-plane area A_w=3621m^2, midship section area A_m=235.60m^2. The ship sailed on the north Pacific, at that time the wind force is 7, significant wave height is 7 m, and wave characteristics of the cycle is 8.7s[1].

Ship's initial speed is 15kn, the initial course is 120°, and the wave to course angle is 60°. Change the ship's speed and course, and calculate the corresponding seakeeping factor value through the spectrum analysis method, as shown in table 3.

Table 3. The seakeeping indexes of four kinds of navigation status

SERIAL	P_1	P_2	P_3	P_4	P_5	P_6	P_7
Course120° Speed15kn	15.2	1.8	1.5	0.16	0.07	0.08	0.05
Course105° Speed15kn	2.8	1.5	1	0.1	0.05	0.04	0.03
Course120° Speed13kn	14.3	2.6	1.6	0.09	0.04	0.04	0.08
Course105° Speed13kn	4.5	2.1	1.3	0.05	0.02	0.02	0.05

Using evaluation model based on SVM to calculate seakeeping safety evaluation value, as shown in table 4.

Table 4. The Safety assessment of seakeeping under four kinds of navigation status

Speed (kn)	15	15	13	13
Course (°)	120	105	120	105
Safety assessment of seakeeping	0.1254	0.4512	0.2876	0.3871

In table 4, the seakeeping safety assessment value is greater, the ship is safer. According to the results of calculation, the ship is safer with the speed of 15 kn and course of 105°.

5   Conclusion

The choice of the course and speed of the ship in the stormy waves is essential to the safety of navigation, which still mainly depends on experiences judgment at sea. This paper evaluates the ship's seakeeping based on support vector mechanism theory, and the evaluation results can provide references for the choice of ship course and speed and have a certain practicality.

This article is just to put forward a solution to the choice of the course and speed, further work is still needed, such as ship form refinement, the establishment of the sample database, the accurate calculation of seakeeping indexes and the determination of index weight, and so on, and eventually establish an accurate evaluation model and make evaluation calculation software in order to guide practice.

Acknowledgements. This paper is supported by the Fundamental Research Funds for the Central Universities (3132013018/3132014083/3132014202), the National Natural Science Foundation of China (Grant No. 51309043), the Applied Basic Research of Ministry of Transport (Grant No. 2014329225020), and the natural science foundation of Liaoning Province (Grant No. 2014025005).

References

1. Li, S.Z., Wang, F.W., Liu, Q., Qi, Z.: SeakeepingEvaluation Based on BP Neural Network. Journal of Dalian Maritime University 38(1), 15–17 (2012) (in Chinese)
2. Wu, Z.Q.: TheResearch on the Evaluation for Investment Risk of Freeway Project Based on Support Vector Machine. Changsha Technical University (2009) (in Chinese)
3. Ai, N., Wu, Z.W., Ren, J.H.: Support Vector Machine and Artificial Neural Network. Journal of Shandong University of Technology 19(5), 45–49 (2005) (in Chinese)
4. Pan, X., Yang, R.Y.: The Research on Neural Networks with Enhanced Generalization and Support Vector Machine. Journal of Anqing Teachers College 13(1), 32–36 (2007) (in Chinese)
5. Bai, P., Zhang, X.B.: Theory of Support Vector Mechanism and the Examples of Engineering Application. Xi'an Electronic and Technology University Press (2008) (in Chinese)
6. Chang, Z., Lu, J.: Application of Support Vector Machine in the Evaluation of Dry Ports Investment Risk. Journal of Dalian Maritime University 38(2), 48–51 (2012) (in Chinese)
7. Xiong, W.H., Mao, X.F., Li, Y.J.: Review on Evaluation Methods and Criteria for Seakeeping of Ships. Ship & Ocean Engineering 36(4), 43–44 (2007) (in Chinese)
8. Vapnik, V.: An Overview of Statistical Learning Theory. IEEE Transaction on Neural Networks 10(5), 988–999 (1999)

Mobile Phone Data Reveal the Spatiotemporal Regularity of Human Mobility

Zihan Sun, Hanxiao Zhou, Jianfeng Zheng, and Yuhao Qin

School of Traffic and Transportation, Beijing Jiaotong University, Beijing, China
sunzihannuli@163.com

Abstract. Recent advance on human mobility are mainly based on mobile phone data since mobile phone records are the most detailed information across a large segment of the population in the modern society. With the spatiotemporal regularity missing in the individual and group level, we investigate the statistics of human mobility pattern using the mobile phone data provided by telecom in Guangdong, finding that the human activity pattern exhibits a heavy-tailed interval time distribution and regression property. We further demonstrate that the spatiotemporal characteristics can contribute to real-time travel prediction of human mobility and be applied in OD survey which is meaningful in traffic planning and management.

Keywords: spatiotemporal regularity, human mobility, Mobile phone data, OD research.

1 Introduction

When it comes to human mobility, we are lost in thought whether our activity pattern is random and unpredictable like the molecule or there exists hidden regularities? Much effort has been devoted to the study of detecting the human mobility pattern [1]. However, the traditional method is characterized by small sample and is hard to represent the group property, so the result is inaccurate and limited. With the inadequate data to quantize the characteristics and describe the microscopic pattern, the scientists have to turn to describe the statistical properties of their group [2]. There is an extraordinary need, therefore, to discover the spatiotemporal characteristics of human mobility.

With the development of the communication technology, we can get magnanimity data ranging from the Facebook, the Twitter, the mobile and etc. The scientists concentrate much on the regularity of human mobility in the individual level. Previous studies have assumed that human activity was randomly and well approximated by Poission process. To explore the regularity, the scientists analyze the distribution of the time intervals. They find that there is increasing evidence that the timing of many human activities follow non-Poisson statistics, characterized by bursts of rapidly occurring events separated by long periods of inactivity [3] The study indicates that there is complex dynamics mechanism in

X.-h. Sun et al. (Eds.): ICA3PP 2014, Part II, LNCS 8631, pp. 359–365, 2014.

human mobility. Immediately, the scientists conduct a series of evidential explorations. They exhibit the burst nature of human behavior and the strong evidence suggests that the human activity pattern exhibits a heavy-tailed interval time distribution. More specifically, Song [4] finds a remarkable lack of variability in predictability, which is largely independent of the distance users cover on a regular basis. These findings contribute to the study on human mobility while the regularity is more than these.

From another dimension, the scientists focus the mobile records themselves to explore the application in traffic. The analysis on mobile data can provide statistic property macroscopically as well as the support to traffic demand prediction. Involved in the characteristic of trip model, path matching and fuzzy identification, the method is validated that it is effective to take use of mobile phone data in splitting of OD survey. However, how to combine the effect of human mobility and the four stages on traffic demand analysis is still a problem for us to solve.

Our goal here is to detect the spatiotemporal characteristics of human mobility and apply the property to traffic planning and management. In this work, we quantify the movement of human mobility information based on the mobile phone data. We investigate the individual spatial distribution, finding that the individual tends to appear the places where they usually appear. And the heavy-tail property is revealed to explain the temporal characteristic in both the individual level and the group. Here we analyze the reason why the burst behavior occurs specifically. These findings are therefore significant to the prediction of human mobility. We believe that it is useful for OD survey and the result can be widely applied to traffic demand analysis.

2   Data

Since the most detailed information on human mobility is collected by mobile phone carriers, we capture part of mobile data collected from the telecom in Guangdong to discover the spatiotemporal characteristics of human mobility. Mobile carriers locate the closet mobile tower, as well as the timestamp, each time the user makes a call or sending a message. The longitude and the latitude of the mobile tower are recorded, allowing us to locate the accurate place the user appears. In order to guarantee data the reliability, we merely retain the continuous record of the users transient location at the preparation period. Meanwhile, we find that a large number of users engaged in infrequent communication and the record cant reflect the real travel activities. To deal with the problem, we capture the random mobile phone users and define them for active users with the criteria [5] that they visit more than two places during the observational period and that their average call or text message frequency f is $\geq 0.5 hour^{-1}$.

3 Result

3.1 Spatial Properties

To analyze the spatial feature of human mobility, we randomly select a typical active user and trying to describe his or her movement in August. We create the Voronoi diagrams based on the signal tower on the map in Guangdong. With the map is divided into several traffic zone by the Voronoi, we establish the corresponding relationship between communication network and geographical location network and the trajectory of the user is shown. (Fig.1a) Thus the travel chain which is the basis of the analysis on the residents travel is obtained. Obviously there exists an area in which the records are relatively concentrated. We capture the concentrated area for detail study. It reflects that the user appear the places frequently (Fig.1b). To investigate whether the frequent appearance signifies the recurrent nature of the individual mobility, we assign the user a mobility network (Fig.1c). From the scaling drawing, we can find that the user qualitatively tends to be in three places, maybe home or workplace. Quantitatively, we calculate the percent of quantities the user make calls or send messages in the particular zone and the result is visually described with the different node sizes. The non-uniform node sizes correspond to the preference to certain locations, indicate the individual mobility has a very significant regularity.

For further study on the distribution of the locations, we make some statistical analysis on the locations where the user appears in the one-month-long observational period (Fig.1d). Here we combine the scattered records under the criteria that the activities occurred within the scope of 4- nearby the respective tower. And on this basis, we respectively explore the probability the user appear in different places under different time sequences (Fig.1e). By rescaling, we find the results are highly integrated. In another word, the result reveals that the individual activity tends to exhibit the characteristics of regression. To some extent, this superposition of three lines in Fig.1e reveals the temporal correlation.

3.2 Temporal Properties

The fact that the individual activity has a very significant regularity in a week suggests us to find the regularity from the time dimension. Here we capture a-week long records and analyze their time distribution. The sequence obviously presents such a statement that there is a stateless period after some high-frequency acuteness activities (Fig.2a). It means the user tends to place most of his or her calls in short burst (Fig.2b). To detect the property of the burst accurately, we analyze the distribution of the time intervals between the users consecutive calls and find that the time intervals approximately follow a power-law. Then we capture abundant data from 2289 users to test whether the property fits the group. Finally we find a wide range of human activity patterns follow non-Poisson statistics. As is shown in Fig.3c, it allow for a long periods without activities that separate bursts of intensive activity. This behavior is characterized by heavy-tailed statistics. And we are amazed to find that there exists an

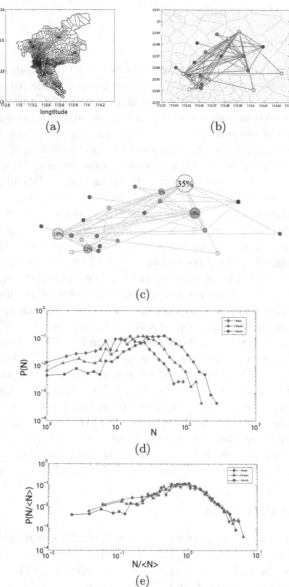

Fig. 1. (a) Trajectory diagram of the active user. Each time the user makes a call or send a message, the approximate location will be recorded shown as the colored dots. Connecting the dots in chronological order, we can get the trajectory or travel chain shown as the colored line. (b) Concentration of the active region. The connecting line represents the movement between two areas, and the different widths of line edges is made to express the frequency of the movement. (c) The mobility network. The proportion of the nodes corresponds to the frequency of calls the user made or the messages they sent in the area. (d) The number distribution of the location the user makes a call or sent a message. The different polygonal lines represent different time sequences: one week, two weeks and a month. (e) The rescaling result in the log-log plot.

obvious peak turns up at about ten hours, which is relative to the physiological period of human: the sleeping time are more or less ten hours. In conclusion, the observed the burst property reflects some fundamental and potentially generic feature of human dynamics and will serve as the basis of our mobility prediction.

We have investigated the spatiotemporal characteristics of human mobility both in the individual and the group level. From the space dimension, we find that human mobility presents the periodic trend. It means the travel places can be predicted. From the time dimension, we find that there exists a significant regularity of travel time. On second thoughts, we can obtain a new tool for travel demand analysis. It is meaningful for future transport planning and management and worth popularizing.

3.3   Application

Traditionally, to grasp the characteristics of traffic demand, we need to do traffic investigations through a series of steps like preparation, personnel training, investigation and etc. Since the late 1970s, home visiting and computer aided telephone interviews have been put into traffic investigations in Shanghai, Beijing and other cities due to the technical maturity. However, they also have some weakness, such as a lot of human cost, small sampling rate, long update cycle, the fact that the data accuracy is highly affected by the subjective factor and etc. Because of the disadvantages, these survey methods has not well adapted to urban transportation planning and the tube in the new period.

Nowadays, with the widespread popularity of the mobile phone market and the development of mobile phone positioning technology, it is possible to detect the characteristic of mobile phone user mobility based on massive amounts of positioning data analysis. According to our study on the spatiotemporal characteristics of human mobility, the conclusion can be applied in OD survey. We imagine an algorithm in which we can obtain all the travel data by prediction based on part of traditional OD data and the human mobility. To prove the accuracy, we can compare it with mobile phone travel data. If the fit is good, the algorithm can be widely used to obtain the group OD data. It will be another revolutionary breakthrough on traffic survey. Meanwhile, with the development of big data, we are provided a new way to correct the predicted result through massive mobile phone data.

Although taking traffic guidance is beyond our goals here, it is possible to obtain the certain place where the travel will go at certain time. Based on the spatiotemporal characteristics of human mobility, we can gain the peoples travel trend. Thus, the real-time traffic prediction can be realized which is significant to the road network analysis. Whats more, the transportation department can guide the traveler a better trip mode and travel rout. It is easy to ease traffic problems and meaningful in traffic planning and management. Here we give an example of OD result in Guangdong (Fig.3a-b) inaccurately to demonstrate our assumption.

364   Z. Sun et al.

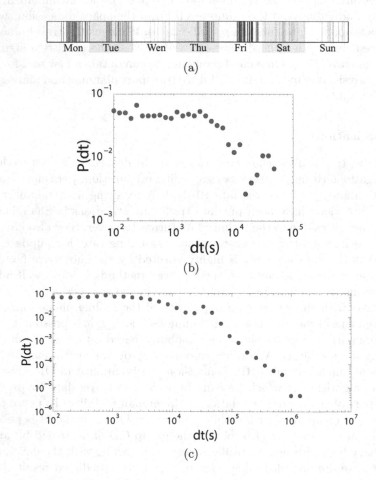

Fig. 2. (a) The call pattern that captures the time-dependent location in a week. Each vertical line represents to a call or message. (b)The distribution of the time intervals between the users consecutive calls during the one-month-long observational period, *dt*, documents the nature of the dynamical pattern as coming in bursts. (c) The distribution of the time intervals among the group, the scatter plot showing the number of calls made or messages sent during a month interval.

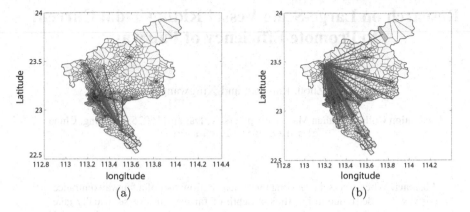

Fig. 3. (a) (b) The OD distribution of an special area in Guangzhou

4   Discussion

Taken together, we have studied the spatiotemporal characteristics of human mobility, and found that the human activity pattern exhibits a heavy-tailed interval time distribution and regression property in space. In summary, the empirical evidence indicates that the human mobility is characterized by a deep-rooted regularity. In the future, we may conduct further study on how to combine the effect of human mobility and the four stages on traffic demand analysis accurately and make traffic planning with instant mobile phone data. We believe the empirical findings in this paper present relevant information that can be used to explain human mobility, and will play an increasing important role in traffic planning and management.

Acknowledgments. This paper is partly supported by National Basic Research Program of China (2012CB725400) and Research Fund for the Doctoral Program of Higher Education of China (20130009120001). My studies depended on the contributions of Jianfeng Zheng. I have also bennifited from discussions with Hanxiao Zhou and Yuhao Qin.

References

1. Gonzalez, M.C., Hidalgo, C.A., Barabasi, A.L.: Understanding Individual Human Mobility Patterns. Nature 453(7196), 779–782 (2008)
2. Brockmann, D., Hufnagel, L., Geisel, T.: The Scaling Laws of Human Travel. Nature 439(7075), 462–465 (2006)
3. Barabasi, A.L.: The Origin of Bursts and Heavy Tails in Human Dynamics. Nature 435(7039), 207–211 (2005)
4. Chaoming, S., Blumm, N.: Limits of predictability in human mobility. Science 327(5968), 1018–1021 (2010)
5. Liang, G.: Song Chaoming: Quantifying Information Flow During Emergencies. Scientific Report (2014)

Research on Large-Scale Vessel Riding Tidal Current to Promote Efficiency of Fairway

Kang Zhou, Ran Dai, and Xingwang Yue

Navigation College, Dalian Maritime University, Dalian 116026, Liaoning, China
zhoukang@dlmu.edu.cn

Abstract. When a vessel is passing through a shallow part of a fairway (entrance fairway included), due to insufficient depth of fairway, the vessel usually take advantage of high tide level to enhance depth of navigable waterway. In normal situation, we only consider rise of tide and increase of waterway depth, and then the under keel clearance is consequently increased. But what we ignore is that the squat would drop due to the diminishment of relative speed between vessel and sea, when the vessel enters the fairway. Calculation of ship's squat when she is riding tidal current in a fairway is a foundation of making sure the under keel clearance of a vessel, thus to enhance efficiency of fairway and optimal use of tidal resource.

Keywords: under keel clearance (UKC), ship's squat, fairway efficiency.

1   Introduce

When a vessel is navigating in shallow water area or anchoring in anchorage,the shallower the water depth is, the more influence the ship will suffer from the fluid force. This would not only give rise to the manoeuvring difficulty, but put her into a dangerous situation when the water is extremely shallow. Hence, to ensure safety passage of vessel, port must keep a certain UKC when vessel is entering into a shallow area(including fairway).Yet the port can't provide the required UKC, vessels need to ride the tide to utilize the rise of tide level. Major way to improve the efficiency of water and tidal resource is to depress UKC.

2   Under Keel Clearance and Factors Considered in Determining UKC

2.1   Under Keel Clearance

For the sake of safety, there exists limitations to depth of shallow water. That is to say, conditions of fairway must be suitable for maneuvering to keep certain depth below her keel. This clearance is called under keel clearance.

X.-h. Sun et al. (Eds.): ICA3PP 2014, Part II, LNCS 8631, pp. 366–375, 2014.

2.2   Factors Considered in Determining UKC

Supposing h_{min} is the smallest depth for ship to pass. Based on research, it could be indicated as

$$h_{min} = d + \sum_1^5 \Delta h_i + \Delta h \qquad (1)$$

where, d, the draft when she is motionless; Δh, the error of draft, including errors from the change of sea state, meteorological condition and depth marked in chart; Δh_1, the change of draft when the vessel is navigating in still water(namely squat); Δh_2, the change of draft due to ship's sway in seawave; Δh_3, the clearance for ship to maintain her maneuverability; Δh_4, the change of draft due to unstable manoeuvre load and the ship's trim and list; Δh_5, the change of draft due to the difference of densities between seawater and freshwater.

The formula above is too detailed to put into use. Merge the term related to velocity in the formula. And we get this:

$$h_{min} = d + \Delta h_1 + \Delta h_2 + \Delta H \qquad (2)$$

In this new formula，Δh_1 and Δh_2 represent the same meanings with the Formula One.ΔH is the mergence of parts of terms in Formula One. Generally speaking, ΔH have few to do with ship's speed and form but the fairway circumstance. Concerning in the field of safety, permanent rectification of water level may be used to provide safety margin. Some document would take it for 0.3m.

So the key to calculating the formula are Δh_1 and Δh_2. Δh_2 could be ignored when the wave and current are not huge. Therefore, the smallest depth of safety passage is totally depending on Δh_1. So grasping the squat is the hinge to determine UKC.

3   The Ship's Squat

It is meaningless to discuss the squat when the depth of fairway is far more deeper than the ship's draft, since there must be sufficient UKC. Only when the depth is limited and even the ship needs to ride tidal current to pass the fairway, Calculating precisely the UKC shall be of great significant. Particularly when she is navigating in shallow water area, the squat may become worse than deep water area.

3.1   Quantity of Navigating Squat

When vessel navigating in shallow water area, Shallow water effect exists, which is, when vessel enters into a shallow water area, the volume of free water under the vessel bottom is diminished and the water is obstructed. Three-dimensional flow gradually in deep water gradually turns himself into two-dimensional flow. Flow speed of water below the keel is relatively increased, water pressure is hence reduced, causing the sinkage of vessel. Vessel would gain her draft, augmentation of draft is the quantity of squat in navigation.

3.2   Analysis of Squat Based on Hydromechanics

According to Archimedes Law, vessel's gravity is supported by vertical component from water pressure. When the ship navigating in shallow water area, three- dimensional flow turns into mainly two-dimensional flow. Relative speed around vessel's hull increases rapidly. Based on Bernoulli equation:

$$z + \frac{p}{\gamma} + \frac{u^2}{2g} = C \qquad (3)$$

where, z, the attitude of each point along the streamline; p, the hydrodynamic pressure of each point along the streamline; γ, the weight of the fluid each volume; u, the speed of each point along the streamline; g, the acceleration due to the gravity; C, the constant of streamline(remain constant along the same streamline).

For the two points along the same streamline, the Bernoulli equation could be written into this form:

$$z_1 + \frac{p_1}{\gamma} + \frac{u_1{}^2}{2g} = z_2 + \frac{p_2}{\gamma} + \frac{u_2{}^2}{2g} \qquad (4)$$

As a result of the increase of relative speed around hull, pressure to the hull will surely decrease. Buoyancy composed from vertical component from water pressure is insufficient to support the vessel's gravity, for this reason the vessel sinks. Moreover, it needs an increase on draft to compensate the lack of buoyancy. Please refer to Fig.1

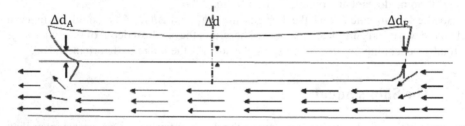

Fig. 1. The chart of three-dimensional flow turning into mainly two-dimensional flow

4   Calculation Method for Squat

Simply, we could calculate squat by using Bernoulli equation. But firstly, we shall conceptively switch the flow to a steady state, and attribute all the motion to the vessel's movement. That is to say, the vessel is taken as in a static condition, while water is within a certain range from vessel and doing uniform motion. Water's velocity and direction are opposite but equal to the vessel.

As to the calculation methods of the squat, theoretically, there are two types, theoretical   algorithm and the experience calculation summarized from models and actual ship experiments. The theoretical algorithm is mainly deduced from one-dimensional theory and slender body theory. Ways to calculate squat are many more. Overwhelming majorities are concluded from the result of experiments after taking ship's particulars in to consideration.

4.1   Details and Comparisons of Empirical Formula about Squat

In the following empirical formula, L, B, d, Δ H, V, C_b, t, s, F_{rh} would in the ship model denote overall length, width, draft, displacement, fairway depth, velocity, the square coefficient, trim, squat,   Froude number, which is defined as:$V / \sqrt{gH}$.

(a) In the early 1960's, Tuck used lender body theory to deducted a general algorithm of squat and trim, which is

$$\frac{s}{L} = C_s F_{rh}^2 / \sqrt{1 - F_{rh}^2} \tag{5}$$

$$\frac{t}{L} = C_t F_{rh}^2 / \sqrt{1 - F_{rh}^2} \tag{6}$$

(b) Hooft raised a functional relationship between displacement and ship's LOA through the result from model experiment and gave the empirical formula as follows:

$$\frac{s}{L} = 1.46 \Delta F_{rh}^2 / L^2 \sqrt{1 - F_{rh}^2} \tag{7}$$

$$t = \Delta F_{rh}^2 / \sqrt{1 - F_{rh}^2} \tag{8}$$

(c) Soukhomel and Zass separated the ratio between depth of water and displacement into two components, and gave the similar formula according to model experiments as follows:

$$s = 12.96 k v^2 \sqrt{\frac{d}{h}} \quad (^d/_h > 0.25) \tag{9}$$

$$s = 12.96 k v^2 \quad (d/h \leq 0.25) \tag{10}$$

$$k = 0.0143 (\frac{L}{B})^{-1.11} \tag{11}$$

(d) Eyuzlu-Hausser's empirical formula

$$s_{max} = 0.113 B \left(\frac{d}{h}\right)^{0.27} (v/\sqrt{gh})^{1.8} \tag{12}$$

(e) Millward's empirical formula

$$\left(\frac{S}{L}\right)^{\%}_{mid} = \frac{38.0C_bF_{rh}^2d}{L\sqrt{1-F_{rh}^2}}$$ (13)

$$\left(\frac{S}{L}\right)^{\%}_{bmid} = \frac{(61.7C_b\frac{B}{L}-0.6)F_{rh}^2}{\sqrt{1-F_{rh}^2}}$$ (14)

(f) Yoshikawa's empirical formula

$$s/L = 1.5(d/L)\left(\frac{C_b}{L/B}\right)F_{rh}^2$$ (15)

$$t/L = 30(d/L)(C_b/(L/B))^3F_{rh}^2$$ (16)

(g) the UK Teddington chart for the fore and astern squat of the puddle estimation

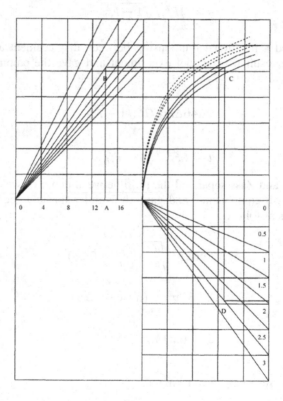

Fig. 2. UK Teddington chart for the fore and astern squat of the puddle estimation

(h) the estimation chart for squat in the China Harbor Engineering Technical Specifications

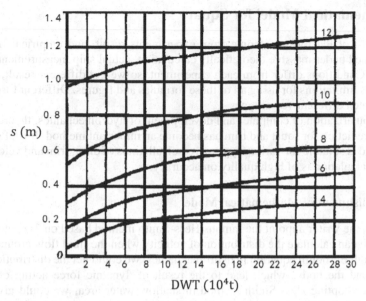

Fig. 3. Estimation chart for squat in the China Harbor Engineering Technical Specifications

4.2   Squat Difference When the Vessel Is Riding the Tidal Stream

We take the flow as in steady state, while water is within a certain range from vessel and doing uniform motion, and water's velocity and direction are opposite but equal to the vessel. But this assumption is given without the consideration of flow's own speed when there is rising tidal stream. When the vessel is navigating in entrance fairway, speed and direction of both vessel and tidal stream are the same. When the stream flows form a open area to a relatively narrow fairway, according to continuity equation of flow motion, the flow speed would be greater than that before it flows into the fairway. Therefore, STW(speed through water) would be slower than SOG(speed over ground) when we calculate squat, and the same thing goes when vessel is in steady water. Please refer to Fig.4.

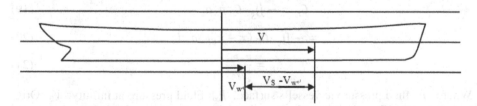

Fig. 4. The chart of the relative motion between the vessel and the tidal current

When the relative speed between the vessel and the water decreases, V in empirical formula would decrease, thus generating the smaller squat.

5   Mathematical Model for Squat

Owing to most of the formulas come from experiments result, and empirical figure being designed under massive theoretically calculation, actual ship measurement and analog tests, Conditions differ from each experiment, so we get different result, thus they generates limitations for using all of these formulas and figures. Different formula and figure match different vessel types.

As the popularization of computer and development of hydromechanics, theoretical calculation prediction for squat and trim has become an important method. It is of great pertinence and is suitable for various type of vessel, all kinds of draft, trim and velocity. Theoretical calculation is of high quality on accuracy.

5.1   Establishment of Mathematical Model

In this article, the writer appoint the famous Hess-Smith method based on 3D potential flow theory. It can calculate the distribution of velocity when the fluid flow around the object. Through Bernoulli equation in hydromechanics, we could get the distribution of pressure around the body, which lead to the result of dynamic force acting on the object. While adopting Hess-Smith method in shallow water area, we could give an assumption, namely "Mirror Effect". After a special procedure, we could calculate the fluid dynamic force and trimming moment when the vessel is navigating in shallow water area by taking the advantage of Hess-Smith method.

The distribution of the fluid pressure can be influenced by the distribution of the current speed on the surface of the vessel. The sum of the pressure and the sinking force can be calculated through integration.

Sinking force,

$$F = \frac{1}{2}\rho V^2 (\frac{L}{2})^2 C_F \tag{17}$$

Trimming moment

$$N = \frac{1}{2}\rho V^2 (\frac{L}{2})^3 C_N \tag{18}$$

Which is:

$$C_F = - \iint_S C_P n_s d_s \tag{19}$$

$$C_N = - \iint_S C_P (x - x_{CB}) n_s d_s \tag{20}$$

$$C_P = \frac{P - P_\infty}{\frac{1}{2}\rho V_0^2} \tag{21}$$

Where, P, fluid pressure at vessel's surface; P_∞, Fluid pressure at infinity; V_0, Original flow speed(Relative speed between vessel and fluid); S , Vessel's merged area Horizontal distance between vessel's centre of buoyancy and any point on the vessel's surface.

5.2   Analysis on Results from Actual Ship Considering the Tidal Current

In this article, we use empirical formula and mathematical model established to calculate the squat at bow for a 300,000 tons of tanker,and use the mathematical model to calculate squat considering the tidal current . Supposed tidal speed is 3kn, the calculation outcome is compared with the outcome of the model test.

(a) Eryuzlu formula（1978）

$$S_{max} = 0.113B(\tfrac{d}{h})^{0.27}(v/\sqrt{gh})^{1.8} \tag{22}$$

(b) Mill ward formula (1990)

$$S = (15.0C_B\tfrac{B}{L} - 0.55) \times \tfrac{F_{rh}{}^2}{1-0.9F_{rh}} \times \tfrac{L}{100} \tag{23}$$

(c) Mill ward formula（1992）

$$S = (61.7 \times C_B\tfrac{B}{L} - 0.6) \times \frac{F_{rh}{}^2}{\sqrt{1-F_{rh}{}^2}} \tag{24}$$

(d) Yoshikawa's empirical formula

$$S/_L = 1.5(d/_L)(\tfrac{C_b}{L/_B})F_{rh}{}^2 \tag{25}$$

The data used in this calculation is shown as Table 1.

Table 1. The ship's particulars

Ship type	L_{BP}	B	d	C_B
Oil tanker	318	56	20.58	0.8272

The outcomes are shown as Fig.5 and Fig.6.

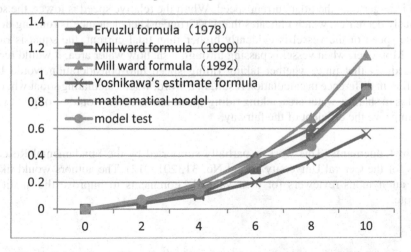

Fig. 5. Comparison of the calculated squat without considering the tidal current

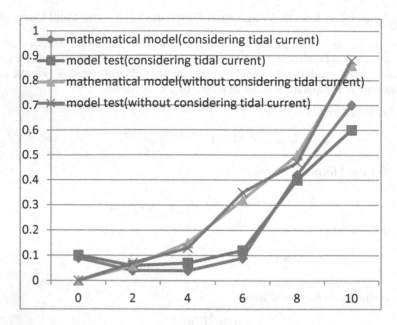

Fig. 6. Comparison of the calculated squat using the mathematical model and model test

6   Conclusion

From the calculation work we could get that it is better to use the empirical formula and mathematical model when the vessel is at low speed. But when the vessel is in fast-speed, those two are no longer agree with each other, and result from mathematical model is closer than actual ship test. if Concerning the riding speed, normally the vessel speed is larger than the tidal current speed. When the relative speed is lower, the squat obviously decreases, which indicates that UKC(under keel clearance)is running down. For the speed of the vessel is evidently higher than tidal current, the squat is rather small. Moreover, when vessel is passing through a shallow water area, it would reduce its speed. At that time, whether taking riding speed into consideration would have magnificent difference in calculation result. In a word, when calculating squat when the vessel is in shallow water area, taking riding speed into account would be of great value as to improve the efficient of the fairway.

Acknowledgements. This work is partially supported by the Fundamental Research Funds for the Central University (Grant No. 3132013012). The authors would like to thank anonymous reviewers for their valuable comments to improve the quality of this note.

References

1. Zheng, H.Y., Han, X.G., Wu, X.: The analysis of the shipping navigation ability in shallow water. Navigation Technology (6), 26–32 (2011)
2. Gu, W.X.: The ship's UKC when navigating in shallow water. World Shipping (5), 54–56 (1995)
3. Dai, R., Jia, C.Y., Sun, L.C.: The field research on the UKC of the ship(under keel clearance), pp. 242–246. Dalian Maritime University
4. Sun, L.C., He, Y.P.: The research on the UKC (under keel clearance) of the extra-large-scale ship in the outter fairway of Xia Zhi Men. Navigation of China,Serial No. 45, 2–5 (1999)
5. Liu, Z.J., Xia, G.Z., Wang, F.C.: The actual empirical calculation of the ship's squat in the restricted water. Journal of Dalian Maritime University 21(4), 9–13 (1995)
6. Ye, Z.B.: The research on the numerical calculation method of the squat of the ship navigating in the shallow water. Dalian Maritime University (2009)
7. Hong, B.G.: The ship's manoeuvring. Dalian Maritime University (2008)
8. Shen, H.: The basic ship dynamics. Dalian Maritime University (2004)

A Vertex-Clustering Algorithm Based
on the Cluster-Clique

Deqiang Wang[1], Bin Zhang[1], and Kelun Wang[2]

[1] Institute of Nautical Science and Technology, Dalian Maritime University, Dalian, China
[2] Department of Mathematics, Dalian Maritime University, Dalian, China
{dqwang,zhangbin,dmu_wkl}@dlmu.edu.cn

Abstract. The vertex-clustering algorithm based on intra connection ratio (MV-ICR algorithm) is a graph-clustering algorithm proposed by Moussiades and Vakali[Clustering dense graph: A web site graph paradigm. Information Processing and Management, 2010, 46:247-267]. In this paper, we propose a new conception called cluster-clique for vertex-clustering of graphs. And based on the cluster-clique and the intra connection ratio, a new vertex-clustering algorithm is proposed. This algorithm is more reasonable and effective than MV-ICR algorithm for some clusters which have the same maximum intra connection ratio.

Keywords: graph, clustering algorithm, cluster-clique, intra connection ratio.

1   Introduction

Clustering (or partition) is a hot research issue in mathematics, computer science, management science and other areas. It is also widely applied in the fields such as pattern recognition, data analysis, communication, biology and other business: monitoring on computer network executive purpose, visualization knowledge based on support of understanding of complex data structure, measurement data cluster, detection source code plagiarism, network data cluster and online community identification [1,3,5,9,10,11]. One of the newly rapidly developed clustering method is the graph-clustering method, the clustering method based on graph theory [2,4,6,8,12,14]. Graph-clustering is a very widely applied research topic, especially in the network research, including e-mail network, social network, gene networks and so on[7,13]. Graph-clustering applies graph theory method to graph classification, and it is a very important variant of data clustering. Unlike ordinary numerical clustering, the clustering based on graph theory has its own particularity, the similarity among data objects in data set is often expressed by a graph.

Generally, clusters of graph-clustering are groups with a higher density of edges within cluster and a lower density of edges between clusters. Moussiades and Vakali proposed a vertex-clustering algorithm based on intra connection ratio (we call the algorithm MV-ICR algorithm) in Ref. [9]. It is the core idea of MV-ICR algorithm that the two clusters with ICR maximum will be merged together. Because the MV-ICR algorithm exists certain irrationality when the maximum ICR values between clusters are more than one, this paper proposes the new concept of "cluster-clique", and gives a vertex-clustering algorithm to solve the merging problem of more than one maximum ICR values between clusters.

X.-h. Sun et al. (Eds.): ICA3PP 2014, Part II, LNCS 8631, pp. 376–385, 2014.
© Springer International Publishing Switzerland 2014

2   Definitions and Notations

Let $G=(V(G),E(G))$ be a simple undirected graph, where $V(G)$ is the set of vertices and $E(G)$ is the set of edges. $\forall v \in V(G)$, the degree of v is denoted as $d(v)$.We denote $\mathscr{C}(G) = \{C_1, C_2, \cdots, C_k\}$ as a clustering of vertices in G into k clusters with $\cup_{C_i \in \mathscr{C}(G)} C_i = V(G)$, $C_i \cap C_j = \varnothing (i \neq j)$.

Definition 1[9]. The connection degree between two clusters $C, S \in \mathscr{C}(G)$, denoted by $d(C, S)$, equals to the number of edges having one endpoint in cluster C and the other in cluster S.

More specifically, for any $C \in \mathscr{C}(G)$ and $v \in V(G)$, the connection degree of C and v is $d(C, \{v\})$, denoted by $d(C,v)$.

Definition 2[9]. The internal degree of cluster $C \in \mathscr{C}(G)$, I_C, equals to the number of edges that have both their endpoints in cluster C(internal edges).

Definition 3[9].The external degree of cluster $C \in \mathscr{C}(G)$, X_C, equals to the number of edges that have only one of their endpoints in cluster C(external edges).

Proposition 1[9]. For any $C \in \mathscr{C}(G)$, $I_C = \frac{1}{2} \sum_{v \in C} d(C,v)$.

Proposition 2[9]. $\forall C, S \in \mathscr{C}(G)$, $I_{C \cup S} = I_C + I_S + d(C,S)$ and $X_{C \cup S} = X_C + X_S - 2d(C,S)$.

Definition 4[9]. The intra connection ratio (ICR) of cluster $C \in \mathscr{C}(G)$, denoted as $icr(C)$, is defined as $\dfrac{\sum_{v \in C} d(C,v)}{\sum_{v \in C} d(v)}$.

Proposition 5[9]. The intra connection ratio value upon merging two clusters $C, S \in \mathscr{C}(G)$ denoted as $\Delta_{ICR}(C,S)$ (Δ_{ICR} for short), is given by

$$\frac{2(I_C + I_S + d(C,S))}{2(I_C + I_S) + X_C + X_S} - \frac{2I_C}{2I_C + X_C} - \frac{2I_S}{2I_S + X_S}.$$

3   MV-ICR Clustering Approach

In this section, we introduce the MV-ICR clustering approach by clustering the vertices in the graph G of Fig. 1.

First, we get the initial clustering of G: $\mathscr{C}_1 = \{\{0\}, \{1\}, \{2\}, \cdots, \{19\}\}$. Then calculate $\Delta_{ICR}(\{i\}, \{j\})(0 \leq i < j \leq 19)$, and find the maximum value:

$$\Delta_{ICR}(\{17\}, \{18\}) = \Delta_{ICR}(\{18\}, \{19\}) = \Delta_{ICR}(\{17\}, \{19\}) = \frac{1}{3}.$$

Choosing one pair of the clusters, for example, $\{17\}$ and $\{18\}$, merging into one cluster, we get the clustering:

$$\mathscr{C}_2 = \{\{0\},\{1\},\{2\},\cdots,\{16\},\{17,18\},\{19\}\}.$$

Calculating $\Delta_{ICR}(C,S)$, where $C,S \in \mathscr{C}_2(G)$, and finding the maximum value $\Delta_{ICR}(\{17,18\},\{19\})$. Then we get the clustering as follows:

$$\mathscr{C}_3 = \{\{0\},\{1\},\cdots,\{15\},\{16\},\{17,18,19\}\}$$

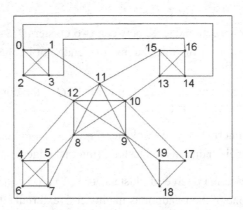

Fig. 1. Graph G

Calculating $\Delta_{ICR}(C,S)$, where $C,S \in \mathscr{C}_2(G)$, and finding the maximum value:

$$\Delta_{ICR}(\{4\},\{6\}) = \Delta_{ICR}(\{5\},\{6\}) = \Delta_{ICR}(\{6\},\{7\}) = \frac{2}{7}.$$

Choosing one pair of the clusters, for example, $\{4\}$ and $\{6\}$, we get the clustering:

$$\mathscr{C}_4 = \{\{0\},\{1\},\{2\},\{3\},\{4,6\},\{5\},\{7\},\{8\},\cdots,\{15\},\{16\},\{17,18,19\}\}.$$

The vertices will be clustered as follows in the same way:

$$\mathscr{C}_5 = \{\{0\},\{1\},\{2\},\{3\},\{4,5,6\},\{7\},\{8\},\cdots,\{15\},\{16\},\{17,18,19\}\},$$

$$\mathscr{C}_6 = \{\{0\},\{1\},\{2\},\{3\},\{4,5,6,7\},\{8\},\{9\},\cdots,\{15\},\{16\},\{17,18,19\}\},$$

$$\mathscr{C}_7 = \{\{0,1\},\{2\},\{3\},\{4,5,6,7\},\{8\},\{9\},\cdots,\{15\},\{16\},\{17,18,19\}\},$$

$$\mathscr{C}_8 = \{\{0,1,2\},\{3\},\{4,5,6,7\},\{8\},\{9\},\cdots,\{15\},\{16\},\{17,18,19\}\},$$

$$\mathscr{C}_9 = \{\{0,1,2,3\},\{4,5,6,7\},\{8\},\{9\},\cdots,\{15\},\{16\},\{17,18,19\}\},$$

$$\mathscr{C}_{10} = \{\{0,1,2,3\},\{4,5,6,7\},\{8\},\{9\},\{10\},\{11\},\{12\},\{13,14\},\{15\},\{16\},\{17,18,19\}\},$$

$$\mathscr{C}_{11} = \{\{0,1,2,3\},\{4,5,6,7\},\{8\},\{9\},\{10\},\{11\},\{12\},\{13,14,15\},\{16\},\{17,18,19\}\},$$

$$\mathscr{C}_{12} = \{\{0,1,2,3\},\{4,5,6,7\},\{8\},\{9\},\{10\},\{11\},\{12\},\{13,14,15,16\},\{17,18,19\}\},$$

$$\mathscr{C}_{13} = \{\{0,1,2,3\},\{4,5,6,7\},\{8,9\},\{10\},\{11\},\{12\},\{13,14,15,16\},\{17,18,19\}\},$$

$$\mathscr{C}_{14} = \{\{0,1,2,3\},\{4,5,6,7\},\{8,9,10\},\{11\},\{12\},\{13,14,15,16\},\{17,18,19\}\},$$

$$\mathscr{C}_{15} = \{\{0,1,2,3\},\{4,5,6,7\},\{8,9,10,11\},\{12\},\{13,14,15,16\},\{17,18,19\}\},$$

$$\mathscr{C}_{16} = \{\{0,1,2,3\},\{4,5,6,7\},\{8,9,10,11,12\},\{13,14,15,16\},\{17,18,19\}\},$$

$\mathcal{C}_{17} = \{\{0,1,2,3\},\{4,5,6,7\},\{8,9,10,11,12,17,18,19\},\{13,14,15,16\}\}$,

$\mathcal{C}_{18} = \{\{0,1,2,3,13,14,15,16\},\{4,5,6,7\},\{8,9,10,11,12,17,18,19\}\}$,

$\mathcal{C}_{19} = \{\{0,1,2,3,13,14,15,16\},\{4,5,6,7,8,9,10,11,12,17,18,19\}\}$,

$\mathcal{C}_{20} = \{\{0,1,2,3,4,5,6,7,8,9,10,11,12,13,14,15,16,17,18,19\}\}$.

According to the above of clustering graph G, MV-ICR clustering algorithm begins from the foundation clustering (i.e. each element as a cluster) with the largest Δ_{ICR} , calculates the Δ_{ICR} between this cluster and its adjacency clusters, gradually merge all vertices into one cluster. This clustering algorithm begins from a small range clustering, gradually extended to the entire graph. Because the maximum(or greater) Δ_{ICR} in a graph certainly is not only one, and the clusters merge with maximum value (or greater) will be more than one. How to choose the first merger is a problem, such as the $\mathcal{C}_1$ in figure 1, the maximum value of Δ_{ICR} is:

$$\Delta_{ICR}(17,18) = \Delta_{ICR}(18,19) = \Delta_{ICR}(17,19) = \frac{1}{3}.$$

Using MV-ICR algorithm, the group randomly selected from $\{17,18\}$, $\{18,19\}$, $\{17,18\}$ will be merged. But no matter how to choose, this group will be merged with the remaining three vertices in the second cycle. For example, the $\{17,18\}$ is merged firstly, then it will merge with $\{19\}$ in the next cycle. The Δ_{ICR} between each pair of $\{17,18,19\}$ are greatest and the relations are most closely linked, if we can merge three points at once in a cycle, it will reduce the clustering step, and the relationships between clusters will be more clear.

4   Improvement of MV-ICR Clustering Approach

Considering an extreme case now, we cluster the vertices of the complete graph K_n with MV-ICR algorithm. Firstly, every vertex in the graph is the clustering $\mathcal{C}_1 = \{\{0\},\{1\},\cdots,\{n-1\}\}$, all Δ_{ICR} between each pair clusters is $\frac{1}{n-1}$. According to the MV-ICR algorithm, optionally two clusters will be merged, let's just take $\{0\}$, $\{1\}$ for example. By calculating the Δ_{ICR} of $\mathcal{C}_2 = \{\{0,1\},\{2\},\{3\},\cdots,\{n-1\}\}$, it will be found that any Δ_{ICR} between each pair clusters is still $\frac{1}{n-1}$. Also, according to the MV-ICR algorithm, optionally two clusters in $\mathcal{C}_2$ will be mergedas well. However, intuitively, according to highly symmetry of vertices in complete graph, each vertex (cluster) has the same status (the same value Δ_{ICR}) at the first clustering, and they should be clustered as one cluster. Namely, there are just two results of the clustering of complete graph: all points are a cluster of $\mathcal{C}_1 = \{\{0\},\{1\},\cdots,\{n-1\}\}$, or $\mathcal{C}_2 = \{\{0,1,\cdots,n-1\}\}$. The MV-ICR algorithm will destroy the vertex symmetry of complete graph by randomly selecting two point to be a cluster. Therefore, it is necessary to improve the clustering strategy of MV-ICR algorithm.

In order to merge more clusters with Δ_{ICR} the maximum at once, it is given firstly including the definition of cluster-clique and the related conclusion of internal degree Ic and external degree Xc of multiple clusters.

Definition 5. Let $\mathscr{C}(G)$ be a clustering of graph G. If $C_1, C_2, \cdots, C_n \in \mathscr{C}(G)$ and $d(C_i, C_j) > 0$, called $\{C_1, C_2, \cdots, C_n\}$ to be a cluster-clique.

Theorem 1. Let $\mathscr{C}(G)$ be a clustering of graph G, and $C_1, C_2, \cdots, C_n \in \mathscr{C}(G)$. If $C = C_1 \cup C_2 \cup \ldots \cup C_n$, the internal degree of cluster Ic is equal to

$$\sum_{i=1}^{n} I_{C_i} + \sum_{i=1}^{n-1} \sum_{j=i+1}^{n} d(C_i, C_j). \tag{1}$$

Proof. We use mathematics induction on n.

For basis $n=1, C = C_1$, the equation (1) holds. For $n=2, C = C_1 \cup C_2$, from Proposition 1, we have

$$I_C = I_{C_1} + I_{C_2} + d(C_1, C_2).$$

The equation (1) holds.

Assume that the equation (1) holds for $n = k-1$, that is

$$I_C = \sum_{i=1}^{k-1} I_{C_i} + \sum_{i=1}^{k-2} \sum_{j=i+1}^{k-1} d(C_i, C_j).$$

For $n=k$. Denote $C^* = C_1 \cup C_2 \cup \cdots \cup C_{k-1}$, then

$$I_C = I_{C^* \cup C_k} = I_{C^*} + I_{C_k} + d(C^*, C_k)$$

$$= \sum_{i=1}^{k-1} I_{C_i} + \sum_{i=1}^{k-2} \sum_{j=i+1}^{k-1} d(C_i, C_j) + I_{C_k} + \sum_{i=1}^{k-1} d(C_i, C_k)$$

$$= \sum_{i=1}^{k} I_{C_i} + \sum_{i=1}^{k-1} \sum_{j=i+1}^{k} d(C_i, C_j).$$

So, the equation (1) holds.

Theorem 2. Let $\mathscr{C}(G)$ be a clustering of graph G, and $C_1, C_2, \cdots, C_n \in \mathscr{C}(G)$. If $C = C_1 \cup C_2 \cup \ldots \cup C_n$, the external degree of cluster Xc is equal to

$$X_C = \sum_{i=1}^{n} X_{C_i} - 2 \sum_{i=1}^{n-1} \sum_{j=i+1}^{n} d(C_i, C_j). \tag{2}$$

Proof. We use mathematics induction on n.

For basis $n=1, C = C_1$, the equation (1) holds. For $n=2, C = C_1 \cup C_2$, from Proposition 3, we have

$$X_C = X_{C_1} + X_{C_2} - 2d(C_1, C_2).$$

The equation (2) holds.

Assume the conclusion holds for $n = k - 1$, that is

$$X_C = \sum_{i=1}^{k-1} X_{C_i} - 2\sum_{i=1}^{k-2}\sum_{j=i+1}^{k-1} d(C_i, C_j) \cdot$$

For $n=k$. Denote $C^* = C_1 \cup C_2 \cup \cdots \cup C_{k-1}$, then

$$X_C = X_{C^* \cup C_k} = X_{C^*} + X_{C_k} - 2d(C^*, C_k)$$

$$= \sum_{i=1}^{k-1} X_{C_i} - 2\sum_{i=1}^{k-2}\sum_{j=i+1}^{k-1} d(C_i, C_j) + X_{C_k} - 2\sum_{i=1}^{k-1} d(C_i, C_k)$$

$$= \sum_{i=1}^{k} X_{C_i} - 2\sum_{i=1}^{k-1}\sum_{j=i+1}^{k} d(C_i, C_j).$$

So, the equation (2) holds

Let $\mathscr{C}(G)$ be a clustering of the graph G. Denote

$$\Delta_{\max\_ICR}\mathscr{C}(G) = \max_{C, S \in \mathscr{C}(G)} \left\{ \Delta_{ICR}(C, S) \right\}.$$

In the following, we will propose an algorithm for merging multi-cluster with maximum ICR based on Theorem 1 and Theorem 2.

Algorithm 1. A graph-clustering algorithm based on the cluster-clique

   Input: Graph $G=(V, E)$

   Output: $\mathscr{C}_k$ $(k = 0,1,\cdots)$

   Initialize: $k=0$, $C_i = \{v_i\}$, $\mathscr{C}_0 = \{C_0, C_1, \cdots, C_{|V|-1}\}$

   FOR $i, j = 1, 2, \cdots, |V| - 1$ $(i \neq j)$ **DO**

   $\{$ $I_{C_i} = 0$, $X_{C_i} = 1$, $X_{C_j} = 1$, $d(C_i, C_j) = 1$; $\Delta_{ICR}(C_i, C_j) = \dfrac{2}{d(v_i) + d(v_j)}$; $\}$

   WHILE $|\mathscr{C}_k| > 1$

   $\{$ Finding cluster-cliques $\mathscr{C}_k^1, \mathscr{C}_k^2, \cdots, \mathscr{C}_k^l \subseteq \mathscr{C}_k$ such that

   $$\forall S_{ti}, S_{tj} \in \mathscr{C}_k^t : \ \Delta_{ICR}(S_{ti}, S_{tj}) = \Delta_{\max\_ICR}(\mathscr{C}_k);$$

   FOR $t = 1, 2, \cdots, l$ **DO**

   $\{$

   $$S_t = \bigcup_{S_{ti} \in \mathscr{C}_k^t} S_{ti},$$

   $$I_{S_t} = \sum_{S_{ti} \in \mathscr{C}_k^t} I_{S_{ti}} + \sum_{S_{ti}, S_{tj} \in \mathscr{C}_k^t (i<j)} d(S_{ti}, S_{tj}), \quad X_{S_t} = \sum_{S_{ti} \in \mathscr{C}_k^t} X_{S_{ti}} - 2 \sum_{S_{ti}, S_{tj} \in \mathscr{C}_k^t (i<j)} d(S_{ti}, S_{tj});$$

   $\}$

   $$\mathscr{C}_k = \left(\mathscr{C}_k - \bigcup_{t=1}^{l} S_t \right) \cup \left(\bigcup_{t=1}^{l} \{S_t\} \right);$$

   $\forall C_i, C_j \in \mathscr{C}_k$, **IF** $d(C_i, C_j) > 0$ **THEN**

$$\Delta_{ICR}(C_i, C_j) = \frac{2(I_{C_i} + I_{C_j} + d(C_i, C_j))}{2(I_{C_i} + I_{C_j}) + X_{C_i} + X_{C_j}} - \frac{2I_{C_i}}{2I_{C_i} + X_{C_i}} - \frac{2I_{C_j}}{2I_{C_j} + X_{C_j}};$$

　　　k++;

　}

END

5　Algorithm Analysis and Examples

5.1　Algorithm Analysis

The original step of this algorithm is to classify the vertex set as meticulous as possible, namely, each vertex is a cluster. Then, the external degree and the internal degree of each cluster, the Δ_{ICR} between each other are given. The next step is to find the cluster-clique with the largest Δ_{ICR} in this clustering to emerge and product a new cluster, and to calculate the internal degree and the external degree of the new cluster. According to Theorem 1 (and Theorem 2), the internal degree (and the external degree) of the new cluster is just the algebraic sum of the internal degree (and the external degree) of those clusters which emerge to the new cluster. So, it is unnecessary to recalculate the internal degree (and the external degree) of the new cluster following the definition of the internal degree (and the external degree), that reduces so much calculation. The third step is to loop the new cluster through the above method until all the vertices are merged into one cluster. Thus, the algorithm follows the clustering principle of "density within clusters and sparsity among clusters", and we can merge multiple vertices at once in each loop step by the idea of cluster-clique and the calculating formula of internal degree, external degree, accordingly improve the clustering efficiency.

5.2　Example

Example 1. We first consider the extreme case of clustering K_n :

　　(1) Initializing a clustering $\mathscr{C}_0$ containing one cluster per vertex of K_n :
$\mathscr{C}_0 = \{\{0\}, \{1\}, \cdots, \{n-1\}\}$.

　　(2) Calculating Δ_{ICR} of $\mathscr{C}_0$, we get the cluster-cliques $\{\{0\}, \{1\}, \cdots, \{n-1\}\}$ (all Δ_{ICR} of clusters $\{i\}$ and $\{j\}$ are equal to $\frac{1}{n-1}$, where $i, j \in \{1, 2, \cdots, n-1\}$ and $i \neq j$). Following Algorithm 1, merging these clusters $\{0\}, \{1\}, \cdots, \{n-1\}$ into one cluster $\mathscr{C}_1 = \{\{0, 1, \cdots, n-1\}\}$.

　　(3) $|\mathscr{C}_1| = 1$. The end.

Example 2. In the following, we cluster the graph G in Fig.1 with Algorithm 1 (based on the cluster-clique).

(1) We first initialize a clustering $\mathscr{C}_0$ of G as $\mathscr{C}_0 = \{\{0\},\{1\},\cdots,\{19\}\}$.

(2) Calculating Δ_{ICR}: the maximum Δ_{ICR} of $\mathscr{C}_0$ is

$$\Delta_{ICR}(17,18) = \Delta_{ICR}(18,19) = \Delta_{ICR}(17,19) = \Delta_{max\_ICR}(\mathscr{C}_0) = \frac{1}{3}..$$

We get a cluster-clique $\mathscr{C}_0^1 = \{\{17\},\{18\},\{19\}\}$ of $\mathscr{C}_0$. Merging $\{17\}$, $\{18\}$ and $\{19\}$ into one cluster, and we get the new clustering (see Fig.2):

$$\mathscr{C}_1 = (\mathscr{C}_0 - \{\{17\},\{18\},\{19\}\}) \cup \{17,18,19\} = \{\{1\},\{2\},\cdots,\{16\},\{17,18,19,\}\}.$$

(3) Calculating Δ_{ICR} of $\mathscr{C}_1$, we get the cluster-cliques as follows:

$$\mathscr{C}_1^1 = \{\{0\},\{1\},\{2\},\{3\}\}, \mathscr{C}_1^2 = \{\{4\},\{5\},\{7\}\}, \mathscr{C}_1^3 = \{\{13\},\{14\},\{15\},\{16\}\}.$$

And we get the new clusters: $\{0,1,2,3\},\{4,5,7\},\{13,14,15,16\}$. Moreover, we have the new clustering (see Fig.3):

$$\mathscr{C}_2 = \left(\mathscr{C}_1 - \{\{0\},\{1\},\{2\},\{3\}\} \cup \{\{4\},\{5\},\{7\}\} \cup \{\{13\},\{14\},\{15\},\{16\}\}\right)$$

$$\cup \{\{0,1,2,3\},\{4,5,7\},\{13,14,15,16\}\}$$

$$= \{\{0,1,2,3\},\{4,5,7\},\{6\},\{8\},\{9\},\{10\},\{11\},\{12\},\{13,14,15,16\},\{17,18,19\}\}.$$

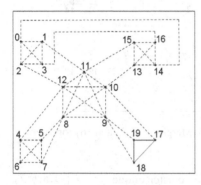

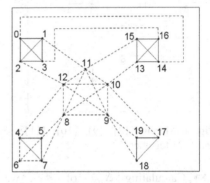

Fig. 2. Merging $\{17\}$, $\{18\}$ and (19) together

Fig. 3. Merging $\{0\}$, $\{1\}$, $\{2\}$ and$\{3\}$ together; $\{4\}$, $\{5\}$ and $\{7\}$together; $\{13\}$, $\{14\}$, $\{15\}$ and$\{16\}$ together

(4)Calculating Δ_{ICR} of $\mathscr{C}_2$, we get the cluster-clique $\mathscr{C}_2^1 = \{\{8\},\{9\},\{10\},\{11\},\{12\}\}$ and the new cluster $\{8,9,10,11,12\}$. Moreover, we have a new clustering (see Fig.4):

$$\mathscr{C}_3 = (\mathscr{C}_2 - \{\{8\},\{9\},\{10\},\{11\},\{12\}\}) \cup \{8,9,10,11,12\}$$

$$= \{\{0,1,2,3\},\{4,5,7\},\{6\},\{8,9,10,11,12\},\{13,14,15,16\},\{17,18,19\}\}.$$

(5) Calculating Δ_{ICR} of $\mathscr{C}_3$, we get the cluster-clique $\mathscr{C}_3^1 = \{\{6\},\{4,5,7\}\}$ and the new cluster $\{4,5,6,7\}$. Moreover, we have a new clustering (see Fig.5):

$$\mathscr{C}_4 = (\mathscr{C}_3 - \{\{6\},\{4,5,7\}\}) \cup \{6,4,5,7\}$$

$$= \{\{0,1,2,3\},\{4,5,7,6\},\{8,9,10,11,12\},\{13,14,15,16\},\{17,18,19\}\}.$$

(6) Calculating Δ_{ICR} of $\mathscr{C}_4$, we get the cluster-clique $\mathscr{C}_4^1 = \{\{8,9,10,11,12\},$ $\{17,18,19\}\}$ and the new cluster $\{8,9,10,11,12,17,18,19\}$. Moreover, we have a new clustering:

$$\mathscr{C}_5 = \left(\mathscr{C}_4 - \{\{8,9,10,11,12\},\{17,18,19\}\}\right) \cup \{8,9,10,11,12,17,18,19\}$$
$$= \{\{0,1,2,3\},\{4,5,7,6\},\{8,9,10,11,12,17,18,19\},\{13,14,15,16\}\}.$$

(7) Calculating Δ_{ICR} of $\mathscr{C}_5$, we get the cluster-cliques $\mathscr{C}_5^1 = \{\{0,1,2,3\},$ $\{13,14,15,16\}\}$ and the new cluster $\{0,1,2,3,13,14,15,16\}$. Moreover, we have a new clustering:

$$\mathscr{C}_6 = \left(\mathscr{C}_4 - \{\{0,1,2,3\},\{13,14,15,16\}\}\right) \cup \{0,1,2,3,13,14,15,16\}$$
$$= \{\{0,1,2,3,13,14,15,16\},\{4,5,7,6\},\{8,9,10,11,12,17,18,19\}\}.$$

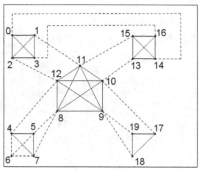

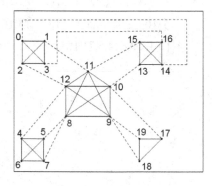

Fig. 4. Merging {8}, {9}, {10}, {11} and {12} together

Fig. 5. Merging{4,5,7} and {6} together

(8) Calculating Δ_{ICR} of $\mathscr{C}_6$, we get the cluster-clique $\mathscr{C}_6^1 = \{\{4,5,6,7\},$ $\{8,9,10,11,12,17,18,19\}\}$ and get the new cluster $\{4,5,6,7,8,9,10,11,12,17,18,19\}$. Moreover, we have a new clustering:

$$\mathscr{C}_7 = \left(\mathscr{C}_6 - \{\{4,5,6,7\},\{8,9,10,11,12,17,18,19\}\}\right) \cup \{\{4,5,6,7,8,9,10,11,12,17,18,19\}\}$$
$$= \{\{0,1,2,3,13,14,15,16\},\{4,5,6,7,8,9,10,11,12,17,18,19\}\}.$$

(9) Calculating Δ_{ICR} of $\mathscr{C}_7$, we get the cluster-cliques $\mathscr{C}_7^1 = \{\{0,1,2,3,13,14,15,16\},$ $\{4,5,6,7,8,9,10,11,12,17,18,19\}\}$ and the new clusters $\{4,5,6,7,8,9,10,11,12,17,18,19\}$. Moreover, we have a new clustering:

$$\mathscr{C}_8 = \left(\mathscr{C}_7 - \{\{0,1,2,3,13,14,15,16\}, \{4,5,6,7,8,9,10,11,12,17,18,19\}\}\right)$$
$$\cup \{\{0,1,2,3,4,5,6,7,8,9,10,11,12,13,14,15,16,17,18,19\}\}$$
$$= \{\{0,1,2,3,4,5,6,7,8,9,10,11,12,13,14,15,16,17,18,19\}\}.$$

(10) $|\mathscr{C}_8| = 1$. The end.

6   Conclusions

From the above two examples, we can conclude that the vertex clustering in the complete graph and the graph in Fig.1 is more reasonable and more efficient than the MV-ICR algorithm in accordance with Algorithm 1.For some special classes of graphs such as regular graphs, the proposed algorithm may be also more reasonable and more efficient than the MV-ICR algorithm. However, it needs further study.

Acknowledgments. The paper is supported by"the Fundamental Research Funds for the Central Universities" (3132014309).

References

1. Alexandros, N., Yannis, T., Yannis, M.: C2P: clustering based on closest pairs. In: Proceedings of the 27th International Conference on Very Large Data Bases, pp. 331–340. Morgan Kaufmann Publishers, Roma (2001)
2. Bradley, P.S., Mangasarian, L.: k-plane Clustering. Journal of Global Optimization 16(1), 23–32 (2000)
3. Brandes, U., Gaertler, M., Wagner, D.: Engineering graph clustering: Models and experimental evaluation. ACM Journal of Experimental Algorithmics 12(1.1), 1–5 (2007)
4. Eades, P., Huang, M.L.: Navigating clustered graphs using force-directed methods. Journal of Graph Algorithms and Applications 4(3), 157–181 (2002)
5. Gomory, R., Hu, T.: Multi-terminal network flows. Journal of the Society for Industrial and Applied Mathematics 9(4), 551–570 (1961)
6. Günter, S., Bunke, H.: Self-organizing map for clustering in the graph domain. Pattern Recognition Letters 23, 401–417 (2002)
7. Kaburlasos, V.G., Moussiades, L., Vakali, A.: Granular graph clustering in the web. In: Proceedingsof the 8th International Conference on Natural Computing, pp. 1639–1645. World Scientific Publishing, Utah (2007)
8. Luo, B., Wilson, R.C., Hancock, E.R.: Spectral embedding of graphs. Pattern Recognition 36(10), 2213–2223 (2003)
9. Moussiades, L., Vakali, A.: Clustering dense graph: A web site graph paradigm. Information Processing and Management 46, 247–267 (2010)
10. Moussiades, L., Vakali, A.: PDetect: A clustering approach for detecting plagiarism in source code datasets. The Computer Journal 48(6), 651–661 (2005)
11. Newman, M.E.J.: Fast algorithm for detecting community structure in networks. Physical Review E 69(066133), 1–5 (2004)
12. Palla, G., Dernyi, I., Farkas, I.: Uncovering the overlapping community structure of complex networks in nature and society. Nature 435(7043), 814–818 (2005)
13. Saha, B., Mitra, P.: Dynamic algorithm for graph clustering using minimum cut tree. In: ICDM Workshops, pp. 667–671 (2006)
14. Serratosa, F., Alquezar, R., Sanfeliu, A.: Synthesis of function-described graphs and clustering of attributed graphs. International Journal of Pattern Recognition and Artificial Intelligence 16(6), 621–655 (2002)

Designed Slide Mode Controller for Ship Autopilot with Steering Gear Saturation*

Gao-Xiaori, Hong-Biguang, Xing-Shengwei, and Li-Tieshan

Navigation College, Dalian Maritime University, No.1 Linghai Road, Dalian, China
gxrdlmu@126.com

Abstract. To design ship autopilot with gear constraints is becoming a hot issue. In this paper, a slide mode control scheme for ship autopilot with the saturation of steering gear was proposed. The MMG ship motion mathematical model was solved for the state of ship nonlinear system. The error between the designed input and the saturation constraints input was approximated by the RBFNN. The stability of the system was proved by selecting the Lyapunov function. The merits of algorithm lie in that the network errors and the external disturbances can be overcome by the robust item of controller and the introduction of the MMG ship model make it closer to the actual conditions. The computer simulation is given by training ship YULONG and validated the effectiveness of the scheme.

Keywords: Input Saturation, Ship Course Control, Slide Mode Control, SMC, RBFNN.

1 Introduction

The ship course system is essential nonlinear system[1,2] and susceptible to a variety of uncertainties and random disturbances. Thus, high-performance autopilot algorithm has always been a hot issue in ship industry[3,4,5]. Following the PID, various control techniques, such as adaptive control[6,7],SMC[8],etc., are applied in this field. These algorithms were validated by the computer simulation and some of them were applied on vessel [3].

However, the steering gear, which is restricted by the maximum steering angle and the maximum steering rate [9,10], is the executing agency of autopilot. Under certain conditions, the gear limitation not only affect the controller's performance, but might weaken the stability of system [1],[11],[12],[13]. Therefore, it is meaningful to achieve autopilot algorithm effectively under such conditions.

In view of input saturation, a SMC controller with the input constraints was achieved by defining assistance system that uses input saturation and error dynamic amplification scheme [14,15]. The constraint of steering gear was considered and adaptive fuzzy control algorithm was developed based on a dynamic surface control

---

* Supported by: the Fundamental Research Funds for the Central Universities(3132013005, 3132014027).

X.-h. Sun et al. (Eds.): ICA3PP 2014, Part II, LNCS 8631, pp. 386–395, 2014.

(DSC) and minimal learning parameter (MLP) for the ship autopilot system by T-S fuzzy system [11]. The algorithm was validated through computer simulation. Stability under input saturation constrains is analyzed with the help of an auxiliary system and training ship simulation demonstrate effectiveness of the proposed scheme [12]. In paper [13], a class strict feedback of ship autopilot was studied by these technologies according to the former research [11,12]. These theoretical researches and scientific achievements have great potential value.

This paper developed a SMC scheme for the ship autopilot with the saturation of steering gear. The MMG ship motion mathematical model was solved for the state of ship nonlinear system. The use of RBFNN makes it possible to approximate the error between the designed input and the saturation constraints input. The stability of the system was proved by selecting the Lyapunov function. The network errors and disturbances can be overcome by the robust item of controller and the introduction of the MMG ship model make it closer to the real world. The computer simulation is given by training ship Yulong.

The contents of paper are organized as follows. In Section 2, the MMG mathematical model with wind disturbances and steering gear dynamic were introduced, meanwhile, the nonlinear ship motion model with input constraints was established. Section 3 briefly described the algorithm of RBFNN and designed controller by SMC method. The simulation results are given in Section 4. Finally, section 5 provides the conclusions.

2   Problem Formulation

2.1   System Description

The block diagram of the ship course control system is shown in Fig.1. The system consists of the SMC course controller, nonlinear ship model, desired reference signal, RBFNN, steering gear saturation and the disturbances.

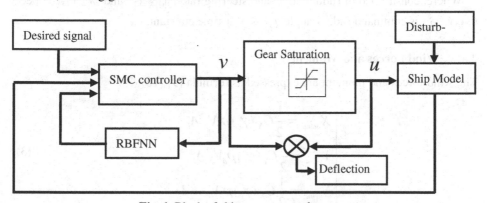

Fig. 1. Block of ship course control system

2.2   Ship Motion Mathematical Model

The 3-DOF (degree of freedom) of MMG ship mathematical model has been introduced [3],[9]. The mathematical model is expressed in formula (1).

$$
\begin{cases}
(m+m_x)\dot{u} - (m+m_y)vr = X_H + X_P + X_R + X_A \\
(m+m_y)\dot{v} + (m+m_x)ur = Y_{HP} + Y_R + Y_A \\
(I_{ZZ} + J_{ZZ})\dot{r} = N_{HP} + N_R + N_A
\end{cases}
\tag{1}
$$

Where m, m_x, m_y are ship's mass and added mass, I_{ZZ}, J_{ZZ} are moment inertia and added moment inertia around mass center, u, v are ship's surge speed and sway speed respectively, r is yaw rate. X, Y, N are external forces and external moment acting on the ship. The variable relevant to hull, propeller, rudder and wind is denoted by subscripts H, P, R and A respectively. Subscript HP denotes the interaction of hydrodynamic force and moment between hull and propeller. The calculation of those variables can be found in paper [9].

Note: The state of ship course nonlinear system was obtained from a group of the MMG ship formulas in order to be much closer to the actual conditions.

2.3 Steering Gear Dynamic Model

To reflect the physical limitations of vessel precisely and improve performance of ship model, the saturation of rudder angle is defined as formula (2).

$$
\begin{cases}
\dot{\delta} = \dfrac{1}{T_E}\delta_E - \dfrac{1}{T_E}\delta \\[2mm]
sat(\delta) = \begin{cases} \mathrm{sgn}(\delta)\cdot\delta_{\max} & if\ |\delta| \ge \delta_{\max} \\ \delta & else \end{cases}
\end{cases}
\tag{2}
$$

Where, constrained of rudder angle and steering rate is $|\delta| \le 35°$ and $|\dot{\delta}| \le 3°/s$ respectively. δ_e is command rudder angle, T_E is gear time constant.

2.4 Wind Forces and Moment

The wind forces and moment are expressed as formula [9],[16] (3).

$$
\begin{cases}
X_{wind} = \dfrac{1}{2}C_X(\gamma_r)\rho_a V_r^2 A_T \\[2mm]
Y_{wind} = \dfrac{1}{2}C_Y(\gamma_r)\rho_a V_r^2 A_L \\[2mm]
N_{wind} = \dfrac{1}{2}C_N(\gamma_r)\rho_a V_r^2 A_L L
\end{cases}
\tag{3}
$$

Where γ_r is the angle of wind relative to ship bow, $C_X(\gamma_r)$ and $C_Y(\gamma_r)$ are the empirical force coefficients. $C_N(\gamma_r)$ is moment coefficient. ρ_a is air density , A_T and A_L are the transverse and lateral projected areas, and L is the overall of ship.

2.5   Descriptions of Nonlinear Systems

The nonlinear model of ship course system [4],[9] is expressed as formula (4).

$$T \cdot \ddot{\varphi} + \dot{\varphi} + \alpha \cdot \dot{\varphi}^3 = K \cdot u + \omega \qquad (4)$$

Where φ is course, u is constraints rudder angle, $T \& K$ are the ship model's parameters, their dimensionless formulas are expressed in paper [9], ω is external disturbance, α is system parameter. Therefore, the group equations of ship course system can be expressed as formula (5).

$$\begin{cases} \dot{\varphi} = r \\ \dot{r} = \alpha_1 \cdot r + \alpha_2 \cdot r^3 + b \cdot u + \omega' \end{cases} \qquad (5)$$

Where $f(x,t) = \alpha_1 \cdot r + \alpha_2 \cdot r^3$, $\alpha_1 = -\dfrac{1}{T}$, $\alpha_2 = -\dfrac{\alpha}{T}$, $b = \dfrac{K}{T}$ is autopilot gain, $\omega' = \dfrac{\omega}{T}$, $|\omega'| \le \kappa$, κ is a positive number.

The reference model with perfect performance can be described as (6).

$$\ddot{\varphi}_m + 2\xi\omega_n\dot{\varphi}_m + \omega_n^2\varphi_m = \omega_n^2\varphi_r \qquad (6)$$

Where φ_m is reference course, φ_r is system's input, ω_n is system's natural frequency, ξ is system's relative attenuation coefficient, $\omega_n \& \xi$ are chosen by designers. The goal is to design controller u which realize $\lim\limits_{t\to\infty}|\varphi - \varphi_m| \to 0$.

3   Design Ship Nonlinear Systems under Input Constraints

3.1   RBF Neural Network

RBF neural network [17] has been proved to approximate any continuous function with arbitrary precision. RBF neural network structure diagram is in fig.2.

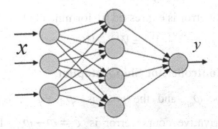

Fig. 2. RBF neural network structure diagram

According to fig.1, the designed input is v and the saturation constraints input is u. The error is $\vartheta = u - v$. Set $u_{\max}$ as the maximum input, then controller with input constraints function $sat(v)$ is expressed as formula (7).

$$sat(v) = \begin{cases} u_{\max}, & |v| > u_{\max} \\ v, & |v| \leq u_{\max} \end{cases} \tag{7}$$

The perfect approximation performance of RBFNN was constructed to approximate the error ϑ. The estimated network output $\hat{\vartheta}(x)$ is obtained by formula (8).

$$\hat{\vartheta}(x) = \sum_{i=1}^{q} \hat{W}_i^T h_i(x) \tag{8}$$

Where x is the network input, $h(x) = (h_1(x), h_2(x), \cdots, h_q(x))^T$ is radial basis vector of RBF network, $h_i(x) = \exp\dfrac{(-\|x - c_i\|^2)}{\sigma_i^2}$ is Gaussian function, c_i is center vector, σ_i^2 is the base width vector of the neural network, q is the number of neural, $\hat{W}$ is the estimated weight of W.

Assume 1. If $\hat{W}$ is bounded, there exists a positive number ϖ which satisfy the mathematical inequality $\|\hat{W}\| \leq \varpi$.

Assume 2. For any given real continuous function $f : B_x \rightarrow R^n$ and arbitrary ε, there exists an optimization weight W^* which satisfy formula (9).

$$\max_{x \in B_x} \|\vartheta(x) - \hat{\vartheta}(x, W^*)\| \leq \varepsilon \tag{9}$$

Set $\Delta\vartheta = \vartheta(x) - \hat{\vartheta}(x, W^*)$, where $\Delta\vartheta$ is the neural network error of $\vartheta(x)$. According to assume 2, $\max\limits_{x \in B_x} \|\Delta\vartheta\| \leq \varepsilon$, therefore

$$\vartheta(x) = \hat{\vartheta}(x, W^*) + \varepsilon \tag{10}$$

And the network weight error is expressed by formula (11).

$$\tilde{W} = W^* - \hat{W} \tag{11}$$

3.2   Design SMC Controller for Ship Autopilot

The desired course is φ_m and the goal is $\varphi \rightarrow \varphi_m$. Define the course error $e = \varphi - \varphi_m$, then derivative course error is $\dot{e} = \dot{\varphi} - \dot{\varphi}_m$. Design the slide mode function $s = c \cdot e + \dot{e}$, where $c > 0$.

Then the derivative slide mode function $\dot{s}$ is expressed as formula (12).

$$\dot{s} = c \cdot \dot{e} + \ddot{e}$$
$$= c \cdot \dot{e} + f(x,t) + b \cdot (v + \vartheta) + \omega' - \ddot{\varphi}_m \qquad (12)$$

Design input v

$$v = \frac{1}{b}\left(-c \cdot \dot{e} - (f(x,t) + \ddot{\varphi}_m - \eta \cdot \text{sgn}(s))\right) - \hat{\vartheta} \qquad (13)$$

Where, η is a designed controller parameter and its value satisfy the formula (14).

$$\eta \geq \kappa + b \cdot \varepsilon_{\max} \qquad (14)$$

Substitute (13) into (12), and then obtain (15)

$$\dot{s} = -\eta \cdot \text{sgn}(s) + b \cdot (\vartheta - \hat{\vartheta}) + \omega'$$
$$= -\eta \cdot \text{sgn}(s) - b \cdot (\widetilde{W}^T \cdot h - \varepsilon) + \omega' \qquad (15)$$

3.3   Stability Analysis

Choose the Lyapunov function candidate (16) for the closed-loop system.

$$V = \frac{1}{2}s^2 + \frac{1}{2}\gamma \cdot \widetilde{W}^T \widetilde{W} \qquad (16)$$

Where γ is the coefficient of NN update weights and $\gamma > 0$. Combined with the formula (15), the differentiating the Lyapunov function with respect to time $\dot{V}$ is expressed as formula (17).

$$\dot{V} = s \cdot \dot{s} + \gamma \cdot \widetilde{W}^T \dot{\widetilde{W}}$$
$$= -\eta \cdot s \cdot \text{sgn}(s) + s \cdot \omega' + s \cdot b \cdot (-\widetilde{W}^T \cdot h + \varepsilon) + \gamma \cdot \widetilde{W}^T \dot{\widetilde{W}} \qquad (17)$$
$$= -\eta \cdot |s| + s \cdot \omega' + s \cdot b \cdot \varepsilon + \widetilde{W}^T \cdot (-s \cdot b \cdot h + \gamma \cdot \dot{\widetilde{W}})$$

Update the adaptive rate $\dot{\hat{W}}$.

$$\dot{\hat{W}} = \frac{1}{\gamma} \cdot s \cdot b \cdot h \qquad (18)$$

Substitute (18) into (17), then simplified equation $\dot{V} = -\eta \cdot |s| + s \cdot (\omega' + b \cdot \varepsilon)$. On the basis of formula (5) and (14), the inequality $\dot{V} \leq 0$ can be analyzed.

4   Simulation Results

In order to validate the performance of the proposed algorithm, the training ship, Yulong, was involved and simulations were performed by Matlab/Simulink. The length, breadth and draft of the ship is 126m,20.8m and 8m respectively. The ship's model parameters are $K'=7.9629$, $T'=13.88$, $\alpha=30$. The wind direction and wind speed is 10°and 20 m/s respectively. The initial speed is 7.2 m/s. The controller parameters are $c=0.2$, $\kappa=0.05$, $\eta=0.1$. The RBFNN structure is 1-5-1 and initial weights are 0. The vector central is $c_i=\pi\cdot[-1/6\ \ -1/12\ \ 0\ \ 1/12\ \ 1/6]$ and the base width is $\sigma_i=1$. The network input is v. The coefficient of NN update weights is $\gamma=0.01$.

4.1   Course-Keep Simulation

The autopilot maintains the ship on a settled course under the external disturbances in this paper. The initial course is 10°and the desired course is 50°. The simulation results were plotted from fig.3 to fig.5. These figures demonstrated that ship can keep the desired course by the proposed algorithm.

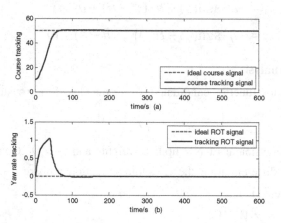

Fig. 3. The historical data of the course tracking and yaw rate tracking

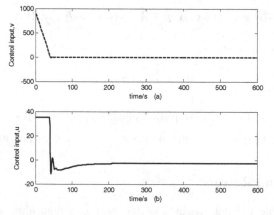

Fig. 4. The historical data of the designed input v and the saturation constraints input u

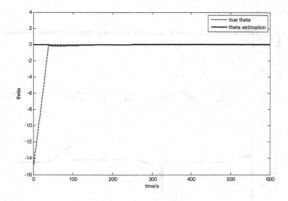

Fig. 5. The data of the error ϑ and $\hat{\vartheta}$ in course-change

4.2   Course-Change Simulation

The autopilot can alter course in accordance with commanded course under the external disturbances. The initial course is $10°$. The desired commanded course system is a two-order settled reference equation and its initial value is $0°$. The other parameters of reference system are as follows. $\xi = 1$, φ_m is square wave with the amplitude $10°$. ω_n is 0.05. The simulation results were plotted from fig.6 to fig.8.

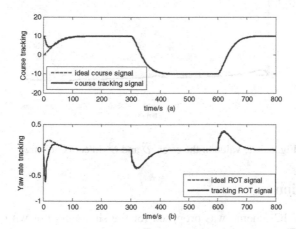

Fig. 6. The historical data of the course tracking and yaw rate tracking in course-change

These figures demonstrated that ship also can track the settled commanded course by the proposed algorithm with the same parameters.

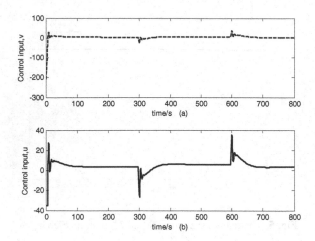

Fig. 7. The historical data of the designed input v and the saturation constraints input u

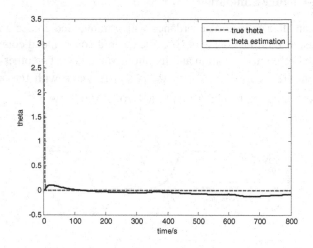

Fig. 8. The value of the error ϑ and $\hat{\vartheta}$ in course-change

5   Conclusion

In this paper, a SMC scheme was proposed for the ship autopilot with the saturation of steering gear. The state of the ship course nonlinear system was solved by a group of the MMG ship motion formulas to be much closer to the actual conditions. The error between the designed input and the saturation constraints input was approximated by the RBFNN. The network errors and the external disturbances were overcome by the SMC method. Take training ship, Yulong, for example, simulation results demonstrate the effectiveness of the proposed scheme.

Although the algorithm can guarantee stability of the system, it is more meaningful to study algorithm with the time and space constraints. Therefore, terminal sliding mode or output feedback control will be the further research.

Acknowledgments. This work is supported by the Fundamental Research Funds for the Central Universities under grant No.3132013005 and 3132014027.

References

1. Sun, N., Fang, Y.C.: A review for the control of a class of under actuated systems. CAAI Transactions on Intelligent Systems 6(3), 200–207 (2011) (in Chinese)
2. Liu, W.J., Sui, Q.M., Xiao, H.R., Zhou, F.Y.: Sliding backstepping control for ship course with nonlinear disturbance observer. Journal of Information & Computational Science 8(16), 3809–3817 (2011)
3. Thor, I.F.: Guidance and control of Ocean vehicles. of Trondheim. John Wiley & Sons Ltd., University of Trondheim Norway (1994)
4. Yang, Y.S., Zhou, C.J., Ren, J.S.: Model reference adaptive robust fuzzy control for ship steering autopilot with uncertain nonlinear systems. Applied Soft Computing 3, 305–316 (2003)
5. Khac, D.D., Pan, J.: Control of ships and underwater vehicles design for underactuated and nonlinear marine systems. Springer, London (2009)
6. Amerongen, J.V.: Adaptive steering of ships—a model reference approach. Automatica 20(1), 3–14 (1984)
7. Du, J.L., Guo, C.: Nonlinear adaptive design for course tracking control of ship without a priori knowledge of control gain. Journal of Control Theory and Applications 22(2), 315–320 (2005) (in Chinese)
8. Bu, R.X.: Nonlinear feedback control of underactuated surface ships. Dalian Maritime University, Dalian (2008) (in Chinese)
9. Jia, X.L., Yang, Y.S.: Ship motion mathematical model. Dalian Maritime University Press, Dalian (1999) (in Chinese)
10. Yang, Y.S., Jia, X.L.: Robust adaptive control algorithm applied to ship steering autopilot with uncertain nonlinear system. Ship Building of China 41(1), 21–25 (2000) (in Chinese)
11. Liu, C., Li, T.S., Chen, N.X.: Dynamic surface control and minimal learning parameter (DSC-MLP) design of a ship's autopilot with rudder dynamics. Journal of Harbin Engineering University 33(1), 1–6 (2012) (in Chinese)
12. Li, J.F., Li, T.S.: Direct adaptive neural network tracking control with input saturation. Journal of Applied Sciences—Electronics and Information Engineering 31(3), 294–302 (2013) (in Chinese)
13. Wei, E.P.: Design ship autopilot with delays and input saturation. Dalian Maritime University, Dalian (2013) (in Chinese)
14. Chen, M., Ge, S.Z.S., Ren, B.B.: Adaptive tracking control of uncertain MIMO nonlinear systems with input constraints. Automatica 47, 452–465 (2011)
15. Liu, J.K.: Sliding mode control design and matlab simulation. Tsinghua University Press, Beijing (2012) (in Chinese)
16. Thor, I.F.: Marine control systems: guidance, navigation and control of ships, rigs and underwater vehicles. Norwegian University of science and technology Trondheim, Norway (2002)
17. Tomaso, P., Federico, G.: A theory of networks for approximation and learning. A.I. Memo No.1140,C.B.I.P. Paper No.31.Massachusetts institute of technology artificial intelligence laboratory and center for biological information processing Whitaker college, Cambridge, Massachusetts (1989)

Automatic Assessment Model for Sailing in Narrow Channel[*]

Wang Delong and Ren Hongxiang

Key Laboratory of Marine Dynamic Simulation & Control for Ministry
of Communications, Dalian Maritime University, Dalian 116026, China
wangdelong1986@sina.com, dmu_rhx@163.com

Abstract. Firstly, analyze the relevant IMO regulations about vessels proceeding along a narrow channel, then establish a evaluation index system combining with the theory of ship handling; secondly, establish membership functions by using the membership function evaluation method for every evaluation index; Thirdly, obtain the weights of evaluation indexes utilizing the expert evaluation method; At last, establish the evaluation procedure and develop the automatic evaluation model for vessels proceeding along a narrow channel by using C++ programming language. This system has been tested preliminarily with satisfied results.

Keywords: narrow channel, automatic assessment model, ship handling, membership function.

1 Introduction

Ship officers maneuver the vessels sailing all over the world depending on their knowledge and experiences. Due to the differences of the education background and the navigating experiences, there are many different method of ship maneuvering, so it comes to the optimization problem. However, it is difficult to evaluate the ship maneuvering skill of a navigator in different environments. Considering the safety issues only, it will be qualified if the ship arrives the designated port with no collisions. But which is the minimum requirements. For in-depth studies, higher request is required. It is necessary to evaluating mariners' maneuvering skills in different situations. For sailing in a narrow channel, firstly consider the restrictions of the channel (breadth, depth and so on); secondly standard the ship maneuvering method; thirdly evaluate the skills of the ship officers' maneuvering; finally, offer the improvement advices according to the detail results. When it achieves the high degree of standardization of ship's maneuvering, the system could apply to the navigating auxiliary system, even could realize the auto-navigation.

---

[*] Foundation item: Supported by "973 Major State Basic Research Development Program "(No. 2009CB320805); "Natural Science Foundation of Liaoning Province"(No. 201202018); "The Fundamental Research Funds for the Central Universities" (No. 01780134).

X.-h. Sun et al. (Eds.): ICA3PP 2014, Part II, LNCS 8631, pp. 396–403, 2014.

2   Evaluation Method

There are lots of ways to establish the evaluation model, for instance, Hypothesis Test[1], Improved TOPSIS[2], Fuzzy comprehensive evaluation method based on grey correlation degree[3], and using a small function curve model[4]. Every methods have their advantages and applied ranges.

In this paper, we adopt the key informant and the fuzzy comprehensive evaluation method.

Because of the uncertainty of some evaluation indexes, apply the fuzzy mathematics to establish the membership function. Acquire the membership value μ_i of single evaluation index according to the results of practical operations. Combine μ_i with the relevant weight value ω_i and sum to get the total score (s). This method is comparatively simple and also could decrease the uncertainty of evaluation indexes.

$$s = \sum_{i=1}^{n}(\mu_i \times \omega_i) \tag{1}$$

Where: n stands for the number of evaluation indexes.

3   Evaluation Index System

The establishment of evaluation indexes system is the fundamental work of evaluation model. There are many factors affecting the ship sailing in the narrow channel, including restriction in fair way, weather condition, the ship and so on. After studied the different factors, this paper get the evaluation indexes system sailing in narrow channel, see figure 1.

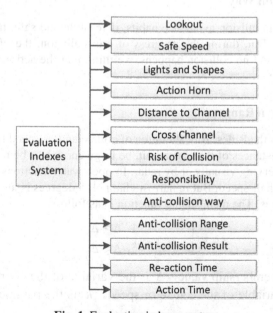

Fig. 1. Evaluation indexes system

After the establishment of evaluation indexes system, we need to establish membership function for each evaluation index. The following are introduced.

3.1   Display of Lights and Shapes

According to the provisions 20-30 of the 1972' International Regulations for Preventing Collisions at sea(short for "The Rules" as follows), display different lights and shapes in different situations. Firstly, get the sailing environment (including day or night, visibility, fairway, navigational status and so on) and the displacement of the ship; secondly, analyze the standard displacement of the ship; finally, contrast them to get the final result.

3.2   Risk of Collision

The minimum distance of the two vessels is the index to judge the risk of collision. For convenience, use the larger Breadth of the two vessels to represent the standard distance. If the distance of the two vessels is smaller than the standard one, the risk of collision exists. We evaluate this index from the action of the ship officer.

3.3   Responsibility

Divide the situations, get the risk of collision, and get the standard responsibility (give-way vessel or stand-on vessel). If the action of the vessel meets the standards, the officer gives the correct answer.

3.4   Anti-collision Way

In accordance with collision avoidance habits, if feasible and safe, try to alter course to avoid collision. But, during the progress of anti-collision, the officer change the speed of the ship, and no collision happens, we think that the action is also qualified, just the score is lower.

3.5   Anti-collision Range

In accordance with the Rules, Any alteration of course and/or speed to avoid collision, shall, if the circumstances of the case admit, be large enough to be readily apparent to another vessel observing visually or by radar. In open waters, actions should be turned 15 degrees and/or half speed. But in narrow channel, 5 degrees is also feasible. So the standard is 5 degrees. The membership function is as follows:

$$\mu = \begin{cases} 1, & \Delta \geq \Delta_s \\ e^{-(\Delta-\Delta_s)^2/k}, & \Delta < \Delta_s \end{cases} \tag{2}$$

Where: μ is a membership value, Δ is the variable of the course or speed, Δ_s is the standard variable of the course or speed, k is the parameter of the membership function.

3.6   Lookout

In accordance with the rule 5 of the Rules, Every vessel shall at all times maintain a proper look-out by sight and hearing as well as by all available means appropriate in the prevailing circumstances and conditions so as to make a full appraisal of the situation and of the risk of collision. The purpose of Lookout is to ensure the safety of navigation. If the officer can find the ship around him as soon as possible use different means, and give the correct judgment of the encounter situation, take corrective action, then the officer lookout can be considered to be qualified, otherwise to be unqualified.

3.7   Re-action Time

After the other vessel is finally past and clear, the vessel taking action should alter course to its original route. The re-action time is very important, if it is earlier, the two vessels may have risk of collision again, if it is later, the vessel taken action should take more time to sailing in the plan route. So, the standard is the time the other vessel is finally past and clear, in open waters, this time may be the time that there are 1 to 2 nm between the two vessels after they are past and clear. In narrow channel, 1.5-2 times ship length is appropriate. The membership function is as follows:

$$\mu = \begin{cases} 1, \ d \geq d_s \\ e^{-(d-d_s)^2/k}, \ d < d_s \end{cases} \tag{3}$$

Where: d is the distance that the vessel begins to take re-action, d_s is the standard that the vessel begins to take re-action.

3.8   Safe Speed

In accordance with the rule 6 of the Rules, Every vessel shall at all times proceed at a safe speed so that she can take proper and effective action to avoid collision and be stopped within a distance appropriate to the prevailing circumstances and conditions. In narrow channel, if there is speed restriction, this speed is the standard value. If not, economic speed is the standard value, by making the appropriate correction according to the environmental conditions and traffic flow conditions. The membership function is as follows:

$$\mu = e^{-(v-v_s)^2/k} \tag{4}$$

Where: v is the average speed, v_s is the standard safe speed.

3.9   Action Horn

In accordance with the Rules relating to the action horn, when the vessel takes action, she needs to use the corresponding action horn. The difficulty is that matching the sailing environment and the relevant provisions of the Rules. As long as the action horn meets the Rules, the evaluation result is out, otherwise is zero.

3.10 Distance to Channel

In accordance with the rule 9 of the Rules, A vessel proceeding along the course of a narrow channel or fairway shall keep as near to the outer limit of the channel or fairway which lies on her starboard side as is safe and practicable. The key issue is the critical distance to the right edge of the fairway. We need to consider the quay effect and the shallow effect, but these two factors are very complex. In assessing, as long as the vessel sails along the right side of the middle line in the narrow channel without these two effects, the evaluation result is out, otherwise is zero.

3.11 Cross Channel

In accordance with the rule 9 of the Rules, A vessel shall not cross a narrow channel or fairway if such crossing impedes the passage of a vessel which can safely navigate only within such channel or fairway. The latter vessel may use the sound signal prescribed in Rule 34(d) if in doubt as to the intention of the crossing vessel. The action meets with it, the evaluation result is out, otherwise is zero. When setting the questions, determine whether the ship should cross the narrow channel, as a basis for evaluation.

3.12 Action Time

There are two key issues for determining the action time; the first one is TCPA while taking action, the second one is the distance between two vessels while taking action. In assessing, consider these two issues separately, then give different weight to each other, finally, weight average to get the final results of the assessment. The membership function is as follows:

$$\mu(T) = \mu(T_{TCPA}) \times \omega_1 + \mu(T_{DIS}) \times \omega_2 \tag{5}$$

$$\mu(T_{TCPA}) = e^{-\left(T - \frac{T_S}{\Delta_S}\right)^2 / k_1} \tag{6}$$

$$\mu(T_{DIS}) = e^{-(D - D_S \times \Delta_S)^2 / k_2} \tag{7}$$

Where: $\mu(T_{TCPA})$, $\mu(T_{DIS})$ is the membership function of $TCPA$ and distance; T is the TCPA while taking action; D is the distance between two vessels while taking action; T_S is the standard TCPA; D_S is the standard distance; ω_1 is the weight of TCPA; ω_2 is the weight of distance.

3.13 Anti-collision Result

The basic requirement is that the other vessel is past and clear. The key issue is the minimum distance between the two vessels. The membership function is as follows:

$$\mu = \begin{cases} 1, & DCPA \geq dDCPA_s \\ e^{-(DCPA - DCPA_S)^2 / k}, & DCPA < DCPA_s \end{cases} \tag{8}$$

Where: $DCPA$ is the distance at closest point of approach, $DCPA_s$ is the standard distance at closest point of approach.

4   Evaluation Model

This article is only evaluated for the case of a ship sailing under good visibility in the narrow channel and collision avoidance with a single target ship. In assessing, determine whether the ship sailing in the obscured area, if it is, judge the action horn is right or not, otherwise, evaluate the sailing in the normal channel. If it comes to ship collision avoidance, evaluate the action of collision avoidance: specific distinction overtaking situation, the head-on situation and the crossing situation, thereby determine the responsibility of the two vessels. According to the responsibility, evaluate the action to avoid collision. The evaluation progress of the automatic evaluation model for sailing in narrow channel is shown in figure 2.

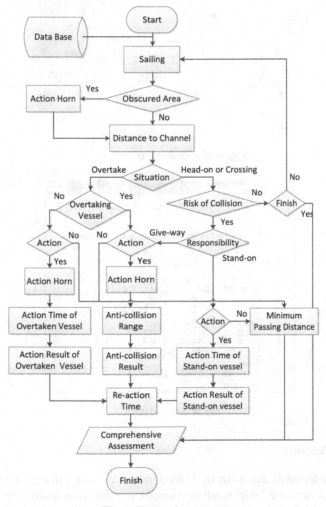

Fig. 2. Evaluation progress

5   Examples

The automatic evaluation model has been established, and tested on ship handling simulator. The following is one of the examples. From the results, the automatic evaluation results are reasonable, meet the actual ship maneuvering. The maneuvering track is shown in figure 3. The score details are shown in figure 4.

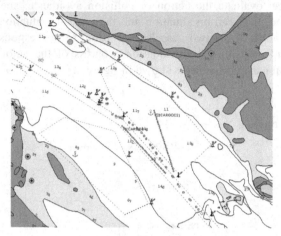

Fig. 3. Maneuvering trajectory

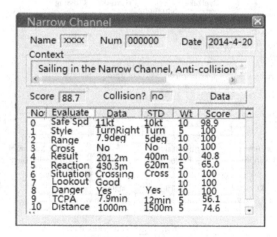

Fig. 4. Score details

6   Conclusions

This paper established an automatic evaluation model for sailing in narrow channel. The model has been tested in ship handling simulator, evaluation results are reasonable. However, the model needs to be further improved, such as this model can be expanded to consider all visibility conditions, and evaluate multi-ship collision avoidance.

References

1. Tao, J., Yin, Y., Lian, J.J.: Research on Assessment of Ship Entering Port in Navigation Simulator. J. Ship Electronic Engineering 2, 119–122 (2011)
2. Yang, Y.F., Fang, Q.G.: Assessment of navigation simulation for marine police in narrow sea-route. J. Journal of Shanghai Maritime University 3, 14–18 (2008)
3. Li, Q.H., Jian, Y.: Evaluation on the Simulator Berthing Training Result Based on Improved TOPSIS. J. Journal of Guangzhou Maritime College 1, 4–7 (2013)
4. Chen, J.B., Wu, G.Y., Ying, S.J.: Evaluation of large-vessel handling simulation based on synthetic grey-fuzzy method. J. Journal of Shanghai Maritime University 4, 1–5 (2008)
5. Chen, L.N., Ren, H.X., Jin, Y.C.: On Ship Radar/ARPA Intelligent Examination System. J. Journal of Chong Qing Jiao Tong University (Natural Science) 30, 1049–1053 (2011)
6. Wang, D.L.: Preliminary Study on the Ship Maneuvering Automatic Evaluation System based on Ship Handling Simulator. Master thesis. Dalian Maritime University (2013)

Bus Arrival Time Prediction and Release:
System, Database and Android Application Design[*]

Junhao Fu[1], Lei Wang[2], Mingyang Pan[1], Zhongyi Zuo[2], and Qian Yang[1]

[1] Navigation College, Dalian Maritime University, Dalian, China 116026
fujunhao2006@126.com
[2] School of Traffic and Transportation Engineering, Dalian Jiaotong University,
Dalian, China 116028

Abstract. The system, facing to passengers, aim to releasing the information of bus arrival time prediction, sends messages to mobile phone directly, saves the travel time and decreases the waiting times and also increases the efficiency. The system runs with the information of bus real-time GPS data, using the computer languages and technologies of Java EE, JSP, MySQL database and Android. The author uses FSM (finite state machine) which is part of servers to handle the bus real-time data, develops a synthetic system centralized, enterprise-level, mobile phone platform and based on requests and responses.

Keywords: Urban Transportation, GPS, Arrival Time Prediction, Java EE, Android.

1 Introduction

With the effect of the reform and opening-up policy, the national economy increasing constantly and the urbanization process of China deepen unceasingly. The city scale expanded quickly, the total of vehicle turned to tremendous. Meanwhile, the conflict between the need of transport, traffic capacity, road using and construction of roads became highlighted. While, it is a necessary path to build high capacity, high load carrying capacity and slight polluted public transportation. Urban public transport systems of China exists some problems of low efficiency of running, low level of information service and so on. With the arrival of information era, computing industry, Internet and communication technology developed a lot. Intelligent Society is near, and also the public needs bus information more and more.

The waiting passenger usually faced with a situation that either no bus arrived or a crowd of buses arrived. The fact could easily causes a series of mental problems such as dysphoric, meanwhile the situation would impacts the next step's judgment and plan of passengers. The aim to research Bus Arrival Time Prediction and Release System is to make travel more convenient and also save passengers' time.

Bring with ITS development, the technologies of bus arrival time prediction and electronic station board have been researched and used widely. Lin and Zeng used real-time GPS data to do some statistical analysis [1], then they came up with a bus

---

[*] Supported by" the Fundamental Research Funds for the Central Universities": No.3132014309.

X.-h. Sun et al. (Eds.): ICA3PP 2014, Part II, LNCS 8631, pp. 404–416, 2014.

arrival predict algorithm which was based on history data. Chien and his colleagues built up an artificial neural network algorithm to predicted bus arrival time [2]. Chen and his colleagues brought APC data to the predict algorithm, in order to increase the accuracy of prediction [3]. Jeong and his colleagues used AVL data to increase the accuracy of vehicles location [4]. Zhou and his colleagues used mobile phone to located bus, in order to predict bus arrival time [5].

Most research of colleges and universities in China have concentrated on theories and Algorithms. Yu and his colleagues came up with a bus arrival time prediction model ,the model, predicting the bus travel time, fully proved that the accurate superiority of optimized Kalman filter which supported vector machine [6][7][8]. Sun and his colleagues used probe vehicle which treated as samples to collect bus travel time data [9], in order to do some prediction. The bus arrival prediction algorithms which is presented by Zuo provided a good thinking in sending bus arrival information to user's mobile phone [10]. But there is nobody published literatures about the design of bus arrival time prediction system till now.

For the application, several cities in China like Suzhou and Xiamen have already covered arrival information prediction of all lines. Such as the crisscrossed traffic network of Suzhou, its search service relied on the line number and station code which had a bad experience in the user surface, also, it could only fetch the number of stations between vehicle and target station and couldn't support the information about the distance or time.

This paper, based on the foundation of the research about bus arrival time predict algorithms, has do some design and realization on the bus arrival time prediction and release system. The article introduced the overall structure of the system in 2, the prediction and the realization of core service in 3, the design of system database in 4, the design of the client based on Android in 4, at last this article summarized the work of design and realization.

2   System Overall Architecture

B/S combined with C/S, application database-middleware-client model, is an architecture which being widely used by information system. The system overall architecture is shown in Fig.1.

The bus information release system includes four parts which is communication interface, servers, and database.

1. Servers

The server which realized the core algorithm and logical operation is the core device. The server handles the data which come from kinds of ports and calculates the result or do some response.

2. Database

The database is used to store a large scale of data which is considered to be a big mount of history data and their calculating results, related information about bus system such as line information and vehicle information.

3. Client

The client is a mobile phone application which is used to release messages to the public. The client and the server communicates through the Internet, the client shows the result which handled by the server to the users directly.

4. Communication interface

The interface does the work of communication between vehicles and servers, it realized the collection of the running state of vehicle data. And also, the interface realized the exchange of information between clients and servers.

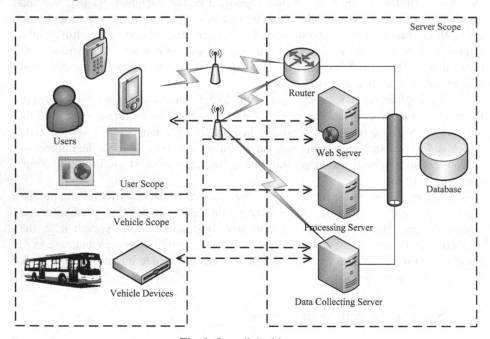

Fig. 1. Overall Architecture

3 Server

3.1 Logical Structure

According to the logical structure of the system, which is the process of business logic, the system service is divided into four function modules named user search function, data collection function, core calculating function and system maintenance function. (See Fig.2.).

1. user search function

The user search function provides to users (public, passengers) the running status of the bus. The system releases the bus running status to the public and response to the query of target vehicle come from the client.

2. data collection function

The data collection function is to collect and store the bus vehicle operating data delivered from the data interface, which conveys the vehicle status online. This function can reserve bus operation history data into the database.

3. Core calculation function

System processes the collected online data and the history data stored in the database in order to export the result information. Core calculation function is composed by two aspects: one is to predict the real-time bus vehicle arrival information which is requested by user query; the other is to collect and store the vehicle online operation status data, which includes such two parts as collecting and storing online and analyzing and processing offline.

4. Management and maintenance function

This function is designed for managing and maintaining some basic information such as route and vehicle information which will be useful for prediction.

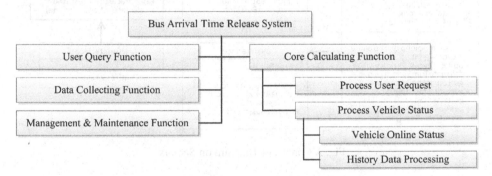

Fig. 2. The Logical Structure of the Server

3.2   Design and Implementation

Based on the service logic on the server scope, we designed the class diagram as shown in Fig.3. The description of several core classes is listed as following:

1. Class Bus: defines the properties and the fundamental methods of bus. Each hypostatic bus vehicle that is operating online will create an instance of class Bus correspondingly, and which will be temporarily stored in an array list called busList in servlet context that has a lifecycle of application scope.
2. Class DataConn: establish the database connection, and keep the connection into the database connection pool, which is aimed to reduce the coupling degree between the server and the database.
3. Class Initialize: response to the initialization operation of the system, then set up the database connection pool, monitor the bus vehicles status and construct and deconstruct the bus objects according to the real-time monitoring bus operating status data.

4. Class Forecast: implement the prediction function.
5. Class BusInterface: response to the request on updating of bus objects according to the bus entities.
6. Class UserInterface: response to the request of users to query information then return the query results.

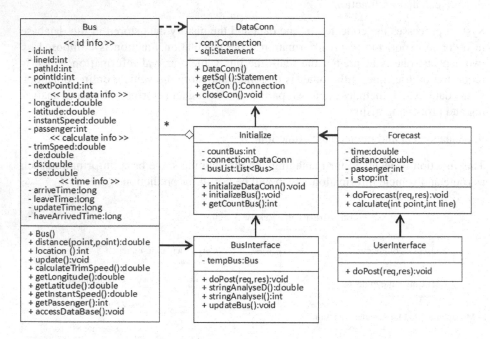

Fig. 3. Core Class Diagram on Servers

Among these classes, class Bus and class Forecast are the basic and core classes of system service. The description on the implementation of these two classes is given as following:

— Class Bus

The main methods in class Bus includes:

- Method Distance: this is the method to calculate the distance between two points, and the returned value is a float value which equals to the distance between the two points those are the parameters of this method.
- Method Location: this is the method to locate a vehicle, i.e., to judge which stop (point) or which link (path) the vehicle is at or on. The implementation flow diagram is shown in Fig. 4.

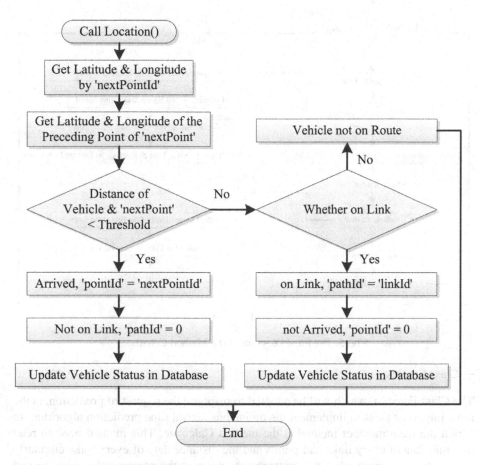

Fig. 4. The Flow Diagram of the Method Location

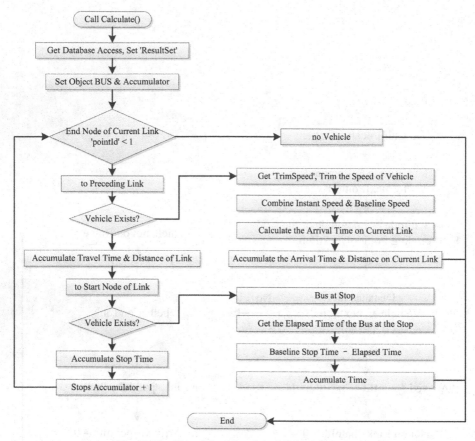

Fig. 5. The Flow Diagram of the Method Calculate

— Class Forecast

The Class Forecast, which will be adopted to response the request of prediction, is the most important class to implement the online bus arrival time prediction algorithm, in which the main member method is the method Calculate. This method need to read the time data of every links and points and the distance data of every links circularly from database, which takes the existence checking of the nearest vehicle as the end mark of the circular processing. The implementation flow diagram is shown in Fig.5.

4   Database

4.1   Composition of Database

The System will apply the database to process including these three aspects: 1) the reference tables for online calculation; 2) the massive history data for offline calculation; 3) management and maintenance data.

Because of the continuous do the prediction computing instantly, huge data size and data processing workload will emerge. Storing the data schema for collecting data, calculating data and basic information managing in a mixture database instance will reduce the efficiency both of the data processing and the information management. For resolving this problem, three independent data schemas are divided, which are responsible for data collection, online data processing and information management. Fig.6 shows the composition of the database.

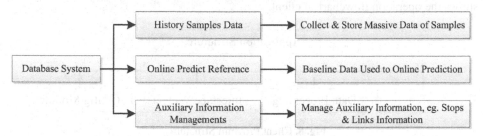

Fig. 6. The Composition of the Database

4.2   Database Design

The database design is a practice on bottom-up approach, which is considered to be an suitable echo to the top-down analyzing approach, i.e., conduct the demand analysis from top to bottom firstly, then proceed the conceptual structure designing from bottom to top, so that an overall conceptual pattern can be aggregated by integrating the minimum elements which are impartible at last. The E-R diagram is shown in fig.7.

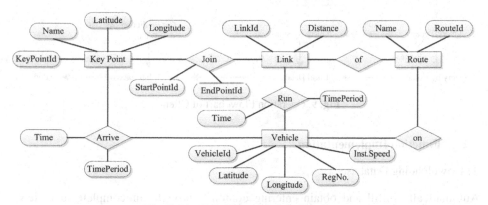

Fig. 7. The E-R Diagram of the Database

5   Client

This paper developed a system with line and station inquiry, arrival time prediction for mobile client, basing on Android platform. Functionally, it inquiry the line details and every probability of this station through the name entering, so as to subjoin the prediction function which can predict the arrival time, distance, remaining station, full load conditions for passengers' convenient travel on the basis of years simple query functions.

5.1   Software Structure

The client program structure showed in Fig.8, it contains Activity module, Data Processing module, Interface control module and Project Configuration module. Fig. 9 shows the operation flowchart of client.

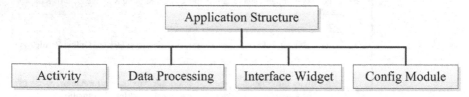

Fig. 8. Client Program Structure

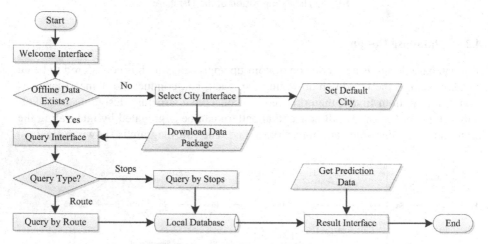

Fig. 9. Operation Flowchart of Client

5.2   Function Implementation

1. Downloading Database

Automatically fulfill and obtain entering contents through autocomplete text view setting, then search database name table and get its English name, calling writeToSDFromInputStream method from Downloader Class and downloading the corresponding database.

2. Record downloading city , urban functions by default

Using ShardPreferences target to create xml files, saving the corresponding data in it.

3. Bus Searching Function

Set interface controls listen for events, access queries of line or station name. Call corresponding method of Class DBgetdata, connecting loaded database as well as searching.

4. Bus Prediction Function

Set interface controls listen for events, access queries of line or station name. Get contact with service via calling getyubao methods of Class Httpgetpost, setting lines and stations names to service for later disposition and obtain the response information through httppost method.

5. Client Local Data Store

This software have three kind of data storage:
  1) downloading database files;
  2) set record file through software;
  3) local database files. Database files located in db file of sd card, set record file located in the path of "data/data/fjh.work.mian/shard_prefs/".
  The main function of local database files is the exchange of Chinese and English, the initial location is apk packbag, and set to mobile along with software and have its path of sd/.

6. The Principle of Software and Server Communication

This software communicate with server through Class HttpURLConnection and Class Httppost, needing the url address of server ,which is the tie of the communication. Figure 10 shows the client software interface and function implementation effect.

(a)   (b)   (c)   (d)

Fig. 10. Client Implementation Effect (a) road query interface; (b) returned result of line query; (c) results prediction and return; (d)station query interface

6   System Experiment

We chose the 18 bus of Lushun, Dalian to test the system of bus information, and the result is showing as following.

6.1   Texting Result

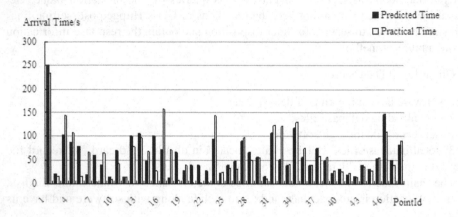

Fig. 11. The Contrast of Prediction Arrival Time and Actual Arrival Time of Key Point

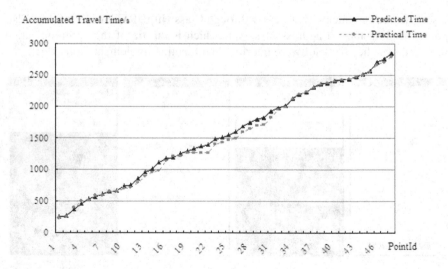

Fig. 12. The Contrast of Prediction Accumulative Time and Actual Accumulative Time of Key Point

6.2   Result Analysis

Due to the limitation of experimental conditions, as we can see from figure 10, we can achieve better accuracy in 18 bus Lushun, Dalian in less number of sample using this system with the main prediction error of 22.6s. Experiments results show that the disturbance between predicted and measured values is large in the subdivision of the small section of the key points, which due to the data acquisition, the degree of subdivision sections, and also with the number of the relevant sample. If we can accumulate more samples in the actual operation will significantly increase its accuracy.

We can see from the figure 11 of accumulative time, the predicted and actual cumulative travel time lines are consistent in the key point. In the condition of longer distances, interval station is more ,the vehicle arrival time is long, will get a better prediction accuracy for this bus line. In other words, the system can better reflect the situation on the bus running the macro and make predictions.

7   Conclusion

This paper started with release bus arrival time prediction information for passengers and intuitively send predicted vehicle arrival information on the situation of the target line to passengers mobile client, designed bus arrival time prediction and information dissemination systems and implement.

This paper precisely expounds the overall system architecture , server design and implementation, database design, and the design and implementation of mobile client based on the Android operating system and use the actual Dalian Port Arthur 18 system been the object of experiment. The results shows that the system can better reflect the situation on the bus running the macro and make predictions.

Currently, the design and implementation of bus arrival time prediction and information dissemination system function is still relatively simple. In subsequent studies, on the basis of the accuracy of predictive algorithm we will strengthening the client application features include electronic map combination, etc., and optimize the user interface, in order to better provide bus arrival time prediction services for travelers.

References

1. Lin, W.H., Zeng, J.: Experimental study of real-time bus arrival time prediction with GPS data: Transportation Research Record. Journal of the Transportation Research Board 1666, 101–109 (1999)
2. Chien, S.I.J., Ding, Y., Wei, C.: Dynamic bus arrival time prediction with artificial neural networks. Journal of Transportation Engineering 128, 429–438 (2002)
3. Chen, M., Liu, X., Xia, J., et al.: A Dynamic Bus-Arrival Time Prediction Model Based on APC Data. Computer-Aided Civil and Infrastructure Engineering 19, 364–376 (2004)
4. Jeong, R., Rilett, L.R.: Prediction model of bus arrival time for real-time applications: Transportation Research Record. Journal of the Transportation Research Board 1927, 195–204 (2005)

416   J. Fu et al.

5. Zhou, P., Zheng, Y., Li, M.: How long to wait?: predicting bus arrival time with mobile phone based participatory sensing. In: Proceedings of the 10th International Conference on Mobile Systems, Applications, and Services, pp. 379–392. ACM (2002)
6. Bin, Y., Zhongzhen, Y., Baozhen, Y.: Bus arrival time prediction using support vector machines. Journal of Intelligent Transportation Systems 10, 151–158 (2006)
7. Yu, B., Lam, W.H.K., Tam, M.L.: Bus arrival time prediction at bus stop with multiple routes: Transportation Research Part C. Emerging Technologies 19, 1157–1170 (2011)
8. Yu, B., Yang, Z.-Z., Zeng, Q.-C.: Bus Arrival Time Prediction Model Based on Support Vector Machine and Kalman Filter. China Journal of Highway and Transport 21, 89–92 (2008)
9. Sun, D.-H., Lai, Y.-B., Liao, X.-Y., et al.: Real-time prediction model of arrival time for floating transit vehicle. Journal of Traffic and Transportation Engineering 11, 84–89 (2011)
10. Zuo, Z.-Y., Wang, L.: Bus Arrival Time Forecasting and Real-time Information Publication Technology. Journal of Transportation Systems Engineering and Information Technology 13, 63–68 (2013)

On Key Techniques of a Radar Remote Telemetry and Monitoring System*

Jiangling Hao, Mingyang Pan, Deqiang Wang, Lining Zhao, and Depeng Zhao

Navigation College, Dalian Maritime Univ. Dalian 116026, China
haojlxn@qq.com

Abstract. In order to monitor those vessels which are not equipped with AIS, a radar remote telemetry and monitoring system which combines radar and ECDIS is proposed. This system consists of data collection layer, processing layer, and presentation layer. Each radar station is installed with MD-3641/3642 radar. Using the 16-bits SCM PIC24 as CPU, an embedded hardware based on ETX PC is designed for radar telemetry. A logic diagram for the embedded radar controller is illustrated. Internet communication technology is adopted to complete the data transmission between center and radar station. A target echo identifying algorithm is presented to denoise the radar image and compute the accurate position of the objects overlaid on the electronic charts. Applied result shows that these techniques and approaches are efficient and feasible.

Keywords: radar remote telemetry and monitoring, ECDIS, embedded technology, target echo identifying algorithm.

1 Introduction

To promote the application of advanced technology in the domestic voyages and to standardize the usage of ECDIS and AIS for navigation safety, China Maritime Safety Administration issued a 'domestic voyages shipboard electronic chart systems and automatic identification system equipment regulations'. According to the specific requirements of the International Maritime Organization concerning, all 300 gross tonnage and above on international voyages and 500 gross tonnage and above and non-international voyages, and all passenger ships should be equipped with AIS.

Electronic Chart Display and Information System (Electronic Chart Display and Information System-ECDIS) is an integrated navigation information system which performs a variety of functions related to the navigation safety in the electronic chart display. It has great many useful functions such as planned route designing, position tracking and display, navigational alarm, sailing records, and other assistant operating decisions. Connecting AIS with ECDIS effectively improves the navigational safety. Now a great number of ships runs by this means.

---

* This work is supported by Fundamental Research Funds for the Central Universities of China (3132014309).

X.-h. Sun et al. (Eds.): ICA3PP 2014, Part II, LNCS 8631, pp. 417–424, 2014.

Those regulation and requirements above provide possible means for monitoring the AIS ships. In article [1], AIS stations are set up on the shore to acquire the real-time information of those AIS ships in the area AIS signal can reach. Article [2] proposes a method that GPRS device is equipped in the ship to transfer the information of own GPS to the center. By this way the center is able to monitor those ships which has GPRS device. Apparently, these methods are not feasible for monitoring the ships un-equipped with AIS or GPRS.

There are over one million and sixty thousands fishing vessels in china, which is the largest number in the world. The equipments and condition in most fishing vessels are worn and dangerous. On the other hand, Ocean fishing vessels are few but coast fishing vessels are many more. Unfortunately, the working area of most vessels are exactly concentrated in the crowded area where great many merchant ships run. Apparently, this brings a terrible threat to navigational safety.

This paper designs a radar remote telemetry and monitoring system based on ECDIS. For promoting vessel traffic management and services, this system fully monitors vessels including those not equipped with AIS and GPRS device. Especially, when some of them are in danger, this system locates their position for rescuing. By these way the blind spots of monitoring is eliminated.

2   System Architecture

The system consists of data collection layer, processing layer, and presentation layer. radar stations is data collection layer. a central monitoring system is processing layer, a web site and user's PC, PAD, smart-phone is presentation layer. The system logical architecture is illustrated in Figure 1.

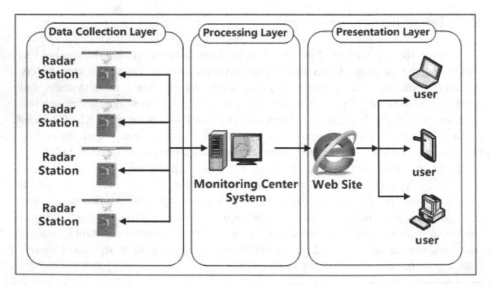

Fig. 1. The system architecture

The key part in radar station is a embedded control unit which obtains the radar video signal via a video capture card and real-timely forms the radar image. Then it sends the compressed image to the center through Internet with the communication technologies such as private Line, ADSL, 2G, 3G. Meanwhile, it receives instructions from the center to control radar[3].

Based on a ECDIS, the central monitoring system is either a data center or a communication control center. It receives the radar images files compressed form the radar stations, then unzips these files and overlays them on the electronic charts. The next procedure is to identify the objects and to calculate their accurate position, speed, course. When these processes are done, the final pictures is published on a web site to provide information for society. Of course, the center is able to remotely control the radar stations by sending control instructions to the radar stations.

The basic platform of the monitoring center system is a ECDIS which accords with international standard. It is able to import the electronic charts of IHO S-57 and display them by IHO S-52 standard.

Conforming to S-52 presentation library, the central monitoring system has the following functions: zoom out and zoom in, roam, layered display, patching without gap, temporary plot (including point, line, circle, polygon, text) and so on. In addition, for improving safety this system completes other functions which are navigational status monitoring, navigational alarm, measure and calculate, making decision to avoid collision (including calculating DCPA/BCPA/TCPA), typhoon and tide informing, geography information query, maps updates and so on.

Radar stations send the image files compressed with a certain period to the central monitoring system. The central monitoring system overlays those image on the electronic charts matching various radar range, scale, and mode of display. Using a target echo identifying algorithm, the center system identifies the objects and calculates their accurate latitude, longitude, speed, course. If some special area need attention, the central system sends remote control instructions to change radar stations' range or frequency of sending images.

3   Embedded Hardware Designed for Remote Telemetry Radar

MD-3641/3642 radar produced by Japan KODEN is chosen in radar station. The radar embedded control unit adopts a 16-bits SCM PIC24 as CPU produced in American Microchip. Hardware development platform is ETX (Embedded Technology extended) PC.

Radar controller is the main component of the radar. The primary function of it is to transmit various control codes to the every subsystem according to the protocols or instructions sent by data processing computer. In addition, it coordinates the synchronization of every subsystem with the timer. It automatically arranges the quick switch of work mode. It implements the monitoring function. It produces the random frequency-hopping. It generates analog signals[4].

Figure 2 is a logic block diagram of the radar controller consisted of ETX PC, receiving controller, instruction distributor and so on. Adapting great many digital signal processing and field-programmable gate array to design modules, the radar controller is a distributed processing system base on a EXT PC.

The descriptions of each module:

(1) Receiving controller: It receives various signals, which are sent by timer, anti-interference, servo, and data processing computer, and puts them into a queues. Finally these signals are carried into ETX PC and instructions distributer to process.

(2) ETX PC: it is the core of radar controller. It real-timely processes various input and output signals. According to the requirements of the radar system, various instructions are assigned to subsystem by distributer. By this way, the processing information speed, capability, flexibility are improved, and performance of radar controller is raised.

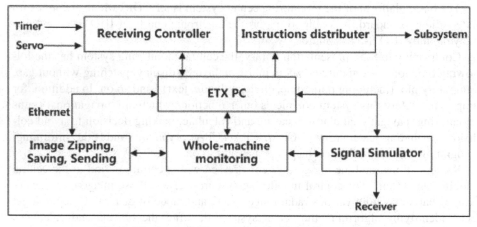

Fig. 2. The Logical diagram of embedded radar controller

(3) Instructions distributer: It receives various information from ETX PC and controller. By certain sequence it distributes macroinstruction and status instruction to subsystem.

(4) Objects simulator: In debug it provides several trails on fixed wave-bit for debugging and checking receiver, signal processing, object extraction, computers and software.

(5)The whole-machine monitoring: All the fault information of each subsystem are analyzed and   summarized. Then these information are displayed in time so that the operator be able to know the working status and the fault conditions. These fault information must be real-timely collected and sent to ETX PC where by analyzing them it is determined whether switch the received channel.

According to the radar controller functional requirements, the network and file processing functions are added. there are four designed tasks: initialization, instructions reorganization and distribution, network reception, data dump. With round robin scheduling mechanism the binary signal lamp is used for synchronization between tasks as well as between task and interrupt. a shared memory is used between tasks communication. a "ping-pong" buffer data structure is designed in storage area[4].

4   A Target Echo Identifying Algorithm

The radar stations sends the zipped image files to monitoring center where these files are unzipped and loaded into memory. First of all is echo identification. This procedure is very important. It directly effects not only the accurate position of objects echo overlaid on the chart but also the correct judgment of the alarm situation. For a bitmap in the memory, the system first filters the radar clutter with a filtering algorithm, then searches the boundary sequence which consists edge points of the object, finally calculates the center position of the boundary sequence (which is considered as a polygon) . In this way the positions of object echoes are obtained—regards the center of boundary as the position of object for each object[5].

Radar image is generally a device-independent bitmap (DIB) with 256 colors or less (including 256 colors). The color value of a pixel is calculated from color palette array and pixel array with the BITMAPINFO structure of DIB.

The paper proposes a target echo identifying algorithm. Before describing the algorithm, the symbols used in the algorithm are showed as bellows:

w , h (in pixels): the width and height of the DIB picture;

C_{ij} : color value of a pixel P_{ij} ($0 \leq i \leq h-1$, $0 \leq j \leq w-1$);

$\overline{C}$, C_{min} : the average and minimal color value of the picture respectively;

IF the color value C_{ij} of a pixel P_{ij} is larger than $\overline{C}$, that is $C_{ij} > \overline{C}$, then call the pixel P_{ij} as bright point, otherwise call it as not bright point.

IF the color value C_{ij} of a pixel P_{ij} equals C_{min} , ($C_{ij} = C_{min}$), then eliminate the pixel.

L : the current scanning row;

S_p : the original point of an echo boundary;

C_p , D_p : normal point of an echo boundary;

E_p : the original point fro next scanning;

R_{list} : the list of boundary point of echo;

N : amount of echoes;

A_{list} : the list of center point of echo (the identifying result)

Algorithm. Target echo identifying algorithm

S1. Let $L = 0$, $E_p = P_{L0}$, $N = 0$, $R_{list} = \varnothing$, $A_{list} = \varnothing$;

S2. IF there is nothing found till the last column, then $L = L + 1$, $E_p = P_{L0}$

   IF L is larger than max row, then go to S9 to end;

   IF P_{ij} is found, then $S_p = P_{ij}$, $R_{list} \Leftarrow S_p$

S3. Judging in sequence whether $C_{i,j+1}$, $C_{i+1,j+1}$, $C_{i+1,j}$, $C_{i+1,j-1}$ is larger than $\bar{C}$;

S4. IF not, then $N = N + 1$, $A_{list} \Leftarrow S_p$, $C_{ij} = C_{min}$;

//here, the point of S_p (P_{ij}) would be eliminated from image.

$E_p = P_{ij+1}$, $R_{list} = \varnothing$, and repeat the processes from S2.

S5. IF yes, mark the bright point as C_p, and $R_{list} \Leftarrow C_p$;

S6. Search next boundary point D_p, in the eight direct of right, right-bottom, bottom, left-bottom, left, left-top, top and right-top of C_p.

IF all neighbors are not boundary point or already contained in R_{list}, then eliminate the C_p and pick-up the last point of R_{list} as new C_p and repeat S6.

S7. IF $D_p = S_p$, then end the searching of the echo boundary;

$N = N + 1$, calculate the average coordinate $(\bar{x}_R, \bar{y}_R)$ of all point in R_{list} ;

// the center of the echo.

$A_{list} \Leftarrow (\bar{x}_R, \bar{y}_R)$, set the color value of the points in R_{list} to be C_{min} ;

//eliminate all points of R_{list} and the points surrounded by from image.

Clean R_{list}, repeat all processes from S2;

S8. IF $D_p \neq S_p$, then $C_p = D_p$, and put C_p into R_{list} ;

Repeat the processes from S6.

S9. Return the amount of echo and the center position A_{list} of all echoes.

S10. End

Annotations:

(1) S1 means that the algorithm is performed from first row and column of radar image.

(2) S2 means that searching rightward from E_p to find the first bright point.

(3) S3 means that the searching is along with the four directions of S_p : right, right-bottom, bottom and left-bottom to find another bright point.

(4) S6 includes two judgment conditions: for a point P, if there is at least one bright point in the top, down, left and right point around it, it would be regarded as a boundary point; for a point D_p, if it isn't contained in R_{list}, it would be regarded to a new boundary point.

5   The Applied Case

The system was applied to monitor fishing vessels in Liaodong bay for protecting jellyfish resources. Nine radar stations was set up on the shore of Liaodong bay. The monitor center was located in Yingkou city. Fig 3 is a radar picture within 3nm-range from Xihekou station overlaid on the electronic chart. Fig 4 is the picture processed with the proposed method. The cluttered points on it was filtered, and the accurate center position of the objects echo (plotted with high bright points) was determined.

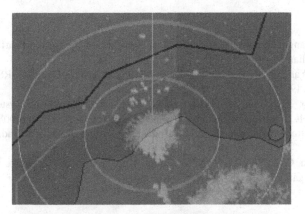

Fig. 3. A initial image from Xihekou radar station

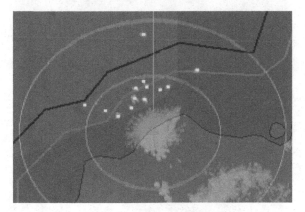

Fig. 4. The processed result

6   Conclusions

Based on the embedded chips, this system not only completes the normal monitoring functions, but also receives the remote instructions, so it extends the ability of remote control.

The approach proposed is different from the general wavelet threshold. It first denoises, then does boundary detection, finally extracts the center position from the boundary sequence. By results analysis it showed that the method improves signal to noise ratio (SNR)of the image.

Combining ECDIS with radar, the whole system founds a distributed radar monitoring system to transmit the image files and instructions through Internet. The next step is to improve the functions and performances of the embedded hardware and software.

References

1. Liu, C.R., Zhang, L.B.: Analysis of AIS Base Stations Design for the Pearl River Delta. J. Journal of Dalian Maritime University. 33(1), 64–66 (2007)
2. Zhou, C.Z., Yang, J.: A Real-time Boat Surveillance System Using GPRS. J. Journal of WUT 28(1), 149–151 (2006)
3. Hao, J.L., Hu, J.F.: Embedded Radar Based Distributed Monitoring System for Inshore Fishing Vessels. J. Journal of Dalian Maritime University 34(1), 83–86 (2008)
4. Zhang, X.P.: Radar Controller Based on Embedded System. J. Modern Radar 26(4), 58–59 (2004)
5. Zhou, L., Hua, C.X.: The Real-time Matching Algorithm for Radar Image with Electronic Chart. J. Navigation of China 69(4), 55–56 (2006)

PSC Ship-Selecting Model Based on Improved Particle Swarm Optimization and BP Neural Network Algorithm

Tingting Yang[1], Zhonghua Sun[1], Shouna Wang[1], Chengming Yang[2], and Bin Lin[3]

[1] College of Navigation, Dalian Maritime University, Dalian China, 116026
[2] College of Transportation Equipment and Ocean Engineering, Dalian Maritime University
[3] College of Information Science and Technology, Dalian Maritime University
yangtingting820523@163.com

Abstract. PSC targeting model has drew much attention recent years. Based on the analysis of PSC targeting mechanisms and algorithms of primary MOU organizations in the maritime society, as 2009/16/EC NIR for instance, a more scientific mathematical targeting model relying on intelligent optimization algorithms is developed in this paper. This algorithm exploits the improved particle swarm-BP neural network mechanism, confronting the weakness of neural network which is easy to drop in local minimum. It could adaptively adjust inertia weights, update speed and position according to premature convergence degree as well as individual fitness value, by exploring improved PSO algorithm to train BP network. The effectiveness and reliability of the algorithm applied to PSC ship-selecting is validated, based on the real cases obtained from the THETIS Inspection database of Paris-MoU. The testing results demonstrate that the proposed PSC ship-selecting model could improve the performance not only on speed of convergence, but also the precision of convergence.

Keywords: Particle Swarm Optimization (PSO), BP Neural Network, PSC ship-selecting.

1   Introduction

2009/16/EC are the newest European PSC (Port State Control) mechanism published by European Congress and Committee in May, 2009. It lays emphasis up on an agreement on ship risk assessment system among Paris MOU Organization, to build up a scientific check procedure and retention management called NIR（New Inspection Regime）[1]. And the Paris Memorandum of Understanding on Port State Control held its 44th Committee meeting in Naples, Italy, May 2011, to discuss its further implementation. The NIR is a risk based targeting mechanism, which will reward quality shipping with a reduced inspection burden and concentrate efforts on high-risk ships. The NIR makes use of company performance and the Voluntary IMO Member State Audit Scheme (VIMSAS) for identifying the risk profile of ships together with the performance of flag State and recognized organization. The NIR is supported by a new information system "THETIS" which is managed and hosted by European

X.-h. Sun et al. (Eds.): ICA3PP 2014, Part II, LNCS 8631, pp. 425–435, 2014.

Maritime Safety Agency (EMSA)[2].But the ship-selecting algorithms just select some representative factors, and simply add each risk value which is scored according to risk factors. They are not comprehensive and scientific, because ship-selecting model should be a non-linear but not linear one.

The existing researches of PSC selecting algorithms mostly focused on fussy comprehensive assessment method and AHP (Analytical Hierarchy Process) method. Some researchers analyzed the main risk factors of ships and employed BP neural network to set up the ship selection model for FSC inspection[3]. But BP neural network needs plenty of samples to train, the convergence speed is lower and it's easy to fall into local optimum value. Zhou introduced and explained the mathematic background of 'Black, Gray and White' Flag State grading system which has been widely used in some regional organizations, and suggested using the same mathematic principle to solve the periodical Matthew Effect and discontinuity problem, by introducing Excess Factor(EF) as revision of the targeting system[4]. But they didn't solve the problem of selecting scientific target factor. PSO (Particle Swarm Optimization) is a kind of Swarm Intelligence optimum method. The idea origins from bird flocks' searching food action, which has applied on optimizing functions and training neural network already. For the purpose of further improving search performance and individual optimizing ability of the basic PSO algorithm, speeding up the convergence efficiency, some literatures have proposed improved algorithm. For example, Shi Y proposed linear decrease progressively weight strategy[5];improved adaptive particle swarm optimization algorithm based on cloud theory[6];cooperative PSO algorithm based on sharing information[7]; Using the strategy of dynamic and self-adaptive inertia weight base on different dimensions and different particles introducing chaotic mutation[8][9].

In this paper, we propose a training BP network by improved PSO algorithm to put forward an algorithm of PSC ship-selecting, with 2009/16/EC NIR be set as research object. The algorithm can adaptively adjust Inertia weight and update speed and position according to premature convergence degree and individual fitness value.

2   Adaptive Swarm Algorithm

2.1   Standard Algorithm and Former Improved Algorithm

Firstly, we randomly initialize M particles in feasible space. Each particle has N dimension, which respectively corresponds to one solution of optimum problem. Then we can determine the fitness value according to the object function. And we can also get the update speed and position with the iteration of following formulas:

$$V_{i,j}^{t} = V_{i,j}^{t-1} + C_1 r_1 (P_{best,i,j}^{t-1} - X_{i,j}^{t-1}) + C_2 r_2 (G_{best,i,j}^{t-1} - X_{i,j}^{t-1})$$

$$X_{i,j}^{t} = X_{i,j}^{t-1} + V_{i,j}^{t}$$

Here, $i = 1, 2, \cdots, N$ indicates dimension of a swarm; $j = 1, 2, \cdots, M$ is the number of swarms; $V_{i,j}^{t}$ and $V_{i,j}^{t-1}$ respectively show the speeds of the t and $t-1$ moment of the ith dimension of the jth particle; $X_{i,j}^{t}$ and $X_{i,j}^{t-1}$ are respectively the speeds of the ith dimension of the jth particle at the t and $t-1$ moment; $P_{best,i,j}^{t-1}$ and $G_{best,i,j}^{t-1}$ are the optimum positions of the jth particle and global particle; C_1 and C_2 are acceleration learning factors.

Shi and Eberhart have proposed inertia weight adjustment method to search speed [10]:

$$V_{i,j}^{t} = \omega V_{i,j}^{t-1} + C_1 r_1 (P_{best,i,j}^{t-1} - X_{i,j}^{t-1}) + C_2 r_2 (G_{best,i,j}^{t-1} - X_{i,j}^{t-1})$$

And Clere has clarified compressed factor can help PSO algorithm fast convergent and get qualified solution, the speed updating equation is :

$$V_{i,j}^{t} = a(V_{i,j}^{t-1} + C_1 r_1 (P_{best,i,j}^{t-1} - X_{i,j}^{t-1}) + C_2 r_2 (G_{best,i,j}^{t-1} - X_{i,j}^{t-1}))$$

$$a = 2 / (\left| 2 - C - \sqrt{C^2 - 4C} \right|)$$

$$C = C_1 + C_2$$

2.2   Improved Adaptive Swarm Algorithm

Improved Inertia Weigh ω

Swarm algorithm has global and local searching abilities, in order to avoid "early mature" convergence, we can change the value of ω to alter convergent speed. Most swarm algorithms proposed linear self-adaptive inertia weight adjustment strategies, but the whole particle searching is a complex non-linear process. Here, we propose a Dynamic Adaptive Particle Swarm Optimization Algorithm (DAPSO), in which the parameter of ω and $V_{i,j}^{t}$ can adaptively adjust according to the Premature Convergence Degree (PCD). We give a definition of PCD, employing the standard difference of probability and mathematical statistics. Definite σ expresses premature convergence degree or disperse degree, as $\sigma = \sqrt{\dfrac{1}{N} \sum_{i=1}^{N} ((f_i - \bar{f}) / \Delta f)^2}$

The scale of particle swarm is N, $\bar{f}$ is current average fitness value of all particles, as $\bar{f} = \dfrac{1}{N} \sum_{i=1}^{N} f_i$; f_i is the fitness value of current iteration number;

$\Delta f = \max\limits_{1 \le i \le N}\{f_i - \bar{f}\}$ expresses maximum difference of current and average fitness. So if Δf lower, the whole swarm can get more premature convergence. We set up a threshold value of σ in advance, if σ is lower than the threshold value, it's recognized that the disperse degree is lower. Then it maybe fall into local optimum, so we should reduce the decrease speed to remain ω a larger value as far as possible; if σ is greater than the threshold value, it's recognized that the disperse degree is larger and its remaining variety to do global research, so should be increase the decrease speed to ensure being convergence quickly.

To satisfy the requirement of above two situations, referring to concave-convex function decrease progressively of ω, we propose an improved adaptive inertia weight according to different PCD.

$$\begin{cases} \sigma < 0.5, & \omega^t = \sqrt{\omega_{min}(1 - \dfrac{\omega_{min}}{\omega_{max}})^{(\frac{T_{max}-t}{T_{max}})^k}} \\[3mm] \sigma \ge 0.5, & \omega^t = (\omega_{min}(1 - \dfrac{\omega_{min}}{\omega_{max}})^{(\frac{T_{max}-t}{T_{max}})^k})^2 \end{cases}$$

Here, ω_{max} and ω_{min} respectively indicate the maximum and minimum value of inertia weight; T_{max} is maximum iteration number; t is current iteration number, k values 3, ω_{max} values 0.9 and ω_{min} values 0.4.

Adaptive Scaling Term $I_{i,j}^t$

Here, we firstly give a definition of $I_{i,j}^t$, indicating the distance between the ith particle and global optimum particle. Then also define two associated parameters: the maximum distance I_{max} and the minimum distance I_{min}. We can find that the distance between the particle and the current optimal position is an important evaluation criterion to PSO, the value of $I_{i,j}^t$ has the equal importance to ω^t. So, it's necessary to consider a dynamic algorithm referring to $I_{i,j}^t$. When $I_{i,j}^t > I_{max}$, $\omega^t = \omega_{max}$; when $I_{i,j}^t < I_{min}$, $\omega^t = \omega_{min}$; when $I_{i,j}^t$ between I_{max} and I_{min}, it will introducing $I_{i,j}^t$. So we can get the following algorithm

$$
\begin{cases}
\sigma < 0.5, & \begin{cases} I_{i,j}^{t} > I_{max}, \omega^{t} = \omega_{max} \\ I_{i,j}^{t} < I_{min}, \quad \omega^{t} = \omega_{min} \\ I_{min} < I_{i,j}^{t} < I_{max}, \omega^{t} = \sqrt{\omega_{min}(1-\dfrac{\omega_{min}}{\omega_{max}})^{(\frac{T_{max}-t}{T_{max}} \cdot \frac{I_{ij}-I_{min}}{I_{max}-I_{min}})^{k}}} \end{cases} \\[2em]
\sigma \geq 0.5, & \begin{cases} I_{i,j}^{t} > I_{max}, \omega^{t} = \omega_{max} \\ I_{i,j}^{t} < I_{min}, \quad \omega^{t} = \omega_{min} \\ I_{min} < I_{i,j}^{t} < I_{max}, \omega^{t} = (\omega_{min}(1-\dfrac{\omega_{min}}{\omega_{max}})^{(\frac{T_{max}-t}{T_{max}} \cdot \frac{I_{ij}-I_{min}}{I_{max}-I_{min}})^{k}})^{2} \end{cases}
\end{cases}
$$

3 PSC Ship-Selecting Model Based on Improved Swarm Optimization-BP Neural Network Algorithm

3.1 BP Neural Network Evaluation Model

(1) Network Structure

According to Kosmogorov theorem, three-layer BP Neural Network can approximate any function. Here, Sigmoid Function is selected to be transmission function.

(2) Input Neural Element Number and Sample Pre-coding

According to risk factor of NIR, select conditional attribute $n = 7$, defined as {TYPE, MARINER, FLAG, CNSM, DEF, DUR, ROUTE}, and they can be pre-coded as follows:

TYPE={other type, bulk, tanker, passenger or dangerous goods
$= \{0.82, 0.84, 0.86\}$

MARINER={No points, 1 times, 2 times, above 2 times }
$= \{0.72, 0.74, 0.76, 0.78\}$

FlAG={flag of convenience, detention rate, flag state approved the convention }
$= \{0.62, 0.64, 0.66\}$

CNSM (Company NSM System)={A class, B class, C class }
$= \{0.52, 0.54, 0.56\}$

DEF (Last 36 months defect number)={ defect number less than or equal 5 in last three inspects, defect number between 5 and 10 in last three inspects, defect number between 10 and 15 in last three inspects, defect number more than 15 }
$$= \{0.42, 0.44, 0.46, 0.48\}$$

DUR (Last detention interval)={0~6 months, 7~12 months, 13 months+}
$$= \{0.32, 0.34, 0.36\}$$

ROUTE={national, international} $= \{0.24, 0.26\}$

(3) Output Neural Element Number

We choose PSC selecting evaluation result to be network output, so the output layer number $m = 1$;

(4) Output factor coding

Define the risk degree value range: Very high risk: $\{0.7, 1\}$; High risk: $\{0.5, 0.7\}$; General risk: $\{0.3, 0.5\}$; low risk: $\{0, 0.3\}$

(5) Hidden Layer Neural Element Number

According to Kosmogorov theorem[11],

$$s = \sqrt{0.43nm + 0.12m^2 + 2.54n + 0.77m + 0.35} + 0.51 = 5$$

3.2   Training and Learning Process Ship-Selecting Analysis

The key point of Particle Swarm optimizing BP Neural Network weigh value is:

(1) Due to the learning process of Neural Network is the weigh updating procession, it can replace the gradient descent method to setup the projection between PSO dimension space and neural network weight, i.e. the weight number of neural network is equal to particle dimension of PSO algorithm.

(2) Employing the mean square error of neural network to be the fitness function of PSO.

Define the kth fitness function to be exponential form $\xi_k = 1 / \exp(E_k)$, here

$$E_k = \frac{1}{2m} \sum_{k=1}^{m} \sum_{t=1}^{n} (y_t^k - c_t^k)^2, \quad m \text{ is sample number, } n \text{ is output Neural Element}$$

number, y_t^k is the tth expected output of kth sample, c_t^k is the tth actual output of kth sample.

The flow of training BP network by improved PSO algorithm is:

(1) Setup BP Neural Network structure, define particle $\vec{x}_m = (x_{m1}x_{m2}\cdots x_{mN})$ are respectively indicate the weights of all neural elements. Here $M = 40$ is the number of particles, and the dimension N can indicated as weight number between input layer and hidden layer+ weight number between hidden layer and output layer + threshold number of hidden layer + threshold number of output layer = $7 \times 5 + 5 \times 1 + 5 + 1 = 46$;

(2) Initialize particle parameter such as position, speed, inertia weight, maximum iteration number;

(3) Calculate fitness and premature convergence degree σ of each particle σ;

(4) Calculate inertia weight adjustment, best position of each particle and global optimum value. Then update position and speed according to above formula;

(5) Output optimum position when precision can satisfy the requirement.

3.3   Selecting Results Analysis

Use Neural Network tool of MATLAB software to provide function and neural class, the Sigmoid function to be transmitted function, the setup in details are:

Self-learning rate net.trainParam.lr = 0.02;
Marquardt adjust parameter net.trainParam.mu=0;
Learning coefficient decreasing factor net.trainParam.mu_dec= 0.9;
Learning coefficient increasing factor net.trainParam.mu_inc=1.05;
Training steps net.trainParam.epochs = 10000;
Training objection net.trainParam.goal1 = 0.01 （BP）；
net.trainParam.goal2 = 0.0001 （PSO-BP）；

We choose 10 groups samples to pre-process and simulation. The accuracy is 10^{-2}. When training step is 7419, the accuracy can satisfy the requirement. Figure 2 indicate the Curve of mean squared error in process of training BP network. And Figure 3 indicate Curve of mean squared error in process of training BP network by improved PSO algorithm When training step is 20, the accuracy can satisfy the requirement of 10^{-4}.

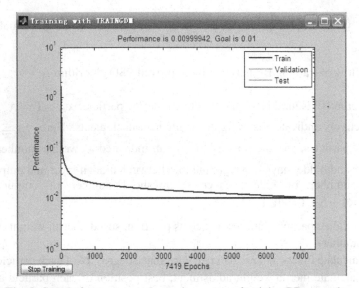

Fig. 1. Curve of mean squared error in process of training BP network

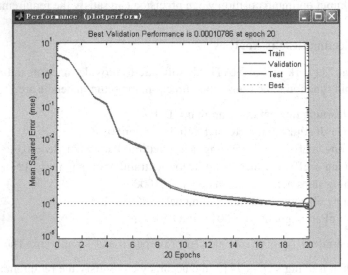

Fig. 2. Curve of mean squared error in process of training BP network by improved PSO algorithm

Table1 are test sample. We can see that the identity errors of the improved PSO-BP algorithm are tiny, which can satisfy the practice requirement. The algorithm has the ability of global search, overcoming the weakness of fall into local minimum value. Test results show that this algorithm improves the speed performance and precision of convergence. It can apply into PSC ship-selecting to improve efficiency and quality.

Table 1. Test samples

sample	TYPE	MARINER	FLAG	CNSM	DEF	DUR2	ROUTE	BP	PSO-BP	Absolute error
1	0.82	0.72	0.62	0.56	0.46	0.32	0.24	0.4362	0.4509	0.0147
2	0.86	0.74	0.64	0.52	0.42	0.34	0.26	0.7035	0.7142	0.0107
3	0.84	0.76	0.66	0.54	0.44	0.36	0.26	0.8164	0.8216	0.0151
4	0.86	0.72	0.64	0.52	0.48	0.34	0.24	0.7120	0.7342	0.0052
5	0.82	0.74	0.62	0.56	0.42	0.32	0.26	0.5287	0.5403	0.0116
6	0.86	0.78	0.66	0.54	0.42	0.36	0.26	0.9041	0.9125	0.0084
7	0.84	0.76	0.62	0.52	0.44	0.32	0.24	0.6713	0.6845	0.0132
8	0.82	0.74	0.64	0.54	0.46	0.34	0.26	0.7369	0.7512	0.0143
9	0.82	0.72	0.62	0.52	0.42	0.32	0.24	0.1382	0.1500	0.0118
10	0.82	0.76	0.66	0.56	0.44	0.32	0.26	0.7824	0.7964	0.0140

Then, we will further validate the performance of the proposed algoithms, based on the real cases obtained from the THETIS Inspection database of Paris-MoU. The 50 sampled vessels with China flag ships are chosen to implement our proposals. Fig. 3 demonstrates the sampled information of China flag ships in THETIS Inspection Database.

	IMO	Name	Flag	Type	Age	Date of Inspection	Type of inspection	Port of inspection	Number of Deficiencies	Result
Details	9601209	HUA HENG 166	China	Bulk carrier	1	04/10/2012	More detailed inspection	Romania - Constanta	0	
Details	9483097	XIANG YUN KOU	China	General cargo/multipurpose	3	28/09/2012	More detailed inspection	Greece - Kavala	5	
Details	9192662	LE YI	China	General cargo/multipurpose	13	25/09/2012	More detailed inspection	France - Dunkerque (GPM)	3	
Details	8700242	ZHEN HUA 25	China	General cargo/multipurpose	25	25/09/2012	More detailed inspection	Norway - Eidfjord	6	
Details	9148465	HAI GONG YOU 302	China	Oil tanker	18	24/09/2012	Expanded inspection	Spain - Las Palmas	6	
Details	9587178	MAPLE FORTITUDE	China	Bulk carrier	2	20/09/2012	Initial Inspection	Lithuania - Klaipeda	0	
Details	9312559	XIN CHANG SHA	China	Container	8	20/09/2012	More detailed inspection	Canada - Delta Port	1	
Details	9337949	XIN DA YANG ZHOU	China	Container	4	19/09/2012	Initial inspection	Netherlands - Rotterdam	0	
Details	9160255	HUANG SHAN HAI	China	Bulk carrier	15	18/09/2012	Expanded inspection	Latvia - Riga	0	
Details	8919568	TAI SHUN HAI	China	Bulk carrier	21	18/09/2012	More detailed inspection	Belgium - Ghent	1	
Details	9133410	HONG XING	China	General cargo/multipurpose	16	14/09/2012	Initial inspection	Netherlands - Rotterdam	0	
Details	9416537	SHENG XING HAI	China	Bulk carrier	7	10/09/2012	More detailed inspection	Spain - Sagunto	2	

Fig. 3. Information of China Flag Ships in THETIS Inspection Database

Instance:

IMO Number：XXX

Vessel Name：XXX

Type：Oil tanker

Tonnage： 2776

Date of construction : 16/9/1994

Mariner: Once

CNSM: C class

Flag :   China

Route :   International

DEF : 6

DUR: 9

Then, we code the input layer of BP network as {TYPE, MARINER, FLAG, CNSM, DEF, DUR, ROUTE} ={0.84, 0.74, 0.62, 0.56, 0.44, 0.34, 0.26}. Inputting the above factors coding set to the trained PSO-BP networks, the assessed value is obtained as 0.7253 which belongs to the range of very high risk that needs extended inspection. The simulation result is identical with PSC-Expanded inspection conclusion.

4   Conclusion

This paper has researched the latest Paris MOU NIR of PSC rules 2009/16/EC, proposing an improved training BP network algorithm by modified PSO algorithm to put forward an algorithm of PSC ship-selecting model. The algorithm can adaptively adjust Inertia weight and update scaling speed and position according to Premature Convergence Degree σ and Adaptive scaling term $I_{i,j}^{t}$, which can avoid the weakness of slower convergence speed and easy to fall into local minimum value. This paper explored the improved PSO algorithm to train BP network and applied to PSC ship-selecting. Test results show that this algorithm can improve the performance on speed of convergence and precision of convergence. It can apply to improve efficiency and quality of PSC ship-selecting. Here we only choose fixed attributes to confirm the algorithm, and then we should consider an adaptive attribute choosing mechanism in the future research.

Acknowledgements. This work was supported by China Postdoctoral Science Foundation under Grants 2013M530900, China Postdoctoral sending plan, Research Funds for the Central Universities, China Scholarship Council, and also supported by NSFC.

References

1. Yi, X.: NIR: A new weapon of Paris-MOU. The Waterborne Safety. China Ship Survey (2009)
2. Fifth IMO Workshop for PSC MoU/Agreement:Update on activities and decisions by the MoU/agreementOutcome of the 44th Committee meeting Submitted by the Paris MoU (2011)

3. Wei, D., Chen, L.L., Zeng, Q.S., Qiu, H.Z.: Research on modeling of ship selection for FSC inspection based on neural network. China Maritime Safety. Maritime Management (2010)
4. Zhou, C.: How to avoid Matthew Effect in selecting target vessels for Port State Control. In: Maritime Workshop on China Maritime Safety, pp. 37–40 (2008)
5. Shi, Y., Eberhart, R.C.: Fuzzy adaptive particle swarm optimization. In: IEEE Congress on Evolutionary Computation Seoul, Korea (2001)
6. Zhang, Y.Q.: Improved adaptive particle swarm optimization algorithm based on cloud theory. Application Research of Computer (2010)
7. Zhang, W.J.: The Research on Cooperative Particle Swarm Optimization and Its Application on Multi-depot Vehicle Routing Problem. East China Normal University (2010)
8. Wang, H.T.: Particle swarm optimization algorithm based on modified inertia weight. Computer Applications and Software 28, 116–122 (2011)
9. Gao, B.K., Li, Y., Xu, M.Z.: Application of particle swarm optimization algorithm in the heating load combination forecasting. Information and Electronic Engineering 9, 58–65 (2011)
10. Eberhart, R.C., Shi, Y.H.: Particle swarm optimization: developments, applications and resources. In: IEEE Congress on Evolutionary Computation, Piscataway, USA, pp. 81–86 (2001)
11. Wikipedia, http://en.wikipedia.org/wiki/Kolmogorov's_theorem

LRPON Based Infrastructure Layout Planning of Backbone Networks for Mobile Cloud Services in Transportation

Song Yingge, Dong Jie, Lin Bin, and Ding Ning

1 Linghai Road, Dalian Maritime University,
Dalian, Liaoning Province, China 116026
binlin@dlmu.edu.cn

Abstract. Driven by fast growing ultra-broadband applications and the advancement of photonic technology, Next Generation Passive Optical Network (NGPON) is positioned as one of the most promising carriers to enable high-speed backbone networks for mobile cloud services in transportation. Long-reach Passive Optical Network (LRPON) is one of the significant directions for the evolution of NGPON. To establish a low-cost deployment of LRPON and achieve the long-distance optical transmission, cascaded optical amplifiers (OAs) are the key to compensate for the optical signals. In this paper, we propose a novel heuristic algorithm for LRPON infrastructure layout planning which focuses not only on the splitter placement, but also on the power awareness and network availability, to maintain LRPON cost-effective competitiveness and mitigate the impacts of various optical losses by fiber transmission and network equipments with specified network availability. The problem has jointly considered the largest possible area coverage while consisting of equipment cost, optical link degradation factors and network stability in a single optimization framework. The heuristic is called Fast-Backward-Seeking (FBS), which can provide deployment solutions for large sized problems fast and effectively. Numerical scenarios are executed to validate and demonstrate the performance and effectiveness of the proposed heuristic. The results have verified the cost-effective performances of the FBS.

Keywords: NGPON, heuristic, network deployment.

1 Introduction

Recently, mobile cloud computing has rapidly emerged as a widely accepted computing paradigm and information technology services in transportation-related applications. It is estimated that 80% of software application will be cloud-based services, and the global cloud-related data traffic will be increased by six times from 2011 to 2016 [1]. Future mobile cloud computing requires stringently on the backbone network infrastructure with ultra-broadband and low latency which can directly affect the Quality of Experience (QoE) of mobile cloud service customers.

X.-h. Sun et al. (Eds.): ICA3PP 2014, Part II, LNCS 8631, pp. 436–446, 2014.

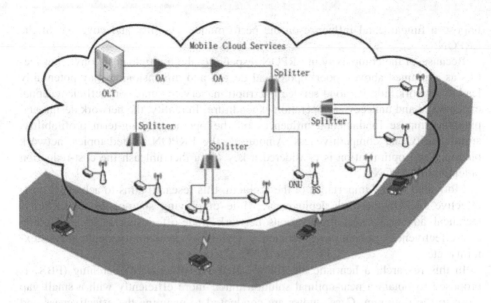

Fig. 1. The LRPON-based backbone network infrastructure for mobile cloud services in transportation

In this paper, we investigate the Infrastructure Layout Planning (ILP) of Long-reach Passive Optical Network (LR-PON), which is one of the most promising candidates for backbone networks for mobile cloud services in transportation, as shown in Fig. 1. Different from traditional PONs, LRPONs combines the capacity of metro and access networks in the last mile of the cloud service provisioning. It can not only serve larger coverage span but also simplify networks by consolidating Central Offices (COs) and network interfaces, thus can significantly reduce the corresponding operational cost of the backbone network and bring great benefit to the operators.

LRPON's longer reach extension (from 20km to 100km and be-yond) and higher capacity is at the price of the following complexities: i) extra means of optical amplification, e.g. active network entities (NEs) using power supply, which will bring extra network capital expenditure (CapEx) in the long run; ii) exploiting more complicated technologies/network entities (NEs) and more diverse topologies, such as TDM, wavelength-division multiplexing (WDM) or hybrid time-division (TDM)/WDM architecture, etc. ; iii) more stringent requirements on differentiated availability to avoid network service outages and to satisfy different FTTx customers service level agreement requirements at the price of extra means of redundancy placements and more intelligent fault tolerance mechanisms.

The topology of traditional PONs has three major characteristics: an OLT located in the central office, multiple Optical Network Unit-Base Stations (ONU-BSs) as mobile user access points, and an optical distributed network (ODN) interconnecting each ONU-BS with the OLT. A LRPON inherits the conventional PON systems and also has a significant evolution. Due to the optical power, noise complexity, more stringent survivability requirements, power awareness and proper availability design impose a fundamental influence on the performance, stability and coverage of the LRPON.

Because of the complexity in LRPON (especially the multiple cost-convicting factors as explained above), poor topological design and dimensioning may potentially lead to network failure, cloud service interruption, service outage or inefficient capital expenditure and unnecessary operation expenditure. In reality, the network design and planning impose fundamental influences on the operators' long-term profitability, sustainability and competitiveness. Among all the LRPON related topics, network planning and optimization is considered a key to further unleash the cost-reduction potential of LRPONs.

Motivated by the importance of the problem, this research aims to achieve a cost-effective LRPON network deployment, while employing state-of-the-art LRPONs technical advances, exploiting various network trade-off design factors including cost-effectiveness, optical power efficiency, scalability, availability, deployment flexibility, etc.

In this research, a heuristic algorithm called Fast-Backward-Searching (FBS) is proposed to obtain a near-optimal solution much more efficiently with a small gap close to the optimum. Case studies are conducted to examine the effectiveness and efficiency of the proposed FBS algorithm, as well as demonstrate its effectiveness to achieve cost-effective LRPON infrastructure deployment.

The remainder of the paper is organized as follows. In Section 2, we review the previous related work. In Section 3, the problem statement is given. The proposed heuristic is described in Section 4. Computational results and case studies are presented in Section 5, respectively. Finally, we conclude the paper in Section 6.

2   Related Work

LRPON has high splitting ratio and OA on top of the conventional PONs to achieve a full-service optical access network [2]. The cascaded splitter topology achieved a cost-effective performance, and an ILP model was proposed to realize the deployment optimization of cascaded PON but without taking account of optical power and noise complexity [3]. [4] proposed a WDM PON design optimization with power loss and splitter selection constraints, but the coverage of PON didn't have a extension. The use of OAs in PONs is investigated in [5], proposed the OA placement strategy in LRPON. In [6], we first propose the study on a comprehensive assessment on the power-aware LRPON ODN topology layout and dimensioning configuration without accounting for network availability. Three survivability policies are expounded in [7] for the tree topologies in GPON. And [8] validated that the availability-guaranteed planning of LRPON directly affects the deployment cost.

Research efforts on PONs have also been extensively reported in deployment heuristic. The planning algorithms proposed in [9] [10] to minimize the total deployment cost just with based on the conventional PON topology. [11] investigated a heuristic to address the minimum cost deployment of a multistage-splitter PON topology however without integrating the power loss concerns. Jaumard and Chowdhury designed a heuristic to selection and placement the splitters and AWGs with the signal attenuation constraints but didn't consider the power compensation in [4]. Only [12] explained a genetic algorithm directly related to the deployment of LRPON also without any power compensation consideration. And all current researches on the ILP or heuristic planning of LRPON infrastructure deployment give no considerations to the availability at the beginning of the LRPON construction.

3   Problem Statement

LRPON Infrastructure Layout Planning (ILP) problem aims at minimizing the total deployment cost of the whole network Infrastructure, and focuses not only on the splitter placement, but also on the power awareness and network availability, as well as to maintain LRPON cost-effective competitiveness and mitigate the impacts of various optical losses by fiber transmission and network equipments with a specified network availability. The ILP problem has jointly considered the largest possible area coverage while consisting of equipment cost, optical link degradation factors and network stability in a single optimization framework.

Moreover, the tree-based network topology has to be constructed for LRPON. The OAs and splitters cannot be deployed anywhere but only some potential sites (PSs) eligible for cabling, construction, and power supply (for OAs). We assume that the cost of deploying a fiber segment between any pair of PSs or between a PS and the OLT (or any ONU-BS) is known in prior. Note that the fibers have to be deployed along the Right of Ways (ROWs), and the total cost of fiber deployment between locations i and j depends not only on the length of the ROW, but also a weight on each unit length denoted as δ_{ij}.

4   Proposed Fast-Backward-Searching (FBS) Algorithm

Let $\vec{G} = (\Omega, \vec{E})$ denote a directed graph where Ω is the set of nodes and $\vec{E}$ is the set of directed edges/links. The OLT is denoted as P. Ω is partitioned into four parts: denoted as Ω_{ONU}, Ω_{PSS}, Ω_{PSA}, and node P, i.e.

$$\Omega = \Omega_{ONU} \cup \Omega_{PSS} \cup \Omega_{PSA} \cup \{P\}$$

$$M = M_A + M_S, \; \Omega_{PS} = \Omega_{PSS} \cup \Omega_{PSA}, \; |\Omega_{PSA}| = M_A, \; |\Omega_{PSS}| = M_S$$

Given:

- The set of fixed ONUs, which are the customer premises equipment (CPE).
- The set of Potential Sites (PSs) for deploying splitters.
- The set of Potential Sites (PSs) for deploying OAs.
- The location of OLT.
- The cost per unit length of fiber ($/km) Cf, including fiber purchase and deployment cost (e.g., fiber bury cost), etc. [3]

- The Manhattan distance between locations i and node j,(d_{ij})
- The cost of splitter of type $t \in T$ (C_t^S)
- The cost of an Optical Amplifier (OA), (C^{OA})
- The power attenuation per unit length of fiber (dB/km) [9]
- The gain of each Optical Amplifier (g^{OA}) is a constant, which is independent of wavelength (e.g., 20dB [5])
- The buried fiber route between any pair of nodes in Ω corresponds to the Manhattan distance.
- The known cost for rights of way (when choosing the route of the fiber network), which consists of annual fees and costs to get permissions.
- The acceptable ONU availability threshold is ζ (e.g. three 9's).

The core idea of the FBS is to construct LRPONs from the ONU-BSs as initiating ends to the OLT, and the FBS quickly provides a LRPON deployment solution in a short period of time with an acceptable cost result which is close to theoretical optimum.

Before explaining the FBS algorithm in detail, we first give some definitions of terms as follows:

Definition 1: A cascaded-splitter incidence matrix $CS=\{CS_{ijk}\}_{(Ms)(Ms+Mo)(3)}$, where $CS_{ijk}=1$, if the PSS_i is selected to be the kth-order splitter and connects to the PSS_j/ONU-BS_j; otherwise $CS_{ijk}=0$. $|\Omega_{ONU-BS}|=M_O$;

Definition 2: A cascaded-OA incidence matrix $CO=\{CO_{ijk}\}_{(Ma)(Ma+1)}$, where $CO_{ijk}=1$, if the PSA_i is selected to be the kth-order OA and connects to the OLT/OA_j; otherwise $CO_{ijk}=0$.

Definition 3: N_{s1}: the least number of the child nodes of the CS_{ij1} when there are several candidate CS_{ij1}s nearby (usually in a 10km radius area) and if one is selected, the child-node number should be larger than N_{s1}, only if there is only one CS_{ij1} near to the ONU-BS, it could be less than N_{s1}.

Definition 4: N_{s2}: the least number of the child nodes of the CS_{ij2} when there are several candidate CS_{ij2}s nearby (usually in a 10km radius area) and if one is selected, the child-node number should be larger than N_{s2}, only if there is only one CS_{ij2} near to the CS_{ij1}, it could be less than N_{s2}.

In addition, we divide a new region called central area as the concentrated area to gather the whole PON where all candidate CS_{ij2}s and CS_{ij3} are located. The central area is a circular region covering the center of the whole PON area with a diameter of half side length of the whole area.

The FBS defines a LRPON architecture that all ONU-BSs link to a central point by third-order-splitters and finally reach to OLT through second-order-OAs, and an OA will be added between the second-order and the third-order splitters if ONU-BS requires extra power compensation. The special LRPON architecture we propose in the FBS inherits from the preceding model and is effective to sustain the whole LRPON considering network survivability. The third-order-splitters can provide an enough large network scale and the two-order-OAs make sure the long-reach transmission and a flexible accessible OA effectively provides a power compensation if necessary.

The placement of OA and splitter and path selection of each ONU-BS to OLT is designed based on the analysis of the availability of ILP deployment solutions. The distributed paths from the center of areas to be covered effectively guarantee similar distances from OLT to each ONU-BS and greatly avoid too long distances between OLT and ONU-BSs so that improve the network stability.

Based on the backward searching, three steps will be executed in order as shown in Algorithm 1. We give detailed descriptions for each step as follows.

Algorithm 1:   Fast-Backward-Seeking (FBS) algorithm

Begin
STEP I
   Connect each ONU-BS to the nearest PSS as corresponding $CS_{ij1}s$;
   Reset All $CS_{ij1}s$ by contrasting to N_{s1} and Redistribution ONU-BSs;
   Connect each CS_{ij1} out of the central area to the nearest PSS as corresponding CS_{ij2};
   Reset All $CS_{ij2}s$ by contrasting to N_{s2} and Redistribution ONU-BSs;
   Connect all $CS_{ij1}s$ in the central area to nearest $CS_{ij2}s$;
   Calculate the central point(CP) of all $CS_{ij2}s$ then find the nearest PSS to CP as CS_{ij3};
STEP II
   Build two-cascaded OAs to achieve the least distance between OLT and CS_{ij3};
   Select CO_{ij1} and CO_{ij2} by $|OA_i, OLT|>=20km$ && $|OA_i, CO_{ij1}|>=20km$ && $Min(|OA_i, CO_{ij1}| + |OA_i, CO_{ij1}|)$;
STEP III
   for each ONU-BS **do**
      Calculate $dline_i$ and $loss_i$ of each ONU;
      if $loss_i \geq \theta$ **do**
         Add a OA between CS_{ij1} and CS_{ij2} associated with ONU_i;
      end if
      Update $dline_i$ and $loss_i$;
   end for
      Calculate the cost for whole LRPON;
Output :
      Output the total cost and executive time;
      for   each ONU-BSs
         Output $dline_i$, $loss_i$ and the path from
         $ONU-BS_i$ to OLT
      end for
   end

- Step 1 The three-order-cascaded splitter structure setup

All ONUs are firstly distributed to the nearest candidate splitters then a redistribution principle will be executed. In this principle, only if a candidate splitter's child-node number is less than N_{s1} and there are other chosen splitters nearby (usually in a 10km radius area) for all ONUs belong to this splitter to choose, all the ONUs should be redistributed to other nearest chosen splitters. All the final chosen splitters are called the CS_{ij1}s.

All the unselected splitters in the central area are considered to the candidate CS_{ij2}s and the CS_{ij1}s out of the central area firstly link to the nearest candidate CS_{ij2}s and then a re-distribution will be executed. Only if the outputs of one chosen candidate CS_{ij2} is less than N_{s2} and there are other chosen candidate CS_{ij2}s nearby (also in a 10km radius area), the CS_{ij1}s under this CS_{ij2} will be redistributed to other nearest chosen candidate CS_{ij2}s and finally all the CS_{ij2}s are located.

We can calculate a geometrical center point for all the CS_{ij2}s and select a candidate splitter which is the nearest to the point as the CS_{ij3}. It's obvious that the CS_{ij3} is the pivot of the LRPON deployment and after that the three-order-cascaded splitter structure is formed.

- Step 2 the two-order-cascaded OA structure setup

To enlarge the transmission distance, we select an OA which is the nearest and at least 20km away from OLT to be CO_{ij1}. After that, an OA should be located between the CO_{ij1} and the CS_{ij3}, which can minimize the sum of the distances to the two ends and set as the CO_{ij2}. The distance between the CO_{ij1} and the CO_{ij2} is also at least 20km. Then the fundamental architecture is then setup.

- Step 3 Loss calculation and power compensation

For each ONU-BS, a distance denoted as $dline_i$ ($i \in \Omega_{ONU-BS}$) is calculated from the ONU-BSi to the OLT. Based on the power budget parameters in Table 2, we can quickly get the $loss_i$ which is the total power loss from one ONU-BSi to the OLT.

Table 1. LRPON Component Cost and Unavailability

Component/Device	Cost ($)	Unavailability
ONU-BS	3 gcu	5.12e-7
Fiber (/km)	1 gcu	3.12e-6
Burying Fiber (/km)	50 gcu	-
1:8 Splitter	4 gcu	1.0e-7
1:16 Splitter	8 gcu	1.0e-7
1:32 Splitter	16 gcu	1.0e-7
1:64 Splitter	32 gcu	1.0e-7
1:128 Splitter	64 gcu	1.0e-7
Optical Amplifier (OA)	18 gcu	4.0e-7

Table 2. LRPON Power Budget parameters

Parameter		Value
σ		20 km
Θ		20dB
Splitting loss	1:8 splitter	9 dB
	1:16 splitter	12 dB
	1:32 splitter	15 dB
	1:64 splitter	18 dB
	1:128 splitter	21 dB

Then the FBS tell whether $loss_i \geq \theta$ or not. If Yes, then an extra OA adds to the LRPON between the corresponding CS_{ij1} and CS_{ij2} in the unimpeded line from $ONU - BS_i$ to the OLT. After executing the three steps, the complete LRPON has setup. The FBS finally outputs the total cost of the deployment scheme which includes each path from $ONU - BS_i$ to the OLT with the path $dline_i$ and $loss_i$.

5   Numerical Results

Without loss of generality, the Manhattan distance of two nodes is used to represent the corresponding edge length of the fiber deployment route, and δ_{ij} is set to 1, i.e., all the fiber segment links have the same weighted deployment costs. The maximum distance between an ONU-BS and OLT is taken as 130km [3]. L_{max}^{S-onu} and L_{max}^{A-A} are set to 40km and 70km. We use Gurobi [13] to solve the ILP formulation as comparison. The optimization is running on a 32-bit windows based work station with an Intel Core i3 3.3GHz processor and 16GB of RAM. We define a generic cost unit (gcu) to evaluate the network costs [14]. The unavailability values of the network components are taken from [8] and [15]. Tables 1 and 2 show the component/device cost and unavailability of LRPON as well as the power budget parameters, respectively.

Table 3. Problem Size of Simulated Scenarios

	Number of nodes		
	ONU-BSs	PSSs	PSAs
Scenario (1)	25	15	6
Scenario (2)	50	20	10
Scenario (3)	100	30	15
Scenario (4)	300	60	30

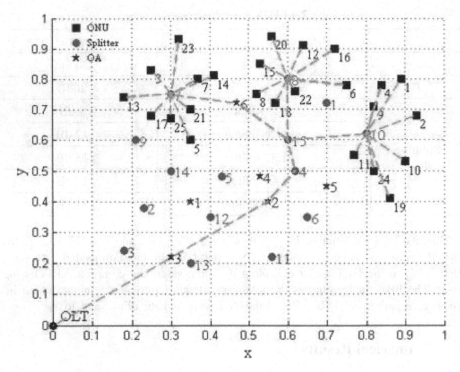

Fig. 2. Results of ILP solution with FBS heuristic

Table 4. Performance Comparison between FBS and Gurobi

		Deployment Cost (gcu)	Running Time(s)	Number of Selected OAs	Number of Selected splitters	Optimization Gap
Scenario (1)	Gurobi	16369.1	4.21	2	5	3.21%
	FBS	16895.2	0.012	3	5	
Scenario (2)	Gurobi	24380.2	51860.86	3	13	8.5%
	FBS	26452.5	0.02	2	14	
Scenario (3)	Gurobi	34574.3	156235.07	2	14	4.12%
	FBS	36001.5	0.064	3	17	
Scenario (4)	Gurobi	CALCULATION OUT OF MEMORY				
	FBS	90879.0	0.093	12	30	

Fig. 2 shows the ILP solution results of FBS which match the tree-based topology. Moreover, we investigate some more scenarios with increasing network scale as listed in Table 4 to prove that our proposed heuristic FBS is superior in performance of efficiency. Scenarios (1), (2), (3) explain that the problem size grows dramatically as the network size increase and the cost-effectiveness can be improved through optimized LRPON ODN topology and dimensioning configuration using power-aware available LRPON placement. Besides, it indicate that, while achieving the objective of minimizing cost and high availability, the FBS greatly reduces the computing time and the solution errors is controlled in about 10% which is perfectly acceptable to employ for the deployment engineering problems.

6   Conclusions

The paper has investigated on the LRPON ILP problem in considerations of minimized cost with proper power budget and network availability constrains simultaneously. A heuristic called Fast-Backward-Seeking (FBS) are proposed to optimize the layout and placement. Numerical scenarios have validated the feasibility and scalability of FBS. And the results have verified the proposed FBS performs excellently in the aspects of the running time and can quickly get an outstanding solution with the network scale increasing comparing with ILP. A quite small error gap between the results of FBS and ILP theoretical optimum is controlled in about 10% which is perfectly acceptable to employ for the deployment engineering problems.

Acknowledgments. This study is sponsored by National Science Foundation of China (NSFC) No. 61371091, No. 61171175 and No. 61301228, Liaoning Provincial Natural Science Foundation of China No.2014025001, the Scientific Research Foundation for the Returned Overseas Chinese Scholars from Ministry of Human Resources and Social Security, and Program for Liaoning Excellent Talents in University (LNET) No. LJQ2013054 and Fundamental Research Funds for Central Universities under grant No.3132014212.

References

1. Cisco Visual Networking Index: Global Mobile Data Traffic Forecast Update (2013–2018), http://www.cisco.com/c/en/us/solutions/collateral/ service-provider/visual-networking-index- vni/white_paper_c11-520862.html
2. Phillips, A.J., Senior, J.M., Mercinelli, R., Valvo, M., et al.: Strategies for a High Splitting Optically Amplified Passive Optical Network. Journal of Lightwave Technology 19(2), 137–149 (2001)
3. Lin, B., Lin, L., Ho, P.H.: Cascaded Splitter Topology Optimization in LRPONs. In: IEEE ICC, Ottawa, Canada, June 10-15 (2012)
4. Jaumard, B., Chowdhury, R.: Selection and placement of switching equipment in a Broadband Access Network. In: 2012 International Conference on Computing, Networking and Communications (ICNC), pp. 297–303 (2012)
5. Sakena, J., Jamro, M.Y., Senior, J.M.: Optical amplifier number and placement in the superPON architecture. In: The 6th International Conference on Advanced Communication Technology, vol. 1, pp. 186–191 (2004)

6. Lin, L., Lin, B., Ho, P.-H.: Power-aware optimization modeling for cost-effective LRPON infrastructure deployment. In: 2013 21st International Conference on Software, Telecommunications and Computer Networks (SoftCOM), pp. 1–5, 18–20 (2013)
7. Gigabit-Capable Passive Optical Networks (G-PON): General Characteristics, ITU-T G.984.1, SG 15 (March 2003)
8. Kantarci, B., Mouftah, H.T.: Availability and Cost-Constrained Long-Reach Passive Optical Network Planning. IEEE Transactions on Reliability 61(1), 113–124 (2012)
9. Li, J., Shen, G.: Cost Minimization Planning for Greenfield Passive Optical Networks. IEEE/OSA Journal of Optical Communications and Networking 1(1), 17–29 (2009)
10. Lv, M., Chen, X.: A kind of planning algorithm for PON and WiMAX convergence network. In: 2010 2nd International Conference on Signal Processing Systems (ICSPS), vol. 2, pp. 83–87 (2010)
11. Eira, A., Pedro, J., Pires, J.: Optimized design of multistage passive optical networks. IEEE/OSA Journal of Optical Communications and Networking 4(5), 402–411 (2012)
12. Liu, X., Gu, R., Ji, Y.: A nested genetic algorithm for topologyoptimization in LRPON. In: 2012 3rd IEEE International Conference on Network Infrastructure and Digital Content (IC-NIDC), pp. 217–221.
13. "Gurobi Optimizer 4.6", Gurobi Optimization Inc. (2012)
14. Chaves, D.A.R., Barboza, E.A., Bastos-Filho, C.J.A., Martins-Filho, J.F.: A Multi-Objective Approach to Design All-Optical and Translucent Optical Networks Considering CapEx and QoT. In: 14th International Conference on Transparent Optical Networks (ICTON), pp. 1–4 (2012)
15. Cankaya, H.C., Lardies, A., Ester, G.W.: Network design optimization from an availability perspective. In: 11th International Telecommunications Network Strategy and Planning Symposium, pp. 359–364 (2004)

Infrastructure Deployment and Dimensioning of Relayed-Based Heterogeneous Wireless Access Networks for Green Intelligent Transportation

Lin Bin, Guo Jiamei, He Rongxi, and Yang Tingting

1 Linghai Road, Dalian Maritime University,
Dalian, Liaoning Province, China 116026
binlin@dlmu.edu.cn

Abstract. Relayed-based Heterogeneous Wireless Access Networks (RHWAN) is envisioned as the promising network architecture for the future Intelligent Transportation (IT) network infrastructure. It is proposed to provide a candidate infrastructure solution for operators to construct intelligent transportation networks in a cost-effective manner. In this paper, we focus on the Infrastructure Deployment and Dimensioning (IDD) problem under the RHWAN architecture. The IDD problem is formulated as a generic integer linear programming (ILP) model which can optimally: (i) minimize the network deploying cost, (ii) identify the locations of BSs, (iii) identify the association relations between RSs and MBSs, (iv) satisfy the mobile coverage requirements so as to allow the mobile IT user access through BSs. We solve the model using Gurobi, which is the newest ILP solver by now. A series of case studies are conducted to validate the optimization framework and demonstrate the solvability and scalability of the ILP model. Computational results show the significant performance benefits of CoMP in RHWAN in terms of lower cost, larger capacity and higher reliability.

Keywords: Heterogeneous, Deployment, Optimization.

1 Introduction

Recent decades have witnessed an unprecedented growth in the numbers of subscribers, terminals, services, and applications in mobile communications market and a more flexible deployment model is needed for operators to improve broadband user experience in a ubiquitous and cost effective way. A more complex architecture consists of heterogeneous wireless technologies, including microcell, pico cell, cooperative relay, will need to be flexibly co-deployed to most efficiently use the dimensions of space and frequency [1]–[3]. With explosive growth in information and communication traffic, the information and communication technology (ICT) industry's contribution to the global carbon footprint is forecast to double over the next ten years [4]. With greater awareness of the industry's impact on the environment, the telecommunications industry has been playing an active role in reducing its impact in this field.

X.-h. Sun et al. (Eds.): ICA3PP 2014, Part II, LNCS 8631, pp. 447–460, 2014.
© Springer International Publishing Switzerland 2014

Apart from the social responsibility aspect, there is also a major economic motivation to reduce energy consumption. Energy consumption in wireless networks is now a major concern due to the potential adverse impact upon the environment and the escalating operating energy costs. ICT is a quickly growing contributor to co2 emissions and energy consumption. One fundamental approach to reduce energy consumption of wireless networks is to adopt new radio access architectures and radio techniques. Recently, the technology of cooperative relaying is as one of the most effective solutions. And the corresponding relay based radio access architecture are recognized as economic, scalable and green network architectures, in which Macro Base Stations (MBSs) and low-power Base Stations (BSs), such as Pico Base Stations (PBSs), and Relay Stations(RSs)in a heterogeneous network as shown in Figure 1.

The PBSs serve as main providers when there is an obstacle, such as a skyscraper hindering the normal service between macro cell and subsequent SSs. The RSs have many advantages over BSs, such as less power consumption, less co_2 emissions, faster and easier installation, lower installation and maintenance cost, and its function is extending the coverage scope of the macro cell. More importantly, cooperative BSs can significantly improve the network throughput and extend the cell coverage. Thus, the Relay-based Heterogeneous Wireless Access Network (RHWAN) is also appealing to infrastructure operators. To fully exploit the advantages of adopting low-power BSs, a foremost critical task is the site planning for low-power BSs, and it has a predominant influence on the subsequent service provisioning, the operator's long-term energy operational cost and even sustainable development.

In the standardization process of the next generation cellular networks, such as 3GPP Long Term Evolution-Advanced (LTE-A), heterogeneous cellular networks are received significant attention and deemed as a cost-efficient way to satisfy the increasing data demand [5–9]. A variety of BSs may coexist in the same geographical area, potentially sharing the same spectrum. PBSs are operator-installed BSs with the same backhaul and access features as MBSs. RSs have the similar sizes of footprints as PBSs. The backhaul link between an MBS and its RS is wireless, so no landline is required. Compared to an MBS, the cost of a low-power BS, including installation cost and maintenance operation cost, is much cheaper. Moreover, due to its lower transmission power and smaller physical size, low-power BSs can offer flexible site acquisitions.

In this paper, we study the Infrastructure Deployment and Dimensioning (IDD) problem in RHWAN, where MBSs, PBSs and RSs are involved. When an MBS is open, its subsidiary RSs can also be selected. When a RS is selected for opening, it consumes a part of radio resource of the donor MBS. The cell planning problem is to select a subset of BSs with minimum cost to supply each demand node the required capacity. To solve the deployment problem, we develop an optimization framework for the IDD problem. The optimization framework provides a formulation with a fine consideration on the affecting factors in the communication environment, such as the wireless propagation environment, the network layout, the locations and minimal traffic demands of a set of Subscriber Stations (SSs), and a set of Candidate Positions (CPs) for deploying BSs. The outputs of interest include the optimal (or near-optimal) locations of BSs, the association between RSs and MBSs, the corresponding total cost.

The remainder of the paper is organized as follows. In Section 2, we review the previous related work. In Section 3, the problem formulation is given, including the network model, the given inputs, variables, constraints, and objective of the ILP model. Computational results and case studies are presented in Section 4, respectively. Finally, we conclude the paper in Section 5.

2   Related Work

We review the recent studies related to network planning and placement. Due to the increasing complexity of state-of-the-art telecommunication networks, the task of planning and dimensioning is essential and full of challenge. It becomes even more sophisticated when the environmental effects are jointly taken into consideration. Heterogeneous cellular networks are three-tier networks, including Macro Base Stations, Pico Base Stations and Relay Stations, which is more flexible and cost-effective. This kind of networks introduces new communication methods into conventional cellular networks to enhance the coverage of dedicated area and also environment-friendly, because heterogeneous cellular network not only is able to significantly improve the system capacity gain and indoor coverage, and lower the whole network power by taking advantage of the lower power stations and comprising cooperative transmissions. In the standardization process of the next generation cellular networks, such as 3rd Generation Partnership Project (3GPP) Long Term Evolution-Advanced (LTE-A), heterogeneous cellular networks are deemed as a cost-efficient way to satisfy the increasing traffic demand and received extensive attention from industry and academia. In order to minimize the total cost of cell planning Zhao introduced an approximation algorithm to tackle the problem in [10]. This approach can surely reduce energy consumption in low traffic time, while on the other, it work out the problem by means of spectrum sharing. Meanwhile, both signal interference statistic characters and network performance analysis methods for dynamic scheduling are presented in [11]. In [12], a GA-Based solution to site planning of relay station in green wireless access network is proposed. An ILP model is formulated to maximize the throughput of an LTE network such that the coverage requirement and radiation limitation can be satisfied given a limited capital expenditure on LTE-BS deployment in[13]. An integer linear programming (ILP) model for the cascaded LRPON topology and network equipment placement, and network dimensioning are proposed in [14].

3   Problem Formulation

3.1   Network Model

In heterogeneous cellular network deployment model, each cell consists of four network entities: Macro Base Stations (MBSs), Pico Base Stations (PBSs), Relay Stations (RSs) and Subscriber Stations (SSs), as shown in Fig. 1. The MBS serves as a central controller in the cell. The PBSs provide service for SSs with a relative small scope. The RSs are responsible for relaying data between the MBS and the associated

SSs through cooperative relaying. The RSs have no direct connections to the wired backbone and are eligible to be deployed at certain outdoor candidate positions (CPs) where uninterrupted power supply can be provided. An SS refers to a fixed site in some densely populated areas such as a hotspot, at which a significant amount of

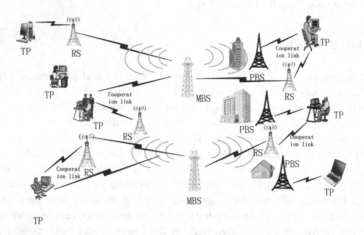

Fig. 1. Relay-based Heterogeneous Cellular Wireless Network deployment model

traffic load demand is imposed. The BS can be multiple accessed simultaneously by different SSs at their assigned frequency band with Orthogonal Frequency-Division Multiple Access (OFDMA) technique. In other words, each transmission between the BS and an SS is inherently an instance of the basic "MBS-RS-SS" three-node relay model, where the MBS-SS, MBS-RS and RS-SS links are assigned the common frequency spectrum. Due to the consideration regarding transmission delay, only two-hop cooperative relaying is assumed. Small scale fading is not explicitly included in the system model since a long-term planning and design is targeted. To test the mobile coverage, we define Test Points (TPs) within the area. The TPs are also used for the test of power intensity for MSs from the associated RSs. In Fig.1, the locations of TPs and MBSs, PBSs, RSs are also illustrated.

3.2   Problem Statement

The Infrastructure Deployment and Dimensioning (IDD) problem can be formulated as follows. Let $\vec{G} = (\Omega, \vec{E})$ denote a directed graph where Ω is the set of nodes and $\vec{E}$ is the set of directed edges/links. Ω is partitioned into four parts, and denoted as ΩTP, ΩMBS, ΩPBS and ΩRS, i.e. $\Omega = \Omega_{TP} \cup \Omega_{MBS} \cup \Omega_{PBS} \cup \Omega_{RS}$.

Given:

The set of fixed TPs, which are the customer premises.

The set of Candidate Sites (CSs) for deploying MBSs.

The set of Candidate Sites (CSs) for deploying PBSs.

The set of Candidate Sites (CSs) for deploying RSs.

The distance matrix.

The maximal transmit power of an MBS, a PBS and a RS.

The cost of an MBS, a PBS and a RS.

The coverage thermal noise power in AOI.

The path loss exponent.

The minimal signal-to-noise-ratio (SNR) requirement for each TP.

The maximal permitted radiation intensity threshold at each TP.

The average minimum required coverage ratio within the AOI.

The average minimum required radiation ratio within the AOI.

Variable:

Five sets of decision variables are defined for the selected locations for deploying MBSs, PBSs and RSs, the assignment of MBSs, PBSs and RSs to SSs, the links from RSs to MBSs, and the directed flow from the MBSs, PBSs and RSs to SSs, respectively. Specifically, we define

The location incidence vector of MBSs A$=(a_m)_{1 \times M}$

$$
a_m = \begin{cases} 1, \text{if } CS_m \text{ is selected to place a MBS;} \\ \\ 0, \text{otherwise;} \end{cases}
$$

The location incidence vector of PBSs B$=(b_p)_{1 \times P}$

$$
b_p = \begin{cases} 1, \text{if } CS_p \text{ is selected to place a PBS;} \\ \\ 0, \text{otherwise;} \end{cases}
$$

The location incidence vector of RSs C$=(c_r)_{1 \times R}$

$$
c_r = \begin{cases} 1, \text{if } CS_r \text{ is selected to place a RS;} \\ \\ 0, \text{otherwise;} \end{cases}
$$

A TP coverage incidence vector Q$=(q_n)_{1 \times N}$, such that

$$
q_n = \begin{cases} 1, \text{if } TP_n \text{ is covered;} \\ \\ 0, \text{otherwise;} \end{cases}
$$

A TP radiation incidence vector F$=(f_n)_{1 \times N}$, such that

$$
f_n = \begin{cases} 1, \text{if the radiation at } TP_n \text{ is greater than threshold;} \\ \\ 0, \text{otherwise;} \end{cases}
$$

The MBS-TP association incidence matrix U$=(u_{mn})_{M \times N}$

$$u_{mn}= \begin{cases} 1, \text{ if the } TP_n \text{is associated with the MBS at } CS_m; \\\\ 0, \text{ otherwise}; \end{cases}$$

The PBS-TP association incidence matrix $V=(v_{pn})_{P \times N}$

$$v_{pn}= \begin{cases} 1, \text{ if the } TP_n \text{is associated with the PBS at } CS_p; \\\\ 0, \text{ otherwise}; \end{cases}$$

The RS-TP association incidence matrix $W=(w_{rn})_{R \times N}$

$$w_{rn}= \begin{cases} 1, \text{ if the } TP_n \text{is associated with the RS at } CS_r; \\\\ 0, \text{ otherwise}; \end{cases}$$

The MBS-RS association incidence matrix $Z=(z_{mr})_{M \times R}$

$$z_{mr}= \begin{cases} 1, \text{ if the he MBS at } CS_m \text{is associated with the RS at } CS_r; \\\\ 0, \text{ otherwise}; \end{cases}$$

Constraints:

The mobile coverage requirement should be satisfied, i.e., the coverage ratio should be larger than a predefined value.

The minimum achievable rate for an SS within the cell should be larger than a rate threshold.

The radiation intensity received at each TP should be less than a predefined threshold value.

3.3   Problem Formulation

(IDD)   Objective: minimize $\displaystyle\sum_{m=1}^{MP}C_m a_m + \sum_{p=1}^{pp}C_p b_p + \sum_{r=1}^{RP}C_r c_m$ .... (1)

Subject To:

$$\sum_{m=1}^{MP}u_{mn} + \sum_{p=1}^{PP}v_{pn} + \sum_{r=1}^{RP}w_{rn} >= 2, \forall n \in \Omega_{TP} \qquad (2)$$

$$\sum_{n=1}^{TP} u_{mn} + \sum_{r=1}^{RP} w_{rn} >= a_m, \forall m \in \Omega_{MP} \tag{3}$$

$$\sum_{n=1}^{TP} u_{mn} + \sum_{r=1}^{RP} w_{rn} <= L \times a_m, \forall m \in \Omega_{MP} \tag{4}$$

$$\sum_{n=1}^{TP} v_{pn} >= b_p, \forall p \in \Omega_{PP} \tag{5}$$

$$\sum_{n=1}^{TP} v_{pn} <= L \times b_p, \forall p \in \Omega_{PP} \tag{6}$$

$$\sum_{n=1}^{TP} w_{rn} >= c_r, \forall p \in \Omega_{RP} \tag{7}$$

$$\sum_{n=1}^{TP} w_{rn} <= L \times c_r, \forall p \in \Omega_{PP} \tag{8}$$

$$\sum_{m=1}^{MP} z_{mr} = c_r, \forall r \in \Omega_{RP} \tag{9}$$

$$\log\left[1 + \frac{1}{N_0}\left(\sum_{m=0}^{M} \frac{u_{mn} \times P_m}{(d_{mn})^\alpha} + \sum_{m=1}^{P} \frac{v_{pn} \times P_p}{(d_{pn})^\alpha} + \sum_{m=0}^{R} \frac{w_{rn} \times P_r}{(d_{rn})^\alpha}\right)\right] >= s_0, \forall n \in \Omega_{TP} \tag{10}$$

$$z_{mr} \times d_{mr} <= L_{m-r}, \forall m \in \Omega_{MP} \forall r \in \Omega_{RP} \tag{11}$$

$$q_n \geq \frac{1}{\frac{1}{N_0}\left(\sum_{m=1}^{M} \frac{P_m}{d^\alpha_{mn}} + \sum_{p=1}^{P} \frac{P_p}{d_{pn}^\alpha} + \sum_{r=1}^{R} \frac{P_r}{d_{rn}^\alpha}\right) - s_0} \left[\frac{1}{N_0}\left(\sum_{m=1}^{M} \frac{u_{mn} P_m}{d_{mn}^\alpha} + \sum_{p=1}^{P} \frac{v_{pn} P_p}{d_{pn}^\alpha} + \sum_{r=1}^{R} \frac{w_{rn} P_r}{d_{rn}^\alpha}\right) - s_0\right], \forall n \in \Omega_{TP} \tag{12}$$

$$1-q_n \geq \frac{1}{\frac{1}{N_0}\left(\sum_{m=1}^{M}\frac{P_m}{d^{\alpha}_{mn}}+\sum_{p=1}^{P}\frac{P_p}{d_{pn}^{\alpha}}+\sum_{r=1}^{R}\frac{P_r}{d_{rn}^{\alpha}}\right)-s_0}\left[s_0-\frac{1}{N_0}\left(\sum_{m=1}^{M}\frac{u_{mn}P_m}{d_{mn}^{\alpha}}+\sum_{p=1}^{P}\frac{v_{pn}P_p}{d_{pn}^{\alpha}}+\sum_{r=1}^{R}\frac{w_{rn}P_r}{d_{rn}^{\alpha}}\right)\right], \forall n \in \Omega_{TP} \tag{13}$$

$$\frac{1}{N}\sum_{n=1}^{N}q_n \geq \eta_1 \times 100\% \tag{14}$$

$$f_n \geq \frac{1}{\frac{1}{N_0}\left(\sum_{m=1}^{M}\frac{P_m}{d^{\alpha}_{mn}}+\sum_{p=1}^{P}\frac{P_p}{d_{pn}^{\alpha}}+\sum_{r=1}^{R}\frac{P_r}{d_{rn}^{\alpha}}\right)-r_0}\left[\frac{1}{N_0}\left(\sum_{m=1}^{M}\frac{a_mP_m}{d_{mn}^{\alpha}}+\sum_{p=1}^{P}\frac{b_pP_p}{d_{pn}^{\alpha}}+\sum_{r=1}^{R}\frac{c_rP_r}{d_{rn}^{\alpha}}\right)-r_0\right], \forall n \in \Omega_1 \tag{15}$$

$$1-f_n \geq \frac{1}{\frac{1}{N_0}\left(\sum_{m=1}^{M}\frac{P_m}{d^{\alpha}_{mn}}+\sum_{p=1}^{P}\frac{P_p}{d_{pn}^{\alpha}}+\sum_{r=1}^{R}\frac{P_r}{d_{rn}^{\alpha}}\right)-r_0}\left[r_0-\frac{1}{N_0}\left(\sum_{m=1}^{M}\frac{a_mP_m}{d_{mn}^{\alpha}}+\sum_{p=1}^{P}\frac{b_pP_p}{d_{pn}^{\alpha}}+\sum_{r=1}^{R}\frac{c_rP_r}{d_{rn}^{\alpha}}\right)\right], \forall n \in \Omega_{TP} \tag{16}$$

$$\frac{1}{N}\sum_{n=1}^{N}(1-f_n) \geq \eta_2 \times 100\ \% \tag{17}$$

$$a_m, b_p, c_r \in \{0,1\}, \forall m \in \Omega_{MP} \forall t \in \Omega_{PP} \forall n \in \Omega_{RP} \tag{18}$$

$$u_{mn} \in \{0,1\}, \forall m \in \Omega_{MP} \forall n \in \Omega_{TP} \tag{19}$$

$$v_{pn} \in \{0,1\}, \forall p \in \Omega_{PP} \forall n \in \Omega_{RP} \tag{20}$$

$$w_{rn} \in \{0,1\}, \forall r \in \Omega_{RP} \forall n \in \Omega_{TP} \tag{21}$$

The objective function in (1) to minimize the total deployment cost of the heterogeneous cellular network. Constraint (2) stipulates that each TP is covered by at least two Stations (including MBSs, PBSs and RSs) which ensure the IDD feature of heterogeneous cellular network. In other words, Constraint (2) ensures the TP has only one parent node in the ΩMPUΩPPUΩRP if it is in the tree. Constraint (3)(4) ensure that the output of each MBS only if am=1, output includes RSs and TPs. Constraint (5)(6) ensure the output of each PBS only if bp=1. Constraint (7) and (8) ensure the output of each RS only if cr=1. Constraint (9) stipulates that a RS is selected; it has only one parental node of an MBS.

Table 1. Definitions of Symbols in the (IDD) Model

Symbol	Definition
Ω_{MP}	The set of Macro Base Stations $\Omega_{MBS} = \{MP_m \mid m = 0,1,\dots,M-1\}$
Ω_{PP}	The set of Pico Base Stations $\Omega_{PBS} = \{PP_p \mid p = 0,1,\dots,P-1\}$
Ω_{RP}	The set of Relay Stations $\Omega_{RS} = \{RP_r \mid r = 0,1,\dots,R-1\}$
Ω_{TP}	The set of TPs $\Omega_{TP} = \{TP_n \mid n = 0,1,\dots,N-1\}$
D	The distance matrix D=$(d_{mn})_{M\times N}$, where d_{mn} is the distance between node m and n.
P_m	The maximal transmit power of an Macro Base Station
P_p	The maximal transmit power of a Pico Base Station
P_r	The maximal transmit power of a Relay Station
C_m	The cost of an Macro Base Station
C_p	The cost of a Pico Base Station
C_r	The cost of a Relay Station
N_0	The coverage thermal noise power in AOI
α	The path loss exponent
s_0	The minimal SNR requirement for each TP
r_0	The maximal permitted radiation intensity threshold at each TP
η_1	The average minimum required coverage ratio within the AOI
η_2	The average minimum required radiation ratio within the AOI
L	The conversion factor which makes the association incidence vector between Base Station and TP equal 0 if there is the location incidence vector equals 0
L_{m-r}	The largest distance between Relay Station and the Macro Base Station which provides service to it.

Constraint (10) ensures that the network satisfy the SNR requirements constraints. Constraint (11) sets an upper bound on the fiber length between MBS and RS in network. Constraints (12) - (14) stipulate the definition of Q. Constraints (15) - (17) stipulate the definition of F. Constraints (18) - (21) state the each entry in A, B, C, U, V,W and Z is binary.

4 Numerical Analysis

4.1 Simulation Settings

We implement the optimization model of Section 3 and solve the ILP models using Gurobi Optimizer [13], which is a state-of-the-art ILP solve. Gurobi is designed from the ground up to exploit modern multi-core processors and the performance is proved to be superior to CPLEX [14].

Table 2 and 3 show the component cost of RHWAN and experimental parameters, respectively. We define a generic cost unit (gcu) [15] to simplify the evaluation of deployment costs in the case studies.

4.2   Validation of the ILP Formulation

To examine the ILP formulation, firstly, a relatively small-size network (so-called Scenario I) is simulated, and the setup of Scenario 0 is show in Fig.2. The coordinates of all the nodes with the area of interest are normalized. Fig.3 shows the corresponding results of network layout in Scenario I. The problem can be solved successfully by ILP solver. We observe that the tree structure in Fig.3 are maintained correctly with the topological features of acyclic, connected and directed. The nodes of MBSs, PBSs, RSs and TPs serve as the root, internal and leaf nodes, respectively. Thus, we can conclude that the IDD formulation is validated.

Secondly, to investigate the effect of CoMP in the network planning strategy, we compare the resulting network layout configuration with and without CoMP technology as shown in Fig.3. We can obverse the difference between Fig.3 (a) and Fig.3 (b). The number of selected MBSs in Fig.3 (a) is more than that in Fig.3 (b).

Table 2. RHWAN Component Cost

Component	Cost(gcu)
C_m	10
C_p	1
C_r	0.7

Table 3. Simulation Parameter Settings

Parameter	Value
α	2.43
P_m	10 W
P_p	1W
P_r	0.7W
s_0	22.8dB
N_0	2mW
L	1000
L_{m-r}	9km
Scale	30km

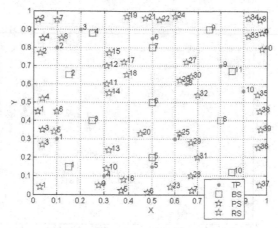

Fig. 2. Experimental Setup of Scenario I before Optimization (Scenario I is set for ILP model verification.)

In the simulations, we randomly select MBSs, PBSs and RSs in the AOI. The problem size, the average computation time, the optimization gap, and the objective values in three scenarios are shown in Table 3. The results verify that the proposed ILP formulation of IDD is correct and solvable. Table 3 indicates that the problem size grows dramatically as the network size increases, and the problem can be solved successfully with Gurobi.

Table 4 show the corresponding computing result of network optimal layout in this scenario. It compares the objective value with, without CoMP and cooperation with MBSs only. Obviously, the total cost of network will be increased greatly without CoMP, and even larger when use MBSs as servers only. In other words, the incorporation of CoMP technology can lead to a significant cost reduction for RHWAN. Besides, the achievable rate at each TP is increased due to multiple wireless links from MBSs, PBSs, RSs, and thus the network capacity and link reliability can be enhanced.

Table 4. Comparisons of IDD Results between With and Without CoMP in Scenario 0

	Without CoMP (s_0=22.8dB)	With CoMP (s_0=22.8dB)	Cooperation With MBSs only
Selected number of MBSs for placement	6MSs	4 MSs	12MSs
Selected number of PBSs for placement	1PS	1PS	0PS
Selected number of RSs for placement	0RS	17RSs	0PS
Obj. Value (gcu)	61	52.9	120
Compute time(s)	0.05	0.26	0.01
Optimality Gap	0.0%	0.0%	0.0%

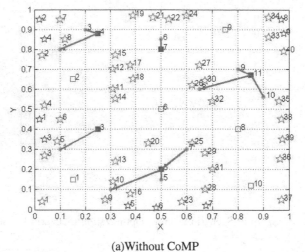

(a)Without CoMP

TP ● Selected MBS ■ Unselected MBS □
Selected PBS★ Unselected PBS☆Selected RS ★Unselected RS ☆

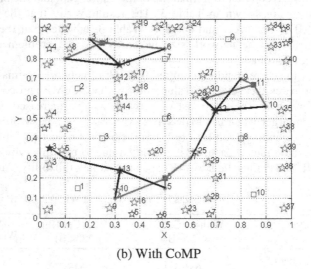

(b) With CoMP

Fig. 3. Network Layout Results in Scenario I

4.3   Feasibility and Scalability of IDD Formulation

Considering that the scale and configuration of a network placement may affect the performance of a network planning, we investigate three scenarios with an increasing network scale as listed in Table 5. With the three cases, we hope to verify the solvability of our formulation. For research convenience, the area is divided into a set of rectangular grids with a uniform size according to the desired accuracy. The MBSs, PBSs, RSs and TPs are defined at rectangular grids in scenario studies.

Table 5. Problem Size of Simulated Scenarios in Scenario I, II, AND III

Scenario	Number of nodes			
	TP	MP	PP	RP
Scenario I	50	11	9	40
Scenario II	102	25	28	32
Scenario III	625	46	33	44

Table 6. Computation Time, Optimality Gap, Objective Value for Gurobi Solving Problem

	Scenario I		Scenario II		Scenario III	
	With CoMP	Without CoMP	With CoMP	Without CoMP	With CoMP	Without CoMP
Time (s)	0.26	0.05	1.06	0.11	86.2	0.08
Cost (gcu)	52.9	61	56.2	111.7	61.4	94.4
Cost (%)	13.28%		49.69%		34.96%	
Optimality Gap	0.0%	0.0%	0.0%	0.0%	0.0%	0.0%

In the simulations, we randomly select MBSs, PBSs, RSs and TPs in the area. The problem size, the average computation time, the optimization gap, and the objective values in three scenarios are shown in Table 6. Note that Scenario III may reflect a practical large-scale network planning task with hundreds of nodes. The results further demonstrate that the proposed IDD formulation is solvable and scalable although the network size increases dramatically.

5   Conclusion

In this paper, we formulate an ILP model to minimize the total deployment cost of the RHWAN such that the coverage requirement can be satisfied given a limited capital expenditure on MBSs, PBSs, RSs deployment and the problem of topology layout with them. We have examined the proposed ILP model via extensive case studies in terms of its feasibility and scalability. The results have demonstrated the performance benefits of CoMP with respect to cost reduction, capacity and reliability enhancement in RHWAN. In the future work, a heuristic algorithm will be proposed to solve the problem more efficiently for even larger scale network planning tasks. The proposed optimization frame work is expected to provide a guideline in the future RHWAN deployment for the operators.

Acknowledgments. This study is sponsored by National Science Foundation of China (NSFC) No. 61371091, No. 61171175 and No. 61301228, Liaoning Provincial Natural Science Foundation of China No.2014025001, the Scientific Research Foundation for the Returned Overseas Chinese Scholars from Ministry of Human Resources and Social Security, and Program for Liaoning Excellent Talents in University (LNET) No. LJQ2013054 and Fundamental Research Funds for Central Universities under grant No.3132014212.

References

1. LTE Advanced: Heterogeneous networks. Qualcomm Inc. White Paper (2011)
2. Zhang, J., Andrews, J.G.: Distributed antenna systems with randomness. IEEE Trans. Wireless Communication 7(9), 3636–3646 (2008)
3. Loa, K., Wu, C.C., Sheu, S.T., Yuan, Y., Chion, M., Huo, D., Xu, L.: IMT-Advanced relay standards. IEEE Communication. Mag. 48(8), 40–48 (2010)
4. http://www.greentouch.org
5. Sydir, J., Taori, R.: An evolved cellular system architecture incorporating relay Stations. IEEE Communications Magazine 47(6), 115–121 (2009)
6. Yang, Y., Hu, H., Xu, J., Mao, G.: Relay technologies for WiMax and LTE-advanced mobile systems. IEEE Communications Magazine 47(10), 100–105 (2009)
7. Yeh, S.P., Talwar, S., Wu, G., Himayat, N., Johnsson, K.: Capacity and coverage enhancement in heterogeneous networks. IEEE Wireless Communications 18(3), 32–38 (2011)
8. Parkvall, S., Furuskar, A., Dahlman, E.: Evolution of LTE toward IMT-advanced. IEEE Communications Magazine 49(2), 84–91 (2011)
9. Guvenc, I.: Capacity and fairness analysis of heterogeneous networks with range expansion and interference coordination. IEEE Communications Letters 15(10), 1084–1087 (2011)
10. Zhao, W., Wang, S.: Cell planning for heterogeneous cellular networks. In: 2013 IEEE Wireless Communications and Networking Conference (WCNC), pp. 1032–1037 (2013)
11. Mukherjee, S.: Distribution of Downlink SINR in Heterogeneous Cellular Networks. IEEE Journal on Selected Areas in Communications 30(3), 575–585 (2012)
12. Lin, B., Lin, L.: Site Planning of Relay Station in Green Wireless Access Networks: A Genetic Algorithm Approach. In: Soft Computing and Pattern Recognition (SoCPaR), Dalian, China, pp. 167–172 (2011)
13. Lin, B., Ho, P.H., Xie, L., Shen, X., Tapolcai, J.: Optimal Relay Station Placement in Broadband Wireless Access Networks. IEEE Transaction on Mobile Computing 9(2) (2010)
14. Lin, L., Lin, B., Ho, P.H.: Power-aware optimization modeling for cost-effective LRPON infrastructure deployment. In: 21st International Conference on Software, Telecommunications and Computer Networks (SoftCOM), pp. 1–5 (2013)

Vessel Motion Pattern Recognition Based on One-Way Distance and Spectral Clustering Algorithm[*]

Wenyao Ma[1,2], Zhaolin Wu[1], Jiaxuan Yang[1], and Weifeng Li[1,**]

[1] Navigation College, Dalian Maritime University, Dalian, Liaoning, China
sddmlwf@163.com
[2] Navigation College, Guangdong Ocean University, Zhanjiang, Guangdong, China

Abstract. Identification of vessel motion pattern from large amount of maritime data can help to high level contextual information and improve the effectiveness of surveillance technologies. Vessel routes belonged to certain motion pattern can provide useful information on daily patterns and transit duration. Therefore an approach to identify motion pattern is presented. In paper, the distance similarity matrix of the trajectory dataset was constructed by using the measurement method in trajectory with one-way distance. The regular motion patterns of vessels were extracted from the trajectories spatial distribution learnt by the spectral clustering algorithm. Finally motion patterns of vessel traveling in Qiongzhou strait was extracted using the proposed method. The results showed that the method has high precision on clustering the vessel trajectories and is applicable to identify movement patterns of vessels in maritime areas such as coastal ports, narrow waterway and traffic complex area.

Keywords: Vessel motion pattern, One-way distance, Spectral clustering, Similarity measure.

1 Introduction

With the coming of maritime cloud date age, a huge database has been formed based on AIS stations network all around the world, so more and more people starts to pay attention on the huge date technology. Use huge marine data to recognize the vessel motion pattern and find high level of situation awareness and anomaly vessel motion pattern are useful to enhance the comprehension to the seasonal difference of the vessel motion pattern [1]. Clustering routes can provide different daily motion pattern and sailing time of different type ships, which can improve the effectiveness of tracking the target ship and maritime monitoring and management technology. There are two important factors which affect the vessel motion pattern recognition, they are high efficiency modeling method and space-time tracks clustering algorithm.

---

[*] This work was supported by the Fundamental Research Funds for the Central Universities under grant 3132013015 and 3132013006.
[**] Corresponding author.

X.-h. Sun et al. (Eds.): ICA3PP 2014, Part II, LNCS 8631, pp. 461–469, 2014.
© Springer International Publishing Switzerland 2014

Some scholars do research on the moving targets of road traffic and propose some algorithms to get motion pattern from the track of the moving targets, but few does on the marine traffic. Hu Hongyu[2] uses improved Hausdorff Distance and spectral clustering algorithm to study the spatial distribution of the vehicles, obtain the classical motion pattern of moving targets. Wen Jia[3] improved the Hausdorff's distance equation with some weighting, which considers the characteristics of the moving vehicle, and obtains the motion pattern of the vehicle, but it is much more complicated compare with others because the characteristics of the track should be calculated. In the reference[4], the author calculates the track similarity of the moving target by one-way distance method, classifies the track and certifies good. Johnson[5] and Sumpter[6] modeling for the track spatial pattern study with the method of self-organized neural network. Hu studies the motion pattern of the moving targets by fuzzy self-organized neural network[7]. But neural network has her own short coming when used to build network, such as much more complicated, slowing studying speed, a lot of settings need to set and it is very complicated to set net weightings.

Non-supervision clustering algorithm is used widely. Atev[8] and Bashir [9] study the track spatial pattern with the method of average K value clustering. Hu obtains the target's motion pattern by average fuzzy value clustering method. But above methods need to standardize the length of the track, and will have some damage to the origin of the track. Biliotti classifies the track by hierarchy clustering method, which may lead unsatisfactory result if one of the hierarchies is broken down [10]. In addition, Junejo obtains the motion pattern by dividing the track collection into many sub-collection [11]. Wang studies the target track motion pattern by spectral clustering method [12].

The paper refers to the motion pattern recognition method on the road traffic, considering the characteristics of ship motion track, provides Vessel Motion Pattern Recognition Based on One-way Distance and Spectral Clustering Algorithm, calculates the similarity of ship track by one-way distance method, obtains the space-time distribution of ship track by spectral clustering algorithm mentioned in reference [12].

2   Similarity of Ship Track

2.1   Pre-processing of Ship Track Data

The ships track are mainly from automatic identification system, which will send own ship's position, speed, course, name, call sign, length and breadth, MMSI and IMO Code information automatically with and interval of 2 or 3 seconds. But sometimes, the track may be incomplete by any reasons such as the fault of AIS device, or the information send by the ship exceed the capacity of the land station receiver or other similar reasons.

All above factors will affect the classification, recognition and analysis of the track. So, it is necessary to preprocessing the date before clustering.

2.2   Measurement of Ship Track Similarity

Classification of ship track is based on the measurement of similarity of ship track. There are a lot of methods to measure the similarity of ship track, such as Euclidean

Distance(ED), dynamic time warping distance (DTW), the longest common subsequence(LCS) and Hausdorff. But ED can only be used to calculate the similarity of equal time track, LCS, Hausdorff Distance and one-way Distance can be used to calculate uneven time interval ship track. In another aspects, the one-way Distance can be used to measure the similarity of track spatial shape and has a high efficiency, so this is the reason to use one-way Distance to measure the similarity of ship track.

2.3   Track Similarity Measurement by One-Way Distance

At first, it is necessary to give a definition of the distance from point P to the track T as shown in equation(1).

$$d(p, T) = \min_{q \in T} d_{ED}(p, q) \tag{1}$$

In the equation (1), q is a point on track T, $d_{ED}(p,q)$ is the Euclidean distance from point p to point q. if there are two tracks T_1 and T_2 in track T, the one-way distance from T_1 to T_2 is defined as following equation (2).

$$d_{owd}(T_1, T_2) = \frac{1}{|T_1|} \left(\int_{p \in T1} d(p, T_2) dp \right) \tag{2}$$

Infect, one-way distance is the distance with direction, here use the average distance of $d_{owd}(T_1,T_2)$ and $d_{owd}(T_2,T_1)$ as the distance from T_1 to T_2.

$$d(T_1, T_2) = \frac{d_{owd}(T_1, T_2) + d_{owd}(T_2, T_1)}{2} \tag{3}$$

The one-way distance, considering the minimum distance from all points on one track to the middle of the other track, has great anti-interference ability to the noise of the track. Then, change the distance in equation (3) to similarity function as shown in following.

$$s(T_1, T_2) = \exp^{-[d(T_1, T_2)/(2\sigma^2)]} \tag{4}$$

In function (4), σ is the dimension parameter, shows the attenuation extent following the increase of the distance. If the distance is bigger, the similarity will be smaller.

3   Ship Track Study Based on Spectral Clustering

After getting the similarity between tracks, the author classifies the high similarity tracks by spectral clustering algorithm and then obtains the spatial distribution of the target track. Spectral clustering algorithm, based on the spectrum theory, can cluster at any shape of the sample and convergence to a best solution overall situation which is the advantage of it. The algorithm define a matrix to express the similarity of the data according to the sample, calculates the feature vector and characteristic value of the matrix, chooses a suitable feature vector to cluster different data, the steps of spectral clustering algorithm are shown as following.

Step 1:express the spatial similarity between tracks by one-way distance for the track collection which includes n tracks Trajectory=$\{T_1, T_2, ..., T_n\}$, constructs $n \times n$ similarity matrix.

$$s_{ij} = \begin{cases} 0, & i = j \\ s(T_i, T_j), & i \neq j \end{cases} \tag{5}$$

Step 2:from similarity matrix S and matrix D to calculate laplacian matrix L, and do decomposition.

Step 3:sort the characteristic values from decomposition $\lambda_1 \leq \lambda_2 \leq ... \leq \lambda_n$, if there is a big difference between the λ_k and λ_{k+1}, choose k to be the number of the motion pattern.

$$k = \arg \max_i |\lambda_{i+1} - \lambda_i| \tag{6}$$

Step 4:calculate corresponding feature vectors from λ_1 to λ_k, they are $x_1, x_2, ..., x_k$, construct $n \times k$ matrix $X=[x_1, x_2, ..., x_k]$;   normalize X, will get feature vector spatial matrix Y.

Step 5: each track T_i is corresponding to the ith feature vector in matrix Y, classifies the tracks into k types by K-means algorithm.

The former algorithm can study the spatial distribution of tracks so that to classify the track samples in the track collection into corresponding track clusters. In order to get ship motion pattern, it is necessary to get the central track of each track cluster, which is use the central track to express the motion pattern. Calculate the average distance from the track T_i in the kth track to other tracks in this cluster.

$$\overline{d}_i = \frac{\sum_{j=1, j \neq i}^{n_k} d(T_i, T_j)}{n_k - 1} \tag{7}$$

Choose the smallest average distance in the kth track cluster to be the central track, which can be used to express the kth moving target's motion pattern in one traffic situation.

4   Experiment Analysis

Verify the effectiveness of the algorithm according to the collected ship tracks in the real traffic situation. The boundary of collection area is (20°01N, 109°55E) and (20°18N, 110°32E) in Qiongzhou strait, collect AIS information in 2011 to get the ship traffic in this area. The area and ship motion tracks are shown in figure 1.

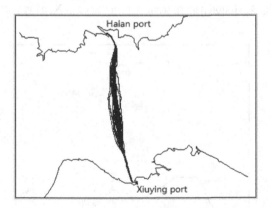

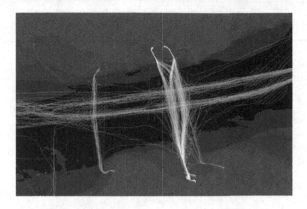

Fig. 1. The researched area and ship tracks

At first, it is necessary to wash AIS data to eliminate some data with errors or lost some parts. Select the tracks entering into Haikou port totally 364 tracks. Figure 2-5 shows the effects after clustering by spectral clustering algorithm. Track collection is divided into 4 types of track clusters according to one-way distance; they are marked by black, blue, red and green colors. The area of each track cluster coincides with the traffic separation scheme in Qiongzhou strait. If the ship is entering into Xiuying port, there are 4 types of classic motion pattern, from new Haian port to Xiuying port pattern (in black), from Haian port to Xiuying port pattern (in blue), from east entrance to Xiuying port pattern (in green), from west entrance to Xiuying port pattern (in red) shown in figure 2, figure 3, figure 4 and figure 5, and figure 6 shows all the motion patterns entering into the Xiuying port.

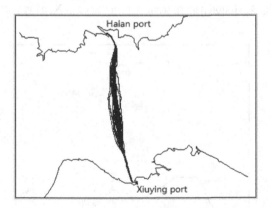

Fig. 2. Motion pattern from HaiAn port to Xiuying port

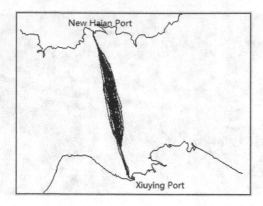

Fig. 3. Motion pattern from new HaiAn port to Xiuying port

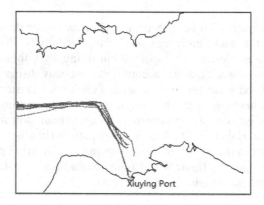

Fig. 4. Motion pattern from west entrance to Xiuying port

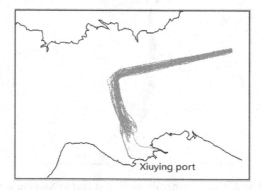

Fig. 5. Motion pattern from east entrance to Xiuying port

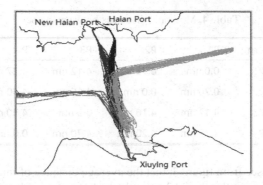

Fig. 6. Motion patterns of vessels entering Xiuying port

It is easy to see that the ship track clustering is reliable from the result of experiment. Table 2 to table5 shows the track clustering statistics of 3 kinds of ship motion patterns. In the table, d1 is Average distance of inner-class, d2 is maximum distance of inner-class, d3 is Average distance of between classes, d4 is maximum distance of between classes.

Table 1. Patterns of vessels entering Xiuying port

NO.	Patterns
P1	Haian Port-Xiuying Port
P2	New Haian Port-Xiuying Port
P3	East entrance to strait-Xiuying Port
P4	West entrance to strait-Xiuying Port

Table 2. Average and maximum distance of inner-class

Pattern	d_1	d_2 nm
P1	0.19 nm	0.27 nm
P2	0.24 nm	0.28 nm
P3	0.25 nm	0.38 nm
P4	0.21 nm	0.34 nm

Table 3. Average distances between classes

Pattern	P1	P2	P3	P4
P1	0.0 nm	1.36 nm	4.73 nm	4.56 nm
P2	1.36 nm	0.0 nm	4.28 nm	4.45 nm
P3	4.73 nm	4.28 nm	0.0 nm	1.26 nm
P4	4.56 nm	4.45 nm	1.26 nm	0.0 nm

Table 4. Minimum distances between classes

Pattern	P1	P2	P3	P4
P1	0.0 nm	0.76 nm	4.12 nm	4.27 nm
P2	0.76 nm	0.0 nm	4.16 nm	4.20 nm
P3	4.12 nm	4.16 nm	0.0 nm	4.30 nm
P4	4.27 nm	4.20 nm	4.30 nm	0.0 nm

It is not hard to see from figure 3, that the average distance of inner-class(d1) of this 4 type of patterns is smaller than 0.3 nm, which shows the inner tracks of patterns are very close to each other, and the biggest maximum distance of inner-class(d2) is 0.38 nm which is smaller than 1/2 width of traffic lane(1.3 nm), which shows most of ships navigate as close as possible to the center of the traffic lane. Table 4 and table 5 show that the average distance between class(d3) is less than 1.26 nm and the smallest value(d4) is 0.76 nm, and they are belonged to pattern p1 and pattern p2. In other words, the patterns from Haian port to Xiuying port and from New Haian port to Xiuying port, which can be seen easily from figure 2 and figure 3, are similar to each other, and most of the ship tracks are very close. Other distance between classes is bigger than 4 nm, so it is easy to separate them.

5   Conclusion

The paper use one-way distance to measure ship track similarity, constructs similarity matrix between tracks, recognizes ship motion pattern by spectral clustering algorithm. Finally, the author takes Haikou port as an example, does experiment to recognize ship motion pattern of entering into Haikou port, obtains 4 kinds of motion pattern, and statistics the distance between these 4 patterns. The result shows the method is reliable and has advantage of high currency, less calculation. It can be used widely in harbor, narrow channel and some other complicated traffic areas for recognition of ship motion patterns.

References

1. Feixiang, Z., Yingjun, Z., Zongjiang, G.: Research on ship behaviors based on data mining. J. Journal of Navigation of China 35, 50–54 (2012)
2. Hongyu, H., Qingnian, W., Zhuhui, L.: Spatial pattern recognition and abnormal traffic behavior detection of moving object. J. Journal of Jilin University 41, 1598–1602 (2011)
3. Jia, W., Wei, C.: Extraction and clustering of vehicle's trajectories from live vedio. J. Computer Engineering and Applications 46, 155–157 (2010)
4. Lin, B., Jianwen, S.: One way distance: for shape based similarity search of moving Object trajectories. J. Journal of GeoInformatica 12, 117–142 (2008)
5. Johnson, N., Hogg, D.: Learning the distribution of object trajectories for event recognition. J. Image and Vision Computing 14, 609–615 (1996)

6. Sumpter, N., Bulpitt, A.J.: Learning spatio-temporal patterns for predicting object behavior. J. Image and Vision Computing 18, 697–704 (2000)

7. Hu, W., Xie, D., Tan, T.: Learning activity patterns using fuzzy self-organizing neural network. J. IEEE Transactions on Systems, Man, and Cybernetics, Part B: Cybernetics 34, 1618–1626 (2004)

8. Atev, S., Masoud, O., Papanikolopoulos, N.: Learning traffic patterns at intersections by spectral clustring of motion trajectories. In: IEEE International Conference on Intelligent Robots and Systems, pp. 4851–4856. IEEE Press, Beijing (2006)

9. Bashir, F.I., Khokhar, A.A., Schonfeld, D.: Object trajectory-based activity classification and recognition using hidden Markov models. J. IEEE Transactions on Image Processing 16, 1912–1919 (2007)

10. Biliotti, D., Antonimi, G., Thiran, J.P.: Multi-layer hierarchical clustering of pedestrian trajectories for automatic counting of people in video sequences. In: Proceedings-IEEE Workshop on Motion and Video Computing, pp. 50–57. IEEE Press, Breckenridge (2007)

11. Junejo, N., Javed, O., Shah, M.: Multi-feature path modeling for video surveillance. In: the 17th International Conference on Pattern Recognition, pp. 716–719. IEEE Press, Washington DC (2004)

12. Wang, L., Hu, W.M., Tan, T.N.: Recent developments in human motion analysis. J. Pattern Recognition 36, 585–601 (2003)

Navigation Safety Assessment of Ship in Rough Seas Based on Bayesian Network

Fengde Qu, Fengwu Wang, Zongmo Yang, and Jian Sun

Navigation College, Dalian Maritime University, Dalian 116026, China
{qufengde,wangfengwu,yangzongmo,sunjian}@dlmu.edu.cn

Abstract. This paper analyzes the rough seas weather which may be encountered during the voyage and its influences on ship's navigation safety. This paper draws lessons from related both domestic and abroad researches about ship's navigation safety, according to the accident causes, analyzes the factors of ship's navigation safety affected by rough seas, determines assessment index system of ship's navigation safety in rough seas, uses Bayesian Network to realize the assessment, and eventually works out which index contributes the most to the marine accidents of ship in rough seas.

Keywords: Ship, Rough Seas, Bayesian Network, Safety Assessment.

1   Introduction

According to statistic of the recorded casualties that happened between 1998 and 2003 which I got from the CASUALTY STATISTICS AND INVESTIGATIONS in the GISIS database of IMO official website, there were totally 2371 marine accidents happened, in which 370 accidents happened in rough seas, which accounts for 15.64%. Thus it can be seen even though the rapid development of the marine technology, marine accidents happen occasionally which result from hostile hydro meteorology [1].

By now, with regard to the researches of ship's navigation safety assessment in Rough seas in China, References [2, 3, 4, 5, 6] use Fuzzy Comprehensive Evaluation, BP Neural Networks, Probabilistic Influence Diagram, Evidence Theory and Rough Set Theory respectively to discuss the navigation safety assessment of different types of ships in rough seas. This paper attempts to use another mathematical method to probe into this issue.

2   Overview of Bayesian Network

Bayesian Network (BN), or Belief Network is a graphical model that describes the dependency relationship of random variables, and it is a combination of probability theory and graphic theory, the main core of it is joint probability calculation. Since late 1980s, Professor Pearl J.[7] from Department of Computer Science, University of

X.-h. Sun et al. (Eds.): ICA3PP 2014, Part II, LNCS 8631, pp. 470–478, 2014.

California, USA, gave the strict definition of BN and established its system info, the effectiveness of BN has been verified in numerous fields including safety management, information fusion, medical diagnosis, system control, bioinformation and so on[8,9].

BN consists of two parts, part one: the structure chart of BN is a Directed Acyclic Graph (DAG), whose nodes represent random variables and edges represent conditional dependencies. Part two: Conditional Probabilities Table (CPT) between nodes. If we can get the CPT of relevant nodes of a BN, then we can calculate any given joint probability, that is to say this BN is inferable. As shown in Fig.1, nodes A, B, C represent variables, we call nodes A, B parent nodes, also we can call them fringe nodes, and node C is the child node. L1 and L2 represent the relationship of variables [10].

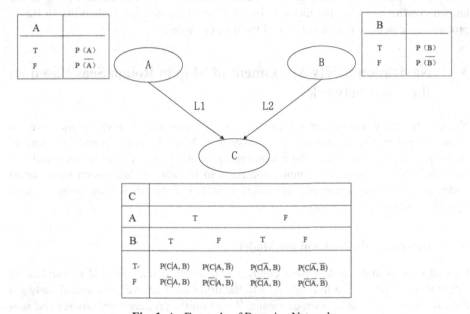

Fig. 1. An Example of Bayesian Networks

If X1,X2,…,Xn are a set of exhaustive events that are incompatible mutually, p(Xi) >0, and A is any event, then the Bayes formula can be described as:

$$p(X_i|A) = \frac{P(X_i)P(A|X_i)}{\sum_{j=1}^{n}P(X_j)P(A|X_j)}$$

(1)

$P(X_i)$, the priori, is the initial degree of belief in X_i;

$P(X_i|A)$, the posterior, is the degree of belief having accounted for A.

According to the Conditional Independence Assumption and d-Separation of BN, the joint probability of BN $p(X_1, X_2, \ldots, X_n)$ can be described as the product of marginal probability of all the nodes:

$$p(X_1, X_2, \ldots, X_n) = \prod_{i=1}^{n} p(X_i | \text{parent}(X_n)) \tag{2}$$

X_i is the ith node of BN;

$\text{parent}(X_n)$ is the nth parent node.

As a matter of fact, the inference of BN is a way to conduct probability calculation. More specifically, when given the conditions of a BN model, according to the known conditions, using the methods of calculating conditional probability in Bayes probability, calculate the probability of the needed nodes.

3   Navigation Safety Assessment of Ship in Rough Seas Based on Bayesian Network

Navigation safety assessment system of ship in rough seas is a comprehensive assessment system which consists of 3 sub-system, Man-Machine (ship)-Environment. In the process of assessment, the conditional probabilities of parent nodes should be given by experts, using BN combination rules to implement data fusion from parent nodes to child nodes, eventually get safety situation of the whole assessment system. Specific procedures as follows:

3.1   Determine the Nodes of the Model

Lots of experts and scholars have conducted in-depth discussion and researches on safety assessment of ship in rough seas in the domestic and overseas, and already got the causes of accidents by various means. Based on the predecessors' studies and several kinds of causes they put forward, this paper removes the factors that have little impact or correlation is not so strong on safety navigation of ship in rough seas, and then determines the nodes of the network model.

3.2   Determine the Range of the Nodes

The range of all the determined nodes in step (1) is [0, 1], 0 means "do not happen" or "have no influence", 1 means "happen" or "have influence", the numerical value between (0, 1) means scope of influence that parent nodes have on the child nodes. Each node has two states, T means the influence degree of "have influence", F means the influence degree of "have no influence".

3.3   Establish the BN Structure of Safety Assessment

Establishing BN structure mainly can be realized by three means. A) According to the experts' knowledge, Establish BN topological structure manually; B) Acquire BN automatically by means of learning database. C) Combination of the two methods above to realize the objective. This paper will use A) to establish the BN structure of navigation safety assessment of ship in rough seas.

3.4   Determine the CPT of Nodes

In the process of modeling of BN, the most difficult job is to determine the CPT of each node. In allusion to this model, because of the less number of the relevant data in database, the CPT of the parent nodes are obtained by means of questionnaire survey from experts. And on the basis of Bayes formula, the CPT of the each child node is eventually calculated.

3.5   Establish BN Model of Safety Assessment

After achieving the four steps above, in the light of the determined BN nodes, establish BN model, shape into the BN of ship's navigation safety assessment in rough seas. By means of the determined CPT of each node, according to the combination rules of BN, infer BN from parent nodes to child nodes to achieve the safety situation of ship's navigation in rough seas.

On account of the bidirection reasoning ability of BN, that is when given the CPT of the fringe nodes, the probability of the top node can be obtained; when given the CPT of the top node, the probability of the fringe nodes can be inferred as well. Therefore if we know that ship's navigation in rough seas is not safe, we can infer from child node to parent nodes, by ways of this kind of backward inference, we can get the dominant factors that affect the navigation safety of ship in rough seas. And then come up with more rational suggestion to guarantee the safety of ship's navigation in rough seas.

4   Instance Analysis

In this paper, training ship MV "YUKUN" of Dalian Maritime University is selected as an example, which is put into use in April 2008, and by now it has been in use for six years, with length over all 116m, breadth 18m, molded depth 8.35m, designed draft 5.4m and total tonnage 6,106tons. Officers on board are all veteran and qualified teachers of Dalian Maritime University. MV "YUKUN" has enough safety and navigation performance, the ship is equipped with integrated bridge system (IBS), AUTO-0 automatic monitoring system in engine control room, retractable fin stabilizers and bow thruster, etc., which have improved the ship's performance. In addition the aspects of stability, separation, fire-fighting, rescue and so on are far beyond regulation requirements. In this case, assumption is made under wind and wave grades 7 to 8.

This paper uses BN analysis of software package "GeNIe (Graphical Network Interface)" to accomplish the navigation safety assessment of MV "YUKUN" in rough seas. "GeNIe" is a software that builds pattern decision theory model which is developed by the Decision Systems Laboratory, University of Pittsburgh [11]. And it utilizes the junction tree algorithm to calculate the established BN model. The network model is shown in Fig.2.

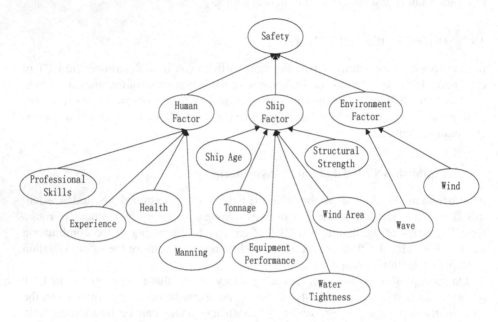

Fig. 2. Bayesian Network of Safety Evaluation of "YUKUN" in Rough seas

According to the relevant data that obtained from the questionnaires that distributed to experts, scholars and experienced navigators, check consistency and remove large-error data, and then fill in the attribute table of the nodes with corresponding conditional probability.

After filling in the CPT into the model, "GeNIe" software can automatically update the network, the results of the navigation safety assessment of MV "YUKUN" in rough seas is shown in Fig.3.

The assessment results of MV "YUKUN" navigating in rough seas can be seen intuitionally from Fig.3, the probability of "T" of the top node "safety" is 94%, that is to say, at this stage, the safety probability of MV "YUKUN" navigating in rough seas is 94%.

Because of the bidirection reasoning ability of BN, assume that the accident occurs, which means the probability of "F" of the top node "safety" is 100%, then by ways of "GeNIe" simulation, we can get the dominant factors that affect the navigation safety of MV "YUKUN" in rough seas, as shown in Fig.4.

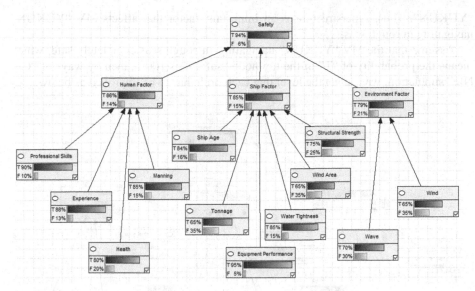

Fig. 3. Navigation Safety Assessment of MV "YUKUN" in Rough seas Based on Bayesian Network

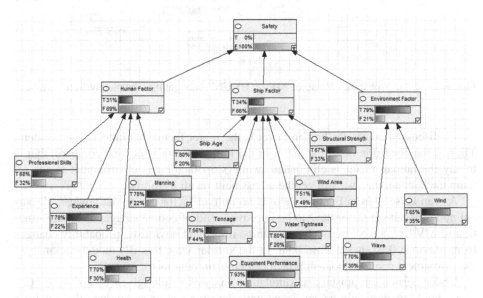

Fig. 4. The Inference of Causation of MV "YUKUN" in Rough seas baesd on Bayesian Network

As can be seen from the Fig.4, assuming the accident occurs, the human factor is the major factor that induces the accident, probability changes from previous 0.14 increases to 0.69, followed by the ship factor, probability changes from previous 0.15 increases to 0.66. Among the nodes, "wind area" node contributes the most on MV

"YUKUN". Thus, superstructure is an important factor that affects MV "YUKUN" navigating in rough seas.

Assume that the MV "YUKUN" navigating in rough seas completely safe, which means the probability of "T" of the top node "safety" is 100%, then by ways of "Ge-NIe" simulation, we can get the level that each node has to be improved as below.

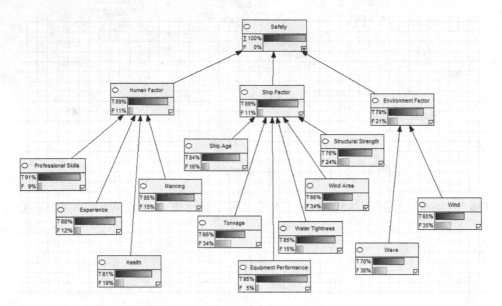

Fig. 5. Posterior Probability Value of MV "YUKUN" Navigating Completely Safe in Rough Seas

As discussed above, the human factor is the major factor that induces the accident. Thus, if the condition of all the factor in the human factor is beyond compare, that is to say the human factor is eliminated, while ship factor and environment factor remain unchanged, then we will get the assessment result as follows.

As can be seen from Fig.6, if there is no human factor during the voyage, all parent nodes of human factor have to be improved, and of course navigation safety situation of MV "YUKUN" in rough seas can be improved obviously, probability changes from previous 0.94 increases to 0.98. In the similar way, this BN model can analyze the assessment result without ship factor or environment factor as well.

Under normal circumstances, simulation analysis results given by software "Ge-NIe" should theoretically be consistent with the practical ones, but here there is little deviation. The three main reasons are: First, when conducting forward reasoning, the priori probability of fringe node is obtained via the questionnaire surveys from experts, even although having taken appropriate adjustments, still subjective; Second, human factors may be contained in the ship factors, such as the inadequate regular checks results in poor equipment performance, etc.; Third, because of the author's knowledge limitation, some factors may not be taken into account, while the factors that do not make big influences on assessment results are not listed .

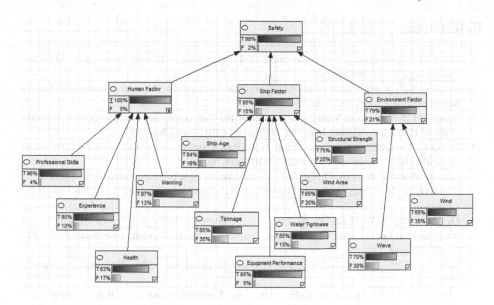

Fig. 6. Assessment Results of Bayesian Network without Human Factors

The simulation model above has great universality. In practice, in allusion to the actual situation of a ship, the corresponding priori probability of fringe nodes can be changed. For example, assumption is made in this paper that wind and wave grade is 7 to 8, if we encounter bigger wind and wave, then we can increase the corresponding priori probability value. In addition, if we want to obtain a more detailed assessment network, we can increase the number of nodes or structural level, then the credibility of the assessment results will be higher and closer to the practice value; however in that case, the scale of network model will be increased, which makes it more complex, and the calculation will become relatively difficult.

5   Conclusion

BN is a technology with huge potential for application across numerous fields. In this paper, BN is adopted as an approach to carry out the assessment of ship's navigation safety in rough seas, modeling and system analysis are settled by software "GeNIe". It provides reference information for vessels navigating in rough seass, helps to improve the safety navigation of ship and reduce accidents at sea, and provides decision basis for captains and ship management sector, which has some practical value.

Acknowledgements. This paper is supported by "the Fundamental Research Funds for the Central Universities" (3132014025).

References

1. Qu, F.D.: Navigation Safety Assessment of Timber Ship in Rough seas. Dalian Maritime University (2012) (in Chinese)
2. Liu, Q.: Safety evaluation of container ship on China-Japan line in storm wave. Dalian Maritime University (2008) (in Chinese)
3. Yang, B.C.: Navigation Safety Assessment of Ro-Pax vessel Sea-keeping ability in Storm wave of Bohai Bay. Dalian Maritime University (2010) (in Chinese)
4. Lu, Q.J.: Navigation safety assessment of Ro-Pax vessel in storm wave based on BP neural network. Dalian Maritime University (2010) (in Chinese)
5. Sun, J., Wang, F.W., Liu, Q., Qu, F.D.: Safety assessment of ships navigating in heavy sea based on evidence theory. Journal of Dalian Maritime University 39(1), 53–56 (2013) (in Chinese)
6. Qi, Z., Wang, F.W., Liu, Q.: Analysis on sea-keeping ability indexes of Ro-Pax vessel navigation in stormy wave of Bohai Bay. Journal of Dalian Maritime University 39(2), 37–40 (2013) (in Chinese)
7. Pearl, J.: Fusion: Propagation and structuring in belief networks. Artificial Intelligence (1986)
8. Maglogiannis, I., Zafiropoulos, E., Platis, A., Lambrinoudakis, C.: Risk analysis of a patient monitoring system using Bayesian Network modeling. Journal of Biomedical Informatics 39(6), 63–64 (2006)
9. Kannan, P.: Bayesian networks: Application in safety instrumentation and risk reduction. ISA Transactions 46(2), 255–259 (2007)
10. Zhou, J.F., Tang, C.Y., Xu, Z.Y.: Application of Bayesian networks to dam risk analysis. Journal of Hydroelectric Engineering 29(1), 92–96 (2010) (in Chinese)
11. GeNIe and SMILE, http://genie.sis.pitt.edu/index.php/about

Optimization of Ship Scheduling Based on One-Way Fairway

Jun Lin[1], Xin-yu Zhang[1,2], Yong Yin[1], Jin-tao Wang[1], and Shun Yao[1]

[1] Key Laboratory of Maritime Dynamic Simulation and Control of Ministry of Transportation,
Dalian Maritime University, Dalian 116026, China
junerlinly@gmail.com
[2] Faculty of Infrastructure Engineering, Dalian University of Technology,
Dalian 116023, China
zhang.xinyu@sohu.com

Abstract. In order to optimize ship scheduling based on One-Way fairway when numerous ships arrive at the port, this paper develops a mathematical model. It aims to minimize the weight of ship's waiting time for the channel in the consideration of the safe navigation. An optimal solution is obtained by applying Genetic Algorithm (GA). The chromosomes are represented as integer permutation, which is applicable for optimizing the ship scheduling. And the Two-Point Crossover is employed in the algorithm. Results show that the 9 ships' waiting time for the channel is 38 minutes and the objective value is 7.937. It demonstrates that the proposed solution has an advantage in improving navigation efficiency and the benefit for the port.

Keywords: One-Way fairway, Optimization priority, Ship scheduling, Genetic Algorithm.

1   Introduction

It may cause a congested situation in the one-way fairway when numerous ships arrive at the port. While there were many researches on ship scheduling, most of them focus on the berth allocation and capacity of channel, few researches were conducted on ship scheduling for the channel. Etsuko (2001) presented a mathematical model to solve the problem of dynamic berth allocation planning for ships in the public berth system [1]. Akio (2003, 2005) presented a heuristic algorithm for the berth allocation with service priority [2] and berth allocation problem in continuous locations [3]. Liang (2009) formulated a multi-objective mathematical model in the consideration of each berth for container ship with quay crane dynamic assignment (QCDA) and number of Quay Crane's Move [4]. Song (2010) analysed the traffic capacity of navigation channel under the influence of navigation duration, and simulated transport ship sailing operation systems by Arena [5]. The results show that the relationship between single-channel transit capacity and shipping navigation duration is negative exponent distribution. Wang (2008) presented a mathematical model on the co-scheduling

X.-h. Sun et al. (Eds.): ICA3PP 2014, Part II, LNCS 8631, pp. 479–486, 2014.
© Springer International Publishing Switzerland 2014

problem to increase the whole passing ability for Three Gorges-Gezhou Dam [6]. However, it is different from ship scheduling on channel without paying attention to shipping navigation duration, thus making their study inappropriate for one-way fairway.

Xu (2008) developed an optimum scheduling model for ships passing through one-way fairway based on the work sorting theory [7]. Factors for each weight in the model are selected according to their influence on the safe of navigation in the consideration of practical operation. The obtained results showed obviously the advantages of improving the navigation efficiency for the channel. The model targets at minimizing the investment time of total ships (including sailing time and the waiting time for the channel availability), which is different from us. In this paper, a mathematical model is proposed to the ship scheduling based on one-way fairway. The goal of the model is to minimize the weight of the ship's waiting time for a channel availability. It takes both the navigation efficiency and the benefit of the port into account, under the premise of navigation safety. To solve the problem above, we employ GA.

2   Description of the Problem

As it is well known, when ships pass through one-way fairway, it is not allowed to overtake other ships. It is necessary to come up with a solution to schedule ship inbound/outbound in the case of numerous ships arriving at the port at a period. It is a typical non-linear integer programming problem: A ship is allowed to access the channel only after it has arrived at the port or it has finished loading and discharging. A distance should be kept to ensure the safety of navigation between two ships inbound/outbound.

3   Formulation of the Ship Scheduling

3.1   Scheduling Priority

It is significant for a port to develop a solution that makes the whole ships pass through the channel as soon as possible, so that clearing the navigation area and reducing the waiting time of the ships at a period. VTS usually offers higher priorities for the ship with well maneuverability in the consideration of safety and navigation efficiency, when the channel is congested. For example, we assume that two ships with different size have just arrived simultaneously, the small one has to wait for long if the large one is scheduled first, while the large waits for a short time if it is scheduled second. In general, maneuverability depends on the following factors: the location of the berth, the size of ship, the type of ship and the draft [8]. On the other hand, according to a survey, large ship preferred to be given a higher priority than small ships when the terminal is busy. In addition, ship with route of international trunk service always has higher priority to be scheduled.

From the above discussion, it is clear that the scheduling priority is critical for ship scheduling, especially in a situation where there are numerous ships to be arranged at a particularly busy port. This paper proposes a priority function for ship scheduling with the factors such as the location of berth, the size of ship, the type of ship, the draft and the route of ship and so on. It is carried out as function (1):

$$p = \mu_1 v^{berth} + \mu_2 v^{size} + \mu_3 v^{type} + \mu_4 v^{draft} + \mu_5 v^{route} + \cdots \tag{1}$$

Where, v^{berth}, v^{size}, v^{type}, v^{draft}, v^{route} denote the location of a berth, the size of a ship, the type of a ship, the draft and the route of a ship; $\mu_1, \mu_2, \mu_3, \mu_4, \mu_5$ are weights for each factor proposed respectively, which are obtained through calculation.

The proposed function is available for the ship scheduling in every port as long as it choose the factors according to their practical situation.

3.2 Assumptions of the Model

In order to simplify the mathematical model, we assume that the ships have already prepared to entry into the channel. That means that they could go on the fairway as long as the channel is available. Furthermore assumptions are shown in details as follows:

1. The channel is idle in initial;
2. The water depth of the channel meets the requirement of the ship to pass through the channel safely;
3. The pilot has boarded if a pilot is needed;
4. There are available berths for ships to call once it has been inbound.

3.3 Formulation of the Ship Scheduling

In formulating the ship scheduling, we define $\forall i (= 1, \cdots, N) \in V$ as the set of total inbound/outbound ships at a given period, and the i is the number of the ship; we set at_i as the arrival time of ship i approaching the channel or the bulwark for the departing ship (there is a conflict on the one-way fairway when ships pass); st_i is the time when the ship i start to be scheduled; wt_i presents the waiting time for the channel availability of ship i ; p_i is the priority weight of the ship i in the scheduling model; t_p is the completion time of a ship for passing through the channel ; t_{gap} is a safe interval between two ships sailing in the channel with the same direction, while t_0 is a safe interval between two ships sailing in the channel with the different direction. The objective function of the ship scheduling can therefore be written as:

$$\text{Minimize} \qquad MinT = \sum_{i}^{N} wt_i * p_i \qquad \forall i (= 1, \cdots, N) \in V \tag{2}$$

Subject to

$$at_i < st_i \qquad \forall i \in V \tag{3}$$

$$st_{i-1} - st_i \geq t_{gap} \qquad \forall i \in V \tag{4}$$

$$st_i - (st_{i-1} + t_{p(i-1)}) \geq t_0 \qquad \forall i \in V \tag{5}$$

$$wt_i = st_i - at_i \qquad \forall i \in V \tag{6}$$

The optimization objective of the ship scheduling is to minimize the weight of waiting time for the channel availability of the N ships at a given period, which is shown in equation (2). Constraint (3) is used to ensure that ship i can be allowed to be scheduled only after it has arrived at the port or it has finished the task in the port to departure. Constraint (4) explains that the interval of the st_i between st_{i-1} must be not less than t_{gap} if the two ships access to the channel in the same direction. Constraint (5) ensures the safety interval of the two ships in the contrary direction, in the condition that a ship should not be scheduled to entry into the channel before it has been clear. Constraint (6) expresses that the waiting time for channel availability of a ship is the difference between its start time and arrival time.

4   Design of GA

To facilitate the solution procedure, we employ a GA [9], which is a random algorithm based on genetic and nature evolution, with the great ability to provide optimal or near optimal solutions. It has been widely used for solving non-linear optimization problem and other complex problems, such as Job-Shop Scheduling problem [10]. This paper designs a Genetic Algorithm, which is applicable for the problem of optimizing ship scheduling.

4.1   Chromosome Representation

We represent the chromosome by using integer permutation in the GA, which represents a solution to the problem clearly and conveniently. The chromosome is divided into N segments for N ships to be scheduled, each of which represents the number of a ship, and the location corresponds to the operation order. They are represented as follows:

$$\begin{array}{cccccccc}
Chromosome & 7 & 3 & 5 & N & \cdot & \cdot & \cdot & 9 \\
Order & 1 & 2 & 3 & 4 & \cdot & \cdot & \cdot & N
\end{array}$$

4.2   Fitness Function

GA searches for the individual with the maximal fitness value for optimizing problem. As to a minimization problem, the smaller the objective function value, the higher must be the fitness value. Therefore, we defined fitness function as shown in function (7), where $ObjV$ denotes the objective function value, according to [1], which is found to be better.

$$F = 100/\left(1 + \exp\left(ObjV/1000\right)\right) \tag{7}$$

4.3 Selection Strategy, Crossover and Mutation

Selection Strategy. In this paper, the criterion used to select individual for reproduction is Roulette Wheel Selection with probability of $GGAP$.

Crossover. The Two-Point Crossover is employed in the GA. We divided the chromosomes into groups with pairs. Every group takes the steps as follows:

1. Step 1: Generate two integers between [1, N] randomly as two crossover points;
2. Step 2: Interchange the two crossover points. The middle fragment genes are exchanged, while the other fragments are reserved and marked as * if they are examined to be the same with the middle genes;
3. Step 3: Repair mechanism. The unknown numbers (with * position) are processed by corresponding with the intermediate fragment of another chromosome. Then we get the feasible children chromosomes. Fig. 1 shows an example how the children chromosomes are created, where we assumed that there are 10 ships and the two crossover points are $r1=4$, $r2=7$.

```
                              2 5 1   3 10 4 9   7 8 6
       Parents chromosomes:
                              10 7 4   6 3 8 5   2 1 9

                              2 * 1   6 3 8 5   7 * *
  Interchanged chromosomes:
                              * 7 *   3 10 4 9   2 1 *

                              2 5 10   6 3 8 5   7 4 2
       Children chromosomes:
                              6 7 8   3 10 4 9   2 1 5
```

Fig. 1. Example of crossover

Mutation. In our procedure, mutation is conducted to select two mutation points between [1, N] randomly and alter their values by interchanging their positions. An instance is shown in Fig. 2, where $N=10$, and $r1=4$, $r2=7$.

```
The chromosome before mutation : 7 5 2 | 6 | 3 8 | 9 | 10 4 1
The chromosome after mutation : 7 5 2 | 9 | 3 8 | 6 | 10 4 1
```

Fig. 2. Example of mutation

5   Experiment and Results

In this section, we conducted an experiment with the data from the center of Dalian VTS. 9 ships inbound/ outbound to Dayao Bay are selected during the time between 18:30-20:30 on July 26 in 2009. Data used in the experiment is shown in Table 1. Where, st is the start time of a ship to be scheduled with the rules of the first come first served (FCFS).

Table 1. Ship scheduling solution for channel with FCFS

No.	I/O	Size	Type	Route	t_p(min)	at	st	wt(min)
1	Out	9587	Container	Trunk	6	18:52	18:52	0
2	Out	65917	Container	Trunk	6	19:29	19:29	0
7	In	9520	Container	Trunk	5	19:30	19:40	10
5	Out	6813	Container	Trunk	4	19:37	19:50	13
9	In	499	Dry Cargo	Feeder	6	19:51	19:59	8
4	In	2997	Container	Feeder	7	20:06	20:10	4
6	Out	7350	Container	Feeder	5	20:08	20:22	14
8	In	90745	Container	Trunk	4	20:12	20:35	23
3	Out	35745	Container	Trunk	7	20:17	20:44	27

Notes:

1. Setting $t_{gap} = 5$ and $t_0 = 5$ according to the practical operation;
2. The completion time for passing through the channel of a ship (t_p) is obtained by dividing the length of the channel and the speed of the ship while passing through the channel. The length of the Dayao Bay channel is 0.8 nm;
3. Size of ship, type of ship and route of ship are selected as factors of ship scheduling priority, according to the situation of the port.

In this paper, the proposed GA was implemented with Matlab to solve the problem. The process in the main function is carried out as follows:

1. Step 1. Read the data from the folder;
2. Step 2.Parameters and Initiation. The size of population is $NIND$=50, the probability of selection is $GGAP$=0.9, the probability of crossover and mutation are Pc =0.9 and Pm=0.01, times of the generation is $MAXGEN$=200;
3. Step 3. Calculate the fitness values of each chromosome and find the best individual in the population;
4. Step 4. Genetic operators with selection, crossover and mutation to obtain a set of offspring;
5. Step 5. If it is carried out by the $MAXGEN$ times, then stop. Otherwise, return to step 3.

We found that it had a satisfactory solution when the weights of the factors for ship scheduling were $\mu_1 = 0.4, \mu_2 = 0.3, \mu_3 = 0.3$, according to tests we conducted with ship scheduling priority function. The scheduling solution is shown in Table 2.

As it is shown in the Table 2, the total waiting time for the channel availability of the 9 ships is 38 minutes, which is less than 99 minutes compared with the solution of FCFS in the Table 1, thus improving the navigation efficiency for the channel obviously. In addition, while ship 8 comes later than ship 6, ship 8 is scheduled before ship 6 for its higher priority than ship 6. It improves the effectiveness of the port for serving an important ship first. The proposed model is proved to be correct by the results.

Table 2. Ship scheduling solution with priority by GA

No.	I/O	Size	Type	Route	Priority	at	st	wt(min)
1	Out	9587	Container	Trunk	0.2605	18:52	18:52	0
2	Out	65917	Container	Trunk	0.4660	19:29	19:29	0
5	Out	6813	Container	Trunk	0.2605	19:37	19:37	0
7	In	9520	Container	Trunk	0.1416	19:30	19:46	16
9	In	499	Dry Cargo	Feeder	0.1405	19:51	19:51	0
4	In	2997	Container	Feeder	0.1405	20:06	20:06	0
8	In	90745	Container	Trunk	0.4660	20:12	20:12	0
3	Out	35745	Container	Trunk	0.3099	20:17	20:21	4
6	Out	7350	Container	Feeder	0.1405	20:08	20:26	18

The evolution of the GA is shown in Fig. 3.

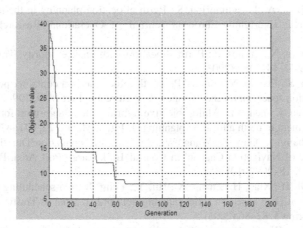

Fig. 3. The evolution of the GA

We find that the objective values have been substantially decline from 38.62 to 7.937. The objective value decreases rapidly while searching an optimal solution in global at early time in the algorithm. It optimizes the solution in the region of local slowly at the medium time in the algorithm. We finally obtain the optimal solution with the minimum objective value, since the algorithm has converged when it runs at 70 gens. Based on the above analysis, it is clear that the proposed algorithm is effective.

6   Conclusions

In this paper, the optimization problem for ship scheduling is discussed in the case of numerous ships arriving at the port. We present a mathematical model for ship scheduling with the use of GA. It is proved to be correct and has an advantage in improving navigation efficiency and the benefit for the port by the experiment. The proposed model is applicable for a port when it is congested with ships. However, ship scheduling is a difficult problem with a continuous procedure and multi-factors influential in practice, which deserves some further consideration. Therefore, we are going to do more researches and present a solution based on further consideration for the proposed problem.

Acknowledgements. This research was financially supported by National Natural Science Foundation of China (Grant No.51309043), Applied Basic Research of Ministry of Transport (Grant No.2014329225020), Fundamental Research Funds for the Central Universities (Grant No.3132014202), China Postdoctoral Science Foundation (Grant No.2014M551095), and Liaoning Provincial Natural Science Foundation of China (Grant No.2014025005).

References

1. Etsuko, N., Imai, A., Papadimitriou, S.: Berth allocation planning in the public berth system by genetic algorithms. European Journal of Operational Research 131, 282–292 (2001)
2. Akio, I., Etsuko, N., Stratos, P.: Berth allocation with service priority. Transportation Research Part B 37, 437–457 (2003)
3. Akio, I., Xin, S., Etsuko, N., Stratos, P.: Berth allocation in a container port: using a continuous location space approach. Transportation Research Part B 39, 199–221 (2005)
4. Liang, C., Guo, J., Yang, Y.: Multi-objective hybrid genetic algorithm for quay crane dynamic assignment in berth allocation planning. J. Intell. Manuf. 22, 471–479 (2009)
5. Song, X., Zhang, J., Guo, Z., Wang, W.: Analysis of Navigation Duration Influence to Trafficability of Navigation Channel in Coastal Bulk Cargo Port Area. Port Engineering Technology 2, 18–20 (2010)
6. Wang, X., Qi, H., Xiao, H., Zhang, X., Hu, Y., Feng, X.: Co-scheduling model of Three Gorges-Gezhou Dam based on series queuing netword. Journal of Traffic and Transportation Engineering 3, 82–86 (2006)
7. Xu, G., Guo, T., Wu, Z.: Optimum Scheduling Model for Ship in/outbound Harbor in One-way Traffic Fairway. Journal of Dalian Maritime University 4, 150–153 (2008)
8. Xu, G., Liu, R., Wu, Z.: Analysis of Sequence Arrangement Weight When Ships Entering or Exiting a Port in One-way Channel. Navigation of China 31, 379–382 (2008)
9. Xi, Y.: The Summary of Genetic Algorithm. Control Theory and Application 13, 697–708 (1996)
10. Fang, H., Ross, P., Corne, D.: A promising Genetic Algorithm Approach to Job-Shop Scheduling, Rescheduling, and Open-Shop Scheduling Problems. In: Proceeding of the Fifth International Conference on Genetic Algorithms, pp. 375–382. DAI Research Paper, Edinburgh (1993)

Research on Virtual Crew Path Planning Simulator Based on A* Algorithm

Huilong Hao, Hongxiang Ren[*], and Dajun Chen

Key Laboratory of Marine Simulation & Control for Ministry of
Communications, Dalian Maritime University, Dalian, China
dmu_rhx@163.com

Abstract. In order to reasonable planning of the virtual crew's walking path in ship-handling simulator, making the virtual crew could walk along a barrier-free path, used OpenSceneGraph, 3D rendering engine, successfully implemented that the simulation of planning about the virtual crew's walking path. A geometric model of the virtual crew met the reality was set up used layered geometric modeling, which was necessary to control the virtual crew's motion by key frame animations. The A* algorithm was studied at the same time, which has been applied to the path planning of the virtual crew. Put forward a method of grid mapping, solved the path planning problem of the accessible obstacles better such as the cab. Through tested in the ship-handling simulator, it can be proved that the work have been done realized the path planning of the virtual crew, and the effect of simulation was good enough.

Keywords: Ship-handling Simulators, Virtual Crew, Path Planning, Geometric Modeling, Motion Controlling, A* Algorithm.

1   Introduction

Joined the virtual crew in ship-handling simulator's visual system and made him to complete a specific action, could meet the demand of authenticity and richness of crew education and training on the ship-handling simulator's visual system. For example, in the training of berthing, if the ship-handling simulator could simulate a serious of operators to the cable of the crew on ship's deck, there is no doubt that it could provide more visual information stimulation and the sense of immersion to users, and increase the effectiveness of the simulator visual system.

In order to accomplish a specific task in ship-handling simulator, virtual crew often needs to walk, but the ship's space is narrow, and there are many obstacles, planning out an barrier-free path which virtual crew can implement a specific task from the start point to target point is a basic question when researching the virtual crew in ship-handling simulator.

The theoretical researches about path planning algorithm were much more than the applications in virtual reality system. Made the geometric modeling, motion control of virtual crew and A* algorithm as the research objects, established the geometric

---

[*] Corresponding author.

X.-h. Sun et al. (Eds.): ICA3PP 2014, Part II, LNCS 8631, pp. 487–495, 2014.

model and realized the motion control of virtual crew, at the same time the A*
algorithm was applied to the virtual crew's path planning simulation. Put forward a
method of grid mapping, solved the path planning problem of the accessible obstacles
better such as the cab.

2   Modeling and Control of Virtual Crew

2.1   Geometry Modeling of Virtual Crew

Geometric modeling of virtual crew is the precondition to realize the virtual crew's
path planning simulation. The modeling methods of virtual crew are: bar model, body
model, surface model and hierarchical model [1, 2]. The methods of bar model and
body model are simple, but they are low fidelity; The fidelity of surface model is
better, but it contains a large amount of data and models slow; Hierarchical model
expresses human body model in bone layer, muscle layer and skin layer, the method
is simple and it has a good fidelity, so this paper chosen hierarchical model to
geometric modeling of virtual crew.

The specific method of hierarchical geometry modeling of virtual crew using 3ds
Max software is: first of all, established a virtual crew's skin layer according to the
appearance of virtual crew characteristics, at the same time, made the UVW unfold
for the skin layer and made the corresponding texture map given to the skin layer,
generated a virtual crew surface profile meet reality; then established the
corresponding bone layer for the skin layer and binding them, adjusted the
parameters of bones, so that it could settle a foundation for the motion control of
virtual crew. Geometric model of virtual crew is shown in figure 1.

Fig. 1. Geometric model of virtual crew

2.2   Motion Control of Virtual Crew

Simulation of virtual crew's walking motions is one of the important contents of
enhancing the reality of the virtual crew's path planning simulation. The main
methods of virtual crew's motion control are: key frame animations method,
kinematics method, dynamics method and motion capture method [3]. Key frame

animations method is simple and intuitive, but this method is tedious; The effect of kinematics method is clear, but this method cannot be used for the simulation of physical reality; The authenticity of dynamics method is strong, but the amount of calculation is large, and its equation is hard to solve; Motion capture method is flexible operated and high efficiency, but there will be a mismatch between the movement data and bone models. Because of the involved walking motion of virtual crew is relatively single, therefore, this paper chosen key frame animations method to realize the virtual crew's walking motion simulation.

Walking motion is a cycle which left and right leg lifts and downs alternately with the right and left hand lifts and downs according to the analysis of human's walking motion [4], so used key frame animations module in 3ds Max software to make a cycle process of virtual crew's walking motion so that it could be called in program. Virtual crew's walking motion is shown in figure 2.

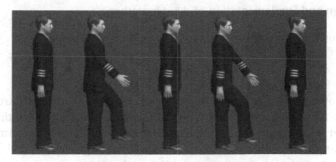

Fig. 2. Virtual crew walking motion

2.3   Virtual Crew File Convert

Converted the geometric modeling and motion control of virtual crew to the format of the file which OSG could recognized after completed, so that OSG could render it. The virtual crew format files which the OSG could identify were divided into two categories: the first type is CAL3D format file, this format file respectively stores the geometric model, skeleton model, texture map, and key frame animations in four independent format file, they are *.CSF format file, *.CMF format file, *.CRF format file and *.CSF format file; The second type is *.FBX format file, this format file could store the geometric model, bone model, texture map, and key frame animations in the same format file, it is more   convenient in practical use. Therefore, the geometric model of virtual crew was selected convent into *.FBX format file in 3ds Max software.

3   Path Planning

3.1   Research Status of Path Planning Algorithm

Path planning mainly divided into global path planning and local path planning [5]. global path planning was also known as static path planning, it is suitable for the path planning which the surrounding environment information was known; Local path planning was also known as dynamic path planning, it is suitable for the path planning which the surrounding environment information was unknown.

Because of the scene which virtual crew's path planning studied was the ship model area, its surrounding environmental information was known, therefore, this paper chosen the global path planning algorithm to plan the path.

Global path planning algorithm derived a lot of intelligent search algorithms based on heuristic search algorithm, such as local optimal algorithm, the best priority algorithm, etc., the most commonly used heuristic search algorithm was the A* algorithm, it used the evaluation function to reasonably choose the development direction of path nodes in A* algorithm, which could improve the efficiency of searching path nodes [6, 7].

3.2   Design and Implementation of A* Algorithm

The evaluation function f(n) of A* algorithm could be represented as:

$$f(n) = g(n) + h(n) \tag{1}$$

The evaluation function f(n) represented the sum costs of a shortest path from the start node s to the target node t by any intermediate node n, g(n) represented the real costs from the start node s to the intermediate node n, h(n) represented the estimation costs of the shortest path from the intermediate node n to the target node t [8, 9].

Designed the following functions according to the above principles:

$$g(n) = \sum_{i=s}^{n-1} [d(i+1) - d(i)] \tag{2}$$

$d(i+1)$-$d(i)$ represented the actual distance between the adjacent nodes. When node i and node (i+1) were in the diagonal position,

$$d(i+1) - d(i) = \sqrt{2} \tag{3}$$

When the node i and node (i+1) weren't in the diagonal position,

$$d(i+1) - d(i) = 1 \tag{4}$$

Estimated costs h(n) selected the Euclidean distance [10, 11]:

$$h(n) = \sqrt{(x_t - x_n)^2 + (y_t - y_n)^2} \tag{5}$$

The x_t and y_t represent the coordinates of the target node t, x_n and y_n represent the coordinates of the current node n.

The implementation process of A* algorithm is shown in figure 3.

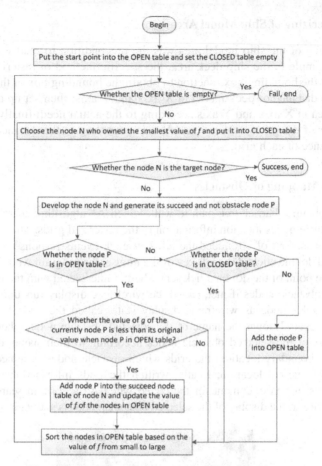

Fig. 3. The implementation process of A* algorithm

4   Implementation of Simulation

Realized the simulation of the virtual crew's path planning based on A* algorithm under the development environment of Microsoft Visual Studio 2010 using the 3d rendering engine OSG.

4.1   Import of Virtual Crew's Model File

Called the file read function to read the geometric model file of virtual crew in program and imported it into the visual system of ship-handling simulator. There would be an uncoordinated between the imported virtual crew's model and the ship model in orientation, location and size, called the matrix transformation function to adjust it.

4.2   Rasterizing of Ship Model Area

The rasterizing of the ship model area was the precondition to realize A* algorithm. Took the example in the ship deck area, the specific method of rasterizing was: first of all, called the bounding box function to obtain the bounding box of the deck model, obtained the distance of deck model in X axis and Y axis; then set up the distance of each grid area in X axis and Y axis according to the actual need; finally, obtained the total number of the grids in X axis and Y axis according to the distance of deck area and the distance of each grid.

4.3   Gird Mapping of Obstacles

In order to obtain a barrier-free path to walk which A* algorithm searched, needed to map the obstacle nodes location information to the raster zed grids. The specific method of mapping was: first of all, added the left key click events response of the mouse in program, and double clicked the left key of the mouse, the program would determine the ray which the point of the double-click sent whether intersected with the obstacle nodes, selected the obstacle nodes if met, called the wireframe display function to present the selected obstacles node as wireframe display state, called the node traverse class to traversal and record down the name of the selected obstacle nodes; then obtained the bounding box of the selected obstacle nodes according to their name, determined the grids of their boundary location, the grids which obstacle nodes occupied contain their boundary and internal location; finally, written the grids information of the selected obstacle nodes in text document for the called when A* algorithm searching the path nodes. The wire frame display of the selected obstacle nodes is shown in figure 4.

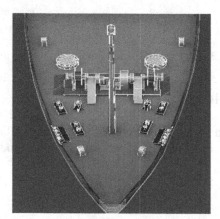

Fig. 4. The wire frame display of the selected obstacle nodes

4.4   Gird Mapping of Accessible Obstacles

There exists accessible obstacles in ship-handling simulator such as cab, the start point or target point of virtual crew's walking path may inside the accessible obstacles, assuming that still uses the grid mapping method of obstacles in section 3.3 at this time, it would lead to fail to plan the walking path of virtual crew. Therefore, this paper puts forward a grid mapping way to fit the accessible obstacles.

Took the grid mapping of the cab as a case to analysis like this:

(1) Set the internal girds of the cab to be not obstacles girds due to the start point or target point of the virtual crew's walking path may be inside the cab.

(2) The path planning method of virtual crew remains the same when the start point and target point of virtual crew's walking path were all inside the cab at the same time.

(3) When the start point and target point of the virtual crew's walking path were inside and outside the cab in the same time, the first thing was found the exit location of the cab if we want to plan the walking path of virtual crew, and then set the girds of the exit location to be not the obstacle grids, so as to ensure the A* algorithm could search the walking path successfully.

Found the exit location by line segment intersection method in this paper, the specific process is shown in figure 5:

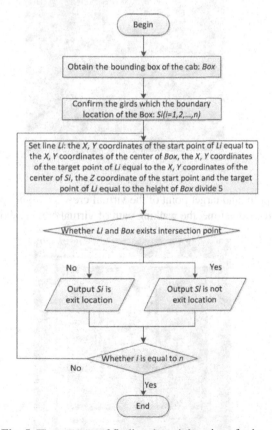

Fig. 5. The process of finding the exit location of cab

4.5   Virtual Crew Walking along Path

Before virtual crew walking along the way to perform a specific task, the program needed to calculate the girds of the start point and target point, and then performed A* algorithm to search the path nodes according to the saved obstacle girds information, called the path animation class to create the critical path when the barrier-free path had been searched, and loop played the key frame animations of the virtual crew's walking motion along the path, stopped the animations when virtual crew reached the target point.

Virtual crew walking along the path is shown in figure 6, green square represented the start point of the walking path, red square represented the target point of the walking path, white squares represented the path nodes of the walking path, the virtual crew walking along the direction of the yellow arrow, when reached the target point virtual crew stopped walking.

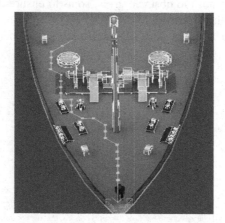

Fig. 6. Virtual crew walking along the path

When the start point and target point of the virtual crew's walking path were inside and outside the cab at the same time, the walking path of virtual crew is shown in figure 7.

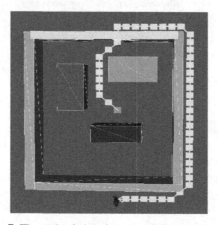

Fig. 7. The path of virtual crew walking out the cab

5   Conclusions

Established the geometric model of virtual crew with the method of hierarchical geometry modeling, achieved the walking motion control of virtual crew through the key frame animations, converted the geometry model and walking motion key frame animations of virtual crew as *.FBX format file and imported it to OSG, at the same time, combined with the study of A* algorithm implemented the simulation of virtual crew's path planning in ship-handing simulator.

The reality of the virtual crew's geometric model is strong, the walking motion of virtual crew is lifelike and virtual crew can walk along a barrier-free path from the start point to target point smoothly. At the same time, founded the exit location girds of accessible obstacles by line segment intersection method and set them to be not obstacle girds, solved the problem of virtual crew's path planning in and out of the accessible obstacles.

Applied the implemented simulation of virtual crew's path planning in ship-handling simulator visual system, enhanced the abundance of the visual system better and settled the feasible foundation for subsequent virtual crew performed a specific task.

Acknowledgment. This work was Supported by 973 Major State Basic Research Development Program(No. 2009CB320805), Natural Science Foundation of Liaoning Province(No. 201202018), The Fundamental Research Funds for the Central Universities (No. 01780134).

References

1. Yang, X.T., Yang, K.J., Yan, C.X.: Research on Methods Geometry Modeling and Motion Control for Virtual Human. Computer and Digital Engineering 8, 132–135 (2008)
2. Wang, J.H., Lv, K.Z.: Comparative Study on Virtual Human Techniques for Art and Design. Computer System and Application 5, 123–127 (2009)
3. Li, S.L., Liang, J.H., Wu, B.: Survey of Virtual Character Motion Generation and Control. Journal of System Simulation 9, 1758–1771 (2011)
4. Chen, M.Z., Chen, J., Xu, C.Y.: Motion Control for Virtual Human Based on IK by Two Phases and Key Frames. Computer Engineering and Design 7, 2760–2765 (2012)
5. Liu, H.: Research and Implementation of the Key Technologies of 3D Character Animation. Central South University (2012)
6. Shi, H., Cao, W., Zhu, S.L.: Application of an Improved A* Algorithm in Shortest Route Planning. Geomatics and Spatial Information Technology 6, 208–211 (2009)
7. Zeng, C., Zhang, Q., Wei, X.: GA-based Global Path Planning for Mobile Robot Employing A* Algorithm. Journal of Computers 2, 470–474 (2012)
8. Qi, Y.H., Yang, Z.P., Huang, Q.H.: Improved Path Planning Algorithm Based on A* Algorithm. Information and Electronic Engineering 4, 326–329 (2009)
9. Wang, H.M., Zhou, X.Z.: Improvement and Realization of Beeline Optimizing A* Algorithm in Shortest Path Problem. Journal of Engineering Graphics 6, 121–126 (2009)
10. He, G.H., Chen, J.Q.: Research on Algorithm of Intelligent Path Finding in Game Development. Computer Engineering and Design 13, 2334–2337 (2006)
11. Ren, B., Zhou, T., Yu, L.: Study on Path Planning for Aircraft Based on Improved A* Algorithm. Systems Engineering and Electronics 2, 324–326 (2010)

Speech Recognition Applied in VHF Simulation System

Dajun Chen, Hongxiang Ren[*], and Huilong Hao

Key Laboratory of Marine Simulation & Control for Ministry of Communications,
Dalian Maritime University, Dalian, China
dmu_rhx@163.com

Abstract. Speech recognition technology can achieve the man-machine dialogue truly, but it has not been application for Marine Simulator. There has an example of VHF of GMDSS simulator to be given to do a briefly introduce from interface, menu design and data input, and then implemented it on the Visual Studio 2010 platform. Based on researching the key technology about speech signal and recognition, the speech recognition system developed with Microsoft Speech SDK, and operated VHF simulator by using this system. It is the first time to application speech recognition technology on marine simulator, and achieved a satisfactory results, it has a good reference for the speech technology used in other marine simulator systems.

Keywords: GMDSS, VHF, Marine Simulation, Speech Recognition, Man-machine Dialogue.

1 Introduction

Marine simulator as an indispensable part of maritime education, it is an increasingly prominent role in the crews' teaching and training. With the rapid development of computer technology and increasingly of the maritime education requirements, the marine simulator and its functions are updating constantly[1,2]. The existing marine simulator includes Ship Handling Simulator, Radar Simulator, Bridge Resource Management Simulator, Marine Cabin Resource Management Simulator, ECDIS Simulator, GMDSS Simulator and so on.

Currently, the speech recognition technology in many areas have been broad applied with several decades of development, such as Mandarin Exams, Automatic Speech Tickets, Phone Voice Dialing etcetera, it greatly improving the efficiency and people's live quality. Bill Gates believes that the user interface of generation operation system and applications will abandon the keyboard and mouse, and instead the man-machine dialogue[3,4,5]. Although the speech recognition technology has not been applied in the marine simulator, however, it has an exciting prospect. As we all know, the GMDSS simulator as an important part of marine simulator, it becomes increasingly significant in the crews' GMDSS teaching and training[6,7]. The VHF(Very High Frequency) is an equipment of the GMDSS system, this paper

---

[*] Corresponding author.

X.-h. Sun et al. (Eds.): ICA3PP 2014, Part II, LNCS 8631, pp. 496–506, 2014.

simulated the VHF which produced by RURUNO, then after studied the key technologies about speech signal and speech recognition, we developed a speech recognition system with Microsoft Speech SDK and applied in the VHF simulator.

2   Design and Implementation of the VHF Simulator System

Currently, the VHF 8800S of FURUNO company is widely used in various types of vessels[8]. In this paper, we have studied this type of VHF, and used Visual Studio 2010 as a development platform to develop the VHF simulator. In order to ensure the simulator consistent with into VHF real device, our development work was divided three main modules, include bitmap processing, operation menus and data input to implement.

2.1   Bitmap Resource Processing

In order to make the manipulation interface of VHF simulation device more realistic, the first step was to take pictures of real device, and using Photoshop or other Image process tools to landscaping treatment appropriately; then using double buffering technology to define several canvas, and put the landscaping bitmaps in the corresponding canvas to display; finally, we have got the simulation interface of VHF (Fig .1).

Fig. 1. Main interface of VHF simulator

Because of the panel of VHF 8800S-type device includes too many buttons and knobs; we just introduced the processed and implemented of knobs in the follows.

1. Bitmap splicing. Generally, almost every knob includes several scales, so we can put different scale images together to form one bitmap (Fig.2), and then according to the scale range to use integer variables I_m to mark which bitmap area should be displayed.

Fig. 2. Bitmap of knobs

2. Determined the direction of rotation. According to judgment the press and release of mouse position to determine the rotation direction[9] (Fig.3).

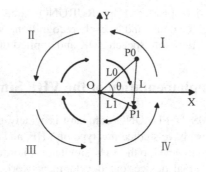

Fig. 3. Judgment of rotation direction

Thus we can count the mouse position changes state about clockwise and counterclockwise in each quadrant. The detailed statistics showed in Tab.1.

Table 1. Judgment of rotation direction

Quadrants	Clockwise	Counterclockwise
I	X+, Y-	X-, Y+
II	X+, Y-	X-, Y-
III	X-, Y+	X+, Y-
IV	X-, Y-	X+, Y+

3. Calculation of integer variables. In the Fig.3, when the mouse was pressed, its position is $P_0(x_0, y_0)$, while released, the position is $P_1(x_1, y_1)$. By calculating the length L of P_0P_1, where

$$L = \sqrt{(x_0 - x_1)^2 + (y_0 - y_1)^2} \tag{1}$$

Likewise, we can calculate the length L_0 of OP_0 and length L_1 of OP_1. So the angle θ of $\angle P_0OP_1$ can be calculated, where

$$\theta = \arccos \frac{L_0^2 + L_1^2 - L^2}{2L_0L_1} \times \frac{180}{\pi} \tag{2}$$

Now, we can calculate the integer variable I_{im} with formula (3) which stated in step 1, and then to show the corresponding bitmap area.

$$I_{im} = \theta \% T_{step} \tag{3}$$

Where T_{step} is a pixel threshold, in this paper, T_{step} is 17.

2.2   Design of Operation Menu

Because of the VHF includes too many operation menus, and the most menus involve select of options, input of data, enter submenus, exist current menus. We can use a data structure which called stack to organize these menus. When need to operating one menu, just to push stack, and if we need to operate a submenu, continue push stack. However, if we need to quit current menu and comeback to the parent menu, just pop stack. Fig. 4 represented the push or pop stack of menus, and the top stack is an operable menus.

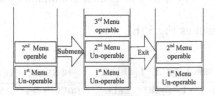

Fig. 4. Push / Pop stack of menus

The main of menus options were shown in Tab.2.

Table 2. Structure of main menus

Main Menus	1st Submenus	Submenus' Number
	ALARM	4
MENU	…	…
	SYSTEM	3
	RCVD ORDINARY	50
LOG	…	…
	TRANSMITTED	50
	COAST CALL	7
CALL	……	…
	DISTRESS	3

2.3   Data Input

The menus about OPSITION, FILE and CALL in the VHF involve the input of digitals and letters, when we need to input characters, we should push them stack, and before this inputting, we can pop the characters stack which locate the top stack, so implemented the function of storing and deleting characters. For the digitals input, we can put the numbers into a variable to store directly in the corresponding numeric key button area. The effect of digitals inputting just as Fig.5(a). Furthermore, for the letters input, since each numeric key corresponding to several(2, 3 or 4) letters, when we when we continuously press the same key, the letters can be switched, as for using a mobile phone to input characters. The first is different uppercases to switch, then lowercases, and in order to archive this effect, we set a timer to control. When a numeric key is pressed, the timer is started simultaneously, it record by t_1, and press this numeric key continue, it record by t_2. The interval of twice to press the same numeric key is Δt, so we can get a formula as follow:

$$|t_2 - t_1| \geq \Delta t, \quad \text{Kill the timer and end letters input}$$

$$|t_2 - t_1| < \Delta t, \quad \text{Starting timer continuously and input letters}$$

The effect of letters input as Fig.5 (b).

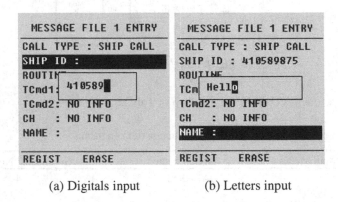

(a) Digitals input   (b) Letters input

Fig. 5. Effect of characters input

3   Speech Signal and Recognition Technology Analysis

Essentially, speech recognition system is a pattern recognition system, it includes some basic units such as feature extraction, pattern matching and reference pattern library[10]. The main methods of speech recognition include DTW (Dynamic Time Warping), HMM (Hidden Markov Models) and ANN (Artificial Neural Network,). DTW have a very good result for isolated word recognition. ANN on the application in speech recognition is still in the research stage. And the HMM is widely used in the field of speech recognition, it have a nice effect in both isolated words and continuous speech recognition. It is the application of relatively sophisticated algorithms, so this paper also uses this algorithm.

The speech recognition basing on HMM, is essentially a pattern matching method, and the speech recognition process of pattern matching method as shown with Fig.6. This paper analyzed the speech recognition technology from the three aspects of pre-processing, feature extraction and model matching.

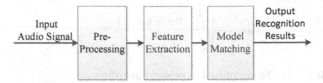

Fig. 6. Flowchart of pattern matching for speech recognition

3.1   Time-Domain Analysis of Speech Signal in Pre-processing Stage

The mainly task in pre-processing stage of speech recognition is processes in time-domain and frequency domain, and one of the most intuitive analysis way is to observe its time-domain waveform, because the waveform can show the speech signal changes with time and the ups and downs of speech energy. Fig.7(a) shows the speech signal original waveform of "Power off" in time-domain.

Through the detection of the speech signal endpoint can determine the start and end position of an isolated word. Before the endpoint detection, we need to analyze the energy of the speech signal, however, the change of speech signal energy with time is very obvious, so we can take short-term energy, short-time average zero-crossing rate and short-term average to describe the feature changes of speech signal [11].

1. Short-term Energy

The speech signal $\{x(n)\}$ at a time of n, its short-term energy is E_n as (4):

$$E_n = \sum_{m=n-(N-1)}^{n} [x(m)\omega(n-m)]^2 \qquad (4)$$

Where N is window-length, set $h(n) = \omega^2(n)$, then the formula (4) can be expressed as (5):

$$E_n = x^2(n)h(n) \qquad (5)$$

It indicates that the short-term energy from the n-th point to add a window-length function is E_n, Fig.7(b) shown the short-term energy waveform of "Power off".

2. Short-time Average Zero-crossing Rate

The short-time average zero-crossing rate means the times of speech signal is zero value in each frame. As the speech signal is a short-time stationary signal, to some extent, the short-time average zero-crossing rate can reflect the nature of the signal spectrum; it can be expressed by follows:

$$Z_n = \left| \text{sgn}[x(n)] - \text{sgn}[x(n-1)] \right| \omega(n) \qquad (6)$$

Where $\text{sgn}[]$ is the sign function, and $\omega(n)$ is a window function. Normally, we should take a rectangle window function in the actual calculation, set the window length is N, and then the window function $\omega(n)$ can be expressed by follows:

$$\omega(n) = \begin{cases} \dfrac{1}{2N}, & 0 \le n \le N-1 \\ 0, & else \end{cases} \tag{7}$$

So the formula (7) can be simplified expressed as follows:

$$Z_n = \frac{1}{2N} \sum_{m=n-(N-1)}^{n} \left| \text{sgn}[x(m)] - \text{sgn}[x(m-1)] \right| \tag{8}$$

As Fig.7(c), it shows the short-time average zero-crossing rate waveform of "Power off".

3. Endpoint Detection

To finish the speech signal analysis about short-term energy, short-term average and short-time average zero-crossing rate, then we should detect the endpoint based on energy and zero-crossing rate, the steps of this algorithm as follows:

① Separation frames processing of the speech signal $\{x(n)\}$, denoted by $S_i(n), n = 1, 2, ..., N$, where n stand by discrete time series, N is the length of frames, i is the numbers of frames;

② Obtained the short frame energy E_i and short-time average zero-crossing rate Z_i per frame from the above calculations.

③ To set a high threshold M_H and a low threshold M_L of the speech signal average energy, then traversal the energy of per frame between M_H and M_L according to time series to determine the current speech endpoint. Fig.7(d) shows the endpoint detection result of "Power off".

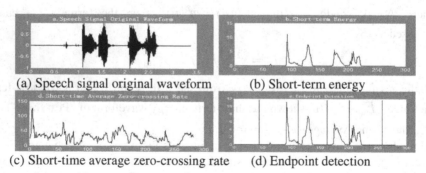

(a) Speech signal original waveform   (b) Short-term energy

(c) Short-time average zero-crossing rate   (d) Endpoint detection

Fig. 7. Wave of speech signal

3.2   Frequency-Domain Analysis of Speech Signal in Feature Extraction Stage

In the time-domain analysis can be visually observed changes to the speech waveform, however, speech signal is a complex signal, in the frequency domain, and we need a deeper understanding of its characteristics change. During the speech recognition, the speech signal characteristic parameters extraction is a very important step, we must find a way to make feature extraction as possible to avoid the effect of noise. Currently, the common feature extraction methods include LPC (Linear Prediction Coefficient), LPCC (Linear Prediction Cepstrum Coefficient) and MFCC (Mel Frequency Cepstrum Coefficient). Where LPCC is the most effective one speech signal analysis technology, it is widely used in speech areas such as speech synthesis and recognition [12].

LPCC is the Cepstrum of LPC, it can be extracted more thorough excitation information in the process of generating a speech signal. Cepstrum coefficient is the inverse z transformation of logarithmic modulus function of signal z transformation. When calculate it, we need to calculate the Fourier transform of the signal and calculate logarithm modulo, then calculate the inverse Fourier transform. In order to simplify the calculation, we can use the recurrence relation of sequence $x(n)$ and its plural Cepstrum coefficient $c(n)$, as follows:

$$\hat{X}(z) = \frac{d \log X(z)}{dz} = \frac{X'(z)}{X(z)} \tag{9}$$

Through the z inverse transform, we can obtain the recursive formula as follows:

$$\hat{x}(n) = \begin{cases} 0, & n \leq 0 \\ \dfrac{x(n)}{x(0)} - \displaystyle\sum_{k=0}^{n-1}(\dfrac{k}{n})\hat{x}(k)\dfrac{x(n-k)}{x(0)}, & n > 0 \end{cases} \tag{10}$$

Scilicet, formula (9) is the recurrence relation of sequence $x(n)$ and its plural Cepstrum coefficient $c(n)$.

3.3   HMM Analysis in Speech Recognition Stage

HMM is a speech recognition model which based on statistical model of time series. It is not observed events correspond with the state, but interconnected each other by a set of probability distribution. The process of HMM is a doubly stochastic process: one is describe the transient characteristics of the signal which can be directly observed, other is describe the dynamic characteristics of short-term statistical characteristics which implicit in the observation sequence.

To the isolated word recognition, it need to prepare an HMM model for each word to describe, this procedure uses a method called VQ (Vector Quantization) to design a series of codebook which the size is M (M is the number of symbols observed), and takes K times for each word model training or learning, so we can obtain the optimal model parameters. Then, to the words which wait for recognition take sub-framing and feature extraction, so we can get a set of random vectors $X_1, X_2, ..., X_T$ (T is the numbers of frames), and process it with VQ to transform into symbol sequence

$O = o_1, o_2, ..., o_T$. Finally, to calculate the output probability of this sequence for each HMM, and the maximum value is the result of recognition. The processing just as Fig.8 is shown.

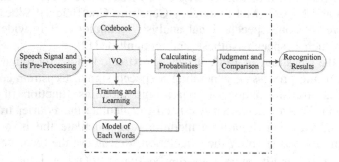

Fig. 8. Processing of HMM speech recognition

4   Implementation of Speech Recognition

In order to achieve the speech recognition function with effectively and efficiently, and reduce the development difficulty, this paper takes Microsoft Speech SDK 5.1 to develop a speech recognition application program [13].   This SDK development kit provides speech application resource package which includes a SAPI (Speech Application Programming Interface), DDI (Device Driver Interface), SR (Speech Recognition) and SS (Speech Synthesis).

When performing specific word recognition, the speech application program which based on Speech SDK used to take CFG (context-free grammars) to analysis the words which need to be identified, that is we should define several waiting for identified words in a XML file, and the structure form of XML as follows:

```
<?xml version="1.0" encoding="Unicode">
<GRAMMAR LANGID="409">
     <DEFINE>
            <ID NAME="Power on" VAL="1"/>
     </DEFINE>
     <RULE ID="Power on" TOPLEVEL="ACTIVE">
            <L> <P>Power on</P> </L>
     </RULE>
</GRAMMAR>
```

In this paper, most operation words of the VHF simulator were defined in a XML file includes 20 operation commands (such as Power on, Daily Test, Menu etc), 10 numbers and 26 letters. Fig.9 shows the process of operating VHF simulator with speech recognition.

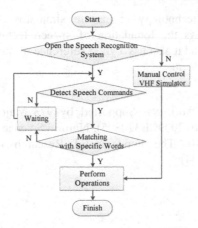

Fig. 9. Flow char of voice operating VHF simulator

This system tests on a software platform of Windows 7, Visual Studio 2010, Microsoft Speech SDK 5.1; the hardware platform includes core-i7 CPU, 4G Memory and SENNHEISER230 Microphone. In the laboratory environment, 10 different people to operate the VHF simulator with several times, and the recognition results were counted in Tab.3.

Table 3. Results of speech operating VHF simulator

Contents	Correct Numbers	Recognition Rate
20 commands	172	86.0%
10 numbers	98	98.0%
26 letters	243	93.4%

Through this test we can visually see that the recognition rate of numbers and letters is very high, and the rate of operation commands is slightly lower. However, with this recognition rate can able to meet the operational requirements of VHF simulator.

5   Conclusions

This paper simulated the VHF of FURUNO from interface, operation and functions, it is very similar to a real VHF device, so it can be applied in the teaching and training of crews. In order to achieve the man-machine dialogue in the marine simulators, this paper analyzed the speech signal state in both time domain and frequency domain, and descripted the recognition process of HMM briefly, then we adopted Microsoft Speech SDK as development kit to develop the speech recognition system of specific vocabulary, finally, it was applied in the VHF simulator device. Through repeated test with different people, we got a nice recognition result that realization the purpose of operating VHF simulator with speech. The works of this paper is the first time used the speech recognition technology in marine simulator, and achieved relatively satisfactory results. It lays the foundation of speech technology apply in marine simulator in the future. And it also has a good reference to speech technology apply in other marine simulator system.

Acknowledgment. This work was Supported by 973 Major State Basic Research Development Program(No. 2009CB320805), Natural Science Foundation of Liaoning Province(No. 201202018), The Fundamental Research Funds for the Central Universities (No. 01780134).

References

1. Jin, Y.C., Yin, Y.: Maritime Simulators: Convention and Technology. Navigation of China 1, 1–6 (2010)
2. Jin, Y.C., Yin, Y.: Development Strategy of Maritime Simulator in Light of the Manlia Amendments to STCW Convention. Navigation of China 3, 5–10 (2012)
3. Juang, B.H.: The Past Present and Future of Speech of Speech Processing. IEEE Signal Processing Magazine 12, 21–27 (1998)
4. Richard, V.C., Candace, A.K., Rabiner, L.R.: Speech and Language Processing for Next Millennium Communications Services. Processing of IEEE 88, 1314–1337 (2000)
5. Huang, X.: Research and Development of Continuous Speech Recognition Based on HTK and Microsoft Speech SDK. Xia Men University (2007)
6. Xiao, F.B., Yin, Y., Jin, Y.C.: Simulation of Maritime Narrow Band Direct Printing Telegraph System. Navigation of China 3, 10–15 (2009)
7. Wei, W.: Development and Application of Martine VHF Radio Simulator. Navigation of China 1, 16–19 (2010)
8. Furuno Operator's Manual - VHF Radio Telephone Model FM-8800D/8800S. Furuno Electric Co., LTD. Inshinomiya (2004)
9. Yu, J.: Study of GMDSS Equipment Operation Simulation Based on FURUNO Series. Dalian Maritime University (2013)
10. Liu, X.H., Song, T.X.: Speech Recognition and Control Application. Science Press, Beijing (2008)
11. Zhang, X.Y.: Digital Speech Processing and Simulate with Matlab. Electronic Industry Press, Beijing (2010)
12. Han, J.Q., Zhang, L., Zheng, T.R.: Speech Signal Processing. Tsinghua University Press, Beijing (2013)
13. Microsoft Corporation. Microsoft Speech SDK Version 5.1, http://www.microsoft.com

The Assessment of Risk of Collision between Two Ships Avoiding Collision by Altering Course[*]

Weifeng Li[1], Wenyao Ma[1,**], Jiaxuan Yang[1], Guoyou Shi[1], and Robert Desrosiers[2]

[1] Navigation College, Dalian Maritime University, Dalian, Liaoning, China
wenyaoma1980@163.com
[2] Chevron Shipping, USA

Abstract. Altering course is the most common and effective method employed by ships to avoid collision. Give-way vessels should take early and substantial action to avoid collision, the effectiveness of a course change is influenced by the distance between the two vessels. In some instances involving more than two vessels are present (special cases), the give-way vessel may not be able to alter course as early as possible. In other instances, the stand-on vessel may be required to take action to due to the failure or inability of the give-way vessel to act. In the event of special cases and action by the stand-on vessel, it is important for navigating officers to be able to determine when a course change alone will avert a collision in order to plan for the worst case scenario. Thus, it is advantageous for navigating officers and masters to quickly and simply model the amplitude and effectiveness of course changes up to the distance between the two ships when course changes will no longer avert a collision. By using existing models of ship movement and maneuvering characteristics, a method will be presented to calculate the extent of risk of collision through reasoning process, provide a quantitative explanation of the effectiveness of course changes and identify the point at which course changes are no longer effective in collision avoidance. A worked example will illustrate the need for navigating officers to make early course changes by demonstrating the decreased effectiveness of course changes at small distances between ships.

Keywords: Risk of collision, Altering course, collision avoidance, Minimum angle alteration.

1 Introduction

A ship at sea can alter her course, change her speed, or alter both her course and change the speed simultaneously to avoid collision. Considering the performance of the main engine and response times while in transit at sea speed, in many instances altering course is the only viable option to execute timely action to avoid collision. The encounter of the ships is a process of approaching and reducing distance from an area of no or minimal potential risk of collision to an area of high potential risk of

---

[*] This work was supported by the Fundamental Research Funds for the Central Universities under grant 3132013015, 3132013004 and 3132013006.
[**] Corresponding author.

X.-h. Sun et al. (Eds.): ICA3PP 2014, Part II, LNCS 8631, pp. 507–515, 2014.

collision. When two vessels are meeting and a risk of collision exists according to the Rules (COLREGS, 1972), there are actions to be taken by the give-way and stand-on vessel. The give-way vessel has the responsibility to take early action to keep clear of the other vessel with a safe distance in an ample time(Zhao Yuelin, 2012). The stand-on vessel may take action if it becomes apparent that the give-way vessel is not taking appropriate action. However, the Rules do not give an quantitative explanation when action should be taken by the give-way (early and substantial action) or stand-on vessel (taking additional action) to avoid a collision.

This paper illustrates two concepts, range of collision avoidance courses θs and the minimum alteration angle $\Delta\varphi$ to assess the risk of collision of ships. A step by step reasoning such as one based on researcher A.S. Lenart's algorithm of the relationship between the speed and course of in case of a constant distance between two vessels, can be applied to the problem(A.S. Lenart, 1983). The result of applying an algorithm is useful to improving navigating officers' comprehension of the risk of collision, while illustrating the need for the give-way vessel need to take early action to avoid collision.

During the process of calculating and reasoning, the assumptions are:

- Own ship and target ship are thought to be an idealized ships;
- The give-way vessel takes altering course action with no change of speed;
- There is no delay from the rudder order to change of course;
- There is no influence to the speed of the ship from the change of the course.

2   Modeling and Calculation

2.1   Calculation of Action to Avoid Collision

In order to understand the algorithm, it is necessary to consider the coordination system to be used. The center of the coordinate system is the ship's directional axis of rotation with X axis represents the direction of true east, and the Y axis represents the direction of true north. The speed of own ship is V_o and course is φ, and the speed of target ship is V_t, the relative speed of target ship to own ship is V_r. The relationship between these elements are shown in equation (1) and equation (2).

$$V_o + V_r = V_t \tag{1}$$

$$\begin{cases} V_{ox} = V_o \sin\varphi \\ V_{oy} = V_o \cos\varphi \end{cases} \tag{2}$$

Here, V_{ox} is the component of own ship speed vector in the X direction, and V_{oy} is the component of own ship speed vector in the Y direction; V_{tx} is the component of target ship speed vector in the X direction, and V_{ty} is the component of target ship speed vector in the Y direction; V_{rx} is the component of target ship relative speed vector in the X direction, and V_{ry} is the component of target ship relative speed vector in the Y direction. Suppose that (X,Y) is the coordinate of target ship in the coordinate system considered in front, and (X_0, Y_0) is the initial position of target ship, the coordinate of target ship position (X,Y) following with time t can be got with equation (3).

$$\begin{cases} X(t) = X_0 + V_{rx}t \\ Y(t) = Y_0 + V_{ry}t \end{cases} \tag{3}$$

Assuming $D(t)$ that is the distance between own ship and target ship, the following relationship should exist as shown in equation (4).

$$D(t) = \sqrt{X^2(t) + Y^2(t)} \tag{4}$$

Derivate $D(t)$ by t and get the following result:

$$D_{min} = \left| \frac{XV_{ry} - YV_{rx}}{V_r} \right| \tag{5}$$

Where D_{min} is the distance of closest point of approach (short for DCPA or CPA) between own ship and target ship. In order to keep a safe passing distance (D_s) between own ship and target ship, it is necessary to let $D_{min} \geq D_s$.

Square equation (4), and get equation (6).

$$V_{rx} = AV_{ry} \tag{6}$$

Then get,

$$A = \frac{X(t)Y(t) \pm D_{min}\sqrt{(X^2(t) + Y^2(t) - D^2_{min}}}{X^2(t) - D^2_{min}} \tag{7}$$

Where,

$$V_o = \frac{AV_{tx} - V_{ty}}{A\sin\varphi - \cos\varphi} \tag{8}$$

Thus, from equation (1), (2) and (7), it can be seen that,

$$V_o = \frac{AV_{tx} - V_{ty}}{A\sin\varphi - \cos\varphi} \tag{9}$$

Then,

$$V_{oy} = AV_{ox} - B \tag{10}$$

Where,

$$B = AV_{tx} - V_{ty} \tag{11}$$

From equation (11), it is the relationship of speeds, and change it into the relationship of distances, multiply both sides by time (Δt) :

$$y = Ax - B\Delta t \tag{12}$$

As it can be seen, the most important factors affecting the risk of collision are distance of the closest point of approach (DCPA) and the time to closest point of approach (TCPA). When DCPA<D_s and TCPA>0 exist simultaneously, the risk of collision exists. If TCPA<0, the two vessels will navigate in opposite directions, thus there is no risk of collision.

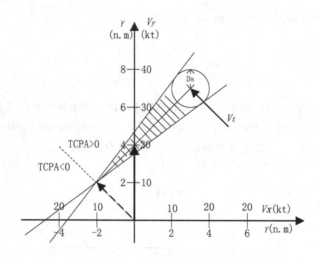

Fig. 1. The relationship between the speed and course (A.S. Lenart)

Equation (12) simply corresponds to the two lines when DCPA=D_s. which will intersect with each other as shown in figure 1. The area on the left side of intersection represents the situation when TCPA<0, with no risk of collision to own ship, and the area on the right side of intersection representing the situation when TCPA>0, where there is no guarantee the passage with a safe distance. Thus, if the vector of own ship is not located in the shaded area, the two ships will pass at a safe distance (D_s).

2.2   Calculation of Range of Collision Avoidance Courses

When an own ship takes action to avoid collision with a target ship by altering course, all the ends of the own ship course vector will form a circle with the center in the middle of the ship and with radius $V_o\Delta t$. This circle will intersect with the shadow area as shown in figure 1, the figure is shown in figure 2. The shaded area in the circle indicates the ship's courses cannot safely navigate with, the angle is θ, the unshaded portions of the circle indicate safe course options, the angle is $(360-\theta)$. Analysis of figure 2 leads the equation of the circle is:

$$X^2 + Y^2 = (V_o \Delta t)^2 \tag{13}$$

From equation (12) and (13),

$$
\begin{cases}
x = \dfrac{A(B\Delta t) \pm \sqrt{A^2(B\Delta t)^2 - (1+A^2)((B\Delta t)^2 - (V_o\Delta t)^2)}}{1+A^2} \\[4mm]
y = \dfrac{\pm A\sqrt{A^2(B\Delta t)^2 - (1+A^2)((B\Delta t)^2 - (V_o\Delta t)^2)} - B\Delta t}{1+A^2}
\end{cases}
\tag{14}
$$

In the equation (8), there are two solutions for A, so does B. So there are four solutions in equation (14), they are (x_i,y_i) $(i=1,2,3,4)$, which corresponds to the four intersections points in figure 2 from the lines of equation (11) and the circle of equation (13). Two of these four points are located in the area corresponding by TCPA<0, which means no effect to passage with a safe distance, but the other two points are located in the area corresponding by TCPA>0, the arc between them is the range which own ship course cannot navigate, and the other part of the circle is the courses that own ship can change to. It is not hard to calculate the length of the arc by equation (15).

$$s = \sqrt{(x_1 - x_3)^2 + (y_1 - y_3)^2} \tag{15}$$

Corresponding degrees is,

$$\theta = 114.64 \arcsin\left(\frac{s}{2V_o \Delta t}\right) \tag{16}$$

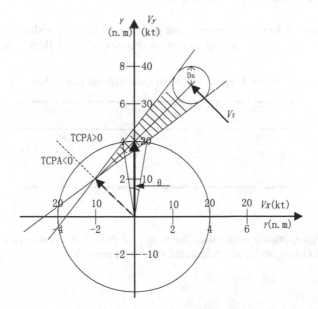

Fig. 2. Schematic diagram of θ and $\Delta\varphi$

Where θ is range of courses which own ship cannot alter course to, and the range which own ship can alter course to θ_s is easy to get by $\theta_s=360°-\theta$, also called range of collision avoidance courses. If the range of collision avoidance courses is bigger, it means that the difficulty to take action to avoid risk of collision by altering course is small, otherwise, is big.

2.3   Calculation of Minimum Alteration Angle

It is not difficult to get the coordinates of the two intersection points (x_1,y_1) and (x_3,y_3) on the side of TCPA>0 according to equation (14). In addition, when there is risk of collision between two vessels in sight of each in a crossing situation, the give-way vessel shall take action in ample time to avoid collision, and avoid crossing ahead of the stand-on vessel. So, the minimum alteration angle is from the initial course of own ship to the vector OB, and the speed vector OB is the new course of the ship. The minimum alteration angle $\Delta\varphi$ can be calculated by the following equation (18).

$$\Delta\varphi = 57.32\arcsin(\frac{x_i}{V_o\Delta t})-\varphi \qquad (17)$$

Here, $\arcsin(\dfrac{x_i}{V_o\Delta t})$ represents the new course, corresponding to the vector OB, changeed degrees; φ is the initial course of own ship.

3   Calculation by an Example

Using researcher S.Lenart's example, the position of the target ship from own ship is (5 n mile, 5 n mile) with own ship and target ship speeds as indicated in table 1.

Table 1. Speed vectors of own ship and target ship

ITEM	V(kt)	X Axis(kt)	Y Axis(kt)
OS	20	0	20
TS	14.1	-10	10
V_r	14.1	-10	-10

As two ships approach each other, the range of collision avoidance courses and the minimum alteration angles are calculated shown in table 2.

Table 2. Results of θ_s, $\Delta\varphi$ and *dif*

D (n mile)	θ_s (°)	$\Delta\varphi$(°)	dif
7.0	343.57237	8.798550	0.045632
6.5	342.29893	9.528705	0.049170
6.0	340.81045	10.39071	0.053304
5.5	339.04709	11.42373	0.058203
5.0	336.92438	12.68411	0.064099
4.5	334.31893	14.25592	0.071336
4.0	331.04284	16.27037	0.080437
3.5	326.79446	18.94415	0.092238
3.0	321.05469	22.66257	0.108181
2.5	312.84017	28.18370	0.131000
2.0	299.99558	37.24150	0.166679
1.5	276.37321	55.00827	0.232297
1.4	268.82391	60.92789	0.253267
1.3	259.42287	68.42934	0.279389
1.2	247.10641	78.43995	0.313593
1.1	229.23033	93.25132	0.363249
1.0	180	135	0.5

- The relationship between the range of collision avoidance courses and distance between two ships is shown in figure 3.

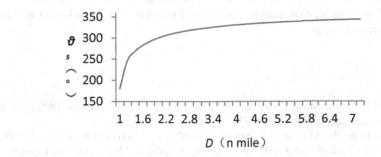

Fig. 3. Relationship between θ_s and D

- The relationship between the minimum alteration angle and the distance between two ships is shown in figure 4.

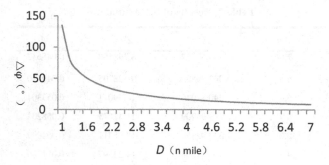

Fig. 4. Relationship between $\triangle\varphi$ and D

4   Conclusion

From the results of calculation in table 2 and the curve in figure 3 and figure 4, it can be seen that:

- When two ships are far away from each other, the range of collision avoidance courses decrease slowly and the minimum alteration angle increase slowly in a linear;
- As the two ships approach each other, especially when the distance is less than 2 times of safe passage distance, the range of collision avoidance courses decrease rapidly and the minimum alteration angle increase rapidly in a exponential way.

When the risk of collision exists when navigating on the sea, if you lost the best chance to alter course by reason of finding the target or taking action too late, the difficulty to keep clear of target ship and the minimum alteration course will rapidly increase, it will give us an explanation why should the give-way vessel need to take action in such an early time.

References

1. Lenart, A.S.: Collision Threat Parameters for a new Radar Display and Plot Technique. J. Journal of Navigation 36, 404–410 (1983)
2. Pedersen, E., Inoue, K., Masanori, T.: Simulator Studies on a Collision Avoidance Display that Facilitates Efficient and Precise Assessment of Evasive Manoeuvres in Congested Waterways. J. The Royal Institute of Navigation 46, 411–427 (2003)
3. Inoue, K.: Evaluation Method of Ship handling Difficulty for Navigation in Restricted and Congested Waterways. J. The Royal Institute of Navigation 53, 167–180 (2000)
4. Xiu-ying, B.: Decision-making on Alert Course Opportunity and Action of Ship's Collision Avoidance and Error Effects on these Results. J. Journal of Guangzhou Ocean University 4, 39–43 (2010)
5. Ming-Cheng, T., Chao-Kuang, H.: The study of ship collision avoidance route planning by ant colony algorithm. J. Journal of Marine Science and Technology 18, 746–756 (2010)

6. Yuelin, Z.: Ships collision avoidance and watch keeping. Dalian Maritime University, Dalian (2012)
7. Szlapczynski, R.: A Unified Measure of Collision Risk Derived From The Concept of A Ship Domain. J. Journal of Navigation 59, 477–490 (2006)
8. Pedersen, E., Inoue, K.: Simulator Studies on a Collision Avoidance Display that Facilitates Efficient and Precise Assessment of Evasive Manoeuvres in Congested Waterways. J. Journal of Navigation 56, 411–427 (2003)
9. Ming-Cheng, T., Sheng-Long, K., Chien-Min, S.: Decision Support from Genetic Algorithms for Ship Collision Avoidance Route Planning and Alerts. J. Journal of Navigation 63, 167–182 (2010)
10. Bi-guang, H.: Ship handling. Dalian Maritime University, Dalian (2012)

The Merging Algorithm of Radar Simulation Data in Navigational Simulator

Shun Yao[1], Xin-yu Zhang[1,2], Yong Yin[1], Xin Xiong[1], and Jun Lin[1]

[1] Key Laboratory of Maritime Dynamic Simulation and Control of Ministry of Transportation,
Dalian Maritime University, Dalian 116026, China
yaoshunyaoshun@gmail.com
[2] Faculty of Infrastructure Engineering, Dalian University of Technology,
Dalian 116023, China
zhang.xinyu@sohu.com

Abstract. In this paper, a method used to generate continuous and complete radar simulation data was described. This new method based on previous radar simulation data, which extracted from different scales S-57 standard electronic navigation charts in navigational simulator. In this work, the clipping buffer in per radar simulation data was set and the boundary line was cut off by forward angle firstly. Then radar simulation data were sort according to scale and area range after deducting clipping buffer from the original chart. Subsequently the redundant data were deleted based on the original scale. Finally, the direct connection was proposed to wave the radar simulation data. Taken charts about waters around Dalian Port as an example, the radar simulation data generated meet the need in navigational simulator.

Keywords: Merging Algorithm, Radar simulation data, Clipping buffer, Forward angle, Direct connection.

1 Introduction

Navigational simulator(certified by Det Norske Veritas, DNV A-class), which researched and developed independently by Dalian Maritime University, generates radar image based on the radar simulation data of the coast line and navigation aid extracted from S-57 standard electronic navigation charts. However, the resulted radar image is inaccuracy or disappears when the position of the simulated ship located the overlapping portion of two charts or outside of the reading chart, as it can only read one radar simulation data from a single chart at a time. So it needs a new method to connect the radar simulation data that extracted from S-57 standard electronic navigation charts with different scales to satisfy the accuracy requirements of the radar image.

There are lots of related researches on how to dissolve problems in segment matching and connecting study in the related fields including Geographic Information System (GIS), cartography, transportation, image processing. Xiong (2000) proposed a

X.-h. Sun et al. (Eds.): ICA3PP 2014, Part II, LNCS 8631, pp. 516–524, 2014.
© Springer International Publishing Switzerland 2014

three-stage algorithm approaching to network matching: node matching, segment matching and edge matching [1]. Du (2004) connected broken contour lines from scanned topographic map based on spatial relationships [2]. Zhao (2004) proposed the trend connection which assigned the connecting error to neighboring points, which smoothed the line and remained the trend basically. Later she presented an algorithm of many maps edge auto matching according to graphic constraints and attribute constraints [3,4]. Pouderoux (2007) reconstructed the gradient orientation field to match end-points and connected the contour lines respecting the tangents at the end-points [5]. Yuan (2007) did research on chart conjoin after coordinate transformation, but it was not conjoint naturally at the level of the element [6]. Y.Zhou (2009) proposed straight merging and curve merging to process 13 kinds of situations that may present according to distance constraints for multi-sheet of digital marine map [7]. Sandhya (2009) used distance matching contour line end-points in topographic maps, then waved the contour lines by intersecting tangents at the matching end-points [8]. Zhang (2010) posed an algorithm of virtual stitching based on ID mapping, however, it did not rebuild the real vector coordinates data, too [9]. Based on the research of Zhao (2004), S.Zhou (2010) proposed edge attenuation algorithm in accordance with distance constraints and attribute constraints [10]. According to the above studies, three common characteristics can be found:

1. The charts have the same scale;
2. The overlapping portion between charts is little or non-existent;
3. The point in the chart contains complete property.

S-57 charts with different scales and navigational applications are selected in different regions according to the need of specific ship sailings. Moreover, the cartography of S-57 charts are based on route planning generally which affected by natural circumstance of sea area and navigational requirement. So the resulted charts inevitably had some problems such as subdivide randomly or the range of overlapping portions is vague. What is more, radar simulation data extracted from S-57 charts are restricted by the original scale. There are few researches related to mergence following radar image generation. Therefore, we adopt the knowledge and algorithm about mergence in GIS, and proposed a procedure to process the radar simulation data, which including all of clipping, deletion, combination and connection, so the radar image could be not only complete but also highly accurate, which was satisfied in navigational simulator.

2   The Algorithm

Radar simulation data from which generating radar image, are a series of feature points of the coast line in accordance with the direction of "while people walking along the coast line, the land is the left-hand side of the people" in S-57 charts. It describes the model of polyline approximation as the real coast line, and it complies with the standard of IHO S-57 and ENC (electronic navigation chart). Radar simulation data are manifest as closed polygon composed of feature points actually.

518   S. Yao et al.

In the process of generating radar image, firstly, all boundary lines were clipped and cut off in every chart. In next step, all of the charts were sorted according to the scale and the range of the chart. Secondly, the redundant data was deleted and the last radar simulation data was connected based on the constraint of the original scale of the coast line and the distance between matching end-points. Finally all radar simulation data was combined into a whole file for generating radar image with highly accurate.

2.1 Clipping

S-57 charts separates the integrated marine geography based on route planning and subdivides randomly. As a result, there are existing some physical cracks on the land in the chart. Thus unnecessary radar simulation data which appears as the boundary line (the outer solid line in Figure 1) closing to the chart border (the outer dashes in Figure 1) will be extracted. As a matter of fact, the boundary is very closed to the chart border, but they do not coincide.

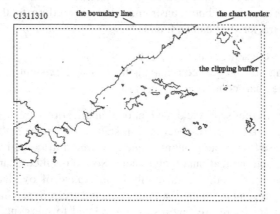

Fig. 1. The chart border, the boundary line and the clipping buffer in C1311310

Fig. 2. C1311310 after clipping

In order to quantize the distance between the boundary line and the chart border, the proportion α is defined: it is the ratio of the distance between the boundary line and the proximate chart border to the char dimension in the same direction.

For example, the proportion α in four directions of six pieces of charts about the waters around Dalian Port are in Table 1:

Table 1. The proportion α of charts about Dalian Port

Number	Chart	Scale	α_{Left}	α_{Bottom}	α_{Right}	α_{Up}
1	C1311900	1:250000	-	0.000006	-	0.00091
2	C1311310	1:150000	-	0.000003	-	0000163
3	C1311370	1:150000	-	-	0.002259	0
4	C1511381	1:40000	-	0.000374	-	0.000266
5	C1511382	1:12500	-	0.000108	0.000203	0.000229
6	C1511385	1:10000	-	0.000365	0.000023	0.009138

The meaning of "-" in Table 1 is that the boundary line in the corresponding position is not in existence.

In order to clip the boundary line quickly and avoid deleting normal radar simulation data, the clipping buffer was set, which including the whole boundary lines and occupied a little space as soon as possible. According to Table 1, it was enough that the value of proportion α equals 0.01.

What was essential to clip the boundary line was distinguishing between the coast line and the boundary line effectively (Figure 2). So the forward angle is defined: the angel between the vector which from the current feature point to next feature point and the X-axis (0°~180°). All the boundary lines were extracted manually from six pieces of S-57 charts of the waters around Dalian Port, then every feature point of the boundary lines was calculated according to the forward angle. It had been drawing a scatter diagram according to the sorted result (Figure 3).

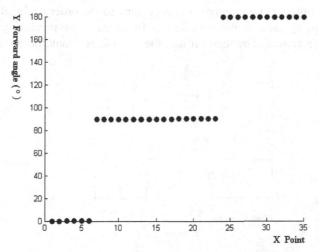

Fig. 3. The scatter diagram of the forward angles

Under statistics, the forward angles of every feature point of the boundary line focused on three special angles: 0°, 90°, 180°, which deviation was less than 0.1°, This is consistent with the conclusion of Figure 1.

All the boundary lines could be clipped according to the forward angle in the clipping buffer. Unfortunately it is inevitable to delete a few radar simulation data erroneously.

2.2   Sorting

In the process of cartography, sometimes it is less accurate and complicated in the small-scale map than the large-scale map for the same target. Therefore the radar simulation data extracted from the large-scale chart should be reserved and the radar simulation data extracted from the small-scale chart at the relevant position should be deleted, while combining the radar simulation data. The S-57 charts are sorted based on two principles:

1. If the scales of S-57 charts are different, the charts are sorted from small to large scale;
2. If the scales of S-57 charts are equal, the charts are sorted from small to large size of the range that chart dimension subtracts the area of the clipping buffer.

2.3   Combination and Deletion

The topological relation between S-57 charts could be divided into three types: disjoint, in, cross (Figure 4). In GIS, it just has the last one type. Besides, the relation of the cross could be divided into two kinds: the edge cross and the corner cross. An irregular multilateral map will be created after the combination of clipped maps. However, it is unnecessary to consider the shape of the created polygon in the combination of radar simulation data, as the blank areas could be filled up to be a rectangle (Figure 5). The process of combination is according to the order declared in Chapter 1.2, if the following radar simulation data is fit to the corresponding position, the blank areas can be covered by them; if not, the areas keep blank, because it declares

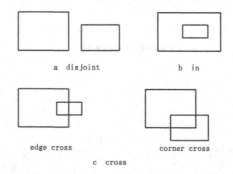

a disjoint   b in

edge cross   corner cross

c   cross

Fig. 4. The topological relation between charts

that this position is not related in the voyage. It simplifies the judgement about the shape of the created chart in the combination of radar simulation data, so the charts could be combined based on the original scale directly, no matter which topological relation is between them.

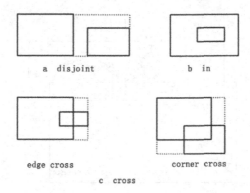

a disjoint   b in

edge cross   corner cross

c   cross

Fig. 5. A new rectangle after filling the blanks

As the accuracy of radar simulation data in the large-scale charts is higher than it in the small-scale charts, the redundant data extracted from the small-scale chart of the overlapping portions should be deleted. The property of radar simulation data is insufficient, so only the original scale could be as the filter.

2.4   Connection

Even though the polygons showed a same land are not total identical in the charts with different scales, they are considered as the same polygon in cartography, because it is significant when the geographic information is abstracted properly.

Due to the coast line in S-57 chart is extracted in accordance with the direction of "while people walking along the coast line, the land are the left-hand side of the people", the terminal point of an unclosed coast line matches the starting point of the other one in the other chart. Whether a coast line connects other one or not, the distance between the starting point (the terminal point) of the coast line and the terminal point (the starting point) of the connected one, is not less than the threshold value, which is determined by the scale of the large-scale chart. The direction connection is proposed to connect the filtered coast line which based on the original scale of radar simulation data in Chapter 1.3 with the connected coastline.

The model of polyline approximation which composed of lots of feature points, is used to describe the real coast line. If the filtered coast line matches the connected coast line, it could be considered that the accuracy of them is equivalent and the way extracting the feature point from S-57 charts is undistinguishable, hence the coast lines are connected directly. This algorithm is easy to be operated and it can meet the accuracy requirement of the radar image.

3   The Experiment

For example, there are six pieces of S-57 charts about the waters around Dalian Port (Figure 6), which scales are in Table 1.

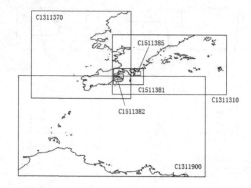

Fig. 6. S-57 charts about the waters around Dalian Port

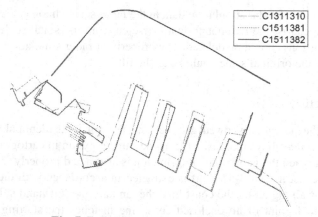

Fig. 7. Dalian Port in the overlapping portion

The radar simulation data about Dalian Port in the overlapping portion among C1311310, C1511381 and C1511382 are combined to generate Figure 7. As the chart above has been displayed, the existence of redundant data are obviously to be detected, and the restore accuracy of radar simulation data extracted from the large-scale chart, for the real coast line is high.

Taken $\alpha = 0.01$, radar simulation data extracted from six pieces of S-57 charts were clipped, deleted, combined and connected by the turns of the serial number in Table 1. Finally the radar simulation data connected are in Figure 8.

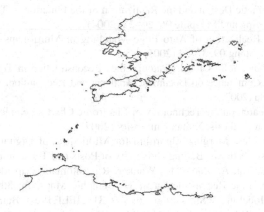

Fig. 8. The waters around Dalian Port after mergence

Contrasting the radar images about the waters around Dalian Port before and after mergence, it is obviously that the radar image got after mergence displays the real coast line accurately.

4   Conclusion and Prospect

Referring to the algorithm of matching maps which scales are equivalent in GIS, the paper described the procedure for the radar simulation data extracted from multi-sheet S-57 charts with different scales in a simulated navigation, the process includes four aspects: clipping, deletion, combination and connection. As a result the radar simulation data became complete and continuous, meanwhile, the radar image was clear and highly accurate as well as meet the actual needs of simulated voyage in the navigation simulator.

The merging algorithm proposed in the paper could be applied to the more fields, like connection of contour lines, generation of three-dimensional visual terrain.

Acknowledgements. This research was financially supported by National Natural Science Foundation of China (Grant No.51309043), Applied Basic Research of Ministry of Transport (Grant No.2014329225020), China Postdoctoral Science Foundation (Grant No.2014M551095), Liaoning Provincial Natural Science Foundation of China (Grant No.2014025005), and Fundamental Research Funds for the Central Universities (Grant No.3132014202).

References

1. Xiong, D.: A three-stage computational approach to network matching. Transportation Research Part C 8, 71–89 (2000)
2. Du, J.Y., Zhang, Y.: Automatic extraction of contour lines from scanned topographic map. In: 2004 IEEE International Geoscience and Remote Sensing Symposium, vol. 5, pp. 2886–2888. IEEE Press, Anchorage (2004)

3. Zhao, J.H.: Arithmetic Design and the Realization of the Function of Trend-edgematching. Bulletin of Surveying and Mapping 06, 26–27 (2004)
4. Zhao, J.H.: The Realization of Auto Edge Matching of Multi-maps in GIS. Bulletin of Surveying and Mapping 09, 32–34 (2005)
5. Pouderoux, J., Spinello, S.: Global Contour Lines Reconstruction in Topographic Maps. In: 9th International Conference on Document Analysis and Recognition, vol. 2, pp. 779–783. IEEE Press, Parana (2007)
6. Yuan, X.Y.: Research on the Technology of Electronic Chart's Seamless Conjoin Display. Unpublished master's thesis, Xidian University (2007)
7. Zhou, Y.W.: Seamless Merging Algorithm for Multi-sheet of Digital Marine Map Data. Unpublished master's thesis, Beijing University of Posts and Telecommunications (2009)
8. Sandhya, B., Agarwal, A., Rao, C.R., Wankar, R.: Automatic Gap Identification towards Efficient Contour Line Reconstruction in Topographic Maps. In: 3th Asia International Conference on Modelling & Simulation, pp. 309–314. IEEE Press, Bali (2009)
9. Zhang, Y., Wang, R.F., Liao, X.J.: Algorithm of virtual stitching on digital maps edge matching. Computer Engineering and Design 16, 3640–3643 (2010)
10. Zhou, S.P., Zhang, J.D., Zuo, Z.J., Wang, P.: Design and achievement of edgematching algorithm of line features in arbitrary scope. Science of Surveying and Mapping 05, 20–22 (2012)

Data Mining Research Based on College Forum

Liming Xue[1], Zhihuai Li[1], and Weixin Luan[2]

[1] Network and Information Center, Dalian Maritime University,
116026 Dalian China
[2] Transportation Management College, Dalian Maritime University,
116026 Dalian China
xuelm@dlmu.edu.cn

Abstract. Forum plays an important role in college information application. As the data of forum increases every moment, finding the valuable rules of forum data makes the point of the attention. This paper studies a college forum of china and combines a data warehouse with data preprocessing, creating time dimensions and other methods. This paper also analyses data with programming mining model. Cluster the forum data with improved Fuzzy C-Means method.

Keywords: forum, cluster, data mining.

1 Introduction

Forum is one of the main applications of Internet, supporting a free exchange platform for the Internet users. Since 1995, there are more than 2,000 online forums opened in China's colleges after the first university forum " SMTH" in Tsinghua University. Right now, there are nearly ten million registered users in college forums. Besides, College Forum has become a useful platform for information releasing, accessing, and processing. Therefore, it is necessary for the researches to analyze and manage the data in College Forum by scientific methods and techniques. After that, the forum will provide reference for the better development and management decisions. On the other hand, Data mining is an effective way to analyze the massive data, identify appropriate rules, and discovery the new knowledge, which has been widely applied in various fields in recent years. Given what has discussed above, we will use the methodologies of data mining to analyze the data of College Forum.

2 Research Object

2.1 Background of Forum

In this paper, we will take an example from a selected college, which includes 20,000 registered students. The forum of this college started form the end of 2001, and accumulated 21,000 users by 2007. There are more than sixty contents in this forum, i.e.,

X.-h. Sun et al. (Eds.): ICA3PP 2014, Part II, LNCS 8631, pp. 525–532, 2014.
© Springer International Publishing Switzerland 2014

Political Economic Review, E-Commerce, Technical Discussions, Literary Arts, and Fashion & Tourism, etc. According to statistics, there are more than 300,000 posts, with 5,000,000 replies. The forum is designed by the PHP programming language and operated on the Linux server. Besides that, in the background of this forum, the database is MySQL, with more than 20 tables, and the biggest table includes more than 5 million records.

We will take two examples of tables to show the structure:

Table 1. User: user

Name	Type	Meaning	Remark
Userid	Integer	The id of user	Primary Key
Username	String	The name of user	
Posts	Integer	The numbers of poster	After posting cleaned
Posts-fic	Integer	The numbers of poster	Since register
Lastact	Integer	Last time for activity	Including browse, post, and view or send message.
Lastpost	Integer	Last time for posting	
Lastvisit	Integer	Last login time	
Jointime	Integer	Time when you register	
Goodnees	Integer	Hot poster	How many hot posters posted by the user
Groupid	Integer	The group id of users	
Birthday	Date	Birthday	
Email	String	Email	

Table 2. Thread: thread

Name	Type	Meaning	Remark
Threadid	Integer	The id of thread	
Title	String	The name of thread	
Lastposttime	Integer	The last posting time of this thread	
Forumid	Integer	The topic id of this thread	
Replycount	Integer	How many replies of this thread.	
Postuser	String	The user name who posting this thread	
Lastposter	String	The user who posting last poster in this thread.	
Dateline	Integer	Posting time	10 digits
Views	Integer	How many times of this thread was reading	
Goodnees	Integer	if hot thread	1-YES, 0-NO

2.2   Supplementary Instruction

The users can post in different sectors with two models. The first one is issued a new poster, and then others can discuss for this topic. The second model is to comment on a existing poster, commonly known as the thread. If the user posts a theme or send a message, and then the user 's overall posts (the column of "posts-fic" in "user" table) will be increased by 1. If the poster was named as hot theme by administrator, and then the numbers of hot poster of a user will increase (the column of "goodnees" in "user" table). At the same time, in the "thread" table, if a theme was viewd, the topic number ("views" in "thread" table) will be increased by 1. If the theme was replied by someone, the number of replies will increase ("rePlycount" in "thread" table). Only the column of "goodnees" was rated as 1, when the theme was labeled as hot poster. In addition, the data type of "time" is a timestamp presented by 10-bit integer, i.e., "dateline", "lastvisit". In Linux, the timestamp of "1 January 1970 GMT 00:00" is 0000000000, so it will increase after each a second time. Therefore, we can locate the time of network behavior occurred, according to timestamp.

3   Data Warehouse

3.1   Data Pre-processing

Data mining is not a automated process. So we should pre-process the raw data before the data mining, and then build a data warehouse according to the data characteristics. In this paper, we firstly import the data from MySQL to SQLServer. While it represents incompatible of data types between these two databases, so we should modify some contents that exported from MySQL in order to meet the requirements of data formats in SQLServer. Besides that, we also need amend the data types and keywords, which do not exist in SQLServer, i.e., "unsigned".

Additionally, we should adjust the raw data tables and the contents in the tables in order to analyze. For instance, the time field is represented by the integers of linux timestamp in the original format, while in the new table, the time should be converted into Beijing time for analysis. While, considering the large amount of data, there will be a huge project to convert all of timestamps into Beijing time, as well as it is no practical significance for the analysis if the time accurate to second. So the timestamp will be simplified when data cleaning and processing, only the foundation of date information will be leaved. On the other hand, this data source was began from 2002 to November 2006, so the time across more than 50 months. Therefore, we should insert a "month" row in the original data table for time data field, the relationship between these two as follows:

In the process of analysis, some other items should be considered, i.e., how long is the online time of user, how long the theme last. Therefore, two fields were inserted into the raw table as "user time" and "thread time". The values of these two rows were calculated by the raw records. For example, the value of "thread time" is the last posting time minus the issued posting time. the value of "user time" is equal to the user last activity time minus user registration time.

Table 3. Relationship of time

Linux timestamp	Value of month
<1017590400	1
1017590400——1020182400	2
1020182400——1022860800	3
……	……
1159632000——1162310400	56
1162310400——1164902400	57

3.2   Create Dimension

Dimension is a measuring unit. The members of dimension can be divided into various metrics levels, which is called hierarchy. In this case, we will construct some dimensions according to the characteristics of users, i.e., user group dimension, user registration time dimension, user online time dimension, user last post time dimension and user last activity time dimension. Besides that, we will also create theme topic dimension, theme issue time dimension and theme duration time dimension, which corresponding to the user behavior patterns. Fortunately, SQLServer provides the appropriate tools for quickly and easily building a data warehouse.

4   Data Mining

Data mining is to find rules that can be interpreted from the instance. These rules can describe and explain the given data, as well as predict trends. There are a variety of data mining models, the actual operation often choose different models based on the data instances and the actual problems. Generally, data mining models include clustering, decision trees, factor analysis, correlation rules etc. We can easily display the data collection by SQLServer tools and analyze the data by conventional models. In this article, we will not specifically introduce these points. Here the author mainly uses Fuzzy C-Means algorithm to design the program on the part of data mining[1].

4.1   Algorithm Description

Fuzzy clustering is to solve the problem of clustering that exists in the objective world without distinct boundaries. Fuzzy C-Means (FCM) algorithm is a commonly used fuzzy clustering algorithm, which applied fuzzy technology in the traditional C-means algorithm.

In Fuzzy C-Means (FCM) algorithm, we set $\{x^i \mid i = 1,2,......,n\}$ is a collection with n samples. k is the number of clusters. $c^1, c^2,...c^k$ are cluster centers. The objective function is:

$$J = \sum_{i=1}^{n} \sum_{j=1}^{k} [u_{ij}]^{a} \left\| x^{i} - c^{i} \right\|^{2}$$

In where, $a>1$ is a blur degree constant, u^{ij} means the membership grade that x^i belongs to j.

$$0 \le u_{ij} \le 1 , \qquad i=1,2,......k ; \qquad k=1,2,......n$$

$$\sum_{j=1}^{n} u_{ij} = 1 , \qquad i=1,2,......h$$

$$0 < \sum_{i=1}^{n} u_{ij} < n , \qquad j=1,2,......k$$

In the iterative process of the FCM, we also used the following formulas to calculate the cluster center:

$$c^{j} = \frac{1}{\sum_{i=1}^{n} u_{ij}^{m}} \sum_{i=1}^{n} [u_{ij}]^{a} x_{ij} , \qquad j=1,2,......k$$

$$u^{ij} = \frac{[\frac{1}{\left| x_{i} - c_{j} \right|^{2}}]^{1/\alpha-1}}{\sum_{j=1}^{k} [\frac{1}{\left| x_{i} - v_{j} \right|^{2}}]^{1/\alpha-1}} , \qquad i=1,2,......n ; \quad j=1,2,......k$$

The steps of FCM is showed as follows:

(1) Initializing a random or a similar $u^{(0)}$; initializing $u^{(0)}$ and calculating $u^{(0)}$. So the iterations is $m=1$, and then select the number of cluster centers k and the index weights a.

(2) Calculating the cluster center. Given $c^{(m)}$, and then calculate the $u^{(m)}$, according to the formula.

(3) Recalculating the membership grade. Given $u^{(m)}$, and then calculate the $c^{(m)}$, according to the formula.

(4) If $\max|u_{ij}^{m} - u_{ij}^{m-1}| \le 3$, then stop the iteration, otherwise $m=m+1$, go to step (2), in which 3 is pre-given positive decimals [2] [3].

4.2   Algorithm Improved

In FCM algorithm, we found that the cluster center is generated randomly. Actually, there are lots of methods for initialization of cluster center, i.e., randomly create the cluster center, manually create the cluster center, as well as some other specific algorithms for setting cluster center. For example, we can use the results of C-means algorithm as the initial cluster centers of FCM algorithm.

Furthermore, the algorithm assumes that the number of clusters, we can quickly obtain the result after input an initial variable, which is the number of customers of class c. While, the initial variable c is very import to the clustering result. Actually, this is the problem of clustering validity, means that the different value of c will produce different clustering results. In this area, we can refer to the literature [4] [5]. Validity function was established for resolving the problem of clustering, which used to measure the clustering tightness and separation. We will use fuzzy clustering validity function in this paper, that the function was proposed by Xie and Beni in 1991.

$$S = \frac{\sum_{i=1}^{c} \sum_{k=1}^{n} \left(u_{ik} \right)^{m} \| X_{k} - V_{i} \|^{2}}{n[\text{mind}_{\text{wij}}]}$$

In this formula, c is the number of clusters, n is the number of data points, u_{ik} represents the membership grade of the point k belongs to the cluster i. X_k is the value of the point k, Vi is the cluster center of cluster i. dwij is the weighted Euclidean distance, means that the average deviation of each point to each cluster center, treated as a measure of the tightness of each cluster. mindwij means the minimum distance of two cluster centers between cluster i to cluster j, which is a measure of the degree of separation. As we know, the best result of clustering is the data points which having the same characteristics should be in a cluster, while the data points having different characteristics should be separated into different clusters. Ideally, the clustering result should be shown as the tightness of the same type of data is smaller, the greater the degree of separation of different types of data, as well as the value of S should be smaller. And then, we will calculate the value of c according to function S, and compare the values of S, take the minimum value of S to confirm the corresponding value of c. Therefore, we can say that the number of clusters c is best clustering result.

Finally, the result of FCM algorithm which discussed above is the membership grade for each individual to cluster. So, we also need a anti-membership fuzzy processing to calculate which individual should belong to clusters. In the anti-fuzzy processing, we will use the median method, the weighted average method, or the maximum membership degree method.

4.3   Program Design

There are five modules in this program.

Data Loading. This module is responsible for the data loaded from the database or data file into memory, make the algorithm is ready for data processing.

Cluster center initialization. This module is charging for initializing the cluster center. Actually, the user can choose their own methods in the initialization process. The program will be designed some initialization methods for users.

FCM calculating. This module is responsible for calculating Fuzzy C-Means clustering, and resulting the cluster centers, as well as the membership grade of each individual to cluster.

Clustering validity evaluation. This module means calculating the validity value of different number of clusters according to the user's need, and then selecting the optimal number of clusters.

Anti-fuzzy processing. This module will ensure that each individual was assigned to different classes, according to the membership grade and the types of anti-fuzzy approach.

4.4   Instance

We chose the data set from the database based on the users whose hot poster is more than 1 and they are not moderators, and then we found there are 273 records of users. The reason for this group of users is that the moderator is a high-quality user among all of registered users, whose online time is always longer and the number of hot posters is bigger than others. Besides that, the users whose hot poster is more than 1 are the potential moderators. As what we have discussed above, we chose this data source for data mining.

In this case, we selected C-Means method to generate the initial cluster centers among a variety of ways. According to the actual situation, it is reasonable for the data were divided into 3-5 categories. And then we calculated the clustering validity function, and got the result is 47.2 when the number of clusters is 3, 39.6 when the number of clusters is 4, and 51.4 when the number of clusters is 5. As we know, 39.6 is the minumum value amount these results, so we chose the number of clusters is 4. After that, we computed cluster centers and the number of samples, and found out that the characteristics of the first sample are closer to moderators. There are 26 users in the first cluster, the hot poster number of this cluster center is 4.45, the online time is 42.16 months. The results were shown in the following figure.

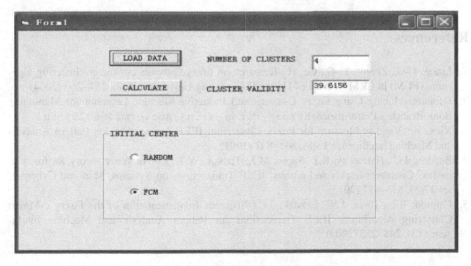

Fig. 1. Computing cluster validity

In determining individual category, we chose the method of maximum degree for the anti-fuzzy processing, the result was shown in the following figure.

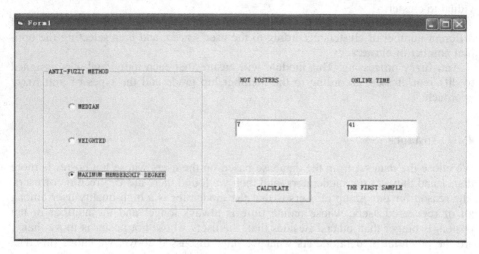

Fig. 2. Determine the user groups

5   Conclusion

This paper described the status of a college student forum, and then combined the data warehouse with data mining technologies to create a time dimension and data warehouse by data preprocessing. After that, we analyzed the users' group by Fuzzy C-Means method. In practical applications, we can analyze data or display data by the tools of data mining software, as well as design their own tools for processing in accordance with the actual situation.

References

1. Liang, J.-G., Zhang, Y.-G., Ge, H.: Research on fuzzy C-means cus-tomer clustering algorithm (FCM) in CRM. Journal of Harbin Engineering University 25(2), 257–260 (2004)
2. Decision Making Using Fuzzy C-means and Inductive Machine Learning for Man-aging Bank Branches Performance, http://citeseer.nj.nec.com/458829.html
3. Xiex, B.: Validity Measure for Fuzzy Clustering. IEEE Transactions on Pattern Analysis and Machine Intelligence 13(8), 841–847 (1991)
4. Bezdek, J.C., Hathaway, R.J., Sabin, M.J., Tucker, W.T.: Convergence theory for fuzzy c-means: Counterexamples and repairs. IEEE Transactions on Systems, Man and Cybernetics 17(5), 873–877 (2013)
5. Cannon, R.L., Dave, J.V., Bezdek, J.C.: Efficient Implementation of the Fuzzy c-Means Clustering Algorithms. IEEE Transactions on Pattern Analysis and Machine Intelligence (2), 248–255 (2009)

Simulation of Maritime Joint Sea-Air Search Trend Using 3D GIS*

Xing Shengwei, Wang Renda, Yang Xuefeng, and Liu Jiandao

Navigation College, Dalian Maritime University, 1 Linghai Road, Dalian, China
navgis@sina.com, wang.renda@gmail.com

Abstract. Joint sea-air search at sea is the search operations which aircrafts and vessels are coordinated, is the most effective way to find maritime targets in distress. Present search and rescue decision-making systems based on 2D GIS (such as ECS, Electronic Chart System) are not intuitive to show three-dimensional search activity, affecting the effectiveness of decision-making. 3D GIS is an intuitive and accurate way to express realistic geographic information, it supports three-dimensional spatial analysis and visualization, so it's suitable for joint sea-air search operations simulation. This paper introduces simulation process of sea-air search trend at sea using 3D GIS, which helps search commander to judge search trend (including search efforts' dynamic and degree of area coverage), improving their capabilities to command search operations.

Keywords: 3D GIS, joint sea-air search, search coverage, search effort, trend simulation.

1 Introduction

Joint sea-air search at sea is the search action coordinated by both sea-surface efforts (vessels) and aeronautical efforts (aircrafts), which is the most effective pattern to find targets in distress at sea[1]. Taking advantage of the naval and air forces at the same time can complete the rapid coverage of sea area and effectively shorten the time to find distress target[2], see Figure 1. It is of great significance for search commander to master all of the search efforts dynamic as well as the extent of coverage in sea area to be searched in real time. However, the traditional search command system based on 2D GIS (such as ECS, Electronic Chart System) can not intuitively demonstrate the search efforts dynamic, especially the aeronautical efforts. In this paper, the process of simulating joint sea-air search using 3D GIS is researched, including: ①creating three dimensional scene of sea area to be searched by geographical data; ② determining the search sub-area according to the searching ability of each search effort; ③calculating search path corresponding to the shape of search sub-area; ④

---

* Supported by the Fundamental Research Funds for the Central Universities (3132014027, 3132013017).

X.-h. Sun et al. (Eds.): ICA3PP 2014, Part II, LNCS 8631, pp. 533–542, 2014.

generating animation tracks through search paths; ⑤ running animation tracks to complete simulation. It can help search and rescue commander to judge the search trend intuitively, as well as to improve their effectiveness of decision-making.

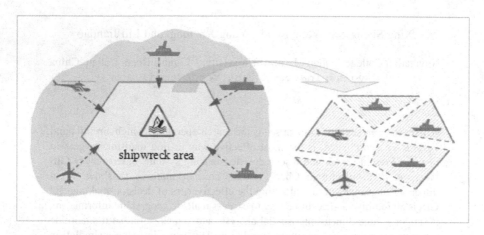

Fig. 1. Quick search coverage by joint sea-air search efforts

2   Creation of 3D Scene

A maritime search action is naturally an activity carried out in a specific geographical space, therefore there needs a 3D scene for visualization and simulation of search process. As shown in figure 2, the 3D scene can be created by overlaying six distinct types of layers, which are search effort 3D model layer, associated important buildings (harbor, airports, etc.) layer, sea area being searched feature layer, navigation aids layer, remote sensing (RS) image layer and terrain model layer. Each layer corresponding related geographic datasets as follows.

1. Raster dataset - Storing remote sensing image data, including sea area remote sensing images as well as flight base remote sensing images onshore;
2. Terrain dataset - Storing terrain data, including the TIN (Triangulated Irregular Network model) and Raster (regular grid model) data. Terrain models can be created using bathymetric data extracted from the electronic chart (e.g. ENC - Electronic Nautical Chart)[3];
3. Important buildings feature dataset - Storing important buildings' spatial data (such as airports, harbors, etc.);
4. Maritime navigation aids feature dataset - Storing navigation aids spatial data of the sea area to be searched;
5. Extent of sea area feature dataset - Storing search area and sub-area's spatial data;
6. Search efforts' initial position dataset - Storing the search efforts' initial position, i.e. the vessel's standby point and aircraft flight base location.

All layers should have the same spatial reference, in order to be overlaid correctly. The accuracy of objects positioning in 3D scene is determined by the quality of spatial data.

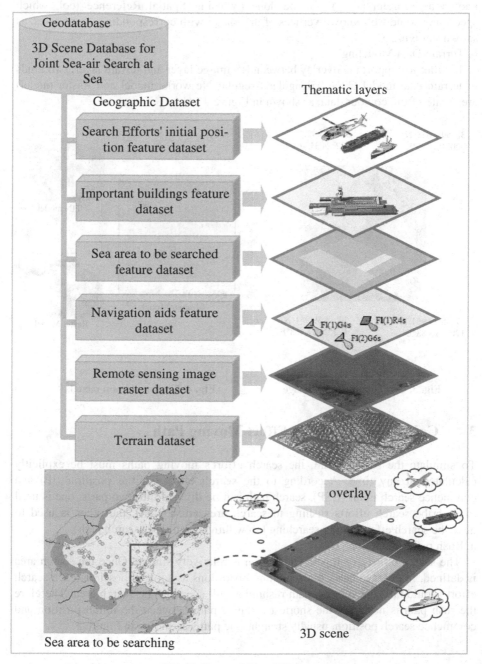

Fig. 2. Composition of 3D scene

a. Georeferencing remote sensing image

If there is no spatial reference information with RS image, it can not be overlaid directly with other layers. Specifying image's spatial reference information (also known as georeferencing), can be done by using Spatial Reference tool, which specifying some well-known vertices of the image with corresponding coordinates, as shown in Figure 3.

b. Terrain Data Modeling

In order to support the overlay between RS image layer and terrain layer, two kinds of terrain data model (TIN, Triangular Irregular Networks model and Raster model) are created from contour data, as shown in Figure 4.

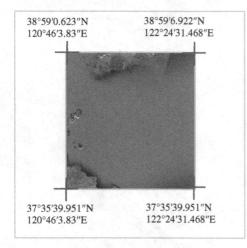

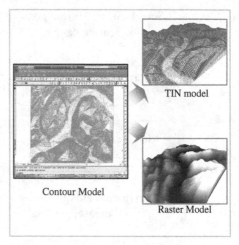

Fig. 3. Georeferencing RS image   **Fig. 4.** Creating terrain models

3   Calculation of Search Effort Moving Path

To simulate the search trend, the search effort's moving paths must be explicitly calculated at any time. According to the search effort's initial position (IP) and commence search point (CSP), search path can be divided into two parts, one is used to describe search efforts rushing to search area (rush path), the other is used to describe search efforts doing searching job within search area (search path).

a. Rush path calculation

The search effort's rush path calculation is relatively simple. Once the search area is defined, in order to carry out searching operations as soon as possible, each search effort should take the shortest path rushing at full speed to the search area. Therefore the rush path is normally the shortest distance path between the initial position and commence search position, usually straight line paths as shown in Figure 5.

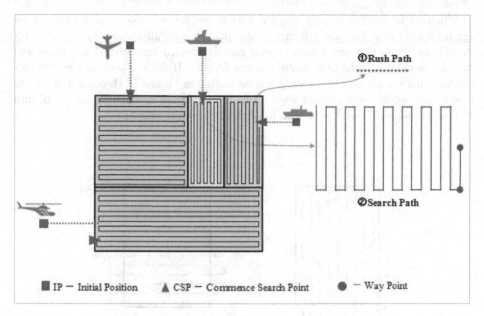

Fig. 5. Search efforts' rush paths and search paths

b. Search path calculation

Each search effort's path within search area depends on the shapes of the search sub-areas assigned. When the search area is very large and many search efforts are available, the whole area should be divided into search sub-areas, and then be assigned among available search facilities to work together in close co-ordination, so as to quickly complete the whole region coverage. Paper[4] present a polygon decomposition algorithm which can be used to divide the whole search area into search sub-areas, according to each search effort's ability of coverage as well as its CSP on the boundary of sub-areas, so as to achieve full coverage of the entire search area. As shown in Figure 6, a search area of 2000 square nautical mile was divided into four non-overlapping sub-areas of 734, 197,184 and 885 square nautical mile.

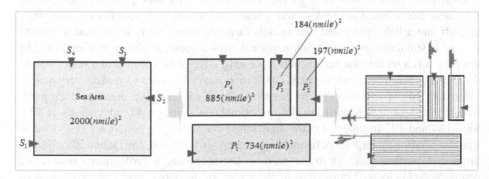

Fig. 6. Search area decomposition

When the location of distress target is very uncertain and needs a uniformly cover-age for a wide area, the most effective search pattern is parallel sweep search (PS). PS should also be used when a large search area is divided into several sub-areas and each of them is assigned to a specific search facility. If the shape of sub-area is rec-tangular, the search path is creeping line as shown in Figure 7. Through making the search line parallel to the longer edge of the rectangle can reduce the number of turn of vessel or aircraft; thereby the search efficiency is improving[5].

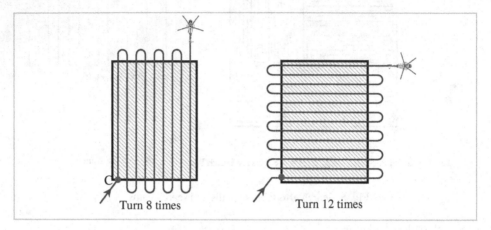

Fig. 7. Search path within rectangular area

4   Search Trend Simulation

While mastering all action paths of search efforts through the entire search process, the search operations can be simulated by demonstrating every search effort's dynam-ic in 3D environment. Paper[6] provides a means of simulating vessel's dynamic by using animation technology from ESRI ArcGIS GIS platform. The aircraft's dynamic can also be simulated by using that technology, which needs to modify the target's (aircraft) elevation parameter to its flight altitude. In this paper, the 3D scene of sea area near Bohai Strait is created, and a search plan with two aircrafts (a fixed-wing aircraft and a helicopter) and two vessels (a professional SAR vessel and a passing vessel) is simulated in the three-dimensional environment, as shown in Figure 9. The sea region is a rectangular area which has a long edge of 50 n mile and a wide edge of 40 n mile, therefore its area equals 2000 (n mile)^2. In order to make every search effort carried out search operation coordinately, this rectangular area has been parti-tioned into four search partition (i.e. partition1 to partition 4), which area is 734, 885, 184 and 197 (n mile)^2. On the start time of searching, a helicopter is located in Penglai ShaHeKou airport; A fixed-wing aircraft, is located in the Dalian ZhouShuiZi airport; A passing vessel is in the north of the scene and a professional search and rescue vessel is located in the east of the scene. In the above search efforts, the heli-copter is responsible for the task of searching partition 1, the fixed-wing aircraft is responsible for the task of searching partition 4, the passing vessel is responsible for the task of searching partition 3 and the professional search and rescue vessel is responsible for the task of searching partition 2. In order to facilitate the observation of the dynamics of the search efforts, every 3D model of search effort is enlarged appropriately.

During the entire joint sea-air search process, the search and rescue command staff must ensure that all search vessels and aircraft to keep a safe distance with each other and to strictly comply with the search pattern have been determined in advance. For aircraft, the search command staff should first consider its safety, by simulating the search efforts' dynamic in search operation before take action, can help the search command staff to judge the aircrafts' safe isolation distance when they meet at the nearest location. If the separation distance can not satisfy the safety requirement, some adjustment could be done (by adjusting the flight altitude and flight path manually) to ensure the safety, as shown in Figure 10.

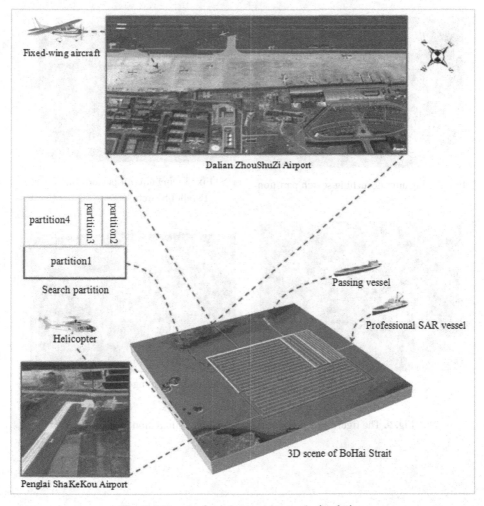

Fig. 8. 3D scene for joint sea-air search simulation

The search trend simulation results are shown in Figure 9.

Helicopter rushing search partition   Helicopter performing Parallel Search

Fixed-wing aircraft rushing search partition   Fixed-wing aircraft performing
Parallel Search

Vessel rushing search partition   Vessel performing Parallel Search

Fig. 9. The figure of search facilities' dynamics simulation in 3D scene

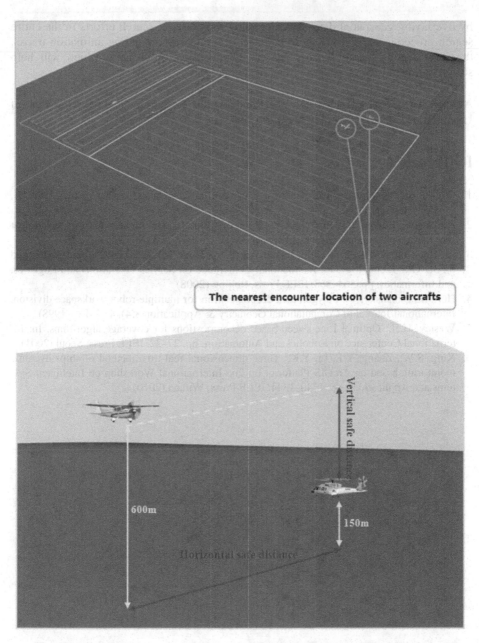

Fig. 10. Adjusting safe separations between the aircraft three-dimensional simulation

5   Conclusion

3D GIS provides an intuitive way to simulate vessel and aircraft's dynamic in joint sea-air search operations at sea. 3D scene for maritime search can be quickly created by overlaying geospatial data. By calculating the paths of search efforts in the entire search procedure, and using these paths to generate corresponding animation tracks, the joint sea-air search process can be demonstrated intuitively, which will help search commander to master the trend of search.

Acknowledgment. Supported by the Fundamental Research Funds for the Central Universities (3132014027, 3132013017).

References

1. IMO/ICAO.: International aeronautical and maritime search and rescue manual, vol. III, London/Montreal (1998)
2. Xing, S.W., Zhang, Y.J., Li, Y.K., Gao, Z.J.: An optimal model for search effort selection at sea. Journal of Dalian Maritime University 38(2), 15–18 (2008) (in Chinese)
3. Li, H., Xing, S.W., Zhang, Y.J.: Inland Waterway Three-Dimensional Visualization Based on 3D-GIS Technology. In: International Conference on Service Operations and Logistics, and Informatics, pp. 564–568. IEEE Press, Beijing (2008)
4. Hert, S., Lumelsky, V.: Polygon area decomposition for multiple-robot workspace division. International Journal of Computational Geometry & Application 8(4), 437–466 (1998)
5. Wesley, H.H.: Optimal Line-sweep-based decompostions for coverage algorithms. In: International Conference on Robotics and Automation, pp. 27–32. IEEE Press, Seoul (2001)
6. Xing, S.W., Zhang, Y.J., Li, Y.K.: Three dimensional real-time method of ships dynamic monitoring based on ArcGIS Platform. In: 2nd International Workshop on Intelligent Systems and Applications, pp. 1340–1344. IEEE Press, Wuhan (2010)

Quantitative Analysis for the Development
of Maritime Transport Efficiency

Wenbo Zhang, Zhaolin Wu, Yong Liu, and Zebing Li

Navigation College, Dalian Maritime University, Dalian 116026, China
{zhangwenbo,wuzhaolin,liuyong,lizebing}@dlmu.edu.cn

Abstract. This paper analyzes the maritime transport efficiency which include ships' quantitative analysis of four main kinds. Nearly 90 percent of the world total trade of goods measured in tons are moved by sea. And vessel's transport efficiency is higher than the other vehicles, so ship is regarded as an epitome of science and technology. The development of ships is achieved by technological innovation, the innovation is the fundament, Now using the principle of transport efficiency to analyze the historical development of transport vehicles is needed .Transport efficiency is the energy efficiency used for transport facilities, which is expressed as $\eta = \frac{1}{h_{fS_{foc}}} \cdot \frac{wv}{p} \cdot \frac{w_p}{w}$. In the historical time, ship's size, speed and engine output power have changed largely. And this paper will discuss base on the basic formulas and statistics of four kinds of ships: bulk carriers , LNG carriers ,oil tankers and container ships.

Keywords: Ship, developing tendency, quantitative analysis, transport efficiency.

1 Introduction

According to different supporting systems, the transport vehicles can be categorized as three types, namely, buoyancy support vehicle, land support vehicle and lift support vehicle. Among them, the buoyancy support vehicle, i.e., ship, has many dominated advantages to transfer large amount cargo over a long distance, because it has much larger capacity and lower transport cost. In another word, vessel's transport efficiency is higher than the other two kinds of vehicles.

With the fast development of high technology and innovation in maritime sector, shipping market is becoming more and more specialized and matured [1]. Within the past several decades, ship's size, speed and engine output power have changed largely. But considering four different types of ships, there are lots of differences of the above items among them [2]. What causes this phenomenon? In this paper, I will use the principle of transport efficiency to analyze the historical development of the four types of ships.

X.-h. Sun et al. (Eds.): ICA3PP 2014, Part II, LNCS 8631, pp. 543–552, 2014.

2   Overview of Principles

Transport efficiency is the energy efficiency used for transport facilities. If we compare two different ships and consider their work necessary for a given transport performance, for example the transportation of 1000 tons of grain from shanghai to Tokyo, this work (fuel consumption) is directly proportional to each ship's specific power output P/(WV). Normally, the higher the value of P/(MV), the lower the transport efficiency η_{TP} will be[3].

Transport efficiency can be expressed as the following formulae:

$$\text{Transport efficiency} = \frac{\text{Payload} \times \text{Distance}}{\text{Energy used for transport}} \tag{1}$$

$$= \frac{\text{Payload (W}_p\text{)} \times \text{Distance (L)}}{\text{Heat Value of Fuel (H}_F\text{)} \times \text{Fuel consumption}} \tag{2}$$

That is:

$$\eta_{TP} = \frac{W_p L}{H_f S_{foc} P(L/V)} \tag{3}$$

$$= \frac{1}{H_f S_{foc}} \cdot \frac{W_p V}{P} = \frac{1}{H_f S_{foc}} \cdot \frac{WV}{P} \cdot \frac{W_p}{W} \tag{4}$$

From formula (4), we can find the relationship between transport efficiency η_{TP} and the specific power output p/wv which is just opposite to each other. When one is high, the other must be low.

In practice, there are many factors that may influence a ship's transport efficiency, such as the ship type, ship particulars, ship engine condition and ship age, etc[4]. In the following part, the historical developing trend of the specific power output of each kind of ship will be list in a table, as well as shown in the K-G diagrams, then the reasons causing the change will be analyzed[5].

3   Instance Analysis

3.1   Bulk Carrier

Bulkers' average engine power increased greatly from 1970s to 1980s, then it dropped a little in 1990s and increased again in 2000s; the average dwt kept continually increasing during this period, and in 2000s, the number was more than 3 times as it was in 1970s, which means the ships' size increased a lot; comparing with this, the speed did not change very much, almost keep stable at around 14 knots. As showing in the right column, the average p/wv of bulk vessels decreased all through this period, especially from 1970s to 1990s, it dropped very quickly. This changing tendency of P/(WV) implies that bulkers' transport efficiency was enhanced a lot from 1970s to 2000s.

The following two charts are about the specific output. Fig.1 includes all bulkers' data, and Fig.2 only shows the average data of four decades.

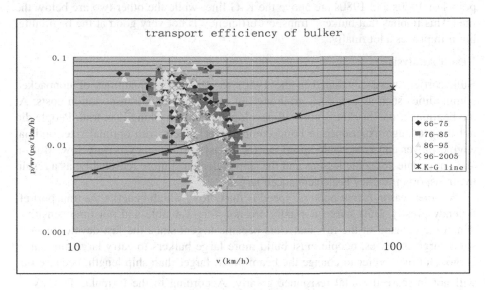

Fig. 1. Data of all bulkers

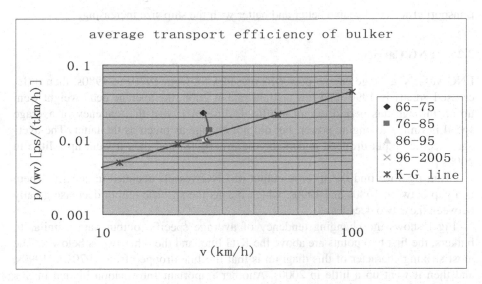

Fig. 2. The average data of four decades

Fig.1 gives us an overall idea that the specific power output became smaller and smaller from 1970s to 2000s. But since there are too many points showed in this same diagram, so the information we get is not very clear and accurate.

Fig.2 reveals the average specific output of each decade. The tendency arrow line dropped continually through this period, which means bulkers' specific power output decreased, and the transport efficiency became higher and higher. In addition, the two points of 1970s and 1980s are above the K-G line, while the other two are below the line. This implies that bulkers' transport efficiency is not very good at the beginning, but it improves a lot finally.

Result Analysis

Bulk carriers were developed in the 1950s to carry large quantities of nonpacked commodities such as ore, coal, grain etc., in order to reduce transportation costs. At the beginning, this market is not well developed, and everything is in trial. People did not have enough experience to build competitive bulkers with optimal size, optimal engine power and reasonable speed, so the transport efficiency is very low. But on and on, people got some lessons and the ship is designed more reasonably, as a result, the transport efficiency is also enhanced largely.

Another reason is that bulkers' speed is fairly low, which benefits the transport efficiency greatly. Bulk cargo normally are not very valuable and not time sensitive. When the demand of the raw materials became urgent since the fast development of some large countries, people must build more large bulkers to carry large amount of cargo. But they prefer to change the beam much larger than ship length, because this will not increase the total resistance greatly. According to the formulae $R = C_1 V^2$ and $P = RV = C_1 V^3$ [6], the engine power will also not change much. So the bulkers' transport efficiency became better and better with the ship size increasing.

3.2   LNG Carrier

LNG vessels' average engine power increased a lot from 1970s to 1980s, then it decreased greatly in 1990s and saw a slight rise in 2000; the average dead weight went up all through this period except a little decline in 1990s; the tendency of average speed is similar to engine power, but did not change as much as the latter. The average specific output dropped remarkably before 1990s, and then it went up a little in 2000s [2].

From fig.3 we find the specific output of LNG vessels declined in general. There is a gap between 1980s and 1990s, which means the specific output decrease greatly between these two decades.

Fig.4 shows the changing tendency of average specific output data. Similar to bulkers, the first two points are above the K-G line, and the other two is below it. The most striking character of this diagram is that the line dropped from 1970s to 1990s, and then it went up a little in 2000s. Another important Information hidden in this diagram is that from 1980s to 1990s [7], the line dropped deeply, which implies there must be some new technology or innovation applied on LNG vessels.

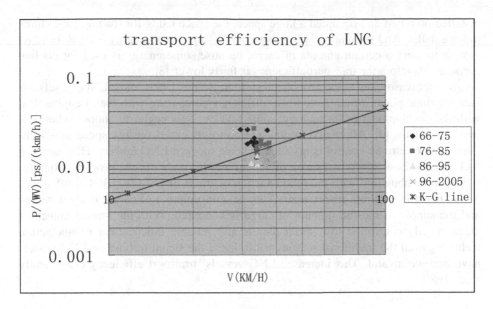

Fig. 3. Data of LNG

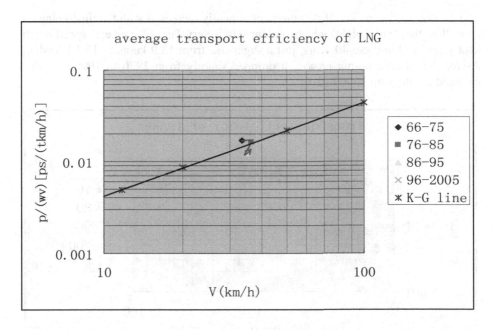

Fig. 4. The average data of LNG

Result Analysis

We all know that LNG vessel is designed to carry liquefied natural gas which is liquid cooled and condensed by natural gas. Due to the large refrigeration system which is installed on board and occupied a large space, the space using for loading cargo turns much smaller. And comparing with other kind of ships, more energy is used for LNG vessels to carry a certain amount of cargo, because some energy is used for cooling purpose. Therefore the transport efficiency is fairly lower [8].

Another reason lies in the propulsion system. Before 1980s, most LNG vessels use steam turbine plants which have lower efficiency comparing with diesel engine. But with the development of technology, some LNG vessels began to choose other propulsion systems [9]. Alternative propulsion concepts based on low speed diesel engines with electronic control is installed in some modern LNG tankers. HFO burning fuel efficient Low Speed two stroke diesel engines in single or twin propeller configuration, in combination with the reliquefaction of the Boil Off Gas (BOG), offer economic benefits for those trades where loss, i.e. consumption of cargo, is not accepted and the supply of the full amount of cargo is honoured. With the market launch of electronically controlled low speed diesels and reliable independent reliquefaction technology, all the traditional reasons not to leave the steam turbine on LNG vessels have become invalid. This increased LNG vessels' transport efficiency dramatically since 1980s.

3.3   Tanker

The average engine power of oil tankers continually increased with the time going on, as well as the dead weight, which also increased very fast; oil tankers' speed nearly kept stable within these 40 years, just a slight rise from 13.9 knots to 15.1 knots[10]. As for the specific output p/(wv), it dropped sharply from 1970 to 1990, and then changed a little from 1990 to 2000.

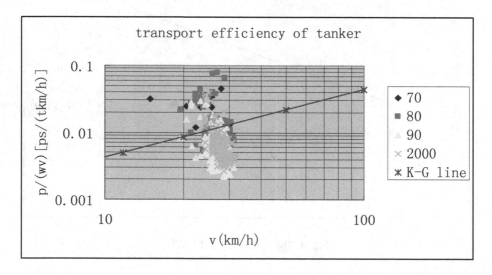

Fig. 5. Data of all tankers

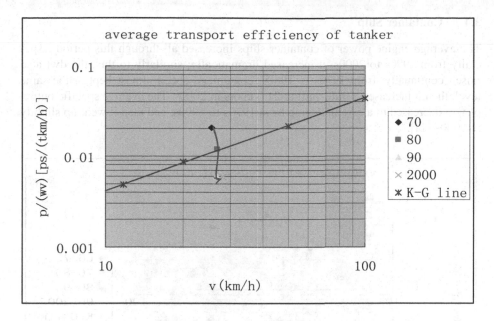

Fig. 6. The average data of tankers

The information we can get from Fig.5 is that the specific power output decreased to a certain degree during this period.

From Fig.6, we can find that the specific output declined quickly from 1970 to 1990, and then it almost kept stable until 2000. The point of 1970 is above the K-G line, in 1980 it is nearly on this line, and the other two is far below the line.

These two figures indicates that tankers transport efficiency became higher and higher.

Result Analysis

The first reason is the large demand of oil production. The tanker market is an increasingly important and attractive transport segment, which, due to the ever increasing global market economy, could be expected to become of even greater importance in the future. Fluctuations in oil production within the OPEC countries and in the world market economy might, of course, in the short term, influence the demand for tanker deadweight tonnage and also the type of tankers being ordered. Because this high demands, oil tanker became larger and larger, especially from 1970 to 1990. This dramatically change in size while speed almost keeping stable result in the steep increase of transport efficiency, just as the bulkers.

Another reason is the development of tanker market. In 1970, large oil tanker is still in trial stage, and people did not know how to build a tanker with optimal size, speed and engine power. But after they got the experience, the transport efficiency became better.

Some other factors, such as double-hull, oil crisis may also affect the specific output to a certain degree.

3.4   Container Ship

The average engine power of container ships increased all through this period, especially from 1990s to 2000s, it increased dramatically; similarly to this, the dwt also raised continually; from 1970s to 1980s, containers' speed almost kept at the same level, then it increased a little until to 21.0 knots in 2000s. The average specific output p/(wv) decreased to a certain degree from 1970s to 1990s, and then it went up slightly in 2000s [11].

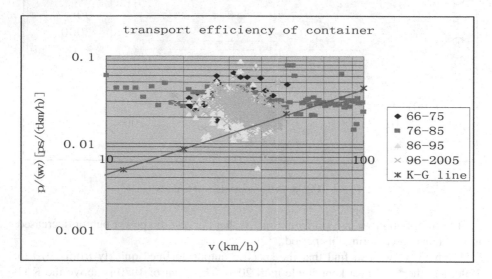

Fig. 7. Data of all containers

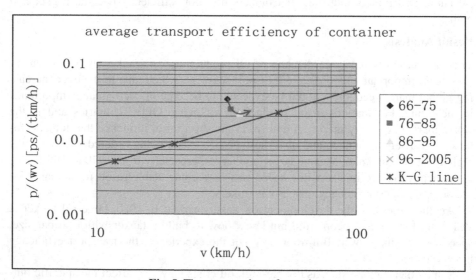

Fig. 8. The average data of containers

From fig.7, we find that most of points are above the K-G line; this implies that container ships' transport efficiency is higher than other kinds of vessel.

Fig.8 also reveals the above information and all the four points are far away from the K-G line. From 1970s to 1990s, the line continually decreased, while it saw a slight rise in 2000s.

Result Analysis

Firstly, the cargo that container vessels carried is more valuable than other cargos like bulk cargo or crude oil, so container ships would like to sail at a high speed. According to the formulae $R=C_1V^2$ and $P=RV=C_1V^3$, we can find that the high speed of container ships will results in a large increase of the ship's engine power, therefore the transport efficiency become lower than other kinds of ships.

Secondly, since container vessels went into the market from 1960s, which is much later than bulkers and tankers. In 1970s this market was still in trial and shaping stage, and this kind of ships did not find the optimal size, speed, power etc, so the transport efficiency starts from a high position. After several years, the ship owners have accumulated some experience and they begin to build some more utilized vessels, so the transport efficiency dropped until to 1990s. In 2000s, the shipping market became prosperous, since large trade business between the east and west, the south and north. To carry more cargo and earn more money, ship owners prefer to increase their container vessels' power and speed exceeding the reasonable level, and definitely, the transport efficiency decreased a little.

4   Conclusion

In a word, transport efficiency is always a very important issue for shipping industry to take into considerations. The General tendency of the transport efficiency in the past decades is improved but not in same level for different types of ship. The transport efficiency of bulk carriers and oil tankers is better than that of container ships and LNG vessels owing to the characteristics of the cargo. Anyway, the improvement of transport efficiency has close relationship with economical issues and technical innovations. Although the transport efficiency is an important issue, the market (or the law of supply and demand) is the decisive factor for marine transport. Economical, political and environmental issues must be considered simultaneously in shipping industry.

Acknowledgements. This paper is supported by "the Fundamental Research Funds for the Central Universities "(3132014032)&(017072) for Ph.D.

References

1. Curt, http://www.intertanko.com/pubupload/curt.pdf
2. Bob, C.: Marine Transportation of LNG (March 29, 2004) (retrieved August)

3. Nakazawa, T.: Impact of maritime Innovation and Technology. Unpublished lecture handout. Dalian Maritime University, Dalian (2005)
4. Wu, Y.: The forever Enchantment of Mechanics and Contribution. Advances in Mechanics 33(1), 41–55 (2003)
5. Ma, S.: Maritime Economics. Unpublished lecture handout. Dalian Maritime University, Dalian (2005)
6. Zhu, R.: Ship-an Epitome of Science and Technology (2005), http://www.tongji.edu.cn/~yangdy/ship/paper9.htm (retrieved August 14, 2005)
7. Liu, H.: Industry Technological and Economical Information of Ships. Development of World LNG Carriers 5, 6 (2000)
8. Morita, K.: Study of Changes in Patterns of LNG Tanker Operation (2003), the World Wide Web: tenth I, http://eneken.ieej.or.jp/en/data/pdf/225.pdf (retrieved August 13, 2005)
9. Lloyd's Register.: The tenth Issue of Lloyd's Register's Marine-focused Technical Publication, Horizons (December 2004), the World Wide Web, http://www.lr.org/image_library/Downloads/Marine/horizons_04dec.pdf (retrieved August 12, 2005)
10. Pan, H.T., Fu, R.H.: Development of world large tankers and scale of China crude oil terminals. Port & Waterway Engineering 375(4), 42–47 (2005), http://www.sspa.se/shipdesign/lng.html
11. Liu, Y.: The Designing Parameter of large Container Ship. The Technology of Port Engineering 1995(2), 42 (1995)

Image Compression Based on Time-Domain Lapped Transform and Quadtree Partition

Xiuhua Ma, Jiwen Dong[*], and Lei Wang

School of Information Science and Engineering, Shandong Provincial Key Laboratory of Network based Intelligent Computing, University of Jinan, Jinan, 250022, China
maxiuhua.qd@163.com

Abstract. We proposed a new image compression system based on quadtree partition and time-domain lapped transform (TDLT) as core transform technology. The system obtained transformation region of different sizes through quadtree partition. And it removed the correlation by utilizing pixel similarity in image regions. The performance of discrete cosine transform (DCT) was improved with the method of pre-filter and post-filter. Superior performance can be achieved in most cases than the fixed block TDLT and DWT about the rate-distortion and subjective visual quality.

Keywords: quadtree partition, DCT, time-domain lapped transform, image compression.

1 Introduction

In two-dimensional image compression, image compression standard JPEG based on DCT is used widely owing to its excellent properties. In order to eliminate the blocking artifacts of compression algorithm based on DCT in the case of low bit rate, researchers designed a variety of filters. Among them, the lapped transform can achieve good result. Usually, in image coding algorithm based on DCT [1], a complete image is first divided into 8x8 pieces, then, DCT transform coefficients are obtained and we achieve the ultimate purpose by quantizing DCT coefficients combined with other related image compression technology. The common feature of such algorithm is that, regardless of the specific content of the image, block size is fixed. Indeed, the main purpose of DCT transform is to remove the correlation between pixels in the image block, which depends on image regional feature and pixel distance. If the image content in a certain region is very similar, the pixels in this region will have strong correlation; on the contrary, if the content of an image area is complicated, the correlation between pixels is relatively weak. Meanwhile, the distance of the pixel will affect the correlation. Typically, the strongest correlation appears around adjacent pixels. As the distance increases, the similarity will be reduced main depending on the extent of the characteristics of the area.

---

[*] Corresponding author.

X.-h. Sun et al. (Eds.): ICA3PP 2014, Part II, LNCS 8631, pp. 553–559, 2014.

Thus it can be seen, the use of a fixed block size coding algorithm mainly considers the influence of the pixel distance. If the texture of the region is not complicated, the DCT coefficients can be still more concentrated, even if the block size is 16x16 or larger.

To improve the algorithm with fixed image block, we proposed quadtree partition transform by taking the characteristics of the image area into consideration to remove the inter-pixel correlation. The basic idea of the algorithm is a kind of top-down recursive quadtree partition segmentation according to the correlation of the original image adjacent pixels, until the consistency of each region to meet the criteria. Each region conducts time-domain lapped transform, then, the coefficients obtained by TDLT are reconstructed in accordance with sub band structure like wavelet. Lastly, it adopts embed bit-plane encoding method for encoding. Experimental results demonstrate the effectiveness of the proposed algorithm.

2   Quadtree Partition

From the view of image features, there are some regions in the image where pixel value is same or similar, which may lead to a lot of spatial redundancy exists. Therefore, the use of block processing of the image is able to make pixel values meet certain conditions and the adjacent pixels appear in the same sub-image block, so that the image block may be handled as a whole.

Quadtree decomposition is an image segmentation method based on the uniformity of detection [2], [3] and [4], and the image size is generally required to be $N = 2n$.

Quadtree decomposition is to meet the compatibility criterion of the image pixel values for sub-block image. The basic process of image quadtree decomposition is as follows. Firstly, the original image is divided into four regions of equal size, then each region is judged whether it satisfy the compatibility criterion. If every region could meet the criteria, image dividing will be end, otherwise, image segment will continue. And each of the divided regions will be judged again until all of the divided regions are met compatibility criterion. The result may contain blocks of different sizes.

Fig. 1(b) shows the processed result of image lena in accordance with the quad-tree decomposition of a certain threshold.

 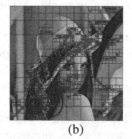

(a)   (b)

Fig. 1. (a) Original image (b) Result of quadtree decomposition

3   Compatibility Criterion

Compatibility criterion is pixel classification standard, and different standards lead to different quadtree segmentations and the compression performance. Through experiments, the paper selected Roberts edge detection method as a criterion [5].

Roberts edge detection operator is the classic image edge detection and image segmentation algorithm. Differential operators for image edge detection can be used as the criteria of quadtree segmentation which can take full advantage of the pixel similarities to achieve better segmentation aim.

For digital images, the first order difference of image is a kind of alternative replaceable means of partial derivatives. Roberts edge detection operator calculate the approximate partial derivatives of image functions f (x, y) for x and y, as shown in (1) and Table 1.

$$g(x,y) \approx \sqrt{[f(x,y)-f(x+1,y+1)]^2 + [f(x,y+1)-f(x+1,y)]^2}$$ (1)

Table 1. 3x3 Templet

$f(x-1,y-1)$	$f(x,y-1)$	$f(x+1,y-1)$
$f(x-1,y)$	$f(x,y)$	$f(x+1,y)$
$f(x-1,y+1)$	$f(x,y+1)$	$f(x+1,y+1)$

In practice, we calculate the image function $f(x,y)$ by equation as shown in (2).

$$g(x,y) \approx R(x,y) = |f(x,y)-f(x+1,y+1)| + |f(x,y+1)-f(x+1,y)|$$ (2)

The quadtree decomposition result will vary from the segmentation threshold. Fig. 3 shows that when the segmentation threshold Q = 7, blocks of the decomposed significantly are more than Q = 10. However, there still exists several blocks, which ensures partial redundancy may be eliminated.

 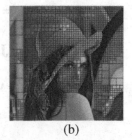

(a)   (b)

Fig. 2. (a) Quadtree decomposition   (Q = 10) (b) Quadtree decomposition   (Q = 7)

4   Time Domain Overlap Transformation Based on Quadtree Partition

Recalling domestic image compression method, transform coding technique is currently the most widely used image compression methods on account of its high compression ratio and easily implementation.

Due to its favorable decorrelation and energy concentration, Discrete Cosine Transform (DCT) has a good application value in image compression. While the two-dimensional image just get locally stationary rather than global stationary, so the DCT is adapted to blocked images. What's more, owing to block transform coding, the blocking artifact often occurs at low bit rates. A variety of filters are designed to remove the block effect based on DCT. The scheme with better performance is proposed by Tran et al [6]. Their time-domain lapped transform algorithm, can effectively eliminate the blocking effect, and can achieve the equivalent performance of JPEG2000 lossy compression.

Overlapped transform can decrease the blocking effect by using overlapping filter in the process of decomposition and reconstruction. Meanwhile, its low complexity compared with the wavelet transform is one of the merits. This paper puts forward the TDLT adapting to quadtree partition.

In short, TDLT consisting of pre-filter and post-filter act before and after the DCT transform [7]. The role of the pre-filter is reduced the correlation between the adjacent blocks to improve the correlation between pixels within the block. Post-filter is a completely inverse transform of pre-filter. Its role is to improve the correlation between the adjacent blocks, thereby eliminating blocking effect between adjacent blocks.

Pre-filter is equivalent to a smoothing unit, which is defined as the formula (3):

$$F = \frac{1}{2}\begin{bmatrix} I & J \\ J & -I \end{bmatrix}\begin{bmatrix} I & 0 \\ 0 & V \end{bmatrix}\begin{bmatrix} I & J \\ J & -I \end{bmatrix} \qquad (3)$$

where I and J are identity matrix and reversal identity matrix, respectively. V is the free control matrix. There are two types of V:

$$V_{LOT} = J(C_{M/2}^{II})^T C_{M/2}^{IV} J \qquad (4)$$

$$V_{LBT} = J(C_{M/2}^{II})^T D_S C_{M/2}^{IV} J \qquad (5)$$

where $C_{M/2}^{IV}$ and $C_{M/2}^{II}$ stand for $M/2$ point type-II and type-IV DCT matrix, respectively; $DS = diag\{s,1,...,1\}$ is a diagonal matrix where $s = \sqrt{2}$ is a scaling factor.

Compression algorithm steps:

1) The input image is divided into blocks according to the appropriate gradient detection threshold, to get the block image smoothing after filter.

2) We conduct DCT transform of different points for the smoothing block image to obtain the transform coefficients, direct current (DC) coefficient and AC (AC) coefficients;

3) Massive distributional transform coefficients are reorganized as wavelet sub-band structure, where DC coefficient interwoven in the low-frequency sub-band and AC coefficients in the high-frequency ones;

4) SPECK coding [8];

5) The output of bit stream file.

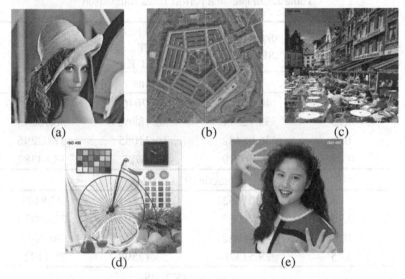

(a)   (b)   (c)

(d)   (e)

Fig. 3. Test images. (a) pentagon1024x1024. (b) lena512x512. (c) cafe2048x2048.   (d) bike2048x2048. (e) woman2048x2048.

5   Results and Analysis

To verify the performance of the algorithm, we tested the images shown in Fig.4 compared with fixed block DCT and DWT. JPEG2000 standard is conducted on Kakadu V6.0 with 9/7FDWT. Experimental images include multiple target characters, scenes, still life, etc. [9]. There are both image with complex texture and single character image. Image size cover three different sizes 512x512, 1024x1024, 2048x2048. Bit per Pixel (BPP) and Peak Signal to Noise Ratio (PSNR) are selected as measure of compression performance.

The compression properties of proposed algorithm are contrasted with the results of fixed block DCT and DWT, and the outcome is shown in Table2:

9/7FDWT adopted by JPEG2000 and algorithm used fixed block DCT belong to floating point type transformation. However, different point affects DCT algorithm's performance in ours algorithm. Experimental data show that in most cases the proposed algorithm outperforms fixed block DCT and DWT performance and fairly, at low bit rates, even better than DWT. In particular, advantages is obvious when comes to the image woman_2048X2048 with single target. Of course, 9/7 FDWT is superior than proposed algorithm in individual cases. However, because the performance of algorithm used quadtree segmentation algorithm is related to the taken threshold which is difficult to determine, the proposed algorithm will be better than 9/7 FDWT once the optimal threshold is fond. There is every reason to believe the optimal performance of the algorithm will be better than the test measured.

Table 2. Compression performance comparison

bpp	9/7FDWT+ SPECK	Fixed block DCT +SPECK	Ours
		lena	
1	40.18385	39.7646	40.13016
0.75	38.72594	38.18862	38.75845
0.5	36.88482	36.21085	37.02296
0.25	33.50219	32.6725	33.84382
		pentagon1024x1024	
1	34.01062	33.61861	33.8103
0.75	32.76068	32.18192	32.49976
0.5	30.98082	30.52891	30.9243
0.25	28.51326	28.17598	28.71929
		cafe_2048X2048	
1	30.38291	29.89533	30.20505
0.75	28.08072	27.52518	28.03781
0.5	25.31767	24.96934	25.42456
0.25	21.91303	21.66586	22.16425
		woman_2048X2048	
1	37.90846	37.90242	38.30017
0.75	35.72063	35.76577	36.15495
0.5	32.95311	32.98756	33.47795
0.25	29.14338	29.37586	29.7957
		bike_2048x2048	
1	38.11787	38.05349	38.2547
0.75	36.08386	36.01494	36.21811
0.5	33.09741	33.13494	33.5181
0.25	28.3971	28.70597	29.22445

6   Conclusion

We designed a new image compression system at the core of TDLT techniques based on quadtree partition. The results suggest that our system's compression performance is equal to or even better than fixed block DCT and DWT. In addition, the proposed algorithm has less memory requirements and lower complexity of hardware implementation compared with DWT [10].

On the downside, tests are only carried out on the image that its size is N = 2n at the present stage [11]. In the meanwhile, there will be more practical significance about experiment and research on the image of any size and superior partition standard.

References

1. Ahmed, N., Natarajan, T., Rao, K.R.: Discrete cosine transform. IEEE Trans. on Computers 23, 90 (1974)
2. Ghadah, A.K.: Image Compression based on Quadtree and Polynomial. International Journal of Computer Applications 76(3), 31–37 (2013)
3. Chung, K.L., Huang, H.L., Lu, H.I.: Efficient region segmentation on compression gray images using quadtree and shading representation. Pattern Recongnition 37, 1591–1605 (2004)
4. Neve, W.D., Deursen, D.V., Lancker, W.V., Ro, Y.M., Walle, R.V.: Improved BSDL-based content adaptation for JPEG2000 and HD Photo (JPEG XR). Signal Processing: Image Communication 24, 452–467 (2009)
5. Pennebaker, W.B., Mitcell, J.L.: JPEG: Still Standard. Van Nostrand Reinhold, New York (1993)
6. Tran, T.D., Liang, J., Tu, C.: Lapped transform via time-domain pre-andpost-processing. IEEE Trans. Signal Process 51(6), 1557–1571 (2003)
7. Wang, L., Wu, J.J., Jiao, L.C., Shi, G.M.: Lossy-to-Lossless Hyperspectral Image Compression Based on Multiplierless Reversible Integer TDLT/KLT. IEEE Geoscience and Remote Sensing Letters 6(3) (2009)
8. Pearlman, W.A., Islam, A., Nagaraj, N., Said, A.: Efficient, Low-ComplexiImage Coding with a Set-Partitioning Embedded Block Coder. IEEE Tran. Circuits and Systems for Video Technology 14, 1219–1235 (2004)
9. http://www.kakadusoftware.com/
10. Antonini, M., Barlaud, M., Mathieu, P., Daubechies, I.: Image coding using wavelet transform. IEEE Transactions on Image Processing 1(2), 205–220 (1992)
11. Sullivan, G.J., Ohm, J.R., Han, W.J., Wiegand, T.: Overview of the High Efficiency Video Coding (HEVC) Standard. IEEE Trans. on Circuits and System for Video Technology (2012)

The Applicability and Security Analysis of IPv6 Tunnel Transition Mechanisms

Wei Mi*

Computer Network Information Center, Chinese Academy of Sciences,
Beijing, China
miwei@cstnet.cn

Abstract. Due to the exhaustion of IPv4 address resources, the transition from IPv4 to IPv6 is inevitable and fairly urgent. Numerous transition mechanisms have been proposed, especially the tunnel scheme which is the focus of research efforts in IETF and academia recently. However, because of the diverse characteristics and transition requirements of practical networks and the lack of applicability analysis, the selection and deployment of transition mechanisms are facing with grand challenges. Targeting at those challenges, this paper investigates the basic issues and key elements of IPv6 tunnel transition mechanisms, and presents its first applicability index system. In particular, we analyze the applicability of existing proposed tunnel techniques based on the presented index system, which has significant guidance in the practical deployment of IPv6 transition. Moreover, as the key factors in realistic working environment, the analysis for the security issues of tunnel transition scheme, which was seldom taken into account before, is provided in this study.

Keywords: IPv6 transition, tunnel mechanisms, applicability, index system, security.

1 Introduction

With the rapid growth of Internet scale, the exhaustion of IPv4 addresses is a significant problem. IPv6 was designed to be an evolutionary step from IPv4, overcoming the problems of IPv4 and promoting the development of Next Generation Internet. Due to the incompatibility in nature, IPv6 transition will face many technical challenges, such as heterogeneous addressing, different semantic, routing isolation, huge size and the transparent to users and to applications. IPv6 transition is a world recognized significant technology problem in the development of Next Generation Internet.

* Supported by the National Key Technology Research and Development Program of the Ministry of Science and Technology of China under Grant No.2012BAH01B00; the National Program on Key Basic Research Project of China (973 Program) under Grant No. 2012CB315800; the Strategic Priority Research Program of the Chinese Academy of Sciences under grant No. XDA06010306.

X.-h. Sun et al. (Eds.): ICA3PP 2014, Part II, LNCS 8631, pp. 560–570, 2014.

Numerous transition mechanisms have been proposed to solve challenging issues of IPv6 transition, which can be divided into dual-stack, translation, and tunnel mechanisms. During the process of IPv6 transition, no matter which network protocol is used, it must support both IPv4 services and IPv6 services, and ensure the transparence to the upper layer applications. Dual-stack mechanisms can support both IPv4 and IPv6, but they bring the high cost on both the hardware upgrading and network operation/management. Translation can be used to achieve direct communication between IPv4 and IPv6, but their algorithms are complicated and destroy the end-to-end features. The Behave Working Group of IETF was focusing on developing and standardizing the translation mechanisms, and ended in October 2013. Compared with dual-stack and translation, tunnel mechanisms possess the merits of expansibility, flexibility and simplified achievement. With the scenarios and requirement of IPv6 transition becoming clearer gradually, the transition technologies are focusing on the tunneling technologies, the IPv6 transition mechanisms research of IETF is focusing on developing and standardizing the tunnel mechanisms in the Softwire Working Group, which has received extensive support from many network operators and equipment markers.

In practical deployment, it is important to find feasible transition mechanisms and make appropriate plan to cover all potential communication scenarios. However, it brings great challenges to the research community of IPv6 transitions. With the diverse characteristics and transition requirements of practical networks and the lack of overall transition architecture, the selection and deployment of IPv6 transition mechanisms are very difficult. Thus, there is a strong need to take the research on the applicability of transition mechanisms. However, the applicability criterion and applicability analysis are lack in the current literature review.

In an effort to push forward the IPv6 transition process, this paper deeply analyzes the basic issues and key elements of IPv6 tunnel transition mechanisms, and presents the first applicability index system and analyze the applicability of existing tunneling techniques. In addition, the security has long been thought to be a key factor impacting the practical deployment, but it was seldom taken into account during the IPv6 translation. Thus, in this paper, the security analysis of tunnel mechanisms is emphatically provided. All of these have guiding significantly in the IPv6 transition process.

The rest of this paper is organized as follows. Section 2 presents the related work. The applicability index system and the applicability analysis of mainstream IPv6 tunnel mechanisms are shown in Section 3 and 4. Section 5 gives the Security analysis of tunnel mechanisms. Finally, Section 6 concludes this study.

2   Related Work

Numerous studies on the evaluation of IPv6 transition mechanisms have been reported in the current literature. Shin et al.[1] showed the impact of IPv6 transition mechanisms on user applications. Law et al. in[2] focused on the performance of dual-stack technologies in terms of various network metrics including network connectivity, hop-count, RTT, throughput, operating systems dependencies and the address configuration latency. The authors in[3, 4] provided the evaluation of tunnel mechanisms with the key performance-related metrics including throughput, delay, jitter, and the CPU usage of transition nodes. AlJa'afreh, Mellor, Awan[5] gave the comparison between the tunneling process and mapping schemes for IPv4/IPv6 transition using end-to-end delay and throughput as the key performance metrics. Guerin and Hosanagar[6] adopted a simple model to illustrate how the connectivity quality affects both IPv6 adoption and the volume of translation traffic, and summarize their implications for IPv6 adoption. The authors in[7] evaluated the dual-stack protocol and tunneling transition based on the metrics of throughput and round-trip delay. Several studies[8–11] presented the comparisons of translation mechanisms with the aspects of operation complexity and scalability, real-time communications, field device, multicast address, and application-layer protocol. The authors in[8] proposed the evaluation of the transition mechanisms including the estimation on the scalability, heterogeneous addressing and application-layer translation, hardware cost, performance and capacity of the equipment, security, end-to-end property, and the influence for developing applications.

Compared with existing studies, in[12], we also provided unified assessment criterion in terms of functionality, applications, performance, development and security to evaluate the mainstream transition mechanisms. The unified evaluation criterion is shown in table 1.

Table 1. The evaluation criterion of IPv6 transition mechanisms

Evaluation criterion	Description
Functionality	Including the transition scenario, transition function, equipment requirements, and IPv4 and IPv6 address requirements .
Applications	The impact on IPv4 or IPv6 application.
Performance	The performance evaluation is mainly for the equipments, such as forwarding performance, and the searching, storage, and computational overhead.
Deployment	Including the implementation cost, and the ease of management and usage.
Security	Including the security issues and concerns.

3   The Applicability Index System

3.1   Basic Problems

Using encapsulation mechanism, tunneling is actually a generic technology. IPv6 tunnel transition mechanisms can achieve communications between IPv6 networks/hosts across an IPv4 network (IPv6-over-IPv4), and communications between IPv4 networks/hosts across an IPv6 network (IPv4-over-IPv6). Its basic operations include encapsulation/de-encapsulation and route discovery between tunnel endpoints. Tunneling operation only affect the network layer.

(1) The basic data operation

Encapsulation/de-encapsulation is the basic data plane operation. For IPv6 transition usage, the encapsulation manners such as IP-IP, GRE (Generic Routing Encapsulation) L2TP (Layer Two Tunneling Protocol), MPLS (Multiple protocol Label Switching), IPsec (Internet Protocol Security) can all be adopted. For a wide selection, network operator can make the decision to select suitable transition mechanism.

(2) The basic control operation

The basic control plane operations include the routing interaction across heterogeneous network, the route discovery between tunnel endpoints, and the encapsulation address mapping by a particular address scheme or address/prefix binding.

(3) The tunnel model

According to the structure of network, the models of IPv6 tunnel transition mechanisms are divided into Hub and Spokes and Mesh[13]. The primary difference between them lies in the number of connections and associated routing between the tunnel ingress endpoint and egress endpoint. Hub and Spokes is composed mainly of multiple tunnel ingress endpoints and a single tunnel egress point. And in Mesh model, there are multiple tunnel endpoints.

3.2   Key Elements

(1) Transition equipment

In tunneling technologies, the tunnel endpoints are the transition equipments. They need to support dual-stack which can be an AFBR (Address Family Border Router) or host equipments. They should support encapsulation/de-encapsulation and routing forward across heterogeneous network and the route discovery between tunnel endpoints. They also maintain the encapsulation address mapping by a particular address scheme or address/prefix binding. Thus, the tunnel transition equipment has requirements in the use of bandwidth, computing and finding, storage.

(2) Encapsulation/de-encapsulation

Encapsulation makes the IPv4/IPv6 packet as a payload of the other IP protocol. It retains the integrity of IP packet information. But it adds the size of packet and may create the fragment reassembly problem.

(3) The routing across heterogeneous networks

Tunnel mechanisms need to support the routing forward across heterogeneous networks. And the border routers should maintain the binding and realizes the transparent data transmission. Thus, tunneling is stateless and lightweight.

(4) The routing discovery between tunnel endpoints

In tunnel mechanisms, the tunnel endpoints need to discover each other. And it involves some problems, such as the selection and dynamic or static configuration of tunnel endpoint, state maintenance.

3.3 Applicability Index System

Based on the analysis of basic problems and key elements, we built the first applicability index system in terms of sustainable, applications, performance and development to evaluate the mainstream tunnel transition mechanisms. The applicability index system is shown in table 2.

Table 2. The applicability index system of IPv6 tunnel transition mechanisms

Applicability criterion			Description
Sustainable	Scenarios and function of transition		Whether meet the needs of transitional scenario.
	The coupling degree between IPv4 address and IPv6 address. The reuse rate of IPv4 addresses resource.		Whether promote the IPv6 deployment and usage.
The support degree of business application.	The support degree of IPv4 application.		Impact on the IPv4 business application.
	The support degree of IPv6 application.		Impact on the IPv6 business application.
Performance	The performance requirements of tunnel endpoint	Maintenance or finding of state table	The capacity of bandwidth, computing and finding, storage.
		Routing discovery	
	Routing scalability	The independence between IPv4 and IPv6 routing	Impact on the scope of deployment.
		The aggregation of IPv6 addresses	
	Robustness		The capacity of redundancy backup.
The cost of development	Technological and industry maturity	The support degree of IETF	The support degree of standard
	Update cost	Impact on application layer.	The impact on the present network.
		Impact on network layer.	
		Impact on end users layer.	
	The cost of operation, management and maintenance	Configuration	The impact on the operator.
		Maintenance	
		Troubleshooting	
Others	Fragmentation and restructuring		The problem of fragmentation and restructuring.

4 The Applicability Analysis

In the early stages of transition from IPv4 to IPv6, IPv4 network has been in the overwhelming dominance. For the operators, supporting IPv6 in the present IPv4 network infrastructure is more attractive than building the IPv6 infrastructure directly. IPv6-over-IPv4 tunnel mechanisms emerged as required.

With the IPv6 development, IPv4 Internet has been gradually replaced. For the low cost, network operators tend to build IPv6 network rather than dual-stack network. In order to ensure the compatibility of legacy IPv4 application, IPv4-over-IPv6 tunnel scheme is provided.

According to the different transition stages, this paper will analyze the applicability of IPv6-over-IPv4 tunnel mechanisms in the early stage and IPv4-over-IPv6 tunnel mechanisms in the middle- to-late-stage.

4.1   The Applicability Analysis of IPv6-over-IPv4 Tunnel Mechanisms

IETF has developed and standardized many IPv4-over-IPv6 tunnel transition mechanisms, such as 6to4[14], 6rd[15], 6over4[16], ISATAP[17], Teredo[18] and 6PE[19]. In this section, we will analyze the applicability of these mechanisms, which is summarized in table 3.

Table 3. The applicability analysis of IPv4-over-IPv6 tunnel mechanisms

	Applicability		6to4	6rd	6over4	ISATAP	Teredo	6PE
Sustainable	Scenarios and function of transition		Connection of IPv6 Domains via IPv4 Clouds	IPv4-only access network provides IPv6 access	Provide the IPv6 access service for dual-stack host who only with IPv4 access		Provide the IPv6 access service for users who behind NAT	Connection of IPv6 host or Domains via IPv4 MPLS
	Coupling degree between IPv4 address and IPv6 address.		1		0 in stateful or 1 in stateless	1		
	Reuse rate of IPv4 addresses		Low		High			Low
The support degree of business application.	Support degree of IPv4 application.		High		Low			High
	Support degree of IPv6 application		High					
Performance	Performance requirement of tunnel endpoints	Maintenance and finding	No need to maintain in stateless encapsulated				The maintenance of NAT state	No need
		Routing discovery	Broadcast the /16 prefix	Using DHCPv6 protocol	Using IPv4 multicast protocol	Using DNS or DHCPv4 protocol	Automatically but need the detection of NAT type	Using MP-BGP protocol
	Routing scalability	Independence between IPv4 and IPv6 routing	Independence by using IPv6-in-IPv4 encapsulation.				Independence by using IPv6-in-UDP encapsulation.	Independence by using IPv6-in-MPLS encapsulation.
		Aggregation of IPv6 addresses	Hard	Easy	Hard	Easy		
	Robustness		Poor	Medium	Poor			Better
The cost of development	Technological/ industry maturity		RFC					
	Impact on application layer.		No impact				ALG is needed.	No impact
	Impact on network layer.		Edge router updates supports tunneling	CPE and BR support tunneling	Tunnel endpoints, across routers support IPv4 multicast	ISATAP Router support tunneling	The high bandwidth of NAT gateway and Teredo Relay are needed.	6PE gateway support tunneling
	Impact on end users layer.		Host supports tunneling	No impact	6over4 Host is dual-stack	Host supports tunneling	Teredo Client is in NAT network.	No impact
	Configuration		High	Low	High	Low	Medium	Low
	Maintenance		Low				Medium	Low
	Troubleshooting		There is no the capacity of redundancy backup.					High
others	Fragmentation and restructuring		Exist					

In 6to4, IPv4 address embedded in IPv6 makes a high coupling degree, which against the network address plan and the deployment of IPv6. The use of a fixed IPv6 prefix and broadcast brings a routing scalability problem. Thus, 6to4 apply to the early-stage of IPv6 transition and will not be a continuable IPv6-over-IPv4 mesh solution.

In 6rd, the use of the network specific IPv6 prefix makes a higher routing scalability. No impact on the IPv4 network and end users layer leads a low deployment cost. Because of its statelessness and simplicity, 6rd apply to the early-stage of IPv6 transition by providing a rapid end site IPv6 deployment in the IPv4 environment. 6rd plays an active role in IPv6 adoption.

The idea of 6over4 is using IPv4 multicast to build the tunneling between IPv6-capable hosts. Therefore, the host and the network infrastructure have to fully support IPv4 multicast, which makes the control plane and data plane are quite complexity. Due to the limited multicast support in todays network, 6over4 does not seem to have much application prospect. ISATAP uses non-multicast router discovery. It is more used in the current deployment. However, both 6over4 and ISATAP can not traverse NAT. The host has to own public IPv4 address when the tunneling endpoint uses public IPv4 address. It failed to ease the IPv4 addresses consumption, and can't promote IPv6 adoption.

Teredo uses IPv6-in-UDP encapsulation. And the encapsulated packets can traverse NAT, which increase the reuse rate of IPv4 addresses resource. Teredo is so far the only IPv6-over-IPv4 solution that survives IPv4 NAT well. But the end-to-end transparency cant ensure. In addition, the control plane functions for traversing NAT brings too much complexity. Therefore, it has less deployment than 6to4 and ISATAP.

6PE can solve the problem of IPv6 networks traversing IPv4 MPLS transit. It needs to upgrade a small amount of equipments. So the cost is small. 6PE uses MP-BGP and IPv6-in-MPLS tunnel for forwarding, which increases the reuse rate of IPv4 network infrastructure and reduces the transition cost. However, 6PE is only applicable to IPv4 MPLS backbone.

4.2   The Applicability Analysis of IPv4-over-IPv6 Tunnel Mechanisms

At present, IETF has been developing and standardizing IPv4-over-IPv6 tunnel transition mechanisms. The mainstream mechanisms include Mesh-based 4over6[20] and Hub and Spokes-based DS-Lite[21], Public 4over6[22], Lightweight 4over6[23] and MAP-E[24]. The applicability analysis of these mechanisms is provided and summarized in table 4.

By extending the MP-BGP protocol, Mesh-based 4over6 mechanism discover the routes between tunnel endpoints. These routes turn into the address bindings between E-IP prefixes and I-IP AFBR addresses on the recipient AFBR, which is per-prefix stateful. So, the size of the binding table will be no larger. And the cost of the binding lookup during encapsulation is acceptable. The encapsulation only involves the outermost layer of IPv4 packets head, which makes 4over6 can be used in NAT scenario. Because of the smaller modify of network, simpler configuration of equipments, higher Sustainable, low cost of maintenance and stronger robustness, 4over6 mechanism has good performance and scalability.

DS-Lite takes the CGN(Carrier-Grade NAT) manner and stateful encapsulation. It only needs to update the CPE equipment (Address Family Transition Router, AFTR). So, the cost of modify is small. But AFTR is required to function as a CGN and perform unified IPv4 private-public translation. The gain is a high multiplexing rate of the address resource. But it also destroys the end-to-end feature which makes the un-support of IPv4 business application, and increases the load of AFTR which affect the performance.

Compared with DS-Lite, Public 4over6 unload CGN from BR, and transfer NAT into CE. The state table of BR is per-user stateful, and the performance would be much better. However, DS-Lite can only assign the full public IPv4 addresses to users. Thus, it does not support the reuse of IPv4 addresses and

Table 4. The applicability analysis of IPv6-over-IPv4 tunnel mechanisms

	Applicability		4over6	DS-Lite	Public 4over6	Lightweight 4over6	MAP-E
Sustainable	Scenarios and function of transition		IPv6-only backbone provides IPv4 transport	Provide the IPv4 access service for IPv6 users			
	Coupling degree between IPv4 and IPv6 address.		0				1
	Reuse rate of IPv4 addresses resource.		Low	High	Low	High.	
Business application.	Support degree of IPv4 application.		High	Low	High	High	
	Support degree of IPv6 application		High				
Performance	The performance requirement of tunneling endpoint	Maintenance and finding of binding table	The 4over6 encapsulation table	The CGN mapping table	The state table in 4over6 BR.	The state table in lwAFTR.	No need to maintain in stateless encapsulated
		Routing discovery	Using MP-BGP protocol	Using DHCPv6 protocol	Using DHCPv4-over-IPv6	Using DHCPv4-over-DHCPv6	Using DHCPv6 protocol
	Routing scalability	Independence between IPv4 and IPv6 routing	Independence by using IPv4-in-IPv6 encapsulation.				
		The aggregation of IPv6 addresses	No impact				
	Robustness		High	Low	Medium	High	Low
The cost of development	Technological and industry maturity		RFC			Group draft	draft
	Impact on application layer.		No impact	ALG is needed.	No impact		
	Impact on network layer.		PE supports tunneling	B4 supports tunneling. CPE supports CGN and tunneling	CE and BR support tunneling	lwB4 and lwAFTR supports tunneling and port embedded	
	Impact on end users layer.		No impact				
	Configuration		Medium	Low	Medium	Medium	Low
	Maintenance		Low	Medium	Medium	Medium	Low
	Troubleshooting		There is no the capacity of redundancy backup.			The capacity of redundancy backup in lwAFTR.	No the capacity of redundancy backup.
others	Fragmentation and restructuring		Exit				

resolve the shortage of IPv4 addresses. By using port-set provision, Lightweight 4over6 extends Public 4over6 to serve the case of address sharing. The amount of port for each user is limited, and the multiplexing rate will not be as high as that in DS-Lite, but 4over6 does not have the ALG issue.

MAP-E takes port-set provision and stateless encapsulation. Compared to DS-Lite and 4over6, MAP-E achieves the great benefit of statelessness, such as better communication efficiency and stability. However, since the higher coupling degree of IPv4 and IPv6 address, the deployment has to be entire-network style rather than on demand style, otherwise some of the coupled IPv4 addresses will be wasted.

5   The Security Analysis

5.1   The Security Analysis of Encapsulation/De-encapsulation

In the tunnel transition mechanism, encapsulated data packets may be needed to some security protection, such as authentication, integrity assurance, encryption or recovery. However, the security requirement of data packet has no relationship with tunnel mechanisms. Therefore, the security of tunnel is the overhead of packet not the payload. And the security consideration of packet overhead mainly reflected in the security of tunnel endpoints.

5.2   The Security Analysis of Transition Equipments

Generally, attacks on equipment mainly have two kinds: attacks on data transmission and routing. And the security of routing relies on the routing information exchange protocol used between tunnel endpoints. Therefore, the security of tunnel transition equipments is mainly focus on data encapsulation. The main attacks include spoofing attack, fake as an endpoint and man-in-the-middle attack.

For example, the IPv6-over-IPv4 tunneling endpoint equipments open a hole for spoofing attack on IPv6 from IPv4, which exists in most tunnel mechanisms. In 6over4, attackers from IPv4 may fake as a 6over4 endpoint. Similarly, a malicious IPv4 host can pretend to be part of the ISATAP link and launch attacks. It also introduces various failure modes and several security risks including man in the-middle attacks at the tunnel equipments.

5.3   The Security Analysis of Routing Or Discovery

The security risk of routing and discovery is mainly from the tunnel model and route discovery mechanism. In Mesh model, the edge routers function as tunnel endpoint and using MP-BGP protocol. Since iBGP has mature security solutions, the control plane of this mechanism is secure. In Hub and Spokes model, due to the tunnel endpoint in the user side is probably the user terminal or CPE, DoS attack and packet amplification attack may be happened.

In 6over4, the main security risk is the attack on the ND protocol. Attackers from IPv4 may inject unicast ND messages to break the ND process. In 6rd, packet amplification attack may arise, which generates traffic of endless loop inside a 6RD domain. The solution is ingress filtering based on the 6RD address scheme. In DS-Lite, the main security issue is DoS attack on CGN. In 4over6, the main security issue is man-in-the-middle attack on DHCP. As a result, ingress filtering and DHCP security solutions should be applied. In MAP-E, Traffic hijacking could happen by man-in-the-middle attack on DHCPv6 which provisions the rules. DHCP Security solution should be deployed.

6   Conclusion

For the consideration of deployment scenarios and address format, numerous tunnel transition mechanisms have been proposed in the past ten years. However, due to a wide range of mechanisms and a lot of overlap and similar functions, no one tunnel mechanism can be used in all transition scenarios. This paper has provided the first applicability index system, and highlighted the applicability and security of all tunnel transition mechanisms to help the operators decide on the development scheme for their IPv6 transition.

We can observe from the applicability and security analysis that Mesh-based 4over6, 6RD, DS-Lite, Lightweight 4over6 and MAP-E are able to cover most cases of the heterogeneous traversing problem and together fulfill different demands under the heterogeneous traversing scenarios in the backbone and access networks.

References

1. AlJa'afreh, R., Mellor, J., Awan, I.: A Comparison between the Tunneling process and Mapping schemes for IPv4/IPv6 Transition. In: International Conference on WAINA 2009, pp. 601–606. IEEE Press, Bradford (2009)
2. Law, Y.N., Lai, M.C., Tan, W.L., Lau, W.C.: Empirical Performance of IPv6 vs. IPv4 under a Dual-Stack Environment. In: IEEE International Conference on ICC 2008, pp. 5924–5929. IEEE Press, Beijing (2008)
3. Aazam, M., Syed, A.M., Khan, I., Alam, M.: Evaluation of 6to4 and ISATAP on a Test LAN. In: IEEE Symposium on ISCI, pp. 46–50. IEEE Press, Kuala Lumpur (2011)
4. Gilligan, R., Nordmark, E.: Transition Mechanisms for IPv6 Hosts and Routers. IETF RFC 1933 (1996)
5. Guerin, R., Hosanagar, K.: Fostering IPv6 Migration Through Network Quality Differentials. ACM SIGCOMM Computer Communication Review 40(3), 17–25 (2010)
6. Wu, Y., Zhou, X.: Research on the IPv6 Performance Analysis Based on Dual-Protocol Stack and Tunnel Transition. In: 6th International Conference on ICCSE, pp. 1091–1093. IEEE Press, Singapore (2011)
7. Jayanthi, J.G., Rabara, S.A.: Transition and Mobility Management in the Integrated IPv4 and IPv6 Network-a systematic review. In: International Conference on ICEIE, vol. 1, pp. 15–162. IEEE, Kyoto (2010)
8. Wu, P., Cui, Y., Wu, J.P., Liu, J., Metz, C.: Transition from IPv4 to IPv6: A State-of-the-Art Survey. IEEE Communications Surveys and Tutorials 99, 1–18 (2012)
9. Wu, P., Cui, Y., Xu, M., Wu, J., Li, X., Metz, C., Wang, S.: PET: Prefixing, Encapsulation and Translation for IPv4-IPv6 Coexistence. In: GLOBECOM 2010, pp. 1–5. IEEE Press, Miami (2010)
10. Miyata, H., Endo, M.: Design and Evaluation of IPv4/IPv6 Translator for IP Based Industrial Network Protocol. In: 8th IEEE International Conference on INDIN, pp. 142–147. IEEE Press, Osaka (2010)
11. Govil, J., Kaur, N., Kaur, H.: An examination of IPv4 and IPv6 networks: Constraints and various transition mechanisms. In: IEEE Southeastcon, pp. 178–185. IEEE Press, Huntsville (2008)
12. Ge, J.G., Mi, W., Wu, Y.L.: The IPv6 Transition Mechanisms: Survey, Evaluation Criteria and Deployment Considerations. Journal of Software 4, 896–912 (2014) (in Chinese)
13. Li, X., Dawkins, R., Ward, D., et al.: Softwire Problem Statement. IETF RFC 4925 (2007)
14. Carpenter, B., Moore, K.: Connection of IPv6 Domains via IPv4 Clouds. IETF RFC 3056 (2001)
15. Despres, R.: IPv6 Rapid Deployment on IPv4 Infrastructures (6rd). IETF RFC 5569 (2010)
16. Carpenter, B., Jung, C.: Transmission of IPv6 over IPv4 Domains without Explicit Tunnels. IETF RFC 2529 (1999)
17. Templin, F., Gleeson, T., Thaler, D.: Intra-Site Automatic Tunnel Addressing Protocol (ISATAP). IETF RFC 5214 (2008)
18. Huitema, C.: Teredo: Tunneling IPv6 over UDP through Network Address Translations (NATs). IETF RFC 4380 (2006)

19. De Clercq, J., Ooms, D., Carugi, M.: BGP-MPLS IP Virtual Private Network (VPN) Extension for IPv6 VPN. IETF RFC 4659 (2006)
20. Wu, J., Cui, Y., Metz, C.: 4over6 transit solution using IP encapsulation and MP-BGP Extensions. IETF RFC 5747 (2010)
21. Durand, A., Droms, R., Woodyatt, J.: Dual-Stack Lite Broadband Deployments Following IPv4 Exhaustion. IETF RFC 6333 (2011)
22. Cui, Y., Wu, J., Wu, P., Metz, C., et al.: Public IPv4 over Access IPv6 Network. IETF RFC 7040 (2013)
23. Cui, Y., Wu, J., Wu, P., et al.: Lightweight 4over6 in access network. IETF draft (2013)
24. Troan, O., Dec, W., Li, X., et al.: Mapping of Address and Port with Encapsulation (MAP). IETF draft (2013)

QOS Performance Analysis for Flexible Workflow Supporting Exception Handling

Xiaoyan Zhu[1], Jingle Zhang[2], and Bo Wang[3]

[1] Software College of Henan University, Kaifeng 475001, China
sfzyan@henu.edu.cn
[2] School of Information Engineering, University of Science and Technology of Beijing,
Beijing 100083, China
Zhangle80@126.com
[3] School of Mathematics and Information Science of Henan University, Kaifeng 457001, China
wangbo@henu.edu.cn

Abstract. The flexible workflow technology is important to workflow management, and Qos performance of network system has become more and more important. One factor that has impacts on flexible workflow performance is exception, which in turn has negative effects on Qos performance of network. Based on the Stochastic Petri Net and the comparison between the old e-commerce systems and the new one, we propose a flexible workflow model in this paper which supports exception handling, and the corresponding Qos performance analysis method. Moreover, we analyze the flexible system's reliability performance parameters. The test results indicate that the method supporting exception is effective.

Keywords: Qos, Flexible Workflow, SPN, Exception process.

1   Introduction

Network Quality of Service (QoS) guarantee is the basic requirement of network and how to provide QoS on the qualitative and quantitative evaluation studies is of great significance[1]. With the maturity and development of Workflow Management research, workflow technology in the manufacturing sector has been widely applied in many fields, which allows companies to achieve business process integration, business process automation and business process management. In response to the development process in many new emerging needs, current workflow technology is experiencing changes from rigid to flexible, and the flexible workflow is characterized by responding to the largest business process that can not be pre-determined by semi-structured and unstructured business processes, for instance, a task change and processes exception. In this premise, it has become one of the main issues of concern whether flexible workflow system can complete the assigned task in a correct, safe, efficient manner, or whether the system can provide reliable services. Based on the analysis of the characteristics of flexible workflow, this paper presents the Flexible Workflow quality of service analysis supporting exception handling and

X.-h. Sun et al. (Eds.): ICA3PP 2014, Part II, LNCS 8631, pp. 571–580, 2014.

presents an *ELMS (E-Business Logistics Management System)* logistics distribution network system modeling and performance analysis on reliability, availability.

Stochastic Petri net, as a result of a more ideal system modeling and performance analysis tool in many areas, has been widely used[2], therefore, this paper will focus on the modeling and performance analysis with stochastic Petri net.

2   Performance Evaluation of QoS

With the development of networks, Web Qos is getting higher and higher quality requirements, so, evaluating the performance of quality of services provided by a network system itself seems even more important. In addition to the quality of service network system performance evaluation done in general, capabilities of providing consecutive   services and resuming the services in specified time should be analyzed when the system is suffered from external attack, or misoperation, environmental impact, as well as hardware failure and software bug. This paper will evaluate the quality of service with reliability, maintainability and availability.

Reliability: the continuity of service provided by system, it can be measured by $R(t)$, which means the probability of the normal service in the time interval of $[0,t]$,supposing the system works at the point of 0[3].

Maintainability: a system's capability to adjust, repair, and to tolerate faults which means the probability of resuming in the time interval t after the failure of system.

Availability: the capability of offering right services by system, it is proposed for the repairable system, is a general description of reliability and maintainability[4].

3   Flexible Workflow Exception Handling

Some existed work[5] believes that the business workflow and its implementation process are not static mainly from internal and external causes. External cause means environmental change in commercial, legal, science and technology. Internal cause means the demand which comes from workflow process itself and unforeseen circumstances of process. Both internal and external factors may cause the deviation of the process execution from the original process definition[6], often referred to as the workflow changes or exception. The ability to deal with change and exception flexibly and dynamically is embodied in the flexible workflow system. This paper focuses on the flexible workflow exception handling.

3.1   Flexible Workflow System Supporting Exception Handling

Exception is the main reason that causes the complexity and limitations of industrial process automation. According to its impact on the scope and the degree of workflow system and whether it can be predicted and so on, exception can be divided into the following types.

The scope of influence: the individual level, group level and organization [7].

The degree of impact: noise, idiosyncratic exceptions and evolutionary exceptions [7].

Whether it can be expected: expected and unexpected[8]. In accordance with the incident arising from the exception, [9] divides the expected exception into exceptional workflow, exceptional data, exceptional timing and external exception.

Excluding the above types, there are other classifications in accordance with the methods, such as: the abstraction levels affected by exception.

3.2   Handling Approach

For exception, [8] thinks the handling of exceptions can be divided into three stages: Detection, Diagnosis and Resolution. Detection is responsible for identifying the trigger conditions which cause exceptional events. Addional, accordance with the trigger conditions, diagnosis process decides some exception handler. Finally, resolution design appropriate processes to implement the exception handler.

4   Exception Handling Flexible Workflow Modeling

In the development process of Web Qos, various analytical techniques and modeling tools are presented in order to improve the quality of service performance, and some mathematical models are established by these tools, which can reflect the system's behavior and nature. Among them, the Stochastic Petri Net has a strong dynamic analysis capabilities of system's concurrency, asynchronism and uncertainty. At the same time, it has advantage of less modeling original language, being in line with intuitive graphical representation. It can describe the system state, also represent the system behavior. Therefore, Petri Net can be applied to evaluate the network Qos. Petri Net can be used to reflect the dynamic nature and service behavior, and can be applied to system modeling and qualitative evaluation of network Qos.

As a powerful tool to analyze discrete event dynamic system, *Stochastic Petri Net (SPN)* is widely used in computer networks[9], resource-sharing systems, as well as parallel and concurrent computing [10] and other fields (Please refer to the relevant literature in detail[11]).

Definition 1. Stochastic Petri Net can be described as a four-tuple $SPN = (P, T, F, \lambda)$, of which:

$P=(p_1, p_2, ..., p_m)$, is a finite place set;

$T = (t_1, t_2, ..., t_m)$, is a finite transition set;

$(P \cap T \neq \Phi), (P \cup T \neq \Phi); F (P \times T) \cup (T \times P)$, is an arc set;

$\lambda = (\lambda_1, \lambda_2, ..., \lambda_n)$, is a set of transition average firing rate.

4.1   Flexible Workflow Model for Exception Handling

As for flexible workflow system supporting exception handling, the basic process includes exceptional Edit, exceptional Diagnosis, exceptional Resolution. The model structure is as follows:

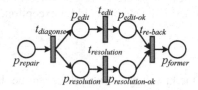

Fig. 1. Exception handling model

In the above figure, symbols are defined as follows:

t_{edit}: the operation of editing and preservation of exception. The operation is to preserve system's exception to analyze easily. When the system experiences the same exception, similar process can be done again.

$t_{diagnosis}$: the operation of diagnosing exception and analyzing the exceptional causes and the treatment methods.

$t_{resolution}$: the exceptional processing operation accordingly.

$t_{re-back}$: the operation of process back to the state before the exception handling.

After simplifying the Exception Handling model above, the simplified model is found:

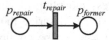

Fig. 2. Simplified exception handling model

According to the existed works, above graph can also be used in simplifying parallel structure model. In this case, using t_{repair} to replace parallel part of original model, the simplified exception handling model is found.

4.1.1   Exception Handling Model of Simple Structure

When exceptions appear in the serial structure, and when there is only one exceptional component, the structure is:

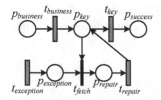

Fig. 3. Exception handling model of Simple structure

In the above graph, p_{key} is on behalf of components in which exception may occur. When exception occurs in system, that is, when $t_{exception}$ is triggered with certain probability, p_{key} will be transferred to exception handling p_{repair}.

4.1.2   Exception Handling Model of Series Structure

When the exception appears in two or more exceptional components, and only when these exceptional components passed the only repairing parts successfully, the system can restore normal exception handling model.

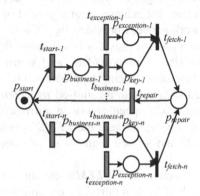

Fig. 4. Exception handling model of series structure

In the above graph, p_{key-1}, p_{key-n} are all palaces in which exception may occurs. When the system is exceptional ,that is, $t_{exception-1}$, $t_{exception-n}$ trigger with certain probability, p_{key-1}, p_{key-n} will be transferred to exception handling p_{repair}.

4.1.3   Exception Handling Model of Parallel Structure

When the exception appears in two or more exceptional components ,and each exceptional part has its own repairing part, the system can restore normal exception handling model after all exceptional parts repairing successfully.

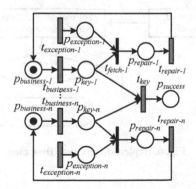

Fig. 5. Exception handling model of parallel structure

In the above graph, p_{key-1} and p_{key-n} are all palaces in which exception may occur. When the system is exceptional, that is, $t_{exception-1}$ and $t_{exception-n}$ trigger with certain probability, p_{key-1} and p_{key-n} will be transferred to respective part of exception handling $p_{repair-1}$ and $p_{repair-n}$.

5   An Example

ELMS (E-Business Logistics Management System) is a new type of e-commerce model. This model makes the logistics system between suppliers and stores no longer establish a direct connection, but achieve a variety need of logistics and distribution system through the network services provided by *ELMS*. In this new model, *ELMS* provides a service platform, which provides information flow, capital flow, logistics and other safeguards for all service providers, and stores to ensure security and a high-performance run of logistics system. Suppliers will be able to release a variety of services provided to the *ELMS* system for unified management, and stores would no longer request for service to a specific service providers and obtain a complete logistics and distribution services through the *ELMS* system. *ELMS* will ensure that the stores service requests and service requests of all suppliers can obtain the best service.

Taking replenishment activities in *ELMS* as an example, we model the replenishment process with *SPN*, then introduce exception handling to model. Finally we compare and analyze the service quality performance parameters of model before and after the introduction of exception handling.

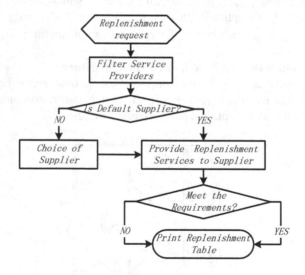

Fig. 6. Replenishment task flow chart

5.1   Process Modeling

Referring to the above flow chart, this paper gives the basic model with *SPN* firstly, and there are not exceptional handling operations in basic model:

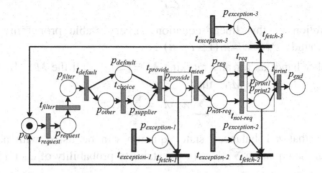

Fig. 7. Simple model of replenishment task

In the above graph, because the exceptional handling operations are not introduced ,the process will re-run when exceptions occur. Then ,this paper gives the process model with introduction of exceptional handling operations. The model as follows:

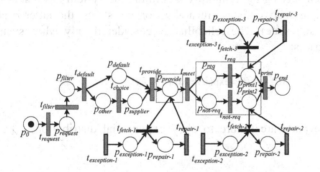

Fig. 8. Exceptional handling model of replenishment task

In the above graph, the model with introduction of exceptional handling units is found in several key palaces.

5.2   Solving of Service Quality Performance Parameters

After modeling of the system's quality of service performance modeling with Stochastic Petri net, the *MC* can be obtained which is isomorphic with *SPN* model. Assuming that the steady-states probability of n-state in *MC* (*Markov chain*) is a row vector $\Pi = (\pi 1, \pi 2, ..., \pi n)$, and each delay of transition subject to exponential distribution function. In accordance with Markov process, the following linear equations can be found:

$$\begin{cases} \Pi \times Q = 0 \\ \sum_{i=0}^{n} \pi_i = 1 \end{cases} \tag{5.1}$$

After solution of this linear equations, every stable probability of reachable marking is found, $P_i(t=\infty)=\pi_i (1 \leq i \leq n)$.

On the other hand, as for any marking $M_i \in [\ M_0 >$, all the M_j, $M_k \in [\ M_0 >$ and $M_i \in [t_j > M_j$, $M_k \in [\ t_k > M_i$, then:

$$(\sum_j \lambda_j)\pi_i = \sum_k \lambda_k \pi_k \tag{5.2}$$

It is clear that n-1 balanced state equation can be listed with above formula, together with the equation $\sum \lambda_j = 1$, the stability probability of each reachable mark can be solved. Based on the above Markov chain and the state transition rate, state transition matrix can be produced and all the steady-state probability of state can be obtained. Then the performance parameters of quality of service further can be analyzed, which are concerned by people.

Next, taking replenishment system as example, the paper will introduce the solution of system's reliability, availability, *MTTR*, *MTBF* and maintenance.

Reliability: When solving the reliability, assuming the system has n states, among which, the first t consecutive states are non-absorbing states, the latter a states are absorbing states (fault state). The reliability is considered only when system is in absorbing states, that is:

$$R(t) = P_0(t) = \exp(\lambda t) = \exp(-\sum_{i=1}^{n} \lambda_i t) \tag{5.3}$$

MTTF : When the parts are failure to obey exponential distribution, $\lambda = \sum_{i=1}^{n} \lambda_i$, then:

$$MTTF = \int R(t)dt = \int_0^\infty \exp(-\sum_{i=1}^{n} \lambda_i t)dt = \lambda^{-1} \tag{5.4}$$

Maintainability: In order to achieve system maintainability of *M(t)*, the system's repairing rate $\mu(t)$ should defined firstly, which means the probability of repairing resources completely in unit time after the resource has not been repaired in time. This can be expressed with a mathematical formula:

$$\mu(t) = \frac{1}{1-M(t)} \frac{dM(t)}{dt} \tag{5.5}$$

then by 5.5 we can obtain :

$$M(t) = 1 - \exp(-\int_0^t \mu(t)dt)$$ (5.6)

when $\mu(t)$ is constant, formula 5.6 is :

$$M(t) = 1 - \exp(-\mu t)$$ (5.7)

MTTR : Means time to repair of the system can be expressed :

$$MTTR = \lambda/\rho = \sum_{i=1}^{n} \lambda_i \Big/ \sum_{i=1}^{n} (\lambda_i/\mu_i) \ (5.8)$$

Among them, $\rho = \sum_{i=1}^{n} \rho_i$ is the system's maintenance coefficient, $\rho_i = \lambda_i/\mu_i$ is i component's maintenance factor.

MTBF : Means time between failures of system is equal to the ratio of normal working hours and the number of failures during this time approximately:

$$MTBF = t/N_f(t)$$ (5.9)

Availability: System's availability is the steady probability of M_0 state:

$$A_s = \pi_0 = \left(1 + \sum_{i=1}^{n} \frac{\lambda_i}{\mu_i}\right)^{-1} = \left(1 + \sum_{i=1}^{n} \rho_i\right)^{-1} = (1 + \rho)^{-1}$$ (5.10)

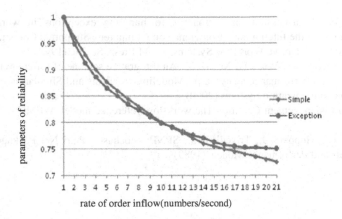

Fig. 9. Comparation of reliability

6   Conclusion

This paper introduced the flexible work flow supporting exception handling operations and its characteristics. Taking the *ELMS* replenishment process as an example, the paper gave a simple process model and a flexible process model which support exception handling with *SPN* modeling. When exception's causes increasing speed, by comparing the services quality of the above models, it is found that with our increasing exception, the performance of the flexible workflow supporting exception handling is superior to common workflow system.

References

[1] Lin, C.: QoS Control of Multimedia Information Networks. J. Journal of Software 10(10), 1016–1024 (1999)
[2] Lin, C., Wang, Y.Z., Yang, Y., Qu, Y.: Research on Network Dependability Analysis Methods Based on Stochastic Petri Net. J. Acta Electronica Sinica 34(2), 322–332 (2006)
[3] Avizienis, A., Laprie, J., Randell, B.: Fundamental Concepts of Dependability. LAAS2CNRS (2001)
[4] Chen, K.W.: Reliability Modeling Method for Network System Using Generalized Stochastic Petri Net. In: The Proceedings of 2012 International Conference on Quality, Reliability, Risk, Maintenance, and Safety Engineering and The 3rd International Conference on Maintenance Engineering (2012)
[5] Han, Y., Sheth, A., Bussl, E.C.: A taxonomy of adaptive workflow management. In: Workshop in Conference on Computer Supported Cooperative Work: Towards Adaptive Workflow Systems. ACM Press, Seattle (1998)
[6] Kammer, P.J., Bolcer, G.A.: Techniques for supporting dynamic and adaptive workflow. J. Computer Supported Cooperative Work 9(3 -4), 269–292 (2000)
[7] Sadiq, S.: On capturing exceptions in workflow process models. In: Proceedings of the 4th International Conference on Business Information Systems, Poznan, Poland. Springer (2000)
[8] Casati, F.: A discussion on approaches to handling exceptions in workflows. In: Proceedings of the International Conference on Computer - Supported Cooperative Work, Workshop on Adaptive Workflow Systems. ACM Press, Seattle (1998)
[9] Lin, C., Sheng, L.J., Wu, J.P., Xu, M.W.: An integrative scheme of differentiated service: modeling and performance analysis. In: Modeling, Analysis and Simulation of Computer and Telecommunication Systems (2000)
[10] Workflow Management Coalition:The workflow reference model. WFMC - TC00 - 1003 (1995)
[11] Ciaodo, G., Muppala, J., Trivedi, K.S.: SPNP: Stochastic Petri Net Package. In: Proc. Petri Nets and Performance Models (1989)

Analysis of Propagation Characteristics
of Variant Worms

Tao Liu[1], Can Zhang[1,2], Mingjing Cao[1,2], and Ruping Wu[1,2]

[1] North China Electric Power University, Baoding 071000, China
[2] National Engineering Laboratory for Information Security Technologies,
Institute of Information Engineering, Chinese Academy of Sciences, Beijing 100093, China

Abstract. The large-scale spread of Internet worm will stimulate users' awareness of security to deploy defense strategy against worms. The game between users' response time and worms' propagation speed affects the range of infection. The paper provides a new kind of worm called "variant worm" which can mutate itself into new forms to implement a secondary propagation. We analyze the necessary conditions of secondary propagation and the propagation characteristics of variant worm in theory.

Keywords: worm, variant worm, response time, variant time, propagation characteristic.

1 Introduction

Internet worm is a kind of malicious program that can propagate in the Internet exploiting system vulnerabilities [1]. The wreak havoc of worms cause large economic losses. Moorish worm breaking out in 1988 infected 6000 university and military computers during several days, which caused in tens of millions of dollars in losses [2]. In 2001, a kind of worm named Code Red worm exploited the Windows IIS vulnerability emerged. It infected 250,000 computers in 9 hours after its outbreak, and resulted in 200 million dollars in losses [3]. In 2010, the famous Stuxnet worm incident occurred. The Stuxnet exploited Microsoft '0 day' vulnerability and spread by USB devices [4]. According to Symantec's statistics, there had been 45,000 networks being infected by the Stuxnet worm until September, 2010. About 60% of infected hosts located in Iran. Bushehr nuclear power plant was attacked by Stuxnet worm, delaying Iran's nuclear program [5]. On June 28, 2011, Sina micro-blog was attacked by Cross-Site attack worm. The whole process lasted about one hour. The worm had significantly strong media attribute and social attribute characteristics of mixed, resulting in a suddenly and rapidly attack. Within ten minutes, hundreds of thousands of garbage consulting messages flood on the Sina micro-blog, "brush screen" appearing [6].

Worm propagates on the Internet in a high speed by replicating itself and infecting specific files [7]. The rapid spread of worm stimulates user's security awareness. Users may take countermeasures against worms, such as anti-virus software, patches, filters or firewalls [8].

X.-h. Sun et al. (Eds.): ICA3PP 2014, Part II, LNCS 8631, pp. 581–589, 2014.

Microsoft has announced that, on April 8, 2014, they will officially end support for Windows XP [9]. Microsoft had stopped providing any services for security patches XP since April 8. XP occupies the market share of approximately 25% in the worldwide, even up to 70% in our country. According to CNCERT/CC reported that Windows XP has nearly 500 million users in the world, the risk of being attacked is increased [10].

This paper studies that variant worm mutates itself into a new kind of worm during the time user deploying defense measures. Through theoretical analysis, the new kind of variant worm can implement a secondary propagation on the Internet, and its propagation model is based on the classical worm propagation model.

The contribution of this paper is as follows :

- Providing a kind of variant worm on the base of classic worm propagation model and modeling its propagation characteristics in theory and mathematic.
- Analyzing the variant worm's propagation characteristics by comparing users' response time and worms' mutating time.

The rest of this paper is organized as follows. Section 2 is related work, in this section we introduce several typical worm propagation models and analysis the advantages and disadvantages of these models. Section 3 describes the mathematical principle of variant worm. Section 4 proposes simulation experiment to verify the correctness of mathematical analysis of variant worm. We draw conclusion in Section 5.

2   Related Work

In this section we analyze and summarize the Internet worm propagation models.

- classic epidemic propagation model

The classic epidemic model is the basic Internet worm propagation model [11].The model assumes that the system is "uniform system". Hosts in the system are in one of two states: susceptible and infectious. The mathematical formula for classic epidemic propagation model is as follows:

$$\frac{dI(t)}{dt} = pI(t)[N - I(t)] \tag{1}$$

where $I(t)$ is the number of infectious hosts at time t, p is the infection probability, N is the total number of hosts on the Internet.

This model doesn't take any other factors such as patches, power off and so on that may affect worm propagation. However, the classic model makes a foundation for analyzing complicated scenario.

- KM model

Based on the classic epidemic model, KM model takes the removal process of infectious hosts into consideration [12].This model assumes that the recovered hosts from infectious are immune to the worm forever. The status is named removed. Hosts in this model stay in one of the three states at any time: susceptible, infectious and removed. The mathematical formula for classic epidemic propagation model is as follows:

$$\begin{cases} \dfrac{dJ(t)}{dt} = pJ(t)[N - J(t)] \\[2mm] \dfrac{dR(t)}{dt} = \gamma I(t) \\[2mm] J(t) = I(t) + R(t) \end{cases} \tag{2}$$

where $J(t)$ is the number of infected host, $I(t)$ is the number of infectious host, $R(t)$ is the number of removed host from infectious host, $J(t) = I(t) - R(t)$, γ is the remove probability.

The disadvantage of this model is that it doesn't take the mutative infectious rate caused by network congestion into consideration.

● Two-factor model

Based on the analysis of KM model, Zou et al [13] analyzed the Code Red worm in detail, taking human countermeasures and the reduced infection rate into consideration. Those two factors affect worm propagation dynamically. The two-factor model can better match the observed data collected the day on which the Code Red broke out. The mathematical formula for classic epidemic propagation model is as follows:

$$\begin{cases} \dfrac{dS(t)}{dt} = -p(t)S(t)I(t) - \dfrac{dQ(t)}{dt} \\[2mm] \dfrac{dR(t)}{dt} = \gamma I(t) \\[2mm] \dfrac{dQ(t)}{dt} = \mu S(t)J(t) \\[2mm] p(t) = p_0[1 - I(t)/N]^{\eta} \\[1mm] N = S(t) + I(t) + R(t) + Q(t) \\[1mm] I(0) = I_0 \ll N \\[1mm] S(0) = N - I_0; \\[1mm] R(0) = Q(0) = 0 \end{cases} \tag{3}$$

These types of typical worm propagation model are aiming at describing a certain type of worm propagate process. The worm propagation characteristic in our study is to describe worm propagation characteristics of "variant worm" before and after the variation. The original worms spread at the beginning of the outbreak in conformity with the general rule. With the massive worm outbreak, it would inevitably cause network congesting, induce security awareness of users. User would adopt security policies to prevent the host from infecting, such as killing the worms, patching vulnerabilities, etc. Worms will mutate during the time of user deploy security strategy, adding new modules, and it will become into a brand-new worms to bypass antivirus software, in order to achieve a secondary propagation.

3   Theory Analysis of Variant Worm Propagation Model

The focus of this paper is to verify the propagation characteristics of variant worm, without considering other factors. The model of variant worm propagation is based on the classic epidemic worm propagation model. All notations used in this paper are listed in Table 1.

Table 1. All Notations Used in This Paper

Notation	Explanation
N	the total number of hosts on the Internet
P	Infection probability
I(t)	The number of Infectious hosts at time t
C	Initially infected, I(0)=C
Tp	Users response time
Tv	Worms variant time

3.1   Worm Modeling Background

The infected rate of classic susceptible – infectious model is as follows:

$$\frac{dI(t)}{dt} = pI(t)[N - I(t)] \tag{4}$$

We solve equation (1) for the number of hosts infected at time t with the initially infected host number C as:

$$I(t) = \frac{N}{1 - \frac{(C-N)}{C}e^{-Npt}} \tag{5}$$

Because of the existence of vulnerability host, when a new worm was first released to the Internet, it will experience a phase of rapid spread. With the employing of human defense strategies and the reduction of vulnerability host, the worm propagation rate will decrease. We define the time that rate start to decreases as critical point Tp, that is to say users' response time. After the users' response time, the infected rate began to decrease as shown in Fig.1.

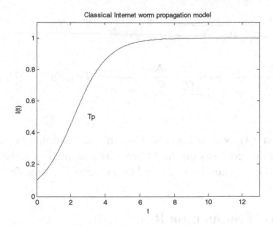

Fig. 1. Classical Internet worm propagation model

3.2   Mathematical Modeling of Variation Worm Propagation Characteristics

The mutated time of variant worm is defined as variant time Tv, meaning that the worm propagation before the variant time worm propagated in accordance with the classic worm propagation model. When $Tv < Tp$, the time of defense strategy deploying is longer than the time of worms mutating, in which case the defense deployment becomes invalid. The variant worm will achieve a secondary propagate. Based on the above analysis, we can derive a formula of relationship between infected worm hosts and t, as shown in equation (3).

$$
I(t) = \begin{cases}
\dfrac{N}{1 - \dfrac{(C-N)}{C} e^{-Npt}} & t < Tv \\[4mm]
\dfrac{N}{1 - \dfrac{(C-N)}{N} e^{-Npt}} & t > Tv\, and\, Tv > Tp \\[4mm]
\dfrac{N}{1 - \dfrac{(C-N)}{C} e^{-NpTv}} + \dfrac{N}{1 - \dfrac{(C-N)}{C} e^{-Np(t-Tv)}} & t > Tv\, and\, Tv < Tp
\end{cases}
\tag{6}
$$

Adjusting equation (3), we can derive the mathematical model of worm propagation as follows:

$$I(t) = \begin{cases} \dfrac{N}{1 - \dfrac{(C-N)}{C} e^{-Npt}} & Tv > Tp \\[4ex] \dfrac{N}{1 - \dfrac{(C-N)}{C} e^{-NpTv}} + \dfrac{N}{1 - \dfrac{(C-N)}{C} e^{-Np(t-Tv)}} & Tv < Tp \end{cases} \qquad (7)$$

From equation (4), we can know that in the assumption that there are only susceptible and infected hosts on the Internet, the number of infected hosts of variant worm just depend on variant time Tv and users' response time Tp.

4   Analysis of Simulation Results

We simulate classic epidemic model and the secondary propagation of variant worm for contradistinction.

To observe the influence of the variant time and user response time to worm propagation, we take different Tv for simulation. The value of the notations used in the simulation is shown in Table. 2.

Table 2. The value of notations used in the simulation

notations	value
N	20000
p	1
C	10
Tp	0.4
Tv	0.2, 0.4, 0.6

Variant worm finish mutation at $Tv = 0.2$, when the defense strategy has not been deployed. The defense strategy is deployed at $Tp = 0.4$, at which time the strategy is not effective to variant worm and the worm can propagate at a second time. While the propagation speed of traditional worm reduced because of the deployment of defense strategy. The time that variant worm exists on the Internet is extended by mutating, which can infect more hosts and cause more serious attack, as shown in Fig.2

Variant worm finish mutation at $Tv = 0.4$, when the defense strategy has just been deployed. The propagation of traditional worm is containment by the defense strategy and the propagation speed decreases gradually. While the defense strategy has no influence on the variant worm, the variant worm can propagate at a second time even infect more hosts. The time that variant worm exist on the Internet is extended by mutating as well, as shown in Fig.3.

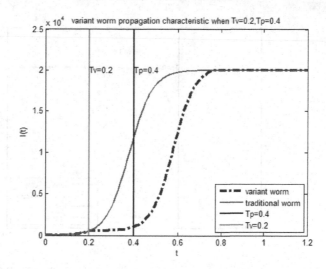

Fig. 2. The curve of variant worm propagation characteristic when Tv=0.2, Tp=0.4

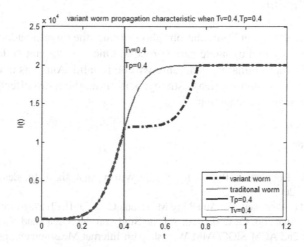

Fig. 3. The curve of variant worm propagation characteristic when Tv=0.4, Tp=0.4.

Variant worm finish mutation at $Tv = 0.6$, while the defense strategy has been deployed at $Tp = 0.4$, which means the variant worm is contained before mutating, and the curve of its propagation is consistent with the traditional worm propagation.as shown in Fig.4.

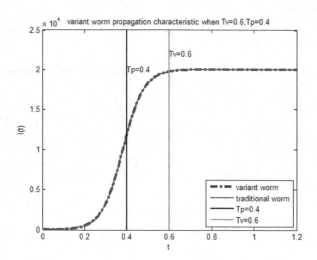

Fig. 4. The curve of variant worm propagation characteristic when Tv=0.6, Tp=0.4

5   Conclusion

Theoretical analysis and simulation show that, the worm attack and defense deployment belong to a dynamic game process. Once the variant code is inserted into the worm code, the original virus defense will be invalid. Analysis in this paper shows that the faster users deploy defense strategies in time, the more effectively containing to worms' secondary propagation.

References

1. Mackie, A., Roculan, J., Russel, R.: Nimda Worm Analysis. J. Incident Analysis Report, Version. 2 (2001)
2. McGraw, G., Morrisett, G.: Attacking Malicious Code. J. IEEE Software 5, 33–41 (2000)
3. Moore, D., Shannon, C.: Code-Red: A Case Study on the Spread and Victims of an Internet Worm. In: 2nd ACM SIGCOMM Workshop on Internet Measurement, pp. 273–284. ACM, New York (2002)
4. Langner, R.: Stuxnet: Dissecting a Cyber-Warfare Weapon. J. Security & Privacy 9(3), 49–51 (2011)
5. Yang, Y., Littler, T., Sezer, S.: Impact of Cyber-Security Issues on Smart Grid. In: 2nd IEEE PES International Conference and Exhibition on Innovative Smart Grid Technologies (ISGT Europe), pp. 1–7 (2011)
6. Sina Micro-blog Encounter XSS Worm Invasion, http://news.xinhuanet.com/2011-06/28/c_121597389.htm
7. Hansman, S., Hunt, R.: A Taxonomy of Network and Computer Attacks. J. Computers & Security 24, 31–43 (2005)

8. Zou, C.C., Gong, W., Towsley, D.: Code Red Worm Propagation Modeling and Analysis. In: 9th ACM Conference on Computer and Communications Security, pp. 138–147. ACM, Washington, DC (2002)
9. Experts on XP Retirement: China Is Heavily Dependent on Foreign Technology, While the Information Security Situation is Grim, http://it.people.com.cn/n/2014/0408/c1009-24847531.html
10. Microsoft, X.P.: System Officially Retired, the World's 500 Million Internet Users at Risk of Attack Large, http://www.cert.org.cn/publish/main/98/2014/20140429140223521706476/20140429140223521706476_.html
11. Grasman, J.: Epidemic modelling: An Introduction (2000)
12. Andersson, H., Britton, T.: Stochastic Epidemic Models and Their Statistical Analysis. Springer, New York (2000)
13. Zou, C.C., Towsley, D., Gong, W.: On the Performance of Internet Worm Scanning Strategies. J. Performance Evaluation 63(7), 700–723 (2006)

A Design of Network Behavior-Based Malware Detection System for Android

Yincheng Qi[1], Mingjing Cao[1,2], Can Zhang[1,2], and Ruping Wu[1,2]

[1] North China Electric Power University,071003 Baoding,China
[2] Institute of Information Engineering,Chinese Academy of Sciences, 100093 Beijing, China

Abstract. In recent years, the number of mobile terminals is increasing sharply. Due to Android's open nature and convenience for surfing, many invaders target on Android. In this paper, we propose a network behavior-based malware detection system for Android which is composed of network behavior monitoring module, anomaly network behavior analyzing module and storage module. We collect the network behavior features of applications, classify them via Bayes algorithm and diagnose whether it is malicious. The priority of the system is that it's aimed the internet characteristics of malware and using network behavior as object of analysis. In theory, the system can detect malware effectively.

Keywords: Android, Network Behavior, Malware, Bayes.

1 Introduction

With the boom of Android, a number of malwares targeted on Android emerged. The Net Qin "Cloud Security" Monitoring Platform diagnosed 134790 malwares, the growth is 106.6% compared with that in 2012. 56,560,000 smartphones have been infected, which increased 76.8% compared with the same period of 2012[1]. Specially, the mobile games and apps that acted as tools were accounting for the major. For instance，in 2013, a malicious app out broke which led signature holes of Android operating system to be implanted Skullkey chargeback Trojan. According to the CNCERT monitoring data, only in An Feng Market, games and tools account for over 60% of the applications infected by Skullkey chargeback Trojan.

Besides, as BYOD spreading, most companies allow their staffs to bring with their mobile devices. However, the WIFI and 3G may bring challenges to the companies ' safety, so the issue has been on the agenda [2].

As the APT (Advanced Persistent Threat) appears, intelligent mobile phone are more likely to be used by the APT attack [3]. The core target of APT attack is human beings. Attackers conduct industrial control or mobile Internet penetration attack by invading the human contact equipment like Android smartphones. The objects of APT attacks can be divided into information theft and behavior disturbance [4].

The malwares on Android platform include virus, worm, Trojans, botnets and spyware [5] which are mainly spread by brush and application market. Almost all the

X.-h. Sun et al. (Eds.): ICA3PP 2014, Part II, LNCS 8631, pp. 590–600, 2014.

popular applications would be packaged again by attackers. The attackers can gain permissions by controlling the mobile phone and even get the contact list, account number, password, photos, text messages and all other information.

There are two kinds of detection methods against malware. One is static signature-based method which is usually used by security software developers. Its weakness is that it can't effectively detect the variants and obfuscation techniques. And it takes a long time to detect if the malware is previously unknown [6]. The other is dynamic behavior-based method which runs programs in an isolated and controlled environment for capturing the traces. It can resolve the former problem.

In this paper, a network behavior-based malware detection system for Android is proposed. The system can monitor network behaviors in real time and classify them by network-based approaches, this system need not to parse the content of data packages. Thus it can protect users' privacy. Also, it makes detecting more efficient. The method has been widely used in software analyzing on PC, but rarely used on Android in domestic.

The work is organized as follows. Section 2 introduces the framework of the detecting system. Section 3 explains the experiment arrange. In section 4 we will conclude our work.

2   Related Work

In order to solve the problems, many researchers have made great efforts. They proposed some detection technologies for Android through a large scale of experiments and researches. These work laid a solid foundation for later research.

Shuaifu Dai et al. [7] proposed a detecting system for Windows Phone which obtains applications' running information by parsing API. According to the Malicious Behavior Feature Library, the system can distinguish the abnormal malware.

Iker Burguera [8] presented a framework to dynamically analyze applications' behavior to detect malware on Android. An application client, Crowdroid, monitors Linux system calls and, after preprocessing, sends them to a central server, which then parses data and creates a system call vector. Finally, each dataset is clustered through a respective clustering algorithm, namely 2-means. These efforts have profound influence for malware detecting study.

Zhenfei Tong and Geng Yang et al.[9] proposed a detection framework for Android malwares. The framework classified behavior features using Nearest Neighbor, Native Bayes and SM0. But the objects of this detection system are static behaviors like ELF files, whose detection ability is weak once variants and fuzzy technology appear.

Wei Zhong [10] proposed a Native Bayes detection model of intrusion based on kernel density, which improved the effectiveness and accuracy of the Bayesian algorithm. This provides new ideas for the future of Bayesian classification algorithm.

Zeting Cai and Mei Jiang [11] proposed an Android malware detection system using Naive Bayes based on permissions. It has achieved a good result by using the similarity between Bayes model characteristics and Android permissions.

Mahinthan Chandramohan [12] has made a survey about mobile malwares. The survey provided a better understanding of the motivations behind mobile malware "in the wild" —the malicious applications available in mobile app markets. Then the survey describes the existing malware detection techniques in detail, including static analysis, dynamic analysis, application permission analysis and cloud-based detection. And, it demonstrated the advantages and disadvantages of each technology, which helps us quickly understand the malware detection technologies.

We have achieved the preliminary research of Android characteristics, summarized the characteristics and harm of smartphone malwares, understood the current situation of the development of anti-malware, and finally found that most of the malicious software harm had a relationship with network behaviors. Besides, we deeply researched the Bayes classification technology and made it suitable for analysis of the mobile terminal data through improving partial parameters.

3   Network Behavior-Based Malware Detection System

3.1   The Framework of Network Behavior-Based Malware Detection System

The architecture of Android includes four layers: Applications, Application Framework, GNU Library and Linux Kernel [13]. Though Android has its own security mechanism, facing more complicated security threat, the mechanism is not enough.

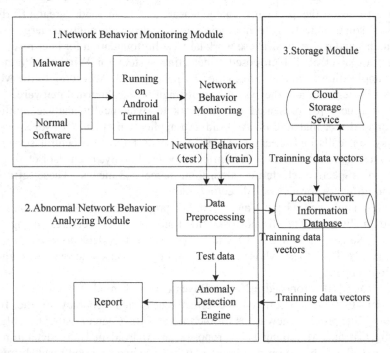

Fig. 1. The Framework of the Network Behavior-Based Malware Detection System.

To make Android phones safe, we design the Network Behavior-Based Malware Detection System which detects malware by analyzing network behaviors. As shown in Figure 1, the system is composed of network behavior monitoring module, abnormal network behavior analyzing module and storage module. The monitoring module is for extracting the features of network behaviors. The analyzing module is for diagnosing the anomaly which includes data preprocessing, anomaly detection engine and report generator. The storage module is for storing the related data such as features and results.

3.2   Network Behavior Monitoring Module

Under normal circumstances, The network information about Android system is stable. But when there is a malicious behavior, the information will be abnormal. To track the anomaly timely, we need to extract valid features. The monitoring module can gain valid network information by analyzing packets.

The main purpose of monitoring module is to obtain network behavior data. We create a feature vector for implying the network behavior characteristics based on both Android's nature and impact on Android phone by malware. As shown in Table 1, the vector contains process ID, the start and end time of the network connection, up/down flow, source/destination IP address, protocol type, source/destination port number. Usually user's information is collected by virus or Trojan and then sent to a specific address. Therefore, the up flow is much more than down flow. So we should monitor the up/down flow. The mobile phones infected by botnet are often connected to the network at a fixed period of time every day, so we need to monitor the start and end time. In particular, the malware usually connects with external via port, so monitoring the port and IP address is also a part of the module.

Data obtaining is divided into two stages. At first, we collect the training data and push them to Cloud storage by tagging with 0(normal) or 1(abnormal). Next, we input the testing data without tag which is directly sent to analyzing module for judgment.

Table 1. The features and the description

Feature	Description
N_PID	Process ID
N_StTime	Start time
N_EdTime	End time
N_UpFlow	Up flow
N_DnFlow	Down flow
N_SIP	Source IP address
N_DIP	Destination IP address
N_Type	Protocol type
N_SPort	Source port number
N_DPort	Destination port number

3.3   Anomaly Analyzing Module

The module includes data preprocessing, anomaly detection engine and report generator.

Data Preprocessing. Preprocessing is mainly about data clearing, transforming and pressing [14]. The validity of data must be ensured before using Bayes classifier for judging. In this system, data clearing and Standardization should be down.

Anomaly Detection Engine. The engine includes two patterns: training pattern and testing pattern. Figure 2 is schematic diagram of this engine. In training pattern, train data is used to train the engine for classifying model with specific parameters. In testing pattern, test data is directly analyzed by the engine.

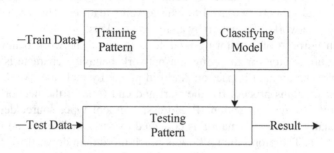

Fig. 2. Principle of Anomaly Detection Engine

The system chooses Bayes classifier in which all the attributes play the potential role, improving the accuracy of the classifier [15]. The principle of Bayes classifier is using the Bayes formula to calculate the posterior probability through prior probability of an object. Then choose the class with maximum posterior probability as the class it belongs to. In this project, we use Naive Bayes.

The classifying process is shown as follows:

(1) Each sample is represented by an n-dimensional vector $X = \{x_1, x_2, \ldots, x_n\}$, describing the n attributes.

(2) Supposing there are m classes. Given an unknown sample data, Naive Bayes distributes the sample to the class with the highest posterior probability. Only if

$$P\left(\frac{C_i}{X}\right) > P\left(\frac{C_j}{X}\right), 1 \le j \le m, j \ne i. \tag{1}$$

(3) The Bayes theorem:

$$P\left(\frac{C_i}{X}\right) = P\left(\frac{X}{C_i}\right)\frac{P(C_i)}{P(X)}, \tag{2}$$

In particular, Naive Bayes has an assumption that each attribute has no relation with each other. Besides, $P(X)$ is a constant for all classes.

(4) Get the maximum:

$$\text{max}=P\left(\frac{X}{C_i}\right)P(C_i).\tag{3}$$

Given the conditions:

$$P\left(\frac{X}{C_i}\right)=\prod_{j=1}^{n}P(\frac{x_j}{C_i})\tag{4}$$

and

$$P(\frac{x_j}{C_i})=\frac{1+n_{ij}}{|V|+n_i}\tag{5}$$

n_{ij} refers to the occurrence number of features . $|V|$ refers to the feature dimens - ion of samples.

Analysis Process of network behavior features by Anomaly Detection Engine.
The anomaly detection engine is divided into training and testing stages. The steps are as follows:

(1) Extract network behavior vectors. We extract network behavior data s_i by the monitoring module which is following extracting vectors automatically. The vector contains ten features such as x = (N_PID, N_StTime, N_EdTime, N_UpFlow, N_DnFlow, N_SIP, N_DIP, N_Type ,N_SPort, N_DPort).

(2) Mark the candidate samples. Each sample is marked by $m_1 = 1$ or $m_2 = 0$. So they are composed of the feature vectors and class variables, just like (X, m_1) and (X, m_2).

(3) Construct the training sample set. We randomly select the normal and abnormal sample to construct data set as following: $D = \{(\vec{x_1}, m_1), (\vec{x_2}, m_2), ..., (\vec{x_{m-1}}, m_1), (\vec{x_m}, m_2)\}, m_1 = 1, m_2 = 0.$

(4) Build the classify model through training, namely, to determine the model parameters.

(5) Extract feature vectors from testing data.

(6) Judge the abnormal network behavior through the classify model ($M = 1$ means abnormal and $M = 0$ means normal).

We now can decide whether the behavior is abnormal using this model. In addition, a monitor report may be generated for further protection of users' mobile security.

3.4   The Storage Module

In this module, we consider what information should be stored and the storage means.

Cloud Storage. Because of the limitation of mobile terminals and the large number of data, the Cloud Storage Server is necessary. It stores the previous or current training data for next training process. As we all know, the storage capacity of cloud is very strong, so that we do not have to worry about the problem of storage. Also, the information in server can be used by other Android mobile phones which have installed in our system.

Local Storage. The Local Network Information Database stores the data recently used in order to promote the efficiency. Local storage has many advantages. The biggest one is for post analysis based on which we can conduct a better texting operation. Compared with the cloud storage, local storage is built on the host being detected. So the data acquisition time is shorter and obviously has a higher efficiency. Similarly, the concerned problem is what information should be storage. Here, we had better choose the information related to testing below, The benefits of doing this is to save local resources.

4   The Experimental and Result

Because of smartphones' mobile nature and the convenient Internet environment, malware is more inclined to attack through network partly. At this point, the network behavior-based detection method highlights its advantages. We create a vector to accurately reflect the network behavior while software is running. What's next, an experiment will be carried out to verify the system's efficiency and accuracy.

4.1   The Experimental Platform

This experimental chooses Samsung I9100G mobile phone as the test platform, which mainly test the monitoring system. The configuration parameters are as shown in Table 2.

Table 2. The configuration parameters of Samsung I9100G mobile phone

Content	Parameter
Hardware	Mali-400MP, 1G Memory
OS	Android 2.3.5
Kernel version	kernel 2.6.35
Network Model	GSM, WCDMA

4.2   Result and Analysis

Firstly, we need to construct a test data set. Zhou Yajin and Jiang Xuxian [16] et al. have done some work. They collected 1260 malwares and divided them into 49 families. We selected 25 families from them (the ones need to connect network) and 25 normal software (shown in Table 3) in Android Market.

The experiments were divided into 5 groups. Each group has 5 normal and 5 malicious applications. Then the system is installed on the testing mobile phone. Once there is a network connection, the system automatically starts the monitoring module and extracts the features vector in real time.

Table 3. The List of Normal Software

ID	Name	Class
1	QQ	Communication
2	WeiXin	Communication
3	WeiBo	Social
4	BaiDu Map	Travel & Local
5	ZhiFuBao	Shopping
6	MoJi Weather	Weather
7	Fruit Slice	Arcade and Action
8	BaiduInput	Tools
9	Google Translate	Tools
10	Chrome Browser	Communication
11	YouDao Dictionary	Books & Reference
12	TTPod	Music & Audio
13	Adobe Reader	Productivity
14	Instagram	Social
15	WanDouJia	Tools
16	BaiDu Cloud	Productivity
17	Google Search	Tools
18	GongShangYinHang for Mobile	Finance
19	Youku-Movie,TV,cartoon,Music	Media & Video
20	YiXin	Social
21	KINGSOFT	Tools
22	TED	Education
23	Netease News	News & Magazines
24	UC Browser	Tools
25	Maps	Travel & Local

Next, we analyze and evaluate the experimental result according to the false negative rate (FNR) , false positive rate (FPR) and accuracy rate (ACC). Besides, we need another four merits, namely, true positive (TP, the number of malware samples detected correctly), false negative (FN, the number of malware samples detected incorrectly), false positive (FP, the number of benign samples detected incorrectly) and true negative (TN, the number of benign samples detected correctly). And, the calculation formula is as follows:

$$FPR = \frac{FP}{FP + TN} \tag{6}$$

$$FNR = \frac{FN}{TP + FN} \tag{7}$$

$$ACC = \frac{TP + TN}{TP + FN + FP + TN} \tag{8}$$

The experiment results are shown in Table 4.

Table 4. The Test Results of Experimental Samples

Group Number	TP	FN	FP	TN	ACC	FPR	FNR
1	3	2	0	5	80%	0	40%
2	4	1	2	3	70%	40%	20%
3	3	2	1	4	70%	20%	40%
4	5	0	1	4	90%	20%	0
5	4	1	1	4	80%	20%	20%

The experimental results show that the detection system can detect the malwares to a certain extent, but it is not particularly desirable. We provide some possible reasons through analyzing. The reason for false negatives is that the server linked by malwares may be invalid, so the malwares cannot conduct network communication. And the reason for false positives is that the training data set is too small, which needs upgrade and expansion in order to reduce the false positive rate. After all, the assumption of Naive Bayes that each attribute has no relation to each other also affects the accuracy.

Performances are analized after the experiment, including cpu usage, free memory and battery power. The Figure 3 shows the comparation of the mobile phone performance before and after the framework. Cpu usage is the average cpu usage without user operation. Free memory means the amount of free memory under the same condition. Battery power means the average power consumption in each hour under the same condition.

The blue bars represent resources before the experiment, and the red bars represent resources after the experiment. We can see from the figure that effects of this system on consumption of resources and the user experience is not so serious. And from this point of view, the system is feasible.

For the further work, we will improve the system. Due to the complexity of malware behaviors, we should collect more network features from emerging malwares to enrich the data set, which aims at optimizing FNR and FPR. Besides, we will adjust the Bayes classifier parameters through repeating tests to achieve the best classification results.

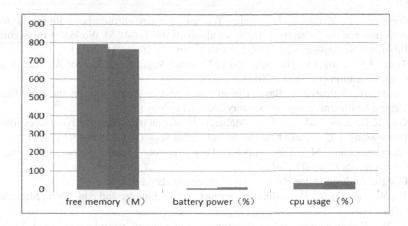

Fig. 3. Resources of the Testing Phone

5   Conclusions

Attacks aimed at Android systems become more sophisticated. The emergence of APT has intensified the threat of the smartphone. More and more convenient Internet environment leaves gaps for attackers. Based on an in-depth analysis of the characteristics of malware, we proposed the network behavior-based detection system which can effectively detect malwares. The work may be a good guide for malware detecting study on Android.

References

1. Net Qin released the 2013 global mobile phone safety report,
   http://finance.chinanews.com/it/2014/02-26/5885596.shtml
2. 2013ISC Experts Detailed: current status and future of network security,
   http://soft.yesky.com/398/35354398.shtml
3. Li, Y., Zhai, L., Wang, Z., Ren, Y.: Control Method of Twitter-and SMS-Based Mobile Botnet. In: Yuan, Y., Wu, X., Lu, Y. (eds.) ISCTCS 2012. CCIS, vol. 320, pp. 644–650. Springer, Heidelberg (2013)
4. Zhai, L.D., Li, Y.: APT Threat Detection and Protection of Network Space. J. Netinfo Security (3), 56–60 (2013)
5. Yi, L.L., Zhang, N., Liu, D.: Current Situation and Development Trend of Mobile Malware. J. Information and Communications Technologies (2), 75–79 (2013)
6. Liu, J.R., Wang, W.J., Liu, B.X.: A Trojan horse detection model based on network behavior analysis. In: The 16th National Conference on Nuclear Electronics and Nuclear Detection Technology Academic Annual Meeting, Mianyang, Sichuan (2012)
7. Dai, S., Liu, Y., Wang, T.: Behavior-based malware detection on mobile phone. In: 2010 6th International Conference on Wireless Communications Networking and Mobile Computing (WiCOM), pp. 1–4. IEEE (2010)

8. Burguera, I., Zurutuza, U., Nadjm-Tehrani, S.: Crowdroid: behavior-based malware detection system for android. In: Proceedings of the 1st ACM Workshop on Security and Privacy in Smartphones and Mobile Devices, pp. 15–26. ACM (2011)
9. Tong, Z.F., Yang, G.: The Detection of Malware Static Behaviors for Android. J. Jiangsu Communication (1), 39–47 (2011)
10. Zhong, W.: Research on Bayes Classification and its Application in Intrusion Detection. Central South University of Forestory and Technology (2008)
11. Cai, Z.T., Jiang, M.: Android Malware Detection of Using Naive Bayes Based on Permissions. J. Computer Knowledge and Technology (14), 3288–3291 (2013)
12. Chandramohan, M., Tan, H.B.K.: Detection of Mobile Malware in the Wild. Computer 45(9), 65–71 (2012)
13. Google. Android Home Page, http://www.android.com
14. Jia, W., Han, M.K.: Data Mining Concepts and Technique, 2nd edn. China Machine Press (2006)
15. Li, W.: The advantages and disadvantages of the commonly used classifiers. J. Technology Trend. (3), 59 (2009)
16. Zhou, Y.J., Jiang, X.X.: Dissecting Android Malware: Characterization and Evolution. In: 2012 IEEE Symposium on Security and Privacy (SP), San Francisco, CA, May 20-23 (2012)

Detection and Defense Technology
of Blackhole Attacks in Wireless Sensor Network

Huisheng Gao[1], Ruping Wu[1,2], Mingjing Cao[1,2], and Can Zhang[1,2]

[1] North China Electric Power University, Baoding 071000, China
[2] National Engineering Laboratory for Information Security Technologies,
Institute of Information Engineering, Chinese Academy of Sciences, Beijing 100093, China

Abstract. The blackhole attack is a typical kind of attack in wireless sensor network (WSN), consisting two types, namely passive attacks and active attacks, of which the latter can cause greater threat. In this paper, considering the principles and characteristics of the active blackhole attacks, an effective approach that can detect and defense active blackhole attacks is presented by improving the AODV routing protocol combining flow analysis. NS2 simulation results confirm the effectiveness of this method.

Keywords: WSN, Blackhole Attack, AODV Protocol, Flow Analysis, NS2 Simulation.

1   Introduction

Wireless sensor network（WSN）which is a new form of wireless network has a quick development and bright look in many application scenarios [1]. WSN technology is the combination of sensor technology, embedded computing technology, distributed processing and communication technologies. It is capable of real-time monitoring and percepting the targets and collecting the information of the environment through the collaboration of a variety of integrated micro-sensors, then processing and transmitting the information to the destination node. WSN can be widely used in many fields, including national defense, national security, environmental monitoring, traffic management, health care, manufacturing, mining, anti-terrorism disaster field and so on. WSN has become the primary means of obtaining information for Internet of things.

Although WSN brought a lot of convenience to people around the world, the characteristics of WSN can't be ignored. The major characteristics consist of the limited processing power, storage capacity, communication bandwidth, and energy of nodes, concentrated and random distribution of nodes, the openness of deployment environment and propagation medium, and so on. The above characteristics of WSN make it vulnerable to a variety of attacks, including the physical layer, data link layer, network layer, transport layer attacks. Among them, the network layer attacks are typical, which is mainly against the network layer routing. This is because the network routing protocol is quite simple and sensitive to attack. AODV (Ad hoc

X.-h. Sun et al. (Eds.): ICA3PP 2014, Part II, LNCS 8631, pp. 601–610, 2014.

on-demand distance vector routing) [2] protocol which is a source-driven routing protocol is commonly used in WSN. When a node needs to transmit information to other nodes in the network, it must first issue a RREQ (Route Request) packet in the form of multicast if there is no route to the destination node. When the neighboring node receives RREQ packet, it will first figure out whether itself is the target node or not. If yes, then the neighboring node sends a RREP (Route response) packet to the originating node; If not, it will first search the routing table to determine if there is a route to the destination node or not. If yes, it will unicast a RREP packet to the source node, otherwise continue forwarding the RREQ packet to find out. Once the source node receives the RREP packet, will immediately send the data packet along the opposite path of the RREP packet, abandoning all the other RREP packets behind the first arrived RREP packet.

Routing attacks in WSN usually include selective forwarding attacks, blackhole attacks, sybil attacks, wormhole attacks, flooding attacks [3]. Among them, blackhole attacks are serious attacks, belonging to a denial of service attack. Usually, there are two kinds of blackhole attacks: passive blackhole attacks and active blackhole attacks [4]. The later are more damaging to the network than the former. We will detail these two attacks in Section 3.1. The active blackhole attacks can get control of network packets by deceiving the routing protocols, and then discard all the packets, thus accomplishing damage to the WSN. It is hard to avoid the active blackhole attacks in AOVD protocol.

For current WSN is vulnerable to blackhole attacks and its effects are harmful, this paper proposes a method to detect blackhole attacks based on the improved AODV protocol and traffic analysis. This method is mainly for the active blackhole attacks, but also can detect the passive blackhole attacks to a certain extent. The remainder of the paper is organized as follows. Section 2 describes blackhole attacks. Section 3 discusses some of the related works. Section 4 describes the proposed scheme. Section 5 presents the simulation results. Finally, Section 6 concludes our work.

2   Related Work

The different detection methods for the blackhole attack have been proposed. The following are some commonly used detection methods.

SAODV proposed by Zapata M G. [5], ad hoc routing protocol security extensions proposed by Papadimitratos P et al. [6], SEAD proposed by Hu et al. [7], SAR proposed by Yi et al. [8], all these secure routing protocols can provide better routing security, including the resolution of the blackhole problem. The above strategies can be formulated into a kind of security strategy based on the encryption algorithm. However, this kind of algorithm need to add complex encryption / decryption algorithm and corresponding protocols in routing protocols, and a strong collaborative relationship between nodes, which will cost too much.

Shurman M et al. [9] proposed a redundant routing method. The source node must find at least three different routes to the destination, and then unicast ping through these three routes. Malicious node and the destination node reply the ping request to the source node which will check these replies, verify whether the node is safe or malicious nodes. This method can be found a safe route reaching the destination, but the delay is high, and there is no corresponding processing on possible malicious node.

Aad I et al. [10] presented a credit node measurement approach. Each node which saves a credit rating of all the nodes in the network will integrate the information and connection reliability of the non-standard node to select out malicious nodes. If a packet successfully propagated through a path, then the credit of all nodes on this path will increase; otherwise reduce the credibility of all the nodes on this path. The credit of the nodes which are not used will do not change. This approach does not consider a situation that malicious nodes may cooperate to improve the credit, and the initial value of credit and the threshold have no reasonable metrics.

Marti et al. [11] presented two new concepts: Watchdog and Pathrater. This method assumes that the network has a symmetrical bidirectional connectivity. In the network, each node is a watchdog of other nodes. When a node forwards the packet, the watchdog will monitor whether the next node forwards this packet. If the next node does not forward the packet, then it will be considered abnormal nodes. Meanwhile, the watchdog compares each packet with the packets in the buffer. If they match, the packet is considered normal transmission, the corresponding data in the cache will be cleared; otherwise keep the data in the cache until the timeout, and then add the sign of packet abnormal forwarding to the node. If the time exceeds a threshold, the node is considered to be malicious too. This method cannot find intentional misstatements of malicious or abnormal circumstances of normal nodes.

Other methods including downstream neighbor node validation method [12], encryption and hops [13], Replying directly to confirm and heuristics method [14] have their flaws, such as high cost with encryption algorithm and wasting a large amount of network link bandwidth.

Blackhole attack prevention and detection method proposed in this paper is mainly for active black hole attacks, aiming at detecting the blackhole attack before it occurred, thus avoiding the destruction caused by the blackhole node. This method also has some effect for passive black hole attack detection. The following describes the specific method.

3   Black Hole Detection Method

3.1   Blackhole Attack

Blackhole attacker claims itself to be the destination node or the nearest path to the destination node in order to attract traffic. When receiving the coming data packets from other nodes, the blackhole attacker will discard all the packets. A black hole that can absorb packets is then formed, and thus the name: blackhole. As mentioned before , there are two kinds of blackhole attacks: passive blackhole attacks and active blackhole attacks [4].

The passive blackhole attack is that a black hole exists in the network, when all the data packets enter into the black hole, they would not come out. This is because that the blackhole node will discard all the packets passing through it. The attacker forward the routing packets passing through itself while drop all the data packets. The passive blackhole attack only attack the network topology without injection of false messages to the network, so it is a passive routing disruptive attack. Fig. 1 (a) shows a schematic diagram of a passive blackhole attack.

The active blackhole attack is a more devastating attack than the passive blackhole attack. After receiving RREQ (Route Request Packet), the malicious node directly replies RREP (Route Reply Packet) to the source node with claiming that "I have a path with only one jump that can make you reach the destination node". By doing like this, the malicious node can attract more data packets sent from other nodes. The source node is likely to receive the false RREP packet from the active blackhole node earlier than the correct RREP packet. According to the AODV protocol, the source

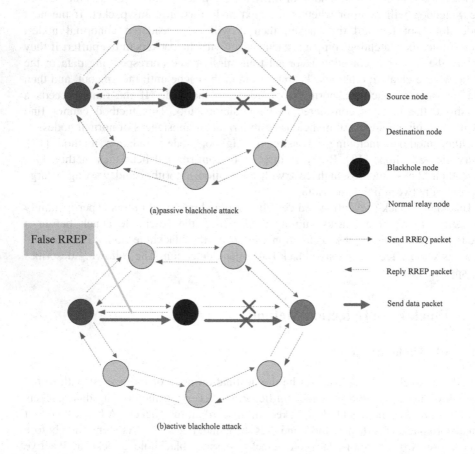

Fig. 1. Diagram of blackhole attacks

node will sent data packets after receiving the first RREP packet, dropping the rest of RREP packets. It is observed that the active blackhole node tampers with the routing information, which disrupts the normal communication and the acquisition of the entire network information, seriously affects the network load. Fig. 1 (b) shows a schematic diagram of an active blackhole attack.

3.2   Blackhole Attack Detection Algorithm

Based on the AODV protocol, we make some improvements. AODV protocol specified, the source node will begin to establish routes and transmit data packets to the destination node after receiving the first RREP packet, the following arrived RREP packets will be abandoned. In this paper, we make some changes to this strategy. By doing some improvement on the AODV protocol, the probability of selecting a route with a blackhole node will be greater reduced. In addition to the above improvement, this paper also introduces the concept of flow analysis. We choose the name mAODV-TA (the modified AODV protocol and Traffic Analysis) for the proposed method, specific information as follows.

When the source node receives the first RREP packet (RREP1), it does not send the packet immediately instead of saving the first received RREP packet. When the second RREP (RREP2) packet arrives, the source node will drop the RREP packets after the second RREP. The two RREP packets both contain information relevant to the neighbor nodes of destination node. As the active black hole attack nodes will falsely claim itself to be the next hop to the destination node in a reply RREP packet to the source node, what's worse, the false RREP sending by malicious node may reach the source node earlier than other nodes, so we cannot directly confirm whether the neighbor nodes are the true and friendly neighbors .It means that the node with next hop to the destination node may be a malicious node. In order to test whether the route contains a black hole or not, this paper will flag the nodes with only one hop to the destination node recording in RREP1 and RREP2 as suspicious. Then the source node will reply a false data packet along the opposite path of RREP1 and RREP2. The false data packet is referred to herein as a probe packet.

Taking into account the characteristics of the blackhole attack, blackhole nodes will directly drop all the data packets sent by source node. Therefore, by sending probe packets, we can discover suspicious nodes whether only have flow input without flow output. If it is, then we can say the suspicious node is a blackhole node. The detection method also has some effect for the passive blackhole detection which is normal in routing process while abnormal in the data transfer process.

The specific process of blackhole detection algorithm is shown in Fig. 2.

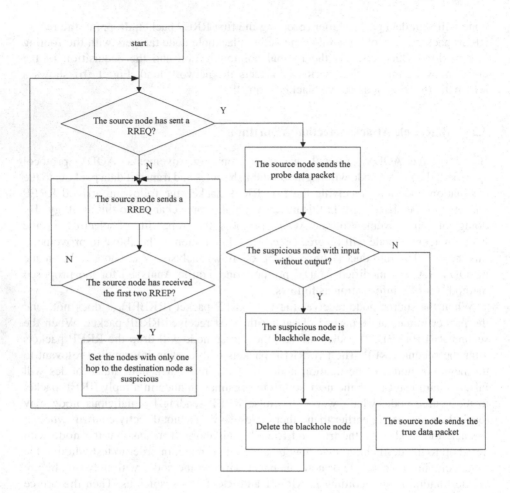

Fig. 2. Flowchart of a blackhole attack detection algorithm

4　Simulation

4.1　Simulation Environment

In order to verify the effectiveness of the proposed scheme, we simulated our proposal using NS2 simulation platform. Our simulation was conducted over a 800m×800m rectangular flat space with randomly distributed sensor nodes. We used constant bit rate (referred to as CBR) traffic source as a communication model. Table 1 presents the simulation environment. The network topology is shown in Fig. 3.

Table 1. Simulation Parameters.

Parameter	Value
Network Area	800m x800m
Number of nodes	50
Node velocity	0
Transmission range	100m
Load size	512Byte
Packet transmission rate	25kbps
The number of Simulation	20

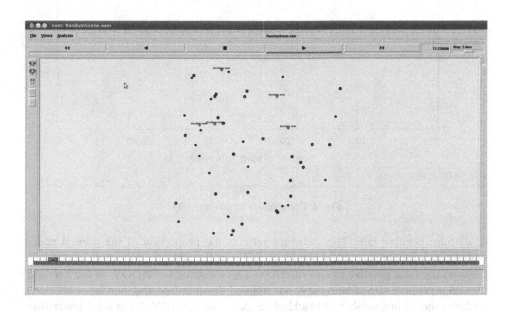

Fig. 3. Network topology

4.2   Simulation Results and Analysis

To compare the performance of mAODV-TA with some related prior work, we chose SAODV [5] as a comparative object. The following two performance indicators was selected to evaluate mAODV-TA .

i) positive rate: This indicator reflects the proportion of the blackhole nodes detected in the all of the blackhole nodes. Fig. 4 shows the positive rate of mAODV-TA compared to SAODV on the average. As shown in the figure below, we can see that mAODV-TA shows very close result to SAODV. It proves that our method is effective. Also, we see that the positive rate increases with the number of blackhole nodes in general. The trends show a decline in a small range. This is because that the network load distribution changed with the number blackhole nodes, thus affecting the routing process.

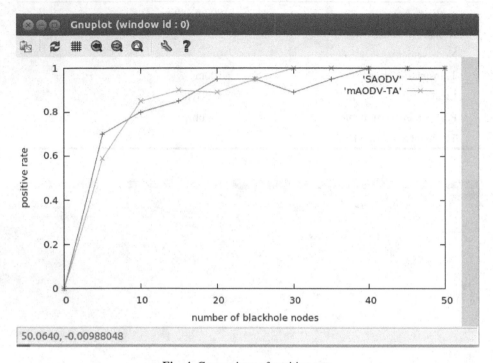

Fig. 4. Comparison of positive rate

ii) false positive rate: This indicator reflects the proportion of the normal nodes which was wrongly accused of blackhole nodes in the all of the blackhole nodes. Fig. 5 shows the false positive rate of mAODV-TA compared to SAODV on the average. The false positive rate of both curve has trended down at first and then level off along with the increasing number of blackhole nodes. The mAODV-TA is a bit lower than SAODV in the aspect of false positive rate. The blackhole detection rate of 100% is not realistic. There are many causes. One reason is that CBR data streams are transmitted in the same frequency in the simulation, thus data congestion tends to conflict resulting in some errors of the detection algorithm.

iii) control overhead: This indicator is an important index to evaluate whether a method practical or not in blackhole detection algorithm. The result of the routing control overhead is shown in Fig.6. The standard AODV is used as a baseline to compare with mAODV-TA and SAODV. As we see, mAODV-TA doesn't change much comparing with the original AODV protocol, while the SAODV shows larger control overhead. So in comparison with SAODV, our method mAODV-TA is more applicable in WSN network with limited energy.

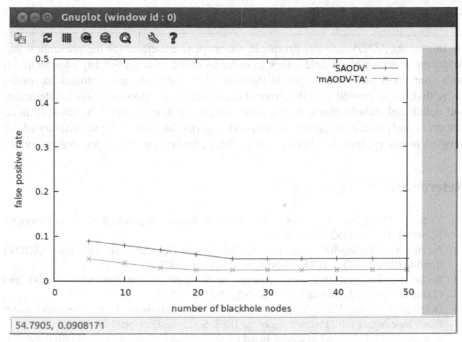

Fig. 5. Comparison of false positive rate

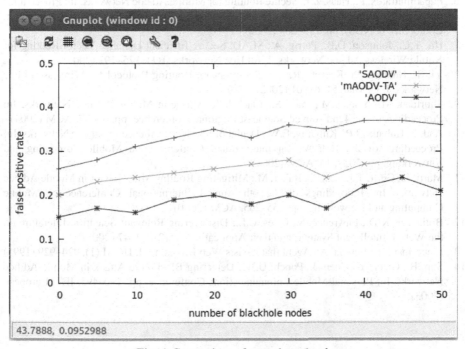

Fig. 6. Comparison of control overhead

5   Conclusion

By improving AODV security protocols, we propose a method for the prevention and detection of active black hole attack in order to reduce the probability of selecting a path containing blackhole nodes in the route discovery process. Simulation results show that the improved AODV protocol combining with flow analysis for detection and defense blackhole attacks is effective. Given the limitations of the network node resources and processing power, limited node energy, as well as the uncertainty of the network topology, there is still room for further optimization for the proposed solution.

References

1. Yick, J., Mukherjee, B., Ghosal, D.: Wireless Sensor Network Survey. J. Computer Networks 52(12), 2292–2330 (2008)
2. Perkins, C., Belding-Royer, E., Das, S.: Ad hoc on Demand Distance Vector (AODV) Routing (RFC 3561). J. IETF MANET Working Group (2003)
3. Karlof, C., Wagner, D.: Secure Routing in Wireless Sensor Networks: Attacks and Countermeasures. J. Ad hoc Networks. 1(2), 293–315 (2003)
4. Dokurer, S., Erten, Y.M., Acar, C.E.: Performance Analysis of Ad-hoc Networks under Black hole Attacks. In: Proceedings of the IEEE SoutheastCon, pp. 148–153 (2007)
5. Zapata, M.G.: Secure Ad hoc on-demand Distance Vector Routing. J. ACM SIGMOBILE Mobile Computing and Communications Review 6(3), 106–107 (2002)
6. Papadimitratos, P., Haas, Z.J.: Secure Routing for Mobile Ad hoc Networks. In: Proceedings of the SCS Commnication Networks and Distributed Systems Modeling and Simulation Conference (CNDS), pp. 193–204 (2002)
7. Hu, Y.C., Johnson, D.B., Perrig, A.: SEAD: Secure Efficient Distance Vector Routing for Nobile Wireless Ad hoc Networks. J. Ad Hoc Networks. 1(1), 175–192 (2003)
8. Yi, S., Naldurg, P., Kravets, R.: A Security-aware Routing Protocol for Wireless Ad hoc Networks. J. Urbana. 51, 61801 (2002)
9. Shurman, M., Yoo, S.M., Park, S.: Black hole Attack in Mobile Ad hoc Networks. In: Proceedings of the 42nd Annual Southeast Regional Conference, pp. 96–97. ACM (2004)
10. Aad, I., Hubaux, J.P., Knightly, E.W.: Denial of Service Resilience in Ad hoc Networks. In: Proceedings of the 10th Annual International Conference on Mobile Computing and Networking, pp. 202–215. ACM (2004)
11. Marti, S., Giuli, T.J., Lai, K., Baker, M.: Mitigating Routing Misbehavior in Mobile Ad hoc Networks. In: Proceedings of the 6th Annual International Conference on Mobile Computing and Networking, pp. 255–265. ACM (2000)
12. Bollacker, K.D., Lawrence, S., Giles, C.L.: Discovering Relevant Scientific Literature on the Web. J. Intelligent Systems and their Applications 15(2), 42–47 (2000)
13. Lieberman, H.: Letizia: An Agent that Assists Web Browsing. J. IJCAI (1), 924–929 (1995)
14. Sun, B., Guan, Y., Chen, J., Pooch, U.W.: Detecting Black-hole Attack in Mobile Ad hoc Networks. In: Personal Mobile Communications Conference, pp. 490–495. IET, European (2003)

An Improved Remote Data Possession Checking Protocol in Cloud Storage

Enguang Zhou and Zhoujun Li

State Key Laboratory of Software Development Environment, Beihang University,
Beijing 100191, China
zhoujun.li@263.net

Abstract. In cloud computing, clients put the large data files on the untrusted cloud storage server, how to ensure the integrity of the outsourced data becomes a big problem.To address this issue, Hao et al. proposed a protocol which supports public verifiability and data dynamics. However, Hao et al.'s protocol suffers from two drawbacks. First, Hao et al.'s protocol is insecure and cannot resist the active adversary. Second, Hao et al.'s protocol only supports fixed-sized blocks as basic unit. As a result, the insertion of short message will cause a considerable waste of storage space. In this paper, we propose an improved remote data integrity checking protocol that can support variable-sized blocks. Besides, the improved protocol can resist the attack of the active adversary, and it is obvious to verify that the improved protocol still preserves the properties of Hao et al.'s protocol such as public verifiability and privacy preserving auditing.

Keywords: cloud storage, data integrity, data security.

1 Introduction

In cloud computing, clients outsource the large data files to the untrusted cloud storage server. As clients no longer possess the local copy of their data, protecting the integrity of outsourced data is important in cloud computing.

Provable data possession (PDP) is a technique for ensuring the integrity of data in outsourced storage services. Ateniese et al. [1] firstly proposed a provable data possession (PDP) model for ensuring possession of files in untrusted remote servers. In their scheme, they utilize RSA-based homomorphic tags for auditing outsourced data without having to download the actual data file. They also presented a dynamic PDP scheme [2] based on symmetric key encryption, however, their scheme does not support block insertions. Hence their scheme does not support fully dynamic data operations. Juels et al. [3] presented proofs of retrievability (POR) model to ensure not only data possession but also retrievability. After that, Sebe et al. [4] proposed a remote data integrity checking protocol. Later, Hao et al. [5] proposed a privacy-preserving remote data integrity checking protocol with data dynamics and public verifiability, which can be considered as an adaptation of Sebe et al.'s protocol.

Erway et al. [6] were the first to propose a dynamic PDP scheme based on the rank-based authenticated skip list (RASL). This scheme was the first PDP

X.-h. Sun et al. (Eds.): ICA3PP 2014, Part II, LNCS 8631, pp. 611–617, 2014.

scheme that can support fully dynamic data operations. Wang et al. [7] proposed a POR scheme based on the Merkle Hash Tree (MHT) [8] that can support public auditing and fully dynamic data operations. Zhu et al. [9] proposed a cooperative Provable data possession (CPDP) scheme which is suitable for a multi-cloud environment. They indicated that CPDP scheme held completeness, knowledge soundness, and zero-knowledge properties. Unfortunately, Wang et al. [10] pointed out that the property of knowledge soundness was not satisfied in Zhu et al.s CPDP scheme, i.e., malicious cloud service provider (CSP) or the malicious organizer can deceive the verifier even if they do not possess clients data. Recently, an efficient dynamic auditing protocol [11] was proposed to support data dynamic operations. Ni et al. [12] pointed out that the protocol in [11] is vulnerable to the attack from the active adversary, i.e., the active adversary can arbitrarily alter the data in the cloud and then is able to generate a valid auditing proof in the auditing process. Liu et al. [13] proposed an authorized dynamic scheme based on BLS signature [14] and ranked Merkle hash tree (RMHT), which can support fine-grained update requests.

Hao et al.'s protocol in [5] supports public verifiability and data dynamics. However, Hao et al.'s protocol suffers from two drawbacks. First, Hao et al.'s protocol in [5] cannot resist the attack launched by an active adversary. Second, in Hao et al.'s protocol, the recommended data block size is 32k bytes. If the client inserts a 140-byte Twitter message, more than 99% of allocated storage is wasted. After many short messages are inserted, huge storage will be wasted. We propose an improved remote data integrity checking protocol that can support variable-sized blocks to resolve above two problems. It is obvious to verify that the improved protocol still preserves the properties of Hao et al.'s protocol such as public verifiability and privacy preserving auditing.

2   Technical Preliminaries

The cloud data storage system involves three different entities: the client, the cloud server, and the third party auditor. The clients store the large data files in the untrusted server. As losing the control over data files, the client needs to verify the integrity of outsourced cloud data without the local copy of data files. The integrity of the data which are stored in the cloud can also be checked by the third party auditor.

Problem Statement. The file F is denoted as m, which is stored in the untrusted server and divided into n blocks of equal lengths. A pseudo-random function $f_K(\cdot)$ is defined as
$$f : \{0,1\}^k \times \{0,1\}^{\log_2(n)} \to \{0,1\}^d,$$
in which k and d are two security parameters.

Homomorphic Verifiable Tags. We explore the concept of a RSA-based homomorphic verifiable tag which is used in Hao et al.'s protocol. $N = pq$ is a public RSA modulus, p and q are two primes. $\{e : e \in Z_n \text{ and } \gcd(e, N) = 1\}$ forms a multiplicative group which is denoted by Z_N^*, Let g be a generator of Z_N^*. Given a message m_i, its RSA-based homomorphic verifiable tag is $T_m = g^{m_i} \bmod N$. Given tags of m_i and m_j denoted by $T_{m_i} = g^{m_i}$ and $T_{m_j} = g^{m_j}$ respectively, anyone can compute a value $T_{m_i+m_j} = T_{m_i} \cdot T_{m_j} = g^{m_i+m_j} \bmod N$, which is corresponding to the messages $m_i + m_j$.

3   On the Security of Hao et al.'s Protocol

In Hao et al.'s protocol, the file m is divided into n blocks $m_1, m_2, \ldots, m_n$. The pseudo-random function $f_K(\cdot)$ is defined as $f : \{0,1\}^k \times \{0,1\}^{\log_2(n)} \to \{0,1\}^d$, in which k and d are two security parameters. Hao et al.'s remote data integrity checking protocol includes the following five functions: **SetUp**, **TagGen**, **Challenge**, **GenProof**, and **CheckProof**.

SetUp$(1^k \to (pk, sk))$. Let $p = 2p' + 1$ and $q = 2q' + 1$ be safe primes, p' and q' are also two primes. Let $N = pq$ be a public RSA modulus. The multiplicative cyclic group QR_N is all the quadratic residues Modulo N. Let g be a generator of QR_N. The public key is $pk = (N, g)$ and the secret key is $sk = (p, q)$.

TagGen$(pk, sk, m) \to \mathcal{D}_m$. For each file block m_i, $i \in [1, n]$, the block tag $D_i = (g^{m_i}) \bmod N$ is calculated by the client. Let $\mathcal{D}_m = \{D_1, D_2, \ldots, D_n\}$, and $\mathcal{D}_m$ is public. After that, the file m is send to the server.

Challenge$(pk, \mathcal{D}_m) \to$ chal. The verifier picks a random group element $s \in Z_n \backslash \{0\}$ and calculates $g_s = g^s \bmod N$. The verifier chooses a random number $r \in [1, 2^k - 1]$ and then sends chal=$< r, g_s >$ to the server.

GenProof$(pk, \mathcal{D}_m, m, \text{chal}) \to R$. After receiving chal=$< r, g_s >$, the server generates a sequence of block indexes $a_1, a_2, \ldots, a_n$ by calling $f_r(i)$ for $i \in [1, n]$ iteratively. Then, the server calculates $R = (g_s)^{\sum_{i=1}^{n} a_i m_i} \bmod N$, and sends the proof R to the verifier.

CheckProof$(pk, \mathcal{D}_m, R, \text{chal}) \to \{\text{success}, \text{failure}\}$. After receiving R , the verifier generates the block indexes $a_1, a_2, \ldots, a_n$ by calling $f_r(i)$ for $i \in [1, n]$, which is the same as the server does in the **GenProof** function. Then the verifier calculates $P = \prod_{i=1}^{n} (D_i^{a_i} \bmod N) \bmod N$ and $R' = P^s \bmod N$. After that the verifier checks whether $R = R'$ is satisfied. If $R = R'$, the verifier outputs "success", otherwise the verifier outputs "failure".

Attack 1: In the **Challenge** step, the client sends a challenge chal=$< r, g_s >$ to the server. An active adversary intercepts the message chal=$< r, g_s >$, and computes a sequence of block indexes $a_1, a_2, \ldots, a_n$ by calling $f_r(i)$ for $i \in [1, n]$ iteratively. Then, the active adversary challenges the server for n times, i.e., the active adversary sends $< r_i, g_s >$ $(i \in [1, n])$ to the server, and receives n valid proofs $R_i = (g_s)^{\sum_{j=1}^{n} a_{ij} m_j} \bmod N$ $(i \in [1, n])$ from the server, where the block indexes $a_{i1}, a_{i2}, \ldots, a_{in}$ are computed by calling $f_{r_i}(j)$ for $j \in [1, n]$ iteratively. Let det$[\cdot]$ be the determinant of a matrix. If

$$\det \begin{bmatrix} a_{11} & a_{12} & \cdots & a_{1n} \\ a_{21} & a_{22} & \cdots & a_{2n} \\ \vdots & \vdots & \vdots & \vdots \\ a_{n1} & a_{n2} & \cdots & a_{nn} \end{bmatrix} \neq 0$$

there exists n integer $\{k_1, k_2, \ldots, k_n\}$, which are not all zero, such that the equation $\begin{pmatrix} a_1 \\ a_2 \\ \vdots \\ a_n \end{pmatrix} = k_1 \begin{pmatrix} a_{11} \\ a_{12} \\ \vdots \\ a_{1n} \end{pmatrix} + \cdots + k_n \begin{pmatrix} a_{n1} \\ a_{n2} \\ \vdots \\ a_{nn} \end{pmatrix}$ is satisfied. The active adversary can compute $R = R_1^{k_1} \cdot R_2^{k_2} \cdots R_n^{k_n}$ and R is the valid proof for the challenge chal$=< r, g_s >$. At last, the active adversary forges a valid proof without possessing the data.

Attack 2: Assume the active adversary modifies data block $m_i^* = m_i + l_i$ for $i \in [1, n]$ and saves the values l_i. In the auditing process, the verifier sends a challenge chal$=< r, g_s >$ to the server. Then the server calculates $R^* = (g_s)^{\sum_{i=1}^n a_i(m_i + l_i)} \bmod N = ((g_s)^{\sum_{i=1}^n a_i m_i} \cdot (g_s)^{\sum_{i=1}^n a_i l_i}) \bmod N = (R \cdot (g_s)^{\sum_{i=1}^n a_i l_i}) \bmod N$ and sends R^* to the verifier. The adversary replaces R^* with $R = (R^*/(g_s)^{\sum_{i=1}^n a_i l_i}) \bmod N = (g_s)^{\sum_{i=1}^n a_i m_i} \bmod N$. Since R is a valid proof, the adversary successfully deceives the verifier and the data owner. This attack is similar to the one in [12]. Ni et al. employed a digital signature scheme to resist the attack of the active adversary, however, we use cryptographic hash function to remedy the weakness, which is more efficient.

4   The Improved Protocol

We improve Hao et al.'s dynamic auditing protocol in this section. We apply the strategy in [13] to support variable-sized blocks. The file m is segmented into $m = \{m_{ij}\}$, $i \in [1, n], j \in [1, l_i], l_i \in [1, l_{\max}]$. Specifically, the number of segments per block will not be more than $l_{\max}$. In other words, the file m includes n data blocks, where the i-th block owns l_i segments. For a block, every segment has the same size.

SetUp($1^k \to (pk, sk)$). Let $p = 2p' + 1$ and $q = 2q' + 1$ be safe primes, p' and q' are also two primes. Let $N = pq$ be a public RSA modulus. The multiplicative cyclic group QR_N is all the quadratic residues Modulo N. Let H be a cryptographic hash function. Let $g_1, g_2, \ldots, g_{l_{\max}}$ be generators of QR_N. The public key is $pk = (N, g_1, g_2, \ldots, g_{l_{\max}})$ and the secret key is $sk = (p, q)$.

TagGen(pk, sk, m) $\to \mathcal{D}_m$. For each file block m_i, $i \in [1, n]$, the block tag $D_i = (g_1^{m_{i1}} \cdot g_2^{m_{i2}} \cdots g_{l_i}^{m_{il_i}}) \bmod N$ is calculated by the client, in which l_i is the number of segments of block m_i. Let $\mathcal{D}_m = \{D_1, D_2, \ldots, D_n\}$, and $\mathcal{D}_m$ is public. After that, the file m is sent to the server.

Challenge($pk, \mathcal{D}_m$) $\to$ chal. The verifier picks a random group element $s \in Z_n \backslash \{0\}$ and calculates $\{\lambda_1 = g_1^s, \lambda_2 = g_2^s, \ldots, \lambda_{l_{\max}} = g_{l_{\max}}^s\}$. The verifier chooses a random number $r \in [1, 2^k - 1]$ and then sends chal$=< r, \lambda_1, \lambda_2, \ldots, \lambda_{l_{\max}} >$ to the server.

GenProof($pk, \mathcal{D}_m, m$, chal) $\to$ R. After receiving chal$=<$ $r, \lambda_1, \lambda_2, \ldots, \lambda_{l_{\max}}$ $>$, the server computes a sequence of block indexes $a_1, a_2, \ldots, a_n$ by calling $f_r(i)$ for $i \in [1, n]$ iteratively. Then, the server calculates $R = H(\lambda_1^{\sum_{i=1}^n a_i \cdot m_{i1}} \cdot \lambda_2^{\sum_{i=1}^n a_i \cdot m_{i2}} \cdots \lambda_{l_{\max}}^{\sum_{i=1}^n a_i \cdot m_{i\lambda_{\max}}} \bmod N)$. If $k > l_i$, let $m_{ik} = 0$. Finally, the server sends the proof R to the verifier.

CheckProof$(pk, \mathcal{D}_m, R, \text{chal}) \rightarrow \{\text{success}, \text{failure}\}$. After receiving R, the verifier generates the block indexes $a_1, a_2, \ldots, a_n$ by calling $f_r(i)$ for $i \in [1, n]$, which is the same as the server does in the GenProof function. Then the verifier calculates P and R' as follows:

$$P = \prod_{i=1}^{n} (D_i^{a_i} \bmod N) \bmod N, R' = H(P^s \bmod N).$$

After that the verifier checks whether $R = R'$ is satisfied. If $R = R'$, the verifier outputs "success", otherwise the verifier outputs "failure".

In the improved protocol, the adversary cannot forge a valid proof due to the properties of the cryptography hash functions, thus, the improved protocol can resist the attack of the active adversary. Besides, all the merits of the original protocol are still preserved.

Data Dynamics. Dynamic data operations (including block modification, block insertion and block deletion) are the same as those of Hao et al.'s dynamic auditing protocol. Therefore, due to space limitation, the detailed description is omitted here.

Correctness. In the improved protocol, as long as both the client and the server honestly execute the protocol, the server can pass the auditing verification. The correctness analysis of the improved protocol can be given by the following theorem:

Theorem 1.If the client and the server honestly execute the protocol, then the server can pass the auditing verification successfully.

If all the data blocks are being correctly stored at the server, we can prove that $R = R'$.

$$
\begin{aligned}
R &= H(\lambda_1^{\sum_{i=1}^{n} a_i \cdot m_{i1}} \cdot \lambda_2^{\sum_{i=1}^{n} a_i \cdot m_{i2}} \cdots \lambda_{l_{\max}}^{\sum_{i=1}^{n} a_i \cdot m_{i\lambda_{\max}}} \bmod N) \\
&= H((g_1^{\sum_{i=1}^{n} a_i \cdot m_{i1}} \cdot g_2^{\sum_{i=1}^{n} a_i \cdot m_{i2}} \cdots g_{l_{\max}}^{\sum_{i=1}^{n} a_i \cdot m_{i\lambda_{\max}}})^s \bmod N) \\
&= H((\prod_{i=1}^{n} g_1^{m_{i1}} g_2^{m_{i2}}, \ldots g_{l_{\max}}^{m_{il_{\max}}})^{a_i \cdot s} \bmod N) \\
&= H((\prod_{i=1}^{n} D_i^{a_i} \bmod N)^s \bmod N) \\
&= H(P^s \bmod N) \\
&= R'
\end{aligned}
$$

5 Performance and Security Analysis

5.1 Security Analysis

We need to prove that the server cannot generate valid proof unless the server possesses the data. In the improved protocol, the security model is the same as those in [5], the details of security proof are highly similar to [5]. Therefore, the detailed security proof is omitted here.

5.2 Communication and Computation

In this section, we analyze the computation and communication costs of the improved scheme. Because algebraic operations and simple modular arithmetic

616   E. Zhou and Z. Li

operations run fast enough [15], the computation cost of those two operations is neglected. The computation cost of an exponent operation is denoted by $\|E\|$. Table 1 presents the comparisons of computation overhead between the improved protocol and Hao et al.'s protocol.

We use $|N|$ to denote the length of N in bits. In Hao et al.'s protocol, the total communication cost (in the Challenge and GenProof steps) is $k + 2|N|$ bits. In the improved protocol, the verifier sends $\{r, \lambda_1, \lambda_2, \ldots, \lambda_{l_{max}}\}$ to the server, then the server sends the proof R to the verifier, the total communication cost is $2k + \lambda_{l_{max}}|N|$ bits.

Table 1. Comparisons between the improved protocol and Hao et al.'s protocol

	The improved protocol	Hao et al.'s protocol
TagGen	$\sum_{i=1}^{n} l_i \|E\|$	$n \|E\|$
Challenge	$l_{max} \|E\|$	$\|E\|$
GenProof	$l_{max} \|E\|$	$\|E\|$
CheckProof	$(n+1) \|E\|$	$(n+1) \|E\|$

6   Conclusion

In this paper, we pointed out the security flaw of Hao et al.s protocol. We propose an improved remote data integrity checking protocol that can support variable-sized blocks. The improved protocol still preserves the properties of the original protocol.

Acknowledgments. This work was supported by the Specialized Research Fund for the Doctoral Program of Higher Education of China (20111102130003).

References

1. Ateniese, G., Burns, R., Curtmola, R., Herring, J., Kissner, L., Peterson, Z., Song, D.: Provable Data Possession at Untrusted Stores. In: 14th ACM Conference Computer and Communications Security, pp. 598–609. ACM Press, Alexandria (2007)
2. Ateniese, G., Pietro, R.D., Mancini, L.V., Tsudik, G.: Scalable and efficient provable data possession. In: 4th International Conference on Security and Privacy in Communication Networks, SecureComm 2008, pp. 1–10. ACM Press, Istanbul (2008)
3. Juels, A., Burton, J., Kaliski, S.: PORs: Proofs of retrievability for large files. In: 14th ACM Conference Computer and Communications Security, pp. 584–597. ACM Press, Alexandria (2007)
4. Sebe, F., Domingo-Ferrer, J., Martinez-Balleste, A., Deswarte, Y., Quisquater, J.-J.: Efficient Remote Data Possession Checking in Critical Information Infrastructures. IEEE Transactions on Knowledge and Data Engineering 20(8), 1034–1038 (2008)

5. Zhuo, H., Sheng, Z., Nenghai, Y.: A Privacy-Preserving Remote Data Integrity Checking Protocol with Data Dynamics and Public Verifiability. IEEE Transactions on Knowledge and Data Engineering 23(9), 1432–1437 (2011)
6. Erway, C.C., Kupcu, A., Papamanthou, C., Tamassia, R.: Dynamic provable data possession. In: 16th ACM Conference Computer and Communications Security, CCS 2009, pp. 213–222. ACM Press, Chicago (2009)
7. Wang, Q., Wang, C., Ren, K., Lou, W., Li, J.: Enabling public auditability and data dynamics for storage security in cloud computing. IEEE Transactions on Parallel and Distributed Systems 22(5), 847–859 (2011)
8. Merkle, R.C.: A Digital Signature Based on a Conventional Encryption Function. In: Pomerance, C. (ed.) CRYPTO 1987. LNCS, vol. 293, pp. 369–378. Springer, Heidelberg (1988)
9. Zhu, Y., Hu, H., Ahn, G.J., Yu, M.: Cooperative Provable Data Possession for Integrity Verification in MultiCloud Storage. IEEE Transactions Parallel and Distributed Systems 23(12), 2231–2244 (2012)
10. Wang, H., Zhang, Y.: On the Knowledge Soundness of a Cooperative Provable Data Possession Scheme in Multicloud Storage. IEEE Transactions Parallel and Distributed Systems 25(1), 264–267 (2014)
11. Yang, K., Jia, X.: An efficient and secure dynamic auditing protocol for data storage in cloud computing. IEEE Transactions on Parallel and Distributed Systems 24(9), 1717–1726 (2013)
12. Ni, J., Yu, Y., Mu, Y., Xia, Q.: On the Security of an Efficient Dynamic Auditing Protocol in Cloud Storage. IEEE Transactions on Parallel and Distributed Systems, doi:10.1109/TPDS.2013.199
13. Liu, C., Chen, J., Yang, L., Zhang, X., Yang, C., Ranjan, R., Ramamohanarao, K.: Authorized Public Auditing of Dynamic Big Data Storage on Cloud with Efficient Verifiable Fine-grained Updates. IEEE Transactions on Parallel and Distributed Systems, doi:10.1109/TPDS.2013.191
14. Boneh, D., Lynn, B., Shacham, H.: Short Signatures from the Weil Pairing. In: Boyd, C. (ed.) ASIACRYPT 2001. LNCS, vol. 2248, pp. 514–532. Springer, Heidelberg (2001)
15. Barreto, P.S.L.M., Galbraith, S.D., O' hEigeartaigh, C., Scott, M.: Efficient pairing computation on supersingular abelian varieties. Designs, Codes and Cryptography 42(3), 239–271 (2007)

Fault Localization of Concurrency Bugs
and Its Application in Web Security

Zhenyuan Jiang[1,2]

[1] State Key Laboratory of Software Development Environment,
Beihang University, Beijing, China
[2] School of Computer Science and Engineering, Beihang University, Beijing, China
jiangzy@nlsde.buaa.edu.cn

Abstract. Concurrent testing is of great importance to web security. This paper presents a new automated edge-labeled communication graph based locating technique, called LUCON, to find buggy memory access pair and to present buggy pattern and to build bug triggering scenario. In LUCON, the buggy pattern gives the essence of the bug and the bug triggering scenario shows how the bug happens. LUCON can discover significant types of concurrency bugs, including order violations and both single-variable and multi-variable atomicity violations. Experimental results prove that LUCON can locate concurrency bugs in real client/server applications such as Mysql and Apache accurately and provide bug reports to help programmer understand the bug.

Keywords: Concurrency Bug, Order Violation, Atomicity Violation.

1 Introduction

As more and more vital data is stored in web applications and the number of transactions on the web increases, web security testing is becoming very important. On the other hand, Concurrency is the main feature of the network environment, its widely used in web applications, real client/server applications, web security protocols, etc. Naturally concurrency bugs have caused many web security issues, such that concurrent testing is an important aspect of web security testing.

Concurrency bugs are difficult to expose and locate because they only occur in rare particular interleavings of memory-access sequences. The non-deterministic behavior of concurrent programs makes it hard to find these particular interleavings [1]. To monitor and investigate all memory accesses is practically impossible since concurrent programs can have potentially astronomically large number of thread interleavings, and since there exists complicated interactions among multiple threads in the manifestation of concurrency bugs, its also hard to understand concurrency bugs.

A variety of fault locating techniques for concurrent programs have been proposed. In early work researchers have focused on finding those involving a single shared variable, these techniques detects data races [2,3], order violations [4] and single variable atomicity violations [5,6]. Although these techniques can successfully find bugs, they can only locate concurrency bugs involving a single variable. Some techniques find multi-variable atomicity violations [7,8], but cannot find some important classes of

X.-h. Sun et al. (Eds.): ICA3PP 2014, Part II, LNCS 8631, pp. 618–630, 2014.

single-variable concurrency bugs, such as order violations. Other techniques report the existence of concurrency bugs involving both single variable and multiple variables [9,10]. However, these techniques cannot provide enough information for programmers to well understand and fix the bug.

Besides the above mentioned techniques, we are particularly interested in Recon, which can locate concurrency bugs involving both single and multiple variables and presents the short fragments of buggy execution schedules that illustrate how and why bugs happened [11]. However, the results provided by Recon are still not enough for programmers to well understand the bugs. For example, for atomicity violation, which usually involves three or more statements, Recon could only give two of them. Actually, the missing statements are also necessary to understand the bugs. In addition, due to the difference of execution contexts, a concurrency bug may be represented by several different edges in different communication graphs. Recon may rank the buggy edges low, which means programmers have to waste time to check useless information.

In this paper we propose LUCON, our approach is based on communication graph technique to locate and understand concurrency bugs. Specifically, by adding two labels for each edge, we extend a communication graph to an edge-labeled communication graph. One label represents whether the edge is relevant with buggy behavior and the other records the edges runtime information. Based on the edge-labeled communication graph, after given some buggy and non-buggy executions, LUCON proceeds in three steps: locate and rank the buggy memory access pair, find bug patterns that contain the buggy memory access pair, build a bug triggering scenario. The buggy pattern gives the essence of the bug and the bug triggering scenario shows how the bug happens which can help programmers well understand the bugs. We have implemented LUCON based on the Recon tool and Pin [12] for testing C/C++ programs. LUCON can deal with significant types of concurrency bugs, including order violation and both single and multiple variable atomicity violation. We provide some case studies to illustrate the utility of our approach such as the real client/server applications Mysql and Apache. The paper makes the following contributions: (1) The presentation of a new technique that handles important classes of concurrency bugs. (2) Implement LUCON for C/C++ programs, and the result of empirical studies show the effectiveness of LUCON.

2 Background

This section elaborates the background knowledge for our technique. We first introduce the notation we use, and then provide the definitions of the concurrency bug types [13] that we address. The execution result of Recon is illustrated at last.

2.1 Notation

For representation, we denote a memory access [14] to a shared variable by $b_{t,s}(x)$: b is the memory access type, either read(R) or write(W); t is the thread that executes the access; s is the corresponding program statement containing the access; x is the shared variable. For example, $R_{1,s_1}(x)$ represents a read access to shared variable x in statement s_1 of thread 1. And when t_1 is different from t_2, memory access pair $(b_{1t_1,s_1}, b_{2t_2,s_2})$ is usually denoted as (s_1, s_2) in brief.

Table 1 lists problematic memory access patterns [14] that represent the concurrency bugs which are considered in LUCON. For example, the pattern $R_{1,s_1}(x)$-$W_{2,s_2}(x)$ means the read access $R_{1,s_1}(x)$ wrongly occurs before the write access $W_{2,s_2}(x)$. Pattern $R_{1,s_1}(x)$-$W_{2,s_2}(x)$-$R_{1,s_3}(x)$ means two memory read accesses $R_{1,s_1}(x)$ and $R_{1,s_3}(x)$ which should be executed atomically, but are wrongly interrupted by the write access $W_{2,s_2}(x)$. Note that one memory access pattern can always be decomposed into one or two memory access pairs. We will introduce how the pairs are used in bug locating and the usage of patterns in Section 3.

Table 1. Memory access patterns considered in LUCON

PID	Memory Access Pattern	PID	Memory Access Pattern
P1	$R_{1,s_1}(x)$-$W_{2,s_2}(x)$	P9	$W_{1,s_1}(x)$-$W_{2,s_2}(y)$-$W_{2,s_3}(x)$-$W_{1,s_4}(y)$
P2	$W_{1,s_1}(x)$-$R_{2,s_2}(x)$	P10	$W_{1,s_1}(x)$-$W_{2,s_2}(y)$-$W_{1,s_3}(y)$-$W_{2,s_4}(x)$
P3	$W_{1,s_1}(x)$-$W_{2,s_2}(x)$	P11	$W_{1,s_1}(x)$-$R_{2,s_2}(x)$-$R_{2,s_3}(y)$-$W_{1,s_4}(y)$
P4	$R_{1,s_1}(x)$-$W_{2,s_2}(x)$-$R_{1,s_3}(x)$	P12	$W_{1,s_1}(x)$-$R_{2,s_2}(y)$-$R_{2,s_3}(x)$-$W_{1,s_4}(y)$
P5	$W_{1,s_1}(x)$-$W_{2,s_2}(x)$-$R_{1,s_3}(x)$	P13	$R_{1,s_1}(x)$-$W_{2,s_2}(x)$-$W_{2,s_3}(y)$-$R_{1,s_4}(y)$
P6	$W_{1,s_1}(x)$-$R_{2,s_2}(x)$-$W_{1,s_3}(x)$	P14	$R_{1,s_1}(x)$-$W_{2,s_2}(y)$-$W_{2,s_3}(x)$-$R_{1,s_4}(y)$
P7	$R_{1,s_1}(x)$-$W_{2,s_2}(x)$-$W_{1,s_3}(x)$	P15	$R_{1,s_1}(x)$-$W_{2,s_2}(y)$-$R_{1,s_3}(y)$-$W_{2,s_4}(x)$
P8	$W_{1,s_1}(x)$-$W_{2,s_2}(x)$-$W_{2,s_3}(y)$-$W_{1,s_4}(y)$	P16	$W_{1,s_1}(x)$-$R_{2,s_2}(y)$-$W_{1,s_3}(y)$-$R_{2,s_4}(x)$

2.2 Concurrency Bug Type

An order violation happens when two memory accesses in different threads execute in an unexpected order and then leads to unintended program behavior. Patterns for order violation (Patterns P1 to P3) consist of two sequential thread accesses to a shared memory location where at least one of the accesses is a write. For example, Figure 1(a) shows an order violation in Transmission, the read access to shared variable *bandwidth* in thread 2 is expected to be executed later than the write access in thread 1, but actually the read access executes firstly, then the program reads an uninitialized null pointer and crashes later. Here the interleaving $R_{1,s_1}(bandwidth)$-$W_{2,s_2}(bandwidth)$ (Pattern P1) belongs to an order violation.

A single variable atomicity violation happens when two memory accesses involving a single variable which supposed to be executed atomically are interrupted by one memory access in other different threads. Figure 2(a) shows an example of a single variable atomicity violation in Mysql. There are two threads in the program. Thread 1 creates a new file, during which *log_type* is temporarily set to CLOSED at s_1 and is set to the original status at s_3. Thread 2 records a transaction into a log if *log_type* is not a CLOSED status at s_2. The two write accesses to the shared variable *log_type* in thread 1 are expected to be executed atomically, but actually the read access in thread 2 occurs between the two write accesses. s_2 reads a CLOSED status and thread 2 mistakenly misses recording a transaction. Here the interleaving $W_{1,s_1}(log\_type)$-$R_{2,s_2}(log\_type)$-$W_{1,s_3}(log\_type)$ (Pattern P6) is a single variable atomicity violation.

A multi-variable atomicity violation is defined as the desired atomicity among several memory accesses involving multiple variables is violated. Atomicity is often referred to as serializability [8], which is satisfied if the result of a concurrent execution

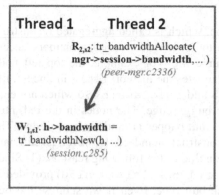

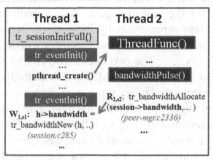

(a) Order violation in Transmission   (b) Bug triggering scenario

Fig. 1. An order violation example

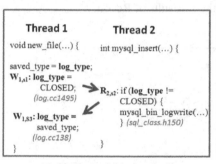

(a) Single-variable involved   (b) Multi-variable involved

Fig. 2. Atomicity violation examples

is the same as that of a serialized execution. Patterns P9 to P16 are unserializable interleaving patterns involving multiple variables. Figure 2(b) shows an example of a multi-variable atomicity violation extracted from simplified version of jsStringLength. There are two shared variables *str* and *len* in program. The two write accesses should be execute atomically to keep the value of *str* and *len* synchronized. For instance, if the value of *str* changed, the program should immediately record the latest length of *str* in *len*. But actually two read accesses to the shared variables occur between the two write accesses. Consequently, the interleaving $W_{1,s_1}(str)$-$R_{2,s_2}(str)$-$R_{2,s_3}(len)$-$W_{1,s_4}(len)$ (Pattern P11) causes $str1$ and $len1$ to become out of sync.

2.3   A Motivating Example

Figure 3 shows the execution result of Recon, which is called aggregated reconstruction, for the bug in Figure 2(a). A node in the reconstruction is an memory access statement represented by its position in source file. For example, the top left node `myopen.c97` means the statement which executes the memory access in line 97, file `myopen.cc`. The two nodes `log.cc1495` and `sqlclass.h150` which are connected by the black bold line constitute the buggy edge. The nodes in the red, blue and purple circles are some memory accesses that happen around the buggy edge. The buggy edge is provided in the aggregated reconstruction indeed. However, its still hard to understand the bug with the result of Recon due to the following reasons: (1) Since there are only two memory accesses (`log.cc1495`, `sqlclass.h150`) provided in the reconstruction. We cannot determine the bug type. Even if we suppose the bug as a single variable atomicity violation, it is very difficult to find the remainder part which is the node `log.cc138` indeed. (2) The aggregated reconstruction mixes the information of several executions without making a distinction. Extracting one concrete execution information from the aggregated reconstruction is impossible. The nodes in reconstruction cannot show useful information about the bug. The programmer cant see the macroscopical bug trigger process from these results of Recon.

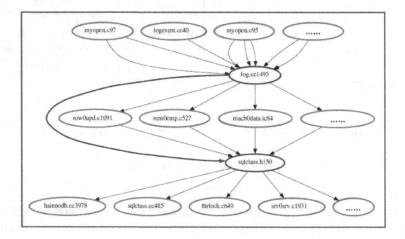

Fig. 3. The result of Recon

3   Methodology

Our method which we call LUCON, is based on communication graph that represents concurrent program execution. LUCON consists of three steps. In Step 1, LUCON inputs a concurrent program P and a test suite T, executes P with T multiple times, and collects some buggy and nonbuggy executions. Calculate the suspiciousness for each memory access pair that appears in the buggy executions. Then rank these pairs by suspiciousness for fault localization. In Step 2, for the top-ranking pairs, LUCON searches for the memory patterns that contain them. In Step 3, by using the information of call stack and thread creation collected during the construction of communication graphs, build bug triggering scenario based on the memory access pattern.

3.1 Locating Buggy Memory Access Pair

In communication graph, nodes represent the memory accesses and edges represent the communications between nodes via shared memory. Edges in the buggy graphs are strongly correlated with the occurrence of buggy behavior. But the lack of runtime information about edges makes it difficult for understanding the bug. Thus we extend the communication graph to an edge-labeled communication graph, which characterizes more properties of communication as follows:

Definition 1. *(Edge-labeled communication graph) An edge-labeled communication graph is a system $G = (V, E, I, F)$, where*
(1) V is a set of nodes and each node $v \in V$ is a tuple (s, ctx), where s is the statement that executes the access and ctx is the execution context of this memory access;
(2) $E \subseteq V \times V$ is a set of edges, each edge $e = (u, v) \in E$ is a communication via a shared memory;
(3) $F : E \rightarrow \{True, False\}$ associates with each edge a truth value to indicate whether its relevant with buggy behavior;
(4) $I : E \rightarrow TS \times T \times B \times TS \times T \times B \times M \times P$ associates with each edge e a tuple, where M is the shared memory, P indicates process pid. For an edge e, $I(e) = (ts_1, t_1, b_1, ts_2, t_2, b_2, m, pid)$ is the runtime information of e, where (ts_1, t_1, b_1) is the execution time, thread id and access type of the source node, (ts_2, t_2, b_2) is the similar information of sink node.

After collecting the buggy and nonbuggy graphs, for each edge e that appears in the buggy executions, we use the method proposed in [11] to counts the edges frequency in the buggy and nonbuggy executions, i.e. $buggyCount[e]$ and $nonbuggyCount[e]$ respectively. These edges compose a set called $edgesInBuggyExecution$. Due to slight difference of the context ctx, there may appear the following situation: One edge is (s_1, ctx_1, s_2, ctx_2) and the other is (s_1, ctx_3, s_2, ctx_4). They appears in different buggy graphs, but correspond to the same buggy behavior, i.e. the buggy communication between memory access s_1 and s_2. Separately calculate their frequency will low their rank, LUCON integrates their frequency to the frequency of their common pair (s_1, s_2). For each edge $e = (s_1, ctx_1, s_2, ctx_2) \in edgesInBuggyEexecution$, the frequency of memory access pair (s_1, s_2) mp is calculated by:

$$freq(mp) = \begin{cases} freq(mp) + buggycount[e], & \text{if } nonbuggycount[e] = 0, \\ freq(mp), & \text{if } nonbuggycount[e] \neq 0. \end{cases} \quad (1)$$

During the integrating process of each mp, when it is updated by an edge e, we associate it with the runtime information $I(e)$ at the same time. At last, for each memory access pair mp LUCON computes the suspiciousness by the following equation:

$$suspiciousness(mp) = \sqrt{freq(mp)^2 + C(mp)^2} \quad (2)$$

$C(mp)$ proposed in [9] is a disparity in communication behavior between buggy and nonbuggy graphs, and then LUCON ranks these memory access pairs in decreasing orderby their suspiciousness.

3.2 Searching Buggy Memory Access Pattern

Concurrency bugs are always depicted in the form of interleaved sequences of operations, i.e. memory access pattern [14] which is called pattern for simplicity in this section. Patterns are important for programmers to well understand concurrency bugs, since they contain all the memory accesses involved and the interleaving orders among these accesses. For the memory access pairs which ranked top, LUCON will search for the possible memory access patterns that contain the pairs.

The problematic memory access patterns that represent the concurrency bugs which are considered in LUCON are listed in Table 1. Given a memory access pair (s_1, s_2) and its runtime information $I(e)$, extracting the access type of (s_1, s_2), LUCON searches the potential patterns that contain (s_1, s_2) in one concrete execution indicated by $I(e)$ by the following steps.

For some memory access pairs, whose one node occurs before main thread creates the first thread, will not cause concurrency bug. These nodes are regarded as deadbeef. In the case of a single shared variable, suppose that the extracted access type is W-R. Firstly we will check whether it is a single variable atomicity violation. If the node contains s_1 is not a deadbeef, the type W-R will be assumed to be a single variable atomicity violation first. Since the type W-R involves in three single variable atomicity violation patterns, LUCON successively searches each of them. For pattern $R_{1,s_1}(x)$-$W_{2,s_2}(x)$-$R_{1,s_3}(x)$, LUCON tries to find the remainder memory access $R_{1,s_1}(x)$ in the following ways: Search from back to front for the latest node occurs before the $W_{2,s_2}(x)$ within the same thread of $R_{1,s_3}(x)$ in one concrete execution, it should be a read access to the shared memory x, and the distance between the two read is in a reasonable range. For the remaining two patterns, LUCON deals with them similarly. After the above searching process, if the remainder memory access cannot be found, the type W-R will be judged as an order violation. And the memory access pattern is just $W_{1,s_1}(x)$-$R_{2,s_2}(x)$.

If the node contains s_1 is a deadbeef, the write access in type W-R is useless. Type W-R will be judged as an order violation with the pattern $R_{1,s_1}(x)$-$W_{2,s_2}(x)$, then LUCON will search for the remainder memory access $W_{2,s_2}(x)$. Nonbuggy executions are used to search for this pattern. Since the read access $R_{1,s_1}(x)$ will cause the program to crash, therefore $W_{2,s_2}(x)$ cannot be found in the buggy executions. Conversely, the nonbuggy edge $W_{2,s_2}(x)$-$R_{1,s_1}(x)$ usually appears in the nonbuggy executions. Then we can search for $W_{2,s_2}(x)$ in the nonbuggy execution with the similar method used while searching atomicity violation patterns.

In the case of multiple variable atomicity violations, suppose that the extracted access type is $W_{1,s_1}(x)$-$R_{2,s_2}(x)$. Since the type W-R involves in six multiple variable atomicity violation patterns, LUCON successively searches each of them. For the first pattern $W_{1,s_1}(x)$-$R_{2,s_2}(x)$-$R_{2,s_3}(y)$-$W_{1,s_4}(y)$, LUCON searches for the access $R_{2,s_3}(y)$ first, according to the following constraints: (1) it should be a read access; (2) it occurs after $R_{2,s_2}(x)$ which can be checked by the timestamp ts; (3) it should belong to the same thread as $R_{2,s_2}(x)$; (4) it should not be too far from $R_{2,s_2}(x)$; After that, LUCON searches for the access $W_{1,s_4}(y)$ according to the following constraints: it should be a write access to the shared memory y, occurs after the $R_{2,s_3}(y)$, belongs to the same thread as $W_{1,s_1}(x)$, it should not be too far from $W_{1,s_1}(x)$. The distance constraints are define as follows: (1) If the two access are in the same function, the distance of code lines should be less than 10; (2) when in different functions, we find the latest function which contains them two, if the max depth of the two nodes from the found function is less than 4, we think this distance is ok. For the remaining five patterns, LUCON searches them in the same way.

3.3 Constructing Bug Triggering Scenario

Memory access pattern gives the essence of the concurrency bug, but it cannot show the detailed bug triggering process. For example, given the memory access pattern in Figure 1(a), it is still difficult for programmers to know how the execution process of thread reaches to the memory access. The thread creation relationship remains unknown either. These two points are important for understanding how the bug happens. For this case, LUCON constructs a bug triggering scenario to help programmers better understand the bugs.

The bug triggering scenario provides call stack information of each memory access in pattern and the creation relationship between threads. The call stack gives the detailed function invoke process from thread start function to the memory access. The thread creation relationship shows whether threads are independent and when the creation happens. LUCON collects these information during the construction of communication graphs. For each thread, every function call and return event is recorded with the timestamp that indicates when the event occurs. According to the timestamp of the memory access, all alive functions from thread start to the current memory access can be found. Simultaneously, the parent thread and the parent threads call stack information when thread creation happens are stored. By recursively searching the parent thread, the relationship between threads can be determined.

From the simplified bug triggering scenario in Figure 1(b), programmers can get the following information. Thread 1 executes to function `tr_sessionInitFull()`, then creates thread 2 by invoking the function `tr_eventInit()` in `tr_sessionIni tFull()`. Thread 2 executes to the read access R_{2,s_2} through several function invokes started from `ThreadFunc()`. After `tr_eventInit()` returns, thread 1 will sequentially execute the write access W_{1,s_1} in function `tr_sessionInitFull()`. But since R_{2,s_2} in the created thread 2 happens before W_{1,s_1} in thread 1, an order violation happened. With the information above, programmers can roughly understand most important events during the bug triggering process.

4 Experiments

There are two components of our evaluation. We show that our ranking technique is effective in finding bugs compared with Recon, the buggy patterns and bug triggering scenario LUCON produces are useful for bug understanding. We implemented LUCON based on Pin [12] and evaluated its ability to detect concurrency bugs using the buggy programs described in Table 2. The first column shows the type of programs in two categories: the bug kernel which are extracted from full versions of Mozilla, the real client/server applications including Transmission, Pbzip2, two versions of Mysql and Apache, which are full applications without any simplification. The second column shows the name of the subject program. The third column lists the size of the program in lines of code. The fourth column shows the type of the concurrency bug.

For the C/C++ extracted programs, we insert sleep primitive into programs to increase the frequency of the bug appearance. For the real client/server programs, we provided inputs to the subjects that can trigger concurrency bugs. Pbzip2 is a compressing tool using bzip2 algorithm with parallel threads. We tested Pbzip2 to compress a large text file with a number of threads. Mysql is the most widely used database application, we concurrently call several queries that can trigger bugs in the database server. We ran all experiments on an 8-core 2.27GHz Intel Xeon with 16GB of memory and Linux 2.6.32. We report results averaged over 10 runs of each experiment.

Table 2. The buggy programs used to evaluate LUCON

Category	Program	LOC	Bug Type
Bug Kernel	httpconnectionw	63	Order Violation
	readwriteproc	60	Order Violation
	BankAcount	136	Single-Variable Atomicity Violation
	jsStringLength	69	Multi-Variable Atomicity Violation
Client/server Application	Transmission	139k	Order Violation
	Pbzip2	2k	Order Violation
	Mysql-3596	415k	Single-Variable Atomicity Violation
	Mysql-791	372k	Single-Variable Atomicity Violation
	Apache	188k	Single-Variable Atomicity Violation

4.1   Effectiveness

Table 3 shows the fault locating result of LUCON and Recon. Experiments of Recon are conducted on the prototype tool provided by the author. For fair comparison to Recon, LUCON collects 25 buggy runs and 25 nonbuggy runs. For all tested programs, LU-CON can handle both single and multiple variable concurrency bugs. LUCON locates the buggy patterns which provide the essence of bugs accurately and ranks all these patterns top.

In contrast, Recon performs not well in some real applications. In some tested programs like Mysql and Apache, the real bugs ranked outside of the top twenty which means that programmers need to check multiple irrelative reconstructions before the real bug. Column 5 and column 7 show the number of edges used in bug locating of LUCON and Recon respectively. The result shows that the number of edges in Recon irrelevant to buggy behavior is rather high in most cases.

Table 3. Results of evaluated programs comparing with Recon

Program	Bug Type	LUCON		Recon	
		Rank	Edges	Rank	Edges
httpconnectionw	$R_{1,s_1}(x)\text{-}W_{2,s_2}(x)$	1	1	2	25
readwriteproc	$W_{1,s_1}(x)\text{-}W_{2,s_2}(x)$	1	1	2	31
Bankaccount	$R_{1,s_1}(x)\text{-}W_{2,s_2}(x)\text{-}W_{1,s_3}(x)$	1	3	24	46
jsStringLength	$W_{1,s_1}(x)\text{-}R_{2,s_2}(x)\text{-}R_{2,s_3}(y)\text{-}W_{1,s_4}(y)$	1	2	1	7
Transmission	$R_{1,s_1}(x)\text{-}W_{2,s_2}(x)$	1	2124	2	4386
Pbzip2	$W_{1,s_1}(x)\text{-}R_{2,s_2}(x)$	1	175	2	484
Mysql-3596	$R_{1,s_1}(x)\text{-}W_{2,s_2}(x)\text{-}R_{1,s_3}(x)$	1	4013	26	5062
Mysql-791	$W_{1,s_1}(x)\text{-}R_{2,s_2}(x)\text{-}W_{1,s_3}(x)$	1	3984	34	5142
Apache	$W_{1,s_1}(x)\text{-}W_{2,s_2}(x)\text{-}R_{1,s_3}(x)$	1	2314	23	3864

4.2 Bug Report

Figure 4 provides the bug report of the bug in Figure 3. There are two components composed the bug report: a summary description of the bug and the bug triggering scenario. The first part (lines 1-6) is the summary description. Line 1 shows that this may be a multi-variable atomicity violation. From line 2 we can get the memory access pattern of the bug is P11: $W_{1,s_1}(x)\text{-}R_{2,s_2}(x)\text{-}R_{2,s_3}(y)\text{-}W_{1,s_4}(y)$. The two shared memories are *str* and *len* which we can know from figure 3. The following four lines give the information about the four accesses contained in this atomicity violation. For example, for the first write access, the position of this access is in line 52 at file `httpconnection.cpp`. The name of the function which executes the access is Activate.

The bug triggering scenario provides call stack information of each memory access in pattern and the creation relationship between threads. The second part (lines 7-9) is the call stack information for the first write access to *str*. It shows that the write access

1: This may be a **multi-variable atomicity violation bug**
2: One possible buggy pattern is: $W_0(x){\to}R_1(x){\to}R_1(y){\to}W_0(y)$
3: Fist access: httpconnection.cpp:52(Activate())
4: Second access: httpconnection.cpp:25(OnHeadersAvailable())
5: Third access: httpconnection.cpp:26(OnHeadersAvailable())
6: Fourth access: httpconnection.cpp:55(Activate())
7: The **first access's** call stack is
8: In httpconnection.cpp:66: main() call Activate()
9: **Start Function of thread 0** is: main()
10: The **second access's** call stack is
11: In httpconnection.cpp:38: thread() call OnHeadersAvailable()
12: **Start Function of thread 1** is: thread()(httpconnection.cpp:36)
13: **pthread_create()**
14: httpconnection.cpp:46 AsyncRead() call above function
15: httpconnection.cpp:51 Activate() call above function
16: httpconnection.cpp:66 main() call above function
17: **Parent thread Id** is: 0
18: The **third access's** call stack is
19: In httpconnection.cpp:38: thread() call OnHeadersAvailable()
20: **Start Function of thread 1** is: thread()(httpconnection.cpp:36)
21: **pthread_create()**
22: httpconnection.cpp:46 AsyncRead() call above function
23: httpconnection.cpp:51 Activate() call above function
24: httpconnection.cpp:66 main() call above function
25: **Parent thread Id** is: 0
26: The **fourth access's** call stack is
27: In httpconnection.cpp:66: main() call Activate()
28: **Start Function of thread 1** is: main()

Fig. 4. The bug report for simplified jsStringLength

is executed in function `Activate()` by thread 0. Since it is in thread 0 without parent thread, it has no thread creation information.

The third and fourth parts (lines 10-25) are the information of call stack and thread creation for the first and second read access to *str* and *len* respectively. These two parts are the same since they are executed in the same thread and function. For these two parts, lines 10-12 and lines 18-20 are the call stack information in the read accesss thread, we should check them from bottom to top. The function invoke process shows how the execution of thread 1 reaches to the read access from the start function `thread()`. Lines 13-17 and lines 21-25 provided the thread relationship. It shows that the parent thread of thread 1 is thread 0. The thread creation process is as follows: In thread 0, `main()` → `Activate()` → `AsyncRead()` → `pthread_create()`.

The fifth part (Lines 26-28) provides the call stack information for the second write access to *len*, which is the same to that of the first write access since they are executed in the same thread and function.

From the call stack information(part2) of the first write access and the thread creation information of thread 1(part3 and part4), we can see that thread 0 created an asynchronous thread(i.e. thread 1) by invoking the function `AsyncRead()` in function `Activate()` of thread 0. After function `AsyncRead()` returns, thread 0 will sequentially execute the second write access in function `Activate()`. But since the two read access in the created thread 1 happen before the second write access in thread 0, the atomicity of the two write accesses is destroyed. This leads to the value of *str* and *len* become out of sync.

As to this bug, Recon only provides the first write and the first read access. It is hard for programmer to find the remaining two memory accesses. Even if all the four accesses are provided, it is hard to get the triggering process of the bug. Since the complicated function invoking and thread creation relationship in the source code makes it hard to understand where the thread is created and how the program executes to the corresponding access. The above bug report shows that LUCON provides the memory access pattern, and further gives a bug triggering scenario to show how the bug happens.

5   Related Work

There is much research on fault analysis and detection for concurrency bugs. In this section, we discuss the most relevant work to our own and compare the LUCON approach with these existing methods.

Falcon [4] collects memory access patterns dynamically and ranks patterns to identify potential concurrency bugs. However, Falcon is limited to concurrency bugs involving a single variable and cannot provide any information about the bug triggering process. DefUse [10] uses communication based strategy to monitor the memory access pairs between threads and report the most suspicious pairs as possible concurrency bugs. Bugaboo [9] collects context-aware communication graphs that contain a list of memory locations between threads and reports the graph with suspiciousness ranking. Recon [11] extends Bugaboo to reconstruct the buggy source and sink locations of two different threads from the communication graphs which aims to help understand the bug. Compared to these approaches, our method can deal with concurrency bugs involving multiple variable and construct bug triggering scenarios to help programmers better understand the bugs.

Among other existing concurrent testing techniques, we are particularly interested in bug eliciting and active testing method which can improve LUCON in terms of concurrency bug detection ability. Since program failures occur infrequently in testing based approaches, bug eliciting techniques can increase the frequency of the bug appearance. Utilizing random delays can increase the possibility of a buggy interleaving [15]. Also, there are some other methods like schemes that control the scheduler to elicit specific interleavings [16], runtime monitoring and synchronization control [17], and some analysis based methods [6]. In LUCON we inject artificial delays into the programs to increase the frequency of the bug appearance. But we have not evaluated it experimentally. An active testing scheduler would try to exercise a suspicious buggy interleaving in a real execution to verify whether it is really a bug or merely a false positive. There are two common ways to perform the validation. One way is to precisely compute an alternate schedule and enforce it to expose the bug [18]. The other way is using heuristics methods to expose predicted buggy interleavings [17].

6   Conclusion and Future Work

Compared with other fault localization techniques, LUCON has two main advantages: (1) Extending detection ability from single variable concurrency bugs to both single and multiple variable concurrency bugs; (2) Presenting buggy patterns and building bug triggering scenarios to help programmers understand the bug. Experimental results show that LUCON is effective for a suite of real client/server programs.

However, there are several areas of future work that will improve it. First, program failures occur infrequently in LUOCN. Thus we need to develop a scheme to increase the frequency of the bug appearance by using bug eliciting technique. Second, by combining active testing technique, we can verify whether the searched patterns are real bugs or merely false positive. In general, we believe these two techniques will enhance the efficiency and accuracy of LUCON.

Acknowledgements. We sincerely thank the anonymous reviewers for their patient review and valuable comments which significantly improve the quality of this paper. Special thanks to He Li for early work on the LUCON infrastructure.

References

1. McDowell, C.E., Helmbold, D.P.: Debugging concurrent programs. ACM Computing Surveys (CSUR) 21(4), 593–622 (1989)
2. Flanagan, C., Freund, S.N.: Fasttrack: efficient and precise dynamic race detection. ACM Sigplan Notices 44, 121–133 (2009)
3. Savage, S., Burrows, M., Nelson, G., Sobalvarro, P., Anderson, T.: Eraser: A dynamic data race detector for multithreaded programs. ACM Transactions on Computer Systems (TOCS) 15(4), 391–411 (1997)

4. Park, S., Vuduc, R.W., Harrold, M.J.: Falcon: fault localization in concurrent programs. In: Proceedings of the 32nd ACM/IEEE International Conference on Software Engineering, vol. 1, pp. 245–254. ACM (2010)

5. Lu, S., Tucek, J., Qin, F., Zhou, Y.: Avio: detecting atomicity violations via access interleaving invariants. In: ACM SIGOPS Operating Systems Review, vol. 40, pp. 37–48. ACM (2006)

6. Park, S., Lu, S., Zhou, Y.: Ctrigger: exposing atomicity violation bugs from their hiding places. ACM Sigplan Notices 44(3), 25–36 (2009)

7. Lucia, B., Ceze, L., Strauss, K.: Colorsafe: architectural support for debugging and dynamically avoiding multi-variable atomicity violations. In: ACM SIGARCH Computer Architecture News, vol. 38, pp. 222–233. ACM (2010)

8. Vaziri, M., Tip, F., Dolby, J.: Associating synchronization constraints with data in an object-oriented language. ACM SIGPLAN Notices 41, 334–345 (2006)

9. Lucia, B., Ceze, L.: Finding concurrency bugs with context-aware communication graphs. In: Proceedings of the 42nd Annual IEEE/ACM International Symposium on Microarchitecture, pp. 553–563 (2009)

10. Shi, Y., Park, S., Yin, Z., Lu, S., Zhou, Y., Chen, W., Zheng, W.: Do i use the wrong definition?: Defuse: definition-use invariants for detecting concurrency and sequential bugs. ACM Sigplan Notices 45, 160–174 (2010)

11. Lucia, B., Wood, B.P., Ceze, L.: Isolating and understanding concurrency errors using reconstructed execution fragments. ACM SIGPLAN Notices 46, 378–388 (2011)

12. Pintool, http://www.pintool.org/

13. Lu, S., Park, S., Seo, E., Zhou, Y.: Learning from mistakes: a comprehensive study on real world concurrency bug characteristics. ACM Sigplan Notices 43, 329–339 (2008)

14. Park, S., Vuduc, R., Harrold, M.J.: A unified approach for localizing non-deadlock concurrency bugs. In: 2012 IEEE Fifth International Conference on Software Testing, Verification and Validation (ICST), pp. 51–60. IEEE (2012)

15. Edelstein, O., Farchi, E., Nir, Y., Ratsaby, G., Ur, S.: Multithreaded java program test generation. IBM Systems Journal 41(1), 111–125 (2002)

16. Sen, K.: Race directed random testing of concurrent programs. ACM SIGPLAN Notices 43, 11–21 (2008)

17. Park, C.S., Sen, K.: Randomized active atomicity violation detection in concurrent programs. In: Proceedings of the 16th ACM SIGSOFT International Symposium on Foundations of Software Engineering, pp. 135–145. ACM (2008)

18. Sorrentino, F., Farzan, A., Madhusudan, P.: Penelope: weaving threads to expose atomicity violations. In: Proceedings of the Eighteenth ACM SIGSOFT International Symposium on Foundations of Software Engineering, pp. 37–46. ACM (2010)

Feature Selection Toward Optimizing Internet Traffic Behavior Identification

Zhenxiang Chen, Lizhi Peng, Shupeng Zhao, Lei Zhang, and Shan Jing

Shandong Provincial Key Laboratory of Network Based Intelligent Computing,
University of Jinan
{czx,plz,nic_zhaosp,nicop8,jingshan}@ujn.edu.cn

Abstract. P2P and multimedia similar applications are seemed as primary bandwidth consume network behaviors. Accurate network traffic behavior identification supports numerous network activities from network management, monitoring and Quality-of-Service(QoS), to forecast and application-specific investigations. Accuracy and performance are the two most important metrics for traffic identification especially for online implementation. In this paper, the optimization of feature selection to traffic identification is demonstrated in two traces which are captured from different time and location. Moreover, this optimization to traffic identification toward various applications are compared and analyzed in online and offline status with C4.5 decision tree algorithm. Our research demonstrated that the optimal features for traffic identification are mainly sensitive to application, time and location. Identifying for the same application behavior on different network location are sensitive to different features. Experiment result shows that the selected optimal feature subset can greatly improve the performance for both online and offline identification. Furthermore, it can improve the online traffic identification implementability in real network condition.

Keywords: Internet traffic, feature selection, behavior identification, online classification.

1 Introduction

Network security, accounting, traffic engineering and Quality of Service(QoS) are network-service facilities which rely on accurate identification of network traffic. Online traffic identification is a potential technique to solve difficult network management problems fundamentally for Internet service providers[1]. Although many research proposed, traffic identification remains a fundamental problem in the network community. Some proposed traffic identification technics include port numbers, application payload, statistical features and host behaviors based methods. Recent years, a lot of attention has been paid on the application of machine learning techniques to traffic identification,which can automatically learn and build a classifier from the given samples and feature set. Then the learned classifier can be used to identify the new captured traffic.

X.-h. Sun et al. (Eds.): ICA3PP 2014, Part II, LNCS 8631, pp. 631–644, 2014.

The machine learning techniques applied in traffic identification, generally can be categorized into supervised ,unsupervised (or clustering) and semi-supervised. The supervised methods[2,3] train a classifier from a set of pre-labeled training samples to classify new traffic flows, while the unsupervised methods[4,5] polymerize the traffic flows that have similar characteristics into clusters. The Traffic clustering does not need any supervised training samples and has the potential of identifying unknown applications, while supervised methods can only classify traffic flows of known applications. Semi-supervised[6] adequately use unlabeled data to train classifier and attract a mess of internet from research communities.

Many research showed that reasonable behavior features are important for accuracy of traffic identification. For online traffic identification, due to rigorous real-time requirement, it is necessary to reduce the number of used features[7,8] for decreasing computational cost and delay. Simply and timely gotten features are also helpful for identification performance. More importantly, identify the same application behavior on different network location are sensitive to selected features. Effectively feature selection can greatly optimize performance of classifier,especially for online traffic identification. For offline identification, in order to search available communication pattern, it is also necessary to cut down irrelevant and redundancy features to improve the performance.

In this paper, the optimization of feature selection to traffic identification is demonstrated in two traces which are captured from the diverse time and location. Moreover, this optimization to traffic identification are compared by online and offline condition. It verified that the optimal features for traffic identification are mainly sensitive to application, time and network location. Experiment result shows that the selected optimal feature subset can greatly improve the performance for both online and offline identification.

The rest of the paper is organized as follows. Section II highlights related work in this field. Section III proposed the foundation of online traffic identification. Section IV focuses on adaptive feature selection toward time, location and applications approaches. In section V, experiment result was compared and analysed. Finally, chapter VI makes some final conclusion on feature selection for traffic identification.

2 Related Work

A feature is a descriptive statistic to characterize an object, and ideally, each object exhibits different feature values depending on the category to which it belongs. Based on the features, models can be established by using machine learning techniques.For Internet traffic, each flow is characterized by a number of features, such as packet size which can describe its behavior. Usually, a flow can be considered as a sequence of share five-tuples source IP address, source Port, destination IP address, destination Port, protocol of transport layer with a timeout of 64 seconds[9].Moore et al investigated 248 traffic features[10] for traffic classification.

Generally, the feature selection techniques share a similar process(as shown in Fig.1) to select a best subset[12], in which the selection process of the best subset has four steps which include: subset generation, subset evaluation, stopping criterion, and final subset validation. Consequently, a feature is selected if additional information is gained when it is added to the previously selected feature set, and discarded in the opposite case since the information obtained is already contained (redundant) in the previous set.

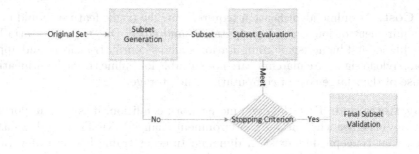

Fig. 1. The generally feature selection process

As the pointed process scheme,Chi-Ho et al[11] present a novel intrusion detection approach to extract both accurate and interpretable fuzzy rules from network traffic data for identification. In addition, the proposed system can also act as a genetic feature selection wrapper to search for an optimal feature subset for dimensionality reduction. Xiaochun et al [13]proposed a hybrid feature selection method for flow identification. It demonstrated that their approach can greatly improve computational performance without negative impact on identification accuracy. Yishi Zhang et al[14] investigated the relation between features and the separate classes instead of only handling the relevance and redundancy analysis from the point of view of the whole class.

Feature selection can improve the performance of identification system on majority classes, but as a cost, it will decrease the accuracy in minority classes. As a result, it brings about the multi-class imbalance problem. To multi-class imbalance problem in Internet traffic identification and applications identification, Zhen LIU et al[15] research the class-dependent misidentification cost to improve the identification performance on the minority class, however, some classes are still hard to be classified.

3   The Foundation of Online Traffic Identification

3.1   Precondition for Online Identification

Due to real-time, fugitiveness, polytrope and nonreversible of Internet traffic, it is difficult to search optimal feature for online traffic identification. A lot of researchers have investigated it deeply[16,17]. It can conclude that online traffic identification need a classifier of low latency(real-time reaction), low cost (computation and storing) and easily be retrained.

Low Latency. For online identification, it is necessary to reduce latency as low as possible, at least, the flows should be classified before it passed away. In other word, it need extract feature information from the first few packets as fewer as possible to obtain enough identification information. Some features such as flow duration and flow length are not suitable for online traffic identification, since they can't be gotten until a complete flow passed away.

Low Cost. As online identification requirement, the traffic feature should meet the requirement of low cost of computation and store. Due to traffic ratio becomes higher and higher,some computation such as Fourier transform and application payload signature matching are not suitable for online traffic identification because of their large cost of computation and storage.

Easily Retrained. Face the dynamic network condition, it is very important to retrain classifier when network environment changed. Xu Tian et al [18]have proved that concept shift exist in dynamic Internet traffic because of various kinds of version in application software and protocol. This situation will badly influence the performance and accuracy of classifier. Therefore, it is necessary to retrain classifier completely or partly in time.

3.2   Online Identification Features Analysis

In the area of traffic identification, various kinds of feature are used to characterize traffic. Moore feature set is seen as origin features and been widely used in recent research. It includes of 248 kinds of flow features, which with application class label. However, not all features are suitable to online traffic identification. If all the 248 statistical features are used for characterize network traffic flows, the computation cost will be a big issue.

For online identification, traffic features should be simple enough for calculation and storing. Some features such as duration of a flow, the length of a flow, and the total number of a flow, which need observing a complete flow to got the effective information, are rejected in this work. More than 100 features such as fast Fourier transform and effective bandwidth based upon entropy that need complex computation are also exclude. Finally, we can get 28 kind of features, which are fit for online traffic identification. TABLE 1 shows a feature subset of Moore feature set[10],which can be calculated on few packets of a flow.

4   Feature Selection toward Time, Location and Applications

4.1   Traces

In this paper, two network datasets are used for validating our methods. One is captured from the real network of Shandong Provincial Key Laboratory of Network Based Intelligent Computing, which is called UJN dataset. The other public one captured from the border router of the University of Auckland, which is called Auckland dataset.

Table 1. The Characters of online traffic identification features

No.	Feature Abbreviation	Feature Description
1	pkt_size_max	The maximum of packet size
2	pkt_size_min	The minimum of packet size
3	pkt_size_mean	The mean of packet size
4	pkt_size_std_dev	The standard deviation of packet size
5	pkt_IAT_max	The maximum of inter-arrival time
6	pkt_IAT_min	The minimum of inter-arrival time
7	pkt_IAT_mean	The mean of inter-arrival time
8	pkt_IAT_std_dev	The standard deviation of inter-arrival time
9	IP_payload_size_max	The maximum of payload size on packet
10	IP_payload_size_min	The minimum of payload size on packet
11	IP_payload_size_mean	The mean of payload size on packet
12	IP_payload_size_std_dev	The standard deviation of payload size on packet
13	TCP_payload_size_max	The maximum of payload size of TCP segments
14	TCP_payload_size_min	The minimum of payload size of TCP segments
15	TCP_payload_size_mean	The mean of payload size of TCP segments
16	TCP_payload_size_std_dev	The standard deviation of payload size of TCP segments
17	window_size_max	The maximum of window size
18	window_size_min	The minimum of window size
19	window_size_mean	The mean of window size
20	window_size_std_dev	The standard deviation of window size
21	TCP_header_size_max	The maximum of head size of TCP segments
22	TCP_header_size_min	The minimum of head size of TCP segments
23	TCP_header_size_mean	The mean of head size of TCP segments
24	TCP_header_size_std_dev	The standard deviation of head size of TCP segments
25	num_URG	The number of packets with URG flag
26	num_ACK	The number of packets with ACK flag
27	num_PSH	The number of packets with PSH flag
28	num_RST	The number of packets with RST flag

UJN Trace. The UJN dataset (TABLE 2) is captured on an all-purpose PC (more than 50) in the LAN of the laboratory which comprises several 1000Base-TX segments routed through a Linux-based server. Each kind of traffic is respectively captured, when the special application separately run in a period of time. Therefore, each flow is labeled with corresponding application ground truth.

The Window system offers a lot of application interfaces for a third part to develop its own driver program, which can capture all user socket calls using winsock interface and make processing at the socket calls before forwarding packets.In order to label packet with applications ground truth, we achieved a labeling platform through Socket Hook and NDIS (Network Driver Interface Specification) Hook on the user hosts (Fig.2)[19].This technology is more effective than that labeling traffic based on port numbers or application payloads.

Auckland Trace. Auckland datasets [20] is captured from Jul. 3, 2000 to Nov. 29, 2001, which are almost 24 hours multiply by 7 days. The volume of total traffic is nearly 359 GB which consist of more than 996 million packets in all. The volume of source dataset size is too large to analyze. For decreasing the size of dataset, two parts of Auckland dataset 20000214-185536-0 and 20000214-185536-1 are selected. In order to get ground truth, each flow is labeled through matching server port to default port in IANA. The statistic information of these traces is represented in TABLE 3.

Table 2. Composition of UJN Dataset

Category	Application	Byte	Packet	Flow
WEB	Web applications	29779475	68746	1126
BULK	FTP	41342040	43678	15
MAIL	IMAP, POP2/3	3220	74	15
ATTACK	Worms, viruses	3632	78	17
CHAT	QQ, MSN	1729268	11319	998
P2P	XunleieDonkey	33341617	46956	3012
MULTIMEDIA	Windows Media Player	2662954	3322	40
VOIP	QQvoice, Ali	22420	478	107
NEWS	NNTP	104	79406	4
GAEMS	Angry birds	15440829	18186	76
DATABASE	MySQL, Oracle	92	2	1
INTERACTIVE	SSH, telnet	76161	720	3
OTHER		875624	13160	427

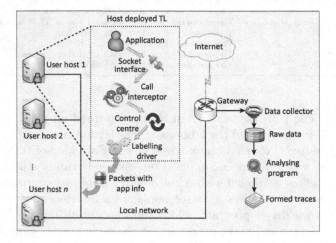

Fig. 2. Architecture of labeling packets with truth ground platform

Table 3. Composition of Auckland Dataset

Traces	Protocol	Packets	Flows	Bytes
20000214-185536-0	TCP	1629765	114085	835.0MB
20000214-185536-0	UDP	201502	-	23.6MB
20000214-185536-1	TCP	1541358	115549	637.4MB
20000214-185536-1	UDP	214371	-	17.3MB

4.2   Computational Platform and Tools

WEKA [21]is a famous experiment toolkit of machine learning, which contains a serial of algorithms for data analysis and predictive modeling. C4.5 algorithm and some feature selection algorithms are selected to build feature selection and identification model in this work. The experiment platform is all-purpose PC which carries on Windows XP operating system, whose CPU is Intel Core(TM) 2-6300, dominant frequency is 1.88 GHz, and Physical memory is DDR-667 2GBytes.

4.3   Feature Selection Algorithm

In this paper, feature selection method is implemented in WEKA, which includes attribute evaluator and search method. The evaluator determines what method is used to assign a worth to each subset of attributes. The search method determines what style of search is performed.

Feature selection is aim to improve the identification performance of the classifier. The feature selection algorithm on WEKA is used to validate our methodology, which is fast correlation-based filter algorithm. This algorithm uses symmetrical uncertainty as the goodness measure whether a feature is relevant to the class. the symmetrical uncertainty can be defined as follows.

$$SU(X,Y) = [\frac{IG(X|Y)}{H(X) + H(Y)}] \tag{1}$$

The $SU(X, Y)$ is the symmetrical uncertainty of variance X and Y in this formula 1. The is the information gain that can be calculated as follows.

$$IG(X|Y) = H(X) - H(X|Y) \tag{2}$$

$$H(X) = -\sum P(x_i)log_2(P(x_i)) \tag{3}$$

$$H(X) = -\sum P(y_i) \sum x_i|y_j log_2(P(x_i)|y_j) \tag{4}$$

It compensates for information gain's bias toward features with more values and normalizes its values to the range [0;1] with the value 1 indicating that knowledge of the value of either one completely predicts the value of the other and the value 0 indicating that X and Y are independent.

4.4   Identification Algorithms

For demonstrating the effectiveness of the methods, C4.5 algorithm is used as a identification model.A test node in the tree represent feature, with branches linked to a sub-tree. A leaf representing the class constitutes the output. To classify real-time using C4.5, the leaf node is searched begin from the tree root to the leaves(the regulation modes). This process will go iteratively into a sub-tree, until it reaches a leaf node with the predicted class. On the other hand, predicting the class of an instance is the key point of tracing the path of nodes and branches to the leaf node.

When building a model, the training set S is consisted of a set of instances which have a fixed set of features (A1, , Ak)T and a class C. The class C represents the application of the network traffic and has the values (c1, c2, , cm). Each feature Aq represents the flow statistics and has the values (a1, a2, , an).The information gain ratio is used to decide which feature should be chosen as a test node. It reflects the correlation between a feature Aq and a class label C, which is calculated by the equation (1). The entropy reflects the impurity of the feature, which is calculated by the equation (3).

$$G_{gainratio}(C|A_q) = \frac{H(C) - H(C|A_q)}{H(C)} \tag{5}$$

Where

$$H(C|A_q) = -\sum_{j=1}^{n} p(a_j) \sum_{i=1}^{m} p(\frac{c_i}{a_i}) log_2 p(\frac{c_i}{a_i}) \tag{6}$$

And

$$H(C) = -\sum_{i=1}^{m} p(c_i) log_2 p(c_i) \tag{7}$$

Where

$$p(c_i) = P[C = c_i] = P[A_q = a_j] and p(\frac{c_i}{a_j}) = P(C = c_i | A_q = a_j)$$

In principle, the process of building model iteratively looks for the best feature to partition the data. The one with highest information gain ratio will be chose as the test node, until the node becomes a leaf node. To classify the instance using C4.5, it just needs to compare the features of the test instance to the node of the tree. Identifying traffic by C4.5 has a low computational cost and can be realized easily for implantation.

4.5   Experiment

In this paper, we want to validate these assumptions as follow:

1) Feature selection can optimize traffic identification by cut redundancy features and irrelevant features. Not only accuracy, precision and recall will be improved, the cost and latency of classifier will be decreased. This kind of optimization is effectual to both online and offline traffic identification.

2) Different applications will produce different traffic, so the feature subset toward various applications will be different. This kind of feature subset will be the fittest one to achieve the optimization.

3) Traffic will change over time in the same network location. For example, the P2P behavior traffic in the day is totaly different from what in the night.

Grasping this discipline will be helpful to optimize classifier with pertinence in special period. A set of experiments are designed to validate above assumptions in Auckland and UJN trace, which are captured from different time and locations. In order to simulate online traffic identification, feature information is extracted from the first few packets of a flow named CFFP[22]. On the contrary, as offline traffic identification, feature information is extracted from entire packets of a flow named CEP in traditional process. On these feature information, features are calculated to form a feature vector that describes a flow.

First of all, fast correlation-based filter algorithm is used to obtain optimal feature subset in Auckland dataset and UJN dataset. Classifier build by online traffic identification feature is compared with classifier build by feature subset. Performance of classifier such as build time, classifier size and any other index are compared in order to illustrate the optimization to traffic identification in different network.

Secondly, feature selection toward various applications is analyzed for identifying single applications category such as P2P. To each application category, traffic identification is considered to identify and classify specific application. Performance of classifier is also compared and analyzed like.

Lastly, in consideration that traffic change over time. The Auckland trace and UJN trace are divided into a series of traces that only includes traffic captured during one hour. That is to say, we observe traffic in each hours. Moreover, we want to know how the feature subset will change when the time passed from one hour to the next. Furthermore, different time granularity should be considered in this observation.

5   Experiment Analysis

5.1   Optimization to Offline and Online Traffic Identification

Duo to various kinds of application categories in our experiment, the identification task is multi-classification. It can analyze and compare experiment result from three points: accuracy, size of identification model and time for building model.

In this part, we adopt symmetrical uncertain attribute set evaluation as attribute evaluator to evaluate which feature subset is best, and use FCBF Search as fast correlation-based filter algorithm to search candidate feature in feature space.It is significant that number of feature after feature selection is less than before in online and offline condition, which is 1 and 4 respectively. Moreover, number of leaves and size of the tree has similar result than number of features, which decrease more than 50% off. It shows that feature selection can retain main structure of identification model and cut down secondary structure.

In same condition, the building model time after feature selection is much less than before. The latter is almost 20 times larger than the former. This character is more important to online traffic identification which need quickly process a great deal of data. From the comparison of accuracy, it can safely conclude that feature selection will not deeply deteriorate the accuracy. It is noting that feature selection also reduce the cost and processing time in extracting feature information. To offline traffic identification, feature selection decreases the volume of storrage. Moreover, it is helpful to find key point to Internet traffic for better network plan and design. Similar with identification result on Auckland dataset, feature selection on UJN dataset also significantly improve the performance of identification system in the number of feature, number of leaves, and the size of the tree, time taken to build model, accuracy and feature number.

Table 4. Identification result on Auckland dataset

	Online traffic identification		Offline traffic identification	
	based on unselected feature	based on selected feature	based on unselected feature	based on selected feature
number of features	28	1	28	4
number of tree leaves	145	62	77	47
size of the tree	289	123	153	93
time to build model	4.92s	0.22s	5.73s	0.34s
accuracy	97.8623%	91.9674%	98.7498%	97.1823%
number in feature list	1-28	9	1-28	1,25.26

Table 5. Identification result on UJN dataset

	Online traffic identification		Offline traffic identification	
	based on unselected feature	based on selected feature	based on unselected feature	based on selected feature
number of features	28	3	28	4
number of tree leaves	173	181	177	101
size of the tree	345	361	353	201
time to build model	1.66s	0.36s	2.19s	0.33s
accuracy	92.4847%	93.7009%	91.2196%	89.7642%
number in feature list	1-28	3,4,17	1-28	20, 25, 18, 19, 28

Comparing with above two experiments result on Auckland dataset and UJN dataset, it has demonstrates that the optimization to traffic identification is very effectual in different dataset, which were captured from different time and location. It means that feature selection could work well in different network environments and it also has the ability of adapting the great change in network environment. In addition to this, new fact attracts our interesting that there are some features in the feature subset no matter in online or offline. It suggests that these features maybe not sensitive to network environment.

It is noting that the FCBF algorithm ranks all feature with corresponding a value. The feature standard deviation of packet size is 0.488 in UJN dataset to offline traffic identification. And the feature maximin of window size is 0.157,which are selected as feature subset. Similarly, the feature minimum of windows size is 0.397 in UJN dataset to online traffic identification. The feature mean of windows size is 0.38 and the number of packets with RST flags is 0.153,which are selected as optimal feature subset. Feature subset to online identification is different from feature subset to offline because sampled packet policies are used in online to implement real time identification. It will lose some information such as feature which is relative with packet size information. To offline traffic identification, all packets of a flow are used to extract feature information. The feature standard deviation of packet size has highest ranked value to demonstrate that this feature is the most valuable to classify traffic. However, it is sensitive to packet sampled to online traffic.

5.2   Feature Selection toward Various Application Categories

Different application category has different feature subset by using same feature selection algorithm in traffic identification for identifying specific applications category. It is effective to research the difference of feature selection toward various application categories. A few feature subsets are selected on Auckland and UJN datasets, which are facing specific application category respectively. Like previous analysis, traffic identification for classify various traffic in mixed traffic in online and offline condition, we deeply analyze performance of identification system from follow metrics: the number of feature, number of tree leaves, size of the tree, time taken to build model, accuracy and feature number. There are some analyses on traffic generated by P2P applications and WWW applications as that are not belong to any applications categories.

No matter offline or online identification, feature selection can significantly decreases the number of selected features as a rate more than 85% off. It will signally cut down the processing delay and storage cost, which is useful to online traffic identification. It is also effective to offline traffic identification for analyzing network tendency. Moreover, the time for building model is also decreased 78% off at least. It can lead to retraining and update classifier timely in order to fit network environment. In additional to above optimization to traffic identification, number of leaves in classifier built by using C4.5 decision tree algorithm, the size of classifier is reduces in different extent. However, the accuracy is reduced little after feature selection as a cost.

Table 6. P2P traffic behavior identification result on Auckland dataset

	Online traffic identification		Offline traffic identification	
	based on unselected feature	based on selected feature	based on unselected feature	based on selected feature
number of features	28	5	28	2
number of tree leaves	53	41	15	11
size of the tree	105	81	29	21
time to build model	3.19s	0.78s	2.56s	0.34s
accuracy	99.3911%	97.2663%	99.8373%	99.7733%
number in feature list	1-28	12, 16, 9, 5, 8	1-28	1, 12, 16, 8, 26

Different application categories are sensitive to different feature subset. It is contrasting that traffic identification toward specific application category has less cost and latency. It is noting that there are more features which are maybe relative with environment. It implies that feature selection toward specific behavior categories are much effectual, which can effectively acquire key feature in different network environments under various requirements.

Table 7. P2P traffic behavior identification result on UJN dataset

	Online traffic identification		Offline traffic identification	
	based on unselected feature	based on selected feature	based on unselected feature	based on selected feature
number of feature	28	2	28	2
number of tree leaves	108	9	4	1
size of the tree	215	17	7	1
time to build model	1.59s	0.08s	0.88s	0.05s
accuracy	97.8384%	79.476%	99.6306%	99.674%
number in feature list	1-28	17,22	1-28	17,24

Table 8. WWW traffic behavior identification result on Auckland dataset

	Online traffic identification		Offline traffic identification	
	based on unselected feature	based on selected feature	based on unselected feature	based on selected feature
number of feature	28	4	28	3
number of tree leaves	117	92	59	40
size of the tree	233	183	117	79
time to build model	4.19s	0.81s	2.78s	0.22s
accuracy	98.6785%	96.6509%	99.1255%	97.4284%
number in feature list	1-28	13,20,7,9	1-28	1,13,26

Table 9. WWW traffic behavior identification result on UJN dataset

	Online traffic identification		Offline traffic identification	
	based on unselected feature	based on selected feature	based on unselected feature	based on selected feature
number of feature	28	5	28	3
number of tree leaves	98	134	81	46
size of the tree	195	267	161	91
time to build model	1.53s	0.28s	1.39s	0.17s
accuracy	98.9626%	96.3428%	97.0444%	88.9275%
number in feature list	1-28	12,21,11,15,17	1-28	15,16,18

6   Conclusion

Motivated by the optimization of feature selection toward traffic behavior identification,our research demonstrated that the optimal features for traffic behavior identification are mainly sensitive to application, time and location. Identifying for the same application behavior on different network location are sensitive to different features. Experiment result shows that the selected optimal feature subset can greatly improve the performance for both online and offline identification, but cost for little accuracy. Furthermore, it can improve the online traffic identification implementability in real network condition.

Acknowledgment. This work was supported by the National Natural Science Foundation of China under Grants No.60903176,the Natural Science Foundation of Shandong Province under Grants No.ZR2010FQ028 and No.ZR2011FL021, and the Program for Youth Science and Technology Star Foundation of Jinan under Grants No.TNK1108.

References

1. Nguyen, T.T.T., Armitage, G.: A survey of techniques for internet traffic classification using machine learning. Communications Surveys and Tutorials 10, 56–76 (2008)
2. Moore, A.W., Zuev, D.: Internet traffic classification using bayesian analysis techniques. ACM SIGMETRICS Performance Evaluation Review 33, 50–60 (2005)
3. Nguyen, T.T.T., Armitage, G.: Training on multiple sub-flows to optimize the use of machine learning classifiers in real-world ip networks. In: 31st Local Computer Networks, pp. 369–376. IEEE Press, New York (2006)
4. McGregor, A., Hall, M., Lorier, P., Brunskill, J.: Flow Clustering Using Machine Learning Techniques. In: Barakat, C., Pratt, I. (eds.) PAM 2004. LNCS, vol. 3015, pp. 205–214. Springer, Heidelberg (2004)
5. Zander, S., Nguyen, T.: ArmitageG.: Automated Traffic Classification and Application Identification using Machine Learning. In: 30th Anniversary of the IEEE Conference on Local Computer Networks 2005, pp. 250–257. IEEE Press, New York (2005)
6. Erman, J., Mahanti, A., Arlitt, M., Cohen, I., Williamson, C.: Offline/realtime traffic classification using semi-supervised learning. Performance Evaluation 64, 1194–1213 (2007)
7. Zhao, J.J., Huang, X.H., Sun, Q., Ma, Y.: Real-time feature selection in traffic classification. The Journal of China Universities of Posts and Telecommunications 15, 68–72 (2008)
8. Zhang, H., Lu, G., Qassrawi, M.T., Zhang, Y., Yu, X.: Feature selection for optimizing traffic classification. Computer Communications 35, 1457–1471 (2012)
9. Callado, A., Kamienski, C., Szab, G., Gero, B., Kelner, J., Fernandes, S., Sadok, D.: A survey on internet traffic identification. IEEE Communications Surveys and Tutorials 11, 37–52 (2009)
10. Moore, A., Zuev, D., Crogan, M.: Discriminators for use in flow-based classification. Queen Mary and Westfield College, Department of Computer Science (2005)
11. Tsang, C.H., Kwong, S., Wang, H.: Genetic-fuzzy rule mining approach and evaluation of feature selection techniques for anomaly intrusion detection. Pattern Recognition 40, 2373–2391 (2007)
12. Liu, H., Yu, L.: Toward integrating feature selection algorithms for classification and clustering. IEEE Transactions on Knowledge and Data Engineering 17, 491–502 (2005)
13. Lei, D., Xiaochun, Y., Jun, X.: Optimizing traffic classification using hybrid feature selection. In: The Ninth International Conference on Web-Age Information Management, pp. 520–525. IEEE Press, New York (2008)
14. Zhang, Y., Li, S., Wang, T., Zhang, Z.: Divergence-based feature selection for separate classes. Neurocomputing 101, 32–42 (2013)
15. Liu, Z., Liu, Q.: Studying cost-sensitive learning for multi-class imbalance in Internet traffic classification. The Journal of China Universities of Posts and Telecommunications 19, 63–72 (2012)

16. Zhang, G., Xie, G., Yang, J., Min, Y., Zhou, Z., Duan, X.: Accurate online traffic classification with multi-phases identification methodology. In: 5th IEEE Consumer Communications and Networking Conference, pp. 141–146. IEEE Press, New York (2008)
17. Che, X., Ip, B.: Packet-level traffic analysis of online games from the genre characteristics perspective. Journal of Network and Computer Applications 35, 240–252 (2012)
18. Tian, X., Sun, Q., Huang, X., Ma, Y.: A dynamic online traffic classification methodology based on data stream mining. In: 2009 WRI World Congress on Computer Science and Information Engineering, pp. 298–302. IEEE Press, New York (2009)
19. Lizhi, P., Hongli, Z., Bo, Y., Yuehui, C., Tong, W.: Traffic Labeller: Collecting Internet traffic samples with accurate application information. Communications, China 11, 69–78 (2014)
20. Micheel, J., Graham, I., Brownlee, N.: The Auckland data set: an access link observed. In: Proceedings of the 14th ITC Specialists Seminar on Access Networks and Systems, pp. 19–30 (2001)
21. Witten, I.H., Frank, E., Kaufmann, E.M.: Data Mining: Practical Machine Learning Tools and Techniques. Morgan Kaufmann series in data management systems, pp. 1046–1698 (2005) ISSN 1046-1698
22. Zhao, S., Yu, X., Chen, Z., Jing, S., Peng, L., Liu, K.: A Novel Online Traffic Classification Method Based on Few Packets. In: 8th International Conference on Wireless Communications, Networking and Mobile Computing (WiCOM), pp. 1–4. IEEE Press, New York (2012)

ID-Based Anonymous Multi-receiver Key Encapsulation Mechanism with Sender Authentication*

Bo Zhang, Tao Sun, and Dairong Yu

School of Information Science and Engineering
University of Jinan, Jinan, P.R. China
zhangbosdu@gmail.com

Abstract. Identity based (ID-based) key encapsulation mechanism (KEM) is used to encapsulate a symmetric key during the construction of hybrid encryption in the identity based setting. In many situations, the receiver does not want to reveal identity information. So anonymous multi-receiver KEM is needed to solve the problem. In this paper, we present the first ID-based anonymous multi-receiver KEM with sender authentication. We formulate its security model and define the security notions. We present an concrete construction from pairings and the construction is provably secure in the random oracle model.

Keywords: key encapsulation mechanism, identity based cryptography, multi-receiver, sender authentication.

1 Introduction

The concept of ID-based cryptosystem were introduced by Shamir [10] in 1984 to remove the extra burden of digital certificates and key management. Its main idea is that the public key of a user can be publicly computed from arbitrary strings corresponding to his identity information such as IP address, social security number, name, telephone number or email address etc while corresponding private key can only be generated by a trusted Private Key Generator (PKG).

In some network applications, we have to distribute same message to several different members. A simple approach for achieving this goal is that the sender encrypts or signcrypts the message for each member of the receiver group respectively (Multiple Single-receiver Encryptions). Obviously, the cost of using the approach in large group is very high. Broadcast encryption and multi-receiver consider this problem of broadcasting digital contents to a large set of authorized users. Such applications include paid-TV systems, copyrighted CD/DVD distributions, and fee-based online databases. The multi-receiver setting for public key cryptography is that there are n receivers. A sender encrypts a message to them at the same time in one logic step. The concept of multi-receiver setting was formalized by Bellare et al [1].

* This work is supported by a Project of Shandong Province Higher Educational Science and Technology Program under Grant No.J13LN21.

X.-h. Sun et al. (Eds.): ICA3PP 2014, Part II, LNCS 8631, pp. 645–658, 2014.
© Springer International Publishing Switzerland 2014

Receiver anonymity or privacy protection means that one can examine whether herself/himself is one of the selected receivers, and nobody in the receiver set knows who the other selected receivers are. For example, in paid-TV systems the privileged set is the set of all users who have paid a subscription to a certain channel. Each customer should have access to that channel using his private key. The problem is that, using the traditional solve method, he has to know who else has paid for the specific subscription which causes serious privacy issues. In recent years, many anonymous MIBE scheme [2], [3], [4], [5]were proposed.

The KEM/DEM hybrid encryption paradigm [6,7]combines the efficiency and large message space of secret key encryption with the advantages of public key cryptography, a natural question is how to design an ID-based anonymous multi-receiver key encapsulation mechanism with sender authentication. In this paper, we answer this question by making the following contributions:

- We specify a security model based on the selective identity attack model in which the adversary commits ahead of time to identities which it intends to attack and formalize three security notions.
- We present a concrete scheme based on some efficient primitives to send a message to multi receivers in a anonymous way.
- We prove that our scheme satisfies the above security notions in the random oracle model.

2 Preliminaries

2.1 Security Problems and Complexity Assumptions

• Computation Diffie-Hellman (CDH) Problem. Given $P, aP, bP \in G_1$ for unknown $a, b \in \mathbb{Z}_q^*$, computing $abP \in G_1$.

Definition 1. *(CDH assumption). Given $P, aP, bP \in G_1$ for unknown $a, b \in \mathbb{Z}_q^*$, the successful advantage of any probabilistic polynomial time adversary $\mathscr{A}$ is presented as $Adv^{CDH} = Pr[A(P, aP, bP = abP)|a, b \in \mathbb{Z}_q^*]$. We say that the (t, ϵ)-CDH assumption holds if there exists no PPT adversary $\mathscr{A}$ with non-negligible advantage ϵ within running time t in solving the CDH problem.*

• Bilinear Diffie-Hellman (BDH) Problem. Given $P, aP, bP, cP \in G_1$ for unknown $a, b, c \in \mathbb{Z}_q^*$, computing $e(P, P)^{abc} \in G_2$.

Definition 2. *(BDH assumption). Given $P, aP, bP, cP \in G_1$ for unknown $a, b, c \in \mathbb{Z}_q^*$, the successful advantage of any probabilistic polynomial time adversary $\mathscr{A}$ is presented as $Adv^{BDH} = Pr[A(P, aP, bP, cP = e(P, P)^{abc})|a, b, c \in \mathbb{Z}_q^*]$. We say that the (t, ϵ)-BDH assumption holds if there exists no PPT adversary $\mathscr{A}$ with non-negligible advantage ϵ within running time t in solving the BDH problem.*

• Decision Bilinear Diffie-Hellman (DBDH) Problem. Given $P, aP, bP, cP \in G_1$ for unknown $a, b, c \in \mathbb{Z}_q^*$, and $R \in G_2$, deciding whether $e(P, P)^{abc} = R$.

Definition 3. *(DBDH assumption). Given $P, aP, bP, cP \in G_1$ for unknown $a, b, c \in \mathbb{Z}_q^*$, and $R \in G_2$, the successful advantage of any probabilistic polynomial time adversary $\mathcal{A}$ is presented as $Adv^{DBDH} = |Pr[A(P, aP, bP, cP, e(P, P)^{abc} = 1)] - Pr[A(P, aP, bP, cP, R) = 1]|$. We say that the (t, ϵ)-DBDH assumption holds if there exists no PPT adversary $\mathcal{A}$ with non-negligible advantage ϵ within running time t in solving the DBDH problem.*

• Gap-BDH problem. Given $P, aP, bP, cP \in G_1$ for unknown $a, b, c \in \mathbb{Z}_q^*$, computing $e(P, P)^{abc} \in G_2$ with the help of the DBDH oracle.

Definition 4. *(Gap-BDH assumption). Given $P, aP, bP, cP \in G_1$ for unknown $a, b, c \in \mathbb{Z}_q^*$, the DBDH oracle means that given (P, aP, bP, cP, R), outputs 1 if $e(P, P)^{abc} = R$ and 0 otherwise. The successful advantage of any probabilistic polynomial time adversary $\mathcal{A}$ is presented as $Adv^{Gap-BDH} = Pr[A(P, aP, bP, cP$*
$= e(P, P)^{abc}|a, b, c \in \mathbb{Z}_q^*]$. *We say that the (t, q_g, ϵ)-Gap-BDH assumption holds if there exists no PPT adversary $\mathcal{A}$ with non-negligible advantage ϵ within running time t by making q_g DBDH-oracle queries in solving the Gap-BDH problem.*

3 ID-Based Anonymous Multi-receiver Key Encapsulation Mechanism with Sender Authentication

3.1 Framework

A generic ID-based anonymous multi-receiver key encapsulation mechanism with sender authentication consists of following probabilistic polynomial time algorithms.

Setup: Given a security parameter l, the Private Key Generator (PKG) generates a master key S and common parameters *Params*. *Params* is made public while S is kept secret.

Extract: Given an identity $ID_u \in \{0, 1\}^*$, the PKG runs this algorithm $Extract(S, Params, ID_u)$ to generate the private key d_u associated with ID_u and transmits it to the user via a secure channel.

Encap: Given multiple receivers choose by the signer with identities $R = \{ID_1, ..., ID_n\}$ and the private key d_s, the sender with identity ID_s runs this algorithm $Encap(d_s, R)$ to generates a pair (K, C), where K is a session key, C is an authenticable encapsulation of K for $ID_i \in R$.

Decap: Given the sender's identity ID_s, the private key d_r for $ID_i \in R$ and the ciphertext C, this algorithm output K or an error symbol $\perp$ indicating that the ciphertext is invalid.

For consistency, we require that if $(K, C) = Encap(d_s, R)$, then $K = Decap(C, ID_s, d_r)$ for all $1 \leq r \leq n$.

3.2 Security Model

Definition 5. *(IND-sMID-CCA) An ID-based anonymous multi-receiver key encapsulation mechanism with sender authentication is said to have the*

*indistinguishability against adaptive chosen ciphertext attacks property if no poly-
nomially bounded adversary has a non-negligible advantage in the following game
played between a challenger $\mathscr{C}$ and the adversary $\mathscr{A}$.*

1. $(params, S) \leftarrow \mathscr{C}^{Setup}(l)$: $\mathscr{C}$ runs the *Setup* algorithm with a security parameter l and obtains common parameters $Params$ and a master key S. He
   sends $Params$ to $\mathscr{A}$ and keeps S to itself.
2. $R^* \leftarrow \mathscr{A}(params)$: After receiving the system parameters, $\mathscr{A}$ outputs target
   multiple identities $R^* = (ID_1^*, ID_2^*, ..., ID_n^*)$, where n is a positive integer.
3. $\mathscr{A}^{\mathscr{O}}(params)$.
4. $(K_1, K_0, C^*) \leftarrow \mathscr{C}^{Encap}(params, ID_s^*, R^*)$: ID_s^* is an arbitrary signer iden-
   tity whose private key is d_s, $(K_\gamma, C) = Encap(d_s, R)$, $\gamma \in \{0, 1\}$, $K_\beta, \beta \in \{0, 1\}$, $\beta \neq \gamma$ is randomly chosen by the challenger from the key space.
5. $\gamma' \in \{0, 1\} \leftarrow \mathscr{A}^{\mathscr{O}}(params, m^*, K_0, K_1, C^*, ID_s^*, R^*)$: $\mathscr{A}$ produces a bit γ'
   and wins the game if $\gamma' = \gamma$.

In stage 3 and 5, the adversary $\mathscr{A}$ can make queries to the key extraction
oracle $\mathscr{O}(Extract)$, the encapsulation oracle $\mathscr{O}(Encap)$ and the decapsulation
oracle $\mathscr{O}(Decap)$ as described below, but subject to the restrictions that $\mathscr{A}$
cannot make queries to $\mathscr{O}(Decap)$ under any identity in the receiver list R^*, nor
to $\mathscr{O}(Extract)$ with an identity in R^*.

$\mathscr{O}(Extract) : d_{ID} \leftarrow Extract(ID)$

$\mathscr{O}(Encap) : (K, C) \leftarrow Encap(ID_s, ID_1, ..., ID_n)$

$\mathscr{O}(Decap) : K/\bot \leftarrow Decap(C, ID_s, ID_1, ..., ID_n)$

The advantage of the adversary $\mathscr{A}$ is defined as:

$$Adv^{IND-sMID-CCA}(A) = |Pr[\gamma' = \gamma] - 1/2|$$

Definition 6. *(EUF-sID-CMA) An ID-based anonymous multi-receiver key encapsulation mechanism with sender authentication is said to be existential un-
forgeability against adaptive chosen message attacks if no polynomially bounded
adversary has a non-negligible advantage in the following game played between
a challenger $\mathscr{C}$ and the adversary $\mathscr{A}$.*

1. $(params, S) \leftarrow \mathscr{C}^{Setup}(l)$: $\mathscr{C}$ runs the Setup algorithm with a security parameter l and obtains common parameters $Params$ and a master key S. He
   sends $Params$ to the adversary and keeps S secret.
2. $ID_s^* \leftarrow \mathscr{A}$:$\mathscr{A}$ outputs the target identity ID_s^* on which he would like to
   challenge.
3. $(K, C, ID_s^*, R = (ID_1, ..., ID_n)) \leftarrow \mathscr{A}^{\mathscr{O}}(params)$, $R^* = (ID_i^*, ..., ID_n^*)$: $\mathscr{A}$
   produces a encapsulation ciphertext C of the key K and n arbitrary receivers'
   identities $(ID_1, ..., ID_n)$.

In stage 3, the adversary $\mathscr{A}$ has access to the same oracles as in the definition
3.1. ID_s^* should be never submitted to $\mathscr{O}(Extract)$, and C^* should be different
from any output of $\mathscr{O}(Encap)$.

$\mathscr{A}$ wins the game if the result of $Decap(C, ID_s^*, d_i)$ for some $i \in [1, n]$ results
in a valid key K and the private key of ID_s^* was not queried. The advantage

of the adversary $Adv(\mathscr{A})$ is defined as the probability $Pr[win]$ that it wins this game.

Definition 7. *(ANON-IND-sID-CCA) An ID-based anonymous multi-receiver key encapsulation mechanism with sender authentication is said to be anonymous indistinguishability against adaptive chosen ciphertext attacks if no polynomially bounded adversary has a non-negligible advantage in the following game played between a challenger $\mathscr{C}$ and the adversary $\mathscr{A}$.*

1. $(params, S) \leftarrow \mathscr{C}^{Setup}(l)$: $\mathscr{C}$ runs the Setup algorithm with a security parameter l and obtains common parameters $Params$ and a master key S. He sends $Params$ to the adversary and keeps S secret.
2. $(ID_1^*, ID_2^*) \leftarrow \mathscr{A}$: $\mathscr{A}$ outputs output a target identity pair (ID_1^*, ID_2^*) on which he would like to challenge.
3. $\mathscr{A}^{\mathscr{O}}(params)$.
4. $(ID_s, ID_3, ..., ID_n) \leftarrow \mathscr{A}$: $\mathscr{A}$ outputs a sender ID_s and a set of identities $ID_3, ..., ID_n$, where $n \geqslant 3$.
5. $(K, C) \leftarrow \mathscr{C}^{Encap}(ID_s, (ID_\gamma^*, ID_3, ..., ID_n))$: $\mathscr{C}$ generates a target ciphertext by chooses randomly a bit $\gamma \in \{1, 2\}$, $d_s = Extract(S, Params, ID_S)$ and $(K, C) = Encap(d_s, (ID_\gamma^*, ID_3, ..., ID_n))$.
6. $\gamma' \in \{0, 1\} \leftarrow \mathscr{A}^{\mathscr{O}}(params, K, C, ID_s, ID_1^*, ID_2^*, ID_3, ..., ID_n)$: $\mathscr{A}$ produces a bit γ' and wins the game if $\gamma' = \gamma$.

In stage 3 and 6, the adversary $\mathscr{A}$ has access to the same oracles as in the definition 3.1 but subject to the restrictions that ID_1^*, ID_2^* should be never submitted to $\mathscr{O}(Extract)$ and it is not allowed to make an Decap query for C under any identity in (ID_1^*, ID_2^*).

The advantage of the adversary $\mathscr{A}$ is defined as:

$$Adv^{ANON-IND-sID-CCA}(A) = |Pr[\gamma' = \gamma] - 1/2|$$

4 The Concrete Scheme

In this section, we propose a concrete ID-based anonymous multi-receiver key encapsulation mechanism with sender authentication based on Tseng et al.'s multiple receiver encryption scheme [5] and Cha et al.'s ID-based signature scheme [8]. The algorithms are as following:

Setup. Given a security parameter l, PKG generates two groups G_1 and G_2 of prime order $q > 2^l$ such that an admissible bilinear map $e : G_1 \times G_1 \rightarrow G_2$ can be constructed and pick a generator P of G_1. The PKG randomly chooses a system secret key $S \in \mathbb{Z}_q^*$ and computes $P_{pub} = S \cdot P \in G_1$ as the system public key. Let H_0, H_1, H_2, H_3 be cryptography hash functions where $H_0 : \{0, 1\}^* \rightarrow G_1$, $H_1 : G_2 \rightarrow \mathbb{Z}_q^*$, $H_2 : \mathbb{Z}_q^* \rightarrow \{0, 1\}^w$ where w is the plaintext block length, $H_3 : \{0, 1^* \times \mathbb{Z}_q^* \times ... \times \mathbb{Z}_q^* \times G_1 \times G_1 \rightarrow \mathbb{Z}_q^*$. The public parameters and functions are presented as $Params = \{G_1, G_2, e, P, P_{pub}, H_0, H_1, H_2, H_3\}$.

Extract. For a given identity $ID \in \{0, 1\}^*$, the PKG computes $QID = H_0(ID)$ and the secret key $d = S \cdot QID \in G_1$. Then, d is transmitted to the user via a secure channel. Without loss of generality, the sender and the receivers' private keys can be expressed as (ID_s, d_s) and $((ID_1, d_1), (ID_2, d_2), ..., (ID_n, d_n))$.

Encap. To generate a encapsulation key k to n receivers with identities $R = \{ID_1, ID_2, ..., ID_n\}$, the sender performs the following tasks:

1. Choose random $r_1, r_2 \in \mathbb{Z}_q^*$, and compute $U = r_1 \cdot P$, $T = r_1 \cdot P_{pub}$ and $v_s = r_2 \cdot QID_s = r_2 \cdot H_0(ID_s)$.
2. Compute $QID_i = H_0(ID_i)$ and $v_i = H_1(e(QID_i, T))$, for $i = 1, ..., n$.
3. Choose a random $k \in \mathbb{Z}_q^*$ and construct a polynomial $f(x)$ with degree t as below: $f(x) = \prod_{i=1,...n}(x - v_i) + k(mod q) = c_0 + c_1 x + ... + c_{n-1} x^{n-1} + x^n$, where $c_i \in \mathbb{Z}_q^*$.
4. Compute $\sigma = (r_2 + h) \cdot d_s$, where $h = H_3(ID_s, c_0, c_1, ..., c_{n-1}, U, v_s)$. Set the result ciphertext to be $C = < ID_s, (c_0, c_1, ..., c_{n-1}), U, v_s, \sigma >$.

Decap. After receive the ciphertext as $C = < ID_s, (c_0, c_1, ..., c_{n-1}), U, v_s, \sigma >$, the receiver with index j in R decrypts the ciphertext as follows:

1. Compute $h = H_3(ID_s, c_0, c_1, ..., c_{n-1}, U, v_s)$.
2. Test whether $e(P, \sigma) = e(P_{pub}, v_s + h \cdot QID_s)$ or not. If it does not hold, output 'reject'.
3. Compute $v_j = H_1(e(d_j, U))$.
4. Set the polynomial $f(x)$ with degree t as $f(x) = c_0 + c_1 x + ... + c_{n-1} x^{n-1} + x^n$ and compute $k = f(v_j)$.

Correctness of Our Scheme. If $C = < ID_s, (c_0, c_1, ..., c_{n-1}), U, v_s, \sigma >$ is a valid ciphertext from a message sender to the receivers list $R = \{ID_1, ID_2, ..., ID_n\}$, then the receiver in receiver list with identity ID_j's Decapsulation is correct because

$$\begin{aligned}
e(P, \sigma) &= e(P, (r_2 + h) \cdot d_s) \\
&= e(P, (r_2 + h) \cdot S \cdot QID_s) \\
&= e(S \cdot P, r_2 \cdot H_0(ID_s) + h \cdot QID_s) \\
&= e(P_{pub}, v_s + h \cdot QID_s)
\end{aligned}$$

and

$$\begin{aligned}
H_1(e(d_j, U)) &= H_1(e(S \cdot QID_j, r_1 \cdot P)) \\
&= H_1(e(QID_j, r_1 \cdot S \cdot P)) \\
&= H_1(e(QID_j, T)) \\
&= v_j
\end{aligned}$$

We have

$$\begin{aligned}
k = f(v_j) &= c_0 + c_1 v_j + ... + c_{n-1} v_j^{n-1} + v_j^n \\
&= \prod_{i=1,...,n}(v_j - v_i) + k \\
&= k(mod q)
\end{aligned}$$

5 Security Analysis

Theorem 1. *In the random oracle, if an adversary $\mathscr{A}$ has non-negligible advantage ε against the IND-sMID-CCA security of our scheme when running in time t and performing q_e extraction oracle, q_{Encap} Encap queries, q_{Decap} Decap queries and q_i queries to oracles $H_i(i = 0, 1, 2, 3)$, then there is an algorithm $\mathscr{B}$ that solves the Gap-BDH problem with probability $\varepsilon' > \varepsilon - q_{Decap}/q$ and within running time $t' \leq t + (q_{Encap} + 2q_{Decap})\mathcal{O}(t_e) + (q_0 + q_e)\mathcal{O}(t_m) + nq_1\mathcal{O}(t_1)$ where t_e denotes the time required for one pairing evaluation, t_m denotes the time required for one scalar multiplication in G_1, t_1 denotes the time required for one DBDH oracle and n is the number of multiple identities.*

Proof. Suppose there exists an IND-sMID-CCA adversary $\mathscr{A}$ for our proposed scheme. We show how to build an algorithm $\mathscr{B}$ that solve the Gap-BDH problem by running the adversary $\mathscr{A}$ as a subroutine. $\mathscr{B}$ plays the role of $\mathscr{A}$'s challenge and works by interaction with $\mathscr{A}$ in the game defined in section 3.

The challenger $\mathscr{C}$ receives an instance (P, aP, bP, cP) of the Gap-BDH problem, in which $P, aP, bP, cP \in G_1$ for unknown $a, b, c \in \mathbb{Z}_q^*$. His goal is to compute $e(P, P)^{abc}$ and he may make at most q_g queries to the DBDH oracle of the Gap-BDH problem.

The challenger $\mathscr{C}$ sets $Q = aP$ and $P_{pub} = bP$. Then $\mathscr{C}$ gives $\mathscr{A}$ the system parameters $Params = \{G_1, G_2, e, P, P_{pub}, H_0, H_1, H_2, H_3\}$. After receive the system parameters, $\mathscr{A}$ outputs target multiple identities $R^* = (ID_1^*, ID_2^*, ..., ID_n^*)$, where n is a positive integer. The hash functions are random oracles controlled by $\mathscr{C}$ and for the adversary $\mathscr{A}$'s queries, $\mathscr{C}$ will maintain four lists $L_i(i = 0, 1, 2, 3)$ to record the results of the hash function $H_i(i = 0, 1, 2, 3)$ respectively.

$\mathscr{C}$ can answer $\mathscr{A}$'s queries as following: • *Query on H_0 for ID_j.* When an element $ID_j \in \{0, 1\}^*$ is submitted to the H_0 oracle for some $j \in [1, q_0]$, $\mathscr{C}$ checks if there exists a tuple (ID_j, u_j, QID_j) in L_0. If such a tuple exists, $\mathscr{C}$ answers with QID_j. Otherwise, $\mathscr{C}$ does the following:

1. Select a random value $u_j \in \mathbb{Z}_q^*$.
2. If $ID_j \in R^*$, then compute $QID_j = u_j \cdot Q \in G_1$; Otherwise, compute $QID_j = u_j \cdot P \in G_1$.
3. Insert the tuple (ID_j, u_j, QID_j) into the list L_0. Then, $\mathscr{C}$ return QID_j to the adversary.

• *Query on H_1 for $X_j \in G_2$.* When an element $X_j \in G_2$ is submitted to the H_1 oracle for some $j \in [1, q_1]$, $\mathscr{C}$ checks if there exists a tuple (X_j, x_j) in L_1. If such a tuple exists, $\mathscr{C}$ answers with x_j. $\mathscr{C}$ checks whether $(P, QID_i^*, P_{pub}, cP, X_j)$ using the DBDH oracle for $i = 1, 2, ..., n$, in which $QID_i^* = u_i \cdot Q \in G_1$ is obtained by issuing H_0 query. If it is, $\mathscr{C}$ return $(X_j)^{u_i^{-1}}$ and terminates the game because $\mathscr{C}$ has obtained the value $e(P, P)^{abc}$. Otherwise, $\mathscr{C}$ selects a value $x_j \in \mathbb{Z}_q^*$ and inserts the tuple (X_j, x_j) into the list L_1. Then, $\mathscr{C}$ returns x_j to the adversary $\mathscr{A}$.

• *Query on H_2 for $k_j \in \mathbb{Z}_q^*$.* When an element $k_j \in \mathbb{Z}_q^*$ is submitted to the H_2 oracle for some $j \in [1, q_2]$, $\mathscr{C}$ first scan the list L_2 to check whether the input was already defined in L_2. If it was, the previously defined value is returned to $\mathscr{A}$. Otherwise, $\mathscr{C}$ randomly picks a bit string $w_j \in \{0,1\}^w$ and inserts the tuple (k_j, w_j) into the list L_2. Then $\mathscr{C}$ returns w_j to the adversary $\mathscr{A}$.

• *Query on H_3 for a tuple $(ID, (c_0, c_1, ..., c_{n-1}), U, v_s)$.* When a tuple $(ID, (c_0, c_1, ..., c_{n-1}), U, v_s)$ is submitted to the H_3 oracle for some $j \in [1, q_3]$, $\mathscr{C}$ first scan the list L_3 to check whether the input was already defined in L_3. If it was, the previously defined value is returned to $\mathscr{A}$. Otherwise, $\mathscr{C}$ randomly picks a value $\lambda_j \in \mathbb{Z}_q^*$ at random and inserts the tuple $(ID, (c_0, c_1, ..., c_{n-1}), U, v_s, \lambda_j)$ into the list L_3. Then, $\mathscr{C}$ returns λ_j to the adversary $\mathscr{A}$.

• *Extraction queries.* Upon receiving this query with $ID_j \notin R^*$, the challenger $\mathscr{C}$ first scans the list L_0 to check whether the tuple (ID_j, u_j, QID_j) was already defined in L_0. If it was, $\mathscr{C}$ computes $d_j = u_j \cdot P_{pub}$. Otherwise. $\mathscr{C}$ randomly selects a value $u_j \in \mathbb{Z}_q^*$, and computes $QID_j = u_j \cdot P$ and $d_j = u_j \cdot P_{pub}$. Meanwhile, $\mathscr{C}$ inserts the tuple (ID_j, u_j, QID_j) into the list L_0. Finally, $\mathscr{C}$ returns d_j to the adversary $\mathscr{A}$.

• *Encap queries.* The adversary $\mathscr{A}$ issues Encap queries for target identities, denoted by (m, ID_s, R^*). $\mathscr{C}$ computes the secret key u_s corresponding to ID_s by making a *extractionquery* and then can simply run the algorithm $Encap(m, d_s, R^*)$. Finally, $\mathscr{C}$ returns the result C to the adversary $\mathscr{A}$.

• *Decap queries.* $\mathscr{A}$ can perform an Decap query for a ciphertext C for a sender ID_s and a receiver $ID_i^* \in R^*$ where $C =< ID_s, (c_0, c_1, ..., c_{n-1}), U, v_s, \sigma >$. Note that the return values of the used hash functions here are obtained from hash queries in the previous phase. $\mathscr{C}$ performs the following tasks:

1. Use $(ID_s, (c_0, c_1, ..., c_{n-1}), U, v_s)$ to scan the list L_3. If it was not found, $\mathscr{C}$ returns 'failure' and halts. Otherwise, $\mathscr{C}$ may get $h = \lambda$ from L_3.
2. Test whether $e(P, \sigma) = e(P_{pub}, (v_s + h \cdot QID_s))$ or not. If it does not hold, output 'reject' indicated that the ciphertext is not valid.
3. Set the polynomial $f(x)$ with degree n as $f(x) = c_0 + c_1 x + ... + c_{n-1} x^{n-1} + x^n$.
4. Use ID_i^* to pick the tuple (ID_i^*, u_i^*, QID_i^*) from the list L_0 to get u_i^* and QID_i^*.
5. For $j = 1, ..., q_1$, do the following:

   (a) Pick the tuple (X_j, x_j) from the list L_1.
   (b) Check whether $(P, QID_i^*, P_{pub}, U, X_j)$ using the DBDH oracle.

6. If some j of the checks above is true, compute $k_j = f(x_j)$, return k_j to $\mathscr{A}$. Otherwise, return $\perp$ indicating that the ciphertext is invalid.

$\mathscr{C}$ randomly chooses ID_s, and performs the following tasks.

1. Scan the list L_0 to check whether the tuple (ID_s, u_s, QID_s) was already defined in L_0. If it was, $\mathscr{C}$ computes $d_s = u_s \cdot P_{pub}$. Otherwise. $\mathscr{C}$ randomly selects a value $u_s \in \mathbb{Z}_q^*$, and computes $QID_s = u_s \cdot P$ and $d_s = u_s \cdot P_{pub}$. Meanwhile, $\mathscr{C}$ inserts the tuple (ID_s, u_s, QID_s) into the list L_0.
2. Choose $r_2 \in \mathbb{Z}_q^*$, set $U = cP$, compute $v_s = r_2 \cdot QID_s = r_2 \cdot H_0(ID_s)$.
3. Choose $z_i \in \mathbb{Z}_q^*$, for $i = 1, ..., n$.

4. Choose a random $k \in \mathbb{Z}_q^*$ and construct a polynomial $f(x)$ with degree n as below: $f(x) = \prod_{i=1,...n}(x - z_i) + k(mod q) = c_0 + c_1 x + ... + c_{n-1}x^{n-1} + x^n$, where $c_i \in \mathbb{Z}_q^*$.
5. Compute $\sigma = (r_2 + h) \cdot d_s$, where $h = H_3(ID_s, c_0, c_1, ..., c_{n-1}, U, v_s)$. Set the result ciphertext to be $C =< ID_s, (c_0, c_1, ..., c_{n-1}), U, v_s, \sigma >$.

$\mathscr{A}$ makes a number of extraction queries, Encap queries and Decap queries. A restriction here is that $\mathscr{A}$ is not allowed to issue the target ciphertext with one of the target identity as Decap query. $\mathscr{A}$ output a guess $\gamma' \in \{0, 1\}$ and wins the game if $\gamma' = \gamma$.

As the simulation above, $\mathscr{C}$ successfully simulates the hash function $H_i(i = 0, 1, 2, 3)$ by random oracles. Meanwhile, the secret key d_u associated to each $ID_u \notin R^*$ created in the key extract query is identically distributed as the key in the real attack environment because of $d_j = u_j \cdot P_{pub} = u_j \cdot S \cdot P = S \cdot u_j \cdot P = S \cdot H_0(ID_j)$. Thus, it is obvious that $\mathscr{C}$ perfectly simulates the key extract query.

In the following, we assess that $\mathscr{C}$'s advantage. For handling the Decap query, if $(c_0, c_1, ..., c_{n-1}), U, v_s)$ cannot be found in L_3, $\mathscr{C}$ returns 'failure' and halts. Thus, it means that $\mathscr{A}$ can guess a right output value of hash function H_3. In this case, there are q_{Decap} queries to the Decap oracle, so the failure probability of is at most q_{Decap}/q. If $\mathscr{A}$ with a non-negligible advantage win the IND-sMID-CCA game, it denotes that $\mathscr{C}$ with a non-negligible advantage has received H_1 queries with some X_j as input, in which one of the DBDH oracle queries with $(P, QID_i^*, P_{pub}, cP, X_j)$ for $i = 1, ..., n$, will return 1. As in H_1 queries, $\mathscr{C}$ may obtain $(X_j)^{u_i^{*-1}} = e(P, P)^{abc}$, in which (ID_i^*, u_i^*, QID_i^*) is obtained from L_0. Hence, assume that the IND-sMID-CCA adversary $\mathscr{A}$ has a non-negligible advantage ϵ against the proposed scheme. Then, the Gap-BDH problem can be solved with a non-negligible advantage $\epsilon' > \epsilon - (q_{Decap}/q)$.

Finally, for answering queries in the simulation game above, the required computation time is $t' \le t + (q_{Encap} + 2q_{Decap})\mathcal{O}(t_e) + (q_0 + q_e)\mathcal{O}(t_m) + nq_1\mathcal{O}(t_1)$ where t_e denotes the time required for one pairing evaluation, t_m denotes the time required for one scalar multiplication in G_1, t_1 denotes the time required for one DBDH oracle and n is the number of multiple identities.

Theorem 2. *In the random oracle, if an adversary $\mathscr{A}$ has non-negligible advantage $\varepsilon \ge 10(q_{Encap} + 1)(q_{Encap} + q_3)/2^l$ against the EUF-sID-CMA security of our scheme when running in time t and performing q_e extraction oracle, q_{Encap} Encap queries, q_{Decap} Decap queries and q_i queries to oracles $H_i(i = 0, 1, 2, 3)$, then there exists an algorithm $\mathscr{B}$ that solves the CDH problem in expected time $t' \le 120686q_3 t/\varepsilon$.*

Proof. Suppose there exists an EUF-sID-CMA adversary $\mathscr{A}$ for our proposed scheme. We show how to build an algorithm $\mathscr{B}$ that solve the CDH problem by running the adversary $\mathscr{A}$ as a subroutine. $\mathscr{B}$ plays the role of $\mathscr{A}$'s challenger and works by interaction with $\mathscr{A}$ in the game defined in section 3.

The challenger $\mathscr{C}$ receives an instance (P, aP, bP) of the CDH problem, in which $P, aP, bP \in G_1$ for unknown $a, b \in \mathbb{Z}_q^*$. His goal is to compute the value of abP.

The challenger $\mathscr{C}$ sets $P_{pub} = aP$. Then $\mathscr{C}$ gives $\mathscr{A}$ the system parameters $Params = \{G_1, G_2, e, P, P_{pub}, H_0, H_1, H_2, H_3\}$. After receive the system parameters, $\mathscr{A}$ outputs a target identity ID_s^*. The hash functions are random oracles controlled by $\mathscr{C}$ and for the adversary $\mathscr{A}$'s queries, $\mathscr{C}$ will maintain four lists $L_i(i = 0, 1, 2, 3)$ to record the results of the hash function $H_i(i = 0, 1, 2, 3)$ respectively.

$\mathscr{C}$ can answer $\mathscr{A}$'s queries as following:

• *Query on H_0 for ID_j.* When an element $ID_j \in \{0, 1\}^*$ is submitted to the H_0 oracle for some $j \in [1, q_0]$, $\mathscr{C}$ checks if $ID_j = ID_s^*$, if it is, $\mathscr{C}$ answers with $QID_j = bP \in G_1$. Otherwise, $\mathscr{C}$ checks if there exists a tuple (ID_j, u_j, QID_j) in L_0. If such a tuple exists, $\mathscr{C}$ answers with QID_j. Otherwise, $\mathscr{C}$ does the following:

1. Select a random value $u_j \in \mathbb{Z}_q^*$, compute $QID_j = u_j \cdot P \in G_1$.
2. Insert the tuple (ID_j, u_j, QID_j) into the list L_0. Then, $\mathscr{C}$ return QID_j to the adversary.

• *Query on $H_i(i = 1, 2, 3)$.* $\mathscr{C}$ produce a random element from the appropriate range, and add both query and answer to the corresponding list.

$\mathscr{A}$ performs a polynomially bounded number of queries adaptively just like in the previous definition.

• *Extraction queries.* Upon receiving this query with $ID_j \neq ID_s^*$, the challenger $\mathscr{C}$ first scans the list L_0 to check whether the tuple (ID_j, u_j, QID_j) was already defined in L_0. If it was, $\mathscr{C}$ computes $d_j = u_j \cdot P_{pub}$. Otherwise. $\mathscr{C}$ randomly selects a value $u_j \in \mathbb{Z}_q^*$, and computes $QID_j = u_j \cdot P$ and $d_j = u_j \cdot P_{pub}$. Meanwhile, $\mathscr{C}$ inserts the tuple (ID_j, u_j, QID_j) into the list L_0. Finally, $\mathscr{C}$ returns d_j to the adversary $\mathscr{A}$.

• *Encap queries.* The adversary $\mathscr{A}$ issues Encap queries for $(m, ID_j, (ID_1, ID_2, ..., ID_n))$ and $\mathscr{C}$ checks if $ID_j = ID_s^*$. IF not, then it computes the private key u_j corresponding to ID_j by running a key extraction query algorithm and then can simply run the algorithm $Encap(m, d_j, (ID_1, ID_2, ..., ID_n))$. Finally, $\mathscr{C}$ returns the result C to the adversary $\mathscr{A}$. In the case when $ID_j = ID_s^*$, it chooses $r, y, h \in \mathbb{Z}_q^*$ randomly and performs the following tasks:

1. Compute $U = r_1 \cdot P$, $T = r_1 \cdot P_{pub}$ and $v_s = y \cdot P - h \cdot H_0(ID_s^*)$.
2. Compute $QID_i = H_0(ID_i)$ and $v_i = H_1(e(QID_i, T))$, for $i = 1, ..., n$.
3. Choose a random $k \in \mathbb{Z}_q^*$ and construct a polynomial $f(x)$ with degree n as below: $f(x) = \prod_{i=1,...n}(x - v_i) + k(mod q) = c_0 + c_1 x + ... + c_{n-1}x^{n-1} + x^n$, where $c_i \in \mathbb{Z}_q^*$.
4. Compute $V = m \oplus H_2(k)$, $\sigma = y \cdot P_{pub}$ and returns the result ciphertext as $C = < ID_s^*, (c_0, c_1, ..., c_{n-1}), U, v_s, \sigma >$.
5. Inserts the tuple $(ID_s^*, (c_0, c_1, ..., c_{n-1}), U, v_s, h)$ into the list L_3.

• *Decap queries.* $\mathscr{A}$ can perform an Decap query for a ciphertext C for a sender ID_j and a receiver $ID_i(i \in 1, 2, ..., n)$ where $C = < ID_j, (c_0, c_1, ..., c_{n-1}), U, v_s, \sigma >$. it computes the private key u_i corresponding to ID_i by making a extraction query algorithm and then can simply run the algorithm $Decap((C, ID_j, d_i)$. Finally, $\mathscr{C}$ returns the result m or $\perp$ to the adversary $\mathscr{A}$.

Finally, $\mathscr{A}$ produces a ciphertext $C^* = (ID_s^*, (c_0^*, c_1^*, ..., c_{t-1}^*), U^*, v_s^*, \sigma^*)$ where t is a position integer. $\mathscr{A}$ wins the game if the result of $Decap(C^*, ID_s^*, ID_i^*)$ for some $i \in [1, t]$ results in a valid message m and the private key of ID_s^* was not queried.

It follows from the forking lemma [9] that if $\mathscr{A}$ is a sufficiently efficient forger in the above interaction, then we can construct another probabilistic polynomial time Turing machine $\mathscr{A}'$ that outputs two ciphertext $C' = <ID_s^*, (c_0, c_1, ..., c_{n-1}),$ $U, v_s, \sigma' >$ and $C'' = <ID_s^*, (c_0, c_1, ..., c_{n-1}), U, v_s, \sigma'' >$ on same message m from the sender with identity ID_s^*. $\mathscr{C}$ decap C' and C'' to obtain the 'signatures' $\sigma' = (r_2 + h') \cdot d_s^*$ and $\sigma'' = (r_2 + h'') \cdot d_s^*$. Now we can apply standard arguments for the outputs of the forking lemma since both σ' and σ'' are valid signatures for the same message m and same random tape of the adversary. Finally, $\mathscr{C}$ obtains the solution to the CDH instance as $(\sigma'' - \sigma')(h'' - h')^{-1}$. We have $(\sigma'' - \sigma')(h'' - h')^{-1} = (h'' - h')d_s^*(h'' - h')^{-1} = d_s^* = abP$.

So, we can see that $\mathscr{C}$ has the same advantage in solving the CDH problem as the adversary $\mathscr{A}$ has in forging a valid ciphertext. Based on the bound from the forking lemma and the above probability of success, if an adversary $\mathscr{A}$ has non-negligible advantage $\varepsilon \geq 10(q_{Encap} + 1)(q_{Encap} + q_3)/2^l$ against the EUF-sID-CMA security of our scheme when running in time t, then $\mathscr{C}$ can solve the CDH problem in expected time $t' \leq 120686q_3t/\varepsilon$.

Theorem 3. *In the random oracle, if an adversary $\mathscr{A}$ has non-negligible advantage ε against the ANON-IND-sID-CCA security of our scheme when running in time t and performing q_e extraction oracle, q_{Encap} Encap queries, q_{Decap} Decap queries and q_i queries to oracles $H_i(i = 0, 1, 2, 3)$, then there is an algorithm $\mathscr{B}$ that solves the Gap-BDH problem with probability $\varepsilon' > \varepsilon - q_{Decap}/q$ and within running time $t' \leq t + (q_{Encap} + 2q_{Decap})\mathcal{O}(t_e) + (q_0 + q_e)\mathcal{O}(t_m) + nq_1\mathcal{O}(t_1)$ where t_e denotes the time required for one pairing evaluation, t_m denotes the time required for one scalar multiplication in G_1, t_1 denotes the time required for one DBDH oracle and n is the number of multiple identities.*

Proof. Suppose there exists an ANON-IND-sID-CCA adversary $\mathscr{A}$ for our proposed scheme. We show how to build an algorithm $\mathscr{B}$ that solve the Gap-BDH problem by running the adversary $\mathscr{A}$ as a subroutine. $\mathscr{B}$ plays the role of $\mathscr{A}$'s challenge and works by interaction with $\mathscr{A}$ in the game defined in section 3.

The challenger $\mathscr{C}$ receives an instance (P, aP, bP, cP) of the Gap-BDH problem, in which $P, aP, bP, cP \in G_1$ for unknown $a, b, c \in \mathbb{Z}_q^*$. His goal is to compute $e(P, P)^{abc}$ and he may make at most q_g queries to the DBDH oracle of the Gap-BDH problem.

$\mathscr{C}$ sets $Q = aP$ and $P_{pub} = bP$. Then $\mathscr{C}$ gives $\mathscr{A}$ the system parameters $Params = \{G_1, G_2, e, P, P_{pub}, H_0, H_1, H_2, H_3\}$. The hash functions are random oracles controlled by $\mathscr{C}$ and for the adversary $\mathscr{A}$'s queries, $\mathscr{C}$ will maintain four lists $L_i(i = 0, 1, 2, 3)$ to record the results of the hash function $H_i(i = 0, 1, 2, 3)$ respectively. After receive the system parameters, $\mathscr{A}$ outputs target identity pair (ID_1^*, ID_2^*). Upon receiving the target identity pair, $\mathscr{C}$ randomly chooses $\gamma \in \{1, 2\}$.

$\mathscr{C}$ can answer $\mathscr{A}$'s queries as following:

• *Query on H_0 for ID_j*. When an element $ID_j \in \{0, 1\}^*$ is submitted to the H_0 oracle for some $j \in [1, q_0]$, $\mathscr{C}$ checks if there exists a tuple (ID_j, u_j, QID_j) in L_0. If such a tuple exists, $\mathscr{C}$ answers with QID_j. Otherwise, $\mathscr{C}$ does the following:

1. Select a random value $u_j \in \mathbb{Z}_q^*$.
2. If $ID_j = ID_i^*$ for some $i \in \{1, 2\}$, then compute $QID_j = u_j \cdot Q \in G_1$; Otherwise, compute $QID_j = u_j \cdot P \in G_1$.
3. Insert the tuple (ID_j, u_j, QID_j) into the list L_0. Then, $\mathscr{C}$ return QID_j to the adversary.

• *Query on H_1 for a $X_j \in G_2$*. When an element $X_j \in G_2$ is submitted to the H_1 oracle for some $j \in [1, q_1]$, $\mathscr{C}$ checks if there exists a tuple (X_j, x_j) in L_1. If such a tuple exists, $\mathscr{C}$ answers with x_j. $\mathscr{C}$ checks whether $(P, QID_i^*, P_{pub}, cP, X_j)$ using the DBDH oracle for $i = 1, 2$, in which $QID_i^* = u_i \cdot Q \in G_1$ is obtained by issuing H_0 query. If it is, $\mathscr{C}$ return $(X_j)^{u_i^{-1}}$ and terminates the game because $\mathscr{C}$ has obtained the value $e(P, P)^{abc}$. Otherwise, $\mathscr{C}$ selects a value $x_j \in \mathbb{Z}_q^*$ and inserts the tuple (X_j, x_j) into the list L_1. Then, $\mathscr{C}$ returns x_j to the adversary $\mathscr{A}$.

• *Query on H_2 for a $k_j \in \mathbb{Z}_q^*$*. When an element $k_j \in \mathbb{Z}_q^*$ is submitted to the H_2 oracle for some $j \in [1, q_2]$, $\mathscr{C}$ first scan the list L_2 to check whether the input was already defined in L_2. If it was, the previously defined value is returned to $\mathscr{A}$. Otherwise, $\mathscr{C}$ randomly picks a bit string $w_j \in \{0, 1\}^w$ and inserts the tuple (k_j, w_j) into the list L_2. Then $\mathscr{C}$ returns w_j to the adversary $\mathscr{A}$.

• *Query on H_3 for a tuple $(ID, (c_0, c_1, ..., c_{n-1}), U, v_s)$*. When a tuple $(ID, (c_0, c_1, ..., c_{n-1}), U, v_s)$ is submitted to the H_3 oracle for some $j \in [1, q_3]$, $\mathscr{C}$ first scan the list L_3 to check whether the input was already defined in L_3. If it was, the previously defined value is returned to $\mathscr{A}$. Otherwise, $\mathscr{C}$ randomly picks a value $\lambda_j \in \mathbb{Z}_q^*$ at random and inserts the tuple $(ID, (c_0, c_1, ..., c_{n-1}), U, v_s, \lambda_j)$ into the list L_3. Then, $\mathscr{C}$ returns λ_j to the adversary $\mathscr{A}$.

• *Extraction queries*. Upon receiving this query with $ID_j \neq ID_i^*$ for $i \in \{1, 2\}$, the challenger $\mathscr{C}$ first scans the list L_0 to check whether the tuple ID_j, u_j, QID_j was already defined in L_0. If it was, $\mathscr{C}$ computes $d_j = u_j \cdot P_{pub}$. Otherwise, $\mathscr{C}$ randomly selects a value $u_j \in \mathbb{Z}_q^*$, and computes $QID_j = u_j \cdot P$ and $d_j = u_j \cdot P_{pub}$. Meanwhile, $\mathscr{C}$ inserts the tuple (ID_j, u_j, QID_j) into the list L_0. Finally, $\mathscr{C}$ returns d_j to the adversary $\mathscr{A}$.

• *Encap queries*. The adversary $\mathscr{A}$ issues Encap queries for target identities, denoted by $(m, ID_s, (ID_1, ID_2, ..., ID_n))$. $\mathscr{C}$ computes the private key u_s corresponding to ID_s by running a key extraction query algorithm and then can simply run the algorithm $Encap(m, d_s, (ID_1, ID_2, ..., ID_n))$. Finally, $\mathscr{C}$ returns the result C to the adversary $\mathscr{A}$.

• *Decap queries.* $\mathscr{A}$ can perform an Decap query for a ciphertext C for a sender ID_s and a receiver $ID_i^*(i \in \{1,2\})$ where $C = < ID_s, (c_0, c_1, ..., c_{n-1}), U, v_s, \sigma >$. Note that the return values of the used hash functions here are obtained from hash queries in the previous phase. $\mathscr{C}$ performs the following tasks:

1. Use $(ID_s, (c_0, c_1, ..., c_{n-1}), U, v_s)$ to scan the list L_3. If it was not found, $\mathscr{C}$ returns 'failure' and halts. Otherwise, $\mathscr{C}$ may get $h = \lambda$ from L_3.
2. Test whether $e(P, \sigma) = e(P_{pub}, (v_s + h \cdot QID_s))$ or not. If it does not hold, output 'reject' indicated that the ciphertext is not valid.
3. Set the polynomial $f(x)$ with degree n as $f(x) = c_0 + c_1 x + ... + c_{n-1} x^{n-1} + x^n$.
4. Use ID_i^* to pick the tuple (ID_i^*, u_i^*, QID_i^*) from the list L_0 to get u_i^* and QID_i^*.
5. For $j = 1, ..., q_1$, do the following:
   (a) Pick the tuple (X_j, x_j) from the list L_1.
   (b) Check whether $(P, QID_i^*, P_{pub}, U, X_j)$ using the DBDH oracle.
6. If some j of the checks above is true, compute $k_j = f(x_j)$ to $\mathscr{A}$. Otherwise, return $\perp$ indicating that the ciphertext is invalid.

$\mathscr{A}$ outputs a sender and a set of identities $ID_s, ID_3, ..., ID_n$, where $n \geq 3$. $\mathscr{C}$ performs the following tasks:

1. Choose $r_2 \in \mathbb{Z}_q^*$, set $U = cP$, compute $v_s = r_2 \cdot QID_s = r_2 \cdot H_0(ID_s)$.
2. For $i = 3, ..., n$, get u_i from the tuples (ID_i, u_i, QID_i) of list L_0 and compute $v_i = H_1(e(U, u_i \cdot P_{pub}))$.
3. Choose random $v, k \in \mathbb{Z}_q^*$ and construct a polynomial $f(x)$ with degree n as below: $f(x) = (x-v) \prod_{i=3,...n}(x-v_i) + k(mod q) = c_0 + c_1 x + ... + c_{n-2} x^{n-2} + x^{n-1}$, where $c_i \in \mathbb{Z}_q^*$.
4. Compute $\sigma = (r_2 + h) \cdot d_s$, where $h = H_3(ID_s, c_0, c_1, ..., c_{n-2}, U, v_s)$. Set the result ciphertext to be $C = < ID_s, (c_0, c_1, ..., c_{n-2}), U, v_s, \sigma >$.

$\mathscr{A}$ makes a number of Extraction queries, Encap queries and Decap queries as in stage 1. A restriction here is that $\mathscr{A}$ is not allowed to issue the target ciphertext with one of the target identity as Decap query. $\mathscr{A}$ output a guess $\gamma' \in \{1,2\}$ and wins the game if $\gamma' = \gamma$.

In the following, we assess that $\mathscr{C}$'s advantage. For handling the Decap query, if $(ID_s, (c_0, c_1, ..., c_{t-1}), U, v_s)$ cannot be found in L_3, $\mathscr{C}$ returns 'failure' and halts. Thus, it means that $\mathscr{A}$ can guess a right output value of hash function H_3. In this case, there are q_{Decap} queries to the Decap oracle, so the failure probability of is at most q_{Decap}/q. If $\mathscr{A}$ with a non-negligible advantage win the ANON-IND-sID-CCA game, it denotes that $\mathscr{C}$ with a non-negligible advantage has received H_1 queries with some X_j as input, in which one of the DBDH oracle queries with $(P, QID_i^*, P_{pub}, cP, X_j)$ for $i = 1, 2$, will return 1. As in H_1 queries, $\mathscr{C}$ may obtain $(X_j)^{u_i^{*-1}} = e(P, P)^{abc}$, in which (ID_i^*, u_i^*, QID_i^*) is obtained from L_0. Hence, assume that the ANON-IND-sID-CCA adversary $\mathscr{A}$ has a non-negligible advantage ϵ against the proposed scheme. Then, the Gap-BDH problem can be solved with a non-negligible advantage $\epsilon' > \epsilon - (q_{Decap}/q)$.

Finally, for answering queries in the simulation game above, the required computation time is $t' \leq t + (q_{Encap} + 2q_{Decap})\mathcal{O}(t_e) + (q_0 + q_e)\mathcal{O}(t_m) + nq_1\mathcal{O}(t_1)$ where t_e denotes the time required for one pairing evaluation, t_m denotes the time required for one scalar multiplication in G_1, t_1 denotes the time required for one DBDH oracle and n is the number of multiple identities.

6 Conclusion

In this paper, we defined the security notions of ID-based anonymous multi-receiver key encapsulation mechanism with sender authentication to simulate attackers' abilities in the real attacking environment. We proposed a concrete scheme based on some efficient primitives and the proposed scheme is secure against the IND-sMID-CCA, EUF-sID-CMA and ANON-IND-sID-CCA attack under several hard problem assumptions.

References

1. Bellare, M., Boldyreva, A., Micali, S.: Public-key Encryption in a Multi-user Setting: Security Proofs and Improvements. In: Preneel, B. (ed.) EUROCRYPT 2000. LNCS, vol. 1807, pp. 259–274. Springer, Heidelberg (2000)
2. Fan, C.I., Huang, L.Y., Ho, P.H.: Anonymous Multireceiver Identity-based Encryption. IEEE T. Comput. 9, 1239–1249 (2010)
3. Chien, H.Y.: Improved Anonymous Multi-receiver Identity-based Encryption. The Comput. J. 4, 439–446 (2012)
4. Hur, J., Park, C., Hwang, S.O.: Privacy-preserving Identity-based Broadcast Encryption. Inform. Fusion. 4, 296–303 (2012)
5. Tseng, Y.M., Huang, Y.H., Chang, H.J.: Privacy-preserving Multireceiver ID-based Encryption with Provable Security. Int. J. Commun. Syst., 12 (2012), doi:10.1002/dac.2395 (Online Version)
6. Shoup, V.: A Proposal for an ISO Standard for Public Key Encryption (version 2.1), http://shoup.net/papers
7. Cramer, R., Shoup, V.: Design and Analysis of Practical Public-key Encryption Schemes Secure against Adaptive Chosen Ciphertext Attack. SIAM J. Comput. 1, 167–226 (2003)
8. Cha, J.C., Cheon, J.H.: An identity-based Signature from Gap Diffie-Hellman Groups. In: Desmedt, Y.G. (ed.) PKC 2003. LNCS, vol. 2567, pp. 18–30. Springer, Heidelberg (2002)
9. David, P., Jacques, S.: Security Arguments for Digital Signatures and Blind Signatures. J. Cryptol. 3, 361–396 (2000)
10. Shamir, A.: Identity-based Cryptosystems and Signature Schemes. In: Blakely, G.R., Chaum, D. (eds.) CRYPTO 1984. LNCS, vol. 196, pp. 47–53. Springer, Heidelberg (1985)
11. Boneh, D., Franklin, M.: Identity-based Encryption from the Weil Pairing. In: Kilian, J. (ed.) CRYPTO 2001. LNCS, vol. 2139, pp. 213–229. Springer, Heidelberg (2001)

Energy Efficient Routing with a Tree-Based Particle Swarm Optimization Approach

Guodong Wang, Hua Wang*, and Lei Liu

School of Computer Science and Technology Shandong University,
Jinan, Shandong Province, China
wangguodong2008@mail.sdu.edu.cn,
{wanghua,l.liu}@sdu.edu.cn

Abstract. In contemporary, the energy waste caused by an un-optimized design of network consumed a large part of limited resource. Reduction of unnecessary energy consumption in wired networks has attracted the public's attention. To save energy without affecting performance, many existing studies classified the problem as Mixed Integer Linear Programming problem, which is NP-complete. Following this idea, we propose a novel energy efficient routing algorithm with tree-based particle swarm optimization (EERTPSO) to get a solution covering all the idle-period communication nodes and minimize the number of nodes or links, considering the constraints of bandwidth, delay and link cost, in order to awake the necessary nodes meanwhile get the idles to sleep. By the above sleep-awake mechanism, algorithm obtains an accepted result satisfied the quality of service requirement. Simulation and analytical results show that our algorithm performs efficiently and effectively.

Keywords: Green networking, energy efficiency, intelligence optimization, particle swarm optimization.

1 Introduction

The current global computer network infrastructures make a surprising amount of energy consumption. Statistics show that according to current growth, by 2025, the average energy consumption in network field of IT industry will reach 13 times of that in 2006[1]. An explosive growth shows up in the energy consumption of Information and Communication Technology (ICT) equipment. For a long period, energy consumption of network equipments is considered to be negligible compared to industry, so few design concepts of network are concerned about power efficiency. Moreover, in order to enhance the robustness or meet the Quality of Service (QoS) requirements, some topological redundancy is designed purposely. These structures consume amount of energy even in idle state, providing opportunity for us to implement some energy saving operations.

---

* Corresponding author.

X.-h. Sun et al. (Eds.): ICA3PP 2014, Part II, LNCS 8631, pp. 659–670, 2014.

In a wired network, links and devices can be shut down independently. Consequently many previous studies concentrate the main idea on switching off the idle parts among that, which is the most straightforward method to reduce power consumption. From this we get a power saving approach that turns off the unnecessary links and nodes, in other words, transferring data with the selected minimum routing nodes while ensuring the QoS request.

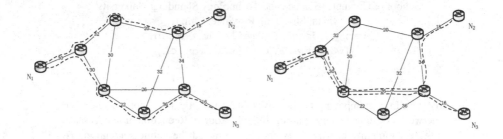

Fig. 1. Optimize the devices and links occupancy

As is simply depicted in Fig.1, N_1 N_2 N_3 are communication members in network idle periods. N_1, like some servers, needs rapidly communicating with the others. It is obviously that the devices and links occupancy of the optimized routing is much fewer than that of the original method. In this way, more devices and links will have the opportunity to be turned into sleep mode for energy saving.

So the key idea of energy-efficient routing is to provide routing service which restricts network traffic to fewer nodes and links in periods of low network utilization, getting high bandwidth utilization and saving energy while meeting network performance. Unused network elements will be shut down or switched into sleep mode. Many scholars have summarized this issue to Mixed Integer Linear Programming (MILP) problem, which proved to be an NP-complete problem[2]. Particle swarm optimization (PSO) is a comprehensive useful swarm intelligent algorithm to solve the NP-complete problem. We adapted a new PSO algorithm based on the tree growth (TPSO) for energy efficient routing problem.

The remaining part of this paper is organized as follows: The section 2 elaborates some related works of similar areas. In Section 3 we formulate network model and problem description. The Section 4 explains and demonstrates energy efficient TPSO algorithm in detail. Then simulation results are depicted and discussed in Section 5. Finally, we provide concluding remarks in Section 6.

2   Related Work

In the research area of energy-efficient networking, several recent novel technologies were summarized by survey[3]. To cope with this problem, two types of approaches have been proposed, what classified as system level and network level. The problem of saving energy consumption in the Internet was earliest proposed by Gupta and Singh[4]. In the follow-on work, some researchers focused on devices and components power management[5], sleeping and rate-adaptation modes were realized on network equipments to reduce the power consumption when network was idle or in lightly loaded state. On network level, energy aware traffic engineering is a common way. Article author in the[6] proposed a method of turning off nodes and links according to a traffic matrix and considering a fully connected network with the traffic constraint. Same on the network level, energy aware routing is another way to save energy. Several heuristic algorithms were modified to solve the energy-saving problem. Author in [7] re-formulated the problem of network energy consumption minimization with the centrality conception and presented an ant colony-based routing scheme to achieve the target. Energy-aware method proposed in [8] saves energy by examining the utilization of switch ports and idles network elements. Heller et al. [9] designed a novel method that chooses the nodes which mustn't to be shut down, then it powers down as many unnecessary links and nodes as possible. Topology-aware heuristic algorithm was used to determine which subset of network elements to be use. In this researching trends, proposing a more effective and efficient routing algorithm is our best orientation.

3   Problem Formulation

Assuming a physical network topology consisting of nodes wired by cable links, the power consumption of each node or link is given. In this architecture we research the energy efficient routing based on sleep-awake mechanism[10]. Our algorithm finds the set of nodes and links that should be powered on, after that, the other nodes and links which not in the solution set will be switched to sleep mode for saving power. Considering that links in a tree structure will be used frequently and so the fixed power consumption of each node or link can be amortized over more communication sessions, our algorithm uses a tree to route all the communication nodes[11]. If new sessions that not in the current routing tree come up, the necessary nodes in sleep state will be waked up to join in the new tree establishing progress. By this thought, we formulate our scheme to a math model which finds a routing tree for all the communication members while minimizes the number of nodes and links on the routing tree and guarantees the QoS requirements.

Definition: Construct a directed graph $G= (V, E)$, where V denotes the set of nodes and E denotes the set of links, while $N=|V|$ and $L=|E|$ are the total number of nodes and links respectively. Let t^{sd} be the bandwidth requirement (traffic demand) from node $s=1$, ... N to node $d=1$, ... N, and b_{ij} represents the bandwidth from node i to j. Let $f_{ij}^{sd} \in [0, t^{sd}]$ denote the amount of flow which is routed through the link from i to j between s to d. Let binary variable x_{ij} $i=1$, ... N, $j=1$, ... N, take the value of 1or 0 depending on whether link from node i to j is power-on state, the same principle applies to binary variable y_i for nodes. Finally, the power consumption of link from node i to j, and of node i are denoted by P_L and P_N respectively.

Based on above definitions, the problem could be formulated as:
Min:

$$\sum_{i=1}^{N}\sum_{j=1}^{N}x_{ij}P_L + \sum_{i=1}^{N}y_iP_N \tag{1}$$

Subject to:

$$\sum_{j=1}^{N}f_{ij}^{sd} - \sum_{j=1}^{N}f_{ji}^{sd} = \begin{cases} t^{sd} & \forall s,d,i = s \\ -t^{sd} & \forall s,d,i = d \\ 0 & \forall s,d,i \neq s,d \end{cases} \tag{2}$$

$$\sum_{s=1}^{N}\sum_{d=1}^{N}f_{ij}^{sd} \leq b_{ij}x_{ij} \quad \forall i,j \tag{3}$$

In this formulation, the objective function (1) is to minimize the total power consumption of network. Constraint (2) ensures the conservation of flow. Constraint (3) ensures the total flow (sum bandwidth required) on each active link to be less than the provided bandwidth. Especially, since P_L and P_N are depended on the actual conditions, in order to facilitate research, we assume P_L is far less than P_N [12], so that the objective for our heuristic algorithm could be converted into finding a solution tree containing as fewer nodes as possible while meeting other conditions.

4   A Tree Based PSO Energy Efficient Algorithm

The PSO algorithm imitates the behaviour of swarm creatures in the real world, which has good performance in NP-c problem optimization[13]. In PSO algorithm, every particle flies to better solution positions by the experience of the individual and its neighbours. This mechanism can be depicted by the formulas below:

$$v_{id} = w \times v_{id} + c_1 \times rand() \times (p_{id} - x_{id}) + c_2 \times Rand() \times (p_{gd} - x_{id}) \tag{4}$$

$$x_{id} = x_{id} + v_{id} \tag{5}$$

Table 1. Parameters of Formula

parameter	meaning
w	inertia weight
v_{id}	particle speed
x_{id}	particle current position
p_{id}	particle historical best position
p_{gd}	global best position
$rand()$ $Rand()$	mutually independent random function
c_1 c_2	study factors

According to each particle's previous speed, historically best position, and overall best position, formula (4) calculates the current particle's velocity. The position of every particle in multi-dimensional space is updated by formula(5).

In accordance with the procedure, algorithm initializes n particles randomly. For each particle a source root tree contained. Particle with the best fitness will be considered as the current global best solution p_g. Then get each particle into the iterative process, in which the step of merging, circle eliminating and edge pruning will be executed. In every loop, QoS constraints are taken into consideration, and a fitness value of each optimized particle is assessed to decide whether to update the global best solution p_g. If the algorithm converges or is beyond the maximum iteration, solution will be obtained. EERTPSO algorithm pseudo code is given as follow:

Algorithm 1. EERTPSO

```
procedure EERTPSO
    input m
    convergestate = FALSE
    for i=0 to n do
    Init_Particle (src, edge)
    end_for
    p_g=Calculate_FitnessofTree (p_tree)
    for i=0 to m do
        k = 0;
        while (k<n) do
            temptree = MergingOfTree (p_g,  p_ld,  particle[k])
            RemoveCircles(temptree, src)
            Prune_IndegreeExcessiveNode (temptree)
            Prune_UselessEdge (temptree)
            if solution tree satistices QoS constraints
            then continue; otherwise repeat
            totalnodes = Count_Nodes (temptree)
            if totalnodes<EERTPSO_SolutionNodes(p_g)
                fitness = FitnessofTree (temptree)
                if fitness > FitnessofTree (p_g)
                p_g = temptree
                end_if
                k++;
            end_if
        end_while
        convergestate = IsConverge (p_g)
        if convergestate = TRUE
            break
        print no solution message
        end_if
    end_for
```

```
    print bestsolution
    print i
end_procedure
```

After the algorithm executes some generations, the solution with minimum amount of nodes and satisfying QoS constraints will be found. PSO Initialization has the advantage of random feature, which ensures good search range. In iterations, each particle is lead by the neighborhood into the favorable direction, by which the algorithm takes a good performance. In the following sections the steps including initialization, tree merging, circle elimination, edge pruning and fitness assessing will be introduced.

4.1   Initialization of PSO Particles

The particle in this paper abandons the traditional way preserving path between source and destination node, maintains a source root tree in n×n matrix instead. In this n-node matrix x, $x[i][j]=1$ indicates link between node i and j is in the source root tree.

At the beginning of process, algorithm constructs a random tree in the following method:

Assuming that all the communication nodes are in the tree members set S, at first there is only the source node s in the set. Construct an array $currentdelay$ recording the delay between source and the other nodes. Randomly search the nodes that are not in S but have edge (assumed e_{mi}) connecting to nodes in S, if the sum of delay on edge e_{mi} (depicted as $Del(m,i)$) and $currentdelay[m]$ is lower than communication tree delay constraint, and the edge e_{mi} has the available bandwidth larger than requirement of communication in tree, then add node i into S while update $currentdelay[i]$ as the sum of $currentdelay[m]$ and $Del(m,i)$. The above random selection will be repeated, if the delay and bandwidth demand are not satisfied, until all the communication nodes are added into S.

After all the communication member nodes are added into the source root tree, the process of pruning leaf nodes not belonging to communication members will be executed. Check each leaf node, if it is not the member and possesses an edge e_{mi} (node m is the parent of i) , then eliminate edge e_{mi} from the tree. Similar inspection will be done on the parent node until a node that is the communication member or its out-degree is bigger than 0. A communication tree that satisfied the delay and bandwidth constraints will be found through the initialization above.

Algorithm 2. Particle Initialization

```
    Procedure Init_Particle (src, edge)
        Init Set S =[src]
        Init currentdelay[n]
        currentdelay[src]=0
        do
            i=0
            while (i<n) do
```

```
        m=0
      while (m<n) do
         if node i is adjacent to node m, and node m is in Set S, and node i is not in
            if (currentdelay[m] + Del(m, i) ≤ Δd and B(m, i) ≥ Bd )
               add node i to Set Candidate
            end_if
         end_if
      end_while
   end_while
i = RandOpt(Candidate)
add node i to Set S
currentdelay[node i]= currentdelay[node m]+ Del(m, i)
while not all of the member nodes contained in set S
Prune_UselessEdge ()
```
End Procedure

4.2 Merging and Optimizing the Tree

Algorithm in this paper optimizes the source root tree with tree shape based method directly instead of the conventional procedure. The main stages are described as follow:

Tree Merging. The source root tree is stored in the form of n×n adjacent matrix. Assuming two trees $T_1 T_2$, their merging can be simply treated as $T = T_1 + T_2$, i.e. $T[i][j] = T_1[i][j] \vee T_2[i][j]$, but this is an intermediate results waiting modification.

Circle Eliminating. It is probable that the result drew from previous stage contains circles or nested loop. We use depth first search(DFS) to eliminate circles. DFS algorithm begins from source node s, DFS($s, deep$), in which the depth of node is denoted as *deep*. Three major arrays, including the node in deep array of tree (*deep*[]), the whether-visited array (*visited*[]), and the finish-searched array(*finished*[]), are kept by the algorithm. By means of these arrays, if algorithm discovers one node i which has been searched but searching procedure is unfinished, it indicated that the graph includes directed circles. In such circumstances, we adopt the approach of deleting the edge returning to node i to solve the problem. After tree merging operation, the nodes on circles or nested loops can be divided into two types: If the edge e_{mi} belongs to both of the two trees, the in-degree of a node i is 1, otherwise the in-degree of node i is more than 1. Circle eliminating does not delete edges shared by two trees but the edges with nodes whose in-degree more than 1, ensuring the connectivity between communication members. Therefore, after the circle eliminating operation, the largest branch of the graph contains all the communication members inevitably.

Eliminating Useless Edges. After the operation of above stages, algorithm could obtain a tree containing all the communication members, but maybe leaves nodes which not belong to the member group are also mixed in, thereupon an operation of eliminating useless nodes and connected edges is necessary. It is the same as the pruning in the initialization section.

4.3   Fitness Evaluating

There are two kinds of fitness evaluations in our algorithm, including edge fitness and the tree fitness. The former aims to eliminate the substandard edges in the stage of circle trimming and over-degree nodes pruning. So the bandwidth and delay constraints are the emphasis of edge fitness evaluation.

$$fitness(e) = \begin{cases} 0 & bandwidth(e) < bw\_req \\ a_1 \times e^{-cost(e)/avgcost} + a_2 \times e^{-delay(e)/avgdelay} & otherwise \end{cases} \tag{6}$$

The edge bandwidth, cost and delay are denoted by $bandwidth(e)$, $cost(e)$ and $delay(e)$ respectively. The bw_req is the bandwidth constraint of an edge, $avgcost$ and $avgdelay$ represent the average cost and delay of the network edge set. The a_1 a_2 are weight value.

In another aspect, the tree fitness evaluation is a compound function related to total cost and delay in the tree. This method of searching optimized solutions is beneficial to seeking a compromise between network performance and energy consumption. We should consider the fitness updating in the meanwhile of nodes minimizing process.

$$fitness(Tree) = a_1 \times e^{-cost()/cbcost} + a_2 \times e^{-del()/cbdelay} \tag{7}$$

In the above formulas, $cost()$, $del()$ stand for the values of the tree's cost and delay, $cbcost$ and $cbdelay$ denote the cost and delay in the current best solution tree. The e is the base of natural logarithm. The a_1 a_2 represent weight variables which can be set to different values according to the requirements, and meet the constraints that $a_1 + a_2 = 1$, $a_1, a_2 \geq 0$. In this paper we assign them to 0.85 and 0.15, respectively.

5   Experiment Results And Analysis

We evaluate the performance of this algorithm in the following section. In our study we adopted MRSIM[14] which is developed by Salama et al. of North Carolina University. The network topology used in the experiment was randomly generated according to the approach of Waxman. The generator randomly distributes nodes over a rectangle area and then creates links between these nodes at random. The edge cost, delay and jitter is set to the distance between its corresponding nodes. This algorithm was programmed with VC6.0 and run on the machine Intel Core2® Duo E7500 2.93GHz, 4GB memories in the operating system of Windows 7.

We have examined the efficacy of our proposed EERTPSO through extensive simulation experiments. The maximum cycling time of our algorithm is set as 30 and the initialization particles number is 30 considering the solution and convergence time. The circulation will be stopped when no evolution occurs in 4 consecutive cycles. When the network is in a low utilization state which provides opportunity for us to exert energy efficient routing algorithm, communication members usually account for 10% to 20% of all the nodes in topology. In order to simulate the real situation, the power consumption of nodes in active and sleep mode are assumed to be 200W and 100W[15] respectively.

To evaluate the performance of our algorithm, we run other two algorithms and record data for comparison. The two algorithms added into comparison are modified Dijkstra least delay algorithm (MDLD) adapted from [16] and ant colony-based self-adaptive energy saving routing algorithm[7] (A-ESR) respectively. We obtained the average solution by running the algorithm 100 times on every testing topology, the data of solution nodes number, power consumption and the convergence time are depicted in the following figures.

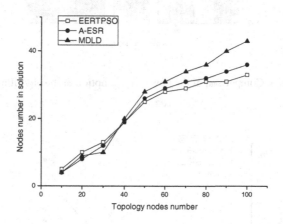

Fig. 2. Comparison of the nodes number of the algorithms

The comparison of nodes number results in solution tree with different algorithms are shown in Fig.2. It can be seen that, taking a better heuristic strategy, our EERTPSO has a good performance slightly better than A-ESR and much better than MDLD. When the communication members are not enough, A-ESR algorithm performs satisfying because of its good unicast feature, but as the members growing, EERTPSO improves quickly. On the contrary, just considering the delay minimization, regardless of the energy efficient, MDLD cannot guarantee the number of nodes in the results.

Fig.3 describes the energy consumption of solutions obtained by different algorithms. As we can see, the energy consumption of each kind of algorithm increases with the network scale increasing. Contrasting the results on each scale level alone, it is shown that, with the network scale increasing, EERTPSO algorithm performs from unsatisfied to the best in energy saving effectiveness. However, the MDLD algorithm, which puts emphasis on low-delay solutions, cannot ensure the nodes number minimization, so it shows worse than the other algorithms.

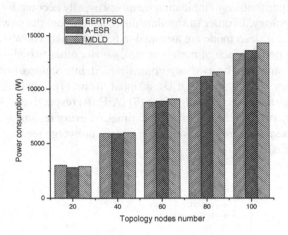

Fig. 3. Comparison of the power consumption of the algorithms

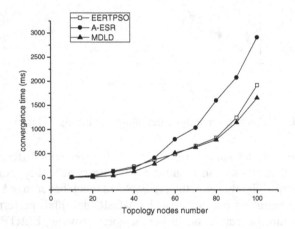

Fig. 4. Comparison of convergence time of the algorithms

As is demonstrated in Fig.4, the convergence time of each algorithm increases with the expanding of network scale. The time consumption speed of A-ESR grows faster than EERTPSO, and when the number of nodes increases over 60, a significant gap of convergence time appears. As the number of communication members becomes larger, EERTPSO is still able to maintain a relatively low convergence time with its tree-based feature, while the A-ESR increase rapidly.

6   Conclusion

In this paper we investigated the power consumption minimizing problem in wired network and proposed an energy-efficient routing derived form tree shape transformation based PSO algorithm. Our method could find an optimized solution containing all the demanding communication sessions with a minimal subset of network nodes while guarantee the bandwidth and other QoS requirements. The idea of tree re-shaping optimized the solution and improved algorithm performance. Through sleep-awake mechanism, fewer necessary network components would be left in awake-state to forward the data flow, and the unnecessary components would be shutdown for energy saving. Experimental results show that the algorithm performs rapidly and effectively.

Acknowledgment. The study is supported by the Natural Science Foundation of Shandong Province (No. ZR2011FM021; ZR2013FM029; ZR2013FQ013), the Science and Technology Development Program of Jinan (No.201303010), the National Natural Science Foundation of China(NSFC No. 60773101), and the Fundamental Research Funds of Shandong University (No. 2014JC037).

References

1. Yun, D., Lee, J.: Research in green network for future internet. Journal of KIISE 28(1), 41–51 (2010)
2. Chiaraviglio, L., Mellia, M., Neri, F.: Minimizing isp network energy cost: Formulation and solutions. IEEE/ACM Transactions on Networking (TON) 20(2), 463–476 (2012)
3. Bolla, R., et al.: Energy efficiency in the future internet: a survey of existing approaches and trends in energy-aware fixed network infrastructures. IEEE Communications Surveys & Tutorials 13(2), 223–244 (2011)
4. Gupta, M., Singh, S.: Greening of the Internet. In: Proceedings of the 2003 Conference on Applications, Technologies, Architectures, and Protocols for Computer Communications (2003)
5. Nedevschi, S., et al.: Reducing Network Energy Consumption via Sleeping and Rate-Adaptation. In: NSDI (2008)
6. Chiaraviglio, L., Mellia, M., Neri, F.: Reducing power consumption in backbone networks. In: IEEE International Conference on Communications, ICC 2009 (2009)
7. Kim, Y.-M., et al.: Ant colony based self-adaptive energy saving routing for energy efficient Internet. Computer Networks 56(10), 2343–2354 (2012)
8. Si, W., Taheri, J., Zomaya, A.: A distributed energy saving approach for Ethernet switches in data centers. In: 2012 IEEE 37th Conference on Local Computer Networks (LCN) (2012)
9. Heller, B., et al.: ElasticTree: Saving Energy in Data Center Networks. In: NSDI (2010)
10. Awerbuch, B., Holmer, D., Rubens, H.: The pulse protocol: Energy efficient infrastructure access. In: Twenty-third Annual Joint Conference of the IEEE Computer and Communications Societies, INFOCOM 2004 (2004)
11. Mumey, B., Tang, J., Hashimoto, S.: Enabling green networking with a power down approach. In: 2012 IEEE International Conference on Communications (ICC) (2012)

12. Gunaratne, C., Christensen, K., Nordman, B.: Managing energy consumption costs in desktop PCs and LAN switches with proxying, split TCP connections, and scaling of link speed. International Journal of Network Management 15(5), 297–310 (2005)
13. Kennedy, J., Eberhart, R.: Particle swarm optimization. In: Proceedings of IEEE International Conference on Neural Networks (1995)
14. Salama, H.F., Reeves, D.S., Viniotis, Y.: Evaluation of multicast routing algorithms for real-time communication on high-speed networks. IEEE Journal on Selected Areas in Communications 15(3), 332–345 (1997)
15. Niewiadomska-Szynkiewicz, E., et al.: Control system for reducing energy consumption in backbone computer network. Concurrency and Computation: Practice and Experience 25(12), 1738–1754 (2013)
16. Jain, S., Fall, K., Patra, R.: Routing in a delay tolerant network, vol. 34. ACM (2004)

A Context-Aware Framework for SaaS Service Dynamic Discovery in Clouds

Shaochong Li[1,*] and Hao-peng Chen[2]

[1] China UnionPay, Shanghai, China
lee.shaochong@gmail.com
[2] School of Software, Shanghai Jiao Tong University, Shanghai, China
chen-hp@sjtu.edfu.cn

Abstract. As Cloud computing and Mobile Computing become more and more prevalent, most of service consumers expect discovery suitable SaaS service in mobile environment. At the same time, in order to economize SaaS service advertisement cost, service provider need recommend SaaS service accurately based on consumer's behavior. Therefore, how to determine a suitable policy of service discovery in mobile environment has become a challenging issue. It is considered that service in mobile environment need involve such contexts: Domain, QoS and Spatial. In this paper, we propose a context-aware framework that benefit for SaaS service discovery and recommend based on service consumer's behavior habit and their context environment. In order to reach this target, we also present a model to describe SaaS service based on context Ontology.

Keywords: Cloud computing, Mobile Computing, Domain, QoS, Spatial, context-aware, Ontology.

1   Introduction

Recently, cloud computing has enough ability to deal with complex and Parallel problems. It virtualized all the resource for everyone who wants to get the suitable service. On the other hand, cloud service identification and discovery remains a tough issue due to different service descriptions, non-standardized naming conventions and diverse features of cloud services [1, 2]. Under such situation, it is hard for consumer to make decision to select service from different service providers due to non-uniform description.

Software as a Service (SaaS) is a software delivery model, which provides customers the functionality of a service that is completely deployed in the cloud environment. It also is a delivery mechanism to provide consumers with the functionality of an application that is deployed in the cloud environment. It is a problem for consumer to choose suitable SaaS from the services with similar functionality. Traditional SaaS service recommended method is based on the service access sequence. It is considered that the more frequent the service is accessed the more chance to recommend. However, it may not be the suitable service for consumer due to consumer's surroundings.

---

* Corresponding author.

X.-h. Sun et al. (Eds.): ICA3PP 2014, Part II, LNCS 8631, pp. 671–684, 2014.

Current personal service recommended mechanism could not consider the factor of context environment. Such as the consumers' habit, information of QoS, their environment and so on.

SaaS service as a resource of cloud, most service providers recommend their services using advertisement or message. In most cases, such method is not effect to attract consumer to use their service and many services they recommend may not suitable for consumer's needs.

In order to address the above limitations, we propose a semantic-based framework that contains cloud SaaS services dynamic recommend based on the context environment achieving the following objectives:

- To provide SaaS service description method based on context-aware ontologies for service consumers and providers.
- To introduce a context-aware framework of service recommend based on the proposed context-aware ontologies.
- To propose a service recommend algorithm to push suitable service for consumer based on consumer behavior.

The remaining paper is structured as follows. In the next section, we discuss related work. Section 3 introduces the SaaS service description based on context ontology. Section 4 introduces our context-aware framework in detail. Section 5 presents the algorithm of service recommend based on consumer's behavior. The simulation details are presented in section 6. Finally, the conclusion and future work are presented in section 7.

2   Related Work

In recent years, the problem of service selection based on cloud computing has received a lot of attention from many researchers. Some researchers describe cloud services with Web Services description language (WSDL), such as paper [3], the authors use BPEL to orchestrate SaaS services which are described as Web Services. But in cloud computing era, the traditional WSDL could not fully meet the requirement of cloud computing services description. Consequently, most researchers expect to describe cloud services based-sematic.

Semantic Web technologies include languages such as RDF [4] and OWL [5] for defining ontologies and describing metadata using these ontologies as well as tools or reasoning over these descriptions. OWL is based on Description Logic (DL) [6] with a representation in RDF. In paper [7] , the authors describe the cloud service based on Ontology. But the authors only give a abstract model which is not describe SaaS service in detail. In [8] sematic matchmaking approach for virtual application deployment in IaaS is proposed with WSML as a language for specifying search requests and service descriptions. However the author only focuses on IaaS service providers. Paper [9] addresses a method of matchmaking for Cloud services and resources. The authors propose a model for reflecting dynamic information in service descriptions. In paper [10], the authors use agent to manage cloud resource. An OWL-S based semantic cloud service discovery and selection system is proposed in [11]. These authors all don't consider the QoS as the factor of service selection.

Based on the semantic web technologies, researchers could build framework for cloud service selection. Paper [12] provides a CloudCmp framework for comparison. The SMICloud framework proposed an Analytical Hierarchy Processing (AHP) ranking mechanism for cloud services selection in paper [13]. But these frameworks could not consider the mobile environment and could not detect context environment.

From the above description, it is noted that current research work exist the following questions :

- SaaS services are not described precisely to satisfy consumer's requirement.
- Service selection Framework doesn't pay attention to the context environment.
- The recommend mechanism is not based on the consumer behavior habit enough.

Consequently, in this paper, we expect to provide a context-ware SaaS service dynamic selection and recommendation framework to benefit for consumer in the mobile environment.

3   Context-Aware SaaS Service Model

Software as a service (SaaS) is a model of software deployment by software vendors (servers) in which their clients use applications through a time subscription or a pay-as-you-go scheme. Most of SaaS services contain the information about function, platform, price, available time and so on. If we consider the context environment, service should include more information about context. In this paragraph, we expect to propose a context ontology model for consumer and provider to describe SaaS service.

The classification method of context is the basis of context ontology. Researchers have proposed various classifications [14 ,15,16,17]. The authors in paper [15] divide the context into Computing Context, User Context and Physical Context. Based on this classification, the author Chen adds Time Context. Dix and Rodden propose a hierarchical classification that contains Infrastructure Context, System Context, Domain Context and Physical Context. For the context, the researchers have different views about the classified method. However, for the SaaS consumer and provider, they pay more attention to the Domain (What the service could do), QoS(How about the service) and Spatial (Which location we can get service).

Considering the characteristic of SaaS service, in this paper, we propose a SaaS service model that contains the three contexts: ***Domain Context, QoS context, Spatial Context.***

3.1   Domain Context

Domain context provides standard ontology for the standard SaaS service. It needs contain various elements related to SaaS service processes of function. The domain context describes SaaS service related field attributes. In this paper, Services domain knowledge was collected from the following resources: the industry ontology standard from FIPA (The Foundation for Intelligent Physical Agents), Business Function Ontology (BFO) framework [18], cloud ontologies [19-20] and industry classification standards. One domain context contains many attributes that need us to record. Here we couldn't describe a complete domain context. The following figure shows a part of domain description based on OWL language:

```
<owl:Class rdf:ID="Restaurant">
    <rdfs:label> Restaurant </rdfs:label>
</owl:Class>
<owl:ObjectProperty rdf:ID="hasClient">
    <rdfs:label> hasClient </rdfs:label>
    <rdfs:domain rdf:resource="#Client"/>
    <rdfs:range rdf:resource="# Restaurant "/>
</owl:ObjectProperty>
```

Fig. 1. A portion of domain description based on OWL language

3.2   QoS Context

Quality of Service (QoS) serves as a benchmark to differentiate service providers and comprises of techniques that aim to bring a balance between the needs of the service consumers and those of the service providers while being constrained by the limited network and server resources. At the same time, QoS should describe consumer and provider extremely concerned attributes, such as price, response time and so on. As an important indication standard for the SaaS service, there are many attributes for it to define the relate standard.

QoS description contains many metrics, such as *response time, availability, interoperability, reliability, connection time.* There are many QoS semantic models to describe QoS. In this paper, we could build QoS model refers to paper [21]. The Qos model contains five parts. The first one relates to various roles in specifying QoS information, QoS description, QoS level, and QoS group. The second one describes main characteristics of QoS properties. The third one defines relationships between and among QoS properties. The fourth one describes QoS metrics. And the last one defines

```
<owl:Class rdf:ID="QoS">
    <rdfs:subClassOf rdf:resource="#Role"/>
    <rdfs:subClassOf rdf:resource="#QoSDescription"/>
    <rdfs:subClassOf rdf:resource="#QoSLevel"/>
    <rdfs:subClassOf rdf:resource="#QoSGroup"/>
    <rdfs:subClassOf rdf:resource="#QoSProperty"/>
</owl:Class>
```

Fig. 2. QoS ontology model based on OWL language

a set of core QoS properties. The Fig 2 shows such QoS model based on OWL language.

3.3   Spatial Context

Spatial context is one kind of the earliest context which researchers paid attention to. Context-aware computing was also originated from LBS (Location Based Services). Consequently, it is no doubt that spatial information such as consumer location and the topological relationship of building is the most important context information. Especially, in the mobile environment, location is the most significant information for SaaS service. Geographic Information Systems and other related domains have proposed many spatial models.

The most representative models are RCC (Regional Connection Calculus)[22], n-intersection model and so on. According to RCC theory, Region is the metadata. It could have any dimension as long as the number of dimension is same as the one of the model based on RCC. Suppose we have two regions x and y. RCC define the connection relationship as $C(x,y)$ which represents the intersection of topological closure between region x and y is not empty. It means that they at least share a same point for these two regions.

The other relationship definitions are based on connection relationship $C(x,y)$. These relationships are always divided into some relationship set in order to form the subset of RCC model. The most common used relationship sets are RCC-5, RCC-8, RCC-15 and so on. In this paper, we put RCC-5 as the spatial information model. RCC-5 includes five topologic relationships between regions: *DR* (discrete), *PO* (partially overlapping), *PP* (proper part), *EQ* (equal), *PPI* (proper part inverse). We use RCC-5 to build a spatial context set which contains information of geographical environment. Each service could find their suitable position. The Fig 3 describes an example model that has DR and PP relationships based on OWL language

```
<owl:ObjectProperty rdf:ID="DR">
    <rdfs:domain rdf:resource="#Region"/>
    <rdfs:range rdf:resource="#Region" />
    <rdf:type rdf:resource=&owl;SymmetricProperty />
</owl: ObjectProperty >
<owl:ObjectProperty rdf:ID="PP">
    <rdfs:domain rdf:resource="#Region"/>
    <rdfs:range rdf:resource="#Region"/>
    <rdf:type rdf:resource=&owl;TransitiveProperty />
</owl: ObjectProperty >
```

Fig. 3. DR and PP relationships based on OWL language

3.4   SaaS Service Model

Based on the above context description, SaaS service could be described as multipleconcepts. One concept contains context information (*Domain Context*, QoS *Context, Spatial Context*). We could define $concept_i$ as the following style:

$$concept_i = \{\Phi(D^C, Q^C, S^C), D^C, Q^C, S^C\} \, (i=0,1,2,3......) \qquad (1)$$

According to the above formula, $D^C = \{D_1, ...D_n\}$, $Q^C = \{Q_1, ...Q_n\}, S^C = \{S_1, ...S_n\}$ represent series sets of elements from *Domain context*, QoS *context* and *Spatial Context* respectively. $\Phi(D^C, Q^C, S^C)$ is the semantic relationship holding among D^C, Q^C, S^C variables, and is represented in the form of OWL triples.

Consequently, one SaaS service could be described as the following style:

$$service_i = Set\{concept^C\} \, (i=0,1,2,3.........) \qquad (2)$$

Where $concept^C = \{concept_1, ...concept_n\}$ represent service contain many concepts come from the context-ontology.

In the next paragraph, we propose a context-aware SaaS service discovery and recommend framework that could benefit for consumer to get service and convenient for provider to push their service based on consumer's behavior.

4   Context-Aware SaaS Service Discovery and Recommend Framework

In this paragraph, in order to utilizing the context information, we put a context-aware framework for service discovery and recommend. Our framework consists of three modules: *SFM (Service foundation module)*, *SLM (Service Library Module)* and *SPM (Service Push Module)*. These modules and their relationships are depicted in Fig 4. *SFM* provide the basic function for SaaS such as LBS and message push based on BaaS [23] and it also could collect the SaaS service description. *SLM* offer a SaaS service library that contains services described by semantic based on context ontology. *SPM* designs a semantic matching mechanism to recommend suitable SaaS service for consumer.

4.1   Service Foundation Module (SFM)

SFM is a module to conduct basic functions that are consist of two sub-modules: BaaS and Cloud Foundation. Backend as a service (BaaS) provides SaaS service backend cloud storage, pushing service, LBS service and other backend services. This module provides base function for SaaS service, SLM and SPM. BaaS module also could record the relate information of SaaS service such as domain, location, price and other attributes. Such information is quite important for SLM to describe a SaaS in its context-aware service library. All SaaS services descriptions are stored as semantic style in SLM. At the same time, BaaS also provide storage function for SPM to storage consumer information and consumer semantic tag. SPM uses push function based on BaaS to recommend user suitable service. Cloud Foundation is another sub module in SFM, it provide the basic cloud functions for BaaS such as IaaS or PaaS. This module also could collect QoS information from SaaS service.

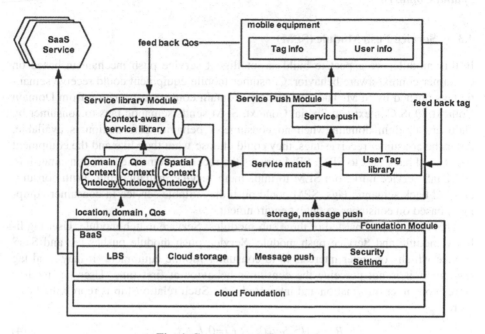

Fig. 4. Context-aware Framework

When a Service Provider proposes a new SaaS service, some related information such as domain and price could be dispatched instantly. All of the result will send to SLM. In the next part, we will describe how the SLM transfer the SaaS information into sematic-information.

4.2   Service Library Module (SLM)

In the SFM, it collects SaaS service related characteristics such as provider name, service name, description, features, application domain, price, SLA. Then SLM map the SaaS features to ontological concepts retrieved from context (***Domain Context***, QoS ***Context, Spatial Context***). The context-aware service library is responsible for the processing of the service semantic-description. It aims at the unification of services descriptions. This module is also responsible for accepting updates of the registered services due to most features of SaaS services are changing in a certain period.

This module is responsible for storing SaaS based on semantic in order to matching service accurately. It contains a set of SaaS services that are described as the following style:

$$Sc = Set\{ \ service_i\} \quad (\ i=0,1,2,3.........) \tag{3}$$

Sc represents a set of SaaS service and $service_i$ represents one specific SaaS service. The service definition had been described in formula (1). All concepts are stored in service library based on three context ontologies (**Domain Context**, QoS **Context**, **Spatial Context**).

4.3   Service Push Module (SPM)

In this module, we expect to build an intelligent service push mechanism based on consumer context-aware behavior. Consumer mobile equipment could receive semantic tags pushed by SPM. The semantic tags contain context information from Domain Context, QoS Context and Spatial Context. SPM sends semantic tags to consumer by choosing random domain when no consumer's behavior information is available. After the consumer receives tags, they could choose what they like and the equipment could send back tags to SPM. SPM utilizes the received semantic tags, consumer info and SaaS service info from SLM to implement service matchmaking. With consumer's fed back semantic tags, SPM could push the suitable service to consumer equipment based on consumer's context environment.

This module is consisted of three sub-modules: Service match module, User tag library module and Service push module. Service push module pushes tag and SaaS service which consumer interests in to consumer mobile equipment. It may send tag random if it is not perceive the consumer behavior at first time. User tag module stores consumer information and interested tags. Such relationship is represented as a pair:

$$R^c = \{ \ U^c, Set\{C_i \ \} \} \ (\ i=0,1,2,3\ldots\ldots) \qquad (4)$$

Where U^c represents the consumer unique identification and $Set\{C_i \ \}$ represents a series of semantic-tags. User tag library store a large number of pairs to record the consumer's interests.

Service match module discovery SaaS service in SLM based on consumer interest semantic tags from User tag library module. At first, it needs match semantic-tags in context-aware ontology and find the similar semantic concepts. It needs matchmaking concept in SLM that we define above and contain three context sets: D^C, Q^C and S^C Context matchmaking method is based on ontology sematic similar computing. In this paper, we use GCSM [24] to compute semantic similarity between two concepts. The formula is defined as the following:

$$GCSM(c_1, c_2) = \frac{depth(c_1)+depth(c_2)}{2*depth(LCA(c_1,c_2))} \qquad (5)$$

Where depth(c) represents the concept c depth in ontology and $LCA(c_1, c_2)$ represents the lowest same ancestor. Based on the method from paper [25], it could use function $Prop(c_1, c_2)$ which represents a set of nodes from concept c_1 to c_2. Consequently, it could define the matchmaking function as the following:

$$Match(c_1, c_2) = \frac{2*|Prop(c_1,LCA)\cap Prop(c_1,LCA)|}{|Prop(c_1,LCA)\cap Prop(c_1,LCA)|+|Prop(c_1,LCA)\cup Prop(c_1,LCA)|} \qquad (6)$$

Then, we could define the context similar function defined as the following formula. w represents as weights.

$$Sim(c_1, c_2) = w * GCSM(c_1, c_2) + (1 - w)Match(c_1, c_2) \qquad (7)$$

In this paper, we use the above formula to compute similarity between two services. Based on formula (2), we could use the following formula to compute similarity:

$$Sim(service1, service2) = \frac{\sum_{i=0}^{n} sim(concept1_i, concept2_i)}{n} \qquad (8)$$

Base on this similarity compute formula, consumer analysis module provides a SaaS service matchmaking mechanism that is described in the following paragraph in detail. Consumer uses their mobile equipment connects to our framework. Their equipment could feedback the QoS of SaaS service to SLM.

As we have described above, our context-aware framework could push consumer interested BaaS services to consumer mobile equipment based on analyzing data. Our framework would accommodate the customer's preference automatically based on context-aware framework. This paper provides a service recommend mechanism based on clustering concepts from consumer selected. In the next paragraph, we will describe it in detail.

5   Service Recommend Algorithm Based on Context

When consumer's interest tags are sent to context-aware framework, the framework would store the semantic description in cloud storage. For the sake of finding consumer interest SaaS services, we focus on how to cluster these services and analyze such data. From what we have described above, our context-aware ontology contains three dimensions: **Domain**, **QoS** and **Spatial**. Since the high-dimension data clustering is a quite complex problem, we use multiple k-means clustering instead. Suppose the number of services we focus on is n. We use k-mean clustering to divide i^{th} services into K_i ranges, thus, the whole data space is divide into $\prod_{i=1}^{n} K_i$ subspaces.

Our service matchmaking algorithm is divided into two steps: at fist, we use k-mean clustering to cluster the service based on context-aware ontology. Consequently, the Services are clustered into $\prod_{i=1}^{n} K_i$ groups. The similarity algorithm use formula (8). The clustering algorithm would be written in the code similar to the Fig 5 pseudo-code. As is described in the Fig 5 algorithm, it iterates each service and each concept in service. All services could be clustered by concepts using k-means algorithm.

```
function clustering(Set services)
    // services:result of all SaaS service
Set <Set> groups ={};
    // groups: the result of clustering
    for each concept_i in services
```

```
        add(groups,{k-mean(concept_i)});
        //k-mean(concept_i):clustering
    end for
    groups = orthogonalize(groups)
    // the final result comes from the groups orthogonalizing
    Map centroidsMap={} ;
    // a map store the relationship between centroid and group
for each group in groups
        for each service_l in group // concept_l is a concept of service
        range = mergeRange(service_l);
        // range: the merged range of service_l
            p = centroid (range);
        // p: the centroid of range,
        // iterate each service in group to get the centroid of range
        end for
    centroidsMap.push(p,group.id)
    // push the relationship between p and group into map
    end for
end function
```

Fig. 5. Cluster Algorithm

The second step uses consumer interest semantic tags to find consumer interest SaaS services. It will find the max similarity cluster for calculating the similarity between sematic tag and centroid from each cluster. And then, we could get a set of concepts that have same similarity from centroid like sematic tags. It is considered that SaaS services contain such concepts in this cluster are the consumer interest services. This algorithm would be written in the code similar to pseudo-code in Fig 6.

Based on the above algorithm, we could get a set of services that are considered related to consumer's behavior. These services are the most suitable for consumer's context environment.

```
function getServices(Set tags )
    // tags: consumer mark tags based on semantic
    for each tag in tags
        for each group in groups
        //groups: the cluster service set, the style is Set <Set>
            p= centroidsMap .get(group.id)
            //p is the centroid in this group
            similarity = Sim(tag,p)
            //compute similarity between tag and p
            if (similarity >simMax){
            simMax =similarity
```

```
            //iterate each tag and store max similarity as simMax
        simGroup = group
            //iterate each tag and store max similarity cluster as
            //simGroup
        }
    end for
  end for
  for each  concept_i in simGroup //iterate each concept in cluster
      μ=Sim (concept_i,p)
          //compute each concept similarity from concert point
      if(μ ≥ simMax )
          // if the similarity larger or equal to simMax, it is target
          services = services  ∪ getServices(concept_i,simGroup)
          // get service by concept and union all services
      end for
  end function
```

Fig. 6. Get Service Algorithm

6   Simulation

In order to implement our simulation, we use BaaS service from StackMob[26] and simulate nealy 1000 SaaS services belong to three domains : travel, sport and accounting. StackMob is a platform that could provide SaaS service conveniently. We use StackMob to simulate our SFM. We use Ontology Lookup Service [27] from web and SaaS service semantic description store in Cloud to implement our SLM. Based on BaaS and ontology lookup service, we build SPM that implement semantic matchmaking and consumer behavior analysis task. As we have described in the above paragraph, we cluster the concepts of service. The following figure shows clustering data based on k-means:

In our simulation, as SaaS service provider, Table 1 shows register simulation SaaS services. Here we only describe SaaS services important elements in these three contexts. Take the first service as example, it shows one SaaS service about restaurant. Consequently, the domain context shows information "{restaurant}". QoS context contains five parts as we have described above: role is "provider", description is "response time", quality level is"Service", group is "QoSUserSystemGroup", QoS Property is "QosMetric". Service 1 Spatial Context information is "{indoor}, {building},{PP}" which means the region is indoor and building. The spatial context relationship is "PP".

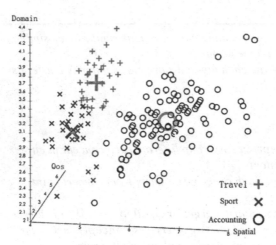

Fig. 7. Three Clusters based on k-means

Table 1. SaaS Service List

SaaS service	Domain cont ect	QoS Context	Spatial Context
Service 1	{restaurant}	{provider, responsetime, Service, QoSUserSystemGroup,QosMetric}	{indoor}, {building}, {PP}
Service 2	{income)	{provier, responsetime, interface, QoSUserGroup,QosWeight}	{indoor} {school} {PO}
Service 2	{basketball}	{provider, responsetime, interface, QoSUserGroup,QosWeight}	{outdoor} {ground} {EQ}
....	....	....	....

After that, we send to consumer several semantic tags that contain different contexts: restaurant, response time, golf, outdoor, income, connection time and so on. Then the consumer selects the "{restaurant, outdoor, response time}" and "{income, connection time}". The table 2 shows the similarity of semantic tags and centroid of each clustering.

Table 2. Similarity

Semantic Tag	Travel cluster	Sport cluster	Accounting cluster
{restaurant,outdoor, response time}	0.8522	0.3321	0.1122
{income, connection time}	0.3567	0.2239	0.6898

Apparently, the max number is the similarity between first semantic tag and travel cluster. At the end, our framework recommends SaaS services that are in travel cluster and the similarity from such cluster centroid is more than 0.8522.

We simulate some consumers connect to our framework and feedback their interest tag. After accumulating more than 100,000 feedback and use service, we find that the most of SaaS service our framework recommend are related to consumer's behavior.

7   Conclusion and Future Work

In this paper, we propose a SaaS service model for consumer and provider to describe their requirement based on context ontology in mobile environment. This model contains three contexts: Domain context, QoS context, Spatial context. And then, we design a context-aware framework for pushing service to consumer and collecting consumer's feedback using semantic tags. Our framework could register SaaS service semantic description and analyzes the consumer behavior to push consumer interest services to them. In our framework, we use k-means algorithm to cluster SaaS services and compute the similarity to recommend suitable services.

In the next work, we expect to cluster consumers based on their interest concepts. This could accelerate the service match rate and make service match more accurately.

References

1. Zhang, M., et al.: Investigating decision support techniques for automating cloud service selection. In: IEEE 4th International Conference on Cloud Computing Technology and Science (CloudCom), pp.759–764 (2012)
2. Höfer, C.N., Karagiannis, G.: Cloud computing services: taxonomy and comparison. Journal of Internet Service Applications (2), 81–94 (2011)
3. Kim, J., Hong, J.E., Choi, J.Y., Cho, J.H.: Dynamic Service Orchestration for SaaS Application in Web Environment. In: Proceedings of the 6th International Conference on Ubiquitous Information Management and Communication (2012)
4. Lassila, O., et al.: Resource Description Framework (RDF) Model and Syntax Specification, W3C recommendation (1999)
5. McGuinness, D., et al.: OWL Web Ontology Language Overview, W3C recommendation (2004)
6. Baader, F., Calvanese, D., McGuinness, D., Patel-Schneider, P., Nardi, D.: The Description Logic Handbook: Theory, Implementation, and Applications. Cambridge Univ. Press (2003)
7. Fortis, T.-F., Munteanu, V.I., Negru, V.: Towards an Ontology for Cloud Services (2012)
8. Dastjerdi, A.V., Tabatabaei, S.G.H., Buyya, R.: An effective architecture for automated appliance management system applying ontology-based cloud discovery. In: IEEE International Symposium on Cluster Computing and the Grid, pp.104–112 (2010)
9. Goscinski, A., Brock, M.: Toward dynamic and attribute based publication, discovery and selection for cloud computing. Future Generation Comp. Syst. 26(7) (2010)
10. Sim, K.M.: Agent-based Cloud computing. IEEE Transaction on Service Computing 5(4) (2012)

11. Kanagasabai, R., et al.: OWL-S based semantic cloud service broker. In: Proceedings of the 19th International Conference on Web Services (ICWS), pp. 560–567 (2012)
12. Li, A., Yang, X., Kandula, S., Zhang, M.: CloudCmp: comparing public cloud providers. In: The 10th Annual Conference on Internet Measurement, pp. 1–14. ACM, New York (2010)
13. Garg, S.K., et al.: A Framework for ranking of cloud computing services. Future Generation Computer Systems (2012)
14. Chen, G., Kotz, D.: A survey of Context-Aware Mobile Computing Research. Technical Report TR2000-381,Hanover: Department of Computer Science, Dartmouth College (2000)
15. Abowd, G.D., Dey, A.K.: Towards a Better Understanding of Context and Context-Awareness. In: Gellersen, H.-W. (ed.) HUC 1999. LNCS, vol. 1707, pp. 304–307. Springer, Heidelberg (1999)
16. Dix, A., Rodden, T., Davies, N., et al.: Exploiting Space and Location as a Design Framework for Interactive Mobile Systems. ACM Transactions on Human Computer Interaction, 285–321 (2000)
17. Krogstie, J.: Requirement Engineering for Mobile Information Systems. In: Proceeding of the Seventh International Workshop on Requirements Engineering: Foundations for Software Quality, Interlaken, Switzerland (2001)
18. Born, M., et al.: Business functions ontology and its application in semantic business process modeling. In: Proceedings of the 19th Australasian Conference on Information Systems, ACIS (2008)
19. Joshi, K., Yesha, Y., Finin, T.: Automating Cloud services lifecycle through semantic technologies. IEEE Transactions on Services Computing (99), 1–14 (2012)
20. Hepp, M.: Eclassowl. The Products and Services Ontology (2013), http://www.heppnetz.de/eclassowl/
21. Tran, V.X.: WS-QoSOnto: A QoS Ontology for Web Services. In: IEEE International Symposium on Digital Object Identifier: Service-Oriented System Engineering, SOSE 2008, pp. 233–238 (2008), doi:10.1109/SOSE.2008.17
22. Randell, C.Z., Cohn, A.: A spatial logic based on regions and connection. In: Nebel, B., Rich, C., Swartout, W. (eds.) Proceedings of the Knowledge Representation and Reasoning, pp. 165–176. Morgan Kaufmann, San Mateo (1992)
23. http://en.wikipedia.org/wiki/Backend_as_a_service
24. Kocaballi, A.B., Kocyigit, A.: Granular Best Match Algorithm for Context-Aware Computing System. In: Proceedings of ACS/IEEE International Conference on Pervasive Services, pp. 143–149 (2006)
25. Ganjisaffar, Y., Abolhassani, H., Neshati, M., et al.: A Similarity Measure for OWL-S Annotated Web Services. In: Proceedings of the 2006 IEEE/WIC/ACM International Conference on Web Intelligence (WI 2006), pp. 621–624 (2006)
26. https://www.stackmob.com/
27. http://www.ebi.ac.uk/ontology-lookup/

Author Index